AF680268

Poultry Health

A Guide for Professionals

Poultry Health

A Guide for Professionals

Edited by

Paul Barrow

University of Surrey

Venugopal Nair

Pirbright Institute

Susan Baigent

Pirbright Institute

Robert Atterbury

University of Nottingham

and

Michael Clark

University of Nottingham

CABI

CABI is a trading name of CAB International

CABI
Nosworthy Way
Wallingford
Oxfordshire OX10 8DE
UK

Tel: +44 (0)1491 832111
Fax: +44 (0)1491 833508
E-mail: info@cabi.org
Website: www.cabi.org

CABI
WeWork
One Lincoln Street
24th Floor
Boston, MA 02111
USA

Tel: +1 (617)682-9015
E-mail: cabi-nao@cabi.org

© CAB International 2021. All rights reserved. No part of this publication may be reproduced in any form or by any means, electronically, mechanically, by photocopying, recording or otherwise, without the prior permission of the copyright owners.

References to Internet websites (URLs) were accurate at the time of writing.

A catalogue record for this book is available from the British Library, London, UK.

Library of Congress Cataloging-in-Publication Data

Names: Barrow, P. A., editor.
Title: Poultry health : a guide for professionals / editors, Paul Barrow, University of Surrey, Venugopal Nair, Pirbright Institute, Susan Baigent, Pirbright Institute, Robert Atterbury, University of Nottingham, Michael Clark, University of Nottingham.
Description: Wallingford, Oxfordshire ; Boston, MA : CAB International, [2021] | Includes bibliographical references and index. | Summary: "Providing a comprehensive overview for small animal veterinarians with poultry clients, this book covers the poultry industry, avian biology, diseases and their agents, infection control, and disease investigation and legislation. Written by international experts, it includes full colour images to aid identification and diagnosis"-- Provided by publisher.
Identifiers: LCCN 2021018814 (print) | LCCN 2021018815 (ebook) | ISBN 9781789245042 (paperback) | ISBN 9781789245059 (ebook) | ISBN 9781789245066 (epub)
Subjects: LCSH: Poultry--Diseases. | Poultry--Physiology. | Poultry--Health.
Classification: LCC SF995 .P683 2021 (print) | LCC SF995 (ebook) | DDC 636.5/0896--dc23
LC record available at https://lccn.loc.gov/2021018814
LC ebook record available at https://lccn.loc.gov/2021018815

ISBN-13: 9781789245042 (paperback)
9781789245059 (ePDF)
9781789245066 (ePub)

DOI: 10.1079/9781789245042.0000

Commissioning Editor: Alexandra Lainsbury
Editorial Assistant: Emma McCann
Production Editor: Tim Kapp

Typeset by SPi, Pondicherry, India

Contents

List of Contributors

Robert Atterbury School of Veterinary Medicine and Science, University of Nottingham, Sutton Bonington Campus, Loughborough, Leicestershire, UK. E-mail: robert.atterbury@nottingham.ac.uk

Susan Baigent Viral Oncogenesis Group, The Pirbright Institute, Woking, Surrey, UK. E-mail: sue.baigent@pirbright.ac.uk

Paul Barrow School of Veterinary Medicine, University of Surrey, Daphne Jackson Road, Guildford, Surrey, UK. E-mail: paul.barrow@surrey.ac.uk

Damer Blake Royal Veterinary College, Hawkshead Lane, North Mymms, Hertfordshire, UK. E-mail: dblake@rvc.ac.uk

Janet M. Bradbury Institute of Infection, Veterinary and Ecological Sciences, University of Liverpool, Leahurst Campus, Neston, UK. E-mail: jmb41@liverpool.ac.uk

Andrew J. Broadbent Department of Animal and Avian Sciences, University of Maryland, College Park, MD 20742, USA. E-mail: ajbroad@umd.edu

Ian H. Brown Animal and Plant Health Agency-Weybridge, Addlestone, Surrey, UK. E-mail: ian.brown@apha.gov.uk

Peter Cargill Wyatt Poultry Services, part of CVS (UK) Ltd., Mortimer Business Park, Hereford, UK. E-mail: peter.cargill@wyattpoultry.com

Vanessa Ceeraz Avian Virology Investigation Unit, Animal and Plant Health Agency-Weybridge, Addlestone, Surrey, UK. E-mail: vanessa.ceeraz@apha.gov.uk

Jens Peter Christensen University of Copenhagen, Department of Veterinary and Animal Sciences, Faculty of Health and Medical Sciences, Frederiksberg, Denmark. E-mail: jpch@sund.ku.dk

Michael Clark School of Veterinary Medicine and Science, University of Nottingham, Sutton Bonington Campus, Loughborough, Leicestershire, UK. E-mail: michael.clark2@nottingham.ac.uk

Jane K.A. Cook Independent Consultant, Huntingdon, Cambridgeshire, UK. E-mail: jane@hough.waitrose.com

Vivien Coward Avian Virology Investigation Unit, Animal and Plant Health Agency-Weybridge, Addlestone, Surrey, UK. E-mail: vivien.coward@apha.gov.uk

Annatachja De Grande Flanders Research Institute for Agriculture, Fisheries and Food, Animal Sciences Unit – Poultry and Rabbit Husbandry, Melle, Belgium. E-mail: annatachja.degrande@ilvovlaanderen.be

Fien De Meyer Livestock Gut Health Team (LiGHT), Department of Pathology, Bacteriology and Avian Diseases, Faculty of Veterinary Medicine, Ghent University, Merelbeke, Belgium.

Evelien Dierick Livestock Gut Health Team (LiGHT), Department of Pathology, Bacteriology and Avian Diseases, Faculty of Veterinary Medicine, Ghent University, Merelbeke, Belgium. E-mail: evelienb.dierick@ugent.be

Richard Ducatelle Livestock Gut Health Team (LiGHT), Department of Pathology, Bacteriology and Avian Diseases, Faculty of Veterinary Medicine, Ghent University, Merelbeke, Belgium. E-mail: richard.ducatelle@ugent.be

Kannan Ganapathy Institute of Infection, Veterinary and Ecology Sciences, University of Liverpool, Leahurst Campus, Neston, Cheshire. E-mail: k.ganapathy@liverpool.ac.uk

Patrick Garland Premier Nutrition, Brereton Business Park, Rugeley, Staffordshire, UK. E-mail: patrick.garland@premiernutrition.co.uk

Evy Goossens Livestock Gut Health Team (LiGHT), Department of Pathology, Bacteriology and Avian Diseases, Faculty of Veterinary Medicine, Ghent University, Merelbeke, Belgium. E-mail: evy.goossens@ugent.be

Hafez Mohamed Hafez Institute of Poultry Diseases, Free University Berlin, Berlin, Germany. E-mail: hafez.mohamed@fu-berlin.de

Rowena Hansen Avian Virology Investigation Unit, Animal and Plant Health Agency-Weybridge, Addlestone, Surrey, UK. E-mail: rowena.hansen@apha.gov.uk

Rüdiger Hauck Department of Pathobiology and Department of Poultry Science, Auburn University, Auburn, Alabama, USA. E-mail: ruediger.hauck@auburn.edu

Grant Hayes Hayes VS Ltd, Little Downham, Ely, Cambridgeshire, UK. E-mail: grant@hayesvs.co.uk

Rikke Heidemann Olsen Department of Veterinary and Animal Science, University of Copenhagen, Frederiksberg, Denmark. E-mail: cava@sund.ku.dk

Richard Jennison Poultry Health Services, Leominster Enterprise Park, Leominster, Herefordshire, UK. E-mail: richard.jennison@poultryhealthservices.com

Michael Jones School of Veterinary Medicine and Science, University of Nottingham, Sutton Bonington, Loughborough, Leicestershire, UK. E-mail: michael.a.jones@nottingham.ac.uk

Richard C. Jones Institute of Infection, Veterinary and Ecological Sciences, University of Liverpool, Leahurst Campus, Neston, Cheshire, UK. E-mail: jonesrc@liverpool.ac.uk

Roberto La Ragione Department of Pathology and Infectious Diseases, School of Veterinary Medicine, University of Surrey, Guildford, UK. E-mail: r.laragione@surrey.ac.uk

Paul McMullin Poultry Health International, Thirsk, North Yorkshire, UK. E-mail: paulmcmullin@poultryhealthinternational.net

Chris Morrow Bioproperties, Ringwood, Victoria, Australia and University of Melbourne, School of Veterinary Science, Victoria, Australia. E-mail: chris.morrow@bioproperties.com.au

Venugopal Nair The Pirbright Institute, Woking, Surrey, UK. E-mail: venugopal.nair@pirbright.ac.uk

David Parsons Poultry Health Centre, Trowbridge, Wiltshire, UK. E-mail: david@poultryhealthcentre.com

Jade Passey Department of Pathology and Infectious Diseases, School of Veterinary Medicine, University of Surrey, Guildford, UK. E-mail: jade.passey@surrey.ac.uk

Androniki Psifidi The Royal Veterinary College, University of London, Hatfield, Hertfordshire, UK. E-mail: apsifidi@rvc.ac.uk

Scott Reid Avian Virology Investigation Unit, Animal and Plant Health Agency-Weybridge, Addlestone, Surrey, UK. E-mail: scott.reid@apha.gov.uk

Joan A. Smyth Department of Pathobiology and Veterinary Science, College of Agriculture, Health and Natural Resources, University of Connecticut, Storrs, Connecticut, USA. E-mail: joan.smyth@uconn.edu

Victoria J. Smyth Avian Virology Unit, Agri-Food and Biosciences Institute (*AFBI*), Stormont, Belfast, UK. E-mail: victoria.smyth@afbini.gov.uk

Barry Thorp St Davids Poultry, Easter Bush Veterinary Centre Roslin, Midlothian, UK. E-mail: barry@stdavids-poultryteam.co.uk

Fiona Tomley Department of Pathobiology and Population Sciences, The Royal Veterinary College, University of London, North Mymms, Hatfield, Hertfordshire, UK. E-mail: ftomley@rvc.ac.uk

Filip Van Immerseel Livestock Gut Health Team (LiGHT), Department of Pathology, Bacteriology and Avian Diseases, Faculty of Veterinary Medicine, Ghent University, Merelbeke, Belgium. E-mail: filip.vanimmerseel@ugent.be

Paul Wigley Department of Infection and Microbiome, IVES, University of Liverpool, Leahurst Campus, Neston, UK. E-mail: wigley@liverpool.ac.uk

Preface

Poultry are one of the most important sources of high-quality meat worldwide for several reasons, including their acceptability to a wide range of cultures and religions, small size and comparative cheapness allowing mass accessibility.

The last few decades have seen great changes in the global poultry industry both economically and geographically and with increasing emphasis on public health in addition to animal health. Production and productivity of the broiler and layer sectors continue to rise, not only in domestic fowl, but increasingly in ducks, turkey, geese and quail.

The centre of gravity of poultry production is inexorably moving east, as standards of living in China and many other regional countries increase, with higher disposable incomes and demand for meat, and also to Brazil and South American countries which are emerging as major exporters. Clearly, these changes bring many advantages in terms of overall human nutrition but may also accompany turbulent changes in local, national and international systems of production and marketing, which can lead to undesirable consequences on the road to progress. Thus, continued production of local birds combined with their sale and slaughter in wet markets, which have been common in the Far East, together with the international movement in humans and animals, has resulted in a number of localized disease outbreaks and the global spread of avian influenza, exacerbated by wild bird migration.

In Asia, intensification and integration of production is increasing and the small producer is fast disappearing, while in Europe and North America intensive production runs in parallel with increased free-range production, as a result of public pressure, combined with increases in backyard hobby/pet birds. These changes increase the risk associated with wild bird contact, frequently exacerbated by – in the case of hobby/pet birds – poor levels of vaccination.

Infection is both a pathological and an evolutionary process which are staple topics for study by poultry veterinarians and researchers, but these processes also ensure that infectious disease problems continue to evolve. This may take the form of natural microbial evolution as occurs with RNA viruses, leading to the appearance of new infectious bronchitis virus strains and avian influenza virus types, or may be expressed as increasing virulence as seen with Marek's disease virus in response to vaccinated hosts. Similarly, widespread use of chemotherapeutic agents to control parasitic and bacterial infections has resulted in extensive resistance, such as that observed in coccidiosis, resulting in the need to manipulate treatment programmes.

The transmissibility of antibiotic resistance in enteric bacteria has been known for more than five decades with huge global concerns for animal welfare and public health as a result of infections becoming increasingly intractable to chemotherapy. This remains an evolving global issue with recent demonstration of transmissible colistin resistance in China followed rapidly by its identification in many other parts of the world. This pressure is leading to some companies rearing birds completely free of antibiotics.

Large outbreaks of food poisoning associated with poultry consumption and increased public pressure in relation to animal welfare have also resulted in increasing national and international legislation to improve these situations. Food-borne pathogens *per se* are a One Health problem, and several countries and the EU have targeted them with some success in the case of *Salmonella*.

The global nature of the industry inevitably has led over the years, via a ripple effect, to changes in one country necessarily being adopted by others.

Working in the poultry industry remains an attractive career decision and it is well known that the emphasis in most veterinary schools on companion animal medicine leaves little room in the curriculum for the extensive training needed for poultry vets to become competent. This deficit affects those entering the intensive poultry world but also veterinarians in private practice who see an increasing number of pet poultry of which they have little experience.

Because of this, the editors realized the need for a readily accessible up-to-date and well-illustrated handbook, rather than a standard text covering all aspects of poultry health. This book will fill a much-needed gap in the market.

There was also a desire amongst the editors to produce a book for the Poultry Health Course, the renowned postgraduate course originally designed for those entering the UK poultry industry, organized first at Houghton Poultry Research Station (Huntingdon), transferred to the Institute for Animal Health (Compton), and most recently run jointly by the Pirbright Institute (Surrey) and the University of Nottingham, School of Veterinary Medicine and Science.

The authors of this book are largely those who have taught on this course, in some cases for almost 40 years, and therefore bring a wealth of expertise in both clinical poultry medicine and research covering the host biology, immune response and genetics, the microbiology, infection biology, epidemiology and control of the pathogens involved, and all relevant aspects of poultry health management.

Paul Barrow
Venugopal Nair
Susan Baigent
Robert Atterbury
Michael Clark

December 2020

1 Basic Anatomy and Physiology

David Parsons*

Poultry Health Centre, Trowbridge, Wiltshire, UK

1.1 Introduction

There are important differences between avian and mammalian anatomy as well as between different avian species. Comparison should be made between the external anatomy of the domestic fowl with that of the domestic turkey, domestic duck and domestic goose. The anatomical differences are matched by adaptations in avian physiology.

Diseases of the alimentary, reproductive and respiratory systems are common. An understanding of the anatomy and physiology of domestic poultry underpins the understanding of the spread of infection within a flock and the pathogenesis of the disease in the individual bird.

The anatomy and physiology of these systems are discussed based on *Gallus gallus domesticus*, the domestic fowl.

1.2 The Respiratory System

The respiratory tract consists of the upper airways: the nostrils, nasal cavity, sinuses and larynx, and lower structures (trachea, lungs and air sacs) (Fig. 1.1).

The nostrils, with the keratinized operculum and cartilaginous lamella, open into the nasal cavity, containing the rostral, middle and caudal conchae. The nasal cavity is separated into two halves by the nasal septum. The choanal cleft is a fissure in the midline of the palate which connects the nasal cavity with the oropharynx. The infraorbital sinus lies laterally and rostroventrally to the eye in the upper jaw. It connects with the nasal cavity ventral to the caudal concha. The nasolacrimal duct opens rostral to the choana and ventral to the middle concha and drains lacrimal secretions from the eye. As in mammals the nasal cavity has important olfaction, air filtration and thermoregulation functions.

Air passes through the choana to the larynx or through the oropharynx in open mouthed breathing to the larynx. The glottis closes reflexly when swallowing to prevent feed entering the trachea. The trachea is made up of about 120 complete signet ring shaped interlocking cartilages that link the larynx to the syrinx which is the voice box and junction with the primary bronchi that connect to the lungs. Branches from the primary bronchi give rise to smaller diameter secondary bronchi, then parabronchi which connects with the atria. The atria are small diverticula that lead to the air capillaries which are the site for gas exchange.

The paired, wedge shaped lungs lie dorsal to the heart. There is no diaphragm. Consequently, the air in the airways of the thoraco-abdomen approximates atmospheric pressure. The lungs are small and non-distensible. The lung can be divided into two parts called the paleopulmo and the neopulmo. In the former, the airflow is unidirectional whilst in the latter it can flow in either direction according to the stage of the respiratory cycle.

The primary bronchus extends to the caudal edge of the lung linking to the ostia from which the abdominal air sac arises. There are nine air sacs in the fowl: a single clavicular and paired cervical, cranial and caudal thoracic and abdominal air sacs (Table 1.1). Their function is ventilation and reducing body weight for flight. The sacs are lined by a single epithelial layer surrounded by connective tissue and are very poorly vascularized. The air sacs arise from secondary bronchi. The exception is the abdominal air sac which has connections with the primary and secondary bronchi.

The cervical air sac lies between the lungs and dorsal to the oesophagus. Diverticula extend into the cervical vertebrae along the neural canal and outside to the level of the axis. The clavicular air sac comprises

*david@poultryhealthcentre.com

© CAB International 2021. *Poultry Health: A Guide for Professionals* (P. Barrow *et al.*)
DOI: 10.1079/9781789245042.0001

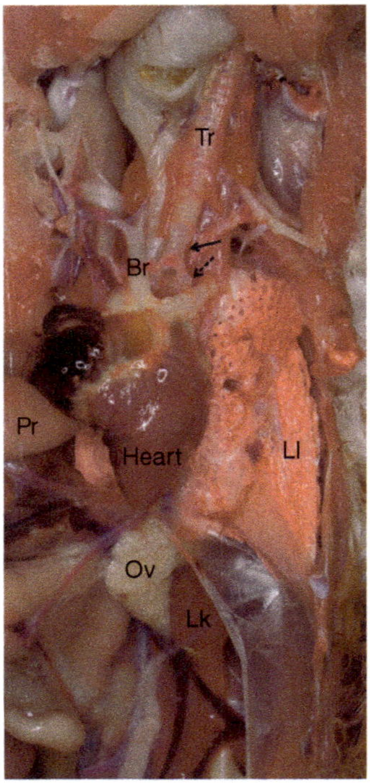

Fig. 1.1. The respiratory tract and other organs visible during initial dissection of the thorax and removal of the rib cage. Tr – trachea; Br – bronchus; L1 – left lung; Pr – proventriculus; Ov – ovary; Lk – left kidney. Small arrow = syrinx. Dotted arrow = primary bronchus. (Author's own image.)

Table 1.1. Air sac volumes in domestic fowl. (Adapted from Sturkie, 1986.)

Air sacs	Volume air (ml) (2.9 kg chicken)
Cervical × 1	20
Clavicular × 1	55
Cranial thoracic × 2	50
Caudal thoracic × 2	24
Abdominal × 2	110
Lungs × 2	35
Skeletal	4
Total	**298**

both intra- (around the heart and along the sternum) and extra-thoracic (between bones and muscles of the thoracic girdle and shoulder joints) diverticula. Oesophagus, syrinx, trachea, associated muscles, nerves and blood vessels are suspended in the clavicular or between the clavicular and cervical air sacs. The cranial and caudal thoracic air sacs have no diverticula. The abdominal air sacs have perirenal diverticula to the kidney, pelvis, synsacrum, free thoracic vertebrae and femoral diverticula to bones and muscles of the pelvic limb.

The poor vascularization and absence of cilia make removal of purulent material and treatment of this area difficult. This also facilitates spread of infection throughout the body via the diverticula or directly across the membrane. Thus, airsacculitis detected at slaughter means rejection of the whole carcass.

The cranial group of air sacs (cervical, clavicular and cranial thoracic) contains almost as much air as the caudal group (caudal thoracic and abdominal). Most respiratory movement occurs caudally. Therefore, on inspiration most air enters the caudal air sacs.

In the domestic fowl, the following are pneumatized: subcutaneous facial planes and between skeletal muscle, humerus, coracoid, sternum, ribs, synsacrum, pelvis, cervical and thoracic vertebrae.

Circulation of air through the respiratory tract requires two breathing cycles. Inspiration draws fresh air into the posterior air sacs (caudal thoracic and abdominal air sacs) and oxygen depleted air into the anterior air sacs (the cervical, clavicular and cranial thoracic air sacs). Expiration pushes fresh air from caudal thoracic and abdominal air sacs into the lungs and oxygen depleted air from the cervical, clavicular and cranial thoracic air sacs into the bronchi and trachea to be breathed out.

It is important to remember that holding a bird upside down or holding a bird too tightly will cause respiratory distress and possibly death.

Breathing (Table 1.2) is controlled by the central nervous system (CNS) with sensory inputs from (i) central chemoreceptors – identified in mammals and probably present in birds; (ii) arterial chemoreceptors; (iii) intrapulmonary chemoreceptors and others including: (iv) air sac mechanoreceptors; (v) thermal receptors in the spinal cord; (vi) upper airway receptors sensitive to irritants, cold and possibly (vii) arterial baroreceptors.

Increasing ambient CO_2 will increase ventilation. However, ventilation is also influenced by exercise, hot or cold temperatures and altitude. There is a balance between the stimulatory and inhibitory drive to ventilate. Hence, in hot weather gular fluttering is important because heat is lost with minimum active ventilation.

Table 1.2. Respiratory parameters in domestic fowl. (Adapted from Sturkie, 1986.)

Species	Weight (kg)	Respirations/min	Haematocrit (%)	Haemoglobin (g%)
Chicken				
Male	4.2	17		
Female	3.4	27	29–45	8.9–12.5
Female	1.6	23		

1.3 The Alimentary System

In addition to its role in nutrition, the alimentary system is also the largest immunological organ (see Chapter 2 this volume) as well as being host to a vast microbiome (see Chapter 17 this volume). The alimentary tract is short and antiperistalsis is an important compensation in digestion. Many growth and developmental changes occur soon after the chick hatches. Managing the development of the alimentary tract to maturity is vital in promoting and maintaining good bird health and welfare. (See Fig. 1.2 for general structure.)

The beak consists of a hard, keratinized epidermal covering which, at its edges, is continually worn away and replaced, and is supplied with extensive sensory innervation, particularly at the tip. The egg tooth is a pointed protuberance on the upper beak which drops off after hatching.

The mouth and pharynx are known as oropharynx. There is no soft palate or pharyngeal isthmus. The choana in the roof of the mouth links oral and nasal cavities. The infundibular cleft behind this is the common opening of the auditory tubes. The salivary glands are located in the roof, cheeks and floor of the mouth. The fowl has about 300 taste buds on the epithelium of the upper beak, and the base and ventrolateral surface on the tongue, with broiler breeds having approximately twice as many as layer breeds.

Food passes along the oesophagus to the crop which is thin walled and distensible. It is a storage organ where bacterial fermentation takes place, reducing the pH to about 4–5.

The proventriculus immediately cranial to the gizzard, produces hydrochloric acid and pepsinogen which is converted to pepsin in the low pH (pH 1–4 depending on food content).

The gizzard (ventriculus) has thick and muscular walls, with a thick yellow to green cuticle on the mucosal surface to protect it from acid and mechanical damage. Finely ground feed – low in fibre – results in poor muscular development while whole grain and high fibre promote good muscular development. Insoluble grit will lodge in the gizzard to facilitate grinding.

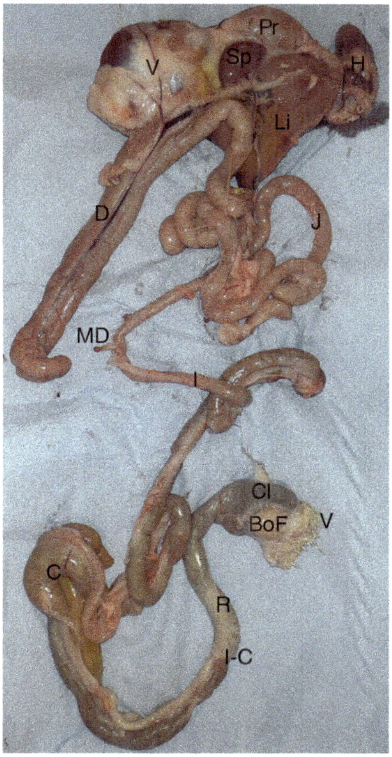

Fig. 1.2. The alimentary tact exposed. Pr – proventriculus; V – ventriculus (gizzard); Sp – spleen; Li – liver; H – heart; D – duodenum; J – jejunum; MD – Meckel's diverticulum; I – ileum; C – caeca; I-C – ileo-caecal junction; R – rectum; Cl – cloaca; BoF – Bursa of Fabricius; V – vent. The crop is not shown but is located immediately caudal to the proventriculus. (Author's own image.)

The U-shaped duodenum is the first section of the small intestine, enclosing the pancreas in the loop and with a pH of 5.7–7.2. The remains of the yolk sac presents as a small stub, Meckel's diverticulum.

which is used as a marker to separate the jejunum from the ileum. Digestion and absorption of carbohydrates, fats, proteins and also water absorption take place in the small intestine.

The large, paired caeca are attached to the intestine via a sphincter at the ileo-rectal junction. A small enlargement in the neck of the caecum is the caecal tonsil which is a lymphoid organ sampling the microorganisms that enter and leave the caeca. The caeca are filled by the convergence of peristaltic contractions from the small intestine and anti-peristaltic contractions from the cloaca and rectum. Liquid only enters the caeca, and the pH varies from 5.7 to 9. The caeca evacuate between one and twelve times daily. Its function is unclear since birds thrive after its removal but some hind-gut fermentation and water reabsorption are thought to take place.

The short rectum has a role in water conservation and carries urine to the caeca by antiperistalsis.

The cloaca is relatively complex for its size with the coprodeum separated from the urodeum which is the smallest chamber into which the urinary and reproductive tracts empty. This is separated by the uroproctodeal fold from the proctodeum which has an external opening through the vent. In the juvenile there is an opening dorsally to the Bursa of Fabricus, the important immunological organ where B cells mature (see Chapter 2 this volume).

Two important additional organs involved in nutrition are the liver and pancreas. The liver is a key organ manufacturing carbohydrates, proteins and fats and is important in detoxification. It also generates heat, raising normal body temperature to 41.5°C for chickens. The body temperatures of turkeys and ducks are similar.

The gall bladder produces bile, aiding lipid uptake, and contains amylase from 4 to 8 weeks of age.

Sick birds that are not eating often have enlarged gall bladders and may excrete green droppings. The green colour in droppings is due to biliverdin. Fowl have very little or no biliverdin reductase for conversion to bilirubin. Brown caecal droppings are possibly due to bacterial breakdown of biliverdin to bilirubin.

The pancreas secretes a number of digestive enzymes and sodium bicarbonate. In the fowl, three pancreatic ducts open into the distal end of the ascending loop of the duodenum on a papilla with the bile ducts.

Transit time depends on whether soluble or insoluble markers are used. Larger insoluble particles are retained longer in the digestive tract. First feed through the digestive tract can be detected in 1.6–2.6 hours but normally the mean retention time is between 5 and 9 hours (Scanes, 2015). Retention time increases with age, amount of fat or protein in the diet and high temperature, whilst cold decreases retention time. Intestinal motility also shows diurnal variation, increasing during the day.

Once hatched, the chick changes from a fat to a carbohydrate-based diet. Early feeding after hatching encourages increased length, weight and enzyme activity when compared to unfed chicks. Villus growth in the duodenum is maximal by 7 days of age and 14 days, at the earliest, for the jejunum and ileum. Enterocyte proliferation occurs along the length of the villus. Migration of enterocytes to the tip of the villus takes about 3 days in four-day-old chicks and 4 days in older chicks.

Absorption of nutrients is not dissimilar to mammals. Volatile fatty acids and uric acid are fermentation products from the caeca.

1.4 Reproductive System

Broilers and layers are genetically different with layers producing high egg numbers on minimal feed consumption and broilers showing rapid growth and good egg production by the parents. Both require different husbandry and management. Parent flocks comprise between 7 and 12% males depending on flock age.

The development and control of the normal functioning of the reproductive tract of the laying hen is affected by a complex combination of factors including temperature, day length, feed and water supply, and the neuroendocrine functions of the hypothalamic–pituitary–gonadal axis.

Unlike mammals, the sex can be reversed prior to gonad differentiation by inhibiting oestrogen production in genetic females resulting in testes development. Temperature during incubation does not determine sex.

Primordial germ cells can be found in the right and left gonads by 2.5 days of egg incubation. Differentiation of the gonads occurs between 6.5 and 7 days. In the male and female, the left gonad is larger. The left ovary and oviduct develop and right ovary regresses. The oviduct consists of the infundibulum, magnum, isthmus, shell gland and vagina. Because there is no connection between the ovary and the oviduct, ova can miss the infundibulum, but these are usually absorbed in the following

48–72 hours, or may be caught by the infundibulum at the next ovulation resulting in double-yolked eggs. But they may also become infected giving rise to egg peritonitis.

1.4.1 Control of sexual maturity and egg laying

The development of sexual maturity and persistence of egg laying is the result of complex interactions between circannual and circadian rhythms, environmental entrainment factors (predominantly photoperiod but also temperature, feed and water availability) and physiological age.

Day length increases at the onset of spring which stimulates reproductive behaviour until the saturation day length is reached. For fowl, the critical and saturation day lengths are about 10 and 15 hours. Chicks are insensitive to day lengths (photorefractory) and modern commercial layers and broiler breeders show significant deviations from these patterns. Selection for egg numbers and the lack of broodiness in commercial layers has resulted in almost complete loss of photorefractoriness. Broiler breeders require restricting feed which delays the dissipation of juvenile photorefractoriness. Commercial husbandry and lighting practices are optimized for the different types of poultry to ensure appropriate physiological development, the best welfare and good production for flocks derived from chicks hatched at any time of the year.

1.4.2 Perception of light

The avian skull is translucent and allows light to penetrate the brain. Photoreceptors are found in the retinae, pineal gland and encephalic photoreceptors situated in the lateral septal organ (LSO), preoptic area and tuberal and mediobasal hypothalamus (MBH). The relative importance of these areas in controlling the reproductive circadian clock is probably species specific. The pineal photoreceptors are sensitive to short and long wavelength light whilst the LSO and MBH on the base of the brain are more sensitive to the long wavelengths. Thus, using orange or red lights to control cannibalism has minimal effect on egg production.

1.4.3 Circadian rhythms

The production of melatonin does not seem to entrain the reproductive photoperiodic response. In fowl, there is a specific period during the circadian rhythm which in fowl occurs about 11.5 hours after dawn, the photoinducible phase. Photostimulation during this phase triggers gonadotrophin releasing hormone (GnRH) resulting in gonad development.

1.4.4 The egg laying cycle

When photostimulated between 16 and 18 weeks of age, all birds in the flock respond and mature sexually together. The increased day length allows the photostimulation during the photoinducible phase of the circadian clock triggering release of GnRH from neurons in the MBH. GnRH triggers release of luteinizing hormone (LH) and follicle stimulating hormone (FSH), produced in the pituitary, that promotes maturation of the testes and ovary. Oestrogens and androgens stimulate the development of the secondary sexual characteristics, both physical and behavioural.

About 2 weeks later the first eggs are laid. Hens are indeterminate layers; if the egg laid one day is removed then she will lay another to replace it. The presence of a cockerel is not needed to stimulate hens to lay. The number of eggs laid in a sequence reflects the time taken to form a shelled egg. The closer to 24 hours, the shorter the time from ovulation to oviposition and the longer the sequence will be. The term sequence is preferred to clutch, the latter being reserved for non-domesticated species, because of the large numbers of eggs laid on consecutive days and the absence of incubation and brooding.

It takes time for the circadian clocks within the brain, ovary and oviduct to become entrained. Thus, for the first two weeks or so after commencement of lay, thin shelled eggs, membrane eggs and double or triple-yolked eggs may be laid.

Ovulation is preceded by an increase in LH, 4 to 6 hours earlier. The LH surge is promoted by an increase in progesterone. There is only one LH surge a day and hence only one egg is laid a day.

The first egg of a sequence is usually laid early in the photophase. Ovulation of the next ovum occurs 15–75 minutes after oviposition. Thus, the egg tends to be laid about an hour later each day associated with an LH surge occurring later during the LH sensitive period known as the 'open period'. Eventually, the next ovulation would be associated with an LH surge that is outside the 'open period'. In this situation, the LH surge does not occur and

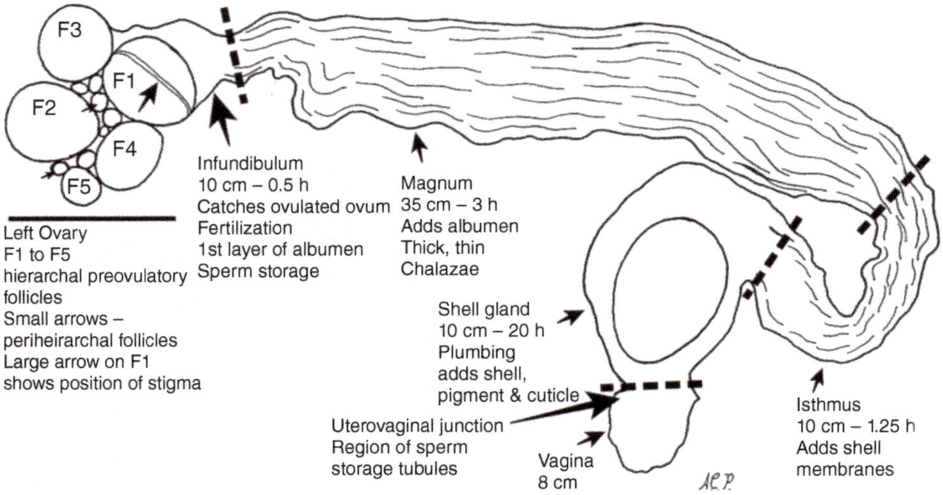

Fig. 1.3. Cartoon of reproductive tract. (Produced by and with permission of A. Parsons.)

the hen does not lay the next day but resumes the day after with the LH surge being associated with the beginning of the 'open period' and the sequence repeats.

Egg formation takes 24 to 28 hours. After ovulation, the ovum (Fig. 1.4) is engulfed by the infundibulum (Fig. 1.3) where the egg will be fertilized, if mating has occurred.

The first albumen is deposited here before the egg passes into the magnum to be coated with more albumen. In the isthmus the egg membranes are formed. On entering the shell gland water is added to the albumen, a process known as plumping, which stretches the egg membranes allowing them to act as a template for the deposition of the eggshell.

Approximately 2–2.5 g of calcium is transported by the shell gland to calcify each egg. Most calcification occurs over night when the hen is not feeding. Whilst most calcium comes from the feed. A proportion (30–40%) of the eggshell calcium is supplied by medullary bone.

Finally, the egg enters the vagina, and under the influence of arginine vasotocin (AVT), oviposition occurs.

Following mating in a breeding flock, spermatozoa become motile and are stored in specialized storage tubules at the uterovaginal junction. Viability is maintained for 7–14 days. Following oviposition, the sperm migrate to storage glands in the infundibulum or directly fertilize the ovum.

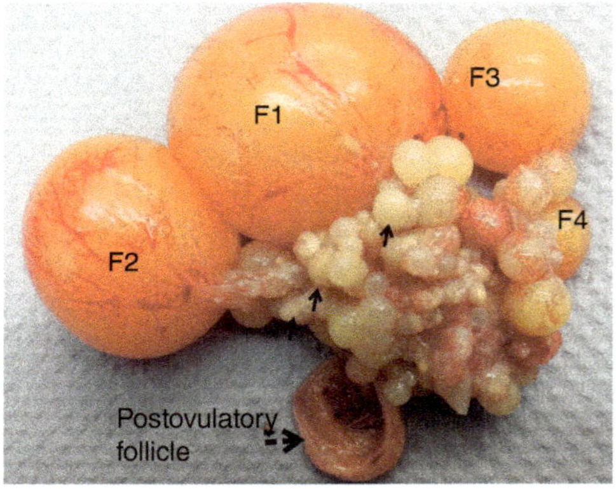

Fig. 1.4. Ovary from laying hen showing follicles F1–F4 in reverse order of maturity. Arrows = small white follicles. (Author's own image.)

Flock egg numbers decrease towards the end of the laying cycle. As the hen ages, fewer follicles are selected into the preovulatory hierarchy and there is an increase in follicle atresia. Fewer follicles receive more yolk and are therefore bigger. The maturation of each follicle also takes longer. This means that the number of eggs in a sequence decreases, and relatively, the number of non-laying days increases coupled with more first sequence eggs that generally have poor shells. As the amount of calcium deposited on each egg remains relatively constant through the laying period, larger eggs will have thinner shells. Consequently, both egg numbers and shell quality decrease with age.

1.5 References

Scanes, C.G. (2015) *Sturkie's Avian Physiology*, 6th edn. Elsevier, London.

Sturkie, P.D. (1986) *Avian Physiology*, 4th edn. Springer-Verlag, New York.

1.6 Further Reading

Bar, A. (2008) Calcium homeostasis and vitamin D metabolism and expression in strongly calcifying laying birds. *Comparative Biochemistry and Physiology Part A* 151, 477–490.

King, A.S. and McLelland, J. (1984) *Birds: Their Structure and Function,* 2nd edn. Baillier Tindall, London.

Lewis, P. and Morris, T. (2006) *Poultry Lighting: The Theory and Practice.* Cambridge University Press, Cambridge, UK.

Nakane, Y. and Takashi, Y. (2018) Seasonal reproduction: photoperiodism, birds. In: Swanson, P and Skinner, M.K. (eds) *Encyclopedia of Reproduction, 2nd edn*, vol. 6. Elsevier, Oxfore, UK, pp. 409–414.

Piper, H. (1887) *Piper's Poultry: A Practical Guide to the Choice, Breeding, Rearing, and Management of All Descriptions of Fowls, Turkeys, Guinea Fowls, Ducks and Geese for Profit and Exhibition*, 5th edn. Groombridge and Sons, London.

Rose, S.P. (1997) *Principles of Poultry Science*. CAB International, Wallingford, UK.

Scanes, C.G. (2015) *Sturkie's Avian Physiology*, 6th edn. Elsevier, London.

2 The Immune System of the Chicken

Paul Wigley*

Department of Infection and Microbiome, IVES, University of Liverpool, Leahurst Campus, Neston, UK

2.1 Introduction

Avian species, of which the chicken is by far the most studied, have a complex immune system that protects against a range of pathogen challenges and which we can exploit to protect against infection through vaccination. Modern mammals and birds are separated by more than 200 million years of evolutionary divergence, so it is perhaps not surprising that although the structure and function of the avian immune system are largely similar to that of humans and mice there are differences that reflect their evolutionary separation. Our knowledge of avian immunology has largely been driven by the development of vaccines to protect the billions of birds reared each year for meat and eggs. As such, our understanding of immune responses is somewhat biased towards commercially important viral and parasitic infections and to foodborne bacteria such as *Salmonella* that may be carried in the chicken's intestinal tract. In recent years there have been more studies on other domesticated species including turkeys and ducks, though our knowledge of other bird species immune systems is limited.

2.2 Overview of the Chicken Immune Response

As in other species, the chicken has broad non-specific intrinsic defences against infection that do not require prior exposure to an infectious agent that we term innate immunity. These can range from simple physical barriers, to secreted antimicrobials through to cells that act to kill invaders. The immune system also has the ability to produce specific cell and antibody responses that have memory that we term adaptive immunity. In general terms innate immunity is rapid and non-specific and does not offer improved protection against the same agent following re-infection, whereas adaptive responses are slower to initiate but offer a much more specific response that is often effective in preventing re-infection. It is this memory or anamnestic response that is the basis of vaccination.

Whilst the overall nature of the mammalian and avian immune response is the same, there are some fundamental differences. In general, the avian immune system is more compact, with less polymorphism in major receptors and fewer classes of antibody. This may seem an unusual strategy in potentially leaving the host more open to infection, but equally it can be argued that the chicken immune system is well-suited to the host, avoiding some of the functional redundancy of the mammalian immune system with a lower physiological cost to the host by reducing some of the complexity.

2.3 Structure of the Avian Immune System

The structure of the avian immune system (Olah *et al.*, 2014) differs somewhat from mammals. The two key differences are the specific primary lymphoid organ the bursa of Fabricius which is the site of B lymphocyte development and the absence of distinct encapsulated peripheral lymph nodes, though in some species such as ducks there are rudimentary structures.

Haematopoesis takes place in bone marrow and foetal liver, with development of T lymphocytes taking place in the thymus and B lymphocyte

*wigley@liverpool.ac.uk

© CAB International 2021. *Poultry Health: A Guide for Professionals* (P. Barrow *et al.*)
DOI: 10.1079/9781789245042.0002

development taking place in the bursa of Fabricius. The bursa is located at the end of the gut near to the cloaca, the common opening for the avian gastrointestinal and urogenitary systems. It is a highly folded structure containing multiple follicles of B lymphocyte development. Haematopoetic stem cells migrate to the bursa from the foetal liver to differentiate and develop into B lymphocytes. The bursa is an active lymphoid organ *in ovo* and in chicks, but atrophies within the first 6 months of life.

The avian secondary lymphoid system differs considerably from mammals, with birds lacking distinct encapsulated peripheral lymph nodes. The avian spleen and liver perform broadly similar functions to mammals as major secondary lymphoid tissues. The structure of the avian spleen is similar to that of mammals though the areas of red pulp, white pulp and the marginal zones are less well defined. The avian spleen also possesses a closed circulatory system. It is the largest lymphoid tissue associated with the generation of systemic immune responses. Germinal centres are follicular structures of B cell development and maturation. In the red pulp, along with the erythrocyte population, are scattered lymphocytes and macrophages. Specialist macrophages called Kupfer cells in the liver are important in phagocytosis of dead cells, cellular fragments and pathogens.

The chicken possesses a number of distinct lymphoid organs in the Harderian gland and the caecal tonsils, the latter of which are small lymphoid structures found at the ileal–caecal junction. Although there are no lymph nodes in the sense found in mammals, for example no distinct Peyer's patch structures in the gut, birds do appear to form looser lymphoid aggregates in the gut and reproductive tract. There is a suggestion that this looser structure allows for a more flexible response to mucosal infection. The Harderian gland is located within the orbit behind the eye and with conjunctiva-associated lymphoid tissue in the lower eyelid forms a distinct eye-associated lymphoid structure. This eye-associated tissue is exploited through the use of eye-drop vaccination. The immune system within the respiratory tract is poorly understood, whilst there are clear lymphoid structures associated with the nasal cavity and bronchus, lung structures are ill defined. In common with mammals are the presence of alveolar macrophages and secreted IgA antibodies in the lungs.

2.4 Cells and Effectors of the Chicken Immune System

2.4.1 Myeloid cells

Heterophils

Heterophils are the most common circulating leukocyte in the chicken. This polymorphonuclear (PMN) cell is the broad equivalent of the mammalian neutrophil and is the main professional phagocytic cell of the avian immune system. Heterophils are a key first line of defense to infection and are efficient phagocytes that are capable of killing pathogens effectively. They survive a short time in circulation.

Monocytes and macrophages

Circulating monocytes and resident macrophages survive much longer than heterophils, up to 80 days following release from bone marrow. They are phagocytic cells that kill pathogens and also act as important antigen-presenting cells with Class II major histocompatibility complex (MHC) expressed on their surface and play a key role in the directing and activating the adaptive immune response through their repertoire of cytokines.

Dendritic cells

Dendritic cells (DCs) are derived from the same myeloid lineage as macrophages. DCs act as professional antigen-presenting cells and also function as accessory cells in adaptive and innate immune responses. Mature DCs primarily reside in lymphoid tissue with several subsets described. Follicular DCs are found primarily around germinal centres and play a key role in presentation to B cells. Interdigitating DCs are found in areas such as the peri-arteriolar lymphoid sheath (PALS) in the spleen and are mostly associated with presentation to T cells. The related Langerhan's cells are antigen-presenting cells (APCs) located in the squamous epithelial layer of the skin. Bursal secreted DCs are found in the bursa and are key to B lymphocyte maturation (Nagy *et al.*, 2016), thymic DCs are also found, but their role is not clear.

Thrombocytes

Thrombocytes, like platelets, have a primary function in haemostasis or blood clotting. Avian thrombocytes are cellular and phagocytic, expressing MHC Class II on their surface. They appear to share basic functions of macrophages both as APCs and in response to infection (Ferdous *et al.*, 2016).

2.4.2 Lymphoid cells

T lymphocytes

T lymphocytes (Smith and Gobel, 2014) are named as they maturate in the thymus. The main T cell receptor is the T cell receptor (TCR). In the chicken there are three TCR variants, αβ1 and αβ2 and γδ. αβ T lymphocytes are those associated with classical adaptive antigen-specific responses, whereas γδ T cells play a bridging role between innate and adaptive immunity.

T lymphocytes play a key role in the development of both humoral (antibody) and cellular adaptive immunity. Broadly all T cells express the CD3 receptor whilst T cells with the CD8 receptor primarily act as cytolytic T cells (CTL) killing infected cells and bind to MHC Class I (MHC Class I restricted). $CD4^+$ cells are associated with acting as T helper (Th) cells directing the immune response into cellular (Th1) and humoral responses (Th2). Regulatory T cells control inflammatory responses and Th17 T cells are key sentinels in protecting mucosal surfaces, wound repair and may be associated with some inflammatory conditions in mammals.

B lymphocytes

B lymphocytes are named from their primary lymphoid organ, the bursa of Fabricius. The main role of B lymphocytes is the production of antibodies, although they may play other regulatory roles and act as antigen presenting cells. The B cell receptor is surface-bound immunoglobulin. B cells mature to form antibody-secreting plasma cells. Like αβ T cells, B cells are antigen specific.

NK cells

Natural killer (NK) cells are large granular lymphocytes that are not antigen specific, and primarily act to kill cells with altered MHC Class I expression.

2.5 Cytokines

Cytokines are small proteins that signal between cells and tissues of the immune system. They are produced by a range of cells and act via receptors on the cell surface to turn cellular functions on and off, to signal for recruitment of cells and the release of inflammatory mediators. Cytokines include interferons, interleukins and small cytokines such as chemokines which are sometimes classified separately. The simplest way to classify cytokines is by their main function, whether pro-inflammatory, regulatory, Th1, Th2 or Th17 as summarized in Table 2.1.

Table 2.1. Major functional groups of cytokines in the chicken.

Cytokine function	Examples	Comments
Pro-inflammatory	IL-1 β, Tumour necrosis factor (TNF) IL-6 Chemokines e.g. CxCLi1, CxCLi2	Produced by multiple cells types Immune activation and inflammation
Macrophage activation	Interferon-γ (IFN-γ)	Produced by NK cells and epithelial lymphocytes as well as Th1 cells
T cell activation	Interleukin-2	Activation of all T cell subsets
Th1	IFN-γ TNF	Activation of CTLs and macrophages
B cell activation/Th2	IL-4 IL-13	
Th17	IL-17 family IL-21	Not fully characterized in chicken
Regulatory/anti-inflammatory	IL-10 family TGF-β family	IL-10 also produced by Th2 cells
Antiviral	Class I (α) and III (κ) interferons	Direct effect and activation of antiviral proteins e.g. viperin

In general, the cytokine repertoire function of the chicken is similar to that of mammals (Kaiser *et al.*, 2005) but several of the key cytokine families have fewer members in the chicken.

2.6 Antibodies

Antibodies are made up of glycoproteins called immunoglobulins. The basic structure is a 'Y' shaped molecule made up of Fc (crystalline fragment) of heavy chains and a Fab (antigen binding fragment) made up of heavy and light chains that branch from the hinge regions. The Fc region possesses a receptor (FcR) that allows phagocytic cells to bind to the antibody. Chickens produce three classes of immunoglobulin. IgM is first produced around 3–4 days after challenge (Ratcliffe and Hartle, 2014). It has relatively low affinity but has a pentameric form with the monomers joined by a 'J' chain and the base of the Fc region which means it is highly efficient at opsonization and fixing complement proteins. IgY is the main class of antibody which is analogous in function to IgG and sometimes labelled as such. IgY has greater affinity and avidity than IgG being highly antigen specific and starts to be produced in increasing amounts around 7 days after challenge. High levels of IgY may also be found in egg yolk and as maternally transferred antibodies in newly hatched chicks. Unlike mammalian IgG, there are no subclasses of IgY. The final immunoglobulin, IgA, which can be found as a monomer but more usually as a secreted dimeric form, is strongly associated with protection at mucosal surfaces.

Antibodies act as the surface receptor of B cells but are also secreted by B cells that have differentiated into plasma cells. Each B cell clone is specific for an individual amino acid epitope. During infection, clonal expansion of antigen-specific B cells occurs that leads to a polyclonal response recognizing multiple antigens of a pathogen. Antibodies protect in a number of ways. They can fix complement via the classical pathway, they may opsonize a pathogen to improve phagocytosis, they may bind phagocytic cells via the FcR which in turn kill the pathogen in a process known as antibody-dependent cell-mediated cytotoxicity, or they may bind to the pathogen surface that prevents it interacting with host cells or binding to cell receptors. This last form of protection is known as a neutralizing antibody and is of particular importance during the response to viral infection.

2.7 Complement

The complement system is a protein cascade system that acts to complement adaptive immunity via the classical pathway or act directly as part of the innate immune system through the alternative pathway. Complement proteins act to bind to pathogens through a mechanism called opsonization that assists in phagocytosis, it can enhance inflammation and acts to kill pathogens through the development of a membrane attack complex (MAC) that disrupts their outer membrane.

The classical pathway is triggered through binding and crosslinking of antibodies with components of the complement system. The alternative pathway is triggered directly through binding to the surface of a pathogen.

2.8 The Immune Response

2.8.1 Innate immunity

Innate immunity is formed of natural barriers, secreted antimicrobials and cells that form the first line of defence to infection. In general, innate immunity lacks 'memory', but there is increasing evidence that prior exposure to some pathogens or vaccines gives rise to a phenomenon called 'trained immunity' in macrophages and NK cells which react more effectively to re-exposure, though much shorter in duration than a classical memory response. The basis of innate immunity in the chicken is summarized in Fig. 2.1.

The simplest protection offered by the host is providing a physical barrier to infection. On mucosal surfaces such as the gut, there are tight junctions between epithelial cells that prevent pathogen entry. In the respiratory tract, mucociliary clearance of pathogens inhibits most infections. Physical barriers also include the acidic pH of the proventriculus and gizzard and lachrymal secretion on the surface of the eyes. In recent years it has also become apparent that the host microbiome, the ecosystem of microbes inhabiting the skin, gut, respiratory tract etc., plays a role in the inhibiting the colonization of pathogens. This is most clearly seen in the intestinal tract where a large population of bacteria can inhibit pathogenic bacteria by competing for nutrients, production of metabolites such as butyrate that are toxic to other species and simply through the physical occupation of a niche through a phenomenon called competitive exclusion. There

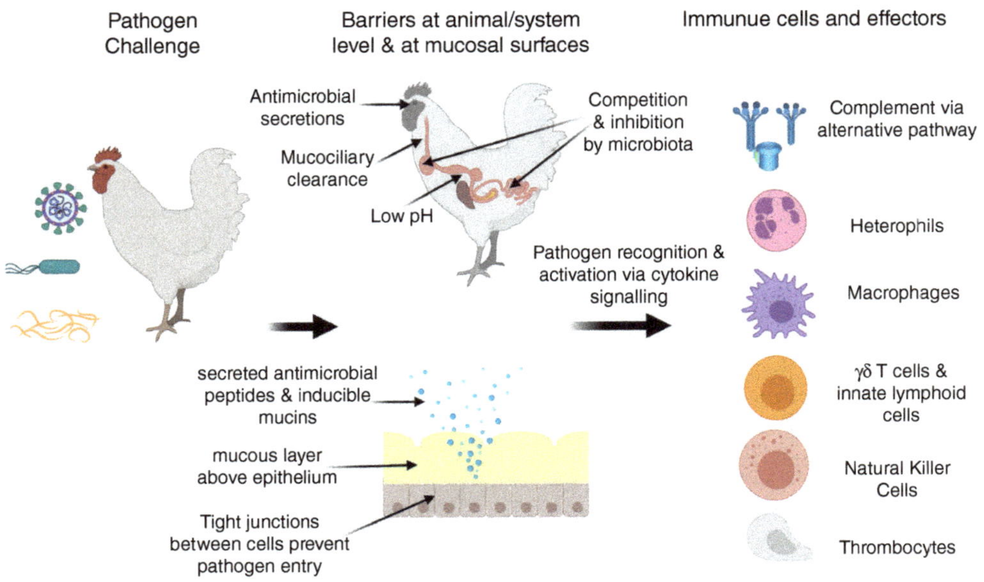

Fig. 2.1. The basis of innate immunity in the chicken. (Author's own work.)

is a growing body of evidence that the microbiome is also a key to immune development and regulation (Broom and Kogut, 2018).

Secretions produced by the bird can also act to inhibit and even kill pathogens. The simplest of these are lysozymes in lachrymal secretions. Many cells secret mucins which are glycoproteins that form a key component of mucus forming a gel structure that can prevent pathogen attachment to epithelial tissues. Some are constitutively produced, though other mucins can be induced as part of an adaptive response. Birds also produce a range of antimicrobial peptides in response to infection including cathelicidins and the β-defensins or gallinacins. β-defensins are also a major mechanism by which heterophils kill pathogens but are also secreted from the respiratory and intestinal epithelium against infection. They are also produced in the female reproductive tract in response to *Salmonella* challenge and specific ovodefensins are also secreted from the oviduct into developing eggs to protect against pathogen growth (Yoshimura, 2015).

If a pathogen penetrates physical barriers, then a range of myeloid and lymphoid cells along with the complement system, via the alternative and lectin activation pathways, may act to protect the host. To activate the response a host must be able to recognize pathogen 'danger' through pattern recognition receptors that bind to conserved molecular patterns of pathogens. These receptors, such as Toll-like receptors (TLR), are highly conserved between species, their structure and function being largely similar to that of mammals (Keestra *et al.*, 2013). The main chicken TLRs and their ligands are shown in Table 2.2.

Whereas TLRs are largely expressed on the cell surface or within intracellular vesicles, a number of cytosolic receptors are also found in chickens including NOD-like receptors and Rig-1-like receptors. A similar array of these receptors are described in ducks.

Recognition via TLRs leads to activation of immune responses through downstream cytokine signalling.

The myeloid cells, heterophils and macrophages, are effective phagocytes and their function has been largely characterized in response to *Salmonella* infection. Depletion of the heterophil population leaves birds highly susceptible to salmonellosis showing their key function in innate protection. Heterophils are thought to kill mainly through the action of antimicrobial peptides but may also produce toxic compounds such as oxidases. They express a range of TLRs on their surface to recognize pathogens. They may also produce extracellular traps, which are akin to a fishing net, to capture bacteria for phagocytosis.

Macrophages are both key effector cells acting as phagocytes and killing through oxidases, superoxides, peroxidases and nitrogen oxide, and as key signalling

Table 2.2. Toll-like receptors (TLR) and other pattern recognition receptors in the chicken.

Receptor	Ligand	Pathogen type recognized
Membrane surface		
TLR2/1	Lipoprotein	Bacteria, protozoa, fungi, virus
TLR4	Lipopolysaccharide (LPS)	Gram negative bacteria
TLR5	Flagellin	Bacteria
TLR15	Protease	Unknown
TLR21	CpG DNA (unmethylated DNA)	Bacteria
Vesicles		
TLR3	dsRNA	Virus
TLR7	ssRNA	Virus
TLR8	ssRNA	Non-functional (pseudogene)
Cytoplasmic		
MDA5 (RIG)	dsRNA	Virus
LPG2 (RIG)	dsRNA	Virus
NOD1	Peptidoglycan	Bacteria
NOD2	Peptidoglycan	Bacteria

cells in activating adaptive immunity through cytokines and as antigen presenting cells. They also play a key 'housekeeping' role in phagocytosis of dead cells and debris.

Natural killer (NK) cells appear to function in birds as they do in mammals. These lymphoid-derived cells function as part of the innate immune system by attacking cells that show an 'altered self' including tumour cells which gave rise to their name and virally-infected cells that show reduced expression of MHC Class I molecules on their surface. NK cells contain cytotoxic granules to kill affected cells directly, can induce apoptosis (programmed cell death) of cells through binding to Fas ligand or can activate a CTL response. The latter of these is important in the activation of anti-viral responses.

γδ T cells are more numerous in birds than many mammalian species and are largely associated with epithelial sites including the gut and the reproductive tract. They have been shown to play an important role in the initiation of cellular responses during *Salmonella* infection (Braukmann *et al.*, 2015). γδ T cells are very much a bridge between innate and adaptive immunity as they possess invariant receptors and are involved in the rapid response to pathogens but are considered to display immunological memory and receptor re-arrangements that are associated with the adaptive response. The function of the large numbers of these cells associated with mucosal tissues especially as they form a large proportion of intraepithelial lymphocytes (IELs) is not yet described, though it is tempting to speculate they are important as an early response to infection and in a sentinel/Th17 role.

2.8.2 Adaptive immunity

MHC and antigen presentation

The major histocompatibility complex (MHC) is a group of polymorphic or variable genes that encode cell surface receptors that present antigens, or more specifically short peptide epitopes, to lymphocytes in the development of adaptive immune responses. The chicken genomic MHC or B locus is considered to be the 'minimal essential MHC' (Kaufman *et al.*, 1999) being considerably more compact than its human equivalent the HLA locus. There are two main forms of classical MHC molecules. MHC Class I molecules bind and present peptides derived from within the cytoplasm (endogenously derived) and are found on most nucleated cell types and are recognized by CD8+, usually cytotoxic, T lymphocytes (CTL). Class II molecules are found only on professional antigen presenting cells like dendritic cells and macrophages. MHC Class II molecules present peptides processed in intracellular vesicles (exogenously derived) to CD4+, mainly helper, T lymphocytes. As such, class I-restricted CTLs act primarily to kill virally-infected cells whereas Class II restricted T helper cells act to induce adaptive responses including antibody production. MHC molecules on the surface of cells are protein heterodimers that form a groove to allow binding of the peptide epitope to the MHC molecule. There is a degree of fit for a peptide based on a series of binding ‘pockets’ in the groove. The peptide bound in the groove is presented to the T cell receptor on the surface of the T lymphocyte.

A consequence of the compact nature of the chicken MHC is the strong linkage between MHC haplotype and resistance or susceptibility to infectious disease most closely seen with Marek’s disease virus (MDV).

Antigen presentation and the role of T lymphocytes

During infection pathogens are taken up by APCs following activation by cytokines produced by the innate response and antigens are processed and expressed in the groove of MHC Class II molecules which bind to naïve T helper (or Th0) cells via the TCR with $CD4^+$ as a co-receptor which helps stabilize the binding. The T helper cells are activated by binding and driven to differentiate into Th1, Th2, Th17 or Treg by the combinations of cytokines produced by APCs and bystander cells (Fig. 2.2).

IL-12 is the main cytokine that drives differentiation into Th1 cells and IL-4 drives the differentiation into Th2 cells. Th1 cells produce inflammatory cytokines and interferon gamma (Interferon γ, IFN gamma, IFN-γ) that lead to the cellular response through macrophage activation and the clonal expansion of antigen-specific cytotoxic lymphocytes (CTLs). These CTLs recognize endogenous antigen presented by MHC class I on cells and act to kill them through the release of compounds such as cytolysins.

Differentiation into Th2 cells drives humoral responses through production of cytokines such as IL-4 and IL-13 that lead to B cell expansion and maturation to produce antibody responses. Th2 cells may also produce regulatory cytokines such as IL-10 that ‘switch off’ inflammatory Th1 responses. Th2 cells are primarily associated with protection against extracellular pathogens.

Th17 cells are a more recently described helper T cell. They are often associated with inflammatory conditions in humans, but their main function appears to be protection at mucosal surfaces where they play a regulatory role when stimulated by members of the microbiome such as segmented filamentous bacteria, but an inflammatory role when stimulated by pathogenic bacteria or fungi. They are named as they are the main producers of IL-17 and related cytokines. Their role in chickens is only

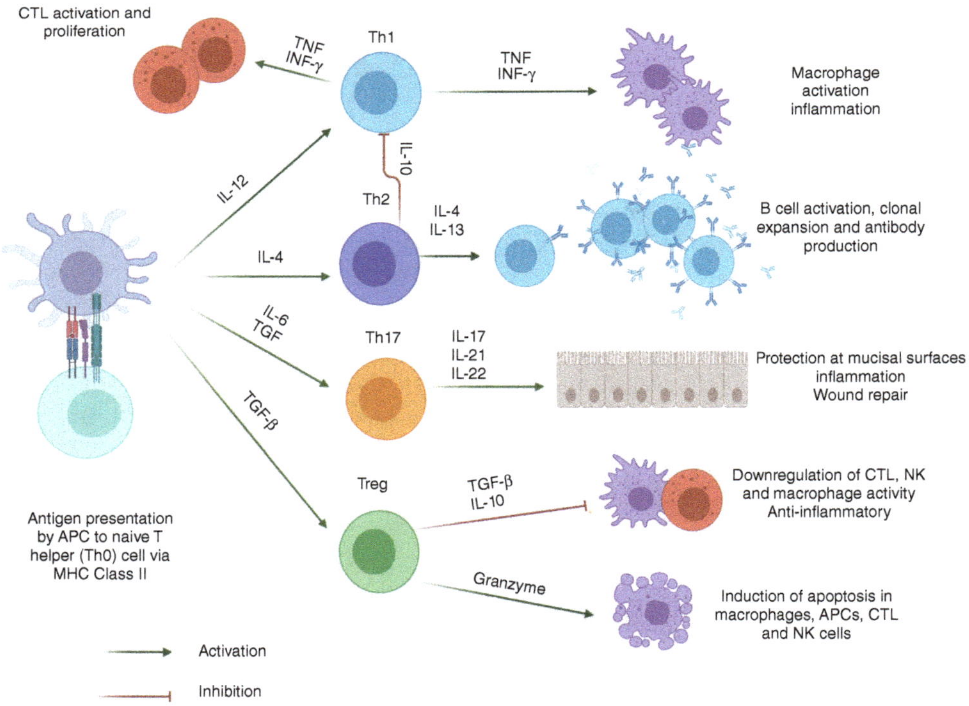

Fig. 2.2. The main roles of T helper subsets in the activation and regulation of immunity. (Author’s own work.)

just beginning to be explored but have been found to play key roles in *Eimeria* and *Campylobacter jejuni* infections (Reid *et al.*, 2016; Kim *et al.*, 2019). Th17 cells are able to recruit macrophages and heterophils to kill extracellular pathogens and act as 'sentinels' in the gut maintaining a barrier, leading to increased expression of tight junction proteins and the production of mucins and antimicrobial peptides.

T regulatory cells

Regulatory T cells (Tregs) formerly called suppressor T cells play a key role in modulating immunity through controlling inflammatory responses and preventing autoimmunity and immune responses to microbiota. Immune responses are regulated through the release of cytokines including TGF-β4 and IL-10 that reduce inflammatory responses (Humphrey *et al.*, 2014). Tregs also regulate effector cells such as CTLs and antigen presenting cells through a range of mechanisms including induction of apoptosis.

Cytotoxic T cell responses

CTL responses are driven via Th1 cytokines. Naïve $CD8^+$ cytotoxic T cells bind to a specific antigen presented via MHC Class1 along with co-involvement of an antigen-presenting cell and differentiate and expand to form a large population of antigen specific CTLs that directly recognize infected or altered cells via Class I MHC. CTLs produce cytokines including IFN-gamma and TNF-alpha that have antimicrobial effects together with inflammatory effects that can lead to pathology. CTLs also release cytotoxic compounds into infected cells from their granules. CTLs also activate caspases within host cells that lead to apoptosis through the 'death receptor' Fas–Fas ligand binding. CTLs are capable of moving from infected cell to infected cell using repeated killing mechanisms. CTLs are highly important in killing intracellular pathogens, most notably viruses.

Antibody responses

B cells may be activated by Th2 cells in lymphoid tissue or through direct binding of the surface expressed IgM. This leads to migration to germinal centres where differentiation of B cells into plasma cells and rapid clonal expansion of the B cell to produce daughter cells occurs. During clonal expansion, mutation and gene re-arrangement lead to development of antibodies/receptors with increased antigen affinity. Upon initial infection IgM antibodies are produced, but usually a process called clonal selection selects clones of higher antigenic specificity that expand and produce the higher affinity IgY and IgA antibodies.

2.8.3 The immune response to viral infection

Immunity to viral infection (Fig. 2.3) and subversion of immunity during viral infection are detailed in their specific chapters, but viruses interact closely with the immune system with many leading to immunosuppression, not least infectious bursal disease (Gumboro disease) (see Chapter 15v, this volume) which destroys the follicular structure of the bursa of Fabricius leading to B cell depletion and poor antibody responses (Gimeno and Schat, 2018). MDV (see Chapter 15xiii, this volume) can lead to transformation of T lymphocytes leading to the development of lymphoma. There is also evidence of viruses producing cytokine, chemokine and receptor-like molecules to alter the immune response to prevent clearance.

Both innate and adaptive responses are key to protection against viral infection. Recognition of viral infection by cells via pattern recognition receptors leads to the production of Type 1 interferons (α, β, κ) and Type III interferons can induce an array of antiviral proteins including ZAP, Mx, PRK and viperin as well as having direct inhibitory effects (Goossens *et al.*, 2013). NK cells in epithelial tissue of the gut and lung appear to play a key role in antiviral activity to influenza, Newcastle disease and Marek's disease (see Chapters 15vii, viii and xiii, this volume) as well as playing a key role, along with innate-associated T cells, in the production of interferon γ in activating a Th1 response leading to production of CTLs. However, these responses are usually accompanied by inflammation associated with pathology of many viral infections (Gimeno and Schat, 2018).

$CD8^+$ CTLs have been shown to offer protection in a number of infections including influenza, Gumboro disease and Marek's disease, though are also likely to play key roles in other infections where the immune response is less-well characterized. The use of live attenuated vaccines generates good CTL responses, but killed and sub-unit vaccines are less effective. Infection with most viruses elicits antibody responses that are frequently used

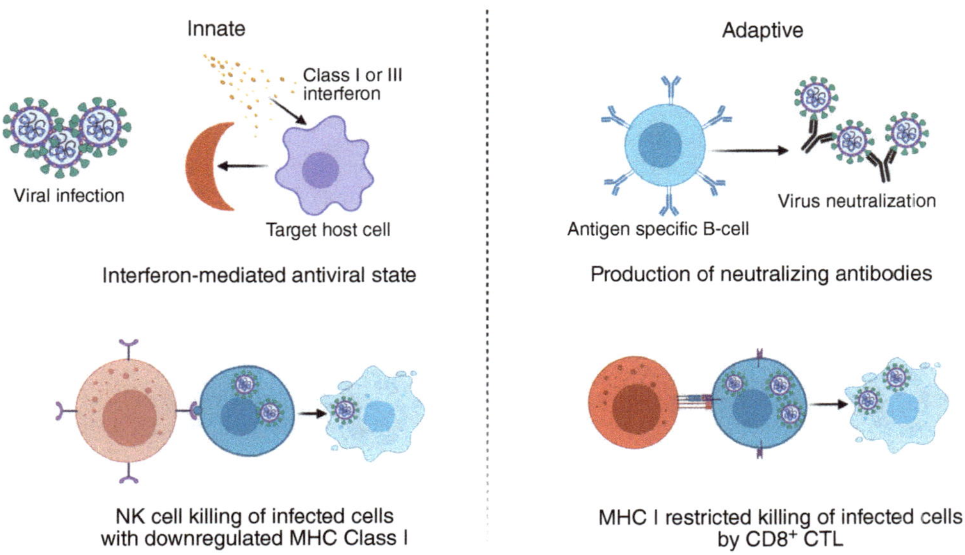

Fig. 2.3. Major immune responses to viral infections. (Author's own work.)

for diagnostics. Neutralizing antibodies are important in clearance and subsequent protection, with the efficacy of killed vaccines showing that they can offer protection without cellular responses. However, antibodies are less effective against intracellular stages of infection and the most effective responses are usually cellular and humoral responses working in concert (Boodhoo *et al.*, 2016).

2.8.4 The immune response to bacterial infection

Vaccine development has been slower for most bacterial infections with the use of antimicrobials more widespread. The exception to this is *Salmonella enterica*, which has been the most studied in terms of immune response in an effort to control infection in the food chain and in reducing systemic infection (see Chapter 14iv, this volume). More recently the function of heterophils, pattern recognition receptors and in particular macrophages in the chicken was largely determined through *Salmonella* challenge models (Wigley, 2014). Salmonellosis also leads to adaptive responses with antibody and specific cellular responses. Although the use of killed vaccines showed the importance of antibody responses, studies in bursectomized chickens and a range of challenge models point to clearance from both systemic sites such as the spleen and liver, and from the gut being driven by Th1 responses which are largely initiated by interferon-γ responses from NK cells or γδ T cells. However, the mechanism by which this is achieved is unclear. *Salmonella* infection is initially highly inflammatory in the gut, though these are regulated by TGF-β 4 and IL-10 produced by putative T regulatory cells (Wigley, 2014).

Salmonella is primarily an intracellular infection of macrophages. One serovar in particular, *Salmonella* Pullorum, is able to persist long-term within macrophages through inhibiting the intracellular killing mechanisms of the cell and through driving a Th2 response rather than a protective Th1 or Th17 response (Tang *et al.*, 2018).

Avian pathogenic *Escherichia coli* (APEC) infection (see Chapter 14ii, this volume) in respiratory tissue leads to inflammation via activation of pro-inflammatory cytokines. Transcriptional studies have characterized responses and identified multiple pathways in several lymphoid organs and cell lines, though despite the availability of a commercial vaccine we know little of the adaptive response, although differential resistance in inbred lines appears to be related to innate immunity. *Clostridium perfringens* (see Chapter 14v, this volume) and *Campylobacter jejuni* (see Chapter 14iii, this volume) are both frequent components of the chicken intestinal tract microflora. *C. perfringens* infection is highly inflammatory and recent evidence points to Th2 and Th17 responses driving this damage with elevated antibody levels and down-regulated expression of the regulatory cytokine TGF-β4 (Fasina and Lillehoj, 2019). *C. jejuni* also elicits Th2 and Th17 responses, though inflammation is well controlled, and these responses are thought to restrict *C. jeuni* to the gut, though not clearance from the caeca (Reid *et al.*, 2016). The adaptive responses to bacterial infection are summarized in Fig. 2.4.

2.8.5 Immune responses to parasitic infection

Immune responses, especially antibody, have been shown in a number of parasitic infections, but most work has focused around intestinal helminth and protozoal infections. The intestinal nematode *Ascardia galli* (see Chapter 16iii, this volume) has been used to demonstrate the Th1/Th2 paradigm in the chicken. *A. galli* infection leads to both cellular and antibody responses but current evidence suggests that Th2-mediated antibody responses are key to protection (Sharma *et al.*, 2019). *Histomonas spp.*, especially *H. meleagridis* (see Chapter 16ii, this volume) are extracellular protozoan parasites infecting turkeys and chicken causing the disease blackhead. To an extent the difference in the high susceptibility of turkeys appears to be the result of a more effective innate response in the gut of chickens. Infection leads to both antibody and cellular responses, although protection appears to be mediated by Th1 responses (Mitra *et al.*, 2018). Given the high prevalence and impact of coccidiosis in chickens and its control, in part through vaccination, have meant *Eimeria* (see Chapter 16i, this volume) is perhaps the best described parasite in terms of immune response. Although an intestinal parasite, protection is considered to be primarily through a combination of Th17- and Th1-mediated responses (Kim *et al.*, 2019).

2.9 Genetic Resistance to Infection

Genetic resistance to a range of pathogens, including *Campylobacter*, APEC and *Eimeria*, has been described in both inbred specific-pathogen free and conventional chickens. In most cases these traits are linked to immune function, though are usually polygenic and difficult to pin to a single gene or protein (see Chapter 3 for more details).

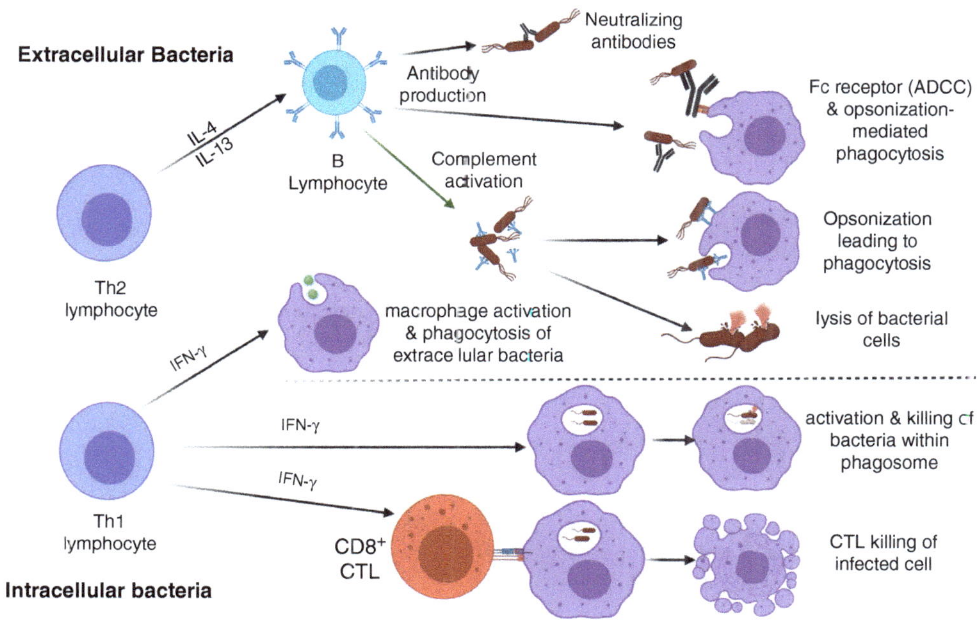

Fig. 2.4. Adaptive immunity to extracellular and intracellular bacterial infections. (Author's own work.)

2.10 Autoimmunity in the Chicken

Detrimental immune responses leading to hypersensitivity and autoimmune conditions are well studied in human immunology but are not well described in the chicken (see Erf, 2014 for further details on autoimmune diseases in the chicken). Delayed-type hypersensitivity (Type IV hypersensitivity) occurs in chickens and was long-used as a tool to assess cell mediated responses. A number of specific chicken lines have been used as a model for several autoimmune conditions. Perhaps the best known is the Obese line chicken that develops a spontaneous autoimmune thyroiditis used as a model of Hashimoto's thyroiditis. UCD200/206 chicken lines developed at the University of California develop scleroderma and the Smyth line develops autoimmune vitiligo.

2.11 Conclusions and Future Perspectives

The last two decades have significantly advanced our understanding of the chicken immune response. Although there are differences in organization, and the immune system generally has less complexity than mammalian biomedical models of immunology, we are finding that function is broadly similar. The need to control disease in the 50 billion or so chickens reared annually across the globe will continue to drive both vaccinology and the need for a better understanding of immune function. We are now beginning to understand how the microbiome shapes immune development and regulation. New tools, most notably transgenic chickens and the use of gene editing, will allow the same approaches used for studies in mice to fully elucidate function. Gene editing also offers up new possibilities in breeding for genetically resistant animals.

2.12 References

Boodhoo, N., Gurung, A., Sharif, S. and Behboudi, S. (2016) Marek's disease in chickens: a review with focus on immunology. *Veterinary Research* 47, 119.

Braukmann, M., Methner, U. and Berndt, A. (2015) Avian CD25(+) gamma/delta (gd) T cells after *Salmonella* exposure. *Veterinary Immunology and Immunopathology* 168, 14–18.

Broom, L.J. and Kogut, M.H. (2018) The role of the gut microbiome in shaping the immune system of chickens. *Veterinary Immunology and Immunopathology* 204, 44–51

Erf, G. (2014) Autoimmune diseases of poultry. In: Schat, K., Kaspers, B., and Kaiser, P. (eds) *Avian Immunology*. Elsevier, London.

Fasina, Y., and Lillehoj, H.S. (2019) Characterization of intestinal immune response to *Clostridium perfringens* infection in broiler chickens. *Poultry Science* 98, 188–198.

Ferdous, F., Saski, C., Bridges, W., Burns, M., Dunn, H., *et al.* (2016) Transcriptome profile of the chicken thrombocyte: new implications as an advanced immune effector cell. *PLoS One* 11, e0163890.

Gimeno, I.M. and Schat, K.A. (2018) Virus-induced immunosuppression in chickens. *Avian Diseases* 62, 272–285.

Goossens, K.E., Ward, A.C., Lowenthal, J.W. and Bean, A.G. (2013) Chicken interferons, their receptors and interferon-stimulated genes. *Developmental and Comparative Immunology* 41, 370–376.

Humphrey, S., Chaloner, G., Kemmett, K., Davidson, N., Williams, N., *et al.* (2014) *Campylobacter jejuni* is not merely a commensal in commercial broiler chickens and affects bird welfare. *MBio* 5, e01364–01314.

Kaiser, P., Poh, T.Y., Rothwell, L., Avery, S., Balu, S., *et al.* (2005) A genomic analysis of chicken cytokines and chemokines. *Journal of Interferon and Cytokine Research* 25, 467–484.

Kaufman, J., Milne, S., Gobel, T.W., Walker, B.A., Jacob, J.P., *et al.* (1999) The chicken B locus is a minimal essential major histocompatibility complex. *Nature* 401, 923–925.

Keestra, A.M., de Zoete, M.R., Bouwman, L.I., Vaezirad, M.M. and van Putten, J.P. (2013) Unique features of chicken Toll-like receptors. *Developmental and Comparative Immunology* 41, 316–323.

Kim, W.H., Chaudhari, A.A., and Lillehoj H.S. (2019). Involvement of T cell immunity in avian coccidiosis. *Frontiers in Immunology* 10, 2732.

Mitra, T., Kidane, F.A., Hess, M. and Liebhart, D. (2018) Unravelling the immunity of poultry against the extracellular protozoan parasite *Histomonas meleagridis* is a cornerstone for vaccine development: a review. *Frontiers in Immunology* 9, 2518.

Nagy, N., Bódi, I. and Oláh, I. (2016) Avian dendritic cells: phenotype and ontogeny in lymphoid organs. *Developmental and Comparative Immunology* 58, 47–59.

Olah, I., Nagy, N. and Vervelde, L. (2014) Structure of the avian lymphoid system. In: Schat, K., Kaspers, B. and Kaiser, P. (eds) *Avian Immunology*. Elsevier, London, pp. 11–44.

Ratcliffe, M. and Hartle, S. (2014) B Cells, the bursa of Fabricius and the generation of antibody responses. In: Schat, K., Kaspers, B. and Kaiser, P. (eds) *Avian Immunology*. Elsevier, London, pp. 65–90.

Reid, W.D., Close, A.J., Humphrey, S., Chaloner, G., Lacharme-Lora, L., *et al.* (2016) Cytokine responses in birds challenged with the human food-borne pathogen *Campylobacter jejuni* implies a Th17 response. *Royal Society Open Science* 3, 150541.

Sharma, N., Hunt, P.W., Hine, B.C. and Ruhnke, I. (2019) The impacts of *Ascaridia galli* on performance, health and immune responses of laying hens: new insights into an old problem. *Poultry Science* 98, 6517–6526.

Smith, A., Gobel, T.W. (2014) Avian T cells: antigen recognition and lineages. In: Schat, K., Kaspers, B. and Kaiser, P. (eds) *Avian Immunology*. Elsevier, London, pp. 91–101.

Tang, Y., Foster, N., Jones, M.A. and Barrow, P.A. (2018) Model of persistent *Salmonella* infection: *Salmonella enterica* serovar Pullorum modulates the immune response of the chicken from a Th17-Type response towards a Th2-type response. *Infection and Immunity* 86, e00307-18.

Wigley, P. (2014) *Salmonella enterica* in the chicken: how it has helped our understanding of immunology in a non-biomedical model species. *Frontiers in Immunology* 5, 482.

Yoshimura, Y. (2015) Avian beta-defensins expression for the innate immune system in hen reproductive organs. *Poultry Science* 94, 804–809.

2.13 Further Reading

de Geus, E.D. and Vervelde, L. (2013) Regulation of macrophage and dendritic cell function by pathogens and through immunomodulation in the avian mucosa. *Developmental and Comparative Immunology* 41, 341–351.

Genovese, K.J., He, H., Swaggerty, C.L. and Kogut, M.H. (2013) The avian heterophil. *Developmental and Comparative Immunology* 41, 334–340.

Kaufman, J. (2015) Co-evolution with chicken class I genes. *Immunology Reviews* 267, 56–71.

Rohde, F., Schusser, B., Hron, T., Farkašová, H., Plachý, J., *et al.* (2018) Characterization of chicken Tumor Necrosis Factor-a, a long-missed cytokine in birds. *Frontiers in Immunology,* 17, 605.

Shanmugasundaram, R. and Selvaraj, R.K. (2011) Regulatory T cell properties of chicken CD4+CD25+ cells. *Journal of Immunology* 186, 1997–2002.

Wigley, P. (2013) Immunity to bacterial infection in the chicken. *Developmental and Comparative Immunology* 41, 413–417.

Wigley, P. (2017) *Salmonella enterica* serovar Gallinarum: addressing fundamental questions in bacteriology sixty years on from the 9R vaccine. *Avian Pathology* 46, 119–124

3 The Genetics of Disease Resistance in Poultry

Androniki Psifidi*

The Royal Veterinary College, University of London, Hatfield, Hertfordshire, UK

3.1 Introduction

High population growth, urbanization and rising incomes have led to increased demands for animal protein. Poultry meat and eggs are now the leading global source of protein for humans, and demand is predicted to increase more in the coming decades. A major challenge is to achieve sustainable poultry expansion and intensification whilst reducing risk to animal and human health. Moreover, improving animal welfare traits is also key for the sustainability of the sector, given the growing concerns of citizens regarding animal production. Recent concomitant changes in management and production systems, namely the reduction in preventive use of antibiotics and the changes from battery cages to free roaming systems, make health issues even more crucial with increased risk of diseases and pathogen spreading.

An attractive strategy to control poultry infectious diseases and zoonoses could be selective breeding aiming to enhance inherent disease resistance. The advantages of breeding strategies, with cumulative effects over generations of selection, could be complementary to other important control strategies such as vaccination, biosecurity, farm management, and treatment. However, disease traits are often difficult to measure, low to moderately heritable, and of complex polygenic architecture. As a result, up to now health related traits have been scarcely taken into account in poultry breeding programmes.

This chapter provides an overview of the advances in genetic, genomic and functional genomic studies of resistance in major infectious bacterial, viral and parasitic diseases in chickens. Section 3.5 then gives an example of how chicken resistance to *Campylobacter* colonization could be enhanced through genetics and breeding. At the end of the chapter, conclusions from this review will be highlighted, paving the way for future trends in research on genetics and genomics of disease resistance in poultry.

3.2 Advances in Genetic Technologies Available for Poultry

For a successful genetic study, a good genome assembly (the process of taking a large number of short DNA sequences and putting them back together to create a representation of the original chromosomes from which this DNA originated) and annotation (the process of identifying the locations of genes in a genome and determining what those genes do) are prerequisites. Considerable improvements in the assembly and annotation of the chicken genome, comprising 39 pairs of chromosomes, have recently been made, facilitating genetic studies of disease resistance. The current version of the chicken genome (galgal6) is much more informative compared to previous versions. Currently, there are further efforts to improve the genome assembly and annotation mainly through the Functional Annotation of Animal Genomes (FAANG) consortium (for more info. see https://www.animalgenome.org/community/FAANG/).

Moreover, the availability of DNA microarrays (a collection of microscopic DNA spots attached to a solid surface such as a glass microscope slide), which are tools used to determine whether the DNA from a particular individual contains specific mutations (single nucleotide polymorphisms

*apsifidi@rvc.ac.uk

© CAB International 2021. *Poultry Health: A Guide for Professionals* (P. Barrow *et al.*)
DOI: 10.1079/9781789245042.0003

(SNPs)) in targeted genes or across the whole genome, have revolutionized genetic studies. Currently, there are multiple DNA microarrays for poultry with lower or higher density of SNPs (up to 600,000 SNPs) which are commercially available and broadly used to genotype (i.e. assess the genetic make-up of an organism) individual chickens. Next-generation sequencing (NGS) technologies for DNA, RNA or epigenetic sequencing are also available for poultry. Although the use of these technologies is very informative, their high costs limit their broad use in both genetic research and breeding programmes in poultry.

3.3 Genetic Studies of Disease Resistance in Poultry

Currently, the most widely implemented method to study the genetic background of poultry diseases is genome-wide association studies (GWAS). GWAS are hypothesis-free methods for identifying associations between genetic regions (SNP markers) and traits (including diseases). Genetic variation between individuals can cause differences in disease susceptibility. These causal variants responsible for the disease, and those which are located in close proximity with the causal variants, are present at higher frequency in cases (individuals with the disease) than in controls (healthy individuals). For a GWAS study, multiple individual birds need to be genotyped using a DNA microarray, and phenotyped (phenotype is a term used in genetics to describe the observable characteristics or traits of an organism) for the specific disease of interest (e.g. estimate for each individual the bacterial load in the blood). Then, a typical GWAS study analyses the genotypic and phenotypic data in order to find out the common genetic variants in individuals, both with and without the disease, across the genome. Variants associated with the disease, or within the same haplotype (a set of DNA variants that tend to be inherited together because they are located in close proximity) with the variant associated with a disease, will be found at a higher frequency in cases than in controls. Statistical analysis is carried out to indicate how likely a variant is to be associated with the disease and, based on this, the most strongly associated SNP markers with the disease are detected.

The benefit of a GWAS study is that the screening for genetic variants associated with the disease is performed across the genome and no previous knowledge of the disease aetiopathogenesis is needed in order to select specific candidate genes to study. On the other hand, GWAS studies require large sample sizes in order to get the required statistical power to identify robust genomic associations. Therefore, these studies are quite costly and require multiple resources: for the experimental challenge of birds with pathogens, the genotyping with the DNA microarrays and the phenotyping (estimation of pathogen load in the main colonized organ or tissue). Inbred chicken lines with different susceptibilities to specific pathogens have been used extensively in order to overcome the requirement of GWAS for very large sample sizes. Inbred chicken lines have been developed through intensive inbreeding programmes. Each line has increased genetic uniformity (increased homozygosity in their genotype), is comprised of birds that are of the same major histocompatibility complex (MHC, is a large locus on DNA containing a set of closely linked polymorphic genes that all together code for proteins essential for the adaptive immune system) type and represent populations of chickens that have immense possibilities in genetic research of disease susceptibility. A limited number of GWAS studies have been conducted using phenotypic data collected from natural disease outbreaks instead of data collected through experimental challenges. These are field studies, where the chickens are naturally infected by multiple pathogens. Compared with controlled challenge experiments, unknown and uncontrolled exposure to infections may reduce the power of a field study but do not constitute a fatal flaw in demonstrating host genetic differences in resistance. In addition, the natural mixed infections and the natural disease outbreaks that characterize field studies offer a more realistic picture of the genetic variation, and yield results that are more relevant to practical genetic improvement programmes in poultry.

Currently, GWAS studies have been performed for almost all the major avian diseases and zoonoses, identifying SNP markers associated with disease resistance and relevant immune responses in inbred chickens, commercial chickens, both pedigree and terminal crosses, as well as African and Asian indigenous chicken populations. Although the inbred chicken line studies are more powerful and require fewer birds, the genetic studies in commercial chickens are more informative since their findings could directly inform breeding programmes. According to these studies, both disease resistance and immune responses are complex polygenic traits affected by both environmental factors and multiple genes with a moderate or small effect on the phenotype. Therefore, a genomic selection approach, which takes into account SNP markers across the genome, would be preferable compared with a markers-assisted selection which focuses only on SNP markers located in genes with a big effect. Host resistance to bacterial, viral and parasitic diseases is a low to moderately heritable trait. Therefore, selective breeding aiming to enhance disease resistance is feasible; however, multiple generations of selection are required in order to improve these traits.

Examples of GWAS studies in inbred chicken line crosses include studies for resistance to *Campylobacter* (phenotype *Campylobacter* level measured in caeca, Psifidi *et al.*, 2016, see Chapter 14iii, this volume), *Salmonella* (Fife *et al.*, 2011, see Chapter 14iv, this volume), Marek's disease (Yan *et al.*, 2015) and coccidiosis (oocysts counts measured in faeces, Boulton *et al.*, 2018b, see Chapter 16i, this volume). Examples of GWAS studies in commercial chickens, layer and broiler, populations include studies for resistance to coccidiosis (Boulton *et al.*, 2018a), *Campylobacter* (Psifidi *et al.*, 2021), *Salmonella* (Psifidi *et al.*, 2018; Li *et al.*, 2019), Marek's disease (Wolc *et al.*, 2013, see Chapter 15xiii, this volume), APEC, Newcastle disease (Rowland *et al.*, 2018, see Chapter 15viii, this volume) and avian influenza (Drobik-Czwarno *et al.*, 2018, see Chapter 15vii, this volume).

3.4 Functional Genomic Studies of Disease Resistance in Poultry

Approximately 95% of genetic variants controlling complex traits such as disease resistance are located not in coding regions of the genes (i.e. the part of the gene that will eventually be transcribed and translated into protein) but in regulatory regions of the genome which control the expression of the genes. Most of the genetic variants identified by a GWAS are located in non-coding regions. Assessing how genetic variation identified by GWAS studies influences phenotype is a fundamental goal of genetics, and using whole genome sequencing (WGS) and RNA-sequencing approaches to collect different levels of molecular data can help accelerate our understanding of the underlying biology, in order to harness the genetic information and use it to inform prevention strategies, drug development and breeding programmes aiming to reduce disease susceptibility. RNA sequencing is a NGS technology that is used to detect the presence and quantity of RNA across the genome in a biological sample at a given moment. Using RNA sequencing, changes in gene expression over time, or differences in gene expression between different groups or treatments can be identified.

Several RNA-sequencing experiments studying gene expression differences in relevant tissues between cases (poultry affected with a pathogen) vs controls (healthy poultry) have been conducted in order to understand which sets of genes are upregulated or downregulated during the infection. In addition, comparisons of gene expression between chicken populations with a diverse resistance to an infectious disease have been conducted in order to identify what makes one chicken population more resistant to the disease compared with the other. RNA-sequencing experiments can be very informative without requiring the large sample sizes of a GWAS. However, gene expression differs among tissues, so the selection of the appropriate tissue to study a disease is important. Spleen, caecal tonsils, gut and liver are the tissues that are usually used to study gene expression associated with infectious disease. The selection of the tissue depends on the disease; for example, caecal tonsils or caecal wall are appropriate tissues for *Campylobacter* infection, while liver or spleen are preferable in the case of fowl typhoid. Similarly, the time point of sample collection is critical since the expression, especially of immunity-related genes, changes rapidly over time after the challenge.

The RNA-sequencing experiments usually identify several hundreds of differentially expressed genes between the different groups. These results attest that disease resistance is a complex trait with multiple genes playing an important role. Moreover, these studies have pointed out that the expression of genes is highly regulated, which results in a cascade of distinct patterns of co-expression of genes forming a network. Identifying and understanding such patterns is crucial in deciphering molecular mechanisms that underlie the pathophysiology of diseases. Network analyses of the differentially expressed genes have shed some light on the underlying molecular mechanisms of susceptibility to multiple poultry diseases, revealing enrichment mainly for innate and adaptive immune response genes, as well as metabolic genes. As in humans, it seems that resistance to infectious disease in chickens is mainly determined by transcriptional regulation (transcription is the process of converting the DNA sequence of a gene into an RNA copy. For a protein-coding gene, the RNA copy (or transcript) carries the information needed to build a protein, and RNA sequencing is a powerful approach to study the genetic architecture of complex polygenic traits.

Examples of RNA-sequencing studies conducted so far in inbred and commercial chicken lines are for resistance to: *Campylobacter* colonization (Connell *et al.*, 2012; Psifidi *et al.*, 2021), Marek's disease (Dong *et al.*, 2017), Newcastle disease (Schilling *et al.*, 2018), avian influenza (Ranaware *et al.*, 2016) and *Eimeria tenella* (Wang *et al.*, 2019).

3.5 An Example: Breeding for Resistance to *Campylobacter* Colonization in Chickens (see Chapter 14iii, this volume)

Campylobacter infection is estimated to cause 95 million illnesses in people worldwide each year. Human infections mostly involve gastroenteritis but can have severe complications. The handling or consumption of contaminated poultry meat is a key risk factor for human campylobacteriosis. The bacteria reach high numbers in the intestines of chickens reared for meat (broilers) and are frequently found on carcasses after slaughter. Effective vaccines against *Campylobacter* are not yet available, and treatments to reduce carcass contamination (e.g. chlorination) are not acceptable in some markets. One alternative is to breed chickens with improved resistance to *Campylobacter* colonization. The scope for genetic control of *Campylobacter* in poultry has been demonstrated in both commercial broiler lines (Connell *et al.*, 2013; Psifidi *et al.*, 2016; Psifidi *et al.*, 2021) and inbred layer lines (Psifidi *et al.*, 2016). A clear path to implement genetic gain exists, as a high proportion of the 75.4 billion poultry, estimated by the Food & Agriculture Organization to be killed for meat per annum, trace their origins to pedigree flocks, the genetics of which are controlled by a small number of companies.

Some studies have suggested that breeding for *Campylobacter* resistance may also benefit chicken intestinal health and productivity. For example, in some commercial broiler chicken lines, *C. jejuni* elicits a prolonged inflammatory response, damage to the intestinal mucosa, diarrhoea and impaired weight gain. Detrimental impacts of *Campylobacter* colonization have also been described on the chicken intestinal barrier function nutrient absorption, and the translocation of *Escherichia coli* from the intestine to extra-intestinal organs.

Genome-wide association studies (GWAS) and analysis of gene expression by RNA sequencing have begun to shed light on potential mechanisms of genetic control of *Campylobacter* in chickens. The resistance to *Campylobacter* colonization has been found to be low to moderately heritable (heritability = 0.11–0.25; heritability is the proportion of observed variation in a particular trait (such as disease susceptibility) that can be attributed to inherited genetic factors in contrast to environmental factors). This heritability is similar to that observed for other livestock pathogens and diseases, such as bovine tuberculosis (heritability = 0.09–0.17) and bovine and ovine mastitis (heritability = 0.10–0.20), where the development of genetic breeding programmes was deemed feasible. Moreover, selection for *Campylobacter* resistance was reported to be compatible with other breeding goals such as broiler growth.

Several quantitative trait loci (QTLs – genomic region containing one or more causative variants) associated with *Campylobacter* colonization resistance have been identified, attesting that this is a complex trait controlled by many mutations and genes with a small or moderate effect. The same QTLs for *Campylobacter* resistance have been identified in different chicken populations (Psifidi *et al.*, 2016; Psifidi *et al.*, 2021). Interestingly, two of these QTLs overlap with two previously identified QTLs for resistance to *Salmonella* colonization in chickens, suggesting that a mechanism of resistance common to both pathogens may exist and a breeding programme aiming to improve resistance to colonization by both pathogens may be feasible (Psifidi *et al.*, 2016; Psifidi *et al.*, 2021). A clear association with the MHC locus on chromosome 16 has been identified in both inbred and commercial chicken lines. This association not surprisingly accounts for most of the genetic variation. The QTLs that have been identified so far account for more than 2 $\log_{10}$ CFU/g difference in the gut *Campylobacter* colonization, sufficient to provide a significant reduction (up to 30%) on the risk of contamination to human health. However, environmental factors, which seem to play a far greater role in determining *Campylobacter* load in the chicken gut, may be more amenable to rapid and effective intervention. A multifactorial approach, addressing both genetic and non-genetic factors, is therefore needed to reduce *Campylobacter* levels in poultry and the incidence of the human disease attributed to this source.

3.6 Conclusion

According to the studies presented in this chapter, significant genetic variation and specific genomic regions play an important role in disease resistance and antibody response traits, indicating that it is possible to genetically improve these traits. However, the genetic architecture of these traits is complex, with both environmental factors and multiple genes with a small or a modest effect controlling them. Further interdisciplinary studies are needed to decipher the underlying mechanisms of disease resistance, the host–pathogen interactions and the role of environmental factors in gene regulation. In conclusion, selective breeding has the potential to provide an accurate, environmentally friendly and cost-effective alternative approach to control poultry diseases and zoonoses. Nevertheless, further interdisciplinary studies are needed to understand the genetics of disease resistance as well as the trade-off of breeding for disease resistance.

3.7 References

Boulton, K., Nolan, M.J., Wu, Z., Psifidi, A., Riggio, V., *et al.* (2018a) Phenotypic and genetic variation in the response of chickens to Eimeria tenella induced coccidiosis. *Genetics Selection Evolution* 50, 63.

Boulton, K., Nolan, M.J., Wu, Z., Riggio, V., Matika, O., *et al.* (2018b) Dissecting the genomic architecture of resistance to *Eimeria maxima* parasitism in the chicken. *Frontiers in Genetics* 9, 528.

Connell, S., Meade, K.G., Allan, B., Lloyd, A.T., Kenny, E., *et al.* (2012) Avian resistance to *Campylobacter jejuni* colonization is associated with an intestinal immunogene expression signature identified by mRNA sequencing. *PLoS One* 7, e40409.

Connell, S., Meade, K.G., Allan, B., Lloyd, A.T., Downing, T., *et al.* (2013) Genome-wide association analysis of avian resistance to *Campylobacter jejuni* colonization identifies risk locus spanning the CDH13 gene. *G3 (Bethesda)* 3, 881–90.

Dong, K., Chang, S., Xie, Q., Black-Pyrkosz, A. and Zhang, H. (2017) Comparative transcriptomics of genetically divergent lines of chickens in response to Marek's disease virus challenge at cytolytic phase. *PLoS One* 12, e0178923.

Drobik-Czwarno, W., Wolc, A., Fulton, J.E., Jankowski, T., Arango, J., *et al.* (2018) Genetic basis of resistance to avian influenza in different commercial varieties of layer chickens. *Poultry Science* 97, 3421–3428.

Fife, M.S., Howell, J.S., Salmon, N., Hocking, P.M., Van Diemen, P.M., *et al.* (2011) Genome-wide SNP analysis identifies major QTL for *Salmonella* colonization in the chicken. *Animal Genetics* 42, 134–40.

Li, X., Nie, C., Liu, Y., Chen, Y., Lu, X., *et al.* (2019) A genome-wide association study explores the genetic determinism of host resistance to *Salmonella pullorum* infection in chickens. *Genetics Selection Evolution* 51, 51.

Psifidi, A., Fife, M., Howell, J., Matika, O., Van Diemen, P.M., *et al.* (2016) The genomic architecture of resistance to *Campylobacter jejuni* intestinal colonisation in chickens. *BMC Genomics* 17, 293.

Psifidi, A., Russell, K.M., Matika, O., Sanchez-Molano, E., Wigley, P., *et al.* (2018) The genomic architecture of fowl typhoid resistance in commercial layers. *Frontiers in Genetics* 9, 519.

Psifidi, A., Kranis, A., Rothwell, L.M., Bremner, A., Russell, K. *et al.* (2021) Quantitative trait loci and transcriptome signatures associated with avian heritable resistance to Campylobacter. *Scientific Reports* 11(1), 1623. DOI: 10.1038/s41598-020-79005-7

Ranaware, P.B., Mishra, A., Vijayakumar, P., Gandhale, P.N., Kumar, H., *et al.* (2016) Genome wide host gene expression analysis in chicken lungs infected with avian influenza viruses. *PLoS One* 11, e0153671.

Rowland, K., Wolc, A., Gallardo, R.A., Kelly, T., Zhou, H., *et al.* (2018) Genetic analysis of a commercial egg laying line challenged with Newcastle disease virus. *Frontiers in Genetics* 9, 326.

Schilling, M.A., Katani, R., Memeari, S., Cavanaugh, M., Buza, J., *et al.* (2018) Transcriptional innate immune response of the developing chicken embryo to Newcastle disease virus infection. *Frontiers in Genetics* 9, 61.

Wang, X., Zou, W., Yu, H., Lin, Y., Dai, G., *et al.* (2019) RNA sequencing analysis of chicken cecum tissues following *Eimeria tenella* infection in vivo. *Genes (Basel)* 10, 420.

Wolc, A., Arango, J., Jankowski, T., Settar, P., Fulton, J.E., *et al.* (2013) Genome-wide association study for Marek's disease mortality in layer chickens. *Avian Diseases* 57, 395–400.

Yan, Y., Yang, N., Cheng, H.H., Song, J. and Qu, L. (2015) Genome-wide identification of copy number variations between two chicken lines that differ in genetic resistance to Marek's disease. *BMC Genomics* 16, 843.

4 The Poultry Industry

Barry Thorp*

St Davids Poultry, Easter Bush Veterinary Centre Roslin, Midlothian, UK

4.1 Introduction

Poultry represents the main source of animal protein for the world's human population in the forms of eggs and meat; both being acceptable to almost all cultures and ethnic groups. Commercial layers and broilers are the main species suppling this global demand, followed by turkeys, ducks and geese. Other species, such as quail, guinea fowl and ostrich, also contribute to global food production, as do some game birds such as pheasants and partridge.

Globally, approximately 14 kg of broiler poultry meat was consumed per person in 2018, although in the USA they eat approximately 48 kg per head. In the same year, 123 million metric tonnes of poultry meat were produced worldwide. In contrast, pork was produced at 120 million metric tonnes, cattle meat at 72 million tonnes, and sheep only at 25 million tonnes. Additionally, the production of poultry meat is predicted to rise by a further 15 million tonnes by 2027. Approximately 10% of poultry meat is globally traded as a frozen commodity. The largest global producer is the USA, which is also a major exporter. The majority of USA export is dark meat from the legs as this type of meat is not popular in the North American market. The dark meat goes to the Far East, of which China is the main importer. China is also the second biggest global producer of poultry meat with the European Union being the third. The EU produces only slightly more than Brazil, which is a major exporter (approx. 3 million tonnes per annum), but this is whole chicken and portions.

4.2 Chickens

Traditionally, live chickens were killed just prior to cooking which would minimize the risk of food spoilage and contamination. Storage is not required, and one chicken provides a family meal. Commercially, chicken carcasses lend themselves to providing portions for popular meat dishes, processing for fast foods and ready meals. Chickens are well suited to being efficiently produced and slaughtered on a commercial scale. Production is relatively efficient with low feed conversion ratio (FCR) and the ability to rapidly multiply populations. Poultry are relatively easy to manage, though to look after large populations correctly and with optimal efficiency requires attention to detail and high standards of husbandry, especially disease control, environmental control and nutrition.

Globally, most broiler meat production is in the hands of 'integrators'; many of these are very large multinational companies and incorporate feed mills, hatcheries, laboratories, poultry farms, abattoirs, processing plants and further processing. In addition, some own large swathes of agricultural land and grow their own cereals for poultry feed. They have contracts for poultry meat products with global fast food and other outlets. The largest global producer of poultry meat in 2018 was JBS S.A. in Brazil who slaughtered 3500 million broilers. Tyson Foods Inc. in the USA rank second with 1844 million broilers slaughtered, and BRF in Brazil rank third. New Hope Liuhe and Wen's Food in China rank fourth and fifth, and CP farms in Thailand rank sixth. The UK poultry industry places about 900 million broiler chicks and slaughters about 860 million at an average weight of 2.2 kg. Just over 6 million broiler breeders, 15 million turkey poults, and 40 million commercial layers are placed annually. Poultry meat production is in the hands of a small and declining number of integrators, some of which are multinational.

*barry@stdavids-poultryteam.co.uk

© CAB International 2021. *Poultry Health: A Guide for Professionals* (P. Barrow *et al.*)
DOI: 10.1079/9781789245042.0004

4.3 Turkeys

After chicken, turkey is the most popular poultry meat. Globally, in 2016, there were 6.2 million tonnes produced. Approximately 40% of global production is in the USA, followed by Brazil (8%), Germany (8%), France (5%) and Italy 4%. In North America and parts of Europe monthly turkey meat production is skewed due to high demand for Thanksgiving and Christmas. This makes efficient production more of a challenge and also effects capital investment in facilities which may be idle for part of the year. Seventeen per cent of turkey meat is a globally traded commodity.

4.4 Ducks

A global total of approximately 4.3 million tonnes of duck meat was produced in 2014. Duck meat is mostly produced in East and South-east Asia, mainly China. Other countries that are major duck meat producers are France, Germany and Poland. The following companies are the key players in the global duck meat market: AJC International, Charoen Pokphand Foods, Maple Leaf Farms, New Hope Liuhe and Pepe's ducks.

4.5 Quail

Quail production is for meat and egg markets. Japanese quail *Coturnix japonica* are a subspecies of *Coturnix coturnix*. They were domesticated in China, which is now the world's largest producer of quail meat (160,000 tonnes of meat per year). Far behind are Spain and France with 9200 and 8100 tonnes, respectively.

4.6 Geese

Geese are farmed for their meat, feathers and down, and to produce fatty livers (goose meat is also notoriously fatty). Ninety-four per cent of the 2.5 million tonnes of goose meat consumed annually (2010 data) worldwide is produced in China (from many different breeds), followed by the Ukraine, Egypt and Hungary. Only 900 tonnes are produced in the US. Geese are very versatile. They were once used in the USA for controlling weeds in several crops (asparagus tobacco, beans and potatoes) and the water hyacinth in waterways. They also serve as 'guard dogs'; Ballantine's whisky bonded warehouse near Glasgow is guarded by geese. After China, Hungary is the largest producer of down and feathers. The geese are plucked three times a year yielding up to 350–400 g down and feathers/bird.

4.7 Egg Production (see also Chapter 6, this volume)

World egg production grew from 37 million metric tonnes to 74 million in 2016. More than 50% of the global egg production is in China, where more than 500 billion eggs are produced annually; the USA is the next biggest producer with just over 100 billion. India is rapidly increasing egg production, more than doubling production from 35 billion eggs in 2000 to almost 80 billion eggs in 2016. The largest egg production companies are in the USA (Cal Maine Foods, 40 million layers; Rose Acre Farms, 22 million layers), Mexico (Proan, 33 million layers) and Thailand (CP Group, 22 million layers). The UK commercial layer sector consists of approximately 40 million brown hens of which about 30% are in enriched cages, 65% free-range, 3% barn and 2% organic.

Eggs are a unique animal protein source in that they are already packaged in a convenient size for easy storage and for feeding individuals and families. Table eggs tend to be sold locally, though there is some trade between neighbouring countries. Processed eggs are a globally traded commodity, and are available as whole eggs, whites, yolks, and various blends. On the basis of products, the egg processing market has been segmented into frozen, liquid and dried products. Frozen and liquid products were the largest egg processing product segments in 2013. Dried products are estimated to witness highest growth rates over the next few years on account of increasing demand for egg proteins and functional foods in international markets. In terms of regional demand, North America dominated the global egg processing and equipment market in 2013. The egg processing market is projected to reach US$29.20 billion by 2020.

The global success of efficient meat and egg production is based on massive genetic improvement, effective vaccine development and disease control, housing with environmental control and advances in nutrition and feed milling.

4.8 Genetic Improvement and Disease Control (see also Chapter 3, this volume)

The genetics of poultry is in the hands of a very small number of primary breeders. In the meat sector, a single pedigree-level hen might have 25,000 parent stock bird descendants, which in turn might produce 3 million broilers. Numerous techniques are used to assess the pedigree stock. For example, birds might be examined with ultrasound or x-rays to study the shape of muscles and bones. The blood oxygen level is measured to determine cardiovascular health. The walking ability of pedigree candidates is observed and scored. Accurate estimates are made of feed intake, and FCR is calculated. In addition, egg production and hatchability are measured. Siblings of the pedigree birds may be put in more challenging environments or on poorer nutrition to assess performance. The end result is a selection index for each individual based on the data from that individual, its siblings and half-siblings, and the birds with the best all round commercial traits are selected for the next pedigree generation. This process needs very high levels of R&D spending and has prompted consolidation within the primary breeder industry. As of 2018, only two sizable breeding groups remained: Aviagen (with the Ross, Hubbard, Arbor Acres, Indian River and Peterson brands) and Cobb-Vantress (with the Cobb, Avian, Sasso and Hybro brands). The primary breeders in the commercial egg sector have also consolidated over recent years and the market is now dominated by three companies: the EW group GmbH (Lohmann and Hyline commercial layer breeds) who also own Aviagen; Hendrix Genetics (Babcock, Bovans, Dekalb, Hisex, ISA and Shaver); and H & N. All three companies supply some commercial layer breeds that lay white eggs and some that lay brown eggs. In recent years, selection characteristics have focused on the FCR of egg production and the longevity of commercial hens. In addition, for some markets, selection has included characteristics for a free-range bird, which has greater disease resilience and less inter-bird aggression.

The control of major diseases in both the meat and egg sector has been brought under control over the last 50 years. Day-old meat parent stock chicks and commercial layer chicks are sold free of vertically transmitted diseases such as mycoplasma (see Chapter 14viii, this volume), notifiable species of *salmonella* (see Chapter 14iv, this volume), leukosis (see Chapter 15xii, this volume), and many more. Modern vaccines effectively control or prevent the diseases that have the potential to kill large numbers of birds, such as Marek's disease (see Chapter 15xiii, this volume), Gumboro (see Chapter 15v, this volume) and Newcastle disease (see Chapter 15viii, this volume), and massively reduce the impact of those diseases that seriously affect production such as infectious bronchitis (see Chapter 15x, this volume). In addition, food safety is enhanced by *Salmonella* vaccines. Modern technology such as '*in ovo*' injection enables modern recombinant and other vaccines to be administered easily and effectively.

Improved genetics, combined with correct management and disease control, has to be combined with the delivery of broiler and layer nutrient requirements with unfailing accuracy, without over- or under-supplying, and is the key to maintaining production efficiency. Detailed research has defined the feed specification requirements of poultry and how those change with age, breed and production system (see Chapter 12, this volume). Nutrition and feed delivery advances include raw and finished feed analysis using methods such as near-infrared spectroscopy (NIR); improved availability of nutrients through enzymes such as phytase; and improvements in milling and pelleting technologies. All these lead to improvements in bird performance, especially FCR, and fewer diseases associated with nutritional imbalances.

The above continual improvement in the efficiency of poultry meat and egg production, combined with further growth of the global human population and the urbanization and improved living standards of humans, is predicted to result in increased poultry meat and egg production.

4.9 Further Reading

Bedford, M. (2018) How NIR Analysis of Poultry Feed Ingredients Increases Output. AB Vista. Available at: https://www.abvista.com/news/January-2018/NIR-poultry-feed-analysis-increases-output.aspx (accessed 21 January 2021).

Bertechini, A.G. (2012) The Quail Production. Available at: http://www.facta.org.br/wpc2012-cd/pdfs/plenary/Antonio_Gilberto_Bertechini_.pdf (accessed 8 March 2021).

Elfick, D. (2012) A Brief History of Broiler Selection: How Chicken Became a Global Food Phenomenon in 50 Years (PDF). Aviagen International. Available at: http://en.aviagen.com/assets/Sustainability/50-Years-of-Selection-Article-final.pdf (accessed 1 July 2012).

Grand View Research (2019) Egg Processing Equipment Market Size, Share & Trends Analysis Report by Application, Regional Outlook, Competitive Strategies, and Segment Forecasts, 2019 to 2025. Grand View

Research. Available at: https://www.grandviewresearch.com/industry-analysis/egg-processing-and-equipment-market (accessed 21 January 2021)

Johnson, R. (2018) Global Turkey Meat Market: Key Findings and Insights. The Poultry Site. Available at: https://www.thepoultrysite.com/news/2018/05/global-turkey-meat-market-key-findings-and-insights (accessed 21 January 2021).

Markets and Markets (n.d.) Egg Processing Market worth 29.20 Billion USD by 2020. Markets and Markets. Available at: https://www.marketsandmarkets.com/PressReleases/egg-processing-equipment.asp (accessed 21 January 2021)

Molnar, S. (2017) Production and Trade of Duck Products in Global View. Annals of the Polish Association of Agricultural and Agribusiness Economists, XIX(3), 199–205. DOI:10.5604/01.3001.0010.3249. Available at: https://rnseria.com/resources/html/article/details?id=151566&language=en

Mordor Intelligence (2020) Processed Egg Market – Growth, Trends, Covid-19 Impact, and Forecasts (2021–2026). Mordor Intelligence. Available at: https://www.mordorintelligence.com/industry-reports/processed-egg-market (accessed 21 January 2021).

Poultry Hub Australia (n.d.) Game Birds. Poultry Hub Australia. Available at: https://www.poultryhub.org/all-about-poultry/species/game-birds (accessed 8 March 2021).

Poultry Hub Australia (n.d.) Goose. Poultry Hub Australia. Available at: https://www.poultryhub.org/all-about-poultry/species/goose (accessed 8 March 2021).

Watt Executive (2018) Watt Executive Guide to World Poultry Trends 2018. Available at: https://www.poultrytrends.com/poultrytrends/poultrytrends2018 (accessed 8 March 2021).

5 The Broiler Industry and Management of Broilers and Broiler Parents

PAUL MCMULLIN*

Poultry Health International, Thirsk, North Yorkshire, UK

5.1 Introduction

Management is the control or organization of an activity. In the context of crop and animal farming operations it is sometimes referred to as husbandry. Figure 5.1 shows one way of looking at a model poultry production system.

We could take all of the known and unknown requirements of the particular bird (species, strain, age, sex) as determined by its genotype and line them up in a stack on the left of the figure. This would provide a 'chart' of its requirements. We could then, for each of these requirements, line up what the natural environment provides on the right of the chart. A gap would be left in the middle. Management is, essentially, everything that we do that tends to 'fill the gap'. It will have a broad range of components: temperature control (heating and, potentially, cooling), ventilation, lighting, formation of groups, feed composition, feed distribution, feeder design, drinker design, and so on. Some of these will be identical or very similar among different classes of poultry; some may require subtle variations even between different strains. The type, intensity and efficiency of management will, inevitably, vary. Factors that will have an impact are basic economics (labour cost, capital cost, product value), climate, season, availability of labour, experience of stock people and production system (e.g. intensive or free-range). Management, at least as conventionally defined, is never perfect. Where farmed poultry are not provided with an environment reasonably close to what they require (taking into account species, breed and age) they tend to be more susceptible to disease and less efficient in producing meat and eggs.

5.2 Origins of Broiler Chickens

Modern broilers, like all farmed chickens, are the result of domestication of Red Jungle Fowl (*Gallus gallus*) although there may have been contributions from other species of Asian junglefowl. Domestication appears to have started around 5000 years ago and, by the mid-19th century Charles Darwin described the large number of varieties then recognized.

Specialized breeding/genetics companies produced hybrid strains for specific commercial uses, from 1940 onward, based on a relatively small number of breeds (Cornish, New Hampshire, Plymouth Rock). Since the 1970s there has been a steady reduction in the number of companies involved in this work, with a corresponding increase in size and geographic spread of the remaining producers. Each of the breeding companies produce 'Management Manuals' for the commercial parent stock, and the broilers they will produce. These are key reference documents for everybody interested in flock management and they are regularly updated in the light of experience.

5.3 Broiler Production Systems

The broiler production pyramid is illustrated in Fig. 5.2.

Specialist primary breeding companies maintain a large population of birds of different strains under high biosecurity and standardized environmental conditions to facilitate accurate assessment and data collection. They will also typically place siblings of selection candidates in conditions representative of commercial production and use the

*paulmcmullin@poultryhealthinternational.net

DOI: 10.1079/9781789245042.0005

Fig. 5.1. Bridging the gap.

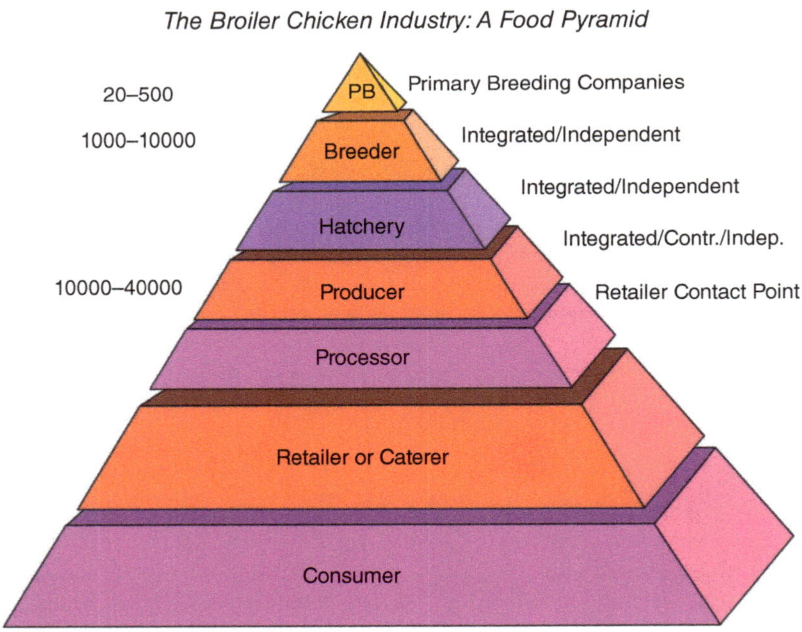

Fig. 5.2. Broiler production pyramid showing primary breeders (PB) at the top, typical group sizes for management purposes on the left and typical type of organization on the right.

data from these in the selection process. The primary breeders will also multiply via grandparents and supply the market with broiler breeders – parents of the commercial broilers. Commercial breeding farms may be part of integrated companies (with their own hatcheries, feed-mills, processing plants) or independent or contracted to larger organizations. Equally, commercial broiler farms may or may not be integrated. Group size for management purpose tends to increase as we go down the levels of the pyramid. Broiler processors act as the main contact point between retailers and food service industries with the production system. All levels of the pyramid pay close attention to consumer demand and can respond relatively rapidly to changing requirements. The process of multiplication from primary breeding selection to the production of broiler chicks takes about 4–5 years. A single family of pure line birds can contribute their genetics to about 50 million broilers.

Selection for broiler production initially focused on weight gain and feed conversion ratio. In recent years the selection criteria have been broadened to include weightings for liveability, conformation, skeletal integrity and other criteria.

5.4 Recent Broiler Production

UK broiler production is approximately 1 billion/year. Figure 5.3 illustrates the production trend in recent years.

5.5 What is Management?

Good management is the provision of an optimal environment for the genotype of the farmed stock to maximize economic return and minimize welfare problems. It is a critically important aspect of modern poultry production because the industry is capital intensive, and margins are very low, so survival and business growth depend on efficient production. In spite of this, when performance tables are compiled for groups of farms, the range from poorest to best producers is substantial. While some of this variation may relate to factors beyond our control, much of it is believed to relate to management.

5.6 Brooding Management

Effective cleaning and disinfection of farms is a key management activity beyond the scope of this chapter (see Chapter 18, this volume). Once this is done, the first task is to ensure that the physical environment is properly set up ahead of chick arrival. It is particularly important to ensure that the required temperature is achieved ahead of chick

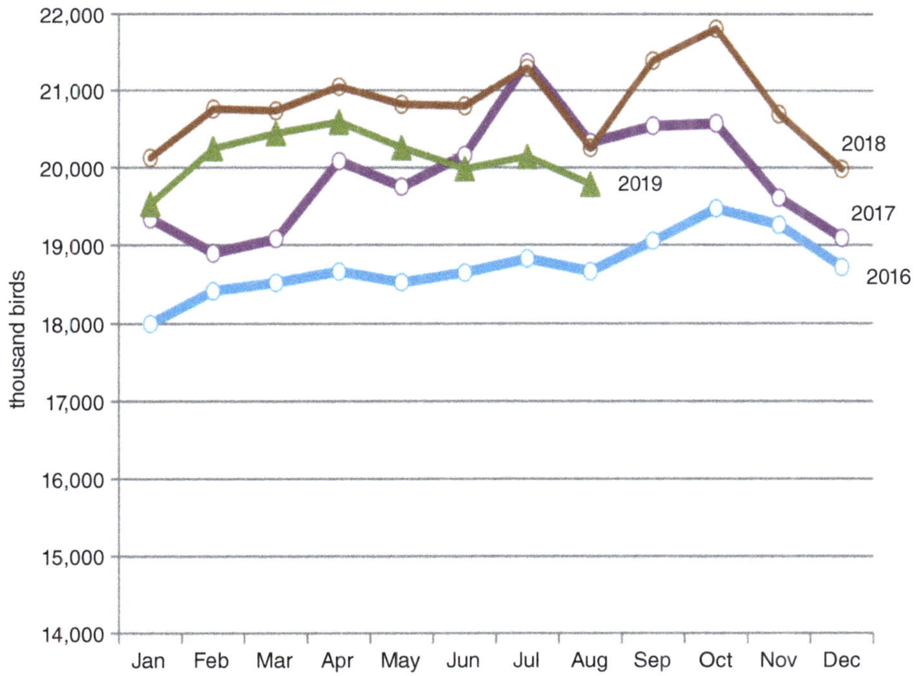

Fig. 5.3. Monthly broiler slaughter in the UK. (From https://www.gov.uk/government/statistics/poultry-and-poultry-meat-statistics.)

arrival. Experienced poultry managers know that a good start lays the foundation for a good production cycle. We simply need to facilitate access to feed and water, and ensure a comfortable environment (temperature and humidity) to achieve early adaptation to the environment with satisfactory feed intake. The chicks need to establish feeding behaviour (i.e. develop appetite) and drinking activity. This can be monitored daily by checking the numbers which are showing ‘crop fill’. The mean bodyweights at 7 days of age are often taken as a good indicator of brooding management, though this can also be affected by the strain, the breeding flock age, feed, disease challenges, and, sometimes, vaccinal reactions. In assessing such data, it is important to compare like-with-like.

The brooding phase is normally considered to be about 10 days, though the period during which supplemental heat will be required varies with the time of year and climate. Because of the steady improvements in growth rates over the years, the brooding period has become an increasing proportion of the total life span of broilers. There is, therefore, less opportunity to recover from issues as a result of poor brooding management.

Brooding temperature is the most critical management parameter and is easy to assess visually in traditional brooding systems with ‘spot brooders’. If the chicks are too cold, they will huddle and stay close to the heat source, and so will not start well. If they are too warm, they tend to migrate away from the heat source, have depressed appetite and become dehydrated. If they survive, they will tend to show slower than normal feathering (replacement of down with normal plumage). Modern broiler houses in temperate climates tend to have whole-house heating systems and, for these, air heaters are gradually being replaced with heat exchangers (with or without heat recovery systems) and boilers using renewable fuels. In whole house heating, low temperatures are associated with chicks forming large ‘rafts’ – groupings making it difficult for them to access feed and water. If temperatures are too high there is little or no grouping of chicks. We should normally be aiming for relative humidity of around 70% RH for the first 3 days to allow the chick to adjust for changes in humidity between hatchery (see Chapter 11, this volume) and farm. Too low humidity (<50%) is seen more frequently in cold climates in winter and can contribute to dehydration and increase the number of chicks that do not establish feeding behaviour. Excess humidity, particularly after the first few days, should be avoided as it will increase the risk of wet litter and damage to the feet (pododermatitis).

Flocks may appear chilled even when the temperature is adequate. This can be associated with inaccurate or wrongly placed thermometers or sensors (should be at chick height), too high air speeds (draughts) or disease challenges that induce fever.

5.7 Ventilation

After the brooding period we need to continue to take care to ensure easy access to feed and water. This is usually very mechanized and equipment has gradually improved over the years to facilitate this process. Effective ventilation is one of the most critical jobs of management after the brooding phase. There is a minimum ventilation requirement to ensure removal of CO_2 and ammonia, and provision of oxygen.

The minimum ventilation in cubic metres per second is 1.95×10^{-4} (m^3/s) per $kg^{0.75}$ bodyweight, so ventilation programmes require that we work out the amount of air needed per bird per hour at their current weight, and then the fan timers and cycles required to achieve this. Modern buildings commonly have computerized panels to facilitate this process. However, it is not just the amount that counts but also its speed and distribution. Efficient systems will direct fresh incoming air to areas of warm air (in the high part of the building), mix the fresh air and warm air, and bring it down to bird height. Ventilation becomes even more important in tropical climates or periods of unusually high temperature in temperate countries.

5.8 Growth Management Programmes

The high feed efficiency and rapid growth rates of modern broilers allows efficient production of high value animal protein. Broiler genetics may be expected to continually evolve in response to market demands. It is sometimes beneficial for health, welfare and fine-tuning of market weights to manage bird growth by adjusting feed availability, nutrient content or day length. If planning to control growth, it is important to first check performance when birds are grown without limits and then establish the objective of the control to be applied. To manage growth, it will be necessary to measure bird weights and feed inputs *accurately*.

One way of improving the predictability of broiler weight/uniformity is to grow males and females separately. If this is done, consideration needs to be given as to whether it is possible to apply different programmes for males and females.

5.9 Broiler Management: Conclusions

Successful broiler management is achieved by matching environment with bird requirements. The brooding period is critical to overall success of production. We must avoid unintentional growth control and ensure that weight monitoring is sufficient for the level of predictability required.

5.10 Management of Broiler Breeders/ Parents

The initial management of broiler parents is similar to that of broilers. They do require extra care in early management, perhaps because they are more likely to be the progeny of young parents, have a longer journey from the hatchery or have been vent-sexed. The males may also have surgical interventions such as comb-dubbing, de-spurring, toe-clipping, and beak-tipping though these have been reduced in recent years. They should only be used where the welfare benefit from their use (usually in terms of less damage of the breeding females) clearly outweighs the welfare challenge of the intervention itself and where it complies with the local animal welfare legislation.

The males and females are each usually crosses, and from distinct lines. Like broilers, their genetics are optimized for rapid growth and weight gain, yet they must be managed in such a way that they can effectively mate and produce fertile eggs from which broilers can be hatched. This is achieved by implementing carefully controlled growth programmes.

The two sexes are reared separately, sometimes in separate houses, sometimes by penning. While day-old-to-death systems are still used in some areas, the young parents will typically be reared from day-old to around 18–20 weeks on specialized rearing farms, and then transferred to laying farms until about 60 weeks of age.

5.11 Growth Control

Growth control must be rigorous and consistent, as excess weight gain results in reduced fertility, reduced egg production, more prolapsed oviducts and more female damage. This is usually achieved by grading birds by weight into groups at 4–5 weeks, then accurate control of feed allowances and rapid distribution. In the UK, the feed allocation is usually spread in the litter automatically using spin feeders. Chain feeders may be used but require fast chain speeds (3 min/group) to allow sufficiently rapid distribution. Weekly weighing is carried out on a sample of birds weighed individually in each pen to adjust overall feed allocation. Results are judged by comparing mean weight against the target and the % coefficient of variation (CV). Visual grading to improve CVs within group is carried out up to about 10 weeks.

5.12 Managing into Lay

It may be necessary to re-draw target bodyweight lines if under- or overweight. Females may be given a feed increase and pre-breeder diet (breeder without the calcium required for eggshell production) at 15 weeks. Females and males are brought together at 18–20 weeks (at transfer if a rear-and-move system). In the laying phase, separate sex feeding is obligatory to manage weight gain appropriately for each sex. This is usually achieved by a grille excluder on the female feeders and having male feeders at a greater height. Careful management of this is required to achieve good control of development and weight gain during the laying phase. Excess weight is not conducive to health and egg production in the females, and excess weight of the males reduces fertility. Weight data may be supplemented with assessments of physiological status, pectoral muscle ‘fleshing’ in the males and sub-cutaneous fat deposition in females to fine-tune decision making. The lighting programme is used to simulate springtime, initiate egg production and synchronize lay. There will be continuing careful attention to male weights, numbers, leg and foot health, and vitality (as we rely on natural mating).

5.13 Egg Collection and Grading

Careful management of daily activities and the nests are required to minimize the occurrence of floor and slat eggs which have a poor microbiological status. Intensive patrolling and collection of floor eggs is particularly important as the flock comes into lay. Thereafter, egg collections should be regular (in the UK this is mainly by roll-away autonest systems). Farm staff carry out grading of eggs, and their suitability for incubation will also be monitored by the hatchery that receives them. Egg storage temperatures will depend on the expected egg age at the point of setting, and care needs to be taken to avoid condensation on egg surfaces at any point.

5.14 Conclusions

Management can be taken to cover all of those activities which adapt the physical environment to meet the needs of the particular livestock. In poultry production, intensive production methods have both advantages and disadvantages. Effective management aims to minimize the disadvantages while maximizing the advantages. The technical efficiency of production is a reasonable rough guide to the quality of management. Production systems and the strains of birds used continue to evolve. Management of broiler parent stock, in particular, is one of the most technically demanding jobs in poultry production.

5.15 Further Reading

There is extensive scientific literature on management of commercial poultry, as well as detailed practical experience among staff at various levels on farms and in associated companies. Detailed management manuals are produced for each type of bird by primary breeding companies and are updated regularly. Manuals routinely used in the UK industry include those produced by Aviagen (for Ross strains) and Cobb-Vantress (for Cobb strains). These are a valuable source of reference for those requiring more detail than is covered here.

6 The Commercial Layer Industry, Management and Disease

Peter Cargill*

Wyatt Poultry Services, part of CVS (UK) Ltd., Hereford, UK

6.1 The Table Egg Industry

Global egg production has increased in the last 50 years by 350% compared with a 2000% increase in broiler meat production. This coincides with a nearly 250% increase in laying hens (estimated at ca. 6.8 billion birds worldwide). The geographical location of production has changed markedly in this time, with most production located in Europe until 1978 when production in Asia overtook Europe. China now dominates production at 37% of global output. Production in Africa, North America and Central and South America has steadily increased during this time (Fig. 6.1.) while it fell in Europe, precipitated by the economic collapse in the USSR post-1989 and again in 2012 after conventional cage production was banned. The majority of global production is of white eggs, with brown eggs being predominant in Europe.

Increases in laying rate are over and above the increase in number of hens, rising from 142 eggs per hen in 1962 to 184 in 2012. Recent changes that extend the economically viable duration of lay enable a total of 350 eggs by 80 weeks and in excess of 420 eggs by 90 weeks of age, and a liveability of 92%. Feed conversion rates have also improved, and mortality has decreased during this period.

Less than 3% of global production is traded internationally, with European countries dominating. The Netherlands is the biggest exporter and Germany the largest importer.

In the UK, production systems have changed with slight falls in intensive production in the last 10 years while free-range production has more than doubled. Barn and organic production are much less and with little change.

6.2 Production Systems and Their Influence on Epidemiology

Birds generally reach sexual maturity at ca. 16 weeks and begin to lay at ca. 18–22 weeks reaching maximum production of in excess of 90% at 6–8 weeks after onset of lay. This gradually reduces to ca. 70% at ca. 70 weeks of age. Moulting of birds in order to increase overall egg production per bird is considered unacceptable and is prohibited in regions such as the EU on welfare grounds but remains in practice in some areas of the world. The moulting process is in itself immunosuppressive and can increase disease susceptibility. In addition, if the total duration of lay is extended, the life of birds may exceed the duration of immunity conferred by the commonly used vaccines. During lay, egg weight is manipulated nutritionally but tends to gradually increase.

Traditional cage systems were prohibited in the EU in January 2012. Elsewhere, farms with traditional cage systems tend to be older multi-aged facilities comprising a small number of large houses with poor internal biosecurity. However, in some countries extremely large farms exist with in excess of 10 million birds in a single location. Cage design may predispose to red mite infestation, but the relatively small number of birds in each cage (4–6) slows the rate of spread of diseases within a house. However, the overall house and cage design limits the extent to which the units can be cleaned and

*peter.cargill@wyattpoultry.com

© CAB International 2021. *Poultry Health: A Guide for Professionals* (P. Barrow *et al.*)
DOI: 10.1079/9781789245042.0006

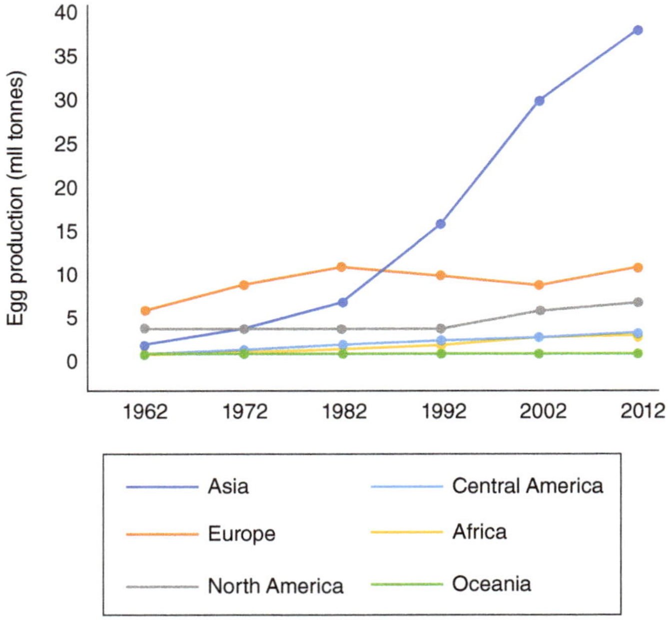

Fig. 6.1. Increase in global egg production in the last 50 years. (Courtesy of International Egg Commission.)

disinfected. Absence of nesting and scratch areas also affects welfare.

Colony cage systems generally involve newer housing, which usually results in improved biosecurity; however, the larger groups of birds involved can lead to a more rapid spread of infection through the house. Farms are mainly multi-age and may be large complexes involving many houses. Depending on the cage design, red mite infestation risk is reduced but is not eliminated. Inclusion of scratch areas increases oro-faecal transmission of disease, and cleaning and disinfection remain challenging due to house design and size.

Free-range production usually involves smaller houses, although farms may include many houses which may be single or multi-aged, and there may be a mixture of both colony and free-range houses within one enterprise. Clearly, there are huge limitations to biosecurity with high risk of infection from exposure to the outside environment from other domestic livestock, wild birds and rodents. Enteric infections, including *Brachyspira* and histomoniasis (blackhead), have an increased incidence and health is influenced by response to stressors including poor weather and predators. Cleaning and disinfection are again difficult.

Barn systems in which birds are housed, but can move freely within the house, are effectively one large cage, from an epidemiological perspective, which facilitates extensive and rapid spread of infection. Generally, they are currently small farms involving small houses where the standards vary widely in terms of the capacity for cleaning and disinfection. However this production system is rapidly increasing in popularity with some large barn houses now in use.

Multi-tier systems occur in barn-style or free-range systems, generally involving small houses. Spread of infection can be rapid, the extensive equipment present leads to difficulties in achieving uniform light intensity which can lead to behavioural problems such as pecking.

6.3 Disease Transmission, Hygiene and Biosecurity

Because of the hardware and variable quality of housing, cleaning and disinfection can be problematic. Cleaning is generally carried out poorly or inadequately, exacerbated by the fact that few sites are single aged. Slats and pits can be particular problems for barn and free-range production. Ideally, houses and hardware should be washed prior to disinfection. Formalin (formaldehyde solution) is one of the most effective disinfectants, although its use does involve health and safety concerns. Care needs to be taken when using formalin and any other disinfectants to ensure that natural water courses are not contaminated. Reference should be made to Chapter 18, this volume for further details of regulating access to farms and houses, cleaning and disinfection and the effects of the presence of organic material. Factors specific to layer farms include difficulties in (i) cleaning the complete house and cages, (ii) cleaning automatic nest boxes and (iii) applying insecticide for mite control.

In considering routes of transmission relevant to infection control, thought needs to be given to transmission within a house and between houses, and whether transmission of the infectious agent is direct (bird-to-bird) as occurs in infectious bronchitis (IB) and infectious laryngotracheitis (ILT) in addition to oro-faecal transmission, and whether it involves an intermediate host (*Histomonas*), persistence of a stage of the life cycle (nematode eggs), or vectors including staff or other personnel.

Direct transmission between birds can involve secretions (nasal, tears or sputum) as occurs with IB, avian rhinotracheitis (ART), ILT, and *Mycoplasma gallisepticum* (MG) and *M. synoviae* (MS); oro-faecal transmission via faeces, water contamination or through pecking as occurs with infectious bursal disease (IBD) and staphylococci; or vertically via the egg as occurs with MG and MS and certain *Salmonella* serovars (Pullorum, Gallinarum and sometimes *S.* Enteritidis).

Routes of transmission between units include airborne infections such as Newcastle disease (ND) and avian influenza (AI), although transmission is in reality generally via fomites, dust or droplets. Wild birds and vermin are particularly important for free-range production and may introduce *Mycoplasma*, *Salmonella* and any of the infectious respiratory disease viruses. However, wild bird behaviour is such that, other than predatory birds, wild birds generally avoid ranging commercial layers, and the risk of introduction of disease by personnel moving wild bird faecal fomites into the bird housing is much greater. Such fomites are often present beneath and around feed bins illustrating the importance of ensuring all feed spillages are removed as soon as possible. Feed can be a source of infection and, although there is relatively tight control on ingredients and preparation within Europe, this is not necessarily the case elsewhere. Staff, visiting contractors and vehicles can spread most avian diseases via fomite translocation. Inadequate cleaning and disinfection can result in pathogens persisting on the site, and these may infect the next batch of birds as may occur with IBD (and any other 'robust' avian viruses), nematode eggs, blackhead (*Histomonas* via *Heterakis* worms) and *Eimeria* oocysts. Persistence can be managed but may depend on the age, condition and state of repair of the fabric of a building and the biosecurity regimen in place and, in free-range production, range management, for example use of rotation and application of high grade activated lime which reacts exothermically with water and reduces contamination in soil. Biosecurity also involves monitoring the health status of the birds that are sourced, for example checking for evidence of *Mycoplasma* or *Salmonella* infection.

6.4 Management Input and Disease

6.4.1 Water

The correct quantity and quality of the water supply is not only vital from the nutritional point of view but has important consequences for infection. Excess water can lead to an overly wet environment which may predispose to enteritis caused by a variety of microorganisms. Insufficient water can reduce productivity and lead to dehydration and kidney failure.

Microbial contamination, whether this is with pathogens or non-pathogens, can lead to reduced or increased water intake. The most likely source is contamination of the header tanks, pipes and drinker systems. Factors affecting the level of contamination include:

- Temperature. The warmer the water, the more microbial multiplication may take place.
- Flow rates. The lower the rate, the better the conditions for microbial multiplication.
- Presence of carcasses (such as wild birds or rodents) in water storage containers.
- The presence of limescale in the pipes or drinkers.
- Faecal contamination in the drinker cups with microbial load, possibly exacerbated by leaking nipples.
- Poor hygiene and lack of cleaning of drinker lines between flocks. This can lead to build up of a microbiological biofilm.

- Presence/absence of water sanitizer.
- Presence of antimicrobials, acids, vitamins, etc., which may act as energy sources for microorganisms.

6.4.2 Feed

This is primarily, although not exclusively, a nutritional issue since correct body weight and condition will affect the general resistance to infection. To this end, intake/consumption should be measured. Feed may be in the form of mash, pellet or crumb. Consistency in manufacturing is important, as is avoidance of carryover of material and contamination from a previous manufactured batch in the feed mill, such as ionophores from broiler feed manufactured previously. It is also common to use old food left over from the previous flock when new birds arrive. This is not good practice.

Feed quality is known to affect eggshell quality although most shell problems are multifactorial. These include low levels of protein, energy and calcium, ionophore contamination and incorrect premixes. Production of a reduced number of eggs may indicate protein and energy levels require attention and a smaller number of large eggs indicates an energy deficit. Poor colouration may indicate that mineral levels are low, that there is ionophore contamination, or the presence of a viral pathogen.

6.4.3 Air quality

Air quality is again important for productivity and health, and is commonly ignored by producers. Many commercial farms are ventilated naturally. Most do not have heating systems, so birds may become cold; automated systems may reduce the total volume of air entering the house, thus increasing dust levels and leading to air-sacculitis and peritonitis. Recirculation fans can be useful as they improve air circulation, particularly in free-range houses when pop-holes are open, but their location is important to avoid exposing birds to drafts. Automated ventilation system failures are also a common predisposing factor to respiratory disease.

6.5 Disease Treatment/Prevention

The almost universal approach to controlling disease by prevention is through vaccination (Chapter 20). Developing a comprehensive vaccination programme requires knowledge of the infection history of the site coupled with the local and national disease picture. The programme must thus be tailored to the particular site.

A common approach is the use of a live priming vaccination programme coupled prior to lay with inactivated vaccines.

A typical standard vaccination programme will include:

1. Marek's disease vaccine at the hatchery.
2. IB, involving usually 2–6 live vaccines of diverse antigenic strains, administered throughout the rearing period, plus an inactivated vaccine prior to the onset of lay.
3. ND programmes are determined by the endemic or non-endemic status of the individual country and can involve 3–6 live vaccines (depending on the prevalence of Newcastle disease virus (NDV)) administered throughout the rearing period, followed by one or two inactivated vaccines prior to the onset of lay.
4. IBD 1–2 live vaccines administered at ca. 25 days of age or the use of a Marek's vectored IBD vaccine either *in ovo* or at 1 day of age.
5. Avian encephalitis (AE) – usually a single dose of live vaccine between 6 weeks of age and at least 4 weeks prior to the onset of lay. Revaccination is commonly required as a result of poor vaccine response. A fowl pox vectored AE vaccine that may be administered at day-old is available in some countries.
6. *Salmonella* vaccination – in the UK, in order to fulfil the Lion Code requirements, a comprehensive auditable stringent programme of infection control and use of vaccination developed by the UK egg industry has helped to reduce *Salmonella* infection (https://www.egginfo.co.uk/british-lion-eggs/lion-code-practice). The use of *Salmonella* vaccines varies greatly on a global basis depending on local requirements or regulations and vaccine availability. Live and inactivated vaccines are available. The live vaccines are administered orally soon after hatch and again on two further occasions during the rearing period. Inactivated vaccines are also commonly used prior to the onset of lay in addition to the live vaccines. In some countries the use of live *Salmonella* vaccines is prohibited
7. Egg drop syndrome (EDS) is controlled by means of a single inactivated vaccine administered prior to the onset of lay.

Common additional vaccines include:

8. Coccidiosis (*Eimeria*) vaccines administered at 1 day of age or in the first few days of life.
9. Avian Metapneumovirus (AMPV) (ART, turkey Rhinotracheitis (TRT), avian pneumovirus (APV)), 1–3 live vaccines administered at some point in the rearing period. Timing is dependent on the administration of other vaccines such as infectious bronchitis virus (IBV) which may interfere with the AMPV vaccine efficacy.
10. ILT, a single live vaccine either at day-old, *in ovo*, in the case of herpes virus of turkeys (HVT)-vectored vaccines, or during the rearing period (in the case of traditional live vaccines). Timing is defined in relation to other vaccines to avoid interference.
11. *Pasteurella* and *Erysipelas*, either one or two doses of inactivated vaccine administered prior to the onset of lay.
12. *M. synoviae* (MS) and *M. gallisepticum* (MG) both live and inactivated vaccines are available. Live vaccines require a single dose during the rearing period and are generally highly protective. Inactivated vaccines ideally require two doses 2–4 weeks apart and, although they can reduce shedding after infection, they are not as protective as live vaccines.

6.6 Key Diseases for Layers

6.6.1 *Mycoplasma* infection (see also Chapter 14viii, this volume)

This involves MG or MS and is often, but not always, associated with multi-age sites and frequently highlights a biosecurity problem. Both are primarily respiratory infections which can result in a reduction in egg production. There is little effect on egg quality, although there is a specific pathotype of MS that can produce a characteristic fragility of the egg apex with absence of respiratory symptoms. In some countries, the majority of multi-age sites may be infected and birds present may be serologically positive without demonstrating any symptoms. However, mycoplasmas are synergistic with most other avian respiratory pathogens and coinfection can lead to clinical disease. Treatment does not eliminate infection but simply reduces the severity of clinical signs, and recrudescence occurs periodically.

6.6.2 Respiratory and other viruses (see also Chapters 15iv, 15viii and 15x, this volume)

The viruses most frequently encountered are NDV, AMPV, IBD and variants of IBV and infectious laryngotracheitis virus (ILTV). Occurrence of clinical disease is associated with shortcomings in biosecurity, ventilation and vaccination. Each disease can result in reduced egg production, and deterioration in shell quality with or without mortality.

AE (see Chapter 15ii, this volume), IBD (see Chapter 15v, this volume) and EDS (caused by an adenovirus, see Chapter 15iii, this volume) produce few problems if birds are vaccinated appropriately. IBD may occasionally cause problems early in rearing, depending on the country and level of IBD field challenge.

Marek's disease (see Chapter 15xiii, this volume) remains a major problem in some countries despite extensive use of vaccination, and may result in as much as 1% mortality per week.

6.6.3 Endoparasites

Amongst the most commonly encountered nematodes are roundworms, *Ascaridia galli*, which are large worms reaching 4 inches (10–12 cm) in length, see Chapter 16iii, this volume. They cause few problems unless infestation is high, when there may be some loss in weight and subsequent effect on hen egg production and egg quality. Roundworm eggs can survive in the environment for up to 4 years where they may be ingested by earthworms, while the adult can survive for as long as the host.

Capillaria spp. are thread-like worms infecting the crop and upper alimentary tract, and can survive in the environment for more than a year.

Heterakis are small thin worms primarily affecting the caeca. *H. gallinarium* is one of the transport hosts for *Histomonas meleagridis*, causing blackhead disease (see Chapter 16ii, this volume. To complicate the life cycle of this parasite, *Heterakis* eggs may be ingested by earthworms when they may be eaten by birds which have access to pasture. Eggs can survive for more than a year in the environment and the adult for the life of the bird.

Syngamus trachea are tracheal worms causing gaping and heavy laboured breathing. They are red in colour and may be identified as a Y shape resulting from permanent copulation between the two sexes. They may also be ingested by earthworms.

The encysted larvae can survive for many months in soil.

Two cestodes (tape worms) are occasionally associated with laying hens. *Davainea* is a microscopically small worm possessing only 1–2 proglottids. Heavy infection can result in reductions in growth rate and poor performance. The life cycle of cestodes is generally complex involving an intermediate arthropod or gastropod host. Detection of the parasites is by microscopy.

Historically, *Eimeria* spp. (coccidiosis, see Chapter 16i, this volume) was a major problem in commercial layers during the rearing period, resulting in poor bodyweight uniformity within flocks; however, the introduction of live *Eimeria* vaccines has transformed the situation. Problems may still be encountered in countries where step down coccidiostat programmes are used, and in birds reared in cages where cycling of the vaccine is hindered. Cage reared birds almost exclusively transfer to colony cage systems where some clinical disease due to *Eimeria* has been experienced; however, the clinical episodes are related to the poor vaccine cycling on the rearing farm rather than influences of the colony cage farms themselves.

H. meleagridis (blackhead, see Chapter 16ii, this volume) tends to have an unpredictable and sporadic incidence that may be influenced by climatic conditions. Clinical blackhead is relatively easy to identify by gross liver lesions on post-mortem examination. Blackhead is often subclinical but has an immunosuppressive effect which may predispose birds to *E. coli* peritonitis. Histopathology on caeca or identification by PCR should be considered in clinical episodes that are unresponsive to antibiotic medication. Efficient worm control is an important component of any blackhead control programme and, although there are few specific anti-blackhead therapeutic products available, the organism is partially sensitive to tiamulin, and oregano-based products and organic acids can be used successfully to control or resolve blackhead outbreaks.

6.6.4 Ectoparasites

The three ectoparasites most commonly encountered are red mite (*Dermanyssus gallinae*), northern fowl mite (*Ornithonyssus bursae*) and scaly leg mite (*Knemidocoptes*).

Red mite is very common and poultry egg production may fall (see Chapter 16iii, this volume).

Northern fowl mite spends its entire life on the bird.

Scaly leg mite produces uneven scales on the legs.

Thorough cleaning is required, including filling cracks and crevices. Disinfection and treatment may involve commercially available insecticides. For backyard flock treatment of the housing and birds, diatomaceous earth can be effective against red mite. Treatment may need to be followed by cleaning and further treatment immediately after depopulation. Scaly leg mite can be treated with avermectins, and in-feed treatment with fluralaner is highly effective for red mite control.

6.6.5 Bacterial infections

E. coli (see Chapter 14ii, this volume) and *Salmonella* (see Chapter 14iv, this volume), especially *S.* Enteritidis, can both be primary infections, with *E. coli* frequently appearing as a secondary infection following infection with a variety of viruses, *Mycoplasma*, *Pasteurella*, *Erysipelas* and *Ornithobacterium*. Peritonitis can be complex, being influenced by physical and hormonal stresses that are brought about by development of the ovaries and increasing light exposure in terms of intensity and duration. Birds with suboptimal bodyweights and flocks with poor uniformity are more susceptible, and measures should be taken to resolve bodyweight issues alongside any antibacterial therapy. In many countries, *S.* Gallinarum (fowl typhoid) in adult birds and *S.* Pullorum in young birds may still be prevalent. There are strict legislative requirements for responding to *S.* Enteritidis, *S.* Typhimurium and group C *Salmonella* serovars in most countries. In-feed organic acids are also effective at controlling new infections. *E. coli* treatment should be based on antibiotic sensitivity testing. However, in some countries there are a limited number of antibiotic active ingredients available, which may compromise choice. Vaccination against *E. coli* can be useful in situations where the primary cause is a highly pathogenic strain of *E. coli*; however, in most cases, underlying management deficiencies or control of concurrent viral and mycoplasma infection should be prioritized over the use of *E. coli* vaccines. Live and inactivated vaccines are available, and the use of autogenous inactivated vaccines is common.

Spirochaetes (see Chapter 14vii, this volume) may cause a frothy diarrhoea with a reduction in performance, although infections can also be asymptomatic. Some organisms are components of the normal flora. Clinical episodes are usually influenced by management factors such as water and house hygiene, and there appears to be a seasonal or weather-related influence as well as an influence from raw material ingredients.

Spotty liver disease is an unpredictable, sporadic condition that is often experienced after hot dry weather that is followed by sudden rainfall and, as such, it is most common in free-range birds where it appears more frequently in spring. Its cause is unclear, and an underlying infection may lead to isolation of *Campylobacter* from the liver. Mortality patterns can mimic those experienced with notifiable disease; however, spotty liver is readily identifiable by means of the gross lesions apparent on and within the liver. Antibiotic followed by organic acid use can be helpful but should be used quickly after identification; however, recurrence is not uncommon.

Other conditions whose cause is uncertain include focal duodenal necrosis associated with poor weight gain and egg production. Antibiotic therapy followed by in-feed organic acid is effective. The condition can be difficult to identify as the characteristic lesions become inapparent in birds that have been dead for 15–20 min, so fresh dead or culls should be examined.

6.6.6 Non-infectious conditions

Cannibalism/pecking. Can be influenced by numerous factors, including diet, light management and lack of behavioural enrichment within the housing. Some breeds are more susceptible than others. It is important to remove carcasses from houses quickly as the presence of carcasses can exacerbate cannibalism/pecking. Treatments should be aimed at resolving the underlying causes, but successful interventions include the use of increased dietary salt levels, the use of nicotinamide and some phytotherapeutic products that appear to have a profound calming effect on birds.

Impactions. This is normally associated with free-range rearing and may involve grass or accumulation of stony material taken in for the gizzard. It is thus a management/environmental problem.

Pale eggs. Can be caused by a large number of factors including physiological and physical stressors. There is a tendency to associate pale eggs with IBV infection, which in general is unjustified, and underlying causes should be investigated systematically. Unusual large events including sudden appearance of loud vehicles or overhead flying objects such as planes and hot air balloons. Owls roosting on the apex of housing, new members of staff, feed and water failures, etc. are all possible stress events that may lead to reduction in egg production, loss of shell colour/quality and predispose birds to secondary bacterial infection.

6.7 Preventative and Reactive Therapy

Some conditions such as endoparasitic and ectoparasitic infestation lend themselves to preventative therapy. There are numerous products available on a worldwide basis; however, local regulatory requirements in some countries limit the range available. Routine strategic worming in feed or in the drinking water is logical in extensively housed birds, but intensive systems can be successfully managed by means of a screening and treatment approach if necessary.

The main global market for antibiotics in commercial layers is related to the high prevalence of mycoplasmas. As such, most registered products are antimycoplasmal but are not always effective against other bacteria such as *E. coli*. Routine use of antibiotics is no longer politically acceptable in most countries and should be avoided on both political and antibiotic resistance grounds. Choice of antibiotic should ideally be based on robust evaluation of antibiotic sensitivity data; dose rates should be calculated on a bodyweight basis and administration of product audited to ensure successful dosing. The effectiveness of some active ingredients with a limited spectrum of activity may be enhanced by combining with other active ingredients such as combining tetracyclines with tiamulin.

7 Backyard (Pet) Poultry

Grant Hayes*

Hayes VS Ltd, Little Downham, Ely, Cambridgeshire, UK

7.1 History and Structure

The pet poultry sector has been one of the fastest growing pet sectors in recent years. Poultry are relatively inexpensive to both purchase and keep. They are relatively self-sufficient, easy to handle and, in particular, can produce a readily accessible food source in the form of eggs. Poultry can fit into family ethics or vision of developing closer links to their source of food and encourage interaction with natural food production. Eggs are a high-quality food source, acceptable to omnivores and vegetarians alike.

Pet or backyard poultry ownership can range from a few hens to a more complex aviary arrangement, housing different breeds and bird types such as so-called fancy breeds, ducks and guinea fowl, often in specific housing in designated or permanent accommodation.

Several factors can influence the health of the pet poultry, including parent stock health and vaccination status, disease status of any previous owner establishment, vaccination history of the birds themselves and local disease status.

Pet poultry rehomed as end-of-lay commercial hybrid birds will have had a comprehensive vaccination and health monitoring programme and specific disease protection will continue into the near future, albeit at lower levels. Pet poultry sourced from fancy fowl breeders are much less likely to have been comprehensively vaccinated and it is likely they will at best have had minimal vaccination and, in some cases, may actually have had no vaccinations performed at all. The latter is not uncommon, due in part to the minimum vaccine vial sizes which are often 1000 doses.

Fancy fowl enthusiasts are often involved in showing and/or breeding. They will often own birds of many different ages, essentially managing a semi-extensive open, multi-age breeding colony of mixed breed birds, with a resulting lower health status. Somewhat like owners of exotic pets, pigeons and ornamental fish, knowledge is often shared by word of mouth or on social media or online forums, with limited professional veterinarian involvement. Advice is often also provided by breeders or retailers supplying replacement birds or to new owners.

7.2 Breeds

Pet poultry can include a wide variety of bird types and breeds from fancy fowl to rehomed end-of-lay commercial layers, but the majority of the recent growth in ownership has specifically been in laying hens, which this chapter will focus on.

7.3 Management

Owners' poultry husbandry knowledge and experience can vary enormously, resulting in a wide range of management standards, with concomitant impact on the health and welfare of the pet poultry.

Management factors influencing bird health would include housing, site security, diet, age range of stock, and quarantine protocols for the introduction of new or re-introduced stock.

Housing can impact bird health by both physical and infectious means (Fig. 7.1).

Lack of adequate ventilation, chilling, draughts, dirty bedding and traumatic wounds can all result from poorly designed, maintained or constructed accommodation, and these factors can all predispose the birds to secondary bacterial infections.

*grant@hayesvs.co.uk

© CAB International 2021. *Poultry Health: A Guide for Professionals* (P. Barrow *et al.*)
DOI: 10.1079/9781789245042.0007

Fig. 7.1. Simple, multi-purpose pet poultry housing that could also be used for other pets such as rabbits.

Parasitic infection can recycle through birds housed in permanent accommodation, both covered and not, and can be introduced into colonies through purchase or lending of second-hand equipment. This is a particular issue for ectoparasites such as red mite and endoparasites such as ascarids and coccidia.

Site security is a particular issue in respect of predation by foxes, but also badgers and household pets such as dogs, cats and ferrets (Fig. 7.2).

Rodents can transmit disease, and rats have been known to bite poultry.

A diet based around a balanced commercially prepared mash or pellet, fed *ad lib*, will be satisfactory whether or not it is supplemented with vegetable household food waste, greenery, worms and insects, whereas nutritional deficiencies can sometimes result from poultry surviving on solely unformulated nutrients (Fig. 7.3).

One of the biggest challenges to bird health is that of introduction of new strains or types of infectious disease transmitted via live birds or fomites. The constant influx of either new, often juvenile, poultry or poultry that have been to shows, borrowed or re-homed, can upset the existing colony physiological and disease equilibrium. Without a period of quarantine, prior to introducing 'new' entrants into an established colony, disease and/or pecking can result. These issues can still result even after adequate quarantine, but are much less likely. The disease outbreaks can be initiated in either the new entrants or in the established colony, dependent on their relative health statuses, but the result can be

Fig. 7.2. Five hens housed at night in a walk-in dog kennel and attached run. The kennel area is blocked off to reduce broodiness developing. The hens are fed and watered in the run and go to 'bed' at dusk and lay eggs on the floor of the kennel.

a full-blown sick colony, often involving multiple pathogens, some of which may have previously been dormant (Fig. 7.4).

7.4 Biosecurity

Biosecurity is an often overlooked, all-encompassing term to describe how bird health status is managed and ideally promoted. It should follow a common sense approach to disease barriers including physical barriers, quarantine procedures, personnel and environmental hygiene. All of these barriers can be implemented in a garden setting.

Biosecurity is an aspect of poultry husbandry that is poorly understood within the pet poultry sector, whose practices are often at odds with the ethos of biosecurity. Within good biosecurity practice, risk assessments and resulting interventions minimize the risk of disease transmission that may otherwise flourish in multi-age flocks, open flocks/sourcing from multiple suppliers and in colonies where limited use of vaccines, disinfectants and protective clothing all compromise hygiene standards. Biosecurity levels on site can never be ideal (Figs 7.5 and 7.6) but they can be optimized in a bespoke manner to minimize the risk of disease introduction and spread.

7.5 Main Disease Issues

The predominant infectious disease conditions experienced by backyard poultry can often reflect the semi-extensive open, multi-age structure of colonies.

Common infectious disease conditions include those caused by mycoplasmas, viruses, bacteria and parasites (ectoparasites and endoparasites).

Fig. 7.3. Pet hens can range over wide areas, constantly scratching and foraging, but particularly like shaded or covered areas like orchards or shrubberies.

Sporadic cases of bacterial infections, secondary to trauma, are also relatively common.

7.5.1 Mycoplasmosis (see Chapter 14viii, this volume)

Mycoplasmosis is relatively common in pet poultry but often lies undiagnosed. It can persistently infect poultry, which can appear asymptomatic. Mycoplasmas can be fully vertically transmitted from breeding birds to the progeny in addition to lateral transmission. Once birds are infected, they remain infected for life and they can act as a reservoir for disease.

Where new poultry are introduced into existing colonies, or where birds are re-introduced into colonies after excursions such as local or national shows, outbreaks of disease such as mycoplasmosis are more common. The clinical outbreak can occur either in the existing colony birds or only in the new birds, depending on their mycoplasma status. If newly purchased birds are mycoplasma positive (infected) they can be asymptomatic, but the stress of handling, transporting and integrating into a new colony can cause a recrudescence of mycoplasmosis, increased shedding and lateral transmission to the existing colony. If the colony is naïve to mycoplasma, infection will likely result in clinical disease. The reverse can also happen in that the newly purchased birds can develop clinical signs of mycoplasmosis if they are naïve to infection but the colony is mycoplasma positive. The severity of infection in either party will depend on the infectious dose, age of the birds, the strain and type of mycoplasma, and any intercurrent disease. Mycoplasmosis can occur in any age of bird.

Mycoplasma gallisepticum (MG) is the most pathogenic mycoplasma. It is infective for all poultry. Infection is often referred as 'chronic respiratory disease' or 'bulgy eye' with snicking and coughing, runny nose and significant swelling around the eyes.

M. synoviae (MS) is also infective to all poultry and classically presents as swollen joints and resulting lameness, but also causes milder respiratory disease than MG.

There are other poultry species-specific status of mycoplasma such as *M. anatis* (in ducks, geese). *M. meleagridis* (in turkeys) that cause similar clinical signs.

Mycoplasmosis can be treated symptomatically in milder cases, but more severe symptoms can be treated with commonly used antimicrobials including macroilides (tylosin, tylvalosin, tilmicosin), pleurmutilins (tiamulin), fluoroquinolones (enrofloxin) and tetracyclines (chlortetracyclines, doxycycline) (being aware of the therapeutic product's licensed egg withdrawal period or it's licensed use in food-producing animals). Medication often results in subsidence of clinical signs but does not consistently

Fig. 7.4. Fancy fowl kept in an enclosed aviary suffered morbidity and mortality in the established flock, due to co-infection with MG and ILT, 2 weeks after introducing younger birds without quarantine. The younger birds remained healthy. The owner liked the distinct appearances of differing breed of fowl.

eradicate infection, resulting in a reservoir of persistently affected asymptomatic birds, so the colony remains infected. Vaccination can be effective particularly against MS. The practicality and cost effectiveness of vaccination can be limited due to the minimum vial size being 1000 doses. Some mycoplasma vaccines are frozen liquid whereas others are freeze dried. Vials can theoretically be re-constituted and an appropriate aliquot administered to the birds to ensure one dose per bird.

7.5.2 Viral diseases

The most common viral diseases affecting pet hens are caused by the herpesviruses Marek's disease virus (MDV) and infectious laryngotracheitis virus (ILTV). These virus infections persist in infected birds and, whilst not truly vertically transmitted, infected birds shed virus intermittently, after initial infection, but also at times of 'stress', acting as a reservoir of infectious virus.

Marek's disease (MD) (see Chapter 15xiii, this volume)

Marek's disease often exhibits clinically in older hens as wasting, and paresis and paralysis affecting one or both legs. The disease is of particular issue in pet hens due to the lower hygiene standards and multi-age nature of the accommodation housing

Fig. 7.5. Fancy fowl in continuous use, multi-age, semi-extensive accommodation, open to wild birds and with limited hygiene and biosecurity.

Fig. 7.6. Platform feeding station in a farmyard setting, which if it functions as designed reduces wild bird and rodent access.

chicks. There is genetic- and age-resistance to infection. Most severe disease is seen in young adult hens after exposure to heavy viral challenge occurring in the first week of life, but the disease can be seen in 'teenage' and older birds. Diagnosis requires post-mortem examination, looking for tell-tale tumour formation, but histopathological confirmation of spleen or sciatic nerve tissues may be required. Once hens are affected, there is no specific treatment other than palliative care.

Vaccination is effective. Administration (as close to day-old as possible) is via sub-cutaneous or intra-muscular injection. Liquid nitrogen stored vaccines offer good levels of protection against MDV. Whilst vaccines are routinely used in commercial hybrid hens, the logistics of the storage mean they are not routinely used in more traditional rearing establishments. The freeze dried HVT vaccines offer much lower levels of protection and still suffer from the same logistics in respect of the minimum vial size of 1000 doses, which often renders vaccination an impractical and overly expensive prevention in backyard poultry.

Infectious laryngotracheitis (ILT) (see Chapter 15iv, this volume)

ILT is likely to be a more common infection in pet chickens and juvenile and adult hens. This is in part related to the persistently infected so-called 'carrier' birds that can appear asymptomatic for long periods, but where virus shedding can recrudesce after periods of 'stress'. In addition to this, some of the live vaccines available for use are less attenuated and can revert to higher virulence levels under certain conditions, resulting in overt signs of ILT, adding to the field virus 'pressure'.

Vaccination is relatively uncommon in pet chickens unless birds are sourced from larger scale or commercial layer rearers. The relative lack of vaccination, combined with more commonly practiced multi-age, openly managed flocks, and sourcing from multiple suppliers, can predispose to both new introductions of ILT and recycling of infection within sites, often from older to younger stock.

Morbidity due to co-infection with, for example, MG is not uncommon and in more typical holdings where ILT has become endemic, depopulation can on occasion be an intervention of last resort on welfare grounds if disease levels become uncontrollable.

Notifiable diseases

Pet Poultry can be at higher risk of both contracting notifiable diseases and of acting as a reservoir of virus, which is reflective of semi-extensive open, multi-age, multi-species structure of colonies, allowing extensive contact with wild birds. Pet poultry that have direct access to ponds or other habitats attractive to wild waterfowl are of particular risk of infection (Fig. 7.7).

In the UK, the two notifiable diseases, namely avian influenza (see Chapter 15vii, this volume) and Newcastle disease (see Chapter 15viii, this volume) can infect all ages of all types of poultry, albeit that the clinical presentations can vary significantly by both strain of virus and age of bird. Commercially reared pet hens will have received a robust vaccination regime against Newcastle disease virus (NDV), but vaccination against avian influenza is not currently available in the UK (Fig. 7.8).

Fig. 7.7. A very tidy, fenced but open-roofed aviary with a central ornamental pond which will be attractive to wild waterfowl.

Fig. 7.8. Layer type chicks purchased as chicks to rear in-house due to the high cost of buying point-of-lay hens. Due to their age, these chicks will have had very limited vaccinations, particularly against NDV.

Other viral infections

A host of other commonly occurring viruses can cause disease, including avian coronavirus (infectious bronchitis, see Chapter 15x, this volume) and avian pneumovirus (see Chapter 15ix, this volume), often with resulting secondary bacterial infection, most commonly with *Escherichia coli*.

7.5.3 Bacterial diseases

Colibacillosis (*E. coli*, see Chapter 14ii, this volume) is the most common bacterial infection. It often occurs secondary to mycoplasmosis, viral infections such as ILT or avian coronavirus, inadequate housing conditions or pecking, cannibalism, red mite or oviposition issues resulting in so called 'egg bind'. It can present as peritonitis, salpingitis, hepatitis, airsacculitis, pneumonia or purulent joint or tendon sheath infections.

Medication can be effective, but the disease can recur if the primary cause is not identified and resolved.

There are several other specific bacterial infections that can arise sporadically in pet poultry. Pasteurellosis (*Pasteurella multocida*), or 'fowl cholera' (see Chapter 14vi, this volume) can be more common in pet hens due to rodent infestation and contact with wild birds. It can present as either sudden death or chronic joint infections, but usually responds well to tetracycline antibiotics. Similar to pasteurellosis, erysipelas (*Erysipelothrix rhusiopathiae*, see Chapter 14ix, this volume) infection can occur sporadically but more commonly presents as sudden death. Infection more often occurs when pet poultry have access to areas where deep excavation has occurred, due to the bacteria surviving in the soil. Penicillins are the medication of choice for infection and can be used to protect birds during an outbreak. Infectious coryza (*Avibacterium paragallinarum*, see Chapter 14vi, this volume) was first seen in the UK a few years ago, but cases are still reported rarely. It presents a similar clinical picture to MG. Salmonellosis (see Chapter 14iv, this volume) rarely causes clinical issues in pet poultry but may colonize birds without disease.

7.5.4 Parasites

Ectoparasites (see Chapter 16iii, this volume)

Mites are the most common ectoparasites. Red mite (*Dermanyssus gallinae*) is the most commonly occurring, infecting new sites and recycling in existing colonies. The red mites can be transmitted on poultry, equipment or people. Their life cycle is very similar to dog and cat fleas hence adult mites can live in empty accommodation for extended periods without feeding. Once fed, the mites are prolific with rapidly maturing juvenile stages. Substantial infestations are common and have a detrimental impact on poultry as a result of both skin irritation and blood feeding activity. The former can contribute to feather pecking and cannibalism and the latter to anaemia, weight loss, morbidity, reduced egg production and mortality.

Treatment and control must be targeted at both poultry but particularly at the poultry environment, where mites reside in the tiniest cracks and crevices. Whilst chemical and physical deterrents are used, there is now a fluralaner product licensed in small pack sizes.

Northern fowl mite is much less common in the UK and can be more easily differentiated from red mite as it is predominantly found around the vent/tail of the bird. They are also blood feeding mites, so cause similar issues. They live permanently on the birds, so treatment options can be aimed solely at birds.

Burrowing mite infections are also relatively common in pet poultry, in particular, *Cnemidocoptes mutans*, the aptly called scaly leg mite. Species specific lice, fleas and tick infestations are also known but appear to be less common.

Endoparasites

Helminth infestation and coccidiosis are common parasite burdens for pet poultry. Ascarids, Capillaria and Heterakis species are the most common roundworm infections with Ascarids predominating particularly in juvenile adult birds (see Chapter 16iii, this volume). Diarrhoea, wasting, pecking/cannibalism and even mortality can result in severe burdens. Benzimidazoles are the most commonly used treatment.

Tapeworms are seen more intermittently and can be incidental findings.

Coccidiosis (see Chapter 16i, this volume) can occur in younger as well as juvenile adults. The age of infection can vary depending on the coccidial strain involved, with *Eimeria necatrix* commonly occuring in older birds. Symptoms are similar to those for worm burden but often more acute onset. Amprolium or toltrazuril treatments are effective.

Flagellate protozoal infections including hexamitiasis and histomoniasis (for the latter, see Chapter 16ii, this volume) are not uncommon in young adults with similar clinical symptoms to helminth coccidial infections. *Hexamita* are thought to have a wild bird reservoir, whereas *Histomonas* use *Heterakis* worms as an intermediate host.

7.5.5 Miscellaneous conditions

Due to the varied nature of both the standards and types of housing and stockmanship of the smallholders or pet owners, non-infectious issues can occur reasonably commonly.

Conditions of this type would include predation, accidental wounds, pecking or cannibalism, relative nutritional deficiencies, egg eating, and dysfunctional ovulations or large egg size resulting in egg-bind.

Pecking and cannibalism can often be secondary to such as parasites or overstocking or competition for feed. Bacterial peritonitis and salpingitis are often sequelae to both vent-pecking and egg-bind.

When presented with a clinical case of backyard poultry, the primary concern is likely to be the health of the pet rather than the requirement to be able to continue to eat the eggs. Egg production will obviously be sacrificed in the event of significant or chronic health challenges. Unfortunately, poultry are a predated species and often appear asymptomatic until they become seriously ill, at which stage mortality rates tend to be high.

7.6 Medication (see Chapter 19, this volume)

Medicinal therapeutics can be a difficulty when managing pet poultry. Within the EU approval status and maximum residue limit (MRL) for drugs used in food-producing animals are listed in European Commission Regulation 37/2010 (https://eur-lex.europa.eu/LexUriServ/LexUriServ.do?uri=OJ:L:2010:015:0001:0072:EN:PDF). The regulation contains a list of 'allowed substances' (Table 1 in the regulations), together with the established MRLs for the specific species and tissues. The regulation also contains a list of 'prohibited substances' (Table 2). From a pragmatic stance, when chickens are kept purely as pets and, providing the vet can justify the prescribing decision, the use of a product not listed in EU Table 1 on welfare grounds may be a consideration. In such a case, the vet must make it very clear to the animal owner that neither the animal nor food products derived from it (such as eggs) can enter the food chain. In reality, it can be difficult to be certain of this (e.g. if chickens are sold or passed on to someone else) as they have no "health passport document" to rely on. As a result, this intervention should be avoided wherever possible. For products authorized for in use chickens, any established withdrawal period for eggs will be stated in the summary of product characteristics (SPC) (e.g. zero days for fenbendazole [Panacur Aquasol SPC]). However, if no withdrawal period for eggs is published, it is the prescribing vet's responsibility to set one based on their own pharmacological research. When medicines are used that have no defined egg withdrawal period, including authorized medicines used in an unauthorized way (for example at a different dose or for a different duration from that authorized), the Veterinary Medicines Regulations define a minimum statutory withdrawal period of 7 days for eggs, unless a longer withdrawal period is stated on the product's SPC. However, as eggs take around 14 days for the yolks to mature, some may decide to err on the side of caution and advise a minimum egg withdrawal of 14 days unless the information gathered to make the decision indicates a longer period. Ultimately, it is the prescribing vet that takes responsibility for medicine selection under the Prescribing Cascade; therefore, if any produce turned up in food for human consumption and was found to have non-compliant residues (i.e. unlisted or 'prohibited substances'), the prescribing vet could be considered liable.

8 The Turkey Industry and Diseases

Richard Jennison*

Poultry Health Services, Leominster, Herefordshire, UK

8.1 Introduction

The modern turkey is descended from wild turkeys (*Meleagris gallopavo*). A number of domestic varieties exist, including white, in which feather shafts are hardly visible if left in the carcass at slaughter. Birds are large, as a result of selective breeding, with females typically reaching 4–8 kg at slaughter age, and males being reared up to around 25 kg, although weight profile also depends on the production system.

Turkeys are highly sociable. Birds have a complex range of vocalizations, with different noises appearing to have different meanings. The most well-known call is a gobbling noise. Aggression in males is common and increases with age.

Males display frequently, fanning tail feathers and drooping wings, erecting feathers including the chest beard. The skin on the naked head and neck becomes red and blue and the snood – the appendage on the head – lengthens and also becomes red. The male birds strut and call.

The genetics of current breeds results in adults that are very heavy, and as a result artificial insemination is typically required.

8.2 The Market: Turkey Production Worldwide

In 2017, over 5.2 million tonnes of turkey meat were produced globally, compared with 90 million tonnes of chicken meat. North America is the biggest producer and consumer, largely for historic reasons, representing over 50% of global production. European production accounts for around 30% of global production. In 2010, 640 million turkeys were killed globally. There is expanding production in South America (Brazil) and Russia. There is a small, but emerging market in North Africa.

In many markets, including the UK, the numbers of birds placed are tending to decline with production increasingly focusing on smaller numbers of larger birds, for example heavy males (stags). In the UK, there is a large seasonal market for turkey meat (Christmas), with smaller amounts of 'all year round' consumption.

In the UK, genetic stock is predominantly supplied by two companies (Aviagen and Hybrid). For additional information, the reader is referred to the websites for these companies. However, there are a number of other companies supplying 'specialist' strains, for example slower-growing birds and for free-range markets.

As with other poultry species, there is a 'breeding pyramid' ranging from elite, great grandparent stock, down to the production generation.

8.3 Rearing Models

Owing to the different growth rates and carcass characteristics of the sexes, with males growing more quickly than females, most turkeys are sexed prior to placement on farm. Some countries will euthanize chicks of one sex or the other (commonly the hens) and only grow one sex. Other countries (or producers) do not allow the killing of chicks and will place all birds that hatch in what is called a 'balanced kill' programme.

In the UK, turkeys are mostly produced in two main growing systems:

1. 'Day-old to death', where birds are placed in a house at day-old, and remain in the same accommodation until they reach slaughter weight. In this case, sexing is not essential. Some producers will sex stags and hens but grow them in separate pens within the same house, then thin/depopulate the hens and continue to grow the stags in the additional space vacated by the hens.
2. 'Brood and move', where birds are placed in one farm at day-old and are grown to around 6 weeks of

*richard.jennison@poultryhealthservices.com

 © CAB International 2021. *Poultry Health: A Guide for Professionals* (P. Barrow et al.)
DOI: 10.1079/9781789245042.0008

age. At this point, they are caught and moved to another farm, where they are grown to slaughter weight.

The 'brood and move' model is mainly used for production of stags, which are grown to heavy weights. However, this model is also used for seasonal production, where a hatchery/brood farm company may supply 6-week-old birds to third party private finishers.

Hens tend to be smaller and slower growing and may be grown on separate 'day-old to death' growing farms.

Birds grown by the integrators are typically sexed. Feed conversion rates (FCR) and carcass characteristics are different in both sexes and this difference increases towards sexual maturity.

Selective breeding has produced a large bird with significant breast meat yield. Male birds (stags) may be around 18–20 (+) kg liveweight at processing (around 19–20 weeks). Female birds (hens) are typically processed at around 4–8 kg liveweight (around 6–15 weeks).

Male carcasses are very large and impractical for whole bird cooking. These are predominantly deboned and used for meat (e.g. breast, thigh, etc). Within the UK and Europe, there are variable preferences: white meat (breast) is preferred within the UK and dark meat (thigh, drumstick) is preferred on the European continent, leading to some import/export trade between the two markets. Female carcasses predominantly tend to be those used for whole bird 'roasting' products but consumer tastes are changing with frozen whole birds being much less popular than in the past, while crowns, saddles and joints are becoming much more popular.

Commercial breeding turkeys typically commence laying at around 30 weeks of age (although fattening hens may show signs of impending sexual maturity as early as 20 weeks). A typical commercial laying cycle may last for 26 weeks. Fertile eggs require 28 days of incubation.

Historically, turkeys have been brooded in 'surrounds' (typically made from wire or cardboard) under canopy brooders (Fig. 8.1).

Fig. 8.1. Surround under-canopy brooder. (Reproduced with permission from Aviagen.)

There is an increase in the use of 'whole house' brooding and alternative heating methods, including indirect biomass heating (Fig. 8.2).

In the brooding stage, turkeys are susceptible to chilling if environmental temperatures are inadequate, leading to inactivity and a risk of starvation. In comparison to chickens, turkeys are 'neophobic' and may respond poorly to changes in the taste, colour or particle size of diets. Turkeys may display similar issues with the drinking water. Strongly flavoured products administered via the water, including drugs, acids or water sanitizers, may be rejected to such an extent as to cause dehydration. It is not uncommon to find ingestion of litter.

8.4 Diseases of Turkeys (refer to appropriate chapters for more detail)

8.4.1 Food-borne zoonoses

Turkeys are susceptible to intestinal colonization by food-poisoning *Salmonella* serovars and *Campylobacter jejuni*, although the level of carriage of *Campylobacter* in turkeys appears to be less than occurs in broilers (see Chapters 14iii and 14iv, this volume).

Diseases affecting turkeys are also dealt with in greater detail in the relevant chapters (see below).

Turkeys are susceptible to the notifiable diseases Newcastle disease and avian influenza.

Some disease and health issues occur more commonly at different stages of life. It is worthwhile to consider these conditions by age.

During the early brooding period (e.g. 0–14 days), the following conditions may be seen: failure to thrive/poor feed intake/starvation, colibacillosis avian metapneumovirus, particularly following day-old vaccination, rotavirus and other enteric viruses and aspergillosis.

During the later-rearing period (e.g. 2–6 weeks), the conditions and pathogens seen may include: rotavirus, colibacillosis, coccidiosis, haemorrhagic enteritis, wet litter (some of which may be associated with enteric viruses) and PEMS (poult enteritis and mortality syndrome).

During the growing period (e.g. 6–20 weeks), the conditions and pathogens seen may include: *Ornithobacterium rhinotracheale* (ORT), pasteurellosis, erysipelas, histomoniasis (also known as blackhead), mycoplasmosis, necrotic enteritis, intestinal parasites (worms) and neoplastic conditions, such as lymphoproliferative disease.

Fig. 8.2. Whole-house brooding. (Reproduced with permission from Aviagen.)

The following diseases are treated in greater depth in the relevant chapters. Here, issues specific for turkey rearing are included only.

8.4.2 Colibacillosis (see Chapter 14ii, this volume)

Escherichia coli is commonly isolated from young poults with yolk sac infection, with contamination occurring at any time throughout egg production and hatching, including via the navel after hatching.

Outbreaks of disease may also occur in older birds associated with underlying stress factors, such as adverse water hygiene, chilling, inadequate ventilation and following turkey rhinotracheitis challenge.

8.4.3 Avian metapneumovirus (turkey rhinotracheitis, TRT, see Chapter 15ix, this volume)

This condition can be a primary cause of mortality in turkeys, but more commonly causes respiratory disease and increases the risk of mortality associated with colibacillosis. Clinical features include swollen heads, sinus discharge and head shaking. Secondary *E. coli* infection can result in air sacculitis.

8.4.4 Rotavirus

Clinical signs associated with rotaviruses are most prevalent in turkey poults around the age of 4–14 days. Birds may present with an acute, watery diarrhoea, vent staining and crusted plumage. Partial vent prolapse and vent pecking may also occur. Mortality associated with dehydration is possible. Secondary infection by the flagellated protozoan *Spironucleus meleagridis* may also occur.

Post-mortem features include dilation of the caecal pouches, and possibly the small intestines, with pale-yellow, markedly watery and often frothy contents. However, these findings are not restricted to rotavirus infection. Confirmation of a diagnosis of rotavirus can be achieved by electron microscopy or gel electrophoresis. Avian rotaviruses are typically Types A and D. Care should be taken in using human or mammalian rapid ELISA (enzyme-linked immunosorbent assay) rotavirus test kits, as these may not react with all avian rotaviruses. Diagnosis of involvement with *S. meleagridis* is by microscopic examination of intestinal scrapes from freshly dead or culled birds.

Management of the infection is through addressing the signs, particularly hydration with oral glucose and electrolytes. Hyper-immune egg powder can reduce the severity of infection. Improved hygiene and management between batches is important.

8.4.5 Turkey coronavirus

Turkey coronavirus has been reported sporadically in birds 9–11 weeks of age showing depression and morbidity with a watery scour, sometimes during winter months with very little mortality.

8.4.6 Astrovirus (see Chapter 15vi, this volume)

Astrovirus can cause severe typhlitis in birds of around 5–10 days old with runting, requiring culling. Post-mortem features resemble those caused by rotavirus. Diagnosis is by PCR on intestinal contents.

8.4.7 Poult enteritis and mortality syndrome (PEMS)

PEMS is a mixed aetiology syndrome involving coronavirus, astrovirus and avian enteropathogenic *E. coli*, causing scouring with mortality in young birds of between 1–4 weeks of age.

8.4.8 'Dysbacteriosis' or 'enteric disturbance' (see Chapter 17, this volume)

This undefined condition can be an important cause of wet litter. It has a number of possible underlying factors, including chilling, nutritional components, parasites, viruses and bacteria.

Gross post-mortem findings can demonstrate watery small intestinal and caecal content, sometimes with reddening of the intestinal wall. Management involves regularly topping up bedding, good water hygiene, a warm atmosphere and ventilation.

8.4.9 Necrotic or ulcerative enteritis (see Chapter 14v, this volume)

This is a relatively recently observed enteric disease of turkeys, principally affecting birds of around 8–10 weeks. Post-mortem examination may indicate pale 'craters' in the wall of the small intestine, which may be visible from the serosal surface.

8.4.10 Aspergillosis (see Chapter 12, this volume)

Aspergillosis is a reasonably uncommon cause of respiratory disease and mortality in turkeys which tends to present in two main ways:

1. A ‘brooder pneumonia’, resulting from inhalation of fungal spores in the hatchery. This is a severe respiratory disease with high mortality and runting/unevenness in first few days of life. It may take a few days for a nodular air sac and lung lesions to develop, after mortality has been evident for a number of days.
2. A severe respiratory disease in older birds, following inhalation of fungal spores from the farm environment such as mouldy straw. Gasping may be evident with high mortality, unevenness and wasting and with severe thickening of air sacs post-mortem. Occasional ‘furry’ green–grey plaques may be evident.

Control is through culling infected birds, removal of contaminated litter, disinfection and proper ventilation of premises.

8.4.11 Coccidiosis (see Chapter 16i, this volume)

All turkeys are likely to be exposed to *Eimeria* to variable extents. Five species of *Eimeria* are known to cause lesions in turkeys.

Eimeria meleagrimitis, affecting the upper small intestine, and *E. adenoides,* affecting the caeca and rectum, are associated with significant disease. Other species include *E. gallopavonis* and *E. meleagridis*, affecting the lower small intestine, rectum and caeca, and *E. dispersa* which is found in the small intestine. Coccidiosis may be underdiagnosed in turkeys.

Depending on the species of coccidia, gross post-mortem findings can be suspicious. For example, *E. meleagrimitis* commonly causes orange mucus in the small intestine and *E. adenoides* may cause caecal cores in the caecal pouches. Diagnosis is confirmed by microscopy performed on intestinal scrapes.

Coccidiosis has been well controlled using in-feed coccidiostats, but resistance is increasing. Shuttle programmes are used increasingly to try to improve control. Anticoccidial sensitivity tests are not as widely available for turkey isolates as they are for chickens. Treatments of choice include toltrazuril, amprolium and sulphonamides. Introduction of ionophores after several weeks with no exposure can lead to toxicity. Drugs such as tiamulin whilst using ionophores increase the risk of toxicity.

Few vaccines are available for coccidiosis in turkeys. A non-precocious vaccine is available in North America; however, importation into the UK/EU is not currently permitted.

‘Nutraceuticals’ such as oregano, cinnamon oils and blends are available, but the efficacy is unknown.

Control by biosecurity is important and anticoccidial disinfectants such as chlorocresol can be effective in reducing environmental levels.

8.4.12 Haemorrhagic enteritis

Haemorrhagic enteritis is a widespread disease caused by turkey adenovirus type II which can result in sudden death, sometimes with blood staining at the vent and bleeding throughout the small intestine with accumulation of blood in the caeca. Maternal immunity probably provides some resistance. The virus is immunosuppressive, and subclinical infections may be followed by *E. coli* infection with mortality. Adenoviruses are resistant and biosecurity is important in control. Effective live vaccines are available, administered via the drinking water.

8.4.13 Blackhead/histomoniasis (see Chapter 16ii, this volume)

Blackhead is an increasingly common cause of severe morbidity and mortality in turkeys with the withdrawal of preventive drugs in the EU and USA being responsible for increases in incidence. Additional paratenic hosts, including slugs and beetles, may be involved.

Treatment may be unsuccessful, as sick birds may not eat or drink the medication, and the parasite may have already reached the liver. Treatment approaches include addressing the *Heterakis* worm burden with a wormer. The antibiotic paromomycin has been shown to possess preventive antihistomonad activity. There are some reports of successful management of cases using nutraceuticals, such as oregano-based products.

Other protozoa, including trichomonads, have been detected from microscopic examination of intestinal smears.

Spironucleus (hexamitiasis) can cause watery diarrhoea but is found most frequently in birds housed outdoors. Co-infection with rotavirus may occur. The small intestines may be dilated post-mortem and the caeca contain frothy, yellow liquid. The actively motile flagellate protozoans are easily demonstrated by microscopic examination of intestinal smears collected from fresh dead or culled birds. Biosecurity and good management are vital in preventing infection. Amoxycillin and tetracyclines have been used to manage the condition.

8.4.14 Bacterial septicaemias

Erysipelas (see Chapter 14ix, this volume) caused by *Erysipelothrix rhusopathiae*, may produce high mortality and male infertility. There appears to be a degree of seasonality with increased incidence in autumn and winter. Treatment with amoxycillin is very effective, but relapses may occur after cessation of treatment. Vaccines are available.

Pasteurellosis (see Chapter 14vi, this volume). Turkeys appear to be more susceptible to infection than chickens. Pasteurellosis is seen in seasonal producers and contact with vermin is considered to be a major risk factor. Gross post-mortem signs are similar to erysipelas. However, unlike erysipelas, pleurisy, pneumonia and purulent arthritis are also features. Fluoroquinolone treatment tends to be effective, but relapses may occur after cessation of treatment. Vaccines are available.

8.4.15 Helminthiasis (see Chapter 16iii, this volume)

The main helminth parasite of turkeys is *Ascaridia dissimilis*. The main risk factors for Ascarid worm burdens appear to be free-range rearing or rearing indoors on earth floors. The *Ascaridia* are of economic significance as they may cause significant organ condemnation at slaughter with livers showing 'milk spot' lesions, and sometimes associated with necrotic enteritis. Worm development begins in the intestine, potentially causing diarrhoea if large numbers of worms are present. There is a risk of anorexia, intestinal obstruction and intestinal inflammation. Aberrant migration of the larvae may result in granulomas in the liver. Immunosuppression may follow.

Turkeys are not regarded as a 'classic' host of *Heterakis gallinarum*, but the nematode has significance to turkeys as a potential vector of blackhead.

8.4.16 Neoplasia (see Chapters 15xii and 15xiii, this volume)

A number of neoplastic conditions exist, including turkey-specific retroviruses (type-C retrovirus), reticuloendotheliosis and Marek's disease. Poor biosecurity, multi-age and multi-species production are risk factors. Pale, enlarged livers and spleens will be evident post-mortem, and other organs, including the proventriculus, kidney, gonads and gut-associated lymphoid tissue, may also be affected. Vaccination is available against Marek's disease, but not for the other lymphoproliferative diseases of turkeys in the UK.

8.4.17 Leg problems

These can be common in turkeys, given their size and rapid growth rates.

Causes of lameness include tibial dyschondroplasia, angular limb deformities and rickets, tendon rupture/'calcified' tendons (see Chapter 13, this volume) and pododermatitis (see also Chapter 14ix, this volume).

In commercial production in the UK, rickets is uncommon. Poor mineralization leads to soft leg bones which tend to bend. Swelling of the costochondral junctions of the ribs can also occur. Severe cases may result in the skull caving in during culling. Management is by ensuring appropriate levels of vitamin D3, calcium and phosphorus in the diet. Shaky leg syndrome is a phenomenon of unknown aetiology. Turkeys between 10 and 15 weeks may be seen standing on toes that are shaking or quivering, especially just after rising. It may affect 20% of the flock, is self-limiting and no signs are detectable post-mortem.

Other infectious causes of lameness include *Mycoplasma*, *Ornithobacterium rhinotracheale* and staphylococcal infections.

8.4.18 *Mycoplasma* (see Chapter 14viii, this volume)

Mycoplasma infections in commercial turkeys are uncommon, since being largely eradicated from commercial breeding flocks. Some mycoplasmas are present in wild avian populations (including released gamebirds), so are always a threat.

8.4.19 ORT/*Ornithobacterium rhinotracheale* (see Chapter 14vi, this volume)

This is the cause of overt respiratory disease, lameness and mortality in commercial stock. Birds can carry the organism subclinically and overt disease can be the result of other factors, such as avian metapneumovirus infection, or another respiratory stressor such as inadequate ventilation.

Respiratory signs may be associated with, or followed by, locomotor signs affecting shoulder joints and legs in turkeys. Antibiotic sensitivity profiles are considered to vary across the world, but chemotherapy may be effective. An inactivated ORT vaccine administered subcutaneously at 28 days is protective.

8.4.20 Septic arthritis (see Chapter 14ix, this volume)

Septic arthritis is a relatively common cause of lameness in turkeys. Purulent hock or stifle joint infection are the most frequent sites, with infection reaching the joints by systemic translocation from other sites of infection. There may also be cases where infection extends from pododermatitis. *Staphylococcus* is the most frequently associated organism, although *E. coli* can also be isolated. Contact with wet litter may be a predisposing factor (Mayne *et al.*, 2007).

8.4.21 Non-infectious conditions include:

Ionophore toxicity

Turkeys are highly susceptible to toxicity, with some ionophore coccidiostats leading to sudden death and recumbent birds, with muscle paralysis leading to dyspnoea. Contaminated feed must be replaced immediately.

Carbon monoxide toxicity

This is an uncommon cause of mortality seen predominantly in young turkeys associated with brood rings under faulty gas brooders. Carbon monoxide is a heavy gas, and the risk is much reduced by indirect heating systems and whole house brooding.

Aortic rupture and renal haemorrhage

Spontaneous blood vessel rupture can occur as a result of fast growth, activity and excitement, typically seen in heavy stags towards the end of the growing cycle. The risk can therefore be reduced by decreasing growth rate and also by reducing activity with adjusting light intensity. Some producers have had success with reducing mortality rates by water supplementation with copper, and possibly other products (e.g. magnesium and nicotinamide).

8.5 Reference

Mayne, R.K., Else, R.W. and Hocking, P.M. (2007) High litter moisture alone is sufficient to cause footpad dermatitis in growing turkeys. *British Poultry Science* 48, 538–545.

8.6 Further Reading

Swayne, D.E. (editor-in-chief) (2013) *Diseases of Poultry*, 13th edn. Wiley-Blackwell, Ames, Iowa.

9 The Duck Industry and Diseases

MICHAEL CLARK*

School of Veterinary Medicine and Science, University of Nottingham, Sutton Bonington, Loughborough, Leicestershire, UK

9.1 The Global Duck Industry

There are approximately 5 billion ducks produced for food consumption globally per annum, of which 80% are farmed in China. The vast majority (>3.8 billion) of these birds are of the Pekin variety.

South-east Asia is a very important area of production and consumption of duck. In the UK, duck production is dwarfed by broiler production with a relatively modest 16 million ducks produced per annum, although there has been a steady increase in production over recent years. Approximately 95% of these birds are reared intensively, with 5% in free range systems. As with other poultry species there is a very well-structured breeding pyramid. The predominant global duck primary breed company is Cherry Valley Ducks (www.cherryvalley.co.uk), providing breeding stock (in conjunction with some joint ventures) for 3 billion commercial ducks per annum. The headquarters for this business are in the UK. The company has two fully pedigreed breeding lines; one in the UK and one in China, with a backup in Australia. There is a grandparent multiplication operation in Germany.

Most breeds of domestic duck are descended from the wild mallard (*Anas platyrhynchos*) and have been domesticated for 2000 years. The exception is the Muscovy duck (*Cairina moschata*), also known as the Barbary duck, which originated from South America and is thought to be the oldest domesticated waterfowl. Mules are an infertile Pekin/Muscovy cross. As ducks are waterfowl, under natural conditions, they will spend large amounts of time in and around water. They also spend considerable time performing complex preening behaviours to clean their feathers and to distribute oil onto themselves from their uropygial gland above their pygostyle. This keeps them waterproof and helps to control their body temperature.

Though ducks are reared predominantly for their meat there are other by-products to consider. Feathers are not the waste product that they are in turkey and chicken production – they are sought after as a thermal filling for products such as duvets. There is some human consumption of duck eggs – they are known to be a good ingredient for sponge cakes – and in the Philippines, balut (cooked embryonated duck eggs), are a delicacy. Duck feet and tongues also enter the food chain. The fatty livers of forced-fed Muscovy ducks are used for foie gras production in France. Foie gras is not produced in the UK, as it would be illegal under current welfare legislation.

9.2 Primary Breeding

Pedigree selection has resulted in proven improvements in Pekin duck in live weight at an age, (Fig. 9.1a), feed conversion rate (FCR) (Fig. 9.1b), lean meat yield and carcass fat levels.

The livestock operational structure is akin to that seen in other poultry species. There are the pedigree lines with a genetic test farm, great grandparent and grandparent farms feeding an elite hatchery. This replenishes the breeding lines and provides day-old parent stock to duck integrated production businesses. The standard layout of a pedigree breeding farm is shown in Fig. 9.2.

*michael.clark2@nottingham.ac.uk

© CAB International 2021. *Poultry Health: A Guide for Professionals* (P. Barrow *et al.*)
DOI: 10.1079/9781789245042.0009

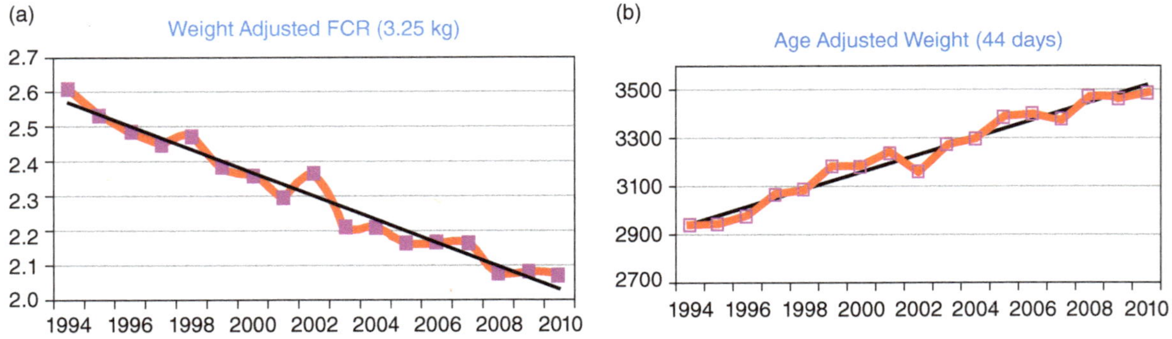

Fig. 9.1. (a) Weight adjusted feed conversion rate (FCR) 1994–2010. (Courtesy of Cherry Valley Ducks.) (b) Age adjusted weight at 44 days 1994–2010. (Courtesy of Cherry Valley Ducks.)

Fig. 9.2. Standard layout of a pedigree duck breeding farm. (Courtesy of Cherry Valley Ducks.)

9.3 Egg Production

Embryonated eggs may be set either with the cuticle on or off. The egg washing protocol for cuticle off is shown in Table 9.1.

UK duck breeding farms are not within the National Control Plan (NCP) for *Salmonella*, unlike broiler and turkey breeder units. However, if they export, they will be part of the Poultry Health Scheme (PHS) and many choose to be members of the Duck Assurance Scheme (DAS). Both the PHS and DAS have protocols for *Salmonella* monitoring that includes the testing of:

Table 9.1. Egg washing protocol. (Courtesy of Cherry Valley Ducks.)

	Egg washing/cuticle off
Temperature	Wash at 38°C/rinse at 48°C
Washing time	7 min
Rinsing time	5 s
Chemicals	Sodium hypochlorite (chorine) and sodium carbonate (washing soda)
Active ingredients in 450 l water	4.68 l 12.5% hypochlorite and 2.75 kg washing soda

- environmental swabs;
- chicks dead on arrival (DOAs);
- litter sampling; and
- hatch papers.

Duck hatcheries operate on the same principle as other poultry hatcheries. After 10 days of incubation, the eggs are candled over a table box light with any clear, early dead or infected eggs removed. After 25 days of incubation the eggs are transferred to hatcher baskets. The total incubation period is 28 days.

On hatch day, the chicks can be vent sexed. The male duckling has a palpable phallus (3–4 mm long). There is never a need for beak trimming or toe removal. In elite hatcheries there may be some means of tagging/identifying individual animals applied as individual bird identification is needed for genetic selection.

9.4 Brooding Ducklings

Ducklings need brooding as when young they are incapable of properly thermoregulating. An initial brood temperature of 30°C is required which can then be tailored back as the birds develop their adult plumage.

9.5 Welfare Considerations Regarding Water Provision

'UK producers do not supply intensively reared ducks with water for swimming. In view of the aquatic nature of all ducks and their need for water to remain healthy, water deprivation represents a serious welfare insult to them' (www.viva.org.uk/ducks-out-water-report-uk-duck-industry).

Though current UK law does not require water to be provided to ducks for anything other than drinking, the Duck Assurance Scheme has strict requirements on provision of water to assured ducks (https://assurance.redtractor.org.uk/contentfiles/Farmers-6922.pdf?_=637311857116592883).

9.6 Major Infectious Diseases Affecting Ducks

9.6.1 Duck viral hepatitis (DVH)

Duck viral hepatitis was first diagnosed in Long Island, USA in 1950. Subsequently it has been identified around the globe and in many areas is endemic. There are three antigenically different small RNA viruses identified as causing duck hepatitis; none of which are known to have public health significance. The causative agent of duck hepatitis A virus type 1 (DHAV-1; formerly DVH type 1) is a virus belonging to the family of *Picornaviridae*. This virus causes an acute, highly infectious disease of ducklings. Birds are generally between 2 days to 3 weeks of age on first infection. Adult ducks are immune to infection as birds have a complete immunity by 7 weeks of age.

9.6.2 Duck astrovirus type 1 (see also Chapter 15vi, this volume)

Duck astrovirus (DAstV-1; formerly duck viral hepatitis type 2 (DVH-2)) is rarer in the UK. In an outbreak of duck hepatitis in 1983–4 in East Anglia (Gough *et al.*, 1985) an astrovirus was identified. Thus, under the classification proposed by Asplin (1965), it was reported as DVH-2, to subsequently be reclassified as DAstV-1. A picornavirus (offering no cross protection to DHAV-1) was classified as DVH type 3 and is now classified as an astrovirus DAstV-2. DHAV-1 is the most widespread and virulent form of the disease. The virus appears more environmentally robust than the agents causing DAstV-1and and DAstV-2, with evidence of it persisting for long periods. There are also two new geno/serotypes of duck hepatitis A virus, DHAV-2 and DHAV-3 that have been identified in China, Taiwan and Korea.

The viability of the picornavirus is significant for disease spread with reports of the virus surviving several months. Susceptible young birds ingest virus-contaminated material spread on equipment, vehicles and people. Once the virus is within a flock there is rapid spread to other susceptible birds. There is no evidence of vertical transmission.

DHAV-1 is a peracute disease with death occurring within 1 h of the onset of clinical signs. Hence birds found dead are often in good bodily condition. Mortality levels within a flock can be up to 90%. Prior to death birds have opisthotonos. In endemic situations, mortality can be at a lower 5–10% level. With DAstV-2 mortality is less than 30%. With these clinical signs it would be reasonable to have duck viral enteritis, bacterial septicaemia and mycotoxicosis on the differential list.

Post-mortem examination of affected birds will reveal hepatomegaly. These diseased livers will have petechial and ecchymotic haemorrhages. In the more chronically affected older birds there may be a concurrent bacterial septicaemia. Fatty infiltration of the kidneys may also be present.

Historically, a definitive diagnosis was made from virus isolation. Direct immunofluorescence on the livers of affected ducks is another means of diagnosis and there are now PCR tests for DVH (DHAV-1).

In areas of the world where DVH is endemic it is difficult to rear ducks in isolation, and vaccination is widespread. Breeding ducks will receive two live attenuated DHAV-1 vaccines during the rearing process prior to the onset of lay followed by an inactivated DHAV-1 vaccine by injection. Commercial ducklings will receive one dose of a live attenuated DHAV-1 vaccine. These vaccines can be administered via water, aerosol spray, foot stab or subcutaneous injection.

9.6.3 Duck virus enteritis (DVE)/duck plague

Duck virus enteritis (DVE) was first diagnosed in the Netherlands in 1949, USA in 1969 and UK in 1972. The disease is caused by anatid herpesvirus-1 (AHV-1) of the genus *Mardivirus*. Outbreaks in commercial ducks and geese are often associated with access to swimming water and contact with wild waterfowl. DVE is a seasonal disease with outbreaks in the Northern Hemisphere usually occurring between April and June.

The main host species for DVE include domestic and feral ducks. Muscovy ducks are very susceptible whereas mallards are more resistant. Geese and swans are also known hosts. Standing water is an important factor in the spread of DVE, with the virus entering hosts orally or cloacally. Epidemiological studies often determine that commercial birds have become infected from wild waterfowl. The risk of disease following infection is heightened if the flock is enduring some form of stress, especially if their stocking rate is high, the birds are breeding, it is springtime and there is a captive/wild bird interaction. It is possible for there to be latent infections in immune carriers. These birds can shed virus for many years.

Diseased birds become ataxic, using their wings to help with walking and swimming. They also have pasted eyelids and photophobia along with rhinitis/nasal discharge. Enteric signs include melena (watery blood-stained diarrhoea), blood-stained vents and penile prolapse in drakes. Usually the dead birds are in good bodily condition as this is an acute disease. This is a vascular disease, which is apparent on post-mortem examination. There will be multiple tissue haemorrhages along with free blood in the coelom. Petechial haemorrhages will be detected on the heart, liver, pancreas, lungs and kidneys. Further investigation will show haemorrhage on the mucosal surface of the gastrointestinal tract, especially the oesophagus. More chronic changes include necrotic foci in the liver and oesophagus.

If a rise in waterfowl mortality occurs in springtime, with a significant egg drop, and the clinical signs and gross lesions previously outlined are seen, one can make a presumptive diagnosis of DVE. Virus isolation is confirmatory. PCR kits have been developed to detect virus in diseased birds and suspected carriers. Serological tests have little value in the diagnosis of acute DVE infections.

Heightened levels of biosecurity on commercial duck units reduce the risk of this disease. DVE is rarely diagnosed in commercial duck flocks in the UK. It is far more frequently seen in ornamental flocks where it is nigh impossible to create a barrier between kept and wild birds. Attenuated live vaccines are available for prophylactic use prior to the spring high-risk time, each year. There is the possibility of reversion to latency of these vaccines in wildfowl but no evidence of reversion to virulence. (https://www.oie.int/fileadmin/Home/eng/Health_standards/tahm/2.03.07_DVE.pdf). For longer-term protection there are also inactivated DVE vaccines.

9.6.4 Avian influenza

Though avian influenza is covered elsewhere in this book (see Chapter 15vii, this volume), below is a short case study on highly pathogenic avian influenza (HPAI) in commercial duck breeders which highlights some of the challenges of this notifiable disease in ducks.

Case Study

Initial contact was made to a private veterinary surgeon on 11 November, due to an egg drop and a very small rise in mortality. The site was 40 years old and contained 12,800 60-week-old duck breeders. Houses 1 to 3 had been depopulated 5 days previously. The 6400 birds housed in sheds 4 to 6 had dropped from 60% egg production to 30% egg production in 3 days. On walking the birds, there was no obvious morbidity but there was decreased feed and water consumption. Birds were necropsied from all three occupied houses and the most prevalent lesions were nodules suggestive of aspergillosis, airsacculitis, salpingitis and egg peritonitis. Samples from heart blood were incubated on blood and MacConkey agar and nodules were incubated on Sabouraud's agar. Serological ELISA testing was performed for Newcastle disease and egg drop syndrome (EDS). Commonly rising EDS titres are seen in breeding ducks with an egg drop. It is a moot point as to whether EDS is a disease of ducks.

On this first day of veterinary investigation the duty vet at the Animal and Plant Health Agency (APHA) was contacted for a telephone case conference. It was agreed that testing to exclude for avian influenza (www.apha.defra.gov.uk/vet-gateway/tte/nad.htm) would be useful, however this is an option for chickens and turkeys only so was not permitted in this case. Following the isolation of *E. coli* from post-mortem examination samples the remaining birds were treated with amoxicillin (20 mg/kg) via the drinking water. Coincidentally there was an initial improvement in appetite and egg production once medicating was instigated. However, these parameters subsequently deteriorated with a rising mortality (120 dead birds on 14 November). By this point it was known that there were low antibody titres to EDS and none to Newcastle disease. Although the presence of aspergillosis and *E. coli* infections had been confirmed the decision was taken to notify APHA of a suspected case of highly pathogenic avian influenza in breeding ducks. That day, a veterinary officer and animal health officer placed the site under restriction and collected samples for submission to APHA Weybridge. By 16 November, Defra confirmed a case of HPAI, later confirmed as H5N8 by normal statutory PCR testing. Control of this disease is by slaughter, and the preferred method is by using mobile gassing chambers. Despite ducks being aquatic birds that can hold their breath for some time, the 60% argon/30% carbon dioxide/10% air mix proved safe and effective causing minimal stress to the birds. Carcass disposal and primary disinfection were unremarkable. By 21 November there was a concern as to what to do with the eggs from the site now residing at the hatchery. There were three classes of eggs in the incubator: (i) eggs from the infected premises, (ii) eggs not from the infected premises and not in contact with affected eggs and (iii) eggs not from the infected premises but in contact with affected eggs. After some deliberation, the decision was made to destroy problem farm eggs and all other eggs that were in close contact. This farm had a link to a primary breed test selection site. Guidance was needed on how to treat this due to its genetic importance. Epidemiologically it would appear that a biosecurity lapse allowing wild bird (or their secretions) incursions was the means of infection. However, biosecurity within the integrated company was good, as although this was the index case of HPAI there was no spread to other units within the business. Important points from this case are:

- Ducks show mild clinical signs to HPAI in comparison with chickens.
- Testing to exclude is not an option for avian influenza in ducks.
- If a breeding site is confirmed with HPAI then by implication a hatchery will be affected.
- Mass euthanasia of ducks has added complexity compared to other poultry species.
- The legislation for avian influenza must be complied with, but for each outbreak there are specific challenges on how to work within that framework.

9.6.5 Newcastle disease (see Chapter 15viii, this volume)

Compared to other poultry species ducks seem relatively immune to Newcastle disease. Though they won't have the same level of mortality (with young birds being asymptomatic), breeders may encounter an egg drop. Despite this, a Newcastle disease infection in ducks is still a notifiable disease. Commercial ducks are rarely vaccinated for Newcastle disease. Breeder birds can receive a live vaccine priming prior to an inactivated Newcastle disease vaccine injection. However, this may not be permitted if the progeny are destined for export.

9.6.6 *Salmonella* infections (see Chapter 14iv, this volume)

European duck flocks are not part of the National Control Plan for *Salmonella*. However, flocks may be routinely tested as part of the Duck Assurance Scheme and/or the Poultry Health Scheme. *Salmonella* Typhimurium (ST) definitive type (DT) 8 and *Salmonella* Enteritidis (SE) phage type (PT) 9b are commonly associated with ducks, but a range of other types can be found (APHA, n.d.). Breeder flocks tend to be vaccinated for *Salmonella* Enteritidis and *Salmonella* Typhimurium. Though the incidence of these serovars is low, the isolation of exotic Salmonellae on routine testing in ducks is common.

9.6.7 *Streptococcus gallolyticus* (formerly *Streptococcus bovis*)

The most commonly diagnosed cause of mortality in commercial intensive ducks is bacteraemia caused by *Streptococcus gallolyticus*. Mortality levels tend to peak between 10 and 21 days of age. The birds die acutely so are in good bodily condition, though on necropsy the viscera are congested. There may be cyanosis, oedematous lungs, hepatomegaly and mottled splenomegaly. Bacteriology on heart blood will reveal the pathogen and invariably *S. gallolyticus* is sensitive to amoxicillin. Metaphylactic treatment at 20 mg/kg for 3 days is the treatment of choice. It has been very difficult to ascertain the predisposing factors in this disease.

9.6.8 *Escherichia coli* (see Chapter 14ii, this volume)

As with other poultry species, pathogenic *E. coli* are frequently isolated from duck post-mortem examinations. Juvenile birds (either breeding stock in rear or commercial birds) commonly have *E. coli* isolated between the ages of 1 to 8 weeks and breeding females, again, frequently have *E. coli* isolated on necropsy.

Whatever the age, the birds present with ill thrift, tucked in heads and incoordination. Gross post-mortem lesions include pericarditis, perihepatitis, airsacculitis, peritonitis and salpingitis (in breeding females). *E. coli* is very easy to isolate from affected organs. The difficulty is knowing whether this is due to contamination (as this is an environmental organism), an incidental finding, a co-infection or the sole pathogen. Hence serotyping is important to determine the presence of an avian pathogenic *E. coli* (APEC). The common pathogenic strains found in ducks are O93, O78 and O92 (Wang *et al.*, 2010).

Though ascertaining which antibiotics are effective against an *E. coli* isolate is important, thought should be given to other interventions before prescribing metaphylactic antibiotics to a flock. As the source of the infection is likely to be due to environmental contamination, there may be much that can be done, for example enhancing water hygiene, improving litter quality, maximizing vermin control to reduce bacterial load. Any intervention that reduces stress in a flock will minimize the extent of the disease. There are no licenced *E. coli* vaccines for ducks, but off-licence use of a chicken *E. coli* vaccine or the development of an autogenous vaccine may be indicated.

9.6.9 *Pasteurella multocida* (see Chapter 14vi, this volume)

If pneumonia is identified as the cause of mortality in ducks, then *Pasteurella* should be high up on the differential diagnosis list. Not only will pasteurellosis cause high levels of mortality and morbidity, there can also be a corresponding high level of carcass rejection when a flock is processed. Vermin control is imperative in getting a disease outbreak under control. Medication is difficult as often the only effective treatment is enrofloxacin, but its use in commercial poultry is undesirable because it is a quinolone and an antibiotic of critical importance. Currently there are no licenced poultry *Pasteurella* vaccines available, though autogenous vaccination is a possibility.

9.6.10 *Riemerella anatipestifer* (see Chapter 14vi, this volume)

As *Riemerella* is a difficult organism to culture (best cultured on blood agar and chocolate agar in 5% CO_2) and the disease is probably more widespread in UK duck flocks than we think. This organism will cause high levels of mortality due to severe polyserositis, with fibrinous exudates covering the serosal surfaces of the body cavity. There can also be lymphoid necrosis of the white pulp of the spleen. Ducks present with weakness, head/neck tremor, ataxia, incoordination, dyspnoea and hyperexcitability. Elsewhere in the world it is a major pathogen. Yet again, poor hygiene is a major contributing factor. If the pathogen is isolated, fortunately in most instances it is found to be sensitive to amoxicillin and chlortetracycline. Prevention hinges on enhancing hygiene and management. As numerous serovars can be present, care should be taken in culture selection for autogenous vaccines.

9.6.11 *Erysipelothrix rhusopathiae* (see Chapter 14ix, this volume)

If a duck flock is encountering high, persistent mortality and especially if they are kept extensively (these bacteria remain viable in soil for long periods) then erysipelas is a differential diagnosis. In erysipelas outbreaks in ducks there is often an association with current or previous keeping of pigs or sheep. As in other host species *E. rhusopathiae* causes bacteraemia in ducks, is easily isolated and is responsive to penicillin treatment. UK commercial and breeder flocks are not vaccinated for this disease.

9.6.12 Chlamydia (*Chlamydophila*, see Chapter 14ix, this volume)

All ages of ducks are susceptible to *Chlamydophila* though it is a rare infection. Clinical signs include conjunctivitis, anorexia and ruffled feathers. The pathogen, *C. psittaci* can be diagnosed on culture and serology. There is zoonotic potential. Tetracyclines have some therapeutic effect.

9.6.13 Aspergillosis

Aspergillus fumigatus can spread vertically through a duck hatchery where contaminated eggs are easily identifiable. There is also a huge horizontal risk with contaminated straw bedding a common source of infection. Clinical signs can be seen from 1-week-old ducklings to adult breeders. Birds present with severe dyspnoea, weight loss, anorexia and death.

9.6.14 Tembusu Virus

Tembusu is a contagious pathogen of ducks causing high fever, inappetence, retarded growth, neurological signs and mortality. This flavivirus has been isolated in Chinese commercial duck flocks and could be an emerging problem in Europe.

9.7 References

Animal and Plant Health Agency (APHA) (n.d.) Better Control of *Salmonella* in Commercial Duck Flocks. *Advice Leaflet*. Available at: http://sciencesearch.defra.gov.uk/Document.aspx?Document=13699_21-Bettercontrolofsalmonella_Advice_leaflet.pdf (accessed 21 January 2021).

Asplin, F.D. (1965) Duck hepatitis. *Veterinary Record* 77, 487–48.

Gough, R.E., Borland, E.D., Keymer, I.F. and Stuart, J.C. (1985) An outbreak of duck hepatitis type II in commercial ducks. *Avian Pathology* 14, 227–236.

Wang, Y., Tang, C., Yu, X., Xia, M. and Yue. H. (2010) Distribution of serotypes and virulence-associated genes in pathogenic Escherichia coli isolated from ducks. *Avian Pathology* 39, 297–302.

9.8 Further Reading

Swayne, D.E. (editor-in-chief) (2013) *Diseases of Poultry*. Wiley-Blackwell, Ames, Iowa.

10 Diseases of Gamebirds

Michael Clark*

School of Veterinary Medicine and Science, University of Nottingham, Sutton Bonington, Loughborough, Leicestershire, UK

10.1 The Game Industry in the UK

The game industry is very lightly regulated making it difficult to glean accurate information regarding its size. It is estimated by the Game & Wildlife Conservation Trust that there are 1.5 million naturally breeding female gamebirds (www.gwct.org.uk). There are thought to be 35–40 million gamebirds reared annually in the UK. Eighty per cent of these birds are pheasants with around 15% being red-legged partridge. Up to 40% of these birds originate from France, arriving in the UK as embryonated eggs, day-old chicks or 6–8-week-old poults. There is some importation of gamebird livestock from Spain and Poland. The British Association for Shooting and Conservation figures suggest there are around 5000 gamekeepers in the UK (https://basc.org.uk).

10.2 Problems with Gamebird Rearing

10.2.1 Egg peritonitis

As the stressors mount (deteriorating body condition, vermin and predator numbers, contamination of the pens) during the breeding season, laying gamebird hens are susceptible to egg peritonitis. This occurs when an ovulating follicle misses the infundibulum and is released directly into the coelom. Foreign material is an irritant causing inflammation which may be sterile or, more commonly, is infected. Egg peritonitis is easily detected on post-mortem examination. Bacteriological examination will identify any pathogens. Commonly, *Escherichia coli* and *Pasteurella* are isolated, as these bacteria grow rapidly as the disseminated yolk material rich in protein and lipids, at body temperature, is an excellent medium. Once vital organs such as the liver and heart are affected, the birds tend not to recover. Thus, a clinical sign for egg peritonitis is increased mortality. In some instances, there is not an egg peritonitis, but infection and inflammation restricted to the oviduct, i.e. a salpingitis, giving rise to a drop in egg production and poor egg quality. Flocks severely affected with egg peritonitis require a veterinary review on interventions that could reduce the stress placed on birds. Supportive therapies such as multivitamins may be indicated. Following culture and testing of the pathogen for antibiotic sensitivity, the prescribing veterinarian may wish to use a suitable antibiotic metaphylactically.

10.2.2 Egg husbandry

Egg hygiene is of the utmost importance in gamebird breeding pens and hatcheries. However, standards are often considerably poorer than their poultry counterparts. Game farmers should have the importance of laying pen hygiene reiterated to them and, though they are often stretched during the breeding season, egg collection should be frequent and diligently carried out. Ideally the operators should wear non-latex disposable gloves or, failing that, ensure their hands are clean and sanitized before handling eggs. Egg washing is an important component of the hatchery functions and should be carried out in accordance with GFA (Game Farmers' Association) recommendations.

10.2.3 Yolk sac infection

If mortality is higher than anticipated in the first 7 days of life, then yolk sac infection is an important differential diagnosis. Peak mortality for this condition occurs between 3 and 5 days. In the brooding

*michael.clark2@nottingham.ac.uk

© CAB International 2021. *Poultry Health: A Guide for Professionals* (P. Barrow *et al.*)
DOI: 10.1079/9781789245042.0010

hut, the stockman may also be aware that the flock is malodourous (a rotten egg smell). On picking up the dead birds, many will also have omphalitis (navel infections). On necropsy birds are often dehydrated and emaciated. The yolk sac is bigger than one would expect for the age of bird (in flourishing chicks it is often virtually reabsorbed by 6 days of age) and discoloured (browny red or green, but no longer golden). If the yolk sac is ruptured, the smell can be overpowering. Even in healthy culled chicks, bacteria can be cultured from yolk material. It is recommended to culture heart blood from chicks with yolk sac infection, to identify the pathogen as, invariably, the infection will have become systemic.

10.2.4 Septicaemia

With yolk sac infections and omphalitis in a flock, there will be a proportion of birds that show septicaemia with congested organs. Once a pathogen has been identified in these cases, it is tempting to reach for an antibiotic to which the isolated bacterium is sensitive. In some cases, this may be justified but, as with commercial poultry chicks, there is a drive to look at alternative therapies and strategies. One option to consider is the use of competitive exclusion products that can be sprayed on the chicks whilst in the chick boxes. The use of organic acids in the drinking water may also be beneficial. If a pathogen such as avian pathogenic *E. coli* (see Chapter 14ii, this volume) is identified, the veterinarian may wish to consider whether there is a way of maximizing maternally derived antibodies through the use of breeder vaccines.

10.2.5 Starve-outs and non-starters

Not all flocks with high mortality have an infectious issue such as yolk sac infection. If mortality is accompanied with morbidity manifested as weakness and lethargy, the chicks could be 'starve-outs'. If after the chicks have been placed in a brood hut with access to food and water, should they die within the first 3–7 days of life and on necropsy have no food material in their gizzards, they are starve-outs. A slightly different manifestation is when a similarly aged dead chick is necropsied and is found to have some food material (or bedding substrate) in the gizzard but pallor to the liver and a reabsorbed yolk sac; this is a non-starter.

Possible causes for these conditions include unhealthy breeding stock, a prolonged hatch window, chilling following hatch, sub-optimal brood temperatures, noxious gas build up and poor food and water distribution in the brood ring.

10.2.6 Enteritis/dysbacteriosis (see Chapter 17, this volume)

It is not uncommon for flocks treated for an enteric protozoal infection to continue to scour. Further laboratory work may show that the protozoal burden is abating but there is now bacterial enteritis. Bacteria such as *Sarcina*, clostridia (see Chapter 14v, this volume) and *Brachyspira* (see Chapter 14vii, this volume) have all been found either concurrent to a protozoal infection or subsequent. Antibiotic treatment may be indicated, amoxicillin being the treatment of choice for Clostridia infections, and tiamulin being the treatment of choice for *Brachyspira*.

10.2.7 Pheasant ataxia

A rare condition seen in birds over 7 weeks of age is pheasant ataxia. Diagnosis is confirmed on histopathology and differential diagnoses include Newcastle disease, fungal encephalitis, cerebral listeriosis, lead poisoning and botulism.

10.3 Specific Diseases of Breeding Birds

10.3.1 Nematode infestations (see also Chapter 16iii, this volume)

In sufficient numbers, worm burdens can cause mortality in gamebirds. At lower levels there are compromises to maintenance of bodyweight and food conversion rates. Breeding birds are either overwintered or caught up from the wild after the cessation of the shooting season. Either way, they are then kept in environments where the stocking level is considerably higher than in the wild, thus negatively impacting on parasitic burdens.

Syngamus trachea (gapeworms)

The adult worms are found in gamebird tracheas. As the name suggests, afflicted birds show signs of dyspnoea (gaping) due to tracheal obstruction. With such clinical signs a presumptive diagnosis can be made if *Syngamus trachea* eggs are detected on faecal analysis of the affected birds. A definitive diagnosis can be made on post-mortem examination. Adult worms can easily be seen attached to the mucosal lining of the trachea. The mouthparts of these red-coloured worms are used for attaching to the tracheal mucosa and the larger female is attached to the smaller male at the genitals in permanent coitus.

Heterakis gallinarum and *Heterakis isolonche* (caecal hair worms)

If nematodes are hair-like in appearance and found in the caeca of birds on post-mortem examination, they are likely to be *Heterakis gallinarum*. Afflicted flocks will have high levels of *He. gallinarum* eggs evident on faecal analysis, though they can be difficult to differentiate from *Ascaridia* spp. eggs. *He. gallinarum* is not especially pathogenic to gamebirds but is a very important nematode as it is the intermediate host for *Histomonas meleagridis*. *He. isolonche* is now considered very rare.

Ascaridia spp.

These large round worms are easily identifiable on gamebird necropsies. If, in the small intestine, there is a mass of writhing worms, looking somewhat like strands of spaghetti, then a diagnosis of *Ascaridia* spp. burden can be made. However, if the flock is seriously ill, this may be an incidental finding as these worms are not thought to be especially pathogenic.

Capillaria spp. (thread worms)

Capillaria spp. eggs are quite distinctive on faecal analysis but the adult worms are so small they can easily be overlooked on post-mortem examination. They are tiny red thread-like worms, but they are the most pathogenic nematode affecting gamebirds.

Amidostomum anseris

The gizzard worm is slim and reddish. It is a parasite of waterfowl, so may be seen in game reared ducks.

Treatment regimes for nematode burdens: Flubenvet 2.5% medicated premixture (flubendazole) is a licenced treatment for nematodes in gamebirds; 2.4 kg of product should be milled per tonne of feed. This is equivalent to 60 mg of flubendazole per kg of feed. There is also Flubenvet 5% available. Both have a 7-day meat withdrawal for gamebirds.

If the cascade principles of prescribing are followed, there are unlicensed flubendazoles and fenbendazoles that are efficacious.

When a flock is affected with nematodes, consideration should also be given to the following:

- whether the stocking level is too high and needs reducing;
- whether it is appropriate to remove faecal material from the pens;
- replacing the substrate used for dust bathing;
- harrowing the grassland; and
- ensuring the pens are not unnecessarily wet.

10.3.2 Histomoniasis (blackhead) (see also Chapter 16ii, this volume)

Blackhead is caused by the protozoan *Hi. meleagridis*. It is seen in both pheasant and partridges, adults and rearing stock. Clinically, the stockman will see an acute rise in mortality. Post-mortem examination will reveal the pathognomonic lesions in the liver. These are multiple necrotizing lesions (numerous black circular lesions with a white ring). These should not be confused with other discrete lesions in the liver such as those seen in ulcerative enteritis. Severe caseous typhlitis will also be present. No further testing is required as the liver lesions provide a definitive diagnosis.

Hi. meleagridis has a complex life cycle, involving either *He. gallinarum* or earthworms as intermediate hosts. There is no licenced treatment for histomoniasis. However, flubendazole treatment is indicated to minimize the impact of the nematodal intermediate host. Tetracyclines, especially doxycycline, are, anecdotally, thought to have a therapeutic effect. Enhanced biosecurity and hygiene are essential in reducing the infectious load.

10.3.3 Spironucleosis and trichomoniasis

Enteric protozoal infections are the bane of gamebird poult rearing. *Spironucleus meleagridis* and *Tetratrichomonas gallinae* cause very similar diseases and can be co-infections. Typically, spironucleosis and trichomoniasis can occur from 3 weeks of age. Both protozoa cause watery diarrhoea which is often yellow and frothy. Sequelae are dehydration, accompanied with weight loss (with birds having prominent keel bones), lethargy and depression and, ultimately, death.

It is recommended that moribund birds are submitted to a suitable veterinary laboratory for diagnosis, as freshly culled birds are required for a useful necropsy. On post-mortem examination the carcasses will be dehydrated and emaciated. Enteritis and typhlitis will be apparent though there are no pathognomonic lesions as there are with coccidiosis in chickens. On microscopy of intestinal scrapes coccidial oocsyts will be evident. Under ×40 magnification, numerous motile protozoa will be seen in affected birds. *Spironucleus* are often described as cigar shaped and have a gentle meandering movement. *Trichomonas* are similarly sized but are more spherical. Long flagella are often visible, giving means of rapid propulsion.

These protozoa are spread in poult pens by the faecal–oral route. Warm damp conditions facilitate protozoal survival. Severe disease outbreaks often have the contributory factors of inclement weather, overcrowding, contaminated pens and other stressors.

There are no licenced treatments for these diseases. Antimicrobials, such as tetracyclines and tiamulin, are thought to have some beneficial effect. Supportive care is important with water soluble electrolytes being indicated. Any enhancement to the birds' environment that reduces the infectious load should be instigated. Focusing on water sanitization, fixing leaks and rectifying poached areas of land will help. Dry germicides, for example Stalosan, are frequently used (www.stalosan.com). Emphasis should be placed on actual stocking levels (i.e. the space the birds really use, not the space that is available). Certain parts of a release pen may not be used as it is too dark and gloomy due to overgrown vegetation, or there is fear of predation in a certain area. It is possible to rectify these issues. Other interventions include increasing the number of available feeders and drinkers and moving them to fresh ground regularly.

10.3.4 Coccidiosis (see also Chapter 16i, this volume)

Eimeria are species specific. Though several species are known to infect pheasant and partridge the most pathogenic species in pheasants is *Eimeria colchici*, and in partridge it is *E. legionensis*. Disease is seen in gamebird poults from 21 days to 16 weeks of age. Again, this is an enteric protozoal disease spread by the faecal–oral route, with birds consuming oocysts on faecally contaminated material. The lifecycle for gamebird coccidiosis is similar to that of other *Eimeria* and will not be covered here. Suffice to say, once a susceptible flock is infected there is a rapid multiplication of protozoa, quickly giving rise to clinical signs. This results in intestinal mucosal cell damage and rapid contamination of the environment. Control is then hampered as environmental oocysts are resistant to desiccation, disinfection, temperature and time. However, they do need warmth and moisture to develop and become infective.

Coccidiosis is impossible to differentiate clinically from a motile protozoal infection, with some birds having coinfections. The clinical signs are similar with the birds having diarrhoea (sometimes whitish droppings), weight loss, lethargy, fluffed feathers, dropped wings, comatosis and death.

Diagnosis can be made on post-mortem examination. Enteritis and typhlitis will be apparent on microscopy (though there are no pathognomonic lesions as there are with coccidiosis in chickens) of intestinal scrapes which will reveal coccidial oocysts. On live birds, faecal analysis may be useful in giving an indication of flock *Eimeria* burdens.

All the management interventions recommended for motile protozoal control are pertinent for coccidiosis control. The licenced treatment is toltrazuril. A 2-day treatment at 1 ml of product per litre of drinking water normally suffices. Amprolium is also efficacious. Meat withdrawal times must be adhered to. Chicken *Eimeria* vaccines are contraindicated as the attenuated vaccine chicken *Eimeria* species provide no cross protection. Lasalocid acid is a gamebird licenced ionophore coccidiostat which has been the mainstay of coccidiosis control for many years. Terminal hygiene is important at the end of the rearing season. It should be stressed to the producer that, following an *Eimeria* challenge, it is essential that a disinfectant known to be efficacious against coccidial oocysts forms part of the disinfection programme.

10.3.5 Mycoplasmosis (see Chapter 14viii, this volume)

A serious bacterial infection of breeding gamebirds requiring veterinary intervention is mycoplasmosis. The most commonly isolated species is *Mycoplasma gallisepticum*, with *M. synoviae* being another important pathogen of gamebirds. *M. gallinaceum*, *M. glycophilum*, *M. iners*, *M. imitans* and *M. pullorum* have also been found. Work by APHA (Welchman, 2016) has shown that there is often concurrent infection with mycoplasmosis, with either more than one *Mycoplasma* species, other bacterial, or viral pathogens being present such as metapneumovirus (see Chapter 15ix, this volume), coronavirus or *Ornithobacterium rhinotracheale* (see Chapter 14vi, this volume).

Mycoplasmas are very small, slow growing bacteria. As they are intracellular bacteria it makes them more difficult to kill with antimicrobials. Very severe conjunctivitis, rhinitis and sinusitis can be seen with a *M. gallisepticum* infection. The birds become dyspnoeic; there is weight loss and also mortality. In breeding birds there can also be a drop in egg production and hatchability. With *M. synoviae* there is less in the way of respiratory signs, but there can be lameness due to tenosynovitis.

Adult gamebirds can become infected horizontally from other afflicted birds in the pen, especially via feeders and drinkers infected with nasal and ocular discharges. Breeding birds are also able to spread infection vertically, as oviducts can be infected with *Mycoplasma* leading to infection of embryos *in ovo*, and ultimately infection of chicks.

Clinical signs are exacerbated by stressors such as transportation of flocks, inclement weather, overstocking, high reproductive output and (as mentioned) concurrent infection. Mild infections may only become apparent to the stockman when data analysis shows poor hen productivity, with lower than anticipated hatchability, fewer chicks per hen and less robust chicks and poults. Thus, mycoplasmosis is of great economic importance and requires veterinary intervention. *Mycoplasma* is endemic in the wild and captive populations of gamebirds in the UK. Many gamekeepers assert that their birds are *Mycoplasma*-free, but the reality is, though birds may not currently be showing signs of disease, they are infected. A major pressure point for veterinarians is when clinically normal birds move from a game farm to a shoot. It is not unknown for birds very soon after transfer to develop mycoplasmosis. The veterinarian needs to make a robust diagnosis and ascertain whether the poults were vertically infected on the game farm from infected breeding stock, or horizontally infected on arrival at the shoot. Also, consideration of the role of stress with regards to catching, transporting and introducing the birds to a new habitat needs to be made.

As breeding birds are frequently caught up from the wild, moved between breeding establishments and are housed in systems open to wild birds, it is very difficult to maintain a flock *Mycoplasma*-free. Historically, and still to this day, prophylactic antibiotic schedules have been used on game farms. Breeding flocks are placed on antibiotics when caught up in February and are regularly treated through lay. Medication is either administered through the feed or via the drinking water. Tylvalosin is the only treatment for *Mycoplasma* licenced in gamebirds. It is dosed at 25 mg/kg. Other antibiotics are known to be efficacious for *Mycoplasma* and are licenced in other species. They include tylosin, tiamulin, tilmicosin and enrofloxacin. Less efficacious, but occasionally used, are tetracyclines and lincocin/spectinomycin. Serious thought should be given as to whether this prophylactic approach is appropriate in an age of responsible use of antibiotics. Prophylaxis will result in the unnecessary use of large amounts of treatment in low/no risk birds. Gamebirds are food animals, so meat residues/withdrawal times are paramount and many of the antibiotics mentioned are on the list of critically important antimicrobials.

Vaccination has been used in breeding gamebirds for mycoplasmosis, but it is challenging. There are reports of adverse vaccine reactions to the live poultry *M. gallisepticum* vaccines. Vaccination of breeding birds, to not only protect them but also to provide protection to their progeny, has been attempted with inactivated *M. gallisepticum* poultry vaccines such as MG-Bacterin. Though difficult and expensive to isolate, if this is achieved with a *M. gallisepticum* flock, then the manufacture of an autogenous vaccine could be considered.

Where there is a poor response to treatment or prevention in a *M. gallisepticum* infected flock, the clinician must be mindful of the role played by any concurrent stress or infection.

10.3.6 Salmonellosis (see Chapter 14iv, this volume)

Gamebirds are not part of the National Control Plan for *Salmonella* (NCP). However, they can be infected with *Salmonella* of concern to public health (*S.* Enteritidis and *S.* Typhimurium), avian pathogens (e.g. *S.* Pullorum) as well as exotic *Salmonellae*. Thus, chicks may be symptomatically or asymptomatically affected. Birds should not be treated with antibiotics if *Salmonella* are isolated on routine bacteriology, and any isolate is reportable to the Animal and Plant Health Agency.

10.3.7 Coronavirus infections

High levels of morbidity and mortality can be seen in breeding flocks of gamebirds due to coronavirus infections. There can also be sudden drops in egg production, with deterioration in egg quality and a corresponding drop in hatchability. Infections due to coronavirus can sometimes be seen in younger birds. On necropsy, many specimens have enlarged, pale kidneys and urate accumulation throughout the coelom (visceral gout). The pathogen is a pheasant-specific coronavirus, distinct from poultry strains. Diagnosis can be confirmed on virus isolation or RT-PCR. Breeding birds have been vaccinated with poultry-licenced live infectious bronchitis vaccines (see Chapter 15x, this volume) containing the Massachusetts, D274 and 793B strains as well as inactivated infectious bronchitis poultry vaccines. Breeder birds tend to be vaccinated in the hope of providing them and their progeny with some cross-protection. The efficacy of these vaccines, for this purpose, is debatable.

10.3.8 Newcastle disease (also see Chapter 15viii, this volume)

Newcastle disease is a notifiable disease of not only poultry but also gamebirds. Outbreaks of Newcastle disease in the UK have involved gamebirds in 1996, 2000 and 2005. Gamebirds show similar clinical signs to poultry, with birds becoming depressed, with diarrhoea, neurological signs (including blindness), egg drops and significant mortality all being possible. No commercially available Newcastle disease vaccines are licenced for gamebirds, but inactivated vaccines have been used in breeder birds, and live vaccines used in both breeders and rearing birds.

10.3.9 Rotavirus

The first reported case of Rotaviral infection in gamebirds in the UK was in 1983. Both infected partridge and pheasant chicks show clinical signs with, in the worst cases, mortality up to 70% from 4 to 14 days of age. Daily mortality often peaks at day 5. Chicks have dropped wings, fluffed feathers, they huddle (as they are pyrexic), closed eyes, ultimately becoming comatose and dying. Grossly there is distension of the intestinal tract and caeca by frothy yellow fluid. There may be secondary bacterial infections.

Rotavirus is an infection of breeding birds, but they are asymptomatic. Though the virus is not vertically transmitted *in ovo*, the disease is passed from parent stock to progeny. Gamebird hen faecal contamination can allow the virus to pass from breeding pen, surviving the incubation process in the hatchery, to the brood hut. Thus, egg hygiene is critically important in controlling the spread of disease. Rotavirus can also be spread horizontally. Later in the rearing season, it is not uncommon for game farmers to use a brood hut for a second batch of chicks. This practice should be discouraged, or requires fastidious cleanout and disinfection, as early season rotavirus-positive chicks are going to pose a risk to later hatches.

Producers can reduce the risk of infection by ensuring very frequent egg collection. High levels of hygiene are required at all points in the breeding cycle: adult breeding pens, egg stores, incubators, hatchers, chick take-off room and brood huts.

There is no licenced veterinary medicine for rotavirus. There is anecdotal evidence that rotavirus antibody egg powder provides some benefit. Sanitization of the water supply with organic acids may also be beneficial in alleviating some of the faecal–oral transmission.

10.3.10 Aspergillosis (also see Chapter 12, this volume)

If chicks or poults show signs of severe dyspnoea, weight loss and mortality, aspergillosis should be a differential diagnosis. A presumptive diagnosis can be made on gross post-mortem examination when numerous whitish/grey nodules can be seen throughout the viscera, especially the lungs and air sacs. Confirmation of the diagnosis is made if these nodules, cultured on Sabouraud's agar, result in the growth of *Aspergillus fumigatus*. Invariably, the source of infection is either contaminated feed or bedding substrate. There is no veterinary medicine treatment, but the affected flock should have the contaminated substrate removed from their environment immediately.

10.4 Reference

Welchman, D. (2016) Diseases in gamebirds: an update. *In Practice* 38, 189–192.

10.5 Further Reading

APHA Avian Expert Group (2015) Common Diseases of Gamebirds in Great Britain. Available at: http://apha.defra.gov.uk/documents/surveillance/diseases/gamebirds-common-diseases.pdf (accessed 21 January 2021).

11 Hatchery Practice

RICHARD JENNISON*

Poultry Health Services, Leominster, Herefordshire, UK

11.1 The Role of the Hatchery

A hatchery should aim to reproduce the environment provided by the broody hen, to her nest of eggs and her young. This is complex, requiring control of temperature, humidity, movement, egg positioning and microbial contamination.

For commercial poultry, the ultimate aim of the hatchery is to produce a 'Grade-A' quality chick for the end user (who may be a broiler farmer, pullet-rearer, breeder-rearer, game farmer, etc).

However, different types of operation may have slightly different objectives.

1. For a commercial hatchery, the saleable product is the live, healthy chick, and the target is therefore to produce as many chicks as possible from the eggs that are set.
2. For a 'broiler' integration, the ultimate objective is the production of kilograms of saleable meat, in the most cost-effective manner. The target is therefore low mortality, high quality chicks, good growth rate and good feed conversion efficiency and low factory rejects. Absolute maximum hatchability may not therefore be the ultimate goal.
3. A breeder flock farmer may be paid on the number of chicks that hatch from the eggs they supplied or even on the number of eggs they supply to the hatchery. This may be very different from the chicks that survive to 7 days or later. The quality of eggs supplied may not be absolutely optimal and it can be challenging to create a disincentive to submitting poorer quality eggs.

At each stage of the process hygiene is a key issue, including egg laying and collection, egg storage, incubation and hatching, and chick assessment and processing.

11.2 The Birds

The production of fertile eggs begins with breeding birds. Producing the maximum number of high-quality eggs with potential for high hatchability requires consideration to be given to:

1. Bird health, since disease can affect egg production, embryo viability and hatchability, negatively.
2. Body condition and nutrition. A number of factors affect embryo viability including feed and water intake, nutritional value and feed particle size, all of which can affect shell quality which can affect moisture loss and gas exchange during incubation, and dietary causes of enteritis which can lead to faecal contamination.
3. The optimal male to female ratio is 1:10–1:12. If this ratio is not optimal, too many males may manifest as aggression. Although this can be interpreted as a good indicator of libido, negative effects can include fighting between males which spend less time mating and injuries to the dorsum in the females. Males may also restrict access to the nest boxes and feeders. Too few males may lead to poor fertility rates.

The vents of males should be inspected for redness and feather wear around the vent as evidence that they are actively mating.

Some breeder flock farmers may part-incubate eggs on the farm for around 5 days, to assess fertility.

The age of the breeder flock can present issues specifically related to age.

There are a number of issues associated with younger (<30 weeks of age) breeder flocks including (i) the birds not using nest boxes correctly leading to increased microbial contamination; (ii) production of small eggs which have a higher

*richard.jennison@poultryhealthservices.com

© CAB International 2021. *Poultry Health: A Guide for Professionals* (P. Barrow *et al.*)
DOI: 10.1079/9781789245042.0011

surface area to volume ratio, leading to increased moisture loss from the egg, increasing the risk of dehydration and nephropathy in the chick; and (iii) leading to smaller chicks. There is perceived to be 'stress' from onset of lay (e.g. hormonal changes, increased metabolic demand, marked changes to calcium homeostasis), which can lead to poorer embryo viability and increased risk of bacterial contamination of the egg contents.

Conversely, older breeders (>50 weeks of age) tend to produce relatively larger eggs leading to larger chicks. With good chick quality and microbial hygiene the performance of larger chicks can be positive. However, larger eggs (i) may have double yolks; (ii) have lower surface area to volume ratio, resulting in a greater challenge dissipating heat from the egg increasing the risk of overheating the embryo, affecting hatchability and chick viability; (iii) commonly show poorer cuticle and shell quality increasing the risk of microbial penetration of the egg, affecting chick health; (iv) have a greater risk of damage; and (v) may interfere with air flow.

11.3 Nest Boxes

Good nest box management is essential in the production of clean eggs with low levels of microbial contamination. It is important to ensure females use the nest boxes and may need training by improving access and providing nest box lights.

Efforts must be made to ensure eggs are laid in nest boxes. Reasons for hens avoiding them include excessive light, interference from males and factors such as red mites.

'Astroturf' as a substrate is easy to clean and replace and, as a result, is more hygienic than natural materials such as straw but hygiene must be managed to ensure minimal microbial contamination. Some breeds show much greater tendency to lay eggs on the floor rather than in the nest boxes. Dwarf breeds enable more birds to be housed per unit area but require more next boxes.

11.4 The Eggs

Broken eggs represent a nutrient rich medium for microbial growth. Damaged eggs should be discarded as soon as possible, as they risk contaminating all parts of the egg collection system. In commercial settings, there are long conveyor systems, with lots of moving parts which can be challenging to clean after egg breakage.

Eggs should be graded. Size should be considered. Eggs which are excessively small are likely to produce very small chicks or with poor viability at increased risk of dehydration. Excessively large eggs should similarly not be set. They may be double yolked, they are at increased risk of damage due to their large size, and they are likely to interfere with air movement around the rest of the tray of eggs.

Shell imperfections may affect hatchability. Cracked eggs should not be set (although fine cracks can be difficult to spot). Cracks pose a significant microbial threat as the shell and cuticle integrity are compromised. Also, cracks affect control of moisture loss. Both are causes of poor hatchability.

Shell quality should be assessed. Chalky shell deposits, for example, can block pores and lead to gas exchange problems. This can be a potential cause of late embryonic mortality.

Some pathogens are transmitted vertically and are not detectable by visual inspection. However, 'pseudo-vertical transmission' can occur, by transmission of infection via eggshell penetration of faecal contamination. Egg shell hygiene is vitally important to reduce egg contamination and infection. Ideally, dirty eggs and eggs laid on the floor of the unit, and which may therefore be contaminated by faeces, should not be set but often are. However, this may also occur if the hen is producing loose faeces as a result of disease or following dietary changes. These can be reduced by good nest box training, by good nest box hygiene and by minimizing nutritional changes to the feed during lay. However, in an attempt to maximize the numbers of 'settable' eggs, there is often a desire to set dirty eggs.

Measures to improve the external appearance of eggs include egg washing as well as 'buffing' ('sanding') the eggshell surface to remove some visible solid contamination. However, buffing affects cuticle integrity. The cuticle is the outermost layer to the shell and is a significant barrier to bacterial penetration of the hatching egg. In theory, it is impervious to bacteria after drying. Physical removal of the cuticle by buffing removes this barrier. There is some evidence that cuticle integrity also reduces as birds age.

Eggs are laid at bird body temperature (around 40°C) and as they cool (storage temperature normally ca. 16°C) the contents contract creating a negative pressure differential which can lead to bacteria being drawn through the shell.

On-farm egg assessment can be quite rudimentary. But is an opportunity to identify issues affecting hatchability as a detailed egg inspection might not happen on receipt of the eggs at the hatchery. Egg Grading charts such as http://en.aviagen.com/assets/Tech_Center/BB_Resources_Tools/Pocket_Guides/Ross-Eggshell-Quality-Booklet2013EN.pdf can provide useful visual aids.

All parts of the operation, from egg collection on the breeding farm to egg storage, must be regarded as part of the whole operation with biosecurity uppermost in the mind of staff.

11.5 Incubation

For incubation, eggs should be placed into the trays, pointed end down, as the chick needs to orientate its head upwards towards the air space (Fig. 11.1). Failure to do this dramatically reduces hatchability in otherwise fertile eggs.

11.5.1 Egg storage

Commercial incubators tend to be large, so 'egg banking' is common practice, to enable incubators to be filled. As a result, eggs may need to be stored, cooled to below 21°C for several days to arrest embryo development. Storage tends to prolong incubation time by 1 h per day of storage with storage for 10–12 days not uncommon although for eggs older than 7 days a 1% drop in hatchability for each additional day of storage can be expected. Short periods of storage may (i) be beneficial to health management in that they may allow pooling of eggs from breeder flocks with known disease/health issues, and (ii) allow pooling eggs into batches by egg weight or breeder age.

Cooling eggs gradually and checking temperature during storage is vital. Suggested temperatures for 3–4 days storage are: 40–41°C (hen body), 24–29°C (house), 21–25°C (egg store), 20–23°C (egg truck) and 19–21°C (hatchery egg room) with cooler temperatures recommended for longer storage. Eggs must be checked during storage for uniformity of temperature, humidity and air circulation to avoid fluctuations and moisture on the egg surface which could increase the risk of bacterial contamination.

11.5.2 At the hatchery

On receipt at the hatchery, eggs will be warmed gradually and may be disinfected by fumigation or fogging.

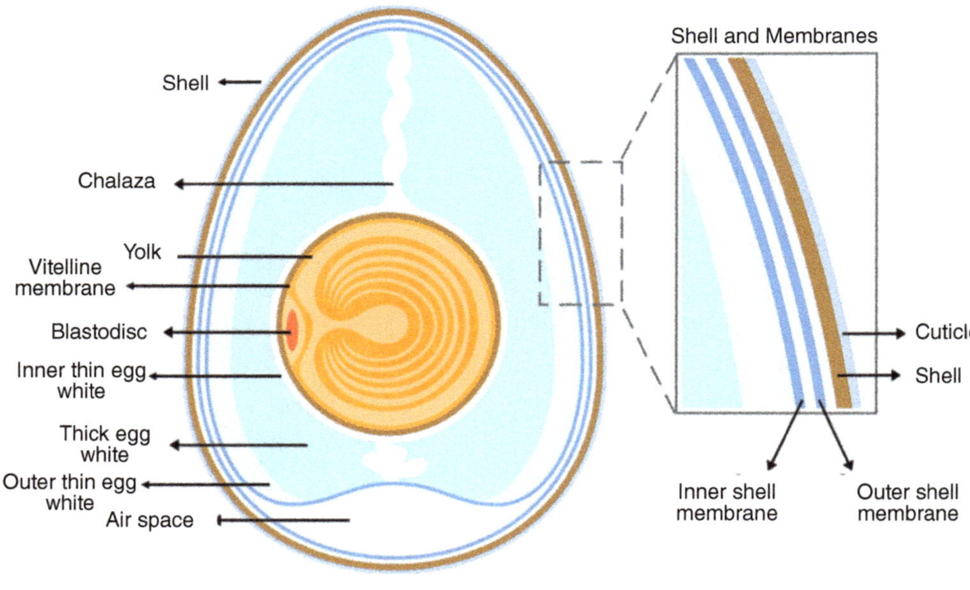

Fig. 11.1. Anatomy of the egg. (Image Courtesy of Wikimedia Commons.)

Incubation

Brood/growing periods for some types of poultry have shortened considerably and continue to shorten, but incubation periods remain unchanged. The incubation period for chickens is 21 days so almost 50% of the life of the broiler, which may be killed at 28–29 days of age, takes place in the egg (Tables 11.1 and 11.2).

Incubation may be single- or multi-stage. In the former, all eggs in the incubator are at the same stage of incubation. The advantages are improved biosecurity from thorough cleaning and disinfection between batches and provision of optimal conditions (temperature, ventilation) for each day of incubation. With multi-stage incubation, the eggs in the incubator are at various stages of incubation with eggs being added or removed continually. The main advantage is reduced cost of operation since the eggs that need to dissipate heat will provide the energy for eggs which require heat. Disadvantages include difficulty in providing optimal conditions for all eggs and increased biosecurity risks.

Effective incubation requires strict control of temperature, humidity, movement, ventilation and microbial contamination.

TEMPERATURE CONTROL Maintaining the optimal temperature for the incubating egg is important to maximize hatch rate (Table 11.3). During incubation and for around 5 days post-hatch the chick is poikilothermic, its rate of development affected by environmental temperature. Variations in incubation temperature affect metabolism and development with fluctuations resulting in embryo stress and reduced hatchability. From about half way through incubation, the embryo changes from a net absorber of heat, to a net producer of heat. The focus of incubation therefore changes from heat supply to heat dissipation.

Table 11.1. Incubation times for different poultry species.

Species	Incubation time (days)
Chicken	21
Turkey	28
Duck	28
Pheasant	24–26
Partridge	23–24
Pigeon	16–19
Goose	28–33
Coturnix Quail	16–18
Muscovy Duck	35

Table 11.2. Hatchability for different poultry species.

Species	Hatchability (%) Good	Hatchability (%) Acceptable	Breeding period/ length of breeding cycle (weeks)
Chicken	85+	78–80	36–52
Turkey	85+	80	26
Pheasant	82+	75–80	12–13
Partridge	82+	75–80	12–13

Shell temperature monitoring may reflect embryo temperature if taken correctly by infrared thermometer at the equator with several readings. Incubator air temperature is not a good indicator of embryo temperature. Opening the incubator for this purpose can reduce temperature and increase mortality. Shell temperatures of 1.1–1.5°C below average can indicate infertile eggs.

Hot and cool spots in the incubator, e.g. due to egg size variability or air movement issues can lead to a larger hatch window and reduced chick viability. Selective breeding for performance has resulted in bigger eggs and bigger embryos with thicker shell/better shell quality. This results in greater heat production from eggs and a greater challenge dissipating the heat with the thicker shell and smaller surface area to volume ratio, creating a significant risk of overheating. Reliance on a constant incubator exhaust temperature as a proxy for embryo temperature may risk overheating the embryo.

A number of leg health issues in poultry can be the result of incubation conditions, even though they may manifest much later in life including tibial length disparity, twisted toes and rotational deformities.

HUMIDITY CONTROL Moisture is lost from the eggs during incubation with loss in egg weight. Thus,

Table 11.3. Impact of incubation temperature on hatchability

Temperature	Comments	Impact on hatch
36.6–37.7°C (98–99.9°F)	Too cold	Slow hatch
37.8–38.0°C (100–100.5°F)	Optimum	
38.1–38.9°C (100.5–102°F)	Too warm	Good hatch, reduced chick quality
39.1–40°C (102.5–104°F)	Too hot	Poor hatch, poor chick quality

although humidity should be based on an analysis of egg weight loss, aiming at humidity levels of 55–60% is a good target. If incubated correctly, eggs lose 11–12% of their weight from laying to day 18 of incubation. Small amounts of moisture loss (ca. 0.5% per week) also occur during storage. Excessively low humidity can result in dehydration and chick nephropathy, kidney failure. Excessively high humidity reduces the air cell size with embryo mortality following pipping into the air cell as the chick cannot inflate its lungs.

EGG TURNING This is essential for proper embryo development and is normally performed by the hen. It has several functions: (i) preventing the embryo adhering to the shell membranes, (ii) promoting better yolk sac and allantois vascular development, (iii) increasing albumen utilization, (iv) increasing hatch weight and (v) improving embryo positioning prior to hatch. Turning is more important in the first week of incubation than in the second week and should occur around 5–6 times per day with a minimum of 3.

VENTILATION CONTROL Air exchange is essential to prevent suffocation from carbon dioxide which is toxic to the embryo. In the avian nest, concentrations are around 0.4–0.6%, which is ten times higher than atmospheric levels. Concentrations of 1% affect hatchability. Air exchange requires careful manipulation since ventilation is also the main method of temperature control for the hatching egg.

MICROBIAL CONTROL If egg-shell quality is good and egg integrity is good, then microbial contamination should reduce during incubation.

Fertility and embryo mortality

Egg fertility can be checked by candling, shining a bright light through the egg in a darkened room. See https://www.raising-happy-chickens.com/candling-eggs.html and http://www.nantahala-farm.com/chicken-duck-incubate-eggs-s.shtml. In investigating a hatchability problem, it is useful to assess when any embryo mortality occurred. In such a case, an embryo development chart (see https://www.cobb-vantress.com/assets/bulkUpload/5299a8f23d/Chick-Embryo-Chart.pdf) can be a useful reference to help identify when embryo death occurred.

Typical 'peaks' of embryo mortality occur at days 0–4 and 18–21 during incubation. Early deaths are commonly associated with egg handling. The late peak is likely to be associated with the switch to pulmonary respiration and related to incubation. Very late embryo mortality is indicated by pipped but unhatched shells.

11.5.3 Hatching

Chicken eggs are transferred from the incubator to the hatcher at 18 days of incubation for the last 3 days. Transfer requires removal of eggs from the incubator trays to hatcher baskets. Automated candling may occur at this stage to remove infertile eggs that are at increased risk of exploding as a result of microbial contamination. Egg turning is no longer required. Humidity tends to be higher, and temperature is cooler.

All eggs in a batch will not hatch at exactly the same time. The period from first to last chick hatching in a batch is called the 'hatch window'.

Chicks should not be hatched for too long prior to removal from the hatcher, as they are at increased risk of dehydration and microbial contamination. Ideally, not more than 25% of chicks should hatch by 24 h prior to removal. If this occurs, it may result from uneven rates of embryo development, possibly as a result of temperature variability during incubation.

Conversely, adequate time is required, after the last chick hatches, for the plumage to dry and the bird be ready for processing (e.g. vaccinating and transporting to farm). Sixty-five to seventy per cent of chicks should be hatched around 12 h prior to removal. Chicks are normally removed from the hatcher when 95–97% chicks are dry.

The shell waste should be checked for excessive meconium contamination of the shells which would indicate that the birds have been left in the hatcher for too long with the increased risk to chick health from bacterial multiplication and contact with a moist navel leading to yolk sac infection. Any exploding contaminated eggs will add significantly to bacterial contamination.

One additional risk to chick health is aspergillosis (brooder pneumonia) arising from inhalation of spores present on shells from the breeding farm. Affected birds may die in respiratory distress or may fail to thrive, diagnosed by the presence of nodular pneumonia or airsacculitis, and confirmation of fungal elements by histology or by culture. Monitoring for mould spores is normal during hatchery hygiene audits. Sequential lung cultures from healthy chicks can be more important since lung fungal counts should decline progressively in the days following hatch.

11.6 Chick Assessment and Grading

Chick Assessment and grading is performed after removal from the hatcher. Chicks should appear visibly normal with no crossed beaks or extra legs (Fig. 11.2).

They should be alert, active, able to stand and should be able to right themselves rapidly if turned over. Pale chicks indicate poor mobilization of yolk pigment. However, care should be taken with this assessment, as the use of formaldehyde can produce yellow colouration to chicks and make pale chicks appear normal in colour.

The core temperature of a chick, measured as rectal temperature (Fig. 11.3), is influenced by the temperature of its environment. This should be 40–40.6°C and temperatures below 39.5°C suggests birds are too cold. Above 41°C other signs of heat stress may be seen, such as panting and wing spreading.

11.7 Sexing

This is required where male and female birds are grown separately. Historically this required inspection for cloacal anatomical difference between the sexes ('vent sexing'), a procedure which is complicated by natural variation between individuals but is required for turkeys. Feather sexing is possible in some breeds/strains of chicken. The process relies on sex chromosome-linked differences in wing feather length at hatching (Fig. 11.4).

Further information of feather sexing can be found at http://en.aviagen.com/assets/Tech_Center/BB_Resources_Tools/AA_How_Tos/AA-How-to-11-FeatherSexDayOldChicks-EN-17.pdf

Colour sexing is possible for some breeds of chicken.

11.8 Vaccines

Vaccines and other products (see Chapter 20, this volume) are commonly administered in hatcheries. Vaccines may be given by spray (e.g. infectious bronchitis virus, Newcastle disease virus) or injection (e.g. Marek's). Injections can be manual or automated. Coccidiosis vaccines and competitive exclusion products (see Chapter 14iv, this volume) may also be given by spray, or by application of gel in a droplet spray.

Fig. 11.2. Abnormal chick with extra leg. (Image produced by author.)

Fig. 11.3. Measurement of rectal temperature with a digital thermometer. (Image produced by author.)

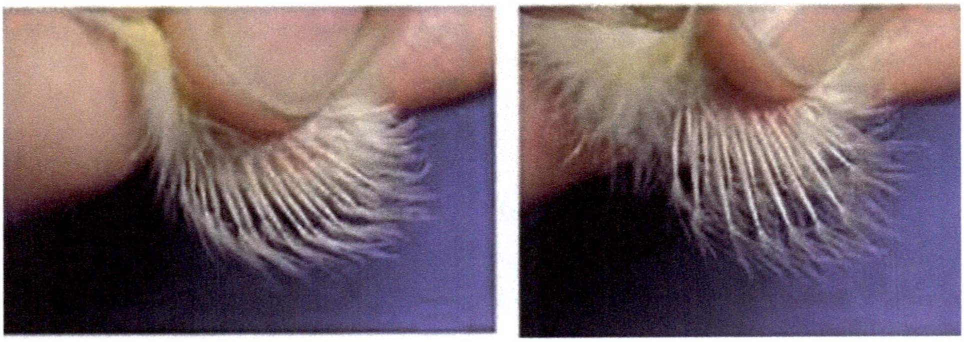

Fig. 11.4. Comparison of the wing feathers of a slow-feathering male (left) and rapid-feathering female (right) at hatch. (With permission from Dr Jacquie Jacob, University of Kentucky.)

11.9 Beak Trimming

Other treatments may or may not be carried out depending on the species and system of production. These include beak trimming/tipping, toe treatment and spur removal in males. Beak trimming can be automated.

11.10 Cleaning and Disinfection

The basic principles are cleanliness prior to disinfection because disinfection alone, including fumigants such as formaldehyde, can cover up weaknesses in hygiene and management. This is improved by good building design to allow access for cleaning. Cleaning involves use of hot water and detergent and includes good cleaning of ducts, fans, etc.

The process must be managed properly with separation of clean from dirty procedures and concentrating cleaning on areas with a high organic load, such as the hatcher. In a multi-stage operation, chicks will be present and washing in these areas should be avoided. Thought should be given to fumigating eggs prior to incubation.

Hazard Assessment Critical Control Point (HACCP) approaches should be used with the aim at reducing bacteria and spore counts. Problem organisms should be identified and targeted (e.g. *Enterococcus* which can persist at alkaline pH) so some disinfectant programmes could, for example, incorporate an acid stage.

Monitoring effectiveness of cleaning and disinfection can be done by swabs and contact plates/dip slides for surfaces and settle plates for aerial organisms and spores. New methods such as adenosine triphosphate (ATP) bioluminescence and oxidation–reduction potential (ORP) for water sources may be included.

11.11 The Future of Hatchery Technology

Technology is moving forward to increase productivity and improve welfare issues. Issues of current interest include:

1. *In ovo* vaccination, although this is currently already in use, for example for Marek's vaccines and vector vaccines, such as Vaxxitek.
2. Targeted incubation. This provides the embryo with what it needs in terms of temperature, oxygen and CO_2 for each day of incubation. This is possible with single stage incubation which is increasingly required by farm assurance schemes.
3. Impact of incubation on yolk absorption, intestinal development and subsequent bird performance.
4. Part brooding birds in the hatchery. Feed and light available in the hatchery with birds moved to the farm at 4–5 days old. See the Hatchtech system (https://www.wattagnet.com/articles/24309-consumer-trends-guide-lagerwey-hatchery-expansion).
5. Hatching birds on the farm involving transporting unhatched eggs to farms for hatching, e.g. Vencomatic X-Treck (https://www.youtube.com/watch?v=cT7rf17ykXc) incorporating an appropriate environment temperature with disposal of unhatched eggs and sick/cull chicks.
6. *In ovo* sexing. This is politically attractive for the laying industry and may resolve the issue of production of surplus males. Some methods require the creation of openings in the shell, which may impact hatchability. The mode of action for one technology is the illumination of extra embryonic circulation with laser light. Blood fluoresces and there is a difference in wavelength of the fluorescence between the sexes (https://www.poultryworld.net/Eggs/Articles/2018/6/Egg-sexing-close-to-market-301797E/).

12 Feeding Poultry and Potential Problems Associated with Diet

Patrick Garland*

Premier Nutrition, Rugeley, Staffordshire, UK

12.1 Introduction

Poultry meat and eggs are a major part of the human diet in all parts of the world and the vast numbers of birds kept for food production purposes has led to a high level of research into the appropriate feeding of poultry.

The ability to mix feed ingredients of known quality to achieve a balanced diet has allowed commercial and hobby flocks to be provided with nutritious diets with less waste and therefore greater efficiency. Feed cost makes up about 70–75% of the production cost for eggs and meat, and striving to optimize feeding efficiency helps with both costs and reducing environmental impact of both large and small flocks.

Genetic selection of chickens, turkeys and ducks has provided efficient and highly productive strains, and each has their own specific feed requirements. This poses a challenge for the hobby or pet poultry keeper in selecting the most appropriate feeds for their chosen wards. Traditional or heritage breeds have different feed requirements to the modern selected strains and this needs to be borne in mind when selecting feeds.

12.1.1 UK poultry population

In the UK, annual livestock feed production is approximately 12 million tonnes, half of which is used in poultry production. Each year, some 1050 million chickens are reared for meat with a little under 8 million breeding hens to produce the offspring needed for this. In the production of table eggs, 38 million hens are in production at any one time, and for turkey meat production, 15.5 million birds are reared each year. In addition, there are some 13 million ducks grown and 45 million game birds. Against this, an estimated 3–4 million birds are kept on smallholdings, as pets or as part of hobby/pure breed flocks (see Chapter 7, this volume). Therefore, feed production is going to be heavily weighted towards the commercial enterprises with major feed mills delivering bulk only products, and that there will be limited manufacture of bagged feeds which meet the needs of the small poultry keeper.

12.1.2 Choice of diet

In the wild, poultry consume a wide range of raw materials to satisfy their nutritional requirements and predominantly eat to satisfy their energy requirement. Poultry, like all other animals, require a variety of nutrients for maintenance, health, growth, development and reproduction. The level and ratio of nutrients needed differs according to the species, age and productive state of the bird. However, all birds require protein, energy, minerals, trace elements, vitamins and water. Apart from water, all these components are provided in manufactured feeds.

Commercially produced feed is designed to deliver a complete ration with the correct balance of nutrients, and the design of feed is based on research for the individual species. These feeds comprise several ingredients of known quality and analysis; they are formulated so that the sum of the ingredients from each raw material in combination meets the detailed requirements for the birds. Feed milling is essentially a simple process of weighing ingredients

*patrick.garland@premiernutrition.co.uk

© CAB International 2021. *Poultry Health: A Guide for Professionals* (P. Barrow *et al.*)
DOI: 10.1079/9781789245042.0012

according to a formulation, grinding, mixing and pelleting. However, the degree of control of the whole process is very detailed both from a manufacturing and regulatory point of view. Within the EU, rigorous controls are in place to ensure that each raw material is from an approved source, transported by approved hauliers and the feed mill complies with both legislative and voluntary codes of practice requirements (see Universal Feed Assurance Scheme). The benefits of these controls are that issues relating to feed having an adverse effect on bird health and performance are fortunately rare when feeds are used as intended. Poultry feed is supplied in either crumb, pellet or mash forms. For young birds, crumb is usually the preferred presentation with growing birds taking pelleted feeds readily. Laying hens normally have a mash or meal feed. It is not advisable to give mash feeds to ducks and geese since the level of fine material causes caking around the beak and tongue which may give rise to local infections and, almost certainly, high water use and consequent dirtying of open drinkers.

As mentioned above, different species have individual feed requirements and, within a species, there will be an influence of age on the precise nutritional needs that must be fulfilled. The selection of appropriate diets is covered by Mackinson and Hodgkin (2019). It can sometimes be difficult to source exact diets for the more unusual breeds of poultry and, therefore, the compromise required needs careful consideration, and expert advice should be sought.

Young growing birds have a higher requirement for protein in their diet; this gradually declines as they get older and reach mature body size, ideally at least two feeds should be used before a maintenance diet is fed for non-productive birds such as ornamental species. Within this, turkeys and pheasants have a higher protein need than chickens and, at the same time, a greater calcium and phosphorus requirement for skeletal development. If birds are kept for egg production, there is a greater need for calcium in the daily ration for eggshell formation; modern commercial hybrid strains need approximately 4% w/w calcium in their feed, so it can be seen that a growing ration which is likely to contain 1% or less of this mineral is not going to be adequate.

Supplementary feeding can be a cause of issues through the use of inappropriate materials or creating a dietary imbalance. Feeding of whole grains, such as wheat, barley or maize, can be a useful means of supplementing energy supply in colder months if birds are exposed to low ambient temperatures. However, feeding excessive amounts without other feeds can lead to deficiencies of essential minerals and vitamins that would be supplied in a proprietary feed. In addition, it should be noted that in the EU the feeding of kitchen scraps is *illegal* and is deemed a potential food safety risk. For further information, refer to the Defra website links provided in the list for further reading.

When using a complete feed, the feeding of supplementary feed/forage, such as whole/mixed grains or vegetables (only permitted when direct from the garden), should be discouraged to avoid an imbalance in nutrient supply. Young, rapidly growing birds and egg-laying birds with a high rate of production are particularly susceptible to an imbalance in nutrient supply. Such supplementary feeding should be limited to no more than 10% of the birds' total daily allowance.

12.2 Vitamin and Trace Mineral Deficiency

This is fortunately rare due to the levels of supplementation of feeds with premixes designed to deliver the appropriate levels of these essential nutrients. The levels of individual vitamins included in premixes considers the absolute requirement of the birds and then overages are added to compensate for losses during feed manufacture. Particularly, if feed is pelleted, where heat damage to some vitamins might occur, additional levels are needed to compensate for increased requirement during periods of stress or illness and potential losses during prolonged feed storage. This is demonstrated in Table 12.1, where contribution from typical ingredients is also taken into account.

However, these actions will not compensate for incorrect diet use or where feed has been stored in sub-optimal conditions. Vitamin deficiencies may manifest when there is poor hatchability and chick viability due to breeding birds not being fed a ration with appropriate level of vitamins. The vitamin requirements of breeding birds, both females and males, are higher than the levels normally used in growing or laying diets. Examples of embryo deficiency symptoms are shown in Table 12.2.

The fat-soluble vitamins (A, D, E and K) are stored in body tissues and short-term inadequate supply can be tolerated, but the water-soluble vitamins (B_1, B_2, B_6, B_{12}, niacin, pantothenic acid, folic

Table 12.1. Minimum vitamin requirement and recommended supplementation per kg of feed. (Adapted from Whitehead and Portsmouth, 1989.)

Vitamin	Requirement	Recommended supplement
Vitamin A IU	1,400	10,000
Vitamin D_3 ICU	400	5,000
Vitamin E mg	10	30
Vitamin K mg	0.4	3
Thiamin (B_1) mg	1.5	–
Riboflavin (B_2) mg	5.0	6
Niacin mg	70.0	60
Pantothenic acid	12	12
Pyridoxine (B_6)	4	3
Biotin µg	180	180
Cyanocobalamin (B_{12}) µg	12	12
Folic acid mg	0.7	1.5
Choline mg	1,300	250

acid, biotin and choline) are rapidly depleted and need to be provided constantly through the diet. As a rule, poultry do not require vitamin C (ascorbic acid (AA)) due to adequate synthesis by themselves. However, under stressful conditions such as high temperatures, AA levels in the adrenal are rapidly depleted and leads to corticosteroid hormone imbalance, immunosuppression and higher mortality. Adding 400 mg/kg of AA to diets may alleviate the symptoms (Whitehead and Portsmouth, 1989).

12.3 Feed Additives

Coccidiosis, caused by a single cell protozoan, is ubiquitous in poultry. Anywhere where chickens and turkeys are kept, there will be a challenge from this intestinal parasite which can lead to poor growth, digestive disorders, scours and bacterial infections of the intestine. Where severe challenges

Table 12.2. Common embryo deficiency symptoms for vitamins and minerals. (Adapted from Whitehead and Portsmouth, 1989.)

Nutrient	Deficiency symptoms
Vitamin A	Early embryo mortality (48 h) with failure to develop circulatory system.
Vitamin D_3	Depending on reserves in dams, stunted chicks and soft bones. Usually associated with shell defects and hence changes in porosity of the shell.
Vitamin E	Usually see early embryo mortality at 1–3 days. Encephalomalacia may be seen in the embryo and exudative diathesis is common.
Vitamin K	Depressed hatchability and signs of haemorrhaging in embryos.
Thiamin (B_1)	Two stages – one very early and the other at 19–21 days. Many dead chicks appear on the trays although there are few, if any, deformed chicks. Mortality can be high for 10–14 days for those chickens that do hatch. Injecting the chicks with thiamin results in an almost instantaneous recovery. Certain types of disinfectants, anticoccidials and poor-quality fish meal have been implicated in thiamin deficiencies. There is also recent evidence to suggest that thiamin requirements are increased in the presence of some Fusarium moulds.
Riboflavin (B_2)	Excessive embryo mortality 9–14 or 17–21 days. Embryos show oedema and/or clubbed down. Chicks may show a curling of the toes.
Niacin	Poor hatchability and bowing of the leg bones in young chicks.
Pantothenic Acid	Subcutaneous haemorrhages in unhatched embryos.
Biotin	Reduced hatch without reduced egg production. Peak in embryo mortality during the first week and last 3 days of incubation. May see skeletal deformities and crooked beaks.
Vitamin B_{12}	Embryo mortality around 8–14 days, with possibly oedema, curled toes and shortening of the beak.
Calcium and phosphorus	As maternal deficiency progresses, embryo mortality shifts from later to earlier stages of incubation. Shortened and thickened legs are seen with shortened lower mandible, bulging forehead, oedema of neck and protruding abdomen. Shell quality is usually affected.
Zinc	Numerous skeletal deficiencies, and feather down may appear to be 'tufted'.
Manganese	Late embryo mortality (18–21 days). Embryos show shortened wings and legs with abnormal head and beak shape. Oedema is common and feather down is usually abnormal.

are faced, mortality can occur. For this reason, commercial poultry operations use either in-feed or vaccine control measures. Where in-feed products are used, the feed declaration ticket will often show 'with ACS' and then give details of the product used.

Whilst the disease can be debilitating, birds will develop immunity over time and by the age of 12–16 weeks most will be immune. Young birds are susceptible, and it is advisable to either provide an oral vaccine or use feed with the appropriate anticoccidial product included; never use both, as the in-feed anticoccidial will impair the effectiveness of a vaccine.

The anticoccidials used are all regulated by EU/UK legislation and specific products are licensed for particular species and ages of birds. Some can have adverse effects in non-target species as outlined in Table 12.3.

It is relevant to point out that studies and reports regarding adverse effects in non-target species are typically limited to commercial poultry strains with little or no information regarding exotic species or heritage breeds. Therefore, the information is incomplete and possible coccidiostat implication should be borne in mind if it transpires that an inappropriate feed has been used.

If an inappropriate additive has been fed to birds destined for meat production or to laying hens, a withdrawal period should be applied before products are used for human consumption.

12.4 Skeletal Defects in Growing Birds (see also Chapter 13, this volume)

From a nutritional perspective, skeletal defects can arise from inadequate supply of protein, macro and trace minerals and vitamins. There can also be issues with imbalances between macro minerals in terms of incorrect ratio of calcium to phosphorus.

As mentioned above, the mineral requirements of turkeys, ducks and pheasants are higher than those for young chickens. Therefore, it is important to ensure that the correct feed is employed at the outset for all species of poultry. In general terms, the ratio between calcium and digestible phosphorus needs to be approximately 2:1, but it is the level of digestible phosphorus that varies between species. For young chickens, a level of 0.43% in a balanced diet should be used, but that for ducks is 0.5% and turkeys 0.7%. Clearly a chicken chick starter ration is not going to be appropriate for turkeys and could be marginal for fast growing duck strains. Fig. 12.1 shows the impact of a phosphorus deficiency in young meat-type birds due to incorrect level in the diet; good recovery was seen upon supplying them with an appropriate diet.

Appropriate protein nutrition is necessary for cartilage development before it becomes mineralized. Insufficient protein will also give poor early growth, and this is more likely to be seen than immediate bone issues which will arise from long-term sub-optimal protein intakes and is unlikely to be seen if diets of 20% protein content are used for young chickens and ducks and 26% for turkeys.

Purchased complete feeds will be supplemented with vitamins and trace minerals. In terms of skeletal development, vitamin D_3, zinc and manganese are important. Typically, the level of D_3 will be at 3000–5000 IU/kg and this will be more than adequate for starting all birds. It is unlikely that deficiency will occur unless feed has been excessively heat processed

Table 12.3. Consequences of incorrect feed use where coccidiostat is included. Based on normal inclusion levels for the approved target species. (Adapted from Fowler, 1995.)

Ionophore coccidiostats	
Monensin	Sudden introduction to turkeys over 12 weeks can lead to morbidity; to breeding turkeys mortality is likely to occur. Guinea fowl show mortality.
Salinomycin and narasin	High mortality in growing and breeding birds. Quail reported to show paralysis and mortality. Breeding and laying hens – reduced appetite, reduced rate of lay, lower hatchability and maternal mortality.
Lasalocid	Some dwarf strains of commercial chicken breeders intolerant, not known if heritage breeds are affected. In breeding birds reduced hatch and fertility and ataxia in chicks.
Chemical coccidiostats	
Nicarbazin	Reduced hatchability and loss of shell colour in brown egg layers.
Robenidine	Almond taint of eggs if fed to laying birds, may also occur in the meat of birds fed robenidine without a withdrawal period.
Halofuginone	Feed refusal by ducks and geese; feed unpalatable to partridge, quail and guinea fowl.

Fig. 12.1. Meat-type chickens affected by phosphorus deficiency in their starter ration. (Author's own photograph.)

or stored for an excessive time or in poor conditions. In this case, the feed is probably going to be unpalatable due to rancidity or mould spoilage.

Trace mineral supplementation will be in the region of 80 ppm or more for zinc and manganese, this will be in addition to the levels derived from the main raw materials used in the formulation of the feed and these levels will be more than sufficient.

Birds with very rapid growth rates can be more prone to skeletal abnormalities and this may occur when management is particularly good and nutrient intake is high. For example, goslings fed a too high a density ration in the first 2–3 weeks may outstrip the ability of their legs to support them if their weight is too high. Again, appropriate diet selection and nutrient intake is important and, for this situation, diets with high energy and protein levels should be avoided.

12.5 Calcium Deficiency in Laying Birds

Egg shell formation requires a much higher level of calcium in the ration than would be used for growing birds, and if egg production commences whilst a grower-type diet is being fed, both shell strength and skeletal strength will be affected, particularly in prolific layers such as commercial hybrid layers and layer ducks. The calcium requirement during shell formation exceeds the supply available from the feed being digested and, therefore, the birds will mobilize medullary bone reserves and then replenish these once the shell has been formed. If there is a low or marginal intake of calcium, bone strength progressively weakens, and this may result in recumbency. At this point, egg production will cease due to low calcium status and inability to access feed and water. Birds can exhibit specific appetites for particular nutrients, and that for calcium is particularly acute. Laying hens with access to calcium sources will actively seek these out in the afternoon as shell formation commences. It can be useful to provide coarse limestone granules or marine shell as a separate supplement to the diet at the rate of 2 g per bird per day if there are concerns about calcium intake. Poorly shelled eggs may not be immediately apparent if they break in the nest and egg eating as a vice may develop.

Weak-shelled eggs may arise from heat stress; it has been shown that laying hens subjected to 33°C will produce poorer quality eggshells for many days after the insult and, therefore, summertime shell issues may not be nutritionally related.

12.6 Wet Droppings and Dirty Eggs

There are many potential causes of scour, leading to wet litter conditions and faecal contamination of eggs in housed birds. The management aspects of adequate ventilation, drinker management, disease, chilling, periods of no feed and poor water quality should not be ignored. Nutritionally, high water consumption (and hence excretion) can be caused by excessive mineral levels in diet, poor quality proteins and fats/oils and anti-nutritional factors leading to poor digestion. In the case of excess minerals, the usual suspects are sodium, potassium and magnesium, and this may be due to a feed manufacture error or from supplementary feeds offered to birds. In the case of sodium, it is mainly supplied as sodium chloride or bicarbonate in the diet to meet the requirement determined, which is usually 0.14–0.18% of the complete feed. The main source of potassium is soya bean meal and levels should not exceed 0.9% in young bird starter feeds, and in layers dietary levels can be in the region of 0.55%. Magnesium can be high in some limestone sources, so free access to limestone grit can provide excess of this mineral.

Excess protein will need to be deaminated by birds, and this has a marked effect on water consumption. It has been reported that in meat-type chickens every 1% of excess protein leads to a 3% increase in water intake. Therefore, it is important not to feed high protein starter type feeds in the later growing or maintenance phases. Poor quality proteins are not well digested, and compound feeds are typically formulated based on digestible amino acids and highly digestible proteins like soya, rape, maize gluten and peas/beans. Again, if additional feedstuffs are available, they may not be particularly well digested. If poorly digested protein is present in the intestinal tract, the pH may become elevated and encourage bacterial overgrowth and then scouring.

Fats and oils used in poultry feed manufacture tend to be of vegetable origin, and the most commonly used will be soya bean oil and blends of soya and palm oils. These are well digested and, unless excessive levels are used, should not cause an issue. In the case of prolonged storage of a high oil diet (greater than 5% total oil), rancidity can occur. If the feed is consumed, since it will not be palatable, digestive disorders can result.

12.7 Drops in Egg Production and Poor Growth Rates

A decline in egg production shortly after peak numbers have been achieved can be related to an inadequate level of nutrition in the period between lighting up and peak. This can be due to either insufficient feed being consumed or a diet that is not sufficient in energy and protein. It is essential for laying birds to be of good body weight prior to the onset of laying, and that they can consume enough feed to support egg output and continued body growth at this critical time. For growing birds, poor growth can be due to diet density or low feed intake.

12.8 Mycotoxins

Wet harvests and poor storage conditions can lead to fungal growth and subsequent mycotoxin development. However, we are fortunate in the UK that problems due to field or storage mycotoxin development are rare. Cereals grown in this country are monitored at harvest and the feed industry check grains visually before acceptance to avoid potential problems. Unfortunately, what is more common is mould growth in feeds after delivery. Storage of all feed must be considered carefully. Dry and cool storage for the minimum possible time is advised; all feeds will have a best-before date and this should be observed. There are a large number of possible mycotoxins and the effects vary widely, and further details can be found in Brown *et al.* (2008).

12.9 Water

This is overlooked in terms of nutrition, but it is the most important nutrient that birds can receive. Clean fresh water must always be available. Drinking systems require good maintenance, should be designed for the type of birds being kept, and be regularly checked and flushed through. Supply pipes need to be cleaned out regularly and there are products available for use during the birds' active use of the system, and other products for when no birds are present that will strip the inevitable biofilm that will develop. Dirty water is a disease risk and will hasten the spread of disease within groups of birds.

Water intake for growing birds is in the region of 1.8 × feed use, for laying chickens over 2 × and for ducks water use can be 5 × feed consumption, although not all of this is actually taken in. Therefore, adequate access to the supply needs to optimized for the type of stock being kept. The Aviagen Water Quality Guide is a useful reference.

12.10 Unintended Feeds

In general, birds tend to avoid toxic plants due to bitter taste. Guidance on which plants to avoid in areas that poultry may access can be found at the Poultry Club of Great Britain website. The list of plants includes rhubarb leaves, rapeseed, yew, laburnum seeds, potato sprouts, sweet pea, ragwort, meadow buttercup, oleander, henbane, moist irises, vetch, clematis, corn cockle, privet, black nightshade, rhododendron, castor bean, common St John's wort and some fungi. However, there are often no specific data or references supporting toxicity for many of these, and their inclusion in the list is based purely on anecdotal evidence.

12.11 References

Brown, T., Jordan, F.T.W. and Wood, A.M. (2008) Fungal diseases. In: Pattison, M., McMullin, P.F., Bradbury, J.M. and Alexander, D.J. (eds) *Poultry Diseases*, 6th edn. Elsevier, Oxford, UK.

Fowler, N.G. (1995) Anticoccidial Compendium (Anticoccidial Information including Safety, Toxicity, Incompatibilities and Associated Matters). Anitec Associates, Canterbury, UK.

Mackinson, I. and Hodgkin, H. (2019) Nutrition. In: Poland, G. and Rafferty, A. (eds) *BSAVA Manual of Backyard Poultry Medicine and Surgery*. British Small Animal Veterinary Association, Gloucester, UK.

Whitehead, C. and Portsmouth, J. (1989) Vitamin requirements and allowances for poultry. Recent advances in animal nutrition. In: Haresign, W. and Cole, D.J.A. (eds) *Recent Advances in Animal Nutrition*. Butterworths, London.

12.12 Further Reading

Kirkpatrick, K. and Fleming, E. (2008) Water Quality. Aviagen Brief. Available at: http://en.aviagen.com/tech-center/download/27/AviagenBrief_WaterQuality_Feb08.pdf (accessed 21 January 2021).

Kleyn, R. (2013) *Chicken Nutrition – A Guide for Nutritionists and Poultry Professionals*. Context, Packington, Leicestershire, UK.

Leeson, S. and Summers, J.D. (2001) *Scotts Nutrition of the Chicken*, 4th edn. University Books, Guelph, Canada.

Leeson, S. and Summers, J.D. (2005) *Commercial Poultry Nutrition*, 3rd edn. Context, Packington, Leicestershire, UK.

Guidance on feeding waste food

Agricultural Industries Confederation (AIC) (2020) Universal Feed Assurance Scheme. Available at: https://www.aictradeassurance.org.uk/ufas/documents/ufas/ (accessed 21 January 2021).

Animal Health and Veterinary Laboratories Agency (2014) Backyard Poultry in Great Britain: General Guidance. Available at: http://apha.defra.gov.uk/documents/surveillance/diseases/backyard-poultry-guidance.pdf (accessed 8 March 2021).

Animal and Plant Health Agency (2017) Press release – APHA warns not to feed kitchen scraps to farm animals because of disease risk. Available at: https://www.gov.uk/government/news/apha-warns-not-to-feed-kitchen-scraps-to-farm-animals-because-of-disease-risk (accessed 16 March 2021).

13 Skeletal Problems

Barry Thorp*

St Davids Poultry, Easter Bush Veterinary Centre Roslin, Midlothian, UK

13.1 Background (Anatomy and Physiology)

A long bone consists of a shaft or diaphysis; at the end there is the articular cartilage. In a growing bird the articular cartilage is on top of a cartilaginous epiphysis, which may contain a secondary ossification centre. The physis (growth plate) is under the cartilaginous epiphysis and is where cartilage cells divide and enlarge to elongate the bone (Fig. 13.1). The growth plate is made up of zones. At the top of the growth plate, under the epiphysis, there is a narrow band of germinal cells. Below this the cells divide, secrete cartilage matrix and then hypertrophy. The cartilage matrix between the hypertrophied cells is then calcified. This makes the cartilage rigid and robust enough for blood vessels from the metaphysis to grow into it and introduce bone cells that lay down bone.

In chickens, the fastest growth of long bones is between 10 and 21 days of age in the proximal tibiotarsus and tarsometatarsus (~1 mm per day in a broiler chicken). Therefore, deficiencies and toxic insults that are likely to affect bone growth are most obvious in these long bone extremities. When bone growth stops, the growth plates close.

The bird skeleton has been modified for flight. Bird bones are specialized to be lighter, and some even have hollow cavities which contain extensions of the airsacs. Another flight-adaptive feature of the avian skeletal system is that there are few articulations. This prevents the incidence of disarticulation during landing. For example, the ankle joint is a simple and robust hinged joint. This is due to fusion of the small ankle (tarsal) bones with the distal tibia to form the tibiotarsus, and fusion with the proximal metatarsus to form the tarsometatarsus. The proximal femur articulates through the hip joint with the pelvis, and also through the antitrochanter/trochanter. This extra hip articulation will reduce load on the femoral neck when landing, reducing the chance of a fracture of the femoral neck. In addition, many spinal vertebrae and pelvic bones are fused.

Skeletal disorders usually present with lameness. Both infectious and non-infectious causes are common and may occur in tandem, often increasing the severity of the problem. Investigation of skeletal problems and lameness requires knowledge of normal gait, bone morphology and how these change during growth. An investigation may require the collection and analysis of samples from age-matched controls from a separate, unaffected flock. Age-matched material from clinically unaffected birds in the problem flock may be unreliable as these birds may be subclinically affected. For example, though some individual birds in a flock may clinically show rickets, most birds will have altered calcium and or phosphorus values in bone ash.

Skeletal problems can induce a lameness in birds. Minor gait abnormalities may not be painful or impact on the ability of a bird to get food and water, and are thus not a welfare concern. However, birds with some skeletal disorders may have painful conditions and also may not be marketable. This is seen as flocks with increased culls due to lameness, or flocks having increased downgrades of carcasses at slaughter due to skeletal issues. Additionally, many farmers find the management of lame birds depressing. Historically, lameness in broilers was often associated with bone deformities and tibial dyschondroplasia (TD). In recent years, the incidence of these types of disorders in meat chickens has been reduced, while infectious and nutritional disorders have become more common.

*barry@stdavids-poultryteam.co.uk

 © CAB International 2021. *Poultry Health: A Guide for Professionals* (P. Barrow *et al.*)
DOI: 10.1079/9781789245042.0013

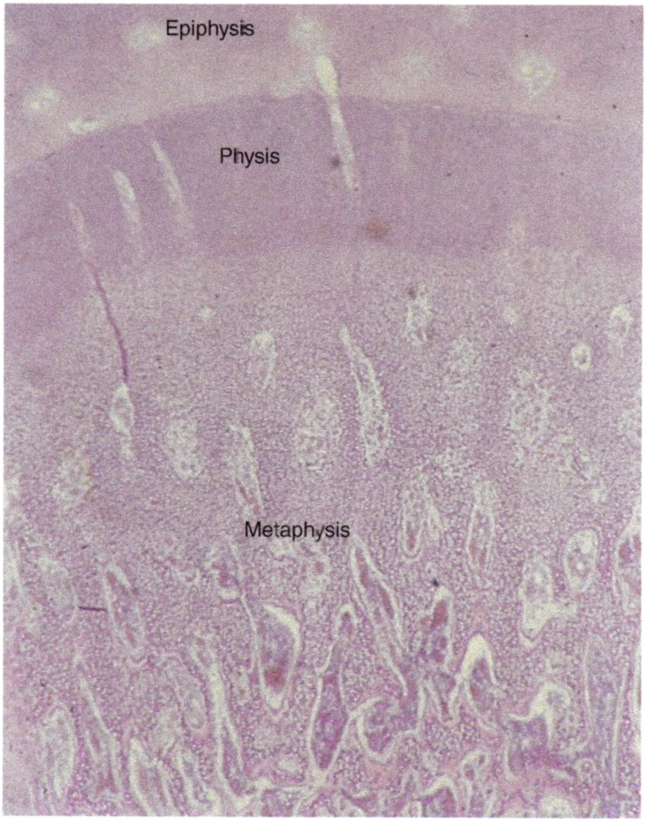

Fig 13.1. Histological section of the growth plate from a 3-week-old broiler chicken. The paler cartilage at the top of the image is epiphyseal hyaline cartilage containing blood vessels, some of which penetrate the darker physeal (growth plate cartilage). In the metaphysis there are metaphyseal vessels eroding into the hypertrophic cartilage below the physis and laying down bone (haematoxylin and eosin staining). (Author's own image.)

Common non-infectious skeletal problems in meat chickens include long bone deformities. Dyschondroplasia and rickets are also seen and may also lead to bone deformities. Infectious disorders are mostly commonly bacterial, though occasionally reovirus (see Chapter 15i, this volume) may be found. *Mycoplasma* (see Chapter 14viii this volume) may cause joint infections (i.e. *M. synoviae*) in broiler chickens despite it being, primarily, a respiratory illness.

13.2 Bone Deformities

Long bones are not perfectly straight; they normally show some torsion and slight medial or lateral deviation, which is of no concern. The most common deformities are in the distal long bones, around the ankle, or in the tarsal joint. These are commonly identified as valgus (lateral) or varus (medial) deformity of excessive external rotation of the distal tibiotarsus. Cartilage is a relatively soft malleable tissue compared with bone. In some conditions, such as rickets or TD, there is an accumulation of non-mineralized cartilage. This excess cartilage will readily deform under load and result in skeletal deformities which persist even after the cartilage is replaced by bone. In addition, deformities may develop if the load bearing on a growing bone is incorrect. This may be a consequence of altered patterns of exercise, deformity in other bones or an incorrect body conformation.

A sudden increase in bone deformities is most often the result of nutritional or mineral absorption problems (see Chapter 12, this volume). A deficiency in circulating calcium, phosphorus or vitamin D can cause rickets. This can be due to failure of absorption (i.e. due to enteritis) or an absolute dietary deficiency. Rickets results in thickened, poorly mineralized growth plates and flexible long bones. Marginal or subclinical rickets can easily be missed on diagnosis, but may manifest as poor chick performance and lead to an increased incidence of bone deformity in the flock as it gets older. In broiler chickens, subclinical rickets occurs typically in the second or third week of age. Diagnosis of rickets is by histopathology of the thickened growth plate. However, it should be noted that in rickets, the accumulated cartilage growth plate can disappear within 24 h of supplying the correct diet. Bone ashing may be of value to estimate the calcium and phosphorus content values. Broiler bones are typically about 45% dry matter and should contain 18% calcium and 9% phosphorus (standard values from different labs can be variable). To prevent rickets, it is important to make sure that the correct ration of calcium to phosphorous is supplied in the feed in a form that can be absorbed. Malabsorption will contribute to problems, as will incorrect estimates of the effect of phytase on mineral availability. Feed mills often operate on a 10% tolerance, and this can cause problems in fast growing broilers with a need for very precise requirement for available calcium and phosphorus. 25-hydroxy vitamin D_3 (25-hydroxy cholecalciferol) may be of some value in treating or preventing rickets.

Dyschondroplasia is most common in the proximal tibiotarsus and is referred to as tibial dyschondroplasia (TD) (Fig. 13.2). In TD there is an accumulation of non-mineralized, avascular, growth plate cartilage extending into the metaphysis of the bone. Factors causing TD include genetic predisposition, incorrect calcium/phosphorus ratios in feed, metabolic acidosis, incorrect acid–base balance and the presence of mycotoxins in the feed. TD leads to bone deformity and may, in some breeds, be a consequence of incorrect calcium phosphorus ratios in feed.

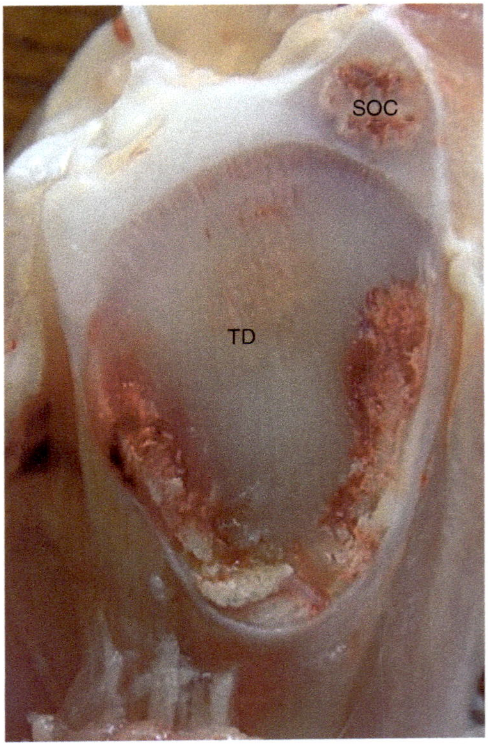

Fig. 13.2. Proximal tibiotarsus from a 3-week-old broiler. A large tibial dyschondroplasia (TD) lesion occupies the metaphysis. The centre of the TD lesion is pale brown indicating necrosis. There is a secondary ossification centre (SOC) in the cartilaginous epiphysis. (Author's own image.)

13.3 Bone Infections

Bone and joint infections in broiler chickens are usually bacterial in nature and are most often caused by either staphylococcus or *Escherichia coli*. Infections are most commonly found in the proximal femur, proximal tibiotarsus, the hock joint and gastrocnemius tendon. The respiratory system is likely to be the entry point for bacteria to seed into the circulation, causing a bacteraemia. As they travel along the small vessels in the cartilaginous growth plate, bacteria adhere to the wall and multiply. This causes formation of thrombi, which block the vessels and protect the bacteria from the immune system and any treatment with antibiotics. Bacterial toxins lead to necrosis and eventual disintegration of the surrounding tissues. Joint infections in broilers are most commonly seen from 22 days of age. Birds of this age may be partially immunosuppressed due to the effects of infectious bursal disease (see Chapter 15v, this volume) or the vaccines used to control it, and/or underlying respiratory disease due to viral infections or 'hot' respiratory vaccines. Sick recumbent birds may also show infected bones or joints, but this can be secondary to a generalized bacterial infection and bacteraemia.

Rickets can also predispose to bacterial infections in bones due to the thickening of the growth plate. A larger growth plate increases the size of the area which bacteria can target for infection. This, combined with a more sluggish circulation due to the greater length of the cartilage canals, will give blood borne bacteria a greater opportunity to lodge in the growth plate.

Hatchery and on-farm hygiene (environment and water supply) in the first few days of a chick's life appears critical to avoiding populating the respiratory system with potentially pathogenic bacteria. In particular, the recent pressure to stop the use of prophylactic antibiotics for day-old chicks has increased the need to maintain high standards of hygiene. Good air quality and absence of respiratory disease or 'hot' respiratory vaccines will help reduce bone and joint infections. The prevention of other stressors, such as coccidiosis infection, may also be associated with a decreased incidence of bacterial bone and joint infections in broiler breeders.

Bacterial infection in bone may also be associated with the airsac of the free thoracic vertebrae. In these cases, *Enterococcus caecorum* is often isolated. This is a slow-growing bacterium most often seen in heavyweight broilers from 40 days of age. The infection leads to vertebral collapse, hind limb paresis and spinal deformity. Enterococcus is also sometimes found in hock and other joint infections, leading to amyloid deposits. This is most frequently seen in commercial layer pullets injected in the leg with Marek's disease vaccine (see Chapter 15xiii, this volume) contaminated with enterococcus. The amyloid appears grossly as an orange deposit in the hock joint of the injected leg.

Other common causes of outbreaks of bone, joint and tendon infections include those caused by *Mycoplasma* and reovirus. *Mycoplasma* is usually seen in joint infections. This illness may be vertically transmitted initially and then spread horizontally through the flock, or may be horizontally spread due to breaches of biosecurity. An outbreak of tenosynovitis in the gastrocnemius muscle may be the result of reovirus infection, which may have been introduced from vertical or horizontal spread.

Pododermatitis is normally associated with poor litter conditions. This may occur as a consequence of inadequate environmental management or due to the birds having excessively wet droppings (i.e. dysbacteriosis, see Chapter 17, this volume). The pododermatitis score for a flock is often used as a welfare outcome measure to assess general enteric health and the environmental hygiene of a flock. Classification systems (0, 1 or 2) are straightforward: 1 if a superficial lesion is present, and 2 if inflammation is found in the underlying dermis when the footpad lesion transected with a scalpel.

In summary, control of bacterial infection in the bones and joints of broilers requires a very high standard of hygiene throughout the system. All inputs, including air quality and water supply, must be considered as sources of pathogenic bacteria. Broilers must be kept free of immunosuppressive diseases and the potentially adverse effects of some vaccines and respiratory pathogens needs to be considered. General health must be good, and rickets, even at the subclinical level, must be avoided.

13.4 Skeletal Problems in Breeders

The most common problems in broiler breeders are hock synovitis and gastrocnemius tendonitis, tenosynovitis and tendon rupture (Fig. 13.3). In meat-

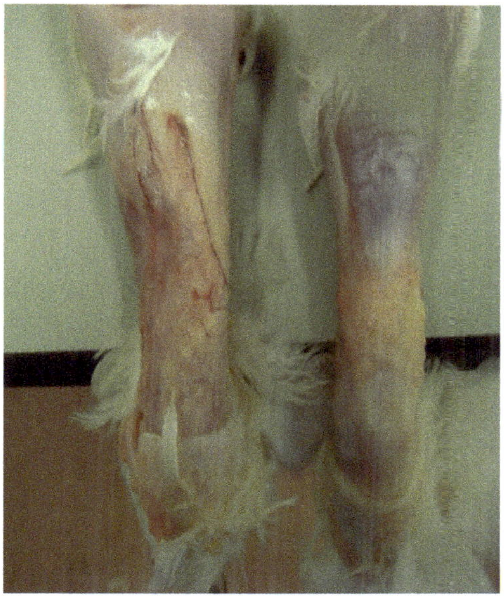

Fig. 13.3. Hock joints and gastrocnemius tendons from an 8-week-old broiler breeder after the skin has been removed. The tendon on the right leg is normal, on the left leg the tendon is thickened as a result of partial rupture. The tendon tissues are inflamed, with obvious 'injected' blood vessels. An indentation is apparent at the site of rupture. (Author's own image.)

type birds, tendons are poorly vascularized which makes healing of lesions difficult and slow. This, in turn, further predisposes to damage and rupture. Problems are most frequently seen in rear during 11–14 weeks of age, and when flocks come into production or at peak production.

Non-infectious tendon issues may be associated with the following: insufficient micronutrients in rear for proper tendon development; inadequate functional load bearing during growth; rapid growth and excessive load bearing; and sudden increase in functional activity usually after moving from a rearing to a laying facility. Functional activity changes may be caused by a longer day length, mating, a different feeding system or the introduction of physical obstacles (slats, nest boxes, etc.). In broiler breeders, the bodyweight of individual birds in a flock can increase from 1.5 kg to almost 3 kg as the birds mature and start production. This places a lot of increased load on the tendons. In birds, the hormonal changes associated with coming into lay enable the tendons and ligaments of the pelvis to slacken to allow eggs to be laid. This may also weaken other tendons predisposing them to damage. It is important to accurately follow the specific breed recommendations for body weight gain in rear and into production, and to maintain a tight coefficient of variation for body weight in the flock.

Bacterial synovitis or tenosynovitis may be the result of bacteria seeding into the circulation from the respiratory system, infected skin wounds or footpads. If the tendon tissue is already damaged due to an underlying tendonitis, it is more likely to become infected. Where birds are immunosuppressed, they are more susceptible to bacterial infections and periods of prolonged bacteraemia which may lead to bacterial tendonitis. One potential cause of immunosuppression is chronic psychological stress and this, especially if combined with physical stress, has the potential to cause damaged and bacterially infected tendons. Chronic stress in a flock may be caused by the simple failure to meet the birds' expectations for water or feed on a regular and frequent daily basis. This can occur with competition over feed or drinking space, and also results in increased frenetic activity when feed is available. Feed should be available equally and adequately to every bird in the house within 3 min of the stimulus of the feed system turning on. There should be no interruptions in feed availability during feeding. Water should be continuously available with no competition for drinkers. Any change in the feeding system or feed availability can promote problems.

Antibiotic medication is likely to be of limited value to treat joint and tendon infection due to the poor blood supply. However, large doses of long-acting antibiotics may benefit some cases and may be worth considering particularly if the birds are of high value (male broiler breeders, for example). Antibiotic medication via feed or water can reduce the occurrence of new cases, presumably by treating the bacteria at the source of the infection. In these cases, a benefit is usually only seen by a reduction in new cases after 4–5 days treatment.

Reovirus may be associated with viral arthritis and tenosynovitis. Reovirus sometimes acts as an opportunistic infection, contributing to a pathology in the face of a different primary clinical challenge. It may, however, be the primary pathogen and histopathology and/or virus isolation should be used for diagnosis. Seroconversion to reovirus, when it coincides with the onset of viral arthritis or tenosynovitis, may help with diagnosis. Maternal immunity to the specific strain of reovirus may be protective in young birds. In some cases, a reovirus vaccine will be protective, though not necessarily against all reovirus strains.

13.5 Osteoporosis in Layers

From the onset of egg production, there is a steady loss of cortical and trabecular bone which eventually leads to thinning of the bone cortex and increased structural bone porosity. This, in turn, results in osteoporosis and potential fracture. The skeleton of the hen contains about 40 g of calcium and the shell of each egg the hen lays will contain about 2 g. She mainly relies on her skeletal calcium as a source for the eggshell during its production. Two weeks before the onset of lay, the hen starts to produce fine spicules of special woven bone (medullary bone) within her medullary cavities and on the endostial surfaces of the cortical and trabecular bone. This medullary bone is highly cellular and provides a supply of calcium by resorption during the 5 h of hard-shell formation. This medullary bone is replaced over the course of the 19 h during which the eggshells are not being made. At this time, the diet is the source of calcium to the hen. From the onset of lay at about 19 weeks, until the end of lay at 72 weeks, there is little or no structural bone formation. Therefore, any structural bone lost as a calcium source for eggshell formation is unlikely to be replaced. This insidious loss of structural bone leads to osteoporosis. In wild birds this is not an issue as the laying period is restricted to, at most, a few weeks at a time.

To minimize osteoporosis in layers, it is important to have a low coefficient of variation (CV) within the flock so that calcium in feed is correctly supplied to all birds at the same stage of reproductive development. Available calcium in the diet should be increased 2 weeks before the first egg is produced and then again from the onset of lay to maintain calcium levels until the end of lay.

13.6 Further Reading

Butterworth, A. (1999) Infectious components of broiler lameness: a review. *World's Poultry Science Journal* 55(4), 327–352.

Edwards, Jr., H.M. (2000) Nutrition and skeletal problems in poultry. *Poultry Science* 79(7), 1018–1023.

Julian, J.J. (2005) Production and growth related disorders and other metabolic diseases of poultry – A review. *The Veterinary Journal* 169, 350–369.

Thorp, B.H. (1994) Skeletal disorders in the fowl: a review. *Avian Pathology* 23, 203–236.

Wideman, Jr., R.F. (2016) Bacterial chondronecrosis with osteomyelitis and lameness in broilers: a review. *Poultry Science* 95, 325–344.

14i *Mycobacterium* and Avian Tuberculosis

Paul Barrow*

School of Veterinary Medicine, University of Surrey, Guildford, UK

14i.1 Introduction

Avian tuberculosis is a chronic bacterial infection whose pathology is not dissimilar to the related disease in humans, cattle and many other animals. It is rarely seen in modern commercial well-managed flocks and is normally associated with birds reared in conditions of poor management. It is a chronic disease and therefore more frequently seen in mature birds. It produces loss in condition and egg production, and can result in serious economic loss. It is also found in wild birds, pigs and rabbits.

14i.2 Microbiology and Taxonomy, and Association with Different Host Species

The mycobacteria are relatively slow-growing bacilli in comparison with other bacterial pathogens. Fast-growing species tend to be less pathogenic and can be cultured within a few days. The species that grow more slowly can require several weeks for production of visible colonies on solid media. *Mycobacterium avium* grows best in the temperature range 39–45°C but can grow at temperatures down to 25°C. Growth is best on specialized media and in the presence of glycerol. Historically, the bacteria have been grown on egg-based solid media such as Löwenstein–Jensen, but improved growth can be obtained by using Middlebrook agars supplemented with glycerol and OADC (oleic acid, albumen, dextrose, catalase) supplement.

The bacteria are acid-alcohol fast when stained with the Ziehl–Neelsen stain. Unlike the mammalian tubercle bacilli, *M. avium* bacterial cells are smooth and can thus be agglutinated by specific sera which can aid in epidemiological investigations.

The bacteria are relatively resistant to disinfectants and antibiotics and survive well for weeks in soil.

The causative agent belongs to a diffuse taxonomic group of related subspecies known as the *M. avium-intracellulare* group (MAIG) which includes *M. intracellulare*, a human pathogen. Within this group the *M. avium* complex (MAC) is itself diffuse, with its members identified by virulence and dissemination, and distinguishable by molecular methods.

The four taxa currently recognized are:

- *M. avium* subsp. *avium* which consists of three serotypes (1–3) which are virulent for birds and some small mammals. Serotypes 1 and 2 are distributed worldwide. Serotype 2 is mainly restricted to Europe and is also the most virulent for birds. Most strains possess insertion sequence IS901, thought to be necessary for virulence, and also IS1245. Some strains isolated from wood pigeons are slower growing and are mycobactin-dependent as is *M. paratuberculosis*. However, serologically they resemble *M. avium* subsp. *avium*. Some of these strains can produce hypertrophic enteritis in calves, similar to mild Johne's disease, indicating the confusing nature of this group.
- *M. avium* subsp. *hominissuis*, which consists of several other serotypes and is largely environmental, but some strains are virulent for birds.
- *M. avium* subsp. *paratuberculosis* which is the cause of paratuberculosis/Johne's disease, a chronic enteritis of cattle, sheep and other ruminants. It is an exceedingly slow-growing organism requiring several months to produce colonies clearly visible to the naked eye.
- *M. avium* subsp. *sylvaticum* is rarely isolated but can be virulent for birds.

*paul.barrow@surrey.ac.uk

 © CAB International 2021. *Poultry Health: A Guide for Professionals* (P. Barrow *et al.*)
DOI: 10.1079/9781789245042.0014

Avian strains from wild birds can frequently infect pigs as a result of their shared environment and may be isolated from their tonsils.

M. avium subsp. *avium* can cause disease in man, although serotypes associated with poultry rarely do so. Other serovars are involved and may be associated with AIDS as a serious secondary infection.

Amongst bird species, domestic fowl are the most susceptible to disease followed by pheasants, guinea fowl, turkeys, geese and ducks. Pigeons are more resistant, which may reflect the very chronic nature of infection in these birds.

14i.3 Epidemiology

Distribution of infections is worldwide although, as indicated, individual serotypes may show a more restricted range. Infection is associated with more temperate regions.

Sources of infection are mainly wild birds, and free-range-reared birds may thus be exposed more than permanently housed birds. The main source of infection is faeces with the organism shed from the gut. In ducks, respiratory infection may be more important.

Factors affecting susceptibility include:

- Age, with older birds presenting greater levels of infection, although this reflects the chronic nature of the disease rather than any specific age-related susceptibility factor.
- Genetics. Some inbred lines of chickens have been shown to have greater levels of susceptibility than others (Bumstead and Barrow, unpublished results). Interestingly, the same lines are also susceptible to systemic salmonellosis indicating a common mechanism.
- Stress, including chilling and wet conditions, which increase susceptibility.
- Sanitation and hygiene, which affect susceptibility, affecting both innate resistance and exposure to infection.

14i.4 Clinical Picture and Pathology

Chronic loss of condition in older birds, with reduced egg production, is typical with an increasingly prominent keel bone. Localization in the joints may cause lameness. Appetite generally remains good. Occasionally, death may be sudden resulting from rupture of the liver or spleen with associated internal haemorrhage.

Unlike bovine or human tuberculosis, which are associated with granulomata in the lungs, the main site of infection appears to be the intestines as a result of infection from the environment by the oral route. Respiratory infection is more common in ducks.

The production of the granuloma is typical for all forms of tuberculosis where the bacteria, which are difficult for leukocytes to kill, are increasingly isolated and walled off by giant cells and other inflammatory cells, and the lesion becomes caseated and calcified. Granulomatous nodules can be seen in the wall of the small intestine and, because of the absence of lymph nodes in birds, also in the liver and spleen (Fig. 14i.1). Ulceration of the intestinal wall occurs, resulting in shedding in the faeces.

14i.5 Diagnosis/Surveillance

The presence of hard miliary lesions in liver or spleen is indicative. Differentiation from cases of leukosis (see Chapter 15xii, this volume) is necessary. Lesions are harder and acid-fast bacteria can be detected by microscopy in the centre of the lesions.

If necessary, a tuberculin test can be carried out involving injection of avian PPD (purified protein derivative) into the wattle, followed by detection of swelling 48 h later. Because of the smooth nature of the bacteria, a serological assay such as an ELISA or agglutination test (see Chapter 22, this volume) can also be carried out.

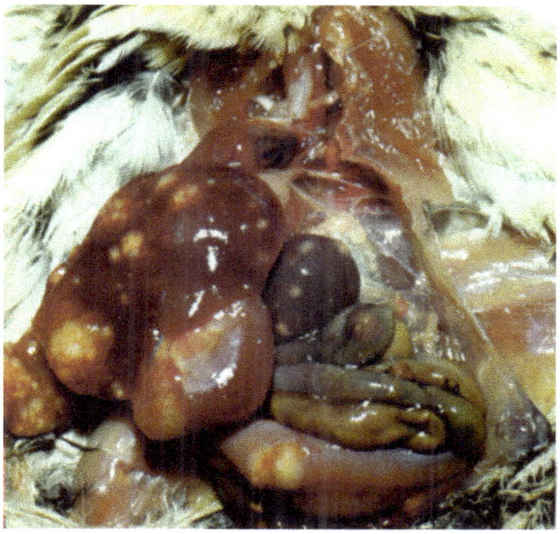

Fig. 14i.1. Avian tuberculosis in the liver (left) spleen (centre) and small intestine (right) of a Japanese quail. (Wikimedia Commons, image produced by Roman Halouzka.)

How far concurrent parasite infection interferes with the tuberculin test is unclear. The tuberculin test is dependent on a Th1-type immune response to the pathogen whereas some parasite infections are associated with a Th2-type infection which may weaken a Th1 reaction. It is known that co-infection of cattle with *M. bovis* and *Fasciola hepatica* weakens the strength of the bovine tuberculin skin test.

14i.6 Control

For most commercial flocks, vaccination and chemotherapy for control are not practical economic options. In housed birds, elimination of infected stock is required with disinfection of premises together with reducing the possibility of reinfection by ensuring no contact with other domestic or wild animals.

In some circumstances, eradication may not be possible and reducing infection, by keeping stock no longer than one laying season, and monitoring for infection with elimination of infected stock is important.

14i.7 Further Reading

Dhama, K., Mahendran, M. Tiwari, R., Singh, S.D., Kumar, D., *et al.* (2011) Tuberculosis in birds: insights into *Mycobacterium avium* infections. *Veterinary Medicine International* 2001, 712369. DOI: 10.4061/2011/712369.

Fulton, R.M. and Sanchez, S. (2020) Tuberculosis. In: Swayne, D.E. (editor in chief) *Diseases of Poultry,* 14th edn. Iowa State University Press, Iowa, pp. 1033–1043.

14ii Avian Pathogenic *Escherichia coli*

Rikke Heidemann Olsen*

Department of Veterinary and Animal Science, University of Copenhagen, Frederiksberg, Denmark

14ii.1 Overview

Escherichia coli is Gram-negative, non-sporing and rod-shaped, found ubiquitously in soil, water and the intestine of most mammals and birds (Dho-Moulin and Fairbrother, 1999). The intestine is considered the primary habitat and source of *E. coli* and although most strains are harmless commensals, pathogenic strains exist that can cause a variety of intestinal and extra-intestinal diseases. Many disease manifestations of extra-intestinal *E. coli* infections in poultry exist which are collectively termed 'colibacillosis'. The host range includes all domestic poultry. Globally, extra-intestinal infections constitute an enormous welfare and economic burden for industrialized poultry production. The total global losses due to *E. coli* is difficult to establish, but one study from the Netherlands reported that a single clinical manifestation of avian *E. coli* infections (*E. coli* peritonitis) led to national losses of approximately €0.4 million, €3.3 million and €3.7 million for the layer-sector, the meat-sector and poultry farming as a whole, respectively (Landman and van Eck, 2015).

Strains of *E. coli* causing extra-intestinal infections in avian species are termed avian pathogenic *E. coli* (APEC). Several studies have aimed to define how a harmless commensal strain may be differentiated from an APEC (Johnson *et al.*, 2008; Silveira *et al.*, 2016; Mohamed *et al.*, 2018). This is not straight forward, as *E. coli* is an opportunistic pathogen. Hence, in cases where the bird is immunocompromised from e.g. concurrent infections (most frequently infectious bronchitis (IB) (see Chapter 15x, this volume), avian pneumovirus (see Chapter 15ix, this volume), Newcastle disease (see Chapter 15viii, this volume) or *Mycoplasma gallisepticum* (see Chapter 14viii, this volume)) or environmental stress such as high ammonia concentration in the poultry house, even low-pathogenic strains of *E. coli* are able to give rise to infections (Vandekerchove *et al.*, 2004). Nevertheless, the APEC strains vary in their pathogenic potential. It has been suggested that a minimum of five virulence genes (*iutA, hlyF, iss, iroN*, and *ompT*) must be present before a strain of *E. coli* should be termed an APEC. It has also been suggested that APEC strains can be further divided into sub-pathotypes, in which the give rise to different pathogenic lesions, e.g. septicaemia, depending on which virulence genes they possess (Silveira *et al.*, 2016). Similarly, certain serotypes of *E. coli* are found more frequently among APEC than other *E. coli* strains, in particular O1:K1, O2:K1 and O78:K80. APEC strains often carry their virulence genes on large plasmids, which may also contain a variety of genes encoding antimicrobial resistance (Mellata *et al.*, 2010).

14ii.2 Epidemiology

E. coli may be transmitted horizontally or vertically (Giovanardi *et al.*, 2005). Horizontal transmission may occur through inhalation of *E. coli* contaminated aerosol or dust particles, or from contaminated drinking water. The vertical transmission can be divided into genuine vertical in which *E. coli* is present in the reproductive system (as clinical or subclinical salpingitis) and the organism is incorporated within the egg during formation, or

*cava@sund.ku.dk

© CAB International 2021. *Poultry Health: A Guide for Professionals* (P. Barrow *et al.*)
DOI: 10.1079/9781789245042.0014

through eggshell contamination, in which the shell is contaminated with *E. coli* in the cloacae during lay. Depending on the quality of the egg, *E. coli* may penetrate the shell (Chousalkar *et al.*, 2010). This can lead to either embryo mortality or colonization of the digestive tract of the embryo *in ovo* yet allowing the embryo to full development and hatch. It has been estimated that in some cases up to 5% of the unhatched eggs contain *E. coli*. These *E. coli*-loaded eggs constitute a risk of severe transmission of *E. coli* in the hatcher as the hatcher-environment provides almost optimal conditions for *E. coli* proliferation and transmission. Such an event may lead to increased first-week mortality among the chicks hatched under a heavy *E. coli* load. Finally, humans, wild animals, insects and rodents can act as vectors of *E. coli* (Nielsen *et al.*, 2004).

14ii.3 Culture and Typing

E. coli grows readily on most types of standard agar, such as blood agar. Most APEC are non-hemolytic. MacConkey's lactose bile agar can be used as a tentative screening for a variety of Enterobacteriaceae (including *Salmonella*, see Chapter 14iv, this volume), with *E. coli* appearing as flat, dry, pink colonies with a surrounding darker pink area of precipitated bile salts. Verification can be done with standard phenotypic tests (fermenting glucose, mannitol and lactose, and not fermenting inositol or producing H_2S in Kligler's medium), *E. coli*-specific PCR (Chen and Griffiths, 1998) or MALDI-TOF mass spectrometry may also be used for strain identification.

Previously, identification of APEC strains to serotype was considered the 'Gold Standard' for strain characterization, with particular focus on the O (somatic) antigen. To document whether an outbreak of colibacillosis was clonal (involving one strain of *E. coli*) or multiclonal (involving several different strains of *E. coli*) pulsed-field gel electrophoresis (PFGE) has been used. One school of thought is that clonal outbreaks is the result of APEC acting as a primary pathogen whereas polyclonal outbreaks indicate that *E. coli* be considered as secondary to another primary infection which is immunocompromising leading to the birds increasing in susceptibility to even low-pathogenic serovars. Defining if an outbreak is primary or secondary is also important when it has to been decided if an autogenously vaccine should by applied, as autogenously based vaccines only have limited cross-serotype protection (Landman and van Eck, 2017; Li *et al.*, 2017). PFGE typing has also been used in tracing outbreak sources (Mohamed *et al.*, 2018) and to document vertical transmission within an integrated broiler operation (Silveira *et al.*, 2016). In the case of the latter, transmission of enrofloxacin-resistant *E. coli* from healthy parents was reported to result in high first-week mortality in the progeny (Petersen *et al.*, 2006), underlining the importance of limiting antimicrobial use of at all levels of the avian production pyramid.

DNA based typing methods have now largely overtaken phenotypic tests. Whole genome sequencing (WGS) can easily predict serotype *in silico* using freely available software, e.g. at https://cge.cbs.dtu.dk/services/SerotypeFinder/. The introduction of multi-locus sequence typing (MLST) with data collected in a public database (https://enterobase.warwick.ac.uk/) has allowed research to compare prevalent sequence type (ST) of APEC between and within countries, for example. This has enabled the recognition of a few STs that are particularly prevalent among APEC worldwide (ST95, ST117, ST140, etc.). It has also become clear that a number of STs are shared between APEC and *E. coli* causing urinary tract infections in humans, e.g. ST131, suggesting that there may be zoonotic potential (or a least a shared niche) between *E. coli* causing extra-intestinal infection in human and avian species (Mellata, 2013). Recently, WGS has also been used to suggest that a large colibacillosis outbreak involving the Scandinavian countries was largely the result of transmission of an *E. coli* ST117 from the breeding company placed outside Scandinavian (Ronco *et al.*, 2017).

14ii.4 Clinical Manifestations

Among the localized infection, omphalitis/yolk sac infection, cellulitis, air sac diseases, salpingitis/peritonitis/salpingo-peritonitis (SPS) are the most frequent manifestation. In addition, less frequently lesions including swollen head syndrome (SHS), venereal colibacillosis and diarrheal diseases may occur albeit less frequently. Because of their importance omphalitis/yolk sac infection, cellulitis, SPS and systemic colisepticaemia will be discussed in more detail.

Omphalitis/yolk sac infection is one of the most common causes of mortality in chicks during the first week of life. Omphalitis is an inflammation of the navel, but because of the close anatomic proximity the yolk sac is also often infected. *E. coli* is the most common pathogen isolated as a primary agent but frequently found together with other bacteria, such as *Bacillus cereus*, staphylococci, *Proteus* spp. and *Pseudomonas aeruginosa*. Some embryos may die in-shell, while hatched but infected chicks appear depressed and have distended abdomens. Macroscopic lesions of the navel, including swelling, redness and necrosis, may be present. In severe cases, the body with overlaying skin may undergo lysis with the chicks appearing dirty and wet (the disease is also referred to as 'mushy chick disease'). Septicaemic carcasses often have a distinctive, putrefying smell on post-mortem examination. A characteristic finding is an unabsorbed yolk sac with the yolk abnormal in colour and consistency.

Cellulitis (or necrotic dermatitis) involves the skin of the lower abdomen to the vent in broilers (Poulsen *et al.*, 2018). This may lead to condemnation or downgrading of carcasses with considerable economic loses. Superficial skin scratches are the most common port of entry, with the cellulitis facilitating haematogenous spread.

Coliform SPS is a common syndrome in laying hens and breeders. The condition may be subacute or chronic. Birds with salpingitis show an inflamed and distended oviduct. As a result of the inflamed and compromised oviduct wall, *E. coli* can spread into the abdominal cavity resulting in concurrent peritonitis (salpingo-peritonitis) with accumulation of caseating exudate in the abdominal cavity. This exudate often has the appearance of coagulated yolk and therefore the condition is commonly named 'egg peritonitis'. The pathogenesis of SPS is still not fully elucidated, but three infection routes have been suggested, namely (i) ascending infection from the contaminated the cloaca, (ii) translocation from the respiratory system (air sacs and lungs) and (iii) translocation from the intestine (Landman *et al.*, 2014), with (i) as the most supported hypothesis. Depending on the virulence of the strain and the immunocompetence of the hen, the acute infection may process to recovery, septicaemia with sudden death or chronicity. Subclinical salpingitis results in lower egg-yield with speculation that it may have wider effect on the industry as a result of vertical transmission (Poulsen *et al.*, 2017).

Localized infection may progress to systemic infections. A generalized *E. coli* septicaemia (colisepticaemia) is the most serious manifestation of colibacillosis. The condition has caused major loses to the broiler industry. It is closely connected with poor management, e.g. high stocking density and poorly ventilated houses. In broilers, the pathogenesis is mainly initiated by inhalation of *E. coli* as aerosols or present on dust particles with subsequent invasion from the respiratory tract. Invasion is much more likely to occur with a concurrent infection involving other respiratory pathogens, such as avian pneumovirus, or in the presence of high dust or ammonia levels as these factors will damage the respiratory mucosa and cilia. Chickens of all ages are susceptible, but most losses occur between weeks 4 and 9. Losses are the direct result of mortality (usually <5%), although the major losses are due to sequalae following from the high morbidity (may be >50%) which leave the flock uneven and with a commercial downgrade in quality after slaughter (Vasdal *et al.*, 2019). At post-mortem the gross lesions are characterized by a polyserositis, which may include combinations of pericarditis, air sacculitis, and peritonitis and perihepatitis. For the latter, a skin of fibrinous material often covers the surface of the liver.

14ii.5 Control

Colibacillosis may be treated with a number of antimicrobial agents, but due to concerns over animal welfare and of antibiotic over- and misuse, prophylaxis is preferred over treatment. Nevertheless, treatment may be required for a severe outbreak but only after susceptibility testing of the *E. coli* strain involved.

As explained above, APEC infections may be primary and secondary infections. For the latter, it is clearly essential to avoid any predisposing factors that will immunocompromise the birds. Vaccination against major viral diseases, such as IB, is important not only to control IB, but also to decrease the risk of *E. coli* related morbidity and mortality. Factors related to management may also influence mortality and morbidity due to *E. coli*. Inappropriate control of bedding/ventilation in the poultry house may cause the ammonia level to rise (see above). In addition, high standards of eggshell disinfection is important to decrease the *E. coli* load in the hatcher. The temperature and humidity of the hatcher provides an excellent environment for *E. coli* to multiply, and the hatching chicks may be exposed to very high doses of *E. coli* if appropriate eggshell hygiene is not performed, which may lead to a high first week chick mortality.

Due to the heterogeneity of APEC, a single vaccine conferring protection against all APEC types has not yet been developed. A spray vaccine (Poulvac® *E. coli*) based on a live O78:K80 *aroA* vaccine-strain has been shown to be highly protective against a homologous challenge strain in broilers (Sadeghi *et al.*, 2018). However, no protection was detectable in broiler parents under experimental settings when the broiler parents were challenged with an *E. coli* O78:H4 strain (Li *et al.*, 2017).

The ideal situation would be the use of a highly immunogenic vaccine administered to the broiler breeder to protect the adults and the progeny through the maternal antibody. Autogenous inactivated vaccines have also been used widely in the poultry industry. If a farm has had *E. coli* problems in consecutive rotations of flock, a single disease-associated isolate can be formalin-inactivated and used as a vaccine for the next flock introduced to the farm. There is reported evidence for the effectiveness of such vaccines although little experimental evidence to support such claims.

Pre- and probiotics have been studied for their potential to protect against APEC infection in addition to their impact on general broiler performance. Some studies have reported reduced mortality in broilers challenged with APEC O78 (Tarabees *et al.*, 2019) and O125 (El-Mawgoud *et al.*, 2020).

14ii.6 References

Chen, J. and Griffiths, M.W. (1998) PCR differentiation of *Escherichia coli* from other gram-negative bacteria using primers derived from the nucleotide sequences flanking the gene encoding the universal stress protein. *Letters in Applied Microbiology* 27, 369–371.

Chousalkar, K.K., Flynn, P., Sutherland, M., Roberts, J.R. and Cheetham, B.F. (2010) Recovery of *Salmonella* and *Escherichia coli* from commercial egg shells and effect of translucency on bacterial penetration in eggs. *International Journal of Food Microbiology* 142, 207–213.

Dho-Moulin, M. and Fairbrother, J.M. (1999) Avian pathogenic *Escherichia coli* (APEC). *Veterinary Research* 30, 299–316.

El-Mawgoud, A.I.A., El-Nahass, E.S., Shany, S.A.S. *et al.* (2020) Efficacy of live attenuated vaccine and commercially available lectin against avian pathogenic *E. coli* infection in broiler chickens. *Veterinary Science* 7, E65. DOI: 10.3390/vetsci7020065.

Giovanardi, D., Campagnari, E., Ruffoni, L.S., Pesente, P., Ortali, G., *et al.* (2005) Avian pathogenic *Escherichia coli* transmission from broiler breeders to their progeny in an integrated poultry production chain. *Avian Pathology* 34, 313–318.

Johnson, T.J., Wannemuehler, Y., Doetkott, C., Johnson, S.J., Rosenberger, S.C., *et al.* (2008) Identification of minimal predictors of avian pathogenic *Escherichia coli* virulence for use as a rapid diagnostic tool. *Journal of Clinical Microbiology* 46, 3987–3996.

Landman, W.J.M. and van Eck, J.H.H. (2015) The incidence and economic impact of the *Escherichia coli* peritonitis syndrome in Dutch poultry farming. *Avian Pathology* 44, 370–378.

Landman, W.J.M. and van Eck, J.H.H. (2017) The efficacy of inactivated *Escherichia coli* autogenous vaccines against the *E. coli* peritonitis syndrome in layers. *Avian Pathology* 46, 658–665.

Landman, W.J.M., Buter, G.J., Dijkman, R. and van Eck, J.H. (2014) Molecular typing of avian pathogenic *Escherichia coli* colonies originating from outbreaks of *E. coli* peritonitis syndrome in chicken flocks. *Avian Pathology* 43, 345–356.

Li, L., Thøfner, I., Christensen, J.P., Ronco, T., Pedersen, K., *et al.* (2017) Evaluation of the efficacy of an autogenous *Escherichia coli* vaccine in broiler breeders. *Avian Pathology* 46, 300–308.

Mellata, M. (2013) Human and avian extraintestinal pathogenic *Escherichia coli*: infections, zoonotic risks, and antibiotic resistance trends. *Foodborne Pathogens and Diseases* 10(11), 916–932.

Mellata, M., Ameiss, K., Mo, H. and Curtss, R. III (2010) Characterization of the contribution to virulence of three large plasmids of avian pathogenic *Escherichia coli chi* 7122 (O78:K80:H9). *Infection and Immunity* 78, 1528–41.

Mohamed, L., Ge, Z., Yuehua, L., *et al.* (2018) Virulence traits of avian pathogenic (APEC) and fecal (AFEC) *E. coli isolated from broiler chickens in Algeria. Tropical Animal Health Production* 50, 547–553.

Nielsen, E.M., Skov, M.N., Madsen, J.J., Lodal, J., Jespersen, J.B., *et al.* (2004) Verocytotoxin-producing *Escherichia coli* in wild birds and rodents in close proximity to farms. *Applied and Environmental Microbiology* 70, 6944–6947.

Petersen, A., Christensen, J.P., Kuhnert, P., Bisgaard, M. and Olsen, J.E. (2006) Vertical transmission of a fluoroquinolone-resistant *Escherichia coli* within an integrated broiler operation. *Veterinary Microbiology* 116, 120–128.

Poulsen, L.L, Thoefner, I., Bisgaard, M., Christensen, J.P., Olsen, R.H., *et al.* (2017) Longitudinal study of transmission of *Escherichia coli* from broiler breeders to broilers. *Veterinary Microbiology* 207, 13–18.

Poulsen, L.L., Bisgaard, M., Jørgensen, S.L., Dideriksen, T., Pedersen, J.R., *et al.* (2018) Characterization of *Escherichia coli* causing cellulitis in broilers. *Veterinary Microbiology* 25, 72–78.

Ronco, T., Stegger, M., Olsen, R.H., Sekse, C., Nordstoga, A.B., *et al.* (2017) Spread of avian pathogenic *Escherichia coli* ST117 O78:H4 in Nordic broiler production. *BMC Genomics* 18, 13. DOI: 10.1186/s12864-016-3415-6.

Sadeghi, M., Tavakkoli, H., Golchin, M., *et al.* (2018) Efficacy and safety of Poulvac *E. coli* vaccine in broiler chickens challenged with *E. coli* serotype O78 and an acute field isolate. *Comparative Clinical Pathology* 27, 1629–1636.

Silveira, F., Maluta, R.P., Tiba, M.R., de Paiva, J.B., Guastalli, E.A., *et al.* (2016) Comparison between avian pathogenic (APEC) and avian faecal (AFEC) *Escherichia coli* isolated from different regions in Brazil. *The Veterinary Journal* 217, 65–67. DOI: 10.1016/j.tvjl.2016.06.007

Tarabees, R., Gafar, K.M., El-Sayed, M.S., Shehata, A.A. and Ahmed, M. (2019) Effects of dietary supplementation of probiotic mix and prebiotic on growth performance, cecal microbiota composition, and protection against *Escherichia coli* O78 in broiler chickens. *Probiotics and Antimicrobial Proteins* 11(3), 981–989.

Vandekerchove, D., De Herdt, P., Laevens, H. and Pasmans, F. (2004) Risk factors associated with colibacillosis outbreaks in caged layer flocks. *Avian Pathology* 33(3), 337–342.

Vasdal, G., Granquist, E.G., Skjerve, E., de Jong, I.C., Berg, C., *et al.* (2019) Associations between carcass weight uniformity and production measures on farm and at slaughter in commercial broiler flocks. *Poultry Science* 98(10), 4261–4268.

14iii Campylobacter

Michael Jones[1]* and Paul Barrow[2]

[1]School of Veterinary Medicine and Science, University of Nottingham, Sutton Bonington, Loughborough, Leicestershire, UK; [2]School of Veterinary Medicine, University of Surrey, Guildford, UK

14iii.1 Introduction

Campylobacter is a genus of Gram-negative bacteria well adapted to life in avian species, frequently without producing obvious disease. They are associated with human food poisoning (campylobacteriosis) causing more individual cases than *Salmonella* (see Chapter 14iv, this volume) and with a very strong association with consumption of poultry meat (but not eggs). Campylobacteriosis has become apparently more significant during the last 40 years mainly as a result of greater awareness and improved culture methods.

14iii.2 Microbiology and Culture

The two main species associated with domestic and wild bird species are *C. jejuni* and *C. coli* with much less frequent isolation of *C. lari*, while *C. coli*, and, less frequently, *C. jejuni* is also frequently isolated from mammalian livestock species such as pigs. They are Gram-negative vibrios (comma or short spiral shapes) which become more coccoid under conditions of stress. They are highly motile through a single flagellum at each end of the bacillus. They do not typically ferment carbohydrates and are microaerophilic and thermophilic, growing optimally at 42°C, thus indicating adaptation to avian species. The genome is relatively small (1.6 Mbp) with a low G+C ratio compared with other Gram-negative bacteria such as *Escherichia coli*.

The related type species *C. fetus* is responsible for abortion and sexually transmitted infections in sheep and cattle.

The presence of *Campylobacter* is generally identified by culture methods, although PCR may also be used. The organisms are fastidious and slow growing, being best cultured in an atmosphere of 5% O_2, 10% CO_2 and 85% N_2. *Campylobacter* is sensitive to atmospheric levels of oxygen and bacterial viability is reduced at ambient temperatures and at atmospheric levels of oxygen. Survival of bacteria is also affected by desiccation and poor temperature management of samples which are best kept cool ca. 4°C in transport.

As a consequence of their susceptibility to killing by oxygen, a charcoal transport medium is recommended for transport of swabs. Campylobacters show similar temperature and disinfectant sensitivities as other Gram-negative bacteria. They are killed by pasteurization and are readily killed by temperatures above 70°C.

Initial culture of stressed bacteria may require preliminary enrichment for 24 h under microaerophilic conditions. Several media are available including modified Exeter broth, a yeast-peptone broth with additional growth factors and defibrinated blood. A number of solid media are also available, most of which contain a number of antibiotics to reduce overgrowth by other contaminating enteric bacteria which may be faster growing. A popular culture medium is CCDA (charcoal-cefoperazone-deoxycholate agar) containing amphotericin B, an antifungal antibiotic.

Colonies are generally visible after 48 h incubation and are small, smooth and grey, and may spread depending on the moisture content of the agar. Presumptive identification can be made by bacterial morphology and motility under phase contrast microscopy. Further identification can be made by biochemistry. For initial presumptive

*Corresponding author: michael.a.jones@nottingham.ac.uk

© CAB International 2021. *Poultry Health: A Guide for Professionals* (P. Barrow *et al.*)
DOI: 10.1079/9781789245042.0014

species identification, *C. jejuni* hydrolyses hippurate whereas *C. coli* does not and *C. lari* strains are generally resistant to nalidixic acid. This is complicated by the extensive use of fluoroquinolones in the last 20 years, which has increased quinolone resistance in *C. jejuni*. Confirmation that the isolates are the genus *Campylobacter* can be achieved by serology, mass spectrophotometry by MALDI-TOF (matrix assisted laser desorption and ionization-time-of-flight) or PCR. In commercial microbiology laboratories MALDI-TOF is taking prominence as the process is robust, rapid and the equipment can also be used to assess other bacterial isolations. It does however require specific equipment and servicing. PCR is relatively robust but requires positive and negative controls to exclude erroneous results.

Historically, an antiserum agglutination-based approach was used for typing strains (Penner typing). This has become displaced by molecular methods including multi-locus sequence typing (MLST) which has been used extensively for epidemiological studies and was central to determining the role of poultry in human food-borne enteritis.

14iii.3 Pathogenicity

The campylobacters are generally regarded as non-pathogenic and commensal for poultry but are well known as a cause of food-borne enteritis in humans, with symptoms manifesting ca. 4 days post-infection, ranging in severity from stomach cramps to bloody diarrhoea. However, there are a number of reports of experimental infections in chickens resulting in diarrhoea, weight loss and death with some evidence also from a limited number of field studies. Colonization correlates with a reduction in feed conversion and increased negative welfare parameters such as hock burn. The fact that it has taken so long to establish a link to production traits and *Campylobacter* colonization is an indicator of the subtle impact these bacteria have on poultry health. Although subtle, the financial impact on productivity over growth cycles is cumulative and as a result, there is a commercial incentive to maintain broilers under *Campylobacter* free conditions.

They colonize the alimentary tract of poultry well, reaching high densities in the caeca, the main site of colonization, of 8–9 Log_{10} mainly as a result of the relatively slow rate of passage of contents through the caeca. Spread in poultry flocks is rapid due to high levels of *Campylobacter* in droppings contaminating feed and water. At slaughter, any damage to the intestinal tissue during evisceration can lead to gross surface contamination of carcass skin and plumage and cross-contamination in poultry processing plants.

Intestinal colonization appears to involve multiplication in the mucous layer in the crypts as occurs with *Vibrio cholerae* in human cholera. Invasion to the spleen and liver may occur in small numbers but without disease. There are also reports of isolation from muscle and this may possibly result from air sac infection.

Several genes have been identified as associated with colonization ability in chickens but their role in intestinal colonization in human enteritis is unclear.

The behaviour of the organisms during colonization is complex because while there is a serological response to the organisms, it does not result in clearance from the gut. Several genes encoding surface structures possess long repetitive tracts of the same nucleic acid base facilitating DNA strand slippage during replication, leading to switching surface epitopes during infection, known as phase variation, and resulting in a single strain comprising several antigenic types during a single infection. The bacteria are thus thought to be able to adapt during infection to avoid immune clearance (Bayliss *et al.*, 2012).

The organisms induce inflammatory responses in the gut indicating a capacity to provoke immune responses. How far these are able to provide protection against secondary infection remains unclear, given the ability to change surface epitopes during infection.

Over the years there has been some indication in the literature that *Campylobacter* produce a vibrionic hepatitis but reports of this in the field are minimal suggesting that it is not a major concern. The role of *Campylobacter* in this is unclear since gross contamination of visceral organs can occur easily during post-mortem examination or slaughter.

14iii.4 Epidemiology

C. jejuni is adapted to the avian intestine and can be isolated from a wide range of wild and domestic birds. They are also found in other domestic animals including pigs and cattle, and also companion animals from which they can be shed from young animals such as puppies in high numbers. The importance of poultry as a source of infection for man has been shown by isolation of identical MLST types from outbreaks of human infection traced back to individual farms. *C. coli* is more commonly isolated from pigs than from poultry, but sheep and cattle can also act as hosts.

Campylobacter are thus found in soil, manure, infected used litter and also in surface water, and their widespread dissemination facilitates infection of domestic poultry.

Levels of infection in free-range poultry can be very high with simultaneous infection with several different strains. This is particularly true for countries with high ambient temperatures where open-sided housing may be the norm. Infection of housed and free-range birds rarely occurs before 2–3 weeks of age, possibly as a result of the protective effects of maternal antibodies. Isolation from very young birds and hatcheries is rare as true vertical transmission does not appear to occur, indicating that control must be at the level of preventing horizontal transmission. Rates of isolation (prevalence) can be very high (>80% of flocks) in countries such as the UK and USA, and are generally much lower (<2%) in Scandinavian countries.

Relaxed biosecurity regimens are risk factors in the introduction of *Campylobacter* to flocks, with frequency of infection increasing with age and increases taking place at thinning associated with introduction by staff involved in this activity. Insects and rodents may also act as vehicles of infection in addition to contaminated drinking water. Insect infection may account for the higher peaks of infection in poultry during summer months and poor-quality housing is thus also a risk factor. Feed is unlikely to be a source of infection as the organisms die rapidly on drying.

Once flocks become infected, transmission within the flock is rapid and birds generally remain infected until slaughter age.

14iii.5 Diagnosis and Public Health Significance

Culture from faecal material is the most frequently adopted approach to identification of flock infection using the cultural methods described above.

Campylobacter accounts for more cases of human enteritis than *Salmonella* and, for both pathogens, poultry are the main source of infection. The highest rates of infection are in children in both developed and developing countries. Person-to-person transmission is rare in developed countries but common in developing countries.

Most cases are self-limiting with resolution after 5–7 days of symptoms which consist of watery or bloody diarrhoea, abdominal pain and sometimes fever. Serious but rare complications can occur mainly with Guillain–Barré syndrome, an autoimmune neurological disorder that can be fatal.

14iii.6 Control

Given the exceptional adaptation of *Campylobacter* to the avian alimentary tract, its high level of colonization and limited immune clearance with rapid horizontal transmission within flocks and numerous sources of infection for poultry flocks, several approaches to control have been explored during the last 30 years.

The high rates of infection in poultry and associated rates of human infection have led national and international governments to a step-wise approach to infection control.

14iii.6.1 Legislation/monitoring

There is currently no legislation relating to *Campylobacter* reduction. Given the high rates of infection in poultry in many countries, approaches to control have been step-by-step, initially involving processing hygiene with sampling neck skins at processing plants with the aim of reducing levels of infection by 50%. Bacterial enumeration has been adopted by individual countries and by the European Union, with expectations in improvement of slaughter hygiene and farm biosecurity where bacterial numbers surpass a specified limit (EU Regulation 2017/1495).

14iii.6.2 Control during and after processing

During processing a number of approaches based on Hazard Analysis and Critical Control Point (HACCP) principles may be used to reduce levels of carcass contamination. These include combining monitoring of flocks with scheduling of flocks for slaughter so that the more contaminated flocks are processed towards the end of the day to prevent gross contamination of the plant equipment and subsequent poults.

In line processes using sonication and steam have been used in some UK factories to reduce surface contamination while not altering the product. In other countries including the US, treatment of carcasses with chlorine rinses or trichloroacetic acid is used, and this reduces levels of infection but does not eliminate it. Irradiation of meat will also prevent human infection, but risks of infection to poultry farm staff and in the processing plant remain.

Campylobacter organisms do not survive freezing, so freezing carcasses eliminates human infection. Similarly, heat treatment by pasteurization of products eliminates infection. The organisms are very infectious, through ingestion of incorrectly cooked meat or from contamination from raw product. Education of the consumer has not been sufficient alone to bring rates of human infection down due to the high frequency of contamination and the variable quality of home food processing. In response to this, retailers, in combination with their suppliers, are working on increased biosecurity and scheduling to reduce contamination at retail.

14iii.6.3 Biosecurity

Keeping flocks clear of *Campylobacter* requires strict attention to biosecurity (see Chapter 18, this volume). This includes maintenance, and thorough cleaning and disinfecting of poultry houses between batches of birds, attention to clean and sanitized water sources, and strict disease security involving visitor control with changes of clothing, and foot dips etc. Thinning should only be carried out with cleaned and disinfected crates.

14iii.6.4 Chemotherapy

Chemotherapy (see Chapter 19, this volume) of flocks should not be used to reduce levels of infection. It is frequently ineffective and increases the risk of resistance selection, not only in the *Campylobacter* organisms but also in other gut bacteria including *E. coli* and *Salmonella*.

14iii.6.5 Vaccination

The potential for vaccination is closely entwined with improving understanding of the immune response to infection and whether protective immunity follows infection, which is still relatively poorly understood. There are no currently available, demonstrably effective vaccines against *Campylobacter*. Serological conversion does occur during colonization, but this does not lead to clearance of the bacteria. It is thought that the potential for alteration of surface epitopes imposes a challenge for vaccine development. Inactivated vaccines have been shown to be ineffective. The partial protective effect of heterologous expressed *Campylobacter* surface antigens, including CjaA (an amino acid transporter), has been shown to reduce colonization in one study, although follow-up work with the same antigen has been less successful, reducing bacterial load by about 2 Log of bacteria. The variability of vaccine responses poses new questions about the providence of birds being vaccinated and the bacterial strains assessed. The absence of a sound understanding of the molecular basis of virulence for humans means that producing a live, attenuated strain which could be used in poultry has not so far been possible.

14iii.6.6 Competitive exclusion

Should live, attenuated strains become available, oral administration to newly hatched chickens should induce a strong protective effect by a form of exclusion as has also been demonstrated between vaccine and wild-type strains of *Salmonella*. Competitive exclusion by the use of gut flora preparation has been less successful, attributed to the very different metabolism and nutritional requirements of *Campylobacter* in the intestine compared with *Salmonella*. Unlike *Salmonella* serotypes, *C. jejuni* strains are able to multiply to very high densities in the gut in the presence of normal flora, so this is perhaps not surprising.

14iii.6.7 Genetic resistance

Genetic resistance is being explored as means to reduce levels of intestinal colonization. In experimental studies using inbred chicken lines, it is interesting that the same lines are more resistant or susceptible to both *Campylobacter* and *Salmonella* suggesting some similarities at least in the mechanism of colonization. Initial genetic analysis has identified a number of quantitative trait loci (QTLs) two of which are common to *Salmonella* resistant lines (see Chapter 3, this volume).

14iii.6.8 Bacteriophages

Experimental work has been carried out on the potential for using lytic bacteriophages to control *Campylobacter*. Oral administration of *Campylobacter*-specific phages has been shown to reduce levels of colonization in the caeca by 100-fold which would translate into substantially reduced levels of carcass contamination. Although there would be problems of variation in genetic susceptibility to phage lysis amongst different strains, as a result of restriction of phage DNA together with the likelihood of co-infection with several strains, phages have been shown to sterilize carcass surfaces through non-specific lysis (lysis from without) when administered in high densities.

The same phase variation mechanisms that lead to change in bacterial antigenicity can also lead to resistance to some phages with resistant sub-types becoming dominant in birds. This has led to the suggestion that phage may be best applied on retail meats to reduce bacterial load where resistant variants would not proliferate.

Other approaches, including probiotics and dietary organic acid incorporation, have also been explored with variable results.

14iii.7 Reference

Bayliss, C.D., Bidmos, F.A., Anjum, A., Manchev, V.T., Richards, R.L., *et al.* (2012) Phase variable genes of *Campylobacter jejuni* exhibit high mutation rates and specific mutational patterns but mutability is not the major determinant of population structure during host colonization. *Nucleic Acids Research* 40, 5876–5889.

14iii.8 Further Reading

Evans, S. and Powell, L. (2008) Campylobacter. In: Pattison, M., McMullin, P.F., Bradbury, J.M. and Alexander, D.M. *Poultry Diseases*, 6th edn. Saunders Elsevier, Philadelphia, Pennsylvania, pp. 181–190.

Ghareeb, K., Awad, W.A., Mohnl, M. and Scatzmayr, G. (2013) Control strategies for *Campylobacter* infection in poultry production. *World's Poultry Science Journal* 69, 57–76.

Humphrey, S., Chaloner, G., Kemmett, K., Davidson, N., Williams, N., *et al.* (2014) Campylobacter jejuni is not merely a commensal in commercial broiler chickens and affects bird welfare. *mBio*, 5(4), e01364-14.

Lin, J. (2009) Novel approaches for *Campylobacter* control in poultry. *Food-borne Pathogen Diseases* 6, 755–765.

Newell, D.G., Elvers, K.T., Dopfer, D., Hansson, I., Jones, P., et al. (2011) Biosecurity-based interventions and strategies to reduce *Campylobacter* spp. on poultry farms. *Applied and Environmental Microbiology* 77, 8605–8614.

Shane, S.M. (2000) *Campylobacter* infection of commercial poultry. *Revue Scientifique Et Technique De L Office International Des Epizooties* 19, 276–395.

World Health Organization (2020) Campylobacter. Available at: https://www.who.int/news-room/fact-sheets/detail/campylobacter (accessed 22 January 2021).

Zhang, Q. and Sahin, O. (2020) Campylobacteriolosis. In: Swayne, D.E. (editor-in-chief) *Diseases of Poultry*, 14th edn. Wiley-Blackwell, Oxford, UK, pp. 754–769.

14iv *Salmonella*

Paul Barrow*

School of Veterinary Medicine, University of Surrey, Guildford, UK

14iv.1 Introduction

Salmonella is a bacterial pathogen associated with food poisoning, largely, but not exclusively, arising from consumption of poultry meat and associated products. It also remains a major cause of morbidity and mortality in birds in many countries where it can be a cause of considerable economic loss.

14iv.2 Microbiology

14iv.2.1 Structure and taxonomy

Salmonella are Gram-negative, rod-shaped, motile bacteria which belong to the *Enterobacteriaceae*, a family of related bacteria including *Escherichia* (*E. coli*), *Klebsiella*, *Shigella*, *Citrobacter* and *Proteus*.

They are facultatively anaerobic and can be cultured equally well with or without oxygen. *E. coli* and *Salmonella* are two of the best studied and understood bacteria in terms of physiology and metabolism, genetics and genomics, and pathogenicity.

The more than 2400 serotypes (serovars) are distinguishable by the combination of O antigens (cell wall lipopolysaccharide, LPS) and H antigens (flagella) which are the immune-dominant surface antigens that historically were identified and differentiated by agglutination with specific antisera. There are many variants of each type of antigen, and, in some cases, multiple epitopes co-exist creating a mosaic of antigens in any one strain. Thus, the antigenic formula of *S.* Typhimurium is O:1,4,5,12, 27, H:i:1,2. Some antigens may or may not be present. Antigen O5 may or may not be present as a result of antigenic conversion resulting from phage infection introducing the relevant gene. The flagella antigens can also exist in one of two phases (in this case i or 1,2) as a result of a gene inversion mechanism allowing either one phase or the other in each bacterial cell. Most serovars have the capacity to express both phases. In some, such as *S.* Enteritidis, the flagella exist in only one phase, O:1,9,12, H:g,m:-. The two avian-specific serovars *S.* Gallinarum and *S.* Pullorum are completely non-motile and serologically identical, O:1,9,12:-:-.

Many of these antigens are shared with *E coli*, *Citrobacter*, etc. in which case culturable and biochemical characteristics are required to differentiate bacteria at the genus level.

Some serovars are distinguishable biochemically, including Gallinarum and Pullorum.

The chromosomes are ca. 4.6 Mb in size. All serovars associated with human and animal disease contain a mosaic of clusters of virulence genes essential for systemic disease and many of which contribute to invasive disease and colonization. Most of these are chromosomal but additional essential virulence genes may be plasmid-mediated, especially in *S.* Gallinarum and *S.* Pullorum and other serovars producing typhoid-like infections. Serovars which produce typhoid-like disease possess more pseudogenes than food-poisoning serovars. Typically, *S.* Gallinarum has 200–300 pseudogenes and *S.* Pullorum has 240–260, whereas *S.* Enteritidis has 113 and *S.* Typhimurium 25.

Historically each *Salmonella* serovar was given species status which did not in any way reflect the high genome sequence identity between serovars. Apart from those serovars which produce characteristic diseases, most serovars were named after the town from which they were first isolated, such as Dublin and Montevideo. Their true taxonomic status was eventually recognized and now serovars are identified as, for example, *Salmonella enterica* subspecies *enterica* serovar Typhimurium or, more conveniently, *S.* Typhimurium, but *S. typhimurium* will still be seen written, as a distinct species.

*paul.barrow@surrey.ac.uk

© CAB International 2021. *Poultry Health: A Guide for Professionals* (P. Barrow *et al.*)
DOI: 10.1079/9781789245042.0014

14iv.2.2 Culture

Most *Salmonella* serovars are prototrophic and grow on minimal medium of glucose and essential salts. The typhoid serovars, including serovars Pullorum and Gallinarum, are auxotrophic and will only grow in minimal medium with added supplements. Even then they are generally slower growing but grow better in or on nutrient medium.

It may be necessary to isolate *Salmonella* from animal feed or other such samples where they may be damaged. Initial culture in a liquid non-selective broth is therefore usually carried out before transferring to selective media.

For culture from tissues and other samples followed by identification, selection against and differentiation from other enteric bacteria, especially *E. coli*, is needed. Selective liquid and solid media are available which also enable differentiation by colony colour. Because *Salmonella* generally do not ferment lactose, solid agar media frequently include lactose with a pH-sensitive dye e.g. MacConkey, Brilliant Green (Fig. 14.1), desoxycholate, XLD agars, to differentiate *Salmonella* from the normally more numerous lactose-fermenting *E. coli*. *Salmonella* colonies may then be picked and tested for agglutination on a slide with a drop of specific antisera to give a presumptive identification as *Salmonella* and even one of the major serovars.

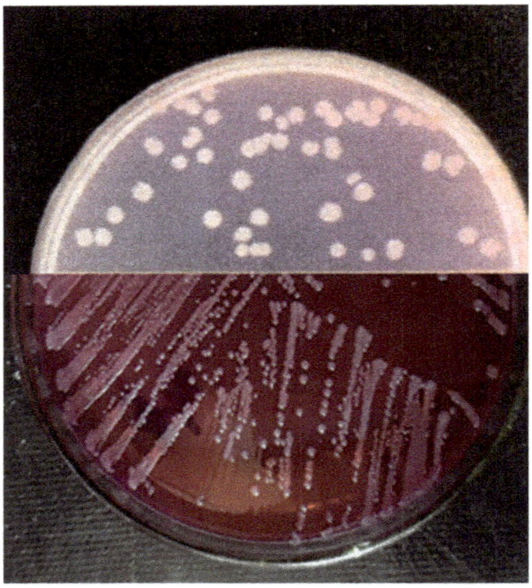

Fig. 14iv.1. Colonies of *Salmonella* Enteritidis on Brilliant Green Agar. (Author's own photograph and with permission of Dr Gulbeena Saleem.)

Some *Citrobacter* strains resemble *Salmonella* culturally on some selective media and may possess similar antigens.

Serovars grow optimally at 37°C but grow well up to 44–45°C (the chicken body temperature is 41.5°C). Other distantly related bacteria, such as *Yersinia pseudotuberculosis*, might be isolated from *Salmonella*-like lesions in the liver, may also appear similar on selective agar and may also agglutinate with sera, but this organism is flagellate only at 22°C and not at 37°C. *Salmonella* flagella agglutinate poorly from selective solid media containing bile salts.

After presumptive identification, biochemical identification may be needed to identify colonies definitively as *Salmonella*. After identification of serovar, these may be sub-divided by their susceptibility to a panel of bacteriophages (phage typing). This is important where a particular serovar is predominant. Strain sequencing and SNP typing can also be used for further epidemiological purposes.

14iv.3 Pathogenicity

The *Salmonella* serovars can be divided into two pathotypes. A small group of serovars typically produce typhoid-like disease in healthy, non-reproducing, non-immunosuppressed adult individuals in a narrow range of host species. The disease is severe and involves intracellular bacterial multiplication in macrophages, largely in spleen and liver. The reproductive tract may become infected. In the absence of clinical disease, they do not normally colonize the alimentary tract, and therefore rarely enter the food chain and produce human infection. In poultry *S.* Gallinarum and *S.* Pullorum fall into this group. Both serovars possess a large plasmid which is essential for virulence in chickens.

Most of the remaining serovars do not typically produce systemic disease in healthy adults and rarely do so in very young animals. They colonize the alimentary tract in a wide range of animal species in a disease-free manner and contaminate carcasses resulting in human food-poisoning/gastroenteritis. Such serovars include *S.* Heidelberg, *S.* Infantis, *S.* Montevideo and many others.

S. Typhimurium and *S.* Enteritidis are unusual in that they produce classic typhoid (in mice), and cause disease and mortality in young chickens belonging to particular genetic lines, but also colonize the poultry gut well and are major serovars causing food-related gastroenteritis.

14iv.3.1 Systemic diseases

Fowl typhoid (S. Gallinarum infection)

This is a severe systemic disease of chickens of all ages, where mortality may reach 100%. It is worldwide in distribution. In countries where intensive indoor rearing has been carried out for decades it has largely been controlled but is still occasionally introduced by different routes such as illegal imports or dirty crates. It remains a major problem in countries where ambient temperatures are high, and open-sided housing is used.

It is likely that horizontal transmission is the major route of spread, at least in susceptible lines of birds. Wild birds can also be sources of infection. The evidence for vertical transmission is epidemiological, i.e. presence of the organism in parent flocks and progeny. Persistent infection can be demonstrated experimentally in more resistant lines of birds but it has been difficult to demonstrate vertical transmission experimentally.

The disease is clinically very similar to human typhoid. Domestic fowl and turkeys are susceptible but most current commercial breeds of ducks are more resistant. Mortality varies with the virulence of individual bacterial strains and also the host genetic background. Some lines of chickens can be so susceptible that <10 bacteria inoculated intravenously (i/v) will produce disease and deaths whereas some lines are completely resistant so that 10^8 bacteria inoculated i/v have no effect whatsoever.

Birds which are clinically ill are lethargic and anorexic with pale wattles and comb, and they produce a green, foul diarrhoea. Substantial drops in egg production only occur in the very late stages of disease.

Bacteria enter orally through the gut and invade macrophages in the spleen and elsewhere where they multiply, resulting in dissemination into the blood, and then disease. During the later stages of clinical disease they re-enter the alimentary tract, from where they are shed.

In the acute phase of the disease, the liver may be enlarged and may have a bronzed appearance immediately and for a short time after opening the body wall. The liver is friable and there may be necrotic lesions in the spleen. Death may occur over a period of weeks and, in more chronic cases, birds may be stunted, and large sterile necrotic lesions may be seen in the myocardium (Fig. 14iv.2).

During the later stages of disease, necrotic areas can be seen in the gut, visible through the gut wall. In all cases, the non-motile bacteria can be isolated from the liver and cultured easily on selective media by direct plating.

Because *S.* Gallinarum (and *S.* Pullorum, below) shows chronic persistent infection and varying degrees of vertical transmission, the chain of infection can be broken by identifying carriers with specific circulating IgG. This can be done either by slide agglutination test using stained Pullorum antigen containing an anticoagulant, or by ELISA, both of which can be done as pen-side tests.

Control of the disease is either by eradication, as indicated above, or by using a live, attenuated vaccine. The vaccine used most frequently is the 9R vaccine which is highly protective. There is some concern over reversion to virulence, although there is little hard evidence for this. Use of antibiotics is not recommended, and unrestricted use in many countries has resulted in multi-resistant strains.

Pullorum disease (S. Pullorum)

Pullorum disease is also clinically very similar to human typhoid but with severe disease, which

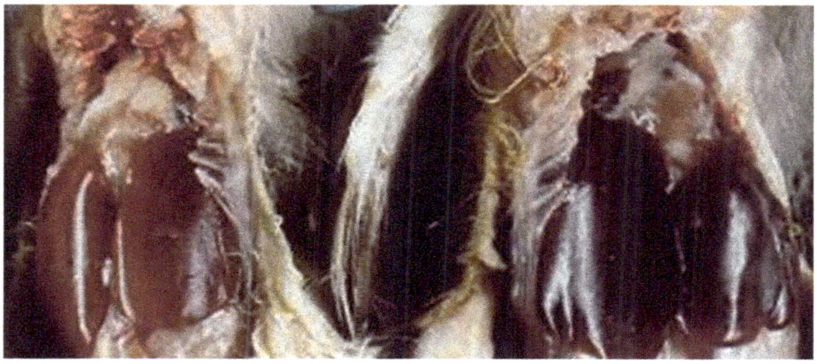

Fig. 14iv.2. Necrotic lesions in myocardium in chronic fowl typhoid. (Author's own photograph.)

can reach 100%, only evident in very young birds. Transmission is faecal–oral in very young birds, frequently originating in the hatchery with chicks also infected by vertical transmission. Mortality varies according to the virulence of individual bacterial strains and host genetic background.

Disease is associated with a diarrhoea and white-caked vents. Generalized inflammation can result in polyserositis. In older birds, necrotic heart lesions similar to those seen in fowl typhoid may be seen. The bacteria can also become localized in the joints and in the reproductive tract, causing malformed ovules. Culture from the liver is relatively easy, yielding non-motile bacteria with colonies smaller than those of *S.* Gallinarum. The two organisms can be differentiated by biochemical and fermentation tests.

Birds that survive may harbour the organism in the spleen without immune clearance, despite the presence of high titre antibody in the serum. Small numbers of bacteria persist until sexual maturity when the increase in levels of sex hormone reduces T lymphocyte responsiveness, resulting in multiplication in the spleen and spread to the reproductive tract. Ovules may be misshapen but sufficient numbers of viable eggs are laid such that hatched chicks shed extensively in the hatchery, repeating the infection cycle (Fig. 14iv.3).

There is evidence that, unlike most *Salmonella* serovars, which induce a strong Th1-type immune response, *S.* Pullorum induces a response more closely resembling a Th2-type response with strong antibody production but with weak cellular immunity, which may thus lead to persistence.

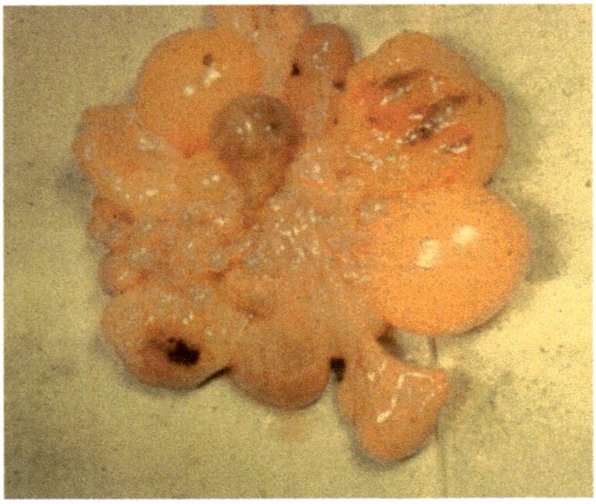

Fig. 14iv.3. Malformed ovules in chronic *S.* Pullorum infection. (Author's own photograph.)

As with *S.* Gallinarum, the chain of vertical infection can easily be broken by identifying carriers by detecting specific circulating IgG either by a slide agglutination test or by ELISA.

Vaccination is generally not used since most mortality occurs in very young birds. Chemotherapy has also resulted in extensive antibiotic resistance.

S. *Typhimurium*, S. *Enteritidis and other food-poisoning serovars*

S. Typhimurium and *S.* Enteritidis are the serovars most frequently isolated from cases of human food poisoning and it is perhaps no coincidence that they are also two of the most virulent non-typhoid serovars (they are also sometimes called paratyphoid or typhoidal). They can produce very high mortality if chicks of less than a few days are infected. In older birds, mortality and morbidity are generally low or non-existent. They do produce typical typhoid disease, but in mice. They also produce invasive enteritis in a number of other livestock including pigs and calves. Most of the other serovars that may be prevalent, such as *S.* Montevideo, *S.* Heidelberg, *S.* Infantis and *S.* Hadar, generally, but not always, produce very little morbidity in birds of any age.

S. Enteritidis has a predilection for the reproductive tract and can infect the ovaries and oviduct with a degree of vertical transmission, resulting in infected eggs, although it is likely that horizontal transmission is more important.

Since the 1990s, monophasic strains of *S.* Typhimurium have appeared first in pig production and more recently in broilers. This phenomenon has appeared in several phage types of this serovar, indicating that it has occurred independently several times. Strains lack phase 2 of the flagella antigen lacking the *fljB* gene. The evolutionary significance is unclear.

Both *S.* Enteritidis and *S.* Typhimurium possess a large virulence plasmid which is essential for virulence in mice, but it plays little role in chickens.

Association with food poisoning

Until the mid-1980s, *S.* Typhimurium was the predominant serovar associated with poultry and human food poisoning. However, there have been early epidemics involving other serovars (*S.* Agona in the 1950s and *S.* Hadar in the 1970s), which entered the turkey industry and transmitted from there into broiler production. In the mid-1980s, several unrelated phage types of *S.* Enteritidis, including phage types 4, 6, 8 and 13a, appeared in different parts of the world. The reason for their simultaneous appearance has been speculated but it is still unclear. It is highly unlikely that this is related directly to the eradication of the serologically related *S.* Gallinarum and *S.* Pullorum. These *S.* Enteritidis phage types never reached Australia where a predominant serovar in poultry was *S.* Sofia which nevertheless was not associated with human infection.

In many countries the epidemic was associated with consumption of eggs and egg products. However, the *S.* Enteritidis strains were also found in the broiler industry (broilers and broiler breeders) where high mortality was observed in very young birds. In this case, heavy infection of the pericardium was found which could lead to gross carcass contamination.

In some countries, including the UK and other European countries, this led to a political crisis resulting in a concentration of effort in controlling food-borne *Salmonella* infections from the poultry industry.

14iv.4 Epidemiology

The major sources of *Salmonella* for intensively reared poultry are (i) the birds themselves, through introduction of stock; (ii) feed, especially unheated feed (protein sources are the main source of contamination; fish meal imported from South America was once dried in the open air facilitating contamination with wild bird and rodent and reptile faeces); (iii) rodents in the poultry house; (iv) man, especially contract staff and vehicles; and (v) housing, from inadequate decontamination between batches of birds and the hatchery. Free-range birds can also be infected by wild birds and other free-range livestock such as pigs.

Birds infected when they are very young, and have little immunity and a simple gut flora, excrete *Salmonella* in larger numbers and for longer periods than when they become infected as adults.

Other factors affecting excretion include ambient temperature (increased stress and shedding at lower temperatures), nutritional status (affecting immunity), crowding (affecting stress and cross-infection), concomitant infections such as with *Eimeria* and necrotic enteritis (releasing blood and iron in the gut) and presence of antibiotics including growth promoters (disrupting and reducing normal flora and increasing *Salmonella* colonization and excretion).

After depopulation and at slaughter, cross-contamination of birds and carcasses occurs. Pooling of meat products or liquid egg for processing also increases the risk of cross-contamination.

14iv.4.1 Surveillance

Surveillance is made at the level of the poultry house rather than individual birds. Surveillance is most easily done by faeces collection, especially fresh caecal droppings or using boot or drag swabs. For invasive serovars such as Typhimurium and Enteritidis, serology may be done using ELISA. Egg yolk gives identical results to sera. Some serovars can be differentiated using LPS and flagella antigens for detection. Sampling statistics are required for a statistically significant result depending on the expected levels of infection.

14iv.5 Control Measures

14iv.5.1 General control – biosecurity and hygiene

The list of sources of infection for poultry flocks above indicates that biosecurity measures need to be put in place to prevent entry by these routes (see Chapter 18, this volume).

Disinfection after depopulation is important both from the point of view of *Salmonella* but also for all other infectious agents and parasites, such as red mite. This includes ensuring that the disinfectant penetrates the small cracks that occur between housing material, particularly in older poultry houses, and is not inactivated by litter and other organic material in the house. Thorough cleaning is therefore essential.

Some disinfectants, including iodophors and quaternary ammonium compounds, are readily inactivated by organic material. Phenolics and aldehydes are more effective in the presence of wood, faeces, feather material, etc. In the UK, all poultry producers are required to use Defra-approved disinfectants.

14iv.5.2 Legislation (see also Chapter 23, this volume)

Following the political problems in the UK arising from the *S.* Enteritidis epidemic, national legislation was introduced to facilitate *Salmonella* infection control. Codes of Practice (CoPs) were available but rarely adhered to and not enforced. The legislation required reporting of *Salmonella* infection of poultry, testing of breeder and layer flocks, hatcheries and animal protein (feed). Free-range rearing was considered a particular risk for infection.

These CoPs were incorporated into European legislation with targets for reducing levels of *S.* Typhimurium and Enteritidis, and also with targets for broiler farms. Vaccination was recommended. An EFSA (European Food Safety Authority) opinion stated that, provided the detection methods were able to differentiate the vaccine strains from wild strains, live vaccines could be used safely throughout the life of the birds, except during the withdrawal period before slaughter and in laying hens during production. Vaccination of layers was considered useful as a measure to reduce shedding and egg contamination, where the purpose is to reduce high prevalence.

In 1998 a UK quality assurance scheme was launched by the egg industry covering all aspects of production including a requirement for vaccination against *S.* Typhimurium and Enteritidis, improved hygiene and welfare standards, and *Salmonella* testing of birds and eggs. In 2017 UK eggs were finally observed to be completely free of *Salmonella*.

Following controls of Typhimurium and Enteritidis other serovars, such as *S.* Infantis, are now showing increases in prevalence in some countries and are also covered by EU legislation.

14iv.5.3 Chemotherapy (see also Chapter 19, this volume)

Antibiotics are used extensively worldwide in poultry production largely because in most countries their use is not regulated. Some may be useful to control systemic disease but the increase in multiresistance in the serovars which produce systemic disease (see above) is reducing effectiveness. Most resistance is transmissible and plasmid-mediated but resistance to furazolidone and quinolones, once thought to be non-transmissible because resistance is chromosomal, is now also increasingly plasmid-mediated.

Nevertheless, chemotherapy is not always effective in reducing *Salmonella* colonization, and withdrawal of the antibiotic can lead to a resurgence in excretion. Chemotherapy also increases the risk of transmission of antibiotic resistance plasmids which may already be present in resistant strains of organisms such as *E. coli*.

The use of chemotherapeutic antibiotics for growth stimulation was banned in the EU in 2006, but they are still used in many other countries. These are also less effective because of increasing resistance. Their use can also increase *Salmonella* shedding.

14iv.5.4 Vaccination

Live, attenuated vaccines are more effective than inactivated vaccines because they stimulate both cellular and humoral immunity. Good protection against fowl typhoid can be obtained with a live *S.* Gallinarum 9R vaccine developed in the 1950s. This is a rough undefined vaccine. It also is protective against the closely related *S.* Enteritidis. Commercial live vaccines are available against *S.* Typhimurium and *S.* Enteritidis. Inactivated vaccines may have some effect when the challenge is small.

Live vaccines administered orally to newly hatched chickens may also provide rapid protection against colonization by a competitive exclusion mechanism.

14iv.5.5 Competitive exclusion

Because adult birds are much more resistant to colonization, as a result of their complex, mature gut flora, commercially available cultures of adult gut flora administered to chicks provide, within 24 h of hatching, a high level of protection against *Salmonella* colonization. However, their use is contraindicated immediately prior to live *Salmonella* vaccines administered orally. They are less effective against *Campylobacter*.

14iv.5.6 Genetic resistance (see also Chapter 3, this volume)

It has been known for years that some lines of chicken are more resistant to systemic salmonellosis than others. Several loci/genes contribute to this including *NRAMP1*, *TLR4* and *SAL1*. Some lines of chicken are also more resistant to *Salmonella* colonization than others and the same lines are resistant to *Campylobacter* colonization (see Chapter 14iii, this volume). There is no relationship between resistance to *Salmonella* and other infectious agents such as *Eimeria* (see Chapter 16i, this volume) and IBV (see Chapter 15x, this volume).

14iv.6 Further Reading

Barrow, P.A. and Methner, U. (2013) *Salmonella in Domestic Livestock*. CAB International, Wallingford, UK, pp. 677–736.

Gast, R., Shivaprasad, H. and Barrow, P. (2013) *Salmonella Infections*. In: Swayne, D.E. (editor in chief) *Diseases of Poultry*, 13th edn. Wiley-Blackwell, Oxford, UK.

Lister, S.A. and Barrow, P. (2008) Enterobacteriaceae. In: Pattison, M., McMullin, P.F., Bradbury, J.M. and Alexander, D. (eds) *Poultry Diseases,* 6th edn. Saunders Elsevier, Philadelphia, Pennsylvania, pp. 110–145.

McMullin, P.F. (2004) *Poultry Health and Diseases – A Pocket Guide*. 5M Enterprises Ltd., Sheffield, UK.

Greenacre, C.B. and Morishita, T.Y. (2015) *Backyard Poultry Medicine and Surgery*. Wiley-Blackwell, Oxford, UK.

14v *Clostridium* and Necrotic Enteritis

Evelien Dierick, Evy Goossens, Richard Ducatelle and Filip Van Immerseel*

Livestock Gut Health Team (LiGHT), Department of Pathology, Bacteriology and Avian Diseases, Faculty of Veterinary Medicine, Ghent University, Merelbeke, Belgium

14v.1 Introduction

Necrotic enteritis (NE) is one of the most important enteric diseases in poultry production affecting both productivity and animal welfare. Its global cost is estimated to exceed US$6 billion annually, equal to a loss of US$0.0625 per bird (Wade and Keyburn, 2015). In the literature NE outbreaks have been reported mainly to affect broiler production systems but the disease has also frequently been observed in the field in turkeys, quail, commercial layer pullets, laying hens and wild birds.

14v.2 Aetiology

Clostridium perfringens is the causative agent of many histotoxic and enterotoxic diseases in production animals in addition to humans. It is a Gram-positive, anaerobic, spore-forming bacillus. Due to their high resilience, bacterial spores are ubiquitous in the environment and can often be found in soil and water samples. Moreover, *C. perfringens* is part of the normal gut microbiota of vertebrates, reaching numbers up to 10^5 cfu/g in intestinal content of healthy chickens. Within this species different toxinotypes have been characterized based on their toxin production profile (Rood *et al.*, 2018). Avian necrotic enteritis is caused by both *C. perfringens* type A and type G, producing alpha toxin or both alpha toxin and NetB toxin, respectively. Only recently, a distinction between both toxinotype-induced NE was proposed based on subtle differences in disease description and histopathological reports in the literature (Goossens *et al.*, 2020). This book chapter focuses on type G-induced non-haemorrhagic NE because of the limited knowledge of type A-induced haemorrhagic NE in broilers.

Dysregulation of the intestinal microbiota can trigger proliferation of a virulent *C. perfringens* strain, eventually followed by massive toxin production. NE outbreaks generally occur in broiler flocks around the age of 3–4 weeks when broilers are most prone to infection. At this stage of life, the immature immune system of the chick is insufficient to replace the declining maternal protective antibodies.

14v.3 Symptoms

Two forms of NE can be distinguished based on disease severity: the clinical and subclinical form. Clinical NE is a peracute disease, in which birds drop dead within one to two hours after showing signs of discomfort. Birds suddenly display a decrease in their overall welfare status, characterized by increased huddling, depression, dullness, decreased appetite, anorexia, dehydration, ruffled feathers and diarrhoea. Post-mortem examination of the carcasses reveals thin-walled intestines and ballooning of the caeca due to increased gas production. Necrotic lesions and ulcers cover the lining of the small intestine (duodenum, jejunum and ileum) leading to the formation of large patches of necrotic tissue (Fig. 14v.1a). No premonitory signs can be seen prior to NE disease development, although some argue wet litter can be a non-specific sign of infection.

Birds suffering from the subclinical form of NE show no signs of discomfort nor elevated mortality rates. However, these birds also suffer from necrotic lesions (Fig. 14v.1b), thin-walled intestines and

*Corresponding author: filip.vanimmerseel@ugent.be

© CAB International 2021. *Poultry Health: A Guide for Professionals* (P. Barrow *et al.*)
DOI: 10.1079/9781789245042.0014

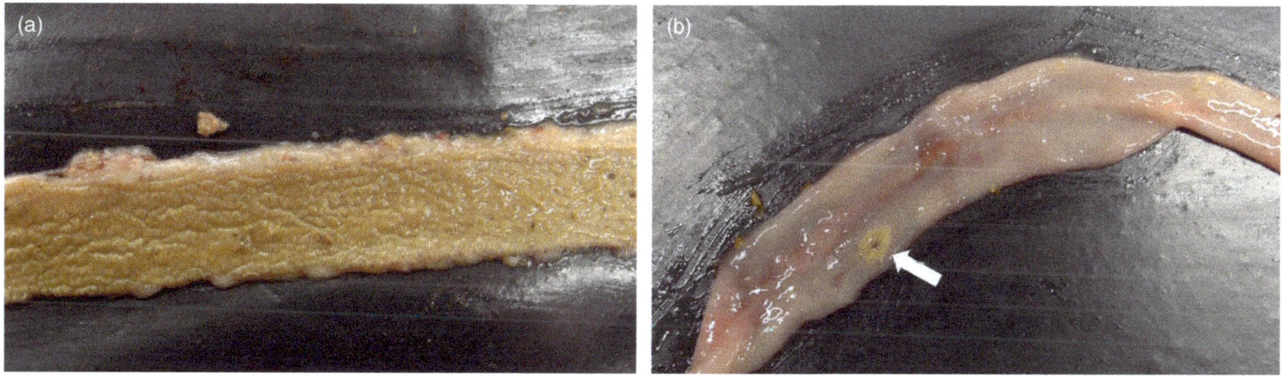

Fig. 14v.1. (a) Photo showing lesions in clinical NE. Necrotic lesions and ulcers cover the lining of the small intestine (ileum) in birds suffering from clinical NE, leading to the formation of large patches of necrotic tissue. (Author's own image.) (b) Photo showing lesions in subclinical NE. Necrotic lesions and ulcers are present on the thin-walled small intestine (ileum) in birds suffering subclinical NE. In contrast to clinical NE, the lesions do not form necrotic patches larger than 2 cm in width. Lesions and ulcers are more often dispersed throughout the small intestine. (Author's own image.)

chronical mucosal damage in the small intestine. Subclinical NE will lead to a reduced feed intake and poor absorption of nutrients resulting in an increased feed conversion ratio (~10%) and drop in body weight gain (~12%) (Skinner *et al.*, 2010). Although mostly undetected due to the absence of clinical manifestation, subclinical NE currently is of considerable economic significance to the poultry industry. Infected flocks have higher feed costs, a lower meat production yield and sometimes costs related to the use of therapeutics to combat the disease. Furthermore, subclinical NE has infrequently been associated with cholangiohepatitis. Bacteria reach the bile duct and portal blood stream, infecting both gall bladder and liver. The liver becomes pale, enlarged and contains a reticular pattern of white and red foci. Simultaneously, fibrinoid necrosis, heterophil and lymphocyte infiltration, bile duct hyperplasia and fibrosis with reticulin fibre proliferation have been observed. This condition may only be noticed after slaughter leading to an increased rate of condemnation.

14v.4 Predisposing Factors

NE is a multifactorial disease in which the presence of the virulent *C. perfringens* strain is insufficient to induce the disease. Many predisposing factors have been described which are able to modify the gastrointestinal environment increasing susceptibility (Fig. 14v.2) (McDevitt *et al.*, 2006; M'Sadeq *et al.*, 2015).

First, NE outbreaks are often associated with coccidiosis. The *Eimeria* parasite has an intracellular reproduction cycle, resulting in damage to the epithelial cells and changes in the immune status of the animal. Plasma proteins leak into the lumen. In addition, mucogenesis is stimulated. Both processes cause a high nutrient input into the gut lumen, resulting in proliferation of the virulent *C. perfringens* strain. Immunosuppression induced by viral infections such as infectious bursal disease, Marek's disease, chicken infectious anaemia and Gumboro disease have also been associated with the development of NE.

Secondly, a wide variety of nutritional factors are associated with NE disease development. Excessive protein levels reaching the lower parts of the gastrointestinal tract can lead to *C. perfringens* proliferation. Proteins of animal origin such as fishmeal appear to be particularly strong triggers for NE. Furthermore, poorly digested proteins can end up in the distal part of the gut, becoming a protein source for pathogenic bacteria after degradation to ammonia and amines. An imbalanced energy-to-protein ratio in the feed can also result in higher intestinal protein levels due to a higher feed intake by the bird in order to fulfil its energy requirements. NE disease development is more common in broilers fed diets containing high amounts of non-starch polysaccharides (NSP) like barley, wheat, rye and oats. The host is not able to hydrolyse NSP. However, it has been suggested that NSP can act as a substrate for pathogenic microbiota. Digesta containing high amounts of NSP have a higher viscosity level. Reduced diffusion of both enzymes and nutrients can cause a decline in nutrient absorption by the host, eventually leaving nutrients for *C. perfringens* growth. Increased digesta viscosity can also induce reverse peristalsis, moving microbial communities from distal to more proximal sites of the gut and prolonging the transit time, enhancing the interaction time between microbiota and substrate. Due to their hydrophilic properties, it is suggested that NSP can increase water content of the digesta. This induces a higher water intake by the birds, leading to wet litter, the ideal environment for *C. perfringens* sporulation. Other dietary compounds that have been shown to predispose broilers to NE are lectins, tannins, protease inhibitors, glucosinolates, alkaloids, terpenes and polyphenols (M'Sadeq *et al.*, 2015). Furthermore, secondary fungal metabolites, mycotoxins, can also initiate predisposing intestinal damage (Antonissen *et al.*, 2014). In addition, physical features of the diet such as particle size can influence NE sensitivity.

Lastly, management related features such as poor temperature control and ventilation, problems with water supply and the nature of the feeding regimes can be related to NE disease outbreaks (Tsiouris, 2016). Rearing the animals under suboptimal conditions can induce stress in young chicks, resulting in a period of elevated NE susceptibility. Even the transition between starter and grower feed can induce a stressful period. Also, high stocking density and rapid growth rate have been proven to predispose broilers to NE.

14v.5 Pathogenesis in Broiler Chickens

Although extensively researched, the pathogenesis of *C. perfringens* type G derived NE in broilers is still not completely understood. However, this book chapter summarizes current knowledge into an overview depicted in Fig. 14v.3.

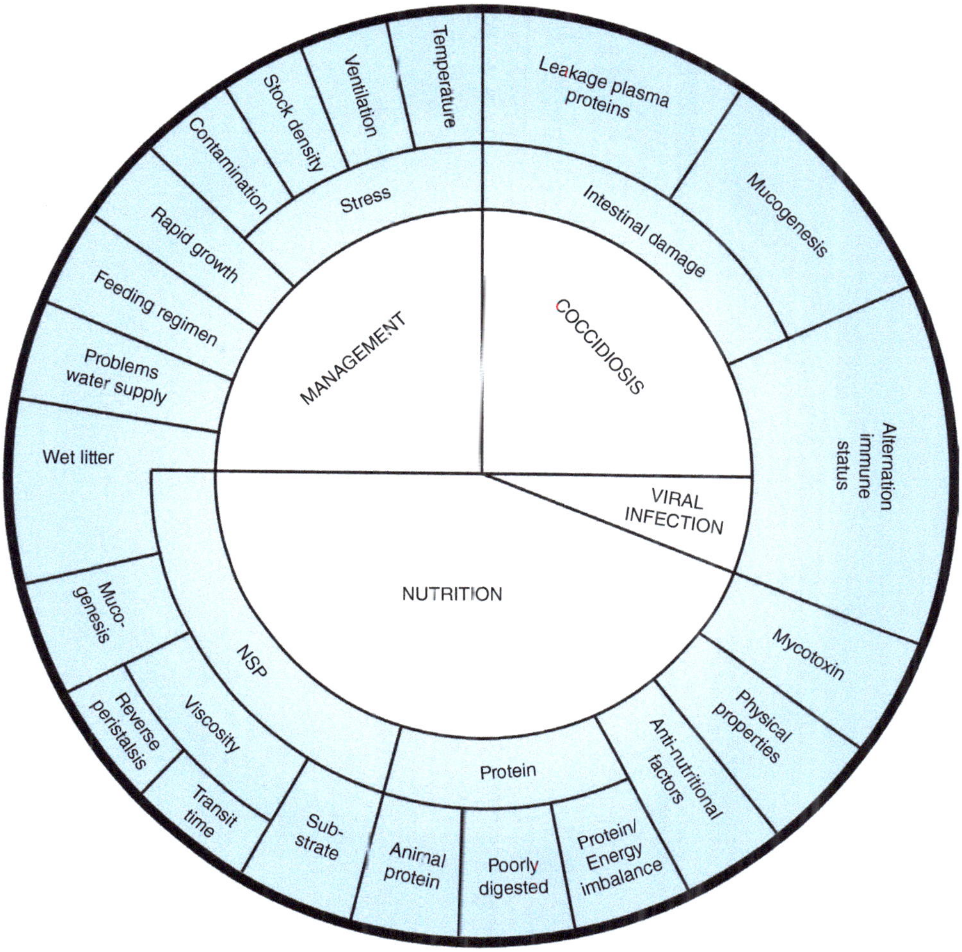

Fig. 14v.2. External factors predisposing broilers to NE. (Author's own image.)

As mentioned above, *C. perfringens* is a member of the normal gut microbiota reaching numbers up to 10^5 cfu/g intestinal content in healthy chickens. A vast array of *C. perfringens* genotypes can be recovered from intestinal content of healthy birds, indicating a large diversity within this bacterial population (Nauerby *et al.*, 2003). All strains produce alpha toxin but only a small fraction of this population is able to produce the all-essential NetB toxin and its associated virulence factors (Keyburn *et al.*, 2010). The intestinal content of diseased animals can contain up to 10^9 cfu *C. perfringens* per gram. Single-strain dominance is observed in contaminated flocks, a process in which only one virulent strain outcompetes all other strains (Nauerby *et al.*, 2003). Inhibition of the closely related strains can be facilitated by bacteriocins, which are proteinaceous toxins produced by bacteria. The ability of virulent *C. perfringens* strains to secrete such growth inhibiting factors has been demonstrated.

NE is a multifactorial disease, necessitating the presence of the virulent *C. perfringens* strain in the gastrointestinal tract in addition to a favourable environment in which the virulent strain can thrive. This environment can be created by an array of predisposing factors, which have been discussed more extensively above. Here, *Eimeria* infection is taken as an example of how the intestinal environment can be altered in favour of the bacterium. The intracellular lifecycle of *Eimeria* parasites is known to induce intestinal epithelial cell damage and thus

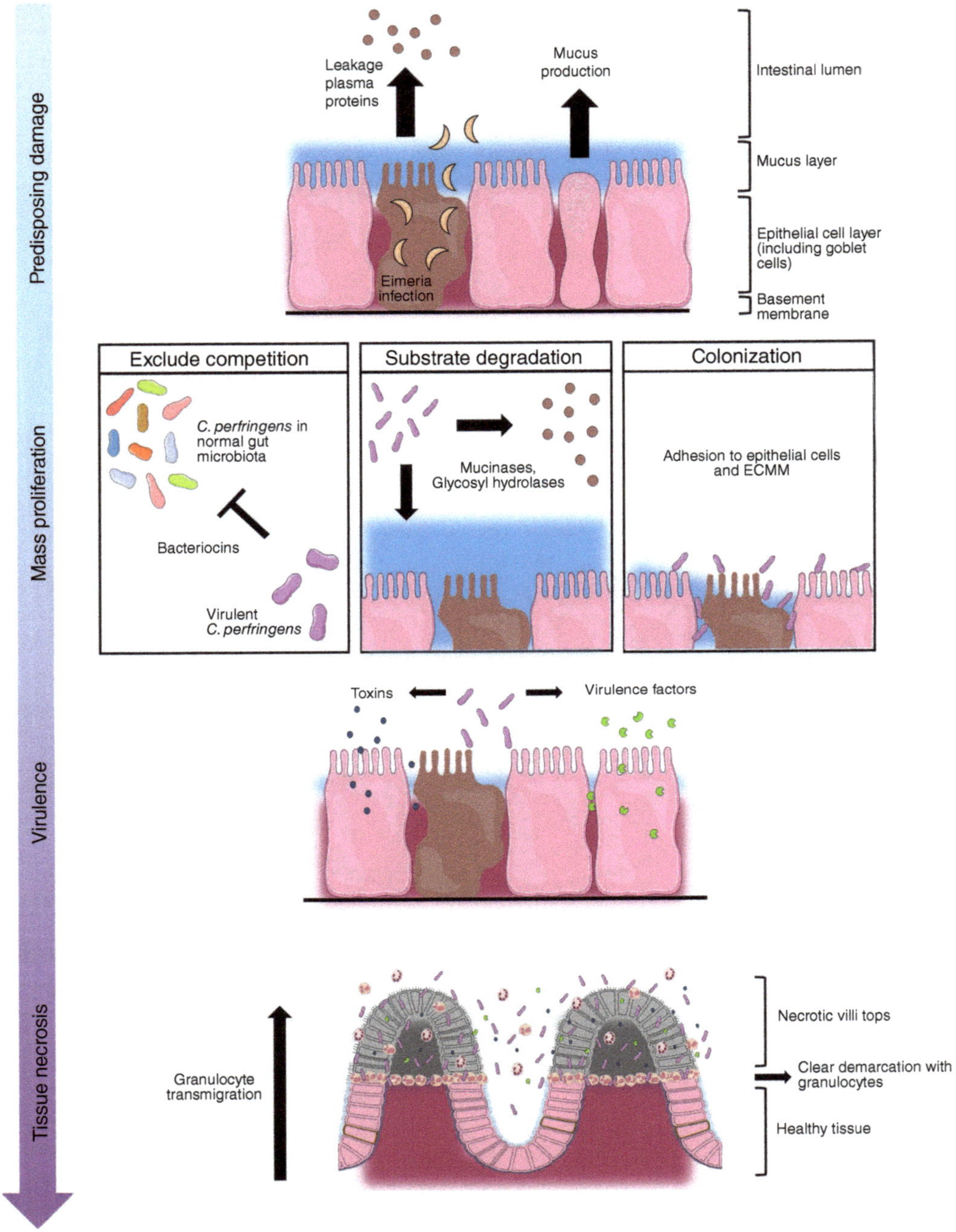

Fig. 14v.3. Pathogenesis of NE in broilers. (Author's own image.)

increase permeability of the intestinal lining. Consequently, plasma proteins leak into the lumen of the chicken gut. Also goblet cells are activated, leading to increased mucogenesis (Collier *et al.*, 2008). Both processes enhance the amount of available nutrients in the gastrointestinal tract that the bacterium can use. *C. perfringens* is auxotrophic, lacking the ability to produce 13 out of 20 essential amino acids. However, *C. perfringens* is able to utilize these newly-available nutrients by producing an array of enzymes including various proteases (Collier *et al.*, 2008). Moreover, genes on plasmid-encoded pathogenicity loci code for mucinases and multiple glycosyl hydrolases like sialidases and chitinase-like proteins, which may play a role in mucin degradation (Lepp *et al.*, 2010; Prescott *et al.*, 2016). Additional research is needed to verify the exact function of these enzymes. However, their key importance during the early stages of pathogenesis is likely. The sudden substrate availability is essential for *C. perfringens* mass proliferation, resulting in a clear disturbance of the microbial balance. Both predisposing damage and the degradation of the protective mucus layer by the bacterium expose numerous binding sites for both *C. perfringens* as well as its toxins and virulence factors. *C. perfringens* is able to bind to both intestinal epithelial cells and exposed extracellular matrix molecules, resulting in colonization of the mucosal surface (Martin and Smyth, 2010).

Mass proliferation might lead to nutrient depletion. In order to circumvent this problem, the bacteria will favour virulence overgrowth when the critical population size is reached. Gene expression can be regulated by quorum sensing, a process in which auto-inducing molecules are produced and perceived by nearby bacteria, indicating their presence when high bacterial densities exist. In *C. perfringens*, quorum sensing is closely linked to the VirR/VirS two-component regulatory system, upregulating the expression of toxins and virulence factors. In the past, alpha toxin was considered the main virulence factor involved in *C. perfringens* pathogenesis. However, in broilers alpha toxin mutants are still able to induce NE, questioning its importance (Keyburn *et al.*, 2006). The *C. perfringens* necrotic enteritis β-like toxin (NetB), a pore forming toxin, has been described to be essential for NE induction (Keyburn *et al.*, 2010). The exact function during pathogenesis and possible binding partners of NetB are still unclear. It has been suggested, however, that NetB will most probably not target intestinal epithelial cells (Prescott *et al.*, 2016). In addition to toxin genes, virulent NetB+ *C. perfringens* strains encode an array of virulence-associated genes (Lepp *et al.*, 2010). Further research is needed to reveal their different functions.

Infiltration of both toxins and other virulence factors (for example sialidases, chitinases, internalin) will further lead to *C. perfringens* migration through the tissue. Literature describing the microscopic lesions of the later stages of NE pathology was combined to establish an overall pathogenesis model (Figs 14v.3 and 14v.4) (M'Sadeq *et al.*, 2015; Prescott *et al.*, 2016). Based on histopathological examinations, it is suggested that damage to the villi is initiated at the basement membrane and the lateral side of the enterocytes, leading to further spreading throughout the lamina propria. Furthermore, granulocyte transmigration is observed. Enterocytes, destroyed extracellular matrix molecules and inflammatory cells become trapped in a fibrin network. Interestingly, it has been suggested that the matrix destruction itself would be responsible for enterocyte degeneration rather than toxin effects. The tips of the villi become necrotic through further destruction of the lamina propria. A clear demarcation line of heterophilic immune cells can be distinguished, dividing the healthy from the necrotic tissue. Blood vessels become congested in both the lamina propria and the submucosa. Although *C. perfringens* accumulates in the necrotic areas, no healthy cells are invaded. Eventually, the superficial layer of the mucosa becomes necrotic and detaches. Cellular degeneration can reach the muscularis mucosa and submucosae in a later stage.

14v.6 Prevention and Control

When there is evidence of NE disease development, the entire flock can be treated using therapeutic antimicrobials. A variety of antimicrobials have been evaluated in disease models and are used in

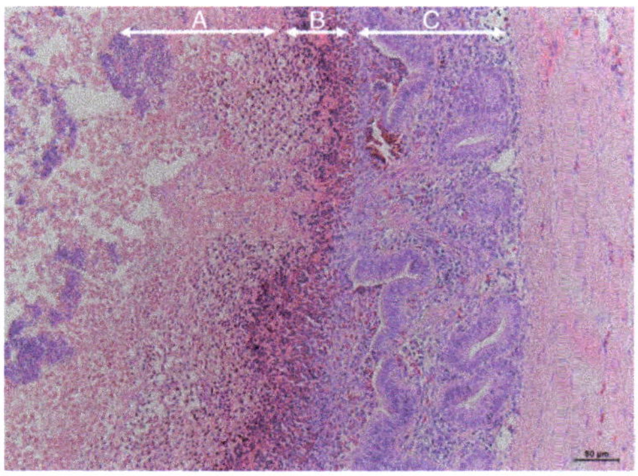

Fig. 14v.4. Histological section of small intestine showing lesions. A clear demarcation line of heterophilic immune cells (B) can be distinguished, dividing the healthy (C) from the necrotic tissue (A). (Author's own image.)

the field in case of a disease outbreak. As preventive measures are clearly much more important, we will not focus on treatment in this chapter.

Antimicrobial growth promoters have been used prophylactically throughout the poultry industry for decades. Due to the increasing concern of antibiotic resistance, their use is prohibited in the European Union and in other parts of the world. Withdrawal of their use has resulted in increasing incidence of NE. Alternative measures are thus in high demand in order to cope with *C. perfringens* infections.

First, optimizing management practices, and specifically on-farm biosecurity and sanitation, can reduce the exposure to possible risk factors (*Eimeria*, viruses, and the causative bacteria themselves). Increasing the hygienic measures can limit the spread of virulent pathogens and subsequently reduce the exposure of the animals (McDevitt *et al.*, 2006). Recycling of litter should be avoided.

Secondly, limiting the effects of predisposing factors can also be a good strategy to reduce NE incidence. The predisposing effect of stress due to management-related factors can be reduced easily by upholding good husbandry practices. Implementing a coccidiosis control program can reduce the initial mucosal gut damage, a key step in NE pathogenesis. *C. perfringens* strains have been shown to be sensitive to ionophore anticoccidial drugs. As a result, restriction of their use also has increased the susceptibility of broiler flocks to NE (McDevitt *et al.*, 2006). The association between both diseases needs to be taken into account when implementing vaccination programmes bearing in mind possible mucosal damage by attenuated vaccine strains. In addition, the predisposing effect of nutritional factors can be reduced by optimizing diet formulations, excluding risky ingredients and controlling mycotoxin levels. Addition of enzymes to the feed has proven to reduce indigestible proteins and carbohydrates in the distal part of the gastrointestinal tracts, eventually reducing the risk of NE outbreaks. Examples of such feed enzymes are xylanases, β-mannanases and proteases.

Another approach to prevent *C. perfringens* proliferation is altering the composition of the intestinal microbiota. Some probiotics, microbial feed supplements improving this microbial balance, are commercially available and have documented activity in disease models. Prebiotics are described as indigestible feed ingredients that selectively stimulate growth and activity of beneficial bacteria that reside in the gut. To date, no prebiotics against NE are commercially available although dietary supplementation of mannooligosaccharides (MOS) has proven partially effective. Next, the oral administration of competitive exclusion products, a suspension of gut microbiota from healthy animals, has been investigated extensively with promising results.

Lastly, development of a vaccination-based strategy against NE is under investigation (Mot *et al.*, 2014). Subcutaneous vaccination (on days 1, 3 and 15) using recombinant alpha or NetB toxoid has proven to be partially protective against experimentally induced NE. In spite of the promising results, implementation of vaccination strategies into the poultry industry is challenging taking into account the dose regimen and the high labour cost. Single day-of-hatch vaccination appears insufficient to protect from NE. Extensive research is required to investigate further the prospects of oral vaccination strategies that are applicable in the field, i.e. the nature of vectors to be used and the optimal combination of antigens.

14v.7 References

Antonissen, G., Van Immerseel, F., Pasmans, F., Ducatelle, R., Haesebrouck, F., *et al.* (2014) The mycotoxin deoxynivalenol predisposes for the development of *Clostridium perfringens*-induced necrotic enteritis in broiler chickens. *PLoS ONE* 9, 1–8.

Collier, C.T., Hofacre, C.L., Payne, A.M., Anderson, D.B. and Kaiser, P. (2008) Coccidia-induced mucogenesis promotes the onset of necrotic enteritis by supporting *Clostridium perfringens* growth. *Veterinary Immunology and Immunopathology* 122, 104–115.

Goossens, E., Dierick, E., Ducatelle, R. and Van Immerseel, F. (2020) Spotlight on avian pathology: untangling contradictory disease descriptions of necrotic enteritis and necro-haemorrhagic enteritis in broilers. *Avian Pathology* 49(5), 423–427.

Keyburn, A.L., Bannam, T.L., Moore, R.J. and Rood, J.I. (2010) NetB, a pore-forming toxin from necrotic enteritis strains of *Clostridium perfringens*. *Toxins* 2, 1913–1927.

Keyburn, A.L., Sheedy, S.A., Ford, M.E., Williamson, M.M., Awad, M.M., *et al.* (2006) Alpha-toxin of *Clostridium perfringens* is not an essential virulence factor in necrotic enteritis in chickens. *Infection and Immunity* 74, 6496–6500.

Lepp, D., Roxas, B., Parreira, V.R., Marri, P.R., Rosey, E.L., *et al.* (2010) Identification of novel pathogenicity loci in *Clostridium perfringens* strains that cause avian necrotic enteritis. *PLoS ONE* 5. DOI: 10.1371/journal.pone.0010795.

M'Sadeq, S.A., Wu, S., Swick, R.A. and Choct, M. (2015) Towards the control of necrotic enteritis in broiler chickens with in-feed antibiotics phasing-out worldwide. *Animal Nutrition* 1, 1–11.

Martin, T.G. and Smyth, J.A. (2010) The ability of disease and non-disease producing strains of *Clostridium perfringens* from chickens to adhere to extracellular matrix molecules and Caco-2 cells. *Anaerobe* 16, 533–539.

McDevitt, R.M., Brooker, J.D., Acamovic, T. and Sparks, N.H.C. (2006) Necrotic enteritis; a continuing challenge for the poultry industry. *World's Poultry Science Journal* 62, 221. DOI: 10.1079/WPS200593.

Mot, D., Timbermont, L., Haesebrouck, F., Ducatelle, R. and Van Immerseel, F. (2014) Progress and problems in vaccination against necrotic enteritis in broiler chickens. *Avian Pathology* 43, 290–300.

Nauerby, B., Pedersen, K. and Madsen, M. (2003) Analysis by pulsed-field gel electrophoresis of the genetic diversity among *Clostridium perfringens* isolates from chickens. *Veterinary Microbiology* 94, 257–266.

Prescott, J.F., Parreira, V.R., Gohari, I.M., Lepp, D., Prescott, J.F., *et al.* (2016) The pathogenesis of necrotic enteritis in chickens: what we know and what we need to know : a review. *Avian Pathology* 45, 288–294.

Rood, J.I., Adams, V., Lacey, J., Lyras, D., McClane, B A., *et al.* (2018) Expansion of the *Clostridium perfringens* toxin-based typing scheme. *Anaerobe* 53, 5–10.

Skinner, J.T., Bauer, S., Young, V., Pauling, G., Wilson, J., *et al.* (2010) An economic analysis of the impact of subclinical (mild) necrotic enteritis in broiler chickens. *American Association of Avian Pathologists* 54, 1237–1240.

Tsiouris, V. (2016) Poultry management : a useful tool for the control of necrotic enteritis in poultry. *Avian Pathology* 45, 323–5.

Wade, B. and Keyburn, A.L. (2015) The true cost of necrotic enteritis. *Poultry World, Oct* 9, 16–17.

14vi *Pasteurella* and Related Organisms

Jens Peter Christensen*

University of Copenhagen, Department of Veterinary and Animal Sciences, Faculty of Health and Medical Sciences, Frederiksberg, Denmark

14vi.1 Introduction

The group of organisms covered in this chapter includes bacteria from the families *Pasteurellaceae* and *Flavobacteriaceae*. The family *Pasteurellaceae* contains more than 19 genera where disease caused by members of *Pasteurella*, *Avibacterium* and *Gallibacterium* will be described here. In addition, close to 100 named species belong to the family and numerous taxa that are not yet named (Christensen *et al.*, 2014).

The family *Flavobacteriaceae* contains more than 90 genera and includes the relevant genera *Ornithobacterium* and *Rimerella* with only one and two species, respectively (McBride, 2014).

This chapter focuses on the following organisms: *Pasteurella multocida* (the cause of fowl cholera), *Avibacterium paragallinarum* (the cause of infectious coryza), *Ornithobacterium rhinotracheale*, *Rimerella anatipestifer* and *Gallibacterium anatis*.

This group of organisms represents a challenge in relation to phenotypic identification as their fermentation patterns are quite similar or utilization of sugars is limited. Further to this, the clinical signs and the pathology caused by some of these organisms are related to the airways and are difficult to differentiate. Consequently, diagnosing these infections requires some experience and caution. However, in the last 10 years molecular methods have improved diagnostics significantly.

14vi.2 *Pasteurella multocida* – Fowl Cholera

Fowl cholera is a contagious, globally occurring bacterial disease that affects domestic and wild birds. It usually occurs as a septicaemia of sudden onset with high morbidity and mortality, but chronic and asymptomatic infections also occur.

14vi.2.1 Aetiology and transmission

P. multocida, the causal agent, is a small, Gram-negative, non-motile rod with a capsule that may exhibit pleomorphism after repeated subculture. A single species status for *P. multocida* has been maintained although extended to include the three subspecies *multocida*, *septica* and *gallicida* (Table 14vi.1).

Subspecies *multocida* is the most common cause of disease but subspecies *septica* and *gallicida* may also cause cholera-like disease. In freshly isolated cultures or in tissues, the bacteria have a bipolar appearance when stained with Wright's stain. Although *P. multocida* may infect a wide variety of animals, strains isolated from non-avian hosts generally do not produce fowl cholera. Strains that cause fowl cholera represent a number of immunotypes (or serotypes), which complicates widespread prevention by using bacterins. Five capsular (A, B, D, E and F) and 16 somatic (1–16) serovars of *P. multocida* are currently recognized. A highly specific multiplex capsular PCR assay and a multiplex PCR assay that can differentiate between different somatic serotypes have been developed enabling less laborious and more specific typing than conventional tests. The organism is susceptible to ordinary disinfectants, sunlight, drying and heat. Turkeys and waterfowl are more susceptible than chickens, older chickens are more susceptible than young ones, and some breeds of chickens are more susceptible than others (Glisson *et al.*, 2013).

*jpch@sund.ku.dk

© CAB International 2021. *Poultry Health: A Guide for Professionals* (P. Barrow *et al.*)
DOI: 10.1079/9781789245042.0014

Table 14vi.1. Characteristics used for identification of subspecies of *Pasteurella multocida.*

	P. multocida		
Characteristics	ssp. *multocida*	ssp. *septica*	ssp. *galliida*
L(+)arabinose	d	–	+
D(–)arabinose	d	d	–
Dulcitol	–	–	+
D(–)sorbitol	+	–	+
L(–)fucose	d	d	–
Trehalose	d	+	–
α-glucosidase (PNPG)	+	+	–

+: 90% or more of the strains positive within 1–2 days
–: 90% or more of the strains negative
d: different from the above

Chronically infected birds and asymptomatic carriers are considered to be a major source of infection. It has been documented that wild birds may introduce the organism into a poultry flock, but different mammals (including rodents, pigs, dogs and cats) may also carry the infection. However, the role of these as a reservoir has not been thoroughly investigated. Dissemination of *P. multocida* within a flock and between houses is primarily by excretions from mouth, nose and conjunctiva of diseased birds that contaminate their environment. In addition, *P. multocida* is resistant enough to be spread by contaminated crates, feed bags, shoes and other equipment. The infection does not seem to be egg-transmitted (Christensen and Bisgaard, 2015).

14vi.2.2 Clinical findings

These vary greatly depending on the course of disease. In acute fowl cholera, the observation of a large number of dead birds without previous clinical signs is usually the first indication of disease. Mortality often increases rapidly. In more protracted cases, depression, anorexia, mucoid discharge from the mouth, ruffled feathers, diarrhoea and increased respiratory rate are usually seen. Pneumonia is particularly common in turkeys.

In chronic fowl cholera, clinical signs and lesions are generally related to localized infections of the sternal bursa, wattles, joints, tendon sheaths and footpads, which are often swollen because of accumulated fibrinosuppurative exudate. There may be exudative conjunctivitis and pharyngitis. Torticollis may result when the meninges, middle ear or cranial bones are infected (Christensen *et al.*, 2008).

14vi.2.3 Lesions

Lesions observed in peracute and acute forms of the disease are dominated by vascular disturbances including general passive hyperaemia and congestion throughout the carcass accompanied by enlargement of the liver and spleen (Figs 14vi.1 and 14vi.2).

Petechial and ecchymotic haemorrhages are common, particularly in subepicardial and subserosal locations. Increased amounts of peritoneal and pericardial fluids are frequently seen. In addition, acute oophoritis with hyperaemic follicles may be observed. In subacute cases, multiple, small, necrotic foci may be disseminated throughout the liver and spleen.

In chronic forms of fowl cholera, suppurative lesions may be widely distributed, often involving the respiratory tract, the conjunctiva and adjacent tissues of the head. Caseous arthritis and productive inflammation of the peritoneal cavity and the oviduct are common in chronic infections. A fibrinonecrotic dermatitis including caudal parts of dorsum, the abdomen and breast, involving cutis, subcutis and the underlying muscle, has been observed in turkeys and broilers. Sequestered necrotic lung lesions in poultry should always arouse suspicion of cholera (Petersen *et al.*, 2001; Bojesen *et al.* 2004) (Fig. 14vi.3).

14vi.2.4 Diagnosis

Although the history, signs and lesions may be helpful in diagnosis, *P. multocida* should be isolated, characterized and identified for confirmation. Primary isolation can be accomplished using media such as

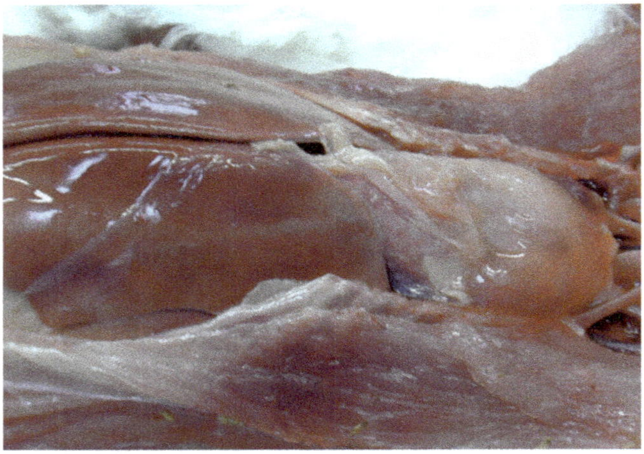

Fig. 14vi.1. Sub-acute *P. multocida* infection with fibrin on the liver and pericardium. (With permission from M. Bisgaard.)

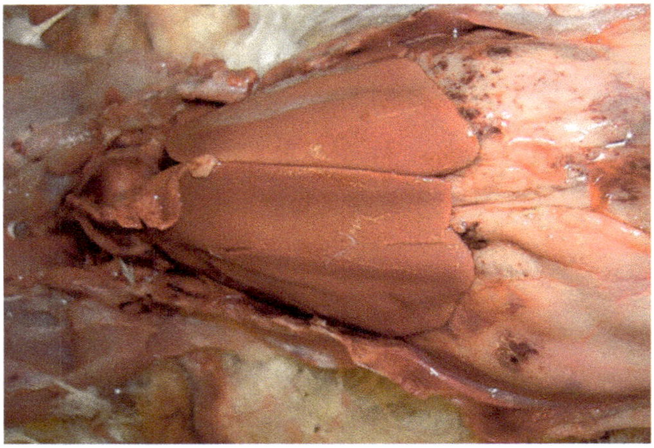

Fig. 14vi.2. Acute fowl cholera with petechial bleeding in the abdominal fat and beginning necrosis of the liver. (With permission from M. Bisgaard.)

blood agar, dextrose starch agar or trypticase soy agar. Isolation may be improved by the addition of 5% heat inactivated serum. *P. multocida* can be readily isolated from viscera of birds dying from peracute/acute fowl cholera, whereas isolation from suppurative lesions of chronic cholera may be more difficult. At necropsy, bipolar microorganisms may be demonstrated by the use of Wright's or Giemsa stains of impression smears obtained from the liver in the case of acute cholera. In addition, immunofluorescent microscopy and *in situ* hybridization have been used to identify *P. multocida* in infected tissues and exudates (Glisson *et al.*, 2013).

Following isolation, classical identification is based on the results of biochemical tests. The most important characteristics for the differentiation of *P. multocida* from other related organisms are shown in Table 14vi.2.

However, simple diagnostic keys do not allow a firm diagnosis within the family *Pasterurellaceae*. For this reason, extended characterization, including the use of reference strains, is recommended. A PCR has been developed and used for the detection of *P. multocida* in pure and mixed cultures and clinical samples (Miflin and Blackall, 2001). Such methods may be helpful for establishing knowledge

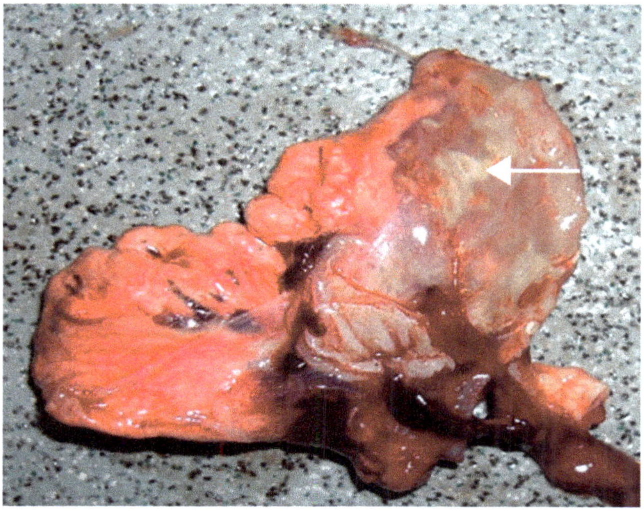

Fig. 14vi.3. Lung lesions caused by *P. multocida* (arrow). (Photograph taken by Christensen and Bisgaard.)

Table 14vi.2. Important characteristics used to separate *Pasteurella multocida* from other relevant taxa.

	P. m.	*Av. g.*	*Av. a.*	*Av. v.*	*Av. p.*	*[P.] l.*	ORT	*R. a.*
Nitrate, red.	+	+	+	+	+	+	–	–
Urease	–	–	–	–	–	–	+	d
Arginine dihydr.	–	–	–	–	–	–	–	(+)
Ornithine decar.	+	–	–	d	–	–	–	–
Indole	+	–	–	–	–	–	–	–
D(+)xylose	+	d	d	d	d	–	–	–
D(–)mannitol	+	–	–	+	+	+	–	–
D(–)sorbitol	d*	–	–	d	+	–	–	–
D(+)galactose	+	+	+	+	–	+	(+)	–
Maltose	–	+	–	+	d	–	(+)	–
Trehalose	d*	+	+	+	–	–	–	–
Dextrin	–	+	–	+	–	–	(+)	–
α-galactosidase	–	–	–	–	–	–	+	+
α-glucosidase (PNPG)	d*	+	–	+	d	–	+	+

P.m.: *P. multocida*; *Av. g.*: *Av. gallinarum*; *Av. a.*: *Av. avium*; *Av. v.*: *Av. volantium*; *Av. p.*: *Av. paragallinarum*; *[P.] l.*: *[P.] langaa*; ORT: *O. rhinotracheale*; *R. a.*: *R. anatipestifer*
+: 90% or more of the strains positive within 1–2 days
–: 90% or more of the strains negative
(+): 90% or more of the strains positive within 3–14 days
*: characteristic used for separation of subspecies of *P. multocida*
d: different from the above

concerning carrier animals within flocks just as the complexities associated with the diagnosis of fowl cholera by conventional methods of isolations and identification may be overcome.

Serological testing can be done by rapid whole blood agglutination, serum plate agglutination, agar diffusion tests and ELISA. Serology may be used to evaluate vaccine responses but has very limited value for diagnostic purposes.

It should be emphasized that several bacterial infections may be confused with fowl cholera based solely on the gross lesions. *E. coli* (see Chapter 14ii, this volume), *S. enterica* (see Chapter 14iv, this volume), *O. rhinotracheale*, Gram-positive cocci (see Chapter 14ix, this volume) and *Erysipelothrix rhusiopathiae* (erysipelas, see Chapter 14ix, this volume) may all produce lesions indistinguishable from those caused by *P. multocida*.

14vi.2.5 Prevention

Good management practices including a high level of biosecurity are essential to prevention. Rodents, wild birds, pets, etc. may be carriers of *P. multocida*, and must be excluded from poultry houses. Adjuvant bacterins are widely used and generally effective; autogenous bacterins may be effective when polyvalent bacterins are found to be ineffective. Attenuated live vaccines are available for administration in drinking water to turkeys and by wing-web inoculation to chickens, but may revert to their virulent forms as the live vaccines currently in use are all undefined attenuated strains. These live vaccines can induce immunity against different serotypes of *P. multocida*.

14vi.2.6 Treatment

A number of drugs will lower the mortality from fowl cholera, but mortality may resume when treatment is discontinued, showing that treatment will not eliminate *P. multocida* from a flock. Thus, in order to eradicate infection from premises the only rational course of action includes depopulation and cleaning, and disinfection of buildings and equipment. Subsequently, the premises should be kept free of poultry for a few weeks. However, sulfonamides and antibiotics are commonly used; early treatment and adequate dosages are important. Sensitivity testing often aids in drug selection. Sulfaquinoxaline sodium in feed or water usually controls mortality, as do sulfamethazine and sulfadimethoxine. Sulfas should be used with caution in breeders because of potential toxicity. High levels of tetracycline antibiotics in the feed (0.04%), drinking water or administered parenterally may be useful. Quinolones are effective against fowl cholera via drinking water, but the use of quinolones cannot be recommended as resistance to this class of drugs may be induced. Thus, many countries do not allow the use of these drugs in food production animals, including poultry. Penicillin is often effective for sulfa-resistant infections. In ducks it has been reported that good effects may be obtained by the combined use of streptomycin and dihydrostreptomycin administered as injections (Christensen, 2016).

14vi.3 *Avibacterium paragallinarum* – Infectious Coryza

Infectious coryza is a globally occurring, acute respiratory disease of chickens. Chronically ill or healthy carriers are the reservoirs of infection.

14vi.3.1 Aetiology and transmission

Av. paragallinarum (previously *Haemophilus paragallinarum*), the causal agent, is a Gram-negative, pleomorphic, non-motile, catalase-negative microaerophilic rod that requires nicotinamide adenine dinucleotide (V-factor) for *in vitro* growth. A staphylococcal nurse colony will provide the V-factor when grown on blood agar. However, V-factor-independent strains have been isolated in Mexico and South Africa. Consequently, these strains can be grown directly on blood agar with no need for a nurse colony.

The Page serotyping scheme groups isolates into three serovars (A, B and C) (no cross protection with the use of inactivated vaccines).

Chronically infected birds and asymptomatic carriers are considered to be the source of infection, and replacement stock has been documented to be the primary source of the infection to farms. Multiple-age farms tend to perpetuate the disease. Chickens of all ages are susceptible to infection, but susceptibility increases with age. Egg transmission does not occur, and transmission is by direct contact, airborne droplets and contamination of drinking water (Blackall, 1999).

14vi.3.2 Clinical findings

Following a short incubation period (2–3 days) nasal discharge, sneezing and oedema of the head may develop. In severe cases, the eyes may get closed by the swelling. In males, swelling of the wattles is not uncommon. If uncomplicated, mortality is usually low. A significant egg drop can develop in laying birds where drops of 10–40% may be seen in uncomplicated cases and egg drop is even higher when concurrent disease is present (Blackall, 1999).

14vi.3.3 Lesions

In acute uncomplicated cases, the lesions are primarily observed in relation to the infra-orbital sinuses where copious, semifluid exudate can be seen. Exudate also runs from the nostrils. Later in the course, and following secondary bacterial infection, the exudate may become consolidated and yellowish. Fibrino-necrotic membranes may also develop (Fig. 14vi.4).

Other lesions reported from adjacent tissues include conjunctivitis, tracheitis and bronchitis. Pneumonia and airsacculitis are rarely observed.

14vi.3.4 Diagnosis

Av. paragallinarum should be isolated, characterized and identified for confirmation. The organism can be grown on sheep blood agar plates at 37°C with a 5–10% carbon dioxide atmosphere (and nurse colony). Table 14vi.2 shows biochemical tests which are useful for the identification of *Av. paragallinarum* and for differentiation from related organisms. However, the definitive diagnosis is best obtained by PCR (directly on samples or cultures) (Chen *et al.*, 1998; Sakamoto *et al.*, 2012). DNA sequencing is another option.

Serology (haemagglutination inhibition test) can be used to evaluate vaccine responses but has limited value for diagnostic purposes.

Several other infections may be confused with coryza based on clinical signs and pathology. Fowl cholera, mycoplasmosis (see Chapter 14viii, this volume), ornithobacteriosis, laryngotracheitis (see Chapter 15iv, this volume), Newcastle disease (see Chapter 15viii, this volume), avian influenza (see Chapter 15vii, this volume) and pneumovirus (see Chapter 15ix, this volume) may all produce disease indistinguishable from coryza.

14vi.3.5 Prevention

All-in-all-out farm programmes should be used in addition to sound management and good biosecurity. Replacement stock should originate from the same farm, or from farms that are free from coryza. Vaccination can be carried out with killed vaccines. However, it is important to determine which serovars are present in the region in order to choose the right vaccine, as no cross-protection will be obtained by the use of a single serovar vaccine.

14vi.3.6 Treatment (see also Chapter 19, this volume)

Erythromycin and oxytetracycline (in the water) will have a beneficial effect on the disease; however, medication will not eliminate the infection from the flock and disease may resume when treatment is discontinued. Quinolones are effective against coryza via drinking water, but the use of quinolones cannot be recommended as resistance to this class of drugs may be induced. Thus, many countries do not allow the use of these drugs to food production animals, including poultry.

14vi.4 *Ornithobacterium rhinotracheale* (ORT)

Ornithobacteriosis is a globally occurring, acute respiratory disease primarily of chickens and turkeys. Although disease is primarily related to the

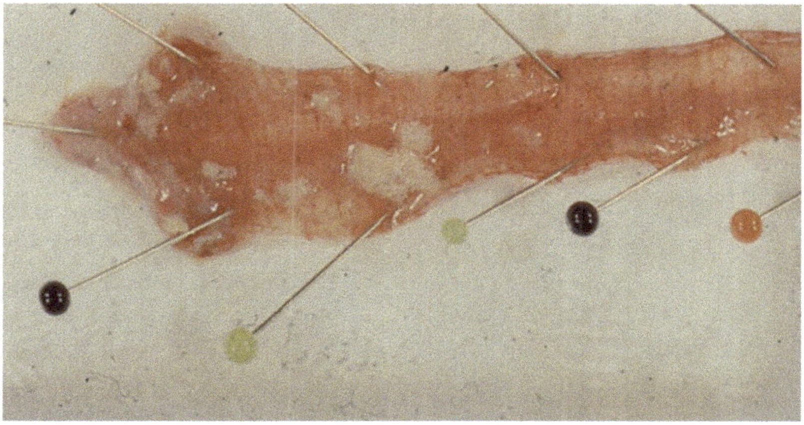

Fig. 14vi.4. Trachea with hyperaemia and fibrino-necrotic membranes following *Av. paragallinarum* infection. (With permission from M. Bisgaard.)

airways, peritonitis, pericarditis and enteritis may be observed.

14vi.4.1 Aetiology and transmission

O. rhinotracheale is slow growing, pleomorphic, Gram-negative, non-motile and non-sporulating. The organism can be grown on sheep blood agar and chocolate agar plates at 37°C where small non-haemolytic colonies will be formed under aerobic, microaerophilic and anaerobic conditions. Table 14vi.2 shows biochemical tests which are useful for the identification of *Av. paragallinarum* and for differentiation from related organisms.

Eighteen serotypes (A–R) are currently recognized, but host specificity of any of the serovars has not been identified. ORT has been isolated from several avian species including chicken, turkey, duck, goose, guinea fowl, pheasant, pigeon, quail, chukar, gull, ostrich, partridge and rook. Serotype A is mainly associated with chickens, whereas serotypes A, B, D and E have often been isolated from turkeys (Gornatti Churria *et al.*, 2012).

The primary mechanism for spread appears to be by horizontal transmission by direct or indirect contact through aerosols or drinking water. Vertical transmission has been suggested but the significance is still unclear.

14vi.4.2 Clinical findings

The clinical signs are extremely variable. Many influencing factors are recognized (ventilation, density, litter conditions, ammonia, concurrent disease, etc.).

In broilers, disease most commonly occurs at 3–4 weeks of age (mortality 2–10%). Depression, decreased feed intake, reduced weight gains, nasal discharge, sneezing and facial oedema are common observations.

In layers and broiler breeders, the disease is often observed between 24 and 52 weeks of age, with mild respiratory disease including egg drop and reduced eggshell quality (Chin and Charlton, 2008).

In turkeys, mostly males over 14 weeks of age are affected with respiratory signs, reduced feed and water intake and with a mortality between 1 and 15%. In breeders, a drop in egg production and increases in the number of unsettable hatching eggs may be observed. Coughing, sneezing and nasal discharge, often progressing to severe respiratory distress, are common in turkeys (Chin *et al.*, 2008).

14vi.4.3 Lesions

The main findings will be in the lungs where oedema, pneumonia with fibrino-purulent exudation, pleuritis and subsequent airsacculitis may be observed. Peritonitis (mainly in broilers) and pericarditis are not uncommon. In turkeys, arthritis may be seen.

14vi.4.4 Diagnosis

ORT should be isolated (from trachea, lungs and air sacs), characterized and identified. The lungs are often the best site for isolation. Serology using commercial ELISA kits (which can detect antibodies against all tested ORT serotypes) can be used as confirmation. PCR (to amplify a 784 bp fragment of 16S rRNA) on samples or pure cultures is also a valuable diagnostic tool.

14vi.4.5 Prevention

Autogenous bacterins and Nobilis ORT Inac (serovar A) can be used as prophylactic measures together with high biosecurity. Inactivated vaccines may be applied to day-old broilers and twice to broilers breeders (at 12 and 18 weeks of age). Inactivated vaccines also may be beneficial for turkeys. It should be remembered that no cross-protection will be obtained with killed vaccines, thus serotyping should be performed before implementation of a specific vaccine (Gornatti Churria *et al.*, 2012).

14vi.4.6 Treatment

Water medication at 3–7 days of age with amoxicillin or better with chlortetracycline has been shown to be quite effective. However, susceptibility testing is needed before medication as ORT isolates are known to vary significantly concerning antimicrobial resistance.

14vi.5 *Rimerella anatipestifer* Infection (New Duck Disease)

R. anatipestifer is globally occurring and primarily affects young ducks (and occasionally turkeys and geese) in the form of septicaemia. It is perhaps the most important disease of ducks. Rarely, other waterfowl, chickens and pheasants are affected. The disease has previously been named; 'anatipestifer syndrome', 'infectious serositis' and 'duck septicaemia'.

14vi.5.1 Aetiology and transmission

R. anatipstifer is a Gram-negative, non-sporulating and non-motile rod. It requires microaerophilic conditions in enriched media to grow. Twenty-one serotypes have been recognized (Bisgaard, 1982).

The mode of transmission is unclear, but infection in ducks is believed to occur via the environment either by the respiratory route or skin lesions mainly of the webbed foot. This is also the case for turkeys. The infection has a tendency to become endemic once introduced onto a farm. Healthy carriers can occur (Sandhu, 2008).

14vi.5.2 Clinical findings

Ducks, usually of the age 1–7 weeks, are affected showing signs of ocular and nasal discharges, coughing and sneezing. In addition, characteristic central nervous system (CNS) signs may develop including tremors of the head and neck, incoordination and, often, the ducklings lie on their backs paddling their legs. Diarrhoea may also be observed. Mortality may range from 2–50%.

Turkeys are often infected at 5–15 weeks old. They often show signs of dyspnoea droopiness, lameness and twisted neck. Mortality is from 5 to 50% (Bisgaard *et al.*, 2008).

14vi.5.3 Lesions

Polyserositis is the main finding which covers fibrinous pericarditis, perihepatitis and airsacculitis (Fig. 14vi.5).

Occasionally, pneumonia and synovitis can be seen. Fibrinous meningitis is often observed. Necrotic dermatitis on the lower back and around the vent may also be observed. Affected birds commonly develop salpingitis.

14vi.5.4 Diagnosis

Clinical signs and pathology may be helpful for diagnosis in case CNS signs are present. However, isolation and identification of the organism (from brain, bone marrow and respiratory tract) should be performed. The organism can be grown on blood agar and chocolate agar in a candle jar or under 5% carbon dioxide conditions. However, as the organism does not ferment sugars and biotyping may be hard to interpret, molecular methods should be implemented for a definitive diagnosis. PCR amplification of a partial region of the *rpo*B gene or the 16S rRNA gene, with subsequent sequencing, is recommended to confirm identification.

14vi.5.5 Prevention

A high level of biosecurity is essential for control. Cleaning and disinfection between flocks is also pivotal. A killed vaccine is available. However, no cross-protection is obtained for other serotypes, and several serotypes may be involved in disease outbreaks on endemically infected farms. Consequently, serotyping of clinical isolates should be performed before choosing the vaccine. A live vaccine, including

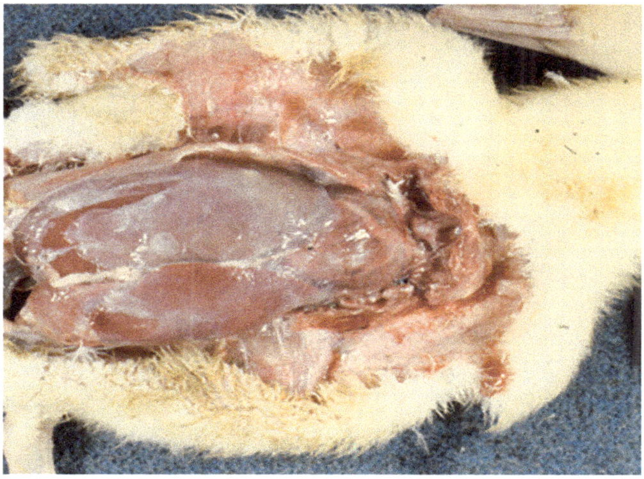

Fig. 14vi.5. Polyserositis in a duckling caused by *R. anatipestifer.* (With permission from M. Bisgaard.)

the three most common serotypes, is available for ducks. Breeder ducks may confer protection to the ducklings following vaccination (up to 2–3 weeks of age) (Bisgaard *et al.*, 2008).

14vi.5.6 Treatment

Penicillin and streptomycin in combination can be used in drinking water or by the intramuscular route. The antimicrobial sensitivity pattern should be obtained before treatment. Quinolones are effective against mortality caused by *Rimerella*, but the use of quinolones cannot be recommended as resistance to this class of drugs may be induced. Thus, many countries do not allow the use of these drugs for food production animals, including poultry.

14vi.6 *Gallibacterium anatis*

G. anatis infection is an emerging disease of poultry. The organism was previously classified as *Actinobacillus salpingitidis*, avian *Pasteurella haemolytica*-like organisms or *Pasteurella anatis*. The infection has been reported from most parts of the world and disease is primarily observed in the reproductive tract.

14vi.6.1 Aetiology and transmission

G. anatis is a Gram-negative, rod shaped, non-motile and facultative anaerobic bacterium. *G. anatis* has two biovars, i.e. a haemolytic biovar, *haemolytica*, and a non-haemolytic biovar, *anatis*. Strains of biovar *haemolytica* form β-haemolytic zones (1–2 mm) around the colonies on agar plates with blood from calf, horse, swine, sheep, rabbit and chicken. More than 20 different biovars have been reported for *G. anatis*. It appears that haemolytic strains are the major disease-causing agents; however, non-haemolytic strains have also been isolated from lesions (Gerlach, 1977, Singh *et al.*, 2016).

Gallibacterium organisms appear to have a wide host spectrum including chickens, turkeys, geese, ducks, pheasants, partridges and various cage bird species and wild birds.

Haemolytic strains of *G. anatis* are common inhabitants of the upper respiratory and lower reproductive tracts of healthy chickens. Only very high levels of biosecurity seem to be able to keep farms free of *G. anatis*.

Horizontal transmission between birds appears to be the main mode of infection. Vertical transmission is a possibility but has not been demonstrated to play a major role in transmission (Persson and Bojesen, 2015).

14vi.6.2 Clinical findings

G. anatis strains are common inhabitants of the upper respiratory and lower reproductive tracts of healthy chickens but the organism has been isolated from a wide range of different pathological lesions, including septicaemia, pericarditis, hepatitis, oophoritis, upper respiratory tract lesions, salpingitis and peritonitis (Figs 14vi.6 and 14vi.7).

Although it is haemolytic, *G. anatis* may act as a primary pathogen mainly of the reproductive tract, and other factors possibly contribute to the outcome of infection (e.g. stress, concurrent infections,

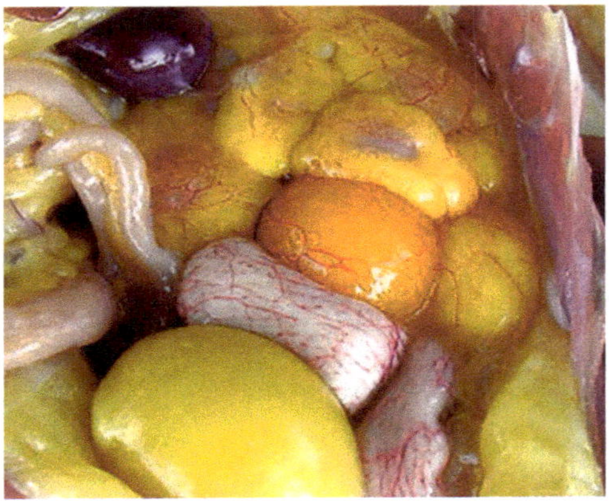

Fig. 14vi.6. Early degeneration of follicles due to *G. anatis* infection (arrow). (With permission from A.M. Bojensen.)

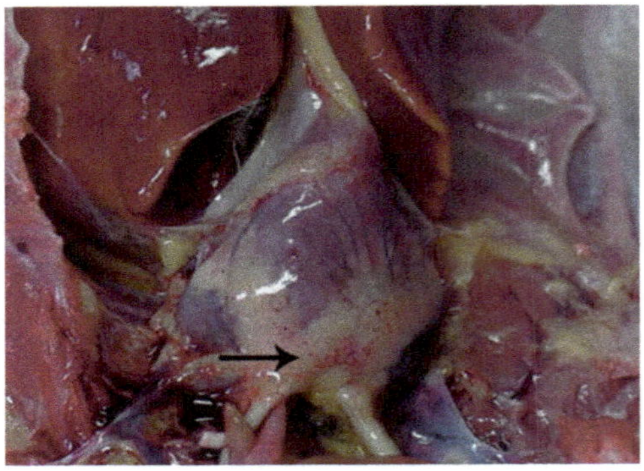

Fig. 14vi.7. Acute septicaemic lesions with petechial bleedings in the coronary fat (arrow) due to *G. anatis* infection. (With permission from A.M. Bojensen.)

hormonal influences, age and a compromised immune system) (Paudel *et al.*, 2013, 2014).

The clinical signs are unspecific and will often include depression, diarrhoea and reduced egg production.

14vi.6.3 Lesions

The lesions typically involve the oviduct, including the ovary where purulent salpingitis and oophoritis may be observed. Chronic cases often involve the peritoneum in the form of purulent peritonitis. Acute septicaemia has been reported where *G. anatis* has been isolated in pure culture from various organs.

14vi.6.4 Diagnosis

The diagnosis should be confirmed by isolation and identification of the causal agent. *G. anatis* grows readily on enriched media. Biochemistry is useful for identification but should be combined with genotypic characterization. A PCR test based on 16S rRNA and 23S rRNA genes has been shown to be of value for cultures and for sample material (Bojsen *et al.*, 2007).

14vi.6.5 Prevention

All-in-all-out production, and general high levels of biosecurity to keep other pathogens out of the farm is recommended. A commercial vaccine is based on three prevalent biovars (1, 2 and 4) (Bojesen *et al.*, 2008).

14vi.6.6 Treatment

Multidrug resistance has been demonstrated in *G. anatis* and it is known that the organism readily acquires resistance. Consequently, the antimicrobial sensitivity patterns should always be established prior to treatment. Tetracycline may be a choice for treatment if susceptibility has been shown.

14vi.7 References

Bisgaard, M. (1982) Antigenic studies on *Pasteurella anatipestifer*, species incertae sedis, using slide and tube agglutination. *Avian Pathology* 11, 341–350.

Bisgaard, M., Bojesen, A.M. and Christensen, J.P. (2008) Riemerella infections. In: Pattison, M., McMullin, P.F., Bradbury, J.M. and Alexander, D.J. (eds) *Poultry Diseases*, 6th edn. Saunders-Elsevier, Oxford, UK, pp 172–175.

Blackall, P.J. (1999) Infectious coryza: overview of the disease and new diagnostic options. *Clinical Microbiology Reviews* 12, 627–632.

Bojesen, A.M., Petersen, K.D., Nielsen, O.L., Christensen, J.P. and Bisgaard, M. (2004) *Pasteurella multocida* infection in heterophil-depleted chickens. *Avian Diseases* 48, 463–470.

Bojesen, A.M., Vazquez, M.E., Robles, F., Gonzalez, C., Soriano, E.V., *et al.* (2007) Specific identification of *Gallibacterium* by a PCR using primers targeting the 16S rRNA and 23S rRNA genes. *Veterinary Microbiology* 123, 262–268.

Bojesen, A.M., Christensen, J.P. and Bisgaard, M. (2008) *Gallibacterium* infections and other avian *Pasteurellaceae*. In: Pattison, M., McMullin, P.F., Bradbury, J.M. and Alexander, D.J. (eds) *Poultry Diseases*, 6th edn. Saunders-Elsevier, Oxford, UK.

Chen, X., Chen, Q., Zhang, P., Feng, W. and Blackall, P.J. (1998) Evaluation of a PCR test for the detection of *Haemophilus paragallinarum* in China. *Avian Pathology* 27, 296–300.

Chin R.P., and Charlton B.R. (2008) Ornithobacteriosis. In: Dufour-Zavala, L., Swayne, D.E., Glisson J.R., Pearson, J.E., Reed, W.M., *et al.* (eds) *A Laboratory Manual for the Isolation, Identification, and Characterization of Avian Pathogens,* 5th edn. American Association of Avian Pathologists, Madison, Wisconsin, pp.75–76.

Chin R.P., van Empel P.C.M., and Hafez, H.M. (2008) *Ornithobacterium rhinotracheale* infection. In: Saif, Y.M, Fadly, A.M., Glisson, J.R., McDougald, L.R., Nolan, L.K., and Swayne, D.E. (eds) *Diseases of Poultry*, 12th edn. Blackwell Publishing Ltd., Oxford, UK, pp.765–774.

Christensen, J.P. (2016) Fowl cholera. In: Aiello, S.E. (ed.) *The Merck Veterinary Manual*, 11th edn. Merck & Co., Inc., pp. 2822–2824.

Christensen, J.P. and Bisgaard, M. (2015) Fowl cholera. In: Brugére-Picoux, J. and Vaillancourt, J-P. (eds) *Manual of Poultry Diseases*. AFAS, France, pp. 316–326.

Christensen J.P., Bojesen, A.M. and Bisgaard, M. (2008) Fowl cholera. In: Pattison, M., McMullin, P.F., Bradbury, J.M. and Alexander, D.J. (eds) *Poultry Diseases*, 6th edn. Saunders-Elsevier, Oxford, UK, pp. 149–155.

Christensen, H., Kuhnert, P., Nørskov-Lauritsen, N., Planet, P.J. and Bisgaard, M. (2014) The family *Pasteurellaceae*. In: Rosenberg, E., DeLong, E.F., Lory, S., Stackebrandt, E. and Thompson, F. (eds) *The Prokaryotes*. Springer Berlin, Heidelberg, Germany, pp. 535–564.

Gerlach H. (1977) Die Bedeutung von *Pasteurella haemolytica* in Hühnerbeständen. *Praktische Tierarzt* 5, 324–325.

Glisson, J.R., Hofacre, C.L. and Christensen, J.P. (2013) Fowl cholera. In: Swayne, D.E., Glisson, J.R.,

McDougald, L.R., Nolan, L.K., Suarez, D.L. and Nair, V. (eds) *Diseases of Poultry*, 13th edn. Wiley-Blackwell, Oxford, UK, pp. 807–823.

Gornatti Churria, C.D., Machuca, M.A., Vigo, G.B. and Petruccelli, M.A. (2012) *Ornithobacterium rhinotracheale* infection in poultry: an updated review. *International Journal of Molecular Zoology* 2, 23–38.

McBride, M.J. (2014) The family *Flavobacteriaceae*. In: Rosenberg, E., DeLong, E.F., Lory, S., Stackebrandt, E. and Thompson, F. (eds) *The Prokaryotes*. Springer, Berlin, Heidelberg, Germany, pp. 643–676.

Miflin, J.K. and Blackall, P.J. (2001) Development of a 23S rRNA-based PCR assay for the identification of *Pasteurella multocida*. *Letters in Applied Microbiology* 33, 216–221.

Paudel S., Alispahic M., Liebhart D., Hess M. and Hess, C. (2013) Assessing pathogenicity of *Gallibacterium anatis* in a natural infection model: the respiratory and reproductive tracts of chickens are targets for bacterial colonization. *Avian Pathology* 42, 527–535.

Paudel S., Liebhart D., Hess M. and Hess C. (2014) Pathogenesis of *Gallibacterium anatis* in a natural infection model fulfills Koch's postulates: 1. Folliculitis and drop in egg production are the predominant effects in specific pathogen free layers. *Avian Pathology* 43, 443–449.

Persson G. and Bojesen A.M. (2015) Bacterial determinants of importance in the virulence of *Gallibacterium anatis* in poultry. *Veterinary Research* 46(1), 57.

Petersen, K.D., Christensen, J.P., Permin, A. and Bisgaard, M. (2001) Virulence of *Pasteurella multocida* subsp. *multocida* isolated from outbreaks of fowl cholera in wild birds for domestic poultry and game birds. *Avian Pathology* 30, 27–31.

Sakamoto, R., Kino, Y. and Sakaguchi, M. (2012) Development of a multiplex PCR and PCR-RFLP method for serotyping of *Avibacterium paragallinarum*. *Journal of Veterinary Medical Science* 74, 271–273.

Sandhu, T.S. (2008) *Riemerella anatipestifer* infection. In: Saif, Y.M., Fadly, A.M., Glisson, J.R., McDougald, L.R., Nolan, L.K. and Swayne, D.E. (eds) *Diseases of Poultry*, 12th edn. Blackwell Publishing Ltd., Oxford, UK, pp. 758–764.

Singh, S.V., Singh, B.R., Sinha, D.K., Kumar, V.O.R., Vadhana, P.A., *et al.* (2016) *Gallibacterium anatis*: an emerging pathogen of poultry birds and domiciled birds. *Journal of Veterinary Science Technology* 7(3), 1000324.

14vii *Brachyspira* – Avian Intestinal Spirochaetosis

ROBERTO LA RAGIONE* AND JADE PASSEY

Department of Pathology and Infectious Diseases, School of Veterinary Medicine, University of Surrey, Guildford, UK

14vii.1 *Brachyspira*

Brachyspira is the sole genus assigned to the Brachyspiraceae family in the order Spirochaetales. The order Spirochaetales contains all spirochaetes which share properties such as a helical morphology, periplasmic flagella and natural resistance to rifampicin. The genus *Brachyspira* has undergone several taxonomic reclassifications, with these organisms originally known as *Treponema*, but were later reclassified in 1991 as a new genus known as *Serpula* and again in 1992 as *Serpulina*. Finally, the genera *Serpulina* and *Brachyspira* were unified as a result of the similarities discovered between *S. hyodysenteriae, S. innocens, S. pilosicoli* and *B. aalborgi.* The genus *Brachyspira* was used instead of *Serpulina* since *B. aalborgi* was proposed as a new genus in 1982.

Brachyspira (brachy 'short' and spira 'coil') are Gram-negative, oxygen tolerant, anaerobic spirochetes that have been isolated from the gastrointestinal tracts of both mammals and birds, including humans, chickens, pigs, dogs and horses (Fig. 14vii.1).

These organisms have also been cultured from the faeces and blood of infected hosts, demonstrating that these bacteria have a wide host range and the potential to cause both enteric and systemic infections.

The genus comprises seven confirmed species of *Brachyspira*, and an additional seven proposed species (Mappley *et al.*, 2014). Of the confirmed species, *B. alvinipulli*, *B. intermedia* and *B. pilosicoli* are considered to be the causative agents of avian intestinal spirochaetosis. *B. innocens* is proposed to be non-pathogenic in avian hosts, although it has been previously associated with reduced productivity in laying hens (Burch *et al.*, 2009).

14vii.2 Virulence Characteristics of *Brachyspira*

Brachyspira has a number of virulence factors which allow it to survive and navigate the gastrointestinal tract of the host in order to cause disease. Disease relies upon these bacteria gaining close proximity to the intestinal mucosa where they can adhere to the gut cells (Fig. 14vii.2).

In order to do this, *Brachyspira* must first move through the viscous mucus of the caeca and/or colon, facilitated by periplasmic flagella and chemotaxis towards mucin. Avian species are also weakly haemolytic. Virulence mechanisms of *Brachyspira* are poorly understood. The severity of disease is dependent on several factors, including the strain of *Brachyspira* involved, health of the host, diet and resident intestinal microbiota.

14vii.3 Avian Intestinal Spirochaetosis (AIS)

Avian intestinal spirochaetosis is an enteric disease resulting from the colonization of the caeca and/or colo-rectum of poultry with spirochaetes such as *Brachyspira.* This disease primarily infects layer hens and broiler breeders over the age of 20 weeks and can vary in the severity of symptoms, but typically presents as delayed onset of lay, watery brown to grey diarrhoea, a 6–10% reduction in egg production, faeces stained eggs and a reduced growth rate (Burch *et al.*, 2006). More severe clinical manifestations can

*Corresponding author: r.laragione@surrey.ac.uk

© CAB International 2021. *Poultry Health: A Guide for Professionals* (P. Barrow *et al.*)

DOI: 10.1079/9781789245042.0014

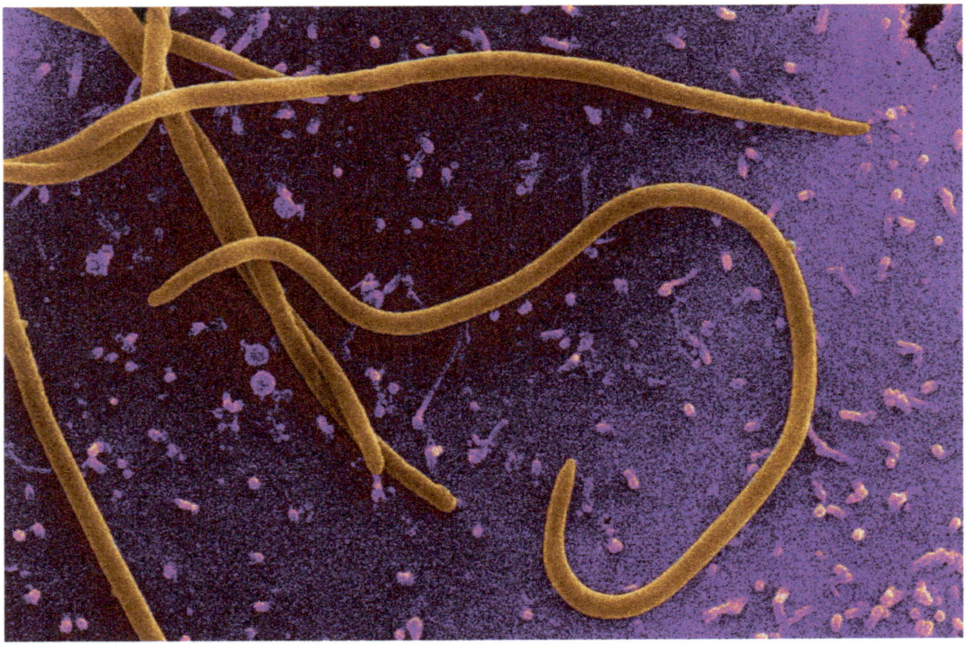

Fig. 14vii.1. Electron micrograph of *Brachyspira* illustrating helical structure (x50,000). (Courtesy of William Cooley, APHA.)

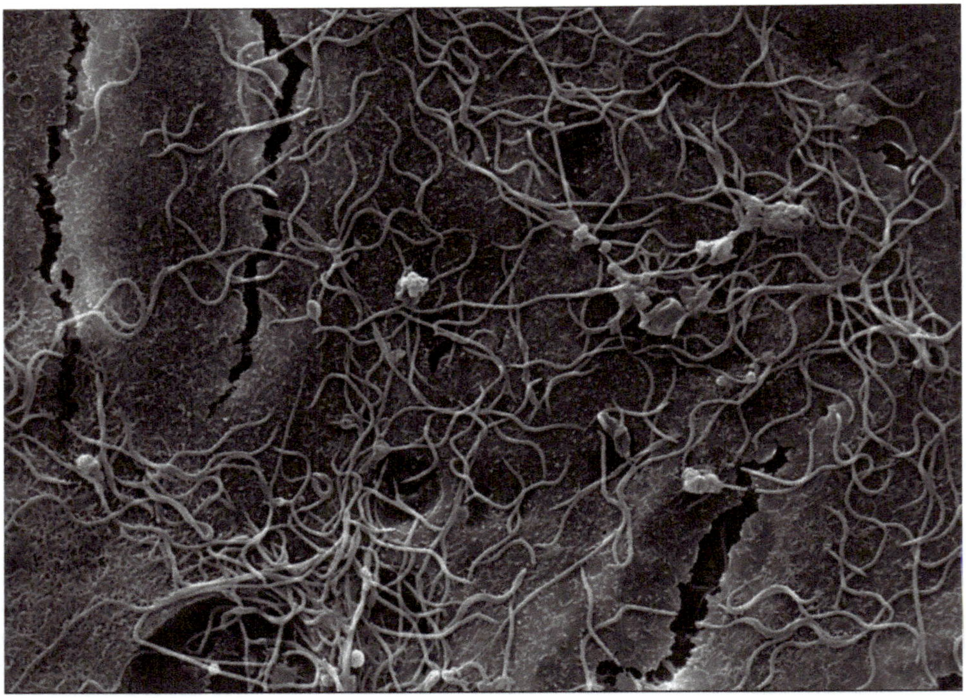

Fig. 14vii.2. Electron micrograph illustrating surface attachment of *Brachyspira* to epithelial cells (x4,000). (Courtesy of William Cooley, APHA.)

include typhlitis and increased mortality rates within flocks. AIS has a significant impact on the UK laying industry, exacerbated by the removal of antibiotic growth promoters from livestock feed in 2006 (Medhanie *et al.*, 2013).

14vii.3.1 Significance of AIS

Since the EU ban of antibiotic growth promoters from livestock feed in 2006, the incidence of AIS has increased significantly and is becoming a growing concern (Medhanie *et al.*, 2013). This disease has a significant economic burden on the UK laying industry, and is estimated to cost £18 million per annum (Mappley *et al.*, 2014). These losses are likely to be similar worldwide, with studies in Australia, Italy and Iran showing similar prevalence to that observed in the UK.

14vii.3.2 Epidemiology of AIS

Host range

Brachyspira colonize the caeca and colo-rectum of many avian species, both domestic and wild. Amongst domestic poultry, known hosts include layer hens, broiler hens, broiler breeder hens and turkeys. Known hosts amongst wild bird species include flamingos, rheas, ducks, swans, grouse, ducks, ostriches and pheasants.

Transmission and infection

Brachyspira are transmitted through flocks via the faecal–oral route. Transmission begins when birds come into contact with vectors, such as wild birds, rodents or environmental reservoirs (Backhans *et al.*, 2010). *Brachyspira* are then shed in the faeces of infected birds and spread rapidly throughout a flock. Furthermore, intensification of farming has led to the close proximity of poultry, facilitating the rapid spread of disease. Wet litter conditions can also promote the proliferation of bacteria and the coprophagic behaviour of chickens in these conditions results in the rapid spread of *Brachyspira* (Mappley *et al.*, 2014).

The infection process begins when the spirochaetes reach the caeca and colo-rectum of the bird. Once these pathogens reach the lower gastrointestinal tract, chemotaxis towards mucin and the strong motility through the mucus enables *Brachyspira* to gain close proximity to the intestinal epithelium. *B. pilosicoli* can form end-on attachments to cells to form a pseudo-brush border. *Brachyspira* can also invade enterocytes and disturb tight junctions, thereby increasing the chances of translocation to the bloodstream and subsequently a systemic infection (Le Roy *et al.*, 2015). Systemic infections have been reported by Mappley *et al.* (2013), with *Brachyspira* isolated from the liver, spleen and reproductive tracts of experimentally infected hens.

Prevalence

Avian intestinal spirochaetosis has been well documented in Europe, North American and Australia, and is thought to be endemic worldwide. The prevalence of *Brachyspira* in UK laying flocks has been estimated to be as high as 100% in barn flocks, 91% in free range flocks, 86% in organic free-range flocks and up to 76% in caged flocks (Burch, *et al.*, 2009). *B. hyodysenteriae* and *B. pilosicoli* have been shown to survive in soil and in contaminated water supplies. The abundance of this bacterium in the environment not only means that infection spreads by direct ingestion, but can also be rapidly spread on farms by vectors such as humans, dogs, rodents and wild birds.

Rodents are major reservoirs of *Brachyspira* on poultry farms, with 83% of rats and 33% of mice carrying the bacterium (Backhans *et al.*, 2010). Wild birds are also known to harbour intestinal spirochaetes asymptomatically. Epidemiological studies have shown that commercial poultry are most frequently infected with *B. intermedia* followed by *B. pilosicoli*, although the prevalence of *B. innocens* is much higher than the pathogenic species (Burch *et al.*, 2009). *B. alvinipulli* has rarely been isolated from commercial poultry in the UK, but has been isolated from poultry in the USA, the Netherlands and Sweden.

Disease incubation period and persistence

The incubation period and persistence of avian intestinal spirochaetosis can be dependent on the dose and species of *Brachyspira* ingested and also the environment of the poultry infected. Clinical symptoms can occur in experimentally infected birds as soon as 5 days post-infection (Mappley *et al.*, 2014), but colonization is most commonly observed after 7 days post infection (Hampson *et al.*, 2002; Mappley *et al.*, 2013). However, significant colonization and disease symptoms can persist several weeks following experimental infection, although this is not true for all experimental infections (Hampson *et al.*, 2002).

Zoonotic potential

Brachyspira species, in particular *B. pilosicoli*, are of potential zoonotic concern. Although human intestinal spirochaetosis in relatively rare, it mostly occurs in immunocompromised patients and those with poor living standards. Biopsies of humans with suspected spirochaetosis show the attachment of spirochaetes to the intestinal epithelium, noted as a false brush border (Hampson, 2018). In rare cases, *B. pilosicoli* has been shown to cause bacteraemia in the elderly and immunocompromised patients (Prim *et al.*, 2011). Furthermore, *B. pilosicoli* can contaminate the meat of infected poultry, which may pose as a zoonotic threat to humans. However, it is important to note, that broiler hens are rarely infected with *Brachyspira* and thus the infection risk most likely comes from the meat of spent laying hens.

14vii.3.3 Clinical disease and sub-clinical colonization

Colonization with intestinal spirochaetes in the absence of clinical disease is most common in wild birds and waterfowl, where they are considered as commensal bacteria. Studies have shown that these birds and their habitats can be reservoirs of infection for both humans and other animals. Subclinical colonization of commercial laying hens and broiler breeders is often associated with infection with *B. innocens* or *B. murdochii*.

Mild to moderate clinical disease is associated with colonization by *B. alvinipulli, B. intermedia* and *B. pilosicoli*, particularly in laying hens and broiler breeders over the age of 20 weeks. Typically, infection is associated with symptoms such as diarrhoea, increased fat content in the faeces, a 6–10% reduction in egg production, reduced growth rates and a delayed onset of lay. Furthermore, eggs may have decreased nutritional value and infected broiler breeders produce weak chicks with retarded growth (Burch *et al.*, 2006).

Severe clinical symptoms are infrequently observed in commercial chicken flocks but may be exacerbated by stress (Stephens and Hampson, 2001). Severe clinical symptoms have been observed in chickens infected with *B. intermedia* and *B. pilosicoli* whereby spirochaetes have penetrated between or below caecal epithelial cells, resulting in erosion or necrosis of the mucosa. Furthermore, the presence of spirochaetes between epithelial cells poses a risk of systemic infection as noted in studies which suggest *B. pilosicoli* can infect multiple organs in laying hens (Mappley *et al.*, 2013). Histological examination of caeca from naturally infected birds has revealed that invasive spirochaetes and typhlitis were associated with *B. intermedia* infections (Stephens and Hampson, 2001).

14vii.3.4 Host immunity

The host immune mechanisms directed against *Brachyspira* are poorly understood. The innate immune response is the first line of defence against *Brachyspira* and infection has been associated with the infiltration of immune cells such as macrophages into the lamina propria (Padmanabhan *et al.*, 1996). Moreover, experimentally infected pigs and mice have been shown to develop varying detectable levels of serum antibodies in response to *Brachyspira* infection (Hampson, 2018).

Brachyspira infection can remain persistent in poultry flocks, which may be attributed to the ability of these bacteria to adhere to the intestinal epithelium which may aid in subverting the immune system or evading an immune response (Hampson, 2018).

14vii.3.5 Diagnosis of AIS

Culture on blood agar (fastidious anaerobic blood agar or *Brachyspira* selective agar) followed by light, phase-contrast or dark-field microscopy to confirm cell morphology and motility, can be used as a preliminary screen for *Brachyspira*. Biochemical testing can be employed to speciate isolates, although the biochemical profiling of avian isolates can be unreliable. Therefore, phenotypic tests that are time consuming and inconsistent, especially with mixed species infections, need to be routinely supported by molecular methods.

PCR primer sequences to identify *Brachyspira* have been designed to target either the 16S ribosomal ribonucleic acid (rRNA) gene or the NADH oxidase (*nox*) gene (Phillips *et al.*, 2006). A major drawback is that there are no current PCR primers to identify *B. alvinipulli* or *B. innocens*. However, with the increased availability of whole genome sequencing, designing PCR assays for less common or non-pathogenic *Brachyspira* strains will become increasingly feasible.

Histological samples can be used to confirm the attachment of *Brachyspira* to the intestinal mucosa using the both haematoxylin and eosin, and Warthin–Starry staining. However, attachment of *Brachyspira* is not observed in all clinical cases, which is why combinations of diagnostic methods must be utilized. Fixed tissue can also be visualized using electron microscopy. Fluorescence *in situ* hybridization (FISH) can also be used as to support diagnosis of intestinal spirochaetosis.

14vii.3.6 Treatment of AIS (see Chapter 19, this volume)

Brachyspira is susceptible to a range of antibiotics, however there are a limited number of antibiotics licensed for use against it. Some of the most common antimicrobials used to treat avian intestinal spirochaetosis include tiamulin, tylosin, chlortetracycline and lincomycin, with tiamulin and tylosin the only licensed antibiotics for use in the UK. Bacteriostatic antibiotics such as tiamulin and tylosin are the most effective against *Brachyspira* and target bacterial protein synthesis, although antimicrobial resistance is emerging. Tiamulin has been used in veterinary medicine for a considerable period of time, primarily in the swine industry. Tiamulin has more recently become available for use in the poultry industry for the treatment of avian intestinal spirochaetosis (Woodward *et al.*, 2015). Another benefit of tiamulin is that it has a zero-day egg withdrawal period, and therefore treatment does not have an adverse effect on the egg industry.

14vii.3.7 Interventions and prevention against AIS

Interventions are required to control the spread of *Brachyspira*, especially as the incidence of this organism can be up to 90% in flocks and the disease is difficult to diagnose. Despite avian intestinal spirochaetosis being easily treated with antibiotics, antimicrobial resistance is emerging and there is an increased consumer demand for antibiotic-free products. Therefore, it is essential to implement measures to prevent disease.

Biosecurity (see Chapter 18, this volume)

Effective biosecurity on farms is essential for controlling the introduction and spread of avian intestinal spirochaetosis. Wild birds and rodent reservoirs require effective controls, usually by physical containment including security fencing, bird-proof netting around openings and rodent traps (Mapgley *et al.*, 2014). Disinfectant foot-dips are utilized to prevent transmission by contaminated boots especially as *Brachyspira* have been shown to have a wide host range. Other disinfectants such as iodine, chlorine, hydrogen peroxide and quaternary ammonium disinfectants have shown efficacy against *Brachyspira* in organic matter (Corona-Barrera *et al.*, 2004).

Vaccines

Autogenous vaccines for *B. pilosicoli* and *B. intermedia* have been tested in pigs and chickens and have demonstrated the ability to elicit antibody responses, although there are no commercially available vaccines. Despite primary and secondary antibody responses, these vaccines have not been able to reduce the intestinal colonization by *Brachyspira*. (Hampson *et al.*, 2000). More recent studies have demonstrated greater success whereby the duration of colonization by *B. pilosciol* was significantly reduced following vaccination with recombinant *B. pilosicoli* membrane protein Bpmp72, which showed potential as a novel vaccine component for *B. pilosicoli* (La *et al.*, 2018).

Essential oils and phytochemicals

More recently the efficacy of essential oils and phytochemicals has been assessed for inhibitory capabilities against *Brachyspira* species. Essential oils such as thymol and cinnamaldehyde are inhibitory against *B. intermedia in vitro* and *in vivo* with the bacterial numbers being significantly reduced compared to experimentally infected controls (Verlinden *et al.*, 2013). Additionally, citrus fruit extracts have demonstrated bactericidal and bacteriostatic activity against *Brachyspira* by damaging the cell membrane and induction of the formation of spherical bodies.

Probiotics to prevent avian intestinal spirochaetosis

Probiotics have been shown to be effective against *Brachyspira* both *in vitro* and *in vivo*. *Lactobacillus rhamnosus* and *L. farciminis* have shown the ability to antagonize the motility of *Brachyspira* through co-aggregation. Scanning electron microscopy (SEM) analysis demonstrated that *Brachyspira* are trapped in a physical network with the *Lactobacillus* (Bernardeau *et al.*, 2009). Furthermore, the production of organic acids such as lactic acid have been shown to elicit stress responses in these pathogens (Bernardeau *et al.*, 2009). Cell-free supernatant has been shown to have a lethal effect on *Brachyspira* cells which was characterized by the perforation of the bacterial cell wall. Other stress responses are indicated by the formation of spherical bodies in response to toxic chemicals and changes in environmental conditions as a result of lactic acid production (Bernardeau *et al.*, 2009). Recent research has demonstrated inhibition of *B. pilosicoli* and *B. innocens* by *L. reuteri* and *L. salivarius* cells and their cell-free supernatant *in vitro* (Mappley *et al.*, 2011). Inhibition of *Brachyspira* was pH dependent and low pH cell free supernatant from *Lactobacillus* species resulted in significant inhibition of *Brachyspira*. Additionally, in agreement with the studies conducted by Bernadeau *et al.* (2009), the motility of *Brachyspira* was shown to be inhibited by both viable and heat-inactivated *Lactobacillus*. *L. reuteri* and *L. salivarius* isolates were also able to significantly reduce the adherence of *Brachyspira* to intestinal epithelium cells *in vitro* and *ex vivo* (Mappley *et al.*, 2011). In addition to these *in vitro* studies, *in vivo* studies aimed to determine if the *L. reuteri* isolate used by Mappley *et al.* (2011) would improve hen health following experimental infection with *B. pilosicoli*. The results showed decreased faecal moisture, decreased faecal staining on eggs, decreased *Brachyspira* colonization and decreased pathology associated with disease, in addition to increased egg weight in birds treated with *L. reuteri* (Mappley *et al.*, 2013).

Note: This chapter is adapted from the following thesis: Passey, J.L. (2018) Lactobacilli probiotics as a potential control for avian intestinal spirochaetosis, PhD thesis, University of Surrey, Guildford, UK.

14vii.4 References

Backhans, A., Johansson, K.E. and Fellström, C. (2010) Phenotypic and molecular characterization of *Brachyspira* spp. isolated from wild rodents. *Environmental Microbiology Reports* 2(6), 720–727.

Bernardeau, M., Gueguen, M., Smith, D.G.E., Corona-Barfrera, E. and Vernoux, J.P. (2009) In vitro antagonistic activities of *Lactobacillus* spp. against *Brachyspira hyodysenteriae* and *Brachyspira pilosicoli*. *Veterinary Microbiology* 138(1–2), 184–190.

Burch, D.G., Harding, C., Alvarez, R. and Valks, M. (2006) Treatment of a field case of avian intestinal spirochaetosis caused by *Brachyspira pilosicoli* with tiamulin. *Avian Pathology* 35(3), 211–216.

Burch, D.G., Strugnell, D., Steventon, A., Watson, E. and Harding, C. (2009) Survey of 222 flocks in Great Britain for the presence of *Brachyspira* species and their effect on production. In: *Proceedings of the 5th International Conference on Colonic Spirochaetal Infections in Animals and Human*. Leon, Spain, 8–10 June 2009.

Corona-Barrera, E., Smith, D.G., Murray, B. and Thomson, J.R. (2004) Efficacy of seven disinfectant sanitisers on field isolates of *Brachyspira pilosicoli*. *Veterinary Record* 154, 473–474.

Hampson, D.J., Robertson, I.D., La, T., Oxberry, S.L. and Pethick, D.W. (2000) Influences of diet and vaccination on colonisation of pigs by the intestinal spirochaete *Brachyspira* (*Serpulina*) *pilosicoli*. *Veterinary Microbiology* 73(1), 75–84.

Hampson, D.J., Oxberry, S.L. and Stephens, C.P. (2002) Influence of in-feed zinc bacitracin and tiamulin treatment on experimental avian intestinal spirochaetosis caused by *Brachyspira intermedia*. *Avian Pathology* 31(3), 285–291.

Hampson, D J. (2018) The spirochete *Brachyspira pilosicoli*, enteric pathogen of animals and humans. *Clinical Microbiology Reviews* 31(1), e00087-17.

La, T., Phillips, N D. and Hampson, D J. (2018) Vaccination of chickens with the 34 kDa carboxy-terminus of Bpmp72 reduced colonisation with *Brachyspira pilosicoli* following experimental infection. *Avian Pathology* 48(1), 80–85.

Le Roy, C.I., Mappley, L.J., La Ragione, R.M., Woodward, M.J. and Claus, S.P. (2015) *Brachyspira pilosicoli*-induced avian intestinal spirochaetosis. *Microbial Ecology in Health and Disease* 26, 1–9.

Mappley, L.J., Tchórzewska, M.A., Cooley, W.A., Woodward, M.J. and La Ragione, R.M. (2011) Lactobacilli antagonize the growth, motility, and adherence of *Brachyspira pilosicoli*: A potential intervention against avian intestinal spirochetosis. *Applied and Environmental Microbiology* 77(15), 5402–5411.

Mappley, L.J., Tchórzewska, M.A., Nunez, A., Woodward, M.J., Bramley, P.M., *et al.* (2013) Oral treatment of chickens with *Lactobacillus reuteri* LM1 reduces *Brachyspira pilosicoli*-induced pathology. *Journal of Medical Microbiology* 62, 287–296.

Mappley, L.J., La Ragione, R.M. and Woodward, M.J. (2014) *Brachyspira* and its role in avian intestinal spirochaetosis. *Veterinary Microbiology* 168(2–4), 245–260.

Medhanie, G.A., McEwen, S.A., Slavic, D. and Guerin, M.T. (2013) *Brachyspira* spp. and avian intestinal spirochaetosis: an epidemiological review. *World's Poultry Science Journal* 69(3), 541–552.

Padmanabhan, V., Dahlstrom, J., Maxwell, L., Kaye, G., Clarke, A., *et al.* (1996) Invasive intestinal spirochetosis: a report of three cases. *Pathology* 28(3), 283–286.

Phillips, Nyree D., La, T. and Hampson, D.J. (2006) Development of a two-step nested duplex PCR assay for the rapid detection of *Brachyspira pilosicoli* and *Brachyspira intermedia* in chicken faeces. *Veterinary Microbiology* 116(1–3), 239–245.

Prim, N., Pericas, R., Español, M., Rivera, A., Mirelis, B. and Coll, P. (2011) Bloodstream infection due to *Brachyspira pilosicoli* in a patient with multiorgan failure. *Journal of Clinical Microbiology* 49(10), 3697–3699.

Stephens, C.P. and Hampson, D.J. (2001) Intestinal spirochete infections of chickens: a review of disease associations, epidemiology and control. *Animal Health Research Reviews* 2(1), 83–91.

Verlinden, M., Pasmans, F., Mahu, M., Vande Maele, L., De Pauw, N., *et al.* (2013) *In vitro* sensitivity of poultry *Brachyspira intermedia* isolates to essential oil components and *in vivo* reduction of *Brachyspira intermedia* in rearing pullets with cinnamaldehyde feed supplementation. *Poultry Science* 92(5), 1202–1207.

Woodward, M.J., Mappley, L., Le Roy, C., Claus, S.P., Davies, P., *et al.* (2015) Drinking water application of Denagard® Tiamulin for control of *Brachyspira pilosicoli* infection of laying poultry. *Research in Veterinary Science* 103, 87–95.

14viii Mycoplasmas

JANET M. BRADBURY[1*] AND CHRIS MORROW[2]

[1]*Institute of Infection, Veterinary and Ecological Sciences, University of Liverpool, Leahurst Campus, Neston, UK.;* [2]*Bioproperties, Ringwood, Victoria, Australia and University of Melbourne, School of Veterinary Science, Victoria, Australia*

14viii.1 Introduction

Mycoplasma infections can cause considerable economic loss to the poultry industries worldwide through reduced production, medication and prevention measures.

Mycoplasmas are very small bacteria belonging to the class Mollicutes. They have evolved over millions of years to possess a minimal genome and, as a consequence, mollicutes do not have a cell wall, are fragile, and have limited ability to survive outside the host, which they rely on for many nutrients. Success of the avian mycoplasmas as poultry pathogens is encouraged by poor husbandry and also by co-infections and synergism with other pathogens, especially those affecting the respiratory tract or resistance of the host.

Although there are currently over 30 different species of *Mycoplasma* in birds, only four are recognized as economically important in chickens and turkeys. Of these, *M. gallisepticum* (MG) has the broadest known host range and, together with *M. synoviae* (MS), is responsible for the most significant infections, while *M. meleagridis* (MM) and *M. iowae* (MI) are mainly turkey pathogens and much less widespread. Economic costs lie not only in suboptimal production of meat and eggs and treatment of disease but also in measures taken to prevent infection and maintain status of mycoplasma-free flocks.

14viii.2 Habitat and Pathogenicity

Mollicutes can be found in humans, animals, arthropods and plants but *Mycoplasma* species are rather host-specific. The primary habitat of pathogenic avian mycoplasmas is the mucosal surface of respiratory and/or urogenital tracts of poultry and other birds; sometimes they may infect conjunctiva, and some can localize in joints. Many non-pathogenic avian *Mycoplasma* species are commensals but may occupy the same niche as the pathogens. The pathogenic species can even behave as commensals until triggered by secondary stress factors or concurrent infections. Occasionally other mycoplasmas, e.g. *M. gallinarum*, *M. gallinaceum* and *M. imitans* are implicated in respiratory disease, especially in co-infections with other pathogens.

Although the main manifestation of mycoplasma disease is often respiratory signs, other systems such as the reproductive or locomotory function can be affected. Infection of flocks in lay may show transitory egg production drops. Some non-specific effects, such as poor weight gain, poorer feed conversion into meat or eggs, and lameness may also occur.

Mechanisms of mycoplasma pathogenicity are not fully understood but adherence to host cells, particularly epithelial cells, is an early stage, usually mediated by specialized terminal-tip structures. Other mechanisms include avoiding host defences by inhibiting respiratory tract ciliary activity, by variable expression of surface antigens and by entering host cells. Infection may cause immunopathological lesions, for example the infiltration of lymphocytes and lymphocytic nodules seen in MG-infected respiratory tract. The importance of mechanisms, such as intracellular invasion or production of biofilms remains to be fully established.

*Corresponding author: jmb41@liverpool.ac.uk

© CAB International 2021. *Poultry Health: A Guide for Professionals* (P. Barrow *et al.*)
DOI: 10.1079/9781789245042.0014

14viii.3 Spread of Infection

Pathogenic avian mycoplasmas can infect embryos and spread vertically to the next generation. Even though a proportion of infected embryos fail to hatch, cross-infection to uninfected chicks or poults could occur at the hatchery and, without strict hygiene, mycoplasmas can survive in egg debris and infect other progeny.

Transmission of mycoplasmas is enhanced by close contact and stress, so poor husbandry, overcrowding and inadequate biosecurity assists dissemination. Spread via infected aerosols or exudates from the respiratory tract is enhanced by coughing/sneezing. MS is thought to spread through flocks more rapidly than MG although experimental evidence is lacking. Artificial insemination can aid transmission of MM and MI as both can infect turkey semen.

Despite poor survival outside the host, mycoplasmas may be protected by mucous exudate or other organic matter and can spread by mechanical transmission between flocks within a farm and further afield, perhaps assisted by human negligence or inadvertent carriage by humans, animals, wild birds, farm equipment, strong winds and proximity of other poultry. Once infected, birds may harbour mycoplasmas for their lifetime.

14viii.4 The Important Pathogenic Species

14viii.4.1 *Mycoplasma gallisepticum*

On a worldwide basis MG remains the most important avian *Mycoplasma* species. Infections are reported in chickens, turkeys, pheasants, partridges, guinea fowl, quail, pigeons, peafowl and also finches and some other wild birds. Infections are reported occasionally in ducks, geese and racing pigeons, but appear rare.

MG is commonly associated with chronic respiratory disease and sub-optimal production in broilers and turkeys, and reduced egg production in layers. Strains of MG vary in virulence, tropism and antigenicity, with young birds being more susceptible and more likely to develop disease. Chickens usually show fewer clinical signs than turkeys or game birds in uncomplicated infection, but all may develop conjunctivitis with frothy ocular exudate, nasal exudate and tracheal rales. Conjunctivitis and swollen infraorbital sinuses are common in turkeys ('infectious sinusitis', Fig. 14viii.1) and in game birds (Fig. 14viii.2) but not in chickens.

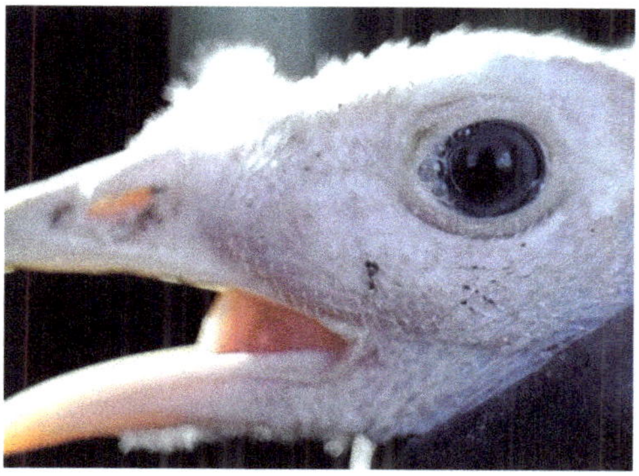

Fig. 14viii.1. *M. gallisepticum* infection in a turkey showing swelling of the infraorbital sinus and frothy ocular exudate. (Original photograph donated by F.T.W. Jordan.)

Infection of embryos can affect hatchability and viability of chicks and turkey poults and airsacculitis may be seen in pipped embryos.

Other disease manifestations are rare, but lameness can occur if MG localizes in hock joints, and salpingitis has also been reported in layers. MG has been implicated occasionally in nervous signs in turkeys due to encephalitis.

In addition to poor husbandry, high stocking density, poor ventilation, accumulation of ammonia or dust, etc., complicating factors are numerous, with the viruses of infectious bronchitis and Newcastle disease (even some live vaccines) exacerbating airsacculitis (Fig. 14viii.3) and overt respiratory disease.

Other concurrent infections such as avian influenza and avian metapneumovirus, can exacerbate disease, and in broilers *Escherichia coli* is notorious for complicating *M. gallisepticum* disease (Fig. 14viii.4).

Mechanisms of protection are not fully elucidated but locally produced antibodies in the respiratory tract are considered more important than humoral antibodies and protection may be overwhelmed in some co-infections. The role of cellular immunity is less well known.

14viii.4.2 *Mycoplasma synoviae*

Once dismissed as relatively unimportant, this mycoplasma is probably more widespread currently than MG in chickens (especially layers) and its role in disease, production inefficiencies and reliance on antibiotics have become more apparent. MS can infect chickens and turkeys, and occasional

Fig. 14viii.2. *M. gallisepticum* in a pheasant has caused bilateral swelling of the infraorbital sinuses. (Author's own photograph.)

hosts may include pheasant, partridge, quail, guinea fowl, duck, goose, pigeon and house sparrows.

MS was originally recognized as the cause of 'infectious synovitis' in broilers and turkeys (Fig. 14viii.5) and considered more likely to cause subclinical respiratory infection than overt disease.

However, it is now known that MS has economic impact and that airsacculitis in broilers may be precipitated by similar factors to those named above for MG. Dutch strains of MS were reported to be associated with amyloid arthritis in some chicken and turkey flocks and with eggshell apex abnormality (EAA) in layers, which results in significant economic loss due to poor shell quality (Fig. 14viii.6).

High prevalence (60–70%) of MS in layers was reported in several countries and EAA seen in many areas including Europe, S. America, Australia and Asia. Also, in layers, MS is believed to increase invasion of *E. coli* and hence mortality due to peritonitis, particularly at the beginning of lay.

14viii.4.3 *Mycoplasma meleagridis (MM)*

MM has been eradicated by major turkey breeding companies but is seen sporadically in commercial birds in Europe and North America. MM has been isolated from guinea fowl and raptors, but is probably rare, as are reports in chickens. Infection with MM can cause dwarfing, chondrodystrophy, crooked necks and abnormal primary wing feathers in young poults, and transient air sac infection in older birds.

Spread resembles MG and MS (i.e. vertical and lateral) but MM can also be spread to turkey hens by artificial insemination with infected semen.

14viii.4.4 *Mycoplasma iowae (MI)*

MI was also eradicated from major primary turkey breeders but is still seen occasionally in commercial turkeys in USA and Europe. Infrequent hosts include chickens and wild birds, and it has been reported in pheasants and partridges in Italy. Under commercial conditions MI can cause 2–10% reduced hatchability, possibly influenced by breed of turkey. There are also sporadic reports of associated leg problems (e.g. USA, Hungary, Italy). MI can spread vertically and horizontally, including the venereal route. Infected birds do not produce detectable antibodies, making serological diagnosis impractical.

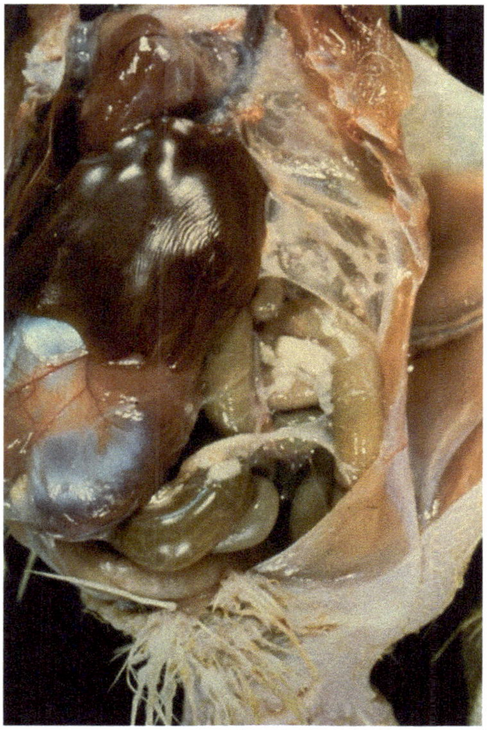

Fig. 14viii.3. Airsacculitis in a broiler chicken with mixed infection of *M. gallisepticum* and infectious bronchitis virus. (Author's own photograph.)

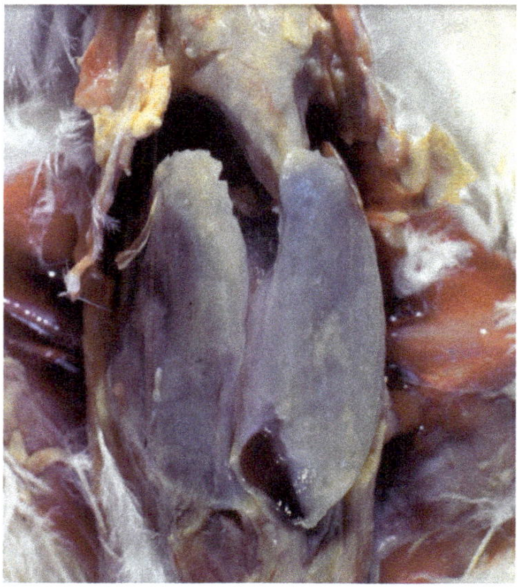

Fig. 14viii.4. *M. gallisepticum*-infected broiler chicken with typical lesions of colisepticaemia (pericarditis, perihepatitis and airsacculitis). (Author's own photograph.)

14viii.4.5 Other species

Other mycoplasmas have been implicated occasionally in poultry disease but *M. anserisalpingitidis* is a clearly established cause of reproductive disorders in geese.

14viii.5 Diagnosis

Respiratory signs and pathological/histopathological lesions are not diagnostic, because there can be other causes. Likewise, agents such as reoviruses and staphylococci may cause lameness.

Diagnosis involves direct detection of the causal *Mycoplasma* species in the pathology by culture and/or PCR, or demonstration of seroconversion.

14viii.5.1 Culture and PCR

Tracheal swabs from live birds are a common sample but swabs can be from choanal cleft, conjunctiva and sinus exudate, depending on disease presentation. Other relevant sites (e.g. air sacs, joints or reproductive tract) can be swabbed post-mortem.

Mycoplasma culture requires a special medium containing serum and yeast extract and can be achieved in a few days but may sometimes take three or more weeks. MM does not grow well on agar medium. Culture and identification may be complicated by over-growth of commensal mollicutes. This applies especially to samples from commercial birds, those on free-range and game birds, and emphasizes the need for chilling samples for rapid transportation to the laboratory. Isolation may be improved by use of a transport medium e.g. swabs moistened with mycoplasma broth or Amies charcoal broth.

After isolation, mycoplasmas are identified by techniques such as immunofluorescence (Fig. 14viii.7), immunoperoxidase or PCR.

Other tests, such as MALDI-TOF, have been investigated for rapid identification of isolates but may be hampered by difficulties in obtaining sufficient quantities of pure cultures.

Nowadays it is more usual to examine swabs or other samples directly by species-specific PCR tests, which can be multiplex, and are generally carried out in real time. Commercial kits are available and pen-side tests are anticipated.

14viii.5.2 Strain typing

In some situations, it is helpful to distinguish between strains of the causal *Mycoplasma*, e.g. a

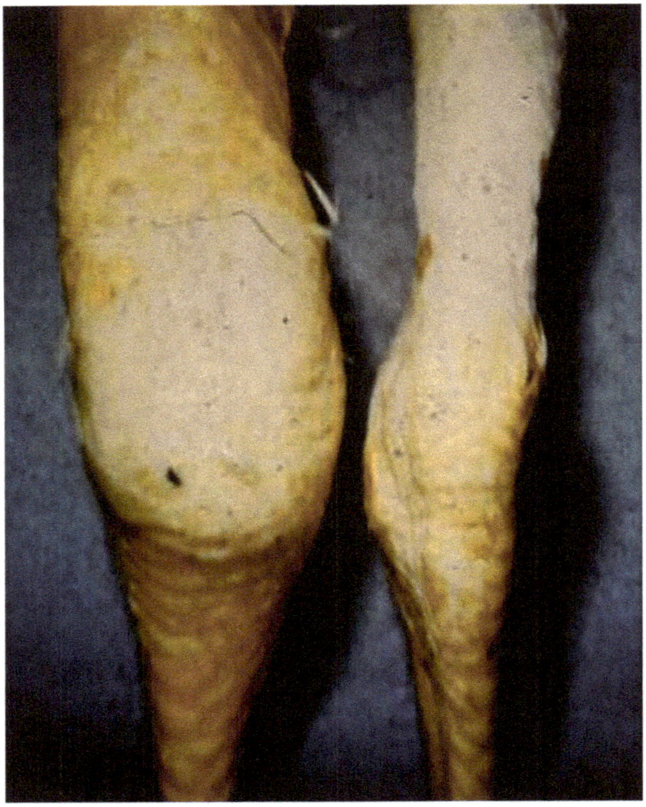

Fig. 14viii.5. Turkey exhibiting unilateral swelling of the hock joint. *M. synoviae* was isolated from joint exudate together with reovirus. (Author's own photograph.)

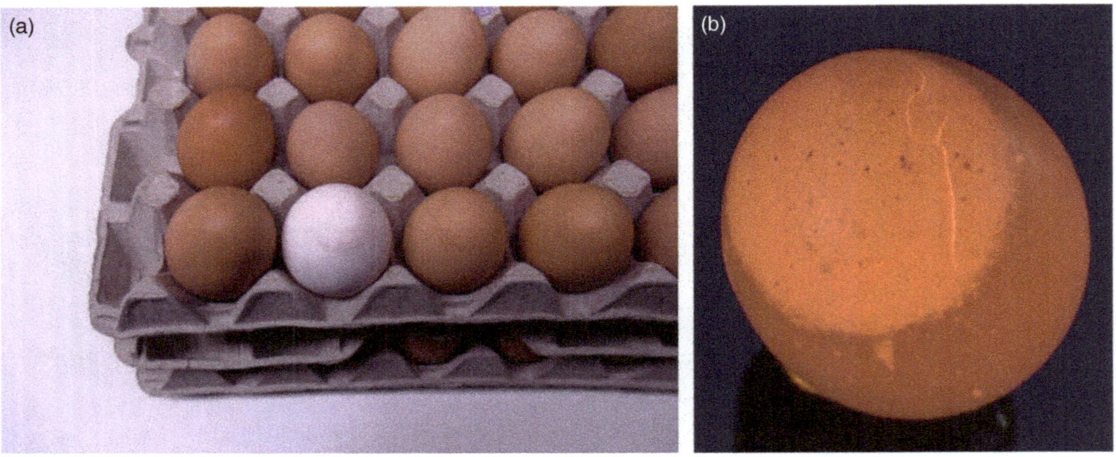

Fig. 14viii.6. Eggshell apex abnormality in eggs from brown and white layers with *M. synoviae* infection of the oviduct. The shells show altered surface, thinning, increased translucency, and the occurrence of cracks and breaks and is more apparent at candling. (Reproduced from Feberwee *et al.*, 2009. Copyright Houghton Trust Ltd, reprinted by permission of Taylor & Francis Ltd, www.tandfonline.com, on behalf of Houghton Trust Ltd.)

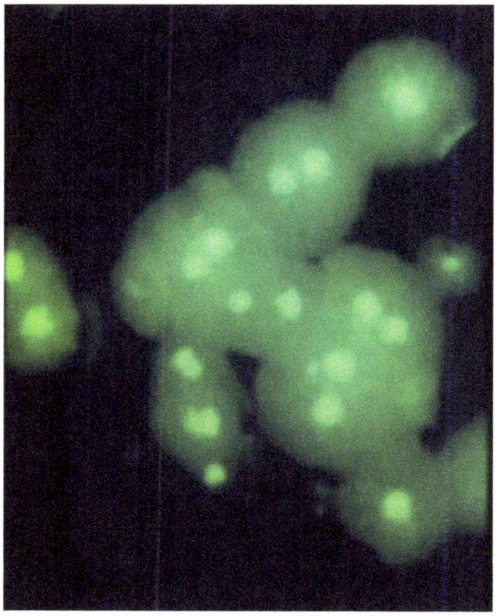

Fig. 14viii.7. *M. gallisepticum* colonies stained positive by indirect immunofluorescence test. (Photograph donated by R.C. Jones.)

client may ask if an isolate is 'wild type' or vaccine, or if a particular strain has spread between flocks. Molecular-based schemes for strain typing are run in specialized laboratories and are proving very helpful (see below). They should become more widely used if value to clients justifies costs.

14viii.5.3 Serology

Flock screening for serum antibodies has been practised widely for many years and stained MG, MS and MM antigens for the 'rapid serum agglutination (RSA) test' are still produced. Equal volumes of antigen and serum are mixed and examined for agglutination. Interpretation is on a flock basis as the test is not reliable for individuals. Commercial ELISAs, after validation, are convenient for screening large numbers of sera, again as a flock test. Serology is unsuitable for flocks that have been vaccinated with live or killed mycoplasma vaccines. Other causes of false serological reactions include chronic bacterial infections (bumble foot or swollen wattles being the most common) and in the case of RSA, abuse of sera (freezing, leaving on clot, etc.).

After infection with wild strains, flocks usually seroconvert within a month and remain sero-positive for life, but antibiotic administration may suppress seroconversion and hence detection.

In freedom programmes monitoring can be as frequent as every 3 weeks; in the past this was by rapid serum agglutination, but ELISA is now used more frequently. Confirmation of infection can be by culture and/or PCR, or demonstration of rising titres at retesting in 2 weeks where access to culture or PCR is limited.

It should be noted that antibodies may be undetectable early in an infection and that some strains of MS may not cause seroconversion. No serological test has yet proved useful for detecting *M. iowae*. Furthermore, serology is not useful for vaccination quality control or assessing protection.

14viii.6 Control Measures

14viii.6.1 Mycoplasma-free flocks

Ideally this is preferred for meat and layer production systems. For broiler breeders it includes MG and MS. For turkeys, freedom from MI and MM is also advantageous. Layer flocks are discussed below. The value of freedom from mycoplasma in other bird industries is less well-defined although respiratory disease in MG-infected game birds is well recognized.

Elimination of MG and MS from breeding programmes has been achieved by multinational breeding companies but some national breeding programmes, especially of local specialist stock, have not eliminated MS. Success in preventing infection in commercial poultry further down the production chain is variable and depends on factors like farm isolation and effectiveness of biosecurity.

Control of MS appears more difficult than MG (possibly due to greater determination to control MG). Control programmes for MG have been guided by the OIE and local implementation of government plans. Eradication of MS is not often operated on a national basis but usually on a commercial poultry integration, industry segment or farm basis. Sectors not participating may become a reservoir (e.g. layer sector as a potential source of infection for breeder sector).

Biosecurity to maintain mycoplasma freedom begins by sourcing mycoplasma-free replacement stock and preventing horizontal entry of field strains. Although mycoplasmas generally have short survival times (measured in days) they can be transmitted mechanically by people and fomites. This might include the nose of people in contact with infected birds. Airborne transmission seems possible, as the authors have, on more than one occasion, detected identical MS vlhA types on epidemiologically unconnected sites more than 2 km apart. Movement of infected birds between sites is hazardous, so mixing donor flocks, especially with eggs sourced from outside, the acquisition of stock from new sources and the 'spiking' of flocks with replacement males are all risky procedures, and pre-testing for infection is essential. Once a multi-age site is infected it will remain so without some intervention.

14viii.6.2 Control at commercial level

MG and MS infections have resulted in poultry production systems worldwide becoming antibiotic dependent over the last 50 years. Antibiotic use has not always been rational, and, for responsible use, prophylactic interventions should be phased out. In many regions, MS in layers is ignored and accompanied by routine antibiotic use during lay. This can hide the impact of infection; furthermore, lack of disease does not eliminate production losses due to MS in this generation (disease, egg production, poorer feed conversion into eggs, increased second quality eggs, cost of antibiotics). Also, antibiotic use seriously compromises the value of serological monitoring for infection.

14viii.6.3 Vaccination

A vaccination programme together with biosecurity may provide a solution, and it is more efficient to adopt a similar strategy for both MG and MS (i.e. freedom or vaccination) although there is no cross-protection between them.

Killed vaccines can decrease clinical signs, especially systemic manifestations. They can decrease tracheal populations and horizontal and vertical transmission, and produce humoral antibody. Maternal antibodies are not considered protective except to prevent mortality in vertically infected embryos. These antibodies disappear quickly (usually by 14 days in broiler stock). Killed autogenous vaccines are permitted in some countries under certain circumstances but may not necessarily prove effective.

There is increasing evidence that protection does not correlate well with humoral antibody and that mucosal antibodies and cell-mediated immunity may be involved. Vaccine properties vary and should be considered in vaccine selection. F strain has been used extensively in USA layers but not in breeders. Outside the USA, studies on progeny of F strain-vaccinated breeders have identified vertical infection, sometimes associated with respiratory disease.

Some infected multi-age sites, especially those with rearing facilities, pose particular challenges for live vaccines because infection may occur before development of adequate vaccinal immunity. This can be solved by remote rearing (which benefits efficacy of many other vaccines, especially Marek's disease). Success of vaccination at transfer has been achieved by antibiotic treatment of the remaining unvaccinated farm flocks around the time of delivery to decrease local challenge. This can cease once all flocks on site are vaccinated. Vaccination at transfer allows pullet rearers who supply multiple customers to vaccinate birds to order.

Live vaccines can be used on multi-age sites as a tool to move from infected to mycoplasma-free status. This can be done in stages, especially if the initial vaccine transmits readily horizontally. Cessation of live vaccination works for well isolated sites with little local challenge, but continued vaccination is preferable in high poultry density areas.

A pox-vectored MG vaccine is also available, but laboratory and field experience are poorly documented.

14viii.6.4 Differentiating vaccinated from infected flocks (DIVA)

Serology is not effective in differentiating vaccinated from infected flocks and currently DNA-based tests are used to confirm both effective vaccine administration and the presence of field strains.

Live vaccines appear to colonize chickens more slowly than wild strains, so the usual time to check vaccine 'take' with PCR is 6 weeks post-vaccination. Some live vaccines may elicit very little serum antibody, but this does not indicate ineffective vaccination and factors that may influence serological response include concurrent tracheitis and bird type. Some vaccines initially inducing a low serological response may, after peak of lay, elicit strong seroconversion. This has been misinterpreted as protection failure, despite subsequent investigations revealing no production problems, clinical signs or field strain colonization. This possibly accounts for the false belief that mild vaccines only protect to 40 weeks and that birds need revaccination with stronger live vaccines or the use of antibiotics.

Strain identification methods for MG and MS have advanced considerably, allowing DIVA testing for vaccine strains on clinical swabs and significantly helping our understanding of live mycoplasma vaccination in poultry. These techniques work best if the gene targets are not under immune or functional pressure. REA (restriction enzyme analysis), RAPD (randomly amplified polymorphic DNA), ALFP (amplified fragment length polymorphism) and HRM (high resolution melting) analysis are now considered unsuitable for use directly on field samples or uncloned cultures. MLST (multi-locus sequence typing) and MVLA (multiple locus variable-number tandem repeat analysis) can be used to confirm relationships between strains and provide good back-up if DIVA test results are ambiguous (see Chapter 22, this volume).

Whole genome sequencing is emerging as a powerful tool and can indicate emergence of antimicrobial resistance (AMR) due to historical use. Detection of known resistance mutations provides evidence of a resistant strain (in clinical swabs or isolates), but absence of known mutations or resistance determinants does not necessarily predict that a strain is sensitive.

These tools suggest that continued protection in flocks receiving live vaccine is associated with continued colonization with vaccine strains. With MG vaccines, tracheal populations after 2 months can be very low and difficult to detect but may increase after peak production. With live MSH vaccination, a DIVA PCR survey showed 93% of flocks (n > 600) vaccinated during rearing were still colonized by the strain at 65 weeks of age (R. Fadavi, personal communication). Where the vaccine is undetectable there is often a history of antibiotic intervention post-vaccination. As with coccidiosis vaccines, continued colonization by the live mycoplasma vaccine is needed to develop and maintain mucosal immunity.

14viii.6.5 Prudent use of antibiotics

Little is known of the interaction between various mycoplasma interventions, but serological monitoring to confirm mycoplasma freedom is not compatible with antibiotic prophylaxis or use of vaccines, and live vaccines are not compatible with antibiotic programmes.

Antibiotic resistance, particularly quinolone resistance in MG and MS has emerged in some countries (usually associated with routine prophylactic programmes) and has disseminated vertically into large sections of the local industry. Antibiotic resistance (minimum inhibitory concentration, MIC) testing is uncommon for MG and MS as results would be unavailable in time to inform treatment of an affected flock. However, testing can be helpful for guiding future antibiotic choice in an area or integration.

There is little evidence of synergy between antibiotics in mycoplasma treatment so combinations of antibiotics should be avoided. AMR consequences should be considered when prescribing antibiotics, bearing in mind that elimination of infection by antibiotic treatment is rare (and apparently expensive). If antibiotics were the total solution for mycoplasma infection in poultry, then control of infection would have been achieved in the early 1960s when antibiotics were first used in food producing animals. Despite this, antibiotics are the only intervention that can be applied once a flock is infected.

14viii.7 Reference

Feberwee, A., de Wit, J.J. and Landman, W.J.M. (2009) Induction of eggshell apex abnormalities by *Mycoplasma synoviae*: field and experimental studies. *Avian Pathology* 38, 77–85. DOI: 10.1080/03079450802662772.

14viii.8 Further Reading

Armour, N.K. (2020) *Mycoplasma gallisepticum* infection. In: Swayne, D.E. (ed.) *Diseases of Poultry*. 14th edn, Vol. II. Wiley Blackwell, Hoboken, New York, pp. 911–923.

El-Gazzar, M. and Bradbury, J.M. (2020) *Mycoplasma iowae* infection. In: Swayne, D.E. (ed.) *Diseases of Poultry*, 14th edn, Vol. II. Wiley Blackwell, Hoboken, New York, pp. 929–933.

Ferguson-Noel, N. (2020) Other mycoplasmal infections. In: Swayne, D.E. (ed.) *Diseases of Poultry*, 14th edn, Vol. II. Wiley Blackwell, Hoboken, New York, pp. 933–939.

Ferguson-Noel, N. and Noormohammadi, A.H. (2020) *Mycoplasma synoviae* infection. In: Swayne, D.E. (ed.) *Diseases of Poultry*, 14th edn, Vol. II. Wiley Blackwell, Hoboken, New York, pp. 924–929

Kempf, I. (2015) Avian mycoplasmosis. In: Brugère-Picoux, J. (ed.) *Manual of Poultry Diseases*. French Association for the Advancement of Science (AFAS), pp. 278–285.

Morrow C. (2018) The cost of mycoplasma infection in poultry. Zootecnica International, 28 July 2018. Available at: https://zootecnicainternational.com/featured/cost-mycoplasma-infection-poultry/ (accessed 8 March 2021).

14ix Miscellaneous Bacterial Infections

Paul Barrow[1]* and Robert Atterbury[2]

[1]*School of Veterinary Medicine, University of Surrey, Guildford, UK;*
[2]*School of Veterinary Medicine and Science, University of Nottingham, Sutton Bonington, Loughborough, Leicestershire, UK*

14ix.1 *Erysipelothrix rhusiopathiae*

This is a pathogen most frequently associated with a sudden onset disease in turkeys, although it can affect many different species, including humans. Because of its zoonotic potential, care should be taken when handling infected birds.

14ix.1.1 Microbiology and culture

E. rhusiopathiae is a Gram-positive, non-motile rod-shaped bacillus which shows a tendency towards filamentation. It can destain easily and appear Gram-negative. It is facultatively anaerobic and grows over a wide range of temperatures between 5 and 42°C. It grows readily but poorly on ordinary media. Growth can be improved by addition of serum to liquid or semi-liquid media, as well as by additional growth supplements such as Tween 80 and glucose.

14ix.1.2 Hosts and epidemiology

The source of infection is direct contact with other animals, or with fomites and material from other animals. Pigs are well known to be infected, but rodents, sheep and other birds can also be infected. Soil can be a source of infection, although this is as a result of contamination with infected material from other animals.

It is most commonly seen in turkeys and less so in chickens. Mature animals are generally infected. It is not known whether factors other than stress might be implicated in infection, but the presence of intestinal parasites may be associated with increased susceptibility.

14ix.1.3 Clinical picture and pathology

The pathogenesis is poorly understood, with the route of infection unclear. Outbreaks have been recorded involving several serovars, suggesting management lapses or faults are involved in the initial infection. Strains vary in their virulence, although the basis of virulence is also poorly studied. Experimental infection produces very variable results. Disease results in infection of a wide range of internal organs.

Onset of disease can be sudden with birds dying after a short acute disease with depression and diarrhoea, and sometimes darkened patches and cyanosis on the skin as occurs in pigs. Mortality can be high in birds which become sick. Loss of condition, lameness and reduced egg production can be chronic in birds that recover.

14ix.1.4 Diagnosis

The organism can be cultured from haemorrhagic lesions and congested liver or spleen. It may also be visualized by Gram-staining and microscopy.

14ix.1.5 Control

Prevention is always better than therapy, and biosecurity measures including prevention of contact with other potentially infected animals are important. Vaccines may be used, but can induce serological cross reactions to *Mycoplasma gallisepticum* and *M. meleagridis* (see Chapter 14viii, this volume). *E. rhusiopathiae* is susceptible to penicillins, but this will not eliminate infection.

*Corresponding author: paul.barrow@surrey.ac.uk

© CAB International 2021. *Poultry Health: A Guide for Professionals* (P. Barrow *et al.*)
DOI: 10.1079/9781789245042.0014

14ix.2 Staphylococcosis

Staphylococcosis is generally caused by *Staphylococcus aureus* but other staphylococcal species, such as *S. epidermidis*, may also be implicated. They produce a variety of infections including septicaemia, arthritis, multiple bone diseases and subdermal abscesses including bumblefoot.

14ix.2.1 Microbiology and culture

Staphylococci are Gram-positive spherical cocci arranged in a 'bunch of grapes formation'. They produce haemolysis on blood agar but unlike mammalian strains, which produce clearing β-haemolysis, avian strains produce α (alpha, greening) or no detectable haemolysis. They are generally resistant to elevated concentrations of NaCl. Strains produce septicaemia and skin infections in man, and mastitis in cattle, and there is huge variation in virulence between strains.

14ix.2.2 Hosts and epidemiology

Since the 1940s, sub-typing methods, including phage-typing and variations in capsule and biomarkers, have been used for epidemiological purposes. The organism is ubiquitous and a normal component of the skin flora of man and animals, especially in areas of skin that remain damp, including the upper respiratory tract.

There is an understandably wide range of routes of infection for a pathogen that is present in the normal flora and the environment. It can be isolated from hatcheries and hatching eggs.

14ix.2.3 Clinical picture and pathology

Infection with disease is thought to occur either following damage to the skin of mucous membranes or following immunosuppression including infection with viruses such as infectious bursal disease (IBD) virus (see Chapter 15v, this volume).

S. aureus produces a wide range of toxins and virulence factors that facilitate survival and resistance to killing by host defence mechanisms and mediating penetration through the tissues, although it remains mainly an intracellular pathogen. The roles of these toxins and factors have mainly been determined for mammalian models of human disease.

A variety of manifestations of infection are observed:

Sub-dermal abscesses (bumblefoot). The foot pad and sternum are most frequently affected, the former leading to lameness sometimes with caseation. It may be seen more often in heavy breeds. This can lead to septicaemia and death.

Arthritis and tenosynovitis. Hock joints are usually affected, causing pain and leading to lameness and depression. The synovial membranes of the tendon sheaths become oedematous and may become caseous.

Osteomyelitis. Spread of infection through the blood can lead to localization in the bone, sometimes leading to femoral head necrosis, although the proximal end of the tibia and also vertebrae may be affected. It is a common cause of lameness in broilers and turkeys.

Dermatitis. Areas of moist gangrenous skin may be seen most frequently on the back or wing tips. *S. aureus* can be frequently isolated simultaneously with clostridial spp.

14ix.2.4 Diagnosis

Culture of the organism, together with the clinical picture, is required although it must be remembered that other contaminating organisms may be present. Gram-staining and microscopy can assist in diagnosis.

14ix.2.5 Control

Bumblefoot abscesses can sometimes be extruded. Other infections are less easy to treat. *S. aureus* strains are frequently resistant to a range of antibiotics. Culling affected birds is sometimes needed in addition to identification and elimination of factors which may have led to immune-suppression and stress.

14ix.3 *Chlamydophila*

The chlamydia are a biologically interesting group of small microorganisms with a life cycle very different from typical bacteria and mycoplasmas. They are known historically as the causative agents of psittacosis, ornithosis in man (a respiratory disease arising from contact with birds) and sexually transmitted diseases in humans.

Recent taxonomic changes have now defined a new genus *Chlamydophila* containing *C. psittaci* causing infection in birds in addition to other species affecting ruminants and other mammals.

14ix.3.1 Microbiology and culture

The chlamydia are a group of very small obligately parasitic microorganisms which multiply within intracellular vacuoles as reticular bodies (400–600 nm in diameter) but are transmitted as resistant elementary bodies (250–300 nm) after ca. 30 h incubation. The elementary bodies are resistant, surviving in faeces for <1 month and in soil for <3 months. Gram-staining is not useful since peptidoglycan has not been identified despite appropriate genes being present. However, a lipopolysaccharide (LPS) very similar to that of the Gram-negative *Enterobacteriaceae* has been identified.

Culturing of chlamydia requires tissue culture, or inoculation of embryonated eggs.

There is variation in virulence between strains, but the details of the virulence determinants are poorly understood.

14ix.3.2 Hosts and epidemiology

Chlamydia are able to infect a wide range of avian species including waterfowl. Carriage and excretion by wild birds can occur without apparent infection. Amongst poultry, turkeys are most susceptible, followed by ducks and pigeons. Chickens are rarely infected, although infection can be detected.

Young birds are more susceptible than older stock. Maternal antibody does provide some protection to progeny.

This is a zoonotic infection, and poultry keepers are at risk if infected birds are in their flocks. Poultry-processing staff are also at risk from infected carcasses.

14ix.3.3 Clinical picture and pathology

The clinical picture varies in terms of severity ranging from mild or no signs, both of which may be the more common presentation, compared with severe respiratory forms of the disease. This is determined by the virulence of the strain involved as well as the age of the birds. The incubation period also varies from 5–10 days in young turkeys infected by a virulent strain to <60 days for adult birds infected with a less virulent strain. In young turkeys a large outbreak may involve 90% of birds being infected with mortality of 5–30%. However, sporadic cases may occur within a flock.

Affected birds show depression and anorexia, with a purulent nasal discharge and conjunctivitis. Diarrhoea may also occur.

Post-mortem, birds show a polyserositis, lung congestion and spleno- and hepatomegaly, with these organs sometimes showing small necrotic lesions.

14ix.3.4 Diagnosis

Respiratory signs are not pathognomonic. PCR is increasingly used for differential diagnosis. It is important to differentiate chlamydiosis from other respiratory infections of turkeys, particularly (i) pasteurellosis (see Chapter 14vi, this volume) from which it can be differentiated by culture, (ii) ORT (see Chapter 14vi, this volume) and *Mycoplasma* (see Chapter 14viii, this volume) for which culture and serology are required, (iii) pneumovirus (see Chapter 15ix, this volume) for which serology or molecular assays such as PCR may be required.

During examination and diagnostic procedures, it is important to remember the zoonotic potential of chlamydia. Biosecurity measures such as the use of gloves and wetting the carcass with alcohol or detergent may reduce aerosols.

14ix.3.5 Control

C. psittaci is susceptible to several antibiotics, and tetracycline and enrofloxacin are the drugs of choice for treatment of infected and in-contact birds. For complete elimination of the pathogen, treatment for 5–6 weeks may be needed.

In addition, improved hygiene and biosecurity, including quarantining of new stock, and cleaning, especially the removal of dust, with disinfection are important.

Vaccines can be effective but are not licensed for use in Europe.

In the UK, infected birds are subject to control under the Psittacosis/Ornithosis Order 1953 requiring isolation of affected birds with cleaning and disinfection required. Control is tighter in the US, and a National Compendium of measures for control of avian chlamydiosis is updated regularly.

14ix.4 *Bordetella avium* (Turkey coryza)

This organism is the cause of a highly infectious respiratory disease, but which is generally associated with low mortality unless other pathogens are present. It is most frequently associated with young turkeys, but may cause disease in young chickens and ducks. Mixed infections with other respiratory pathogens such as pneumoviruses (see Chapter 15ix, this volume), *Mycoplasma* (see Chapter 14viii, this volume), *Pasteurella* and *Ornithobacterium* (see Chapter 14vi, this volume) can produce more severe disease and *Escherichia coli* may be a secondary pathogen leading to pneumonia.

14ix.4.1 Microbiology and culture

The organism is a Gram-negative, aerobic, motile, rod-shaped bacillus producing small smooth, glistening colonies on blood or Brain Heart Infusion (BHI) agar. It does not grow or survive well at temperatures above 40°C which may explain its restriction to the respiratory tract. It survives for up to a month in faeces at lower temperatures and humidity.

14ix.4.2 Hosts and epidemiology

Although primarily associated with turkeys, *B. avium* is also a significant pathogen of chickens, and domestic ducks and geese. It is also found in wild birds including duck and geese species. Although closely related to the causative agent of pertussis (*B. pertussis*), it is not known to infect humans. There is some evidence that heavier breeds of turkey are more susceptible, associated with poorer cellular immunity.

It is highly infectious with a low infectious dose and easily transmitted by litter or water infected with nasal mucus. Rapid transmission through a flock can result in an almost 100% infection rate.

14ix.4.3 Clinical picture and pathology

The incubation period varies according to the degree to which transmission is direct, and varies between 4 and 10 days. The disease is an uncomplicated respiratory infection in which the bacteria adhere to the tracheal epithelial cells and produce toxins inducing ciliostasis. Necrotic lesions are produced, the quantity of which varies with the strain involved.

The clinical picture is thus one of initial sneezing in a high percentage of the flock, followed by a clear nasal discharge which may become encrusted with time. This may be accompanied by mouth breathing, dyspnoea and altered vocalization. Post-mortem changes in the trachea include excess mucus and secondary infection, sometimes leading to pneumonia.

14ix.4.4 Diagnosis

The clinical signs are not dissimilar to those of avian pneumovirus infection. Isolation of the pathogen is therefore important. Other faster growing bacteria such as *E. coli* (see Chapter 14ii, this volume) may be present and early sampling both in an outbreak and immediately after culling from the mid-trachea is essential.

Serological assays including ELISA are available.

Differentiation from other pathogens including pneumovirus, NDV (see Chapter 15viii, this volume), *Mycoplasma* and ORT should be done.

14ix.4.5 Control

The highly infectious nature of the disease indicates the absolute importance of rigorous hygiene measures during depopulation, with litter disposal, cleaning and disinfection. Water and feed delivery systems should also be disinfected. Antibiotics such as a combination of sulfonamide and trimethoprim or quinolones can be effective, but cessation of treatment frequently results in relapse as a result of reinfection from the environment.

Vaccination of hens produces maternally derived resistance for the first 2–3 weeks of life of the progeny chicks. Given that infection can occur in birds at this age, vaccination of the poults does not give enough time for full immunity to develop.

14ix.5 Further Reading

Pattison, M., McMullin, P.F., Bradbury, J.M. and Alexander, D.J. (2008) *Poultry Diseases*, 6th edn. Butterworth Heinemann, Edinburgh, UK.

Swayne, D.E. (editor-in-chief) (2013) *Diseases of Poultry*, 13th edn. Wiley-Blackwell, Danvers, Massachusetts, USA.

15i Avian Reoviruses – Viral Arthritis

Richard C. Jones*

Institute of Infection, Veterinary and Ecological Sciences, University of Liverpool, Leahurst Campus, Neston, Cheshire, UK

15i.1 Introduction

Avian reoviruses are ubiquitous in commercial poultry flocks. They are global in distribution although the virulence of these viruses appears to differ between different regions. Most strains are non-pathogenic and appear to survive harmlessly in the intestine whereas others have been found in association with several disease conditions including malabsorption and other enteric disorders, hydropericardium and occasionally respiratory disease. In many instances the association between a reovirus and disease is uncertain. An exception to this is viral arthritis or tenosynovitis (Fig. 15i.1).

This is because it can be produced experimentally by infecting birds with the virus alone. This section will concentrate on viral arthritis because it is the most important manifestation of reovirus infection.

15i.2 Avian Reoviruses

Avian reoviruses (ARV) are non-enveloped and possess a double-stranded, segmented ribonucleic acid (RNA) genome. They are members of the family Reoviridae, subfamily Spinareovirinae and genus Orthoreovirus (Fig. 15i.2).

There are ten different segments that have been identified and classified based on their electrophoretic mobility: L1–L3, M1–M3 and S1–S4. The S1 segment encodes for three viral proteins, including the minor capsid protein σC. This particular protein plays a key role during early stages of infection, mediating the interaction between the virion and the host cell, and elicits type-specific neutralizing antibodies. Amplification and sequencing analysis of the portion of the S1 gene that encodes the σC protein has been commonly used as a genetic marker for the characterization and classification of ARV isolates. To date, five and six genotypes have been described based on Lu and Kant's classification, respectively (cited by Egaña-Labrin *et al.*, 2019). Avian reoviruses are distinct from mammalian reoviruses. They can easily be cultivated in chick embryonic cell culture or fertile chicken eggs, so easily in fact that, occasionally, they have been implicated in disease conditions where they had no role.

15i.3 Species Affected

Reoviruses have been isolated from many avian species of wild birds but are most important in chickens, turkeys and Muscovy ducks where they cause a severe disease with high mortality. In turkeys, they have been associated with enteric disease but only recently identified in the USA as the cause of viral arthritis resembling that seen in chickens. The ten-segmented genome of the virus allows genetic reassortment to occur, resulting in the emergence of different types and causing difficulties in control by vaccination.

15i.4 Epidemiology

Reoviruses can be egg transmitted and horizontal transmission is via the faecal–oral route, although respiratory transmission and infection through broken skin in the feet have also been demonstrated. Reoviruses are relatively resistant away from the host on the surface of items found in the poultry house, particularly in the presence of organic material, but can be inactivated by strong commercial disinfectants.

*jonesrc@liverpool.ac.uk

© CAB International 2021. *Poultry Health: A Guide for Professionals* (P. Barrow *et al.*)
DOI: 10.1079/9781789245042.0015

Fig. 15i.1. Broiler breeders affected by viral arthritis, preferring to sit near feed troughs. (Author's own photograph.)

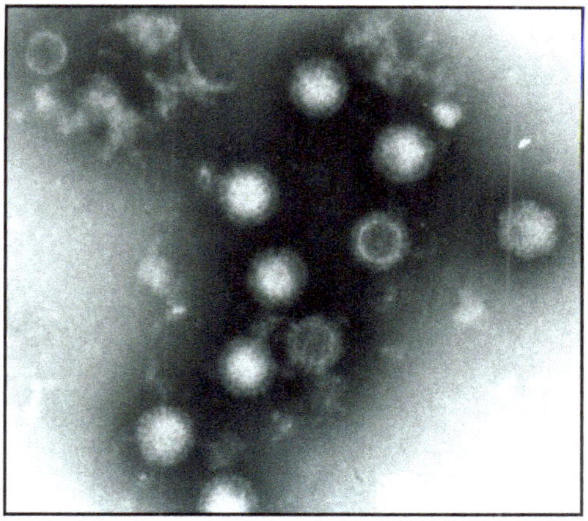

Fig. 15i.2. Electron micrograph of avian reoviruses. Negative staining. ×50,000. (Author's own photograph.)

15i.5 Disease

This chapter will concentrate on viral arthritis, being the most economically important disease caused by avian reoviruses. Following oral infection, reoviruses replicate in the gut, induce a viraemia and then may inflict damage in the liver in young chicks and the hock joints, where localization results in viral arthritis. In young chicks infected with high doses of virus, acute hepatitis may result. Paradoxically, though extensive replication occurs in the gut at the tips of the villi, reovirus replication induces little organ damage at that site.

A nucleus of chicks infected transovarially will transfer infection to hatch mates via the faecal–oral route. The disease is seen commonly in broiler breeds and is uncommon in lighter egg-layers.

Viraemic virus localizes in the hock joints and the slow disease process becomes evident through lameness though lesions may not be seen until 5 or 6 weeks of age. The hock joint (tibiotarsal tarsometatarsal) being the main load-bearing joint in the chicken, is the most severely affected, though virus may be detected in other leg joints. Lame birds prefer to remain recumbent due to painful and warm hock joint swelling, mainly seen above the joint. Sometimes the shank is swollen. Effects are due to swelling of gastrocnemius and digital flexor tendons, sometimes causing an effect called 'green leg', due to extravasation of blood above the hock (Figs 15i.3 and 15i.4).

In the most severe cases, there is rupture of the gastrocnemius and flexor tendons and erosion of the cartilage in the hock joint (Figs 15i.5 and 15i.6).

Lameness may be seen in up to 15% of badly affected flocks and mortality is usually low, although severely affected individuals may be trampled on by healthier birds. Losses are due to poor growth, tramplings and condemnations at slaughter. In laying flocks, there may be a transient loss of production and hatchability.

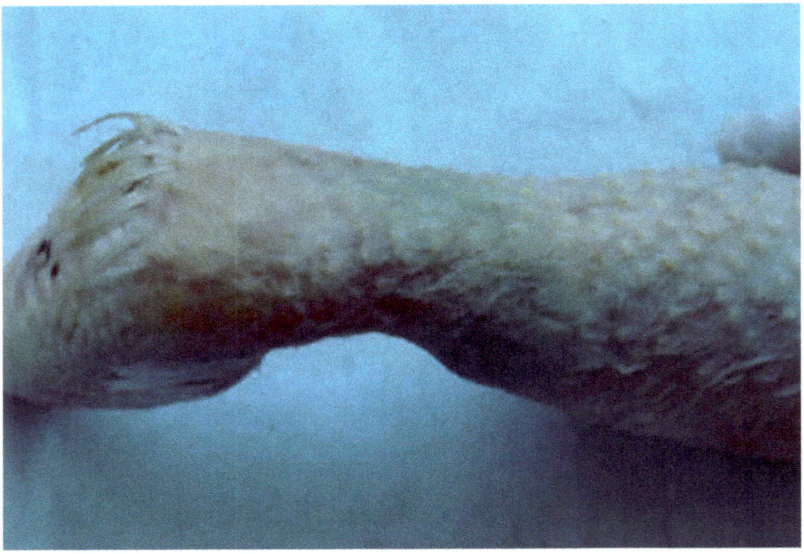

Fig. 15i.3. 'Green leg' appearance due to leakage of blood under the skin due to gastrocnemius tendon rupture. (Author's own photograph.)

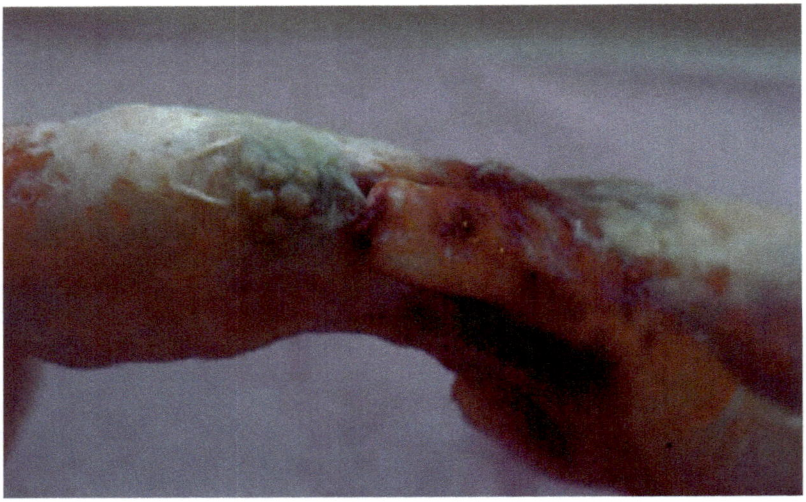

Fig. 15i.4. As Fig. 15i.3, revealing tendon rupture. (Author's own photograph.)

Histologically, there is aggregation of lymphocytes and macrophages around the tendons at the hypotarsal sesamoid with oedema and heterophil accumulations. Heterophil aggregates are also present in the synovial membrane. Cartilage erosion is accompanied by an increase in the numbers of small blood vessels. These changes are not pathognomonic.

15i.6 Other Factors

Several factors can influence the severity of viral arthritis. Oral infection of chicks after about 4–5 weeks of age rarely develops into disease and chicks immediately post-hatch are the most susceptible. Occasional outbreaks of swollen hocks, sometimes accompanied by tendon rupture in broiler-breeders

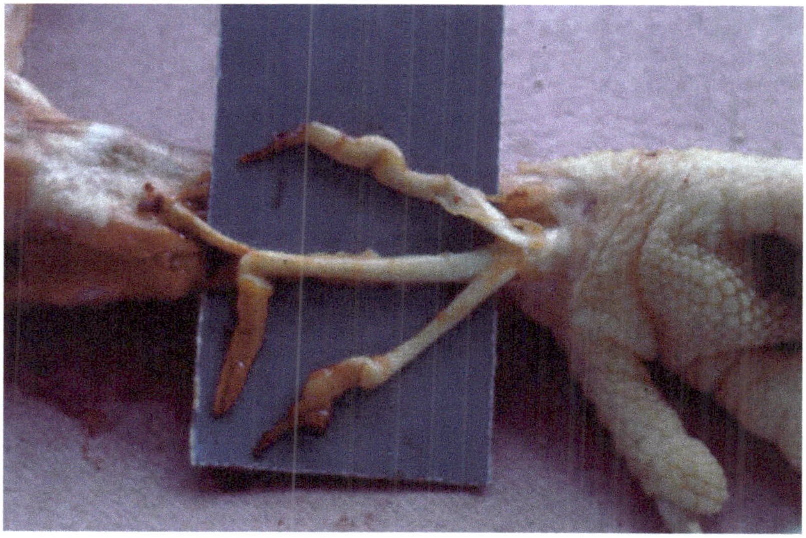

Fig. 15i.5. Ruptured digital flexor tendons in the shank. (Author's own photograph.)

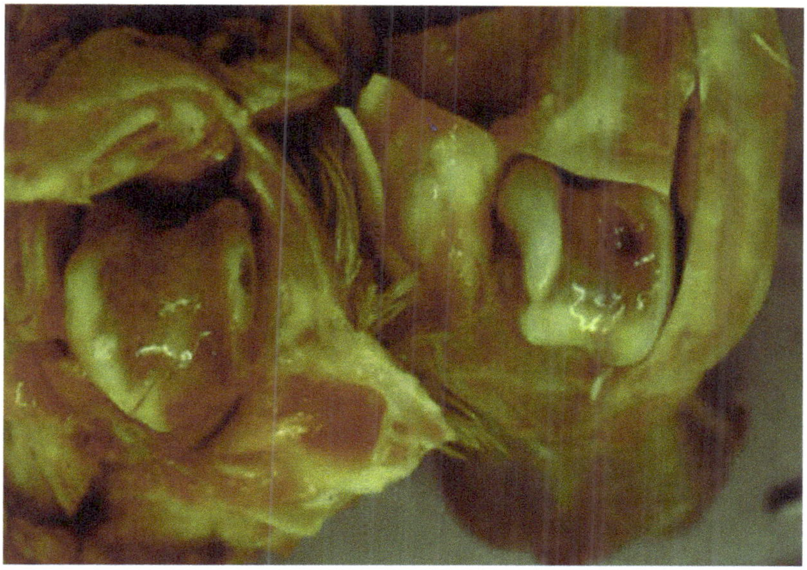

Fig. 15i.6. Erosion of articular cartilage in the hock joint. (Author's own photograph.)

around point of lay, have never satisfactorily been explained unless there is persistence of virus in some organ which is reactivated by hormonal action at sexual maturity. Broiler breeds have been shown to be more susceptible than light breeds. Exacerbating factors in the joints can be *Mycoplasma synoviae* (see Chapter 14viii, this volume), *Escherichia coli* (see Chapter 14ii, this volume) and *Staphylococcus aureus* (see Chapter 14ix, this volume). Immunosuppressive viruses, in particular, infectious bursal disease (see Chapter 15v, this volume) and chicken anaemia viruses (see Chapter 15xi, this volume) can result in more severe disease and increased mortalities.

15i.7 Diagnosis

While the lameness and joint swellings are characteristic, they are not diagnostic and may resemble similar lesions caused by *M. synoviae* or *S. aureus*. Diagnosis depends on detection of virus in the affected tissues. This can be achieved by isolation from joint tissue or swabs in cell culture such as chick embryo liver cells, when multinuclear syncytia are produced, or in chick embryos, which causes death and liver lesions. Identification of virus then depends on virus neutralization, electron microscopy or PCR. In the early stages of infection, immunostaining can be effective on joint sections. It must be remembered that reoviruses occur harmlessly in the intestine of most birds, so detection in the gut is unlikely to be significant.

Once the presence of virus is detected, genetic typing of the σC protein is undertaken for epidemiological purposes.

Reovirus antibodies can be detected in serum by virus neutralization or more commonly by ELISA, although interpretation of results may be difficult in view of the common occurrence of reoviruses in healthy chicken flocks. Serological monitoring is helpful in monitoring vaccine uptake.

15i.8 Viral Arthritis in Turkeys

Until 2012, it was accepted that viral arthritis was a disease of chickens and attempts to induce similar hock joint disease in turkeys with the chicken viruses had no effect. About that time, first reports appeared describing disease in 14 week or older turkeys in Iowa, Minnesota, North Dakota, South Dakota, Arizona and Missouri of lameness with swollen joints, closely resembling viral arthritis, from which reoviruses were isolated. These viruses proved serologically different from the common chicken types and furthermore, commercial vaccines against the chicken strains were ineffective against experimental infection with them in turkeys. Their sudden appearance cannot be explained except by suggesting that they arose through genetic reassortment.

15i.9 Control

Avian reovirus infections (but not necessarily disease) are ubiquitous. The virus can be transmitted both vertically and horizontally and, because of its resistance to inactivation, may be frequently carried by mechanical means. In view of these properties, maintaining freedom from infection in modern intensively housed chicken flocks appears to be virtually impossible. Though the main approach to control of viral arthritis in chickens is vaccination, good management and biosecurity procedures including the use of validated disinfectants which minimize reovirus infections, especially in young chickens, is essential.

For many years reovirus vaccines were derived from the American S1133 strain but because of the emergence of many variants in different parts of the world, relevant vaccines have been developed for local use. Vaccines of one serotype may give poor or no protection against other types. Reovirus vaccination of breeding stock can be done with live or inactivated vaccines or combinations of both to protect the progeny. Inactivated vaccines are more efficacious if preceded by the use of live vaccines. Care is needed if live reovirus vaccine is given simultaneously with Marek's disease vaccine, since the former may interfere with the latter. More recent approaches include *in ovo* vaccination and incorporation of reovirus genes into an engineered Newcastle disease vaccine which confers protection against both infections.

15i.10 Further Reading

Egaña-Labrin, S., Hauck, R., Figueroa, A., Stoute, S., Shivaprasad, H.L., *et al.* (2019) Genotypic characterization of emerging avian reovirus genetic variants in California. *Scientific Reports*, 9, 9351.

Jones, R.C. (2000) Avian reovirus infections. *Revue Scientifique et Technique* 19, 614–25.

Jones, R.C. (2013) Reovirus infections. In: Swayne, D.E. (editor-in-chief) *Diseases of Poultry*. Wiley-Blackwell, Danvers, Massachusetts, pp. 351–373.

Sellers, H.S. (2017) Current limitations in control of viral arthritis and tenosynovitis caused by avian reoviruses in commercial poultry. *Veterinary Microbiology* 206, 152–156.

Sharafeldin, T.A., Mor, S.K., Bekele, A.Z., Verma, H., Goyal, S.M., *et al.* (2014) The role of avian reoviruses in turkey tenosynovitis/arthritis. *Avian Pathology* 43, 371–378.

15ii Infectious Avian Encephalomyelitis

Richard C. Jones*

Institute of Infection, Veterinary and Ecological Sciences, University of Liverpool, Leahurst Campus, Neston, Cheshire, UK

15ii.1 Introduction

Infectious avian encephalomyelitis (IAE) is a viral nervous disease of young chicks, turkeys, Japanese quail, pheasants and pigeons. Turkeys are less susceptible to natural infection and develop a milder disease than chickens. Ducklings and guinea fowl are susceptible to experimental infection. Neurological signs result from infection of the central nervous system with a picornavirus. Traditionally, the disease has been known as 'epidemic tremor' though this is not the most appropriate name since tremor may be transient and not affect all birds. There is a very strong age-linked susceptibility since clinical signs are seen in chicks between the ages of 1 and 5 weeks. In adults, the disease is asymptomatic, resulting in a loss in egg production of not usually more than 5%, lasting no more than 2–3 weeks. The virus is egg transmitted.

15ii.2 Aetiology

The causative virus is Tremovirus A in the genus *Tremovirus* of the family *Picornaviridae* which are tiny, robust RNA viruses (Fig. 15ii.1).

It exists as a single serotype though there are variations in tissue tropism. Natural field strains are enterotropic with faecal shedding and cause nervous signs in chicks. A well-known embryo-adapted strain is neurotropic and has been used to determine virus-neutralizing antibodies in chick sera using chick embryo infection models. Infection occurs via vertical transmission from the infected hen to the embryo, and horizontal transmission via the faecal–oral route from chicks to hatch mates. If a breeder flock becomes infected during egg production, the virus is vertically transmitted to the offspring, and a major outbreak occurs. The virus is very resistant away from the host and may survive in the environment in faeces and fomites for several weeks.

15ii.3 Disease

Disease is usually initiated by vertical transmission from an infected flock for 3–4 weeks and some of the progeny chicks develop signs after hatching. Some of these chicks will die but virus will spread to hatch mates within the hatchery and cause a second bout of mortalities after about 2–4 weeks. The episode may be over when the birds are 5 weeks old. There is no convincing evidence of a carrier state, though there may be prolonged excretion of virus in some individuals. Frequently, disease is seen in a series of flocks hatched from the same breeder flock.

The incubation period in horizontally infected chicks may be 2–7 days, and those infected as embryos will show signs within a week. Clinical signs will comprise depression, ataxia, tremors during the first week ('epidemic tremor' – not to be confused with trembling when chicks are exposed to low temperature), prostration and paralysis (Fig. 15ii.2).

Tremor can be detected by cupping the chick in the hands. Badly affected chicks may be trampled on, while those with mild signs may recover. Some of the survivors develop cataract lesions in the eyes. Morbidity is usually about 15% but may be as high as 50%, and mortalities of a similar level will be seen in two waves, according to the method of infection. Fresh cases are rarely seen in chicks over 5 weeks of age. In hens with some immunity, chick mortalities will be lower.

*jonesrc@liverpool.ac.uk

© CAB International 2021. *Poultry Health: A Guide for Professionals* (P. Barrow *et al.*)
DOI: 10.1079/9781789245042.0015

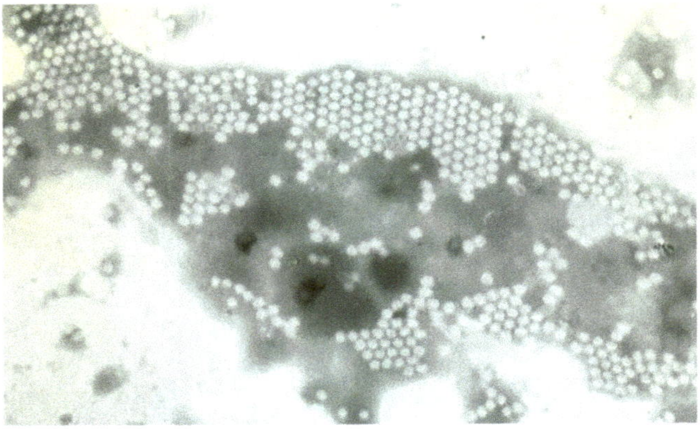

Fig. 15ii.1. Electron microscope image of IAE picornavirus virions. Negative staining. ×25,000. (Author's own image.)

Fig. 15ii.2. Prostrate chicks affected with IAE. (Author's own image.)

In egg-laying birds, production may drop about 5–10% but return to expected levels after about 2 weeks. The fall in egg production is not accompanied by a deterioration in shell quality. Hatchability in breeders may be reduced by 5%.

15.ii.4 Clinical Picture and Lesions

There are no gross lesions with IAE in affected chicks, though whitish foci are sometimes observed in the proventriculus. Lens opacity occurs in some birds (Fig. 15ii.3).

Histological examination is necessary to show the microscopic effects of IAE. The changes in the brain and spinal cord are particularly important for diagnosis. These consist of degeneration and necrosis

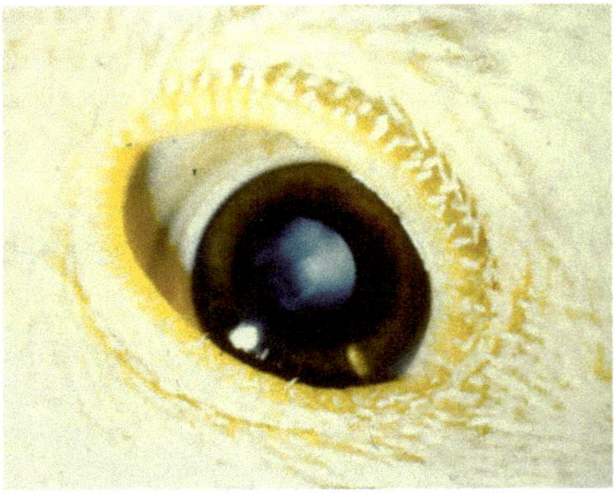

Fig. 15ii.3. Eye of a chick affected with IAE, showing opacity of the lens. (Author's own image.)

of neurons, perivascular lymphocytic cuffing and gliosis with formation of glial nodules. In the cerebellum, there are areas of necrosis or loss of Purkinje cells and replacement by glial nodules that extend into the molecular layer of the grey matter. Neuronal lesions of central chromatolysis, shrinkage and increased basophilia, satellitosis, and neuronophagia are found in neuron clusters in the brain stem, *arbor vitae* of the cerebellum and lateral horn (grey matter) of the spinal cord. Central chromatolysis of neurons is characterized by rounding of the cell contour and displacement of Nissl granules to the periphery. Dorsal root ganglia have multifocal nodular collections of lymphocytes.

A common microscopic lesion outside the central nervous system (CNS) is diffuse or nodular lymphocytic infiltration in the gizzard muscle, muscular layer of the oesophagus and proventriculus, myocardium and pancreas. Apart from cataracts, microscopic lesions generally are not found in infected adults unless they are showing nervous signs, in which case they will have CNS lesions similar to those in young birds.

15ii.5 Diagnosis

Diagnosis of IAE is based on detailed history of the parent flock, the appearance of typical clinical signs in young birds and characteristic histopathologic lesions in the brain and spinal cord as described. The diagnosis can be confirmed by isolation and identification of the virus. Tissues collected for virus detection in fertile eggs must include the brain and duodenum with the pancreas. Demonstration of IAE viral antigen in the brain, spinal cord, and other tissues by immunofluorescent or immunoperoxidase staining (see Chapter 22, this volume) is a reliable and relatively rapid method of diagnosis and can be effective when applied to brain smears.

For differential diagnosis, other neurological disorders in young chicks must be considered, and include bacterial or mycotic encephalitis caused by *Salmonellae* (see Chapter 14iv, this volume) or *Aspergillus* (see Chapter 12, this volume). Marek's disease (see Chapter 15xiii, this volume) and Newcastle disease (see Chapter 15viii, this volume) will also cause neurological signs. Rickets and nutritional deficiency (see Chapter 13, this volume) may also be borne in mind, although the clinical manifestations of these diseases differ from those in IAE.

In adults, serologic testing of acute and convalescent sera to demonstrate an increase in antibody titres helps establish a diagnosis and, in particular, to differentiate from other more important causes of loss of egg production such as infectious bronchitis (see Chapter 15x, this volume), egg drop syndrome (see Chapter 15iii, this volume) and Newcastle disease.

15ii.6 Control

Since IAE is primarily a disease of young chicks and the virus is egg transmitted, the main approach to control is to vaccinate broiler-breeder pullets, normally at least 4 weeks before the onset of lay, so the chicks are protected by maternal antibodies. The commercial vaccine is a chick embryo-attenuated live enterotropic virus given in the drinking water after 8 weeks of age. The vaccine is usually combined with a fowlpox vaccine and can be given by wing web stab. There is also a recombinant ILT/IAE vectored vaccine (see also Chapter 15iv, this volume). The vaccines give long-lasting immunity.

Since the tremovirus is particularly stable away from the host, it is essential that strict biosecurity measures are applied, in particular, disinfection of premises after a disease outbreak with destruction of carcasses.

15ii.7 Further Reading

Abdul-Aziz, T. (2018) Avian encephalomyelitis. In Aiello, S.E. (ed) *The Merck Veterinary Manual*, 12th edn. Merck and Co., Kenilworth, NJ.

Suarez, D.L. (2020) Avian encephalomyelitis. In: Swayne, D.E. (editor-in-chief) *Diseases of Poultry*, 14th edn. Wiley-Blackwell, Danvers, Massachusetts, pp. 520–527.

15iii Adenoviruses

JOAN A. SMYTH*

Department of Pathobiology and Veterinary Science, College of Agriculture, Health and Natural Resources, University of Connecticut, Storrs, Connecticut, USA

15iii.1 Introduction

In the past, all of the adenoviruses of poultry were classified as members of the genus *Aviadenovirus* of the family *Adenoviridae*. Based upon DNA sequence information, the adenoviruses that infect poultry are now found in three of the five genera currently in the family *Adenoviridae*. Thus, the 12 former Group I adenoviruses (FAdV-1 to FAdV-8a and FAdV-8b to FAdV-11) remain within the genus *Aviadenovirus* (see Table 15iii.1), the former Group II avian adenoviruses (marble spleen disease virus, turkey haemorrhagic enteritis virus and avian splenomegaly virus) are now classified as one species *Turkey siadenovirus A* and have been moved to a new genus, *Siadenovirus,* while the former Group III avian adenoviruses (the egg drop syndrome '76 viruses) now belong to one species, *Duck atadenovirus A*, in the genus *Atadenovirus* (see Table 15iii.1). Features that are common to all of the adenoviruses of poultry are considered collectively in this chapter.

The economically important diseases caused by the different adenoviruses are quite distinct, so the clinical signs and pathological features of each major disease are considered by species and disease syndrome.

15iii.2 Importance

Adenovirus infections are ubiquitous in poultry. Given the facts that disease occurs much less commonly than infection, and, with a few notable exceptions, experimental infections with adenoviruses usually result in mild or inapparent disease, most of the adenoviruses of poultry have been considered insignificant as pathogens. Among the notable exceptions are the viruses that cause turkey haemorrhagic enteritis (THE), marble spleen disease of pheasants (MSD), quail bronchitis (QB), egg drop syndrome '76 (EDS'76) in chickens, inclusion body hepatitis (IBH) and hydropericardium/hepatitis syndrome (HPS) in chickens, and gizzard erosion and ulceration syndrome (GEU) in chickens. THE, MSD, QB, IBH and HPS are diseases that are usually associated with high mortality rates. In contrast, EDS'76 is important because it causes production of abnormally shelled eggs, leading to a loss of settable hatching eggs for the broiler and breeding industries, as well as a loss of table eggs produced by the commercial egg sector. GEU has emerged as an important cause of subclinical losses as well as low-grade mortality in chickens of all ages. There are sporadic reports of some of the adenoviruses contributing to, or causing, a variety of other diseases e.g. an EDS'76 virus (*Duck atadenovirus A*) caused an outbreak of severe respiratory disease in geese, but such sporadic conditions are beyond the scope of this chapter. Several adenoviruses have been reported to cause immunosuppression.

Adenoviruses are common contaminants in cell cultures and egg derived materials, which is of importance to vaccine manufacturers and diagnostic laboratories (see below).

15iii.3 Viruses, Transmission and Distribution

The adenoviruses are non-enveloped icosahedral DNA viruses measuring 70–90 nm in diameter. The adenovirus genome is a linear double stranded DNA molecule that varies in length from ~26 kb (siadenoviruses), ~30 kb (atadenoviruses), and ~43–45 kb (aviadenoviruses).

*joan.smyth@uconn.edu

 © CAB International 2021. *Poultry Health: A Guide for Professionals* (P. Barrow *et al.*)
DOI: 10.1079/9781789245042.0015

Table 15iii.1. Classification of the adenoviruses of poultry and the diseases they produce.

Genus	Species	Serotypes	Disease
Aviadenovirus (formerly Group I avian adenoviruses)	*Fowl aviadenovirus A*	Fowl adenovirus 1 (FAdV-1)	GEU in chickens, quail bronchitis
	Fowl aviadenovirus B	Fowl adenovirus 5 (FAdV-5)	ND
	Fowl aviadenovirus C	Fowl adenovirus 4 (FAdV-4)	HPS/IBH in chickens, ducks and geese
		Fowl adenovirus 10 (FAdV-10)	IBH in pigeons
	Fowl aviadenovirus D	Fowl adenovirus 2 (FAdV-2)	IBH in chickens
		Fowl adenovirus 3 (FAdV-3)	ND
		Fowl adenovirus 9 (FAdV-9)	non-pathogenic
		Fowl adenovirus 11 (FAdV-11)	IBH in chickens
	Fowl aviadenovirus E	Fowl adenovirus 6 (FAdV-6)	IBH in chickens, pigeons and falcons
		Fowl adenovirus 7 (FAdV-7)	Immunosuppression
		Fowl adenovirus 8a (FAdV-8a)	IBH in chickens
		Fowl adenovirus 8b (FAdV-8b)	IBH in chickens
	Duck aviadenovirus B	Duck adenovirus 2 (DAdV-2)	mortality
		Duck adenovirus 3 (DAdV-3) proposed	Swelling and haemorrhagic liver disease in ducks
	Goose aviadenovirus A	Goose adenovirus 1	ND
		Goose adenovirus 2	ND
		Goose adenovirus 4	ND
		Goose adenovirus 5	ND
	Turkey aviadenovirus B	Turkey adenovirus 1 (TAdV-1)	ND
		Turkey adenovirus 2 (TAdV-2)	ND
	Turkey aviadenovirus C	Turkey adenovirus 4 (TAdV-4)	ND
	Turkey aviadenovirus D	Turkey adenovirus 5 (TAdV-5)	ND
		Turkey adenovirus 3 *(proposed)*	ND
	Pigeon aviadenovirus A	Pigeon adenovirus 1 (PiAdV-1)	ND
	Pigeon aviadenovirus B	Pigeon adenovirus 2 (PiAdV-2)	One of many agents in young pigeon disease syndrome
Siadenovirus (formerly Group II avian adenoviruses)	*Turkey siadenovirus A*	Turkey adenovirus 3 (TADV-3)	THE, MSD, avian spenomegaly
	Pigeon siadenoviruses	Pigeon adenovirus 4 and 5 (*proposed*)	ND
Atadenovirus (formerly Group III avian adenoviruses)	*Duck atadenovirus A*	Duck adenovirus 1 (DAdV-1)	EDS'76 in chickens, respiratory disease in geese

EDS'76 – egg drop syndrome '76
GEU – gizzard erosion and ulceration syndrome
HPS – hydropericardium syndrome
IBH – inclusion body hepatitis
MSD – marble spleen disease
ND – not yet proven to cause disease
THE – turkey haemorrhagic enteritis

All of the adenoviruses can be transmitted vertically and horizontally, and some strains can become latent. Vertical transmission and latency are of particular importance with respect to *Duck atadenovirus* A which causes EDS' 76 in chickens, as the virus can remain latent until hens reach sexual maturity and those hens either fail to reach peak egg production and/or produce abnormally shelled eggs. Vertical transmission leads to the relatively common inadvertent finding of adenoviruses in embryonated materials used for virus isolation procedures or vaccine production; indeed, it has long been suspected that the virus that causes EDS'76 in chickens was introduced to chickens through a contaminated vaccine. Adenoviruses are frequently present in droppings, and in the case of *Duck atadenovirus A* (the virus that causes EDS'76), the virus effectively spreads horizontally through eggs and materials used for handling eggs e.g. egg trays and trolleys. Many of the adenoviruses can replicate in the respiratory tract and so the potential for aerosol transmission exists. In fact, there has been a recent report of aerosol transmission of FAdV-4, the cause of HPS.

Adenoviruses of most types have been found in most countries that have examined for them. Interestingly, *Duck atadenovirus A* infection and egg drop syndrome were only reported in chickens in the USA for the first time in 2019.

15iii.4 Clinical Signs, Post-mortem and Histological Findings in the Major Adenoviral Diseases of Poultry

As mentioned above, many of the adenoviruses that infect poultry produce asymptomatic infections, but some of the adenoviruses are primary pathogens that cause significant disease. The major primary disease syndromes are discussed separately below, in the order of diseases in chickens, turkeys, pheasants, quail, pigeons, ducks and geese. The current classification of the adenoviruses of poultry and the disease syndromes with which they are associated are summarised in Table 15iii.1.

15iii.4.1 Major adenoviral diseases in chickens

Inclusion body hepatitis

Several types of aviadenoviruses can cause IBH. FAdV-2, -8A, -8B and -11 (see Table 15iii.1) are the most commonly reported isolates, but there is geographical variation in prevalence.

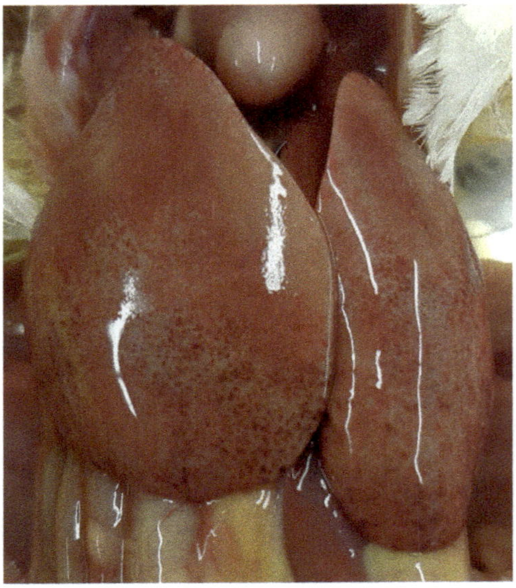

Fig. 15iii.1. Liver in a 10-day-old broiler with inclusion body hepatitis. The liver is enlarged and pale. (Courtesy of Grant Hayes.)

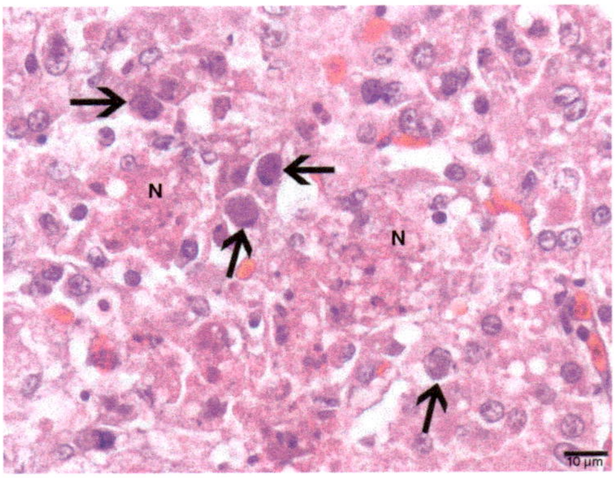

Fig. 15iii.2. Foci of necrosis (N) and numerous large basophilic intranuclear inclusions (arrows) within hepatocytes in a 3-week-old broiler chicken with inclusion body hepatitis. Haematoxylin and eosin stain (H&E). Bar = 10 µm. (Author's own photograph.)

IBH is most commonly seen in broiler chickens between 2 and 5 weeks of age but it has occurred in younger and older chickens, and in layers and breeders. Affected chickens may be dull, reluctant to move or may be found dead. Mortality rate is commonly between 2 and 10% but up to 30% has been reported.

On post-mortem examination, the liver is the consistently affected organ. Commonly it is pale pink to tan in colour, mildly to moderately enlarged and may have petechial to ecchymotic haemorrhages (Fig. 15iii.1).

Histologically there is multifocal hepatic necrosis with intranuclear inclusions within hepatocytes; the inclusions are usually most evident at the periphery of the necrotic foci (Fig. 15iii.2).

In the first described outbreaks of IBH, the nuclear inclusions were eosinophilic while in outbreaks over the last three decades, basophilic inclusions are usually found. The reason for this difference is unknown. Other findings may include mild hydropericardium, pale kidneys and necrotizing pancreatitis with basophilic intranuclear inclusions similar to those in the liver.

Hydropericardium/hepatitis syndrome

HPS is caused by virulent FAdV-4 strains. Disease outbreaks most commonly affect 3–6-week-old broiler chickens, but as with IBH, there have been some outbreaks in layers and broiler breeders. This disease has many similarities to IBH, but the disease course is more acute, mortality rates are much higher (20–80%), and hydropericardium with accumulation of up to 10 ml of serous fluid in the pericardial sac is a striking gross feature. Histologically, as in IBH, there is a marked necrotizing hepatitis with intranuclear inclusion bodies in hepatocytes. Additionally, there is viral tropism for lymphoid tissues with degeneration of lymphoid organs and lymphocyte depletion.

Gizzard erosion and ulceration syndrome

GEU caused by FAdV-1 has emerged in the last 20 years as a significant cause of economic losses in broilers and has also been reported in pullets during rear and in broiler breeder and commercial egg laying flocks. This disease can occur sporadically or as outbreaks following vertical transmission from an actively infected breeding flock. Losses are due to reduced growth rate, increased mortality rates and condemnation of affected gizzards in the slaughterhouse. Affected gizzards may be dilated and/or contain brown sanguineous fluid. There are variably sized brown–black discoloured areas of koilin, with erosions, ulceration and inflammation of the koilin (Fig. 15iii.3) that extends to the deeper mucosa (Fig. 15iii.4).

Basophilic intranuclear inclusions typical of adenoviruses are commonly, but not always, detectable in the glandular epithelial cells upon histological examination (Fig. 15iii.5).

Egg drop syndrome '76

EDS'76 is caused by *Duck atadenovirus A*. In contrast to most other adenoviral diseases of poultry, infection does not cause death of chickens. Clinical signs can include transient dullness and watery droppings, which are actually the result of excessive fluid secretion from the oviduct, but the main sign is either failure to reach peak egg production in flocks that were infected vertically, or the production of pale, thin-shelled, soft-shelled or shell-less eggs (Fig. 15iii.6) by laying flocks that have become infected horizontally.

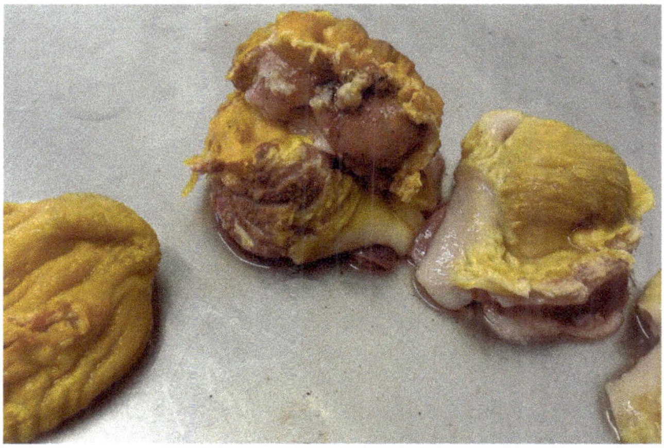

Fig. 15iii.3. Gizzards from approximately 27-day-old broiler chicken with gizzard erosion and ulceration syndrome (GEU). There are multiple erosions and ulcers in all, with extensive loss of the koilin layer in the middle gizzard. (Courtesy of Henrietta Kodilinye-Sims.)

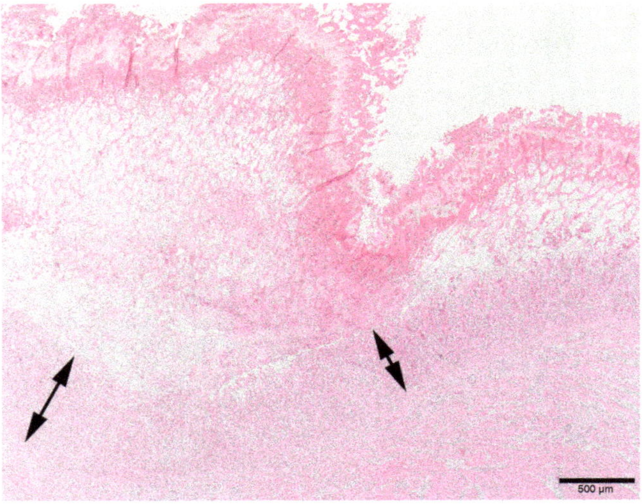

Fig. 15iii.4. Histological section of gizzard from a young layer chicken with GEU. The mucosa is denoted by double-headed arrows. There is thickening and vacuolation of the overlying koilin layer due to inflammation and degeneration. This is most pronounced at the left side of the image where there is also thickening and inflammation of the mucosa. H&E. Bar = 500 µm. (Author's own photograph.)

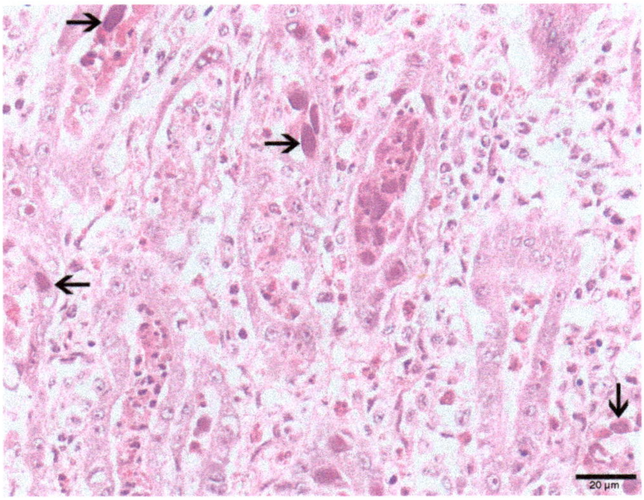

Fig. 15iii.5. Higher magnification of the gizzard in Fig. 15iii.4. Several mucosal glands contain a mixture of sloughed epithelial cells and degenerate inflammatory cells, and there are areas of attenuation of the lining epithelium. Several of the glandular epithelial cells have markedly enlarged nuclei containing basophilic intranuclear inclusions (arrows). The lamina propria is expanded by a mixture of heterophils, mononuclear inflammatory cells and oedema. H&E. Bar = 20 µm. (Author's own photograph.)

Egg production rate can drop precipitously, reflecting simultaneous infection of a large number of birds, but in such flocks, recovery is usually faster. Misshapen shelled eggs are not a feature of EDS'76 virus infection, and if present, then infection or co-infection by infectious bronchitis virus must be considered (see Chapter 15x, this volume). In the absence of co-infecting pathogens, flock egg production usually recovers, but it can take 4–10 weeks for the virus to pass through all birds in large flocks.

Mucosal oedema, heterophilic exudate and numerous basophilic intranuclear inclusion bodies

Fig. 15iii.6. Eggs produced by brown egg layers infected with *Duck atadenovirus* A (egg drop syndrome virus). There is a mixture of normal eggs, cracked eggs, pale eggs, soft shelled eggs (SS), shell-less eggs (S) and egg membranes (M). Note that misshapen or ridged eggs are not a feature of a drop syndrome '76. (Author's own photograph.)

develop in the surface epithelium of the shell gland, but as the changes are transient, such lesions are rarely found in hens in naturally infected flocks. This is due to difficulty in identifying recently infected birds within a large flock. Infected hens have seroconverted by the time they start to produce the abnormal eggs, and this can be useful diagnostically (see below).

15iii.4.2 Adenoviral diseases in turkeys

Turkey haemorrhagic enteritis

This is an important disease of turkeys that usually occurs between 6 and 12 weeks of age. It is caused by *Turkey siadenovirus A*. Mortality rate may approach 60% but is more usually in the range of 10–15%. Affected turkeys may be depressed and pass heavily blood-stained droppings. At post-mortem examination, the carcass may appear pale and there is diffuse haemorrhagic enteritis (Fig. 15iii.7) and a mottled spleen (Fig. 15iii.7), which is usually enlarged.

Large lightly basophilic intranuclear inclusion bodies are found in cells in the spleen (Fig. 15iii.8) and in the lamina propria of the intestine.

Aviadenovirus associated diseases in turkeys

Aviadenoviruses have been isolated from turkeys with respiratory disease, poult enteritis complex and inclusion body hepatitis. However, the pathogenicity of aviadenoviruses in turkeys remains unclear at present.

15iii.4.3 Adenoviral diseases in pheasants

Marble spleen disease of pheasants

MSD is an important disease of pheasants that usually strikes between 3 and 8 months of age. It is also caused by *Turkey siadenovirus A* (Table 15iii.1). The mortality rate can approach 100% when flock management is poor. Affected pheasants are often found moribund or dead, but depression and/or ruffled feathers may be noted. At post-mortem examination, a striking feature is an enlarged red/grey mottled spleen (which gives rise to the name of the disease) and marked pulmonary congestion and oedema; the lungs may appear almost black. The disease can be confirmed histologically by the presence of the characteristic pale basophilic adenoviral inclusions in the spleen that are similar in appearance to those found in turkeys with THE (Fig. 15iii.8).

15iii.4.4 Adenoviral diseases in quail

Quail bronchitis

QB is an important highly contagious respiratory disease of young bobwhite quail, caused by FAdV-1

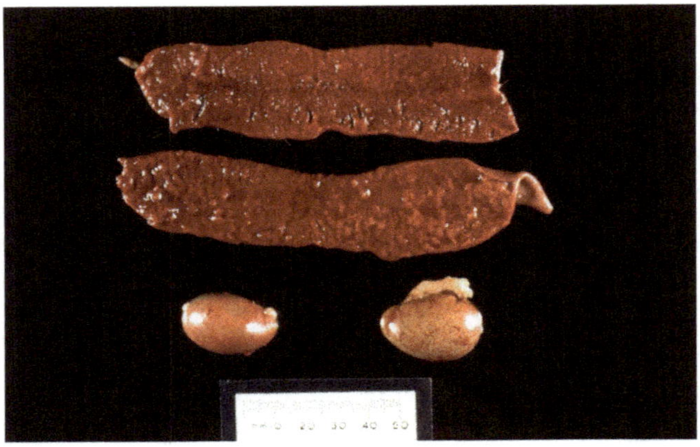

Fig. 15iii.7. Small intestine (mucosal surfaces) and spleen from two 6-week-old turkeys that died from turkey haemorrhagic enteritis. Note the diffusely haemorrhagic mucosa and the pale mottled spleens. (Author's own photograph.)

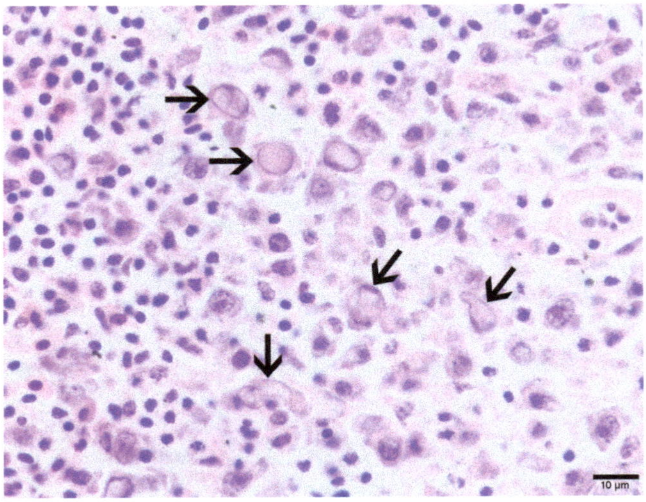

Fig. 15iii.8. Spleen from a 10-week-old turkey that died from turkey haemorrhagic enteritis (THE). There are several cells with enlarged nuclei (arrows) that contain very pale basophilic inclusions that marginate the chromatin. These large pale inclusions are typical of those seen in THE, and in the spleen of pheasants with marble spleen disease. (Author's own photograph.)

(*Fowl aviadenovirus A*). The disease occurs worldwide and mortality rates in excess of 50% have been reported in quail less than 6 weeks old. The virus causes necrotizing tracheitis and bronchitis with typical adenoviral intranuclear inclusions developing in tracheal and bronchial epithelium. Oculonasal discharge and pneumonia also commonly develop. Multifocal necrosis and occasional intranuclear inclusion bodies may also occur in the liver and spleen.

Inclusion body hepatitis

FAdV-1 has been reported to cause inclusion body hepatitis in quail.

15iii.4.5 Adenoviral diseases in pigeons

Inclusion body hepatitis

FAdV-6 and -10 have been recovered from herpesvirus-free pigeons that had IBH. The association (if any) of PiAdV-1 and PiAdV-2 (Table 15iii.1) infection and IBH is less clear. Gross and histological lesions in pigeons with IBH can resemble those of IBH in chickens. However, it should be noted that herpesvirus infections may also cause IBH in pigeons that is virtually indistinguishable from that caused by adenoviruses.

Classical adenovirosis of pigeons

This syndrome was first recognized in Belgium. It was reported as an enteric disease of young racing pigeons, so it is not further discussed in this chapter.

15iii.4.6 Adenoviral diseases in ducks

Outbreaks of hydropericardium syndrome caused by FAdV-4 that resembles the disease seen in chickens, have been reported in ducks in China.

A novel disease was reported in Muscovy ducks in China in 2018–19. This was characterized by swollen tan-coloured liver and kidneys with petechiation. It has been reproduced experimentally using duck adenovirus 3 (*Duck aviadenovirus B*) isolated from naturally occurring outbreaks of the disease. Morbidity ranged from 40 to 55%, and mortality ranged between 35 and 43%.

15iii.4.7 Adenoviral diseases in geese

Hydropericardium syndrome associated with FAdV-4 has recently been reported in geese in China.

An outbreak of respiratory disease in geese was attributed to *Duck atadenovirus A* infection.

15iii.5 Diagnosis

15iii.5.1 General approaches

As adenovirus infections are so common in poultry, and are often asymptomatic, detection of adenovirus by PCR, antigen capture or virus isolation, and/or detection of antibodies against adenoviruses other than EDS'76, is insufficient for disease diagnosis.

With the exception of IBH in pigeons and EDS'76 in chickens (see specific diagnostic approaches below), the adenoviral diseases described above can usually be diagnosed by histopathological examination of affected organs because of the presence of characteristic inclusion bodies within the lesions. For IBH in chickens, HPS, quail bronchitis, THE and MSD, such inclusions are usually readily detected, especially if several of the moribund and/or freshly dead birds are examined.

In the past, confirmatory testing for THE and MSD was performed by agar gel immunoprecipitation or fluorescent antibody testing for detection of antigen in affected tissues or virus isolation, but nowadays, PCR or other molecular diagnostic techniques such as *in situ* hybridization are usually employed, especially if the specific type of adenovirus involved needs to be determined (see Chapter 22, this volume).

15iii.5.2 Specific diagnostic approaches needed for some adenoviral diseases

Diagnosis of adenoviral IBH in pigeons

As mentioned in Section 15iii.4.5 'Clinical signs, post-mortem and histological findings', IBH in pigeons can be caused by both adenoviruses and herpesviruses and it is very hard if not impossible to distinguish between the two based on histological appearance alone. Thus, once intra-hepatocytic inclusions have been identified in pigeons, it is important to perform additional testing on the liver to definitively determine which type of virus was involved.

Diagnosis of EDS'76

EDS'76 virus infection may be diagnosed in non-vaccinated flocks by the detection of specific antibodies. Serological testing is best done on birds that are laying the abnormal eggs, as infected hens have seroconverted by the time they start to produce the abnormal eggs, a fact that can be used to diagnostic advantage in caged birds. Cages in which hens have produced abnormal eggs can be identified by inspection before the belts are switched on. All hens in a few such cages should be bled. If the problem is due to EDS'76 infection, then at least some of the hens will have detectable antibody. In flocks housed on the floor, blood samples should be collected from 20–30 hens distributed throughout the flock. Many poultry breeding companies collect and store bloods harvested at 16–18 weeks of age, and these can be tested retrospectively to determine pre-lay antibody status. Seroconversion during lay together with failure to reach peak egg production or a drop in egg production with production of pale, thin-shelled, soft-shelled and shell-less eggs enable a diagnosis of EDS. Detection of the virus either by PCR or virus isolation is also useful because chickens are not the natural host for this virus.

15iii.6 Control, Prevention and Treatment of Disease

Adenoviruses are very resistant viruses that can be transmitted both vertically and horizontally. This makes prevention of infection very challenging. Since the virus that causes EDS'76 is actually a duck virus that apparently was inadvertently introduced into chicken flocks, it is possible to eradicate this infection from chickens. However, where infection has become endemic in chickens, or if there is a risk of exposure to waterfowl (the virus is commonly found in ducks and geese), vaccination is often practiced. EDS'76 vaccines have been available for many years and when administered before onset of lay, they are very effective in preventing disease. Vaccines are available for prevention of THE in turkeys, and there are reports of successful use of avirulent vaccines to prevent MSD in pheasants. Some of the live THE vaccines are reported to cause some degree of immunosuppression. Before vaccines were available, THE was treated successfully by subcutaneous or intramuscular injection of 0.5–1.0 ml of serum derived from flocks that recovered from an outbreak.

Until the emergence of HPS in Pakistan, India and China, and IBH in Australia there had been relatively limited interest in developing vaccines against the aviadenoviruses, mainly because infections were widespread and the viruses were not considered to be major pathogens of poultry. Inactivated vaccines derived from natural outbreaks of IBH or HPS, or from *in vitro* grown viruses are available in some countries. Such vaccines carry major risks should inactivation be incomplete. Laboratory grown virus vaccines are more costly to produce. Also problematic for successful vaccination is that several serotypes can be involved in producing disease, for example, IBH can be caused by several types of FAdVs. A live vaccine based on FAdV-8b has been in use in Australia for many years, and at least some outbreaks of disease there in recent years have been due to FAdV-11. Wild-type aviadenoviruses have been used to vaccinate breeders with successful protection of the 14-day-old progeny, but again, use of virulent viruses carries risks e.g. inadvertent administration to susceptible flocks. There is now strong demand and effort to produce safer vaccines against FAdV-4, the cause of HPS.

15iii.7 Further Reading

Fitzgerald, S.D., Hess, M., Smyth, J.A., Rautenschlein, S., Mahsoub, H.M., *et al.* (2020) Adenovirus infections. In: Swayne, D.E., Boulianne, M., Logue, C.M., McDougald, L.R., Nair, V., and Suarez, D.L. (eds) *Diseases of Poultry*, 14th edn. Wiley-Blackwell, Ames, Iowa, pp. 321–363.

Harrach, B. (2021) Available adenovirus sequences. Available at: https://sites.google.com/site/adenoseq/.

International Committee on Taxonomy of Viruses (ICTV) (2018) Virus Taxonomy: 2018b Release. Available at: https://talk.ictvonline.org/taxonomy/.

Schachner, A., Matos, M., Grafl, B. and Hess, M. (2018) Fowl adenovirus-induced diseases and strategies for their control – a review on the current global situation. *Avian Pathology* 47, 111–126.

Smyth, J.A. and McFerran, J.B. (2000) Avian adenoviruses. *Revue Scientifique et Technique* 19, 589–601.

Smyth, J.A. and McNulty, M.S. (2008) Adenoviridae. In: Pattison, M., McMullin, P.F., Bradbury, J.M. and Alexander, D.A. (eds) *Poultry Diseases,* 6th edn. Elsevier, Oxford, UK, pp. 367–381.

15iv Infectious Laryngotracheitis

Richard C. Jones*

Institute of Infection, Veterinary and Ecological Sciences, University of Liverpool, Leahurst Campus, Neston, Cheshire, UK

15iv.1 Introduction

Infectious laryngotracheitis (ILT) is a highly contagious viral respiratory disease of chickens and pheasants resulting, in the most acute form, in apnoea with frequent high mortality, increased feed conversion and a transient fall in egg production and quality in layers. The disease is worldwide particularly affecting countries with intensively kept poultry, but has particular importance and is endemic in parts of the USA and Australia.

15iv.2 Aetiology

ILT is caused by a DNA virus, *Gallid herpesvirus-1 (Iltovirus)* (Fig. 15iv.1) which characteristically causes intranuclear inclusions in the trachea of affected birds and on the chorioallantoic membrane of fertile hens' eggs.

There is only one serotype but different strains can be differentiated by molecular methods. ILT virus, like other herpesviruses, becomes latent in the affected chicken where it remains for life. Under conditions of stress, the virus may be reactivated. The virus appears to spread more slowly than other respiratory viruses such as infectious bronchitis virus or Newcastle disease virus. The virus is not egg transmitted.

15iv.3 Disease

ILT is more commonly seen in older rather than younger birds and may be present in acute or mild forms. In the acute form, between 5–10 days after exposure, disease is characterized by rattling, coughing and extreme difficulty in breathing, with some birds dying through asphyxiation. The effort of clearing tracheal obstruction by neck extension causes blood and caseous material to be coughed up which stains the feathers, litter and walls of the house. Expectoration of blood is not found with any other respiratory disease of poultry and is pathognomonic and may be sufficient for a positive diagnosis. The acute form is likely to be accompanied by high mortality, sometimes exceeding 50%.

In the mild form, birds may show respiratory signs similar to other generally milder respiratory diseases such as infectious bronchitis, low virulence Newcastle disease or mycoplasma infection. There may be coughing, head shaking, lachrymation and general depression. Respiratory signs usually subside by 14 days of onset, though some individuals may show signs for longer, particularly if other respiratory pathogens are present.

In laying flocks, there may be a transient loss of production and egg quality with a return to normal when the disease has subsided. There is no apparent permanent effect on the oviduct as there is in, for example, infectious bronchitis. The virus appears to be a pathogen principally of the respiratory tract.

Birds that have recovered will carry latent virus throughout life in the trigeminal ganglia. This virus may be reactivated by stress such as movement, especially after mixing of a latently infected flock with new birds, and at the time of sexual maturity. Reactivated virus may not result in disease in the latently infected individuals but can cause disease after contact with previously unexposed birds. Live ILT vaccines have been shown to result in latency in the same way as virulent field viruses.

*jonesrc@liverpool.ac.uk

© CAB International 2021. *Poultry Health: A Guide for Professionals* (P. Barrow *et al.*)

DOI: 10.1079/9781789245042.0015

15iv.4 Diagnosis

An acute respiratory disease, often with significant mortality accompanied by the expectoration of blood and caseous material, is pathognomonic for acute ILT. No other respiratory disease of poultry shows such dramatic signs. Lachrymation and conjunctivitis are likely to be present. At autopsy, those birds dying from acute disease will show the presence of streaks and clots of blood and mucus in the trachea, frequently accompanied by variable amounts of solid caseous material, sometimes completely blocking the airway (Figs 15iv.2. and 15iv.3). Caseous material in the trachea can closely resemble the diphtheritic or 'wet' form of fowlpox (see Chapter 15xiv this volume) so the causative virus must be identified. The author has encountered at least one outbreak of ILT in which fowlpox virus was also detected in the trachea.

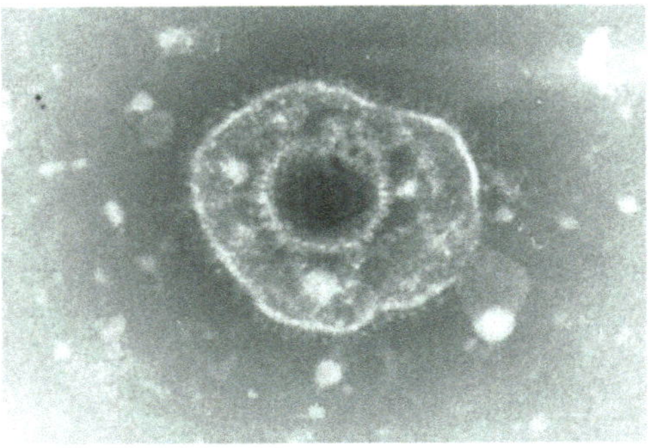

Fig. 15iv.1. ILT Herpesvirus virion. Electron microscope, negative staining. ×50,000. (Author's own image.)

In flocks with mild ILT, where disease is moderate, laboratory methods will be required to demonstrate the virus and confirm the diagnosis. In these cases, there may be excess amounts of mucus with only traces of blood or no blood. There may be clear or turbid nasal exudate. Sometimes, ILT may appear asymptomatic, and few signs are seen at autopsy.

Examination of histology of the tracheal epithelium of affected birds during the first few days of the disease allows the detection of epithelial cells containing blue-stained Cowdry type-A intranuclear inclusion bodies after haematoxylin and eosin (H&E) staining (Figs 15iv.4 and 15iv.5). These are pathognomonic but may be absent or hard to find later in the disease course. It is recommended that longitudinal sections are examined.

Immunostaining is also a rapid means of identifying the virus in sections or smears of infected tracheal epithelial cells in the early stages of infection. The nuclei of infected cells stain brightly due to the virus presence.

Where available, the use of negative staining by electron microscopy (EM) is a valuable method of recognizing the virus in tracheal scrapings (Fig. 15iv.1). This technique can allow the characteristic icosahedral herpesvirus to be seen within 20 min of receipt of clinical material. This is the only disease where herpesvirus can be detected in tracheal mucus. EM diagnosis is convenient and rapid where at least 3.0 $\log_{10}$ per gram of virus is present in the sample.

Isolation of virus may be achieved from respiratory tissues – mainly trachea and lung but also

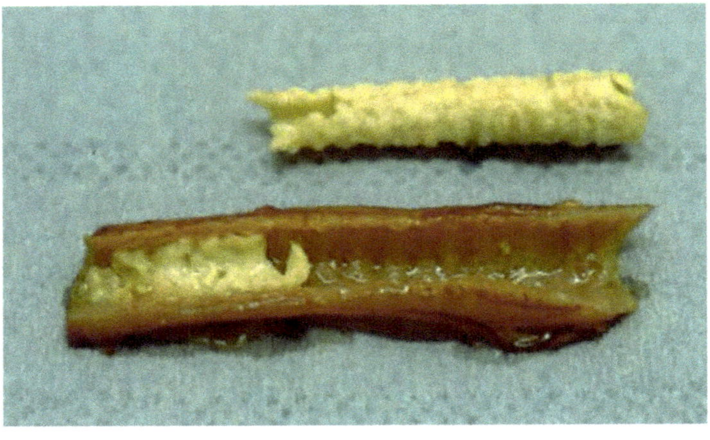

Fig. 15iv.2. Caseous material blocking the tracheal airway. Acute ILT. (Author's own image.)

conjunctiva. Supernatant from macerated tissue is inoculated onto the dropped chorioallantoic membrane (CAM) of fertile eggs after 11 days of embryonic development. After a further 3–4 days of incubation, the virus will cause the appearance of discrete pocks on the CAM. Sometimes, more than one passage may be necessary. Alternatively, ILT virus can be isolated on cell cultures prepared from chick embryo kidney or the more sensitive liver cells, where typical multinucleate syncytia are formed after 4–6 days incubation. Viruses isolated by these methods need further confirmation of identity by immunostaining or PCR. In all cases, the trachea is the best tissue for attempting virus detection as it is the primary site for viral replication.

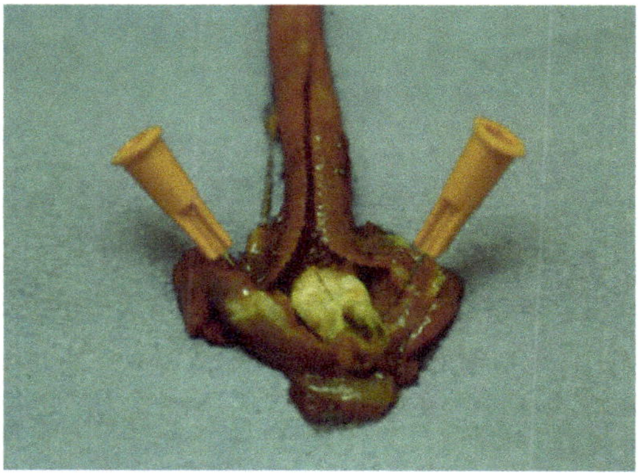

Fig. 15iv.3. Caseous mass in the larynx and blood in the trachea. Acute ILT. (Author's own image.)

Nowadays, molecular methods, and especially PCR, are used for identifying ILT virus in clinical samples and material after passage in cell culture or eggs. Single or multiple areas of the virus genome can be used, and field and vaccine strains can now be differentiated and classified in this way.

From time to time, other agents may be present in an outbreak of ILT, such as other respiratory viruses or mycoplasmas (see Chapter 14viii, this volume).

Antibodies to ILT virus can be detected by serum neutralization tests in cell culture or fertile eggs. Using either system is laborious and time-consuming, taking several days. Rapid screening of large numbers of serum samples is done conveniently and cheaply using commercially available ELISA kits. Serological tests can be used to monitor the success of vaccination though their value is limited in that they cannot distinguish between vaccinated and carrier birds. However, where recombinant ILT vaccines are administered, the use of glycoprotein-specific ELISAs would be able to differentiate the two types of antibody.

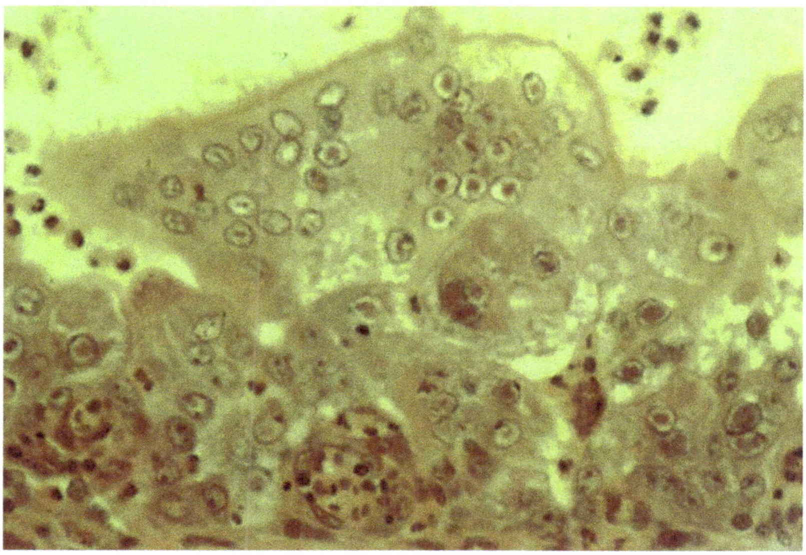

Fig. 15iv.4. Cowdry-type A intranuclear inclusion bodies in an ILT-infected trachea. H&E. (Author's own image.)

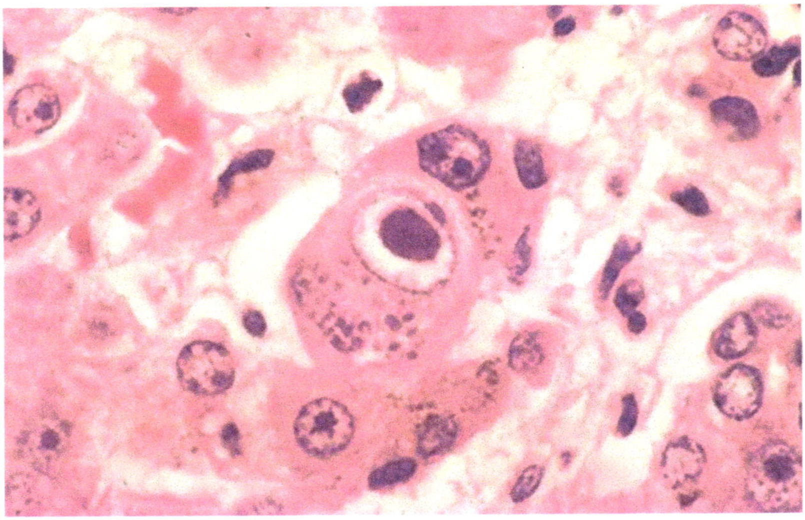

Fig. 15iv.5. Single ILT-infected tracheal cell with an intranuclear inclusion body. H&E. (Author's own image.)

15iv.5 Control

There is no treatment for ILT, and control is achieved by the implementation of rigorous biosecurity measures and the use of live vaccines. The herpesvirus can persist on all fomites – inanimate articles – as well as the personnel in contact with infected chickens. ILT virus infectivity can persist for weeks to months in tracheal mucus or carcasses.

The fact that ILT exists as a single serotype is an advantage for diagnosis and also vaccine development and use. The lack of vertical transmission of the virus from the hen to the chick is also an advantage. Indeed, it has been proposed in Australia, that an eradication system could be carried out in a specified area, taking into account these properties and using a marker ELISA that only recognizes vaccinal antibodies. An additional factor which would be helpful is that there is apparently no obvious wildlife host.

Live vaccines have been developed from virulent field strains by attenuation in chick cell culture or chick embryos and have been used for many years. These vaccines are administered by eye drop or intranasally or by mass delivery in the drinking water. They are usually given after four weeks of age and especially in areas of high risk. They are frequently used routinely in areas where there is an 'afraid to stop' mentality. Work has shown that the tissue culture derived vaccines are safer but need eye drop application, while the chick embryo vaccine is more immunogenic and can be given in the drinking water or by spray. These traditional ILT vaccines have been shown to be capable of becoming latent like the virulent strains and, under certain circumstances of stress, these vaccines may reactivate and cause disease especially if vaccinated birds are mixed with uninfected birds. Thus, mixing of healthy vaccinated birds with unvaccinated birds may be dangerous.

Recombinant vaccines that express immunogenic proteins of ILT have been developed in fowlpox and turkey herpesvirus (see Chapter 15xiii, this volume) and these need administration *in ovo*, subcutaneously or by the wing web method. *In ovo* delivery in the turkey herpesvirus vector gives the advantage of lifelong protection from a very early age.

The regional nature of reservoirs of ILT virus-infected flocks will tend to interact unfavourably with widely varying ILT control practices in the poultry industry, so as to periodically result in sporadic and unexpected outbreaks of ILT in intensive poultry industry populations.

A landmark study in Australia showed that, sometimes, the use of two different live attenuated vaccines can result in recombination to form virulent viruses. The work was done with commercial ILT vaccines but indicates the potential danger which may arise from this practice.

15iv.6 Further Reading

Garcia, M. (2017) Current and future vaccines and vaccination strategies against infectious laryngotracheitis (ILT) respiratory disease of poultry. *Veterinary Microbiology* 206, 157–162.

Guy J.S. and Garcia, M. (2013) Laryngotracheitis. In: Swayne, D.E. (editor-in-chief) *Diseases of Poultry*, 13th edn. Wiley-Blackwell, Danvers, Massachusetts, pp. 161–180.

Sang-Won, L., Markham, P.F., Coppo, M.J.C., Legione, A.R., Markham, J.F., *et al.* (2012) Attenuated vaccines can recombine to form virulent field viruses. *Science* 337(6091), 188–188.

15v Infectious Bursal Disease

ANDREW JAMES BROADBENT*

Department of Animal and Avian Sciences, University of Maryland, College Park, Maryland, USA

15v.1 Introduction

In 1962, in Gumboro, Delaware, there were the first recorded cases of a disease in chickens that was initially described as 'Gumboro Disease'. Pathological changes were seen in the bursa of Fabricius (BF), and the disease subsequently became known as infectious bursal disease (IBD), with the virus responsible termed infectious bursal disease virus (IBDV). The first IBDV outbreaks were caused by 'classical' strains, responsible for between 1 and 2% flock mortality, and the virus was discovered to be immunosuppressive (van den Berg *et al.*, 2000). The infection continued to spread throughout the USA, Europe, the Middle East, Africa, Asia and Australia and, by the mid-1980s, 'variant' strains had also emerged in the US that escaped vaccine-induced immunity and necessitated the development of new vaccines to bring them under control. In the late 1980s, there was the emergence of so-called 'very virulent' (vv) strains that had an elevated mortality of around 60% in commercial flocks and up to 100% in specific pathogen free (SPF) birds, for reasons that remain poorly understood (Eterradossi and Saif, 2020). Since their emergence, vv strains have spread across the globe and now classical and vv strains co-circulate in many countries. Moreover, evolution of the virus continues, vaccine failures are still reported, and reassortment continues to complicate the epidemiology. Consequently, IBD remains among the top five infectious diseases of poultry in almost every country surveyed. Given its importance, IBDV has been the subject of several excellent reviews providing a comprehensive summary of the pathogen and disease for experts (van den Berg *et al.*, 2000; Muller *et al.*, 2012; Ingrao *et al.*, 2013; Alkie and Rautenschlein, 2016; Jackwood, 2017; Qin and Zheng, 2017; Eterradossi and Saif, 2020). Rather than repeating this literature in detail, the present chapter aims to be of use to veterinarians in practice and poultry health professionals in the field.

15v.2 Nature of the Pathogen

IBDV is a member of the *Birnaviridae* family, which are non-enveloped viruses with a genome comprised of double-stranded (ds) RNA that is divided into two segments, A and B (Fig. 15v.1).

Segment A encodes a polyprotein that is cleaved into viral protein (VP) 2, VP3 and VP4 by the viral protease, VP4. Segment A also encodes another non-structural protein, VP5, via an overlapping reading frame that is thought to be involved in apoptosis and viral egress. Segment B encodes VP1, the viral polymerase. The virus capsid is of icosahedral symmetry and is comprised of a single layer of the VP2 protein. VP3 coats the dsRNA genome, binds and activates the polymerase, and binds the VP2 protein, acting as a scaffolding protein for the assembly of the capsid (Eterradossi and Saif, 2020).

The virus initially binds a receptor on the plasma membrane, the identity of which depends on the cell type that is infected, with candidate proteins including: IgM, HSP90 and integrins. Following receptor binding, the virus particle is taken up into an endosome, where the pH and calcium concentration drops, causing a conformational change in the capsid releasing a small peptide (pep46) that forms pores in the endosome membrane. It is currently thought that the genome exits the endosome through these pores to enter the cytoplasm and set up a replication complex where the polymerase replicates the genome and transcribes the genome into mRNA that is subsequently translated into viral proteins by the host cell ribosomes. Newly assembled virions form paracrystalline arrays in

*ajbroad@umd.edu

© CAB International 2021. *Poultry Health: A Guide for Professionals* (P. Barrow *et al.*)
DOI: 10.1079/9781789245042.0015

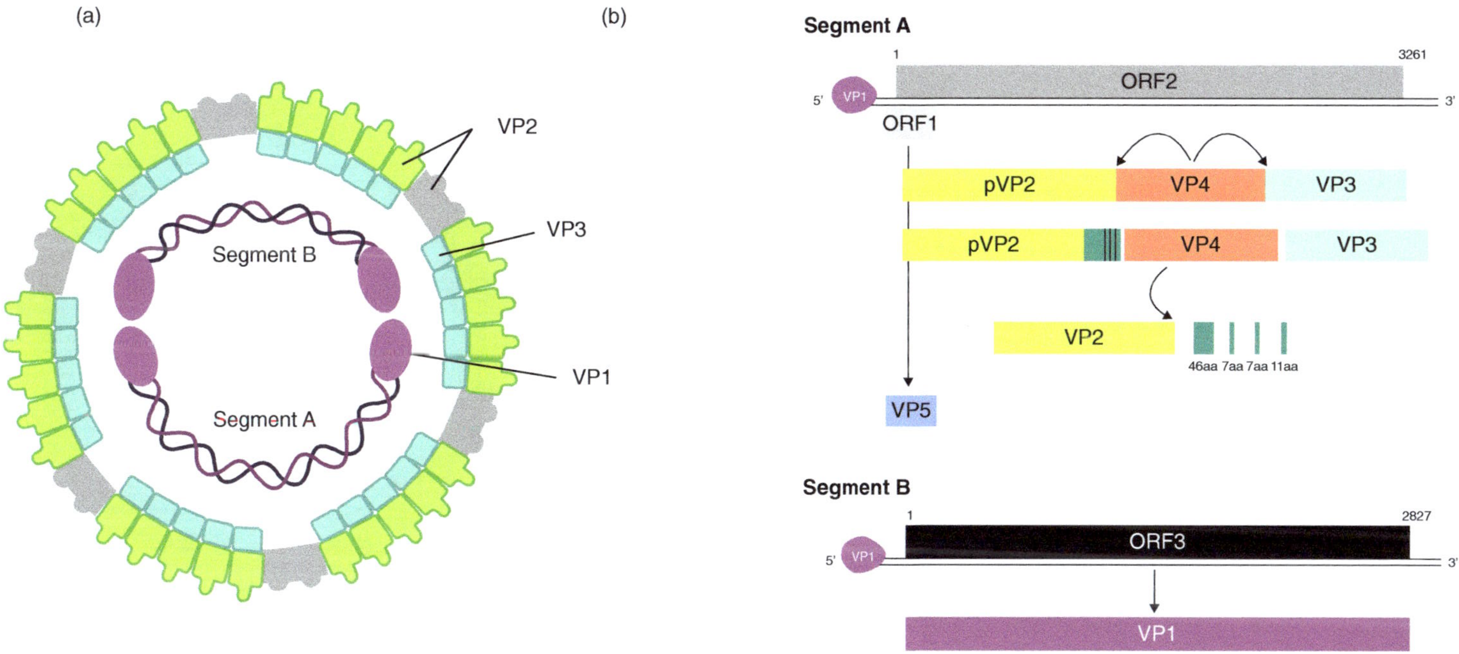

Fig. 15v.1. IBDV virus and genome. (a) IBDV is a non-enveloped virus with a capsid comprised of a single layer of VP2, and genome comprised of double stranded (ds) RNA that is divided into two segments, A and B. VP3 coats the genome, binds the VP1 polymerase and the capsid. (b) Segment A has two open reading frames. One encodes a polyprotein that is cleaved into VP2, 4 and 3 and the other encodes VP5. Segment B encodes VP1. (Schematics adapted from viralzone.expasy.org by [15] and reproduced with permission.)

the cytoplasm, the majority of which are released when the cell lyses, although a smaller number may exit by an egress mechanism mediated by VP5 (Qin and Zheng, 2017).

Cells sense they are infected though pattern recognition receptors (PRRs), which trigger innate antiviral defences, leading to the production of type I interferon (IFN) and pro-inflammatory cytokine responses (Dulwich *et al.*, 2017). In the case of IBDV, the presence of the dsRNA genome in the cytoplasm is sensed by a PRR known as MDA5. However, multiple copies of VP3 coat the dsRNA genome, which masks detection by MDA5. Furthermore, additional viral proteins, for example VP4, have been shown to antagonize the induction of type I IFN responses in infected cells, favouring viral replication (Qin and Zheng, 2017).

15v.3 Pathobiology

Birds become infected through contact with contaminated feed, bedding or water, and infected birds shed the virus from the cloaca. There is no known vertical transmission. Virus particles may be inhaled and/or ingested and may also infect birds via the conjunctiva. If IBDV is ingested, the first cells to be infected are macrophages and lymphoid cells in the gut (Eterradossi and Saif, 2020). The preferred tropism of the virus is for B-lymphocytes, the majority of which reside in the BF. Within the BF, the virus infects and lyses B cells, causing inflammation with associated oedema and influx of macrophages and T cells. It is thought that macrophages phagocytose infected and dying cells, and CD8+ cytotoxic T lymphocytes (CTLs) destroy infected cells using perforin and granzyme. Moreover, CD4+ Th1 cells infiltrating the BF secrete IFNγ, which may provide T cell help to the CTLs and macrophages to further the cell-mediated immune response that plays an important role in clearance of the virus and recovery. However, cell mediated immunity can also contribute to immunopathology (Ingrao *et al.*, 2013).

Birds that recover from infection are left immunosuppressed and more susceptible to secondary infections and more refractory to vaccination programmes against other diseases. Immunosuppression is a complex phenotype. It is thought to principally be the result of B cell lysis, causing a widespread loss of humoral immunity. However, IBDV also causes impairment to cell mediated responses, with T cells failing to respond to stimuli through mechanisms that remain poorly understood. Additionally, in convalescing birds, there is repopulation of the BF with B cells. However, many follicles remain small and lack the distinct structure of mature follicles and it is thought that the BF never fully recovers to its original architecture. Paradoxically, despite the widespread immunosuppression caused by IBDV infection, there is evidence that infected birds do generate lasting immunity against the IBDV infection itself. While the underpinning mechanism is not fully understood, it is thought that IBDV preferentially targets immature B cells, preventing the birds from mounting adaptive humoral immunity to future infections, while more mature B cells, capable of inducing protective responses against the current infection, are less impaired (Ingrao *et al.*, 2013).

15v.4 Nature of the Disease

15v.4.1 Clinical presentation

The incubation period is typically short, with clinical signs that have a sudden onset apparent after 2–3 days of incubation. A spectrum of clinical signs exists. In mild cases, birds may have ruffled feathers, a hunched posture, drooping wings, half-closed eyes, and a pale comb and wattles. In more severe cases, they may fail to eat and drink so will lose weight and become dehydrated. Their crops may be empty, and they may have evidence of diarrhoea and/or soiled vent feathers as a consequence. They may also fail to show signs of normal social interaction with the rest of the flock and, in severe cases, they may be found prostrate and have difficulty in breathing (Fig. 15v.2).

Symptoms usually peak 3–5 days post-infection, whereupon they subside, and birds that do not die are usually clinically well after a couple of weeks. Mortality usually begins on day 3 post-infection, peaking and receding 5–7 days post-infection. It should also be noted that subclinical IBDV infections also occur (Eterradossi and Saif, 2020).

The severity of disease and the outcome of infection depends on many factors, including the breed and age of the bird, the presence of maternal antibodies, and the infecting strain of IBDV. Layer birds are typically more susceptible to severe disease than broiler breeds, for reasons that are poorly understood, and the period of greatest susceptibility is 3–6 weeks of age. The clinical progression of disease caused by vv and classical IBDV strains is similar; however, vv IBDV causes a greater mortality

(a) (b)

Fig. 15v.2. IBDV clinical signs. (a) Mock-infected White Leghorn chicken at 2–3 weeks of age. (b) vvIBDV-infected White Leghorn chicken at 2–3 weeks of age displaying some typical signs of IBDV, for example hunched posture, ruffled feathers, closed eyes and prostration. (Author's own photographs.)

percentage within a flock (classical strains have been reported to cause up to 50% mortality, and vv strains have been reported to cause up to 100% mortality) (Eterradossi and Saif, 2020). Finally, owing to the segmented nature of the genome, viral reassortment also occurs in the field. When reassortment occurs between a vv strain and a non-vv strain, this can produce an infection with a reduced pathogenicity (Eterradossi and Saif, 2020).

The economic impact of IBDV to the poultry industry is due to morbidity and mortality of the infection and due to immunosuppression that exacerbates secondary infections and makes birds less responsive to other vaccination programmes (van den Berg *et al.*, 2000). Secondary infections known to be exacerbated by IBDV are numerous and include potentially zoonotic pathogens of public health importance, for example *Campylobacter jejuni*, *Salmonella enteritidis*, *Escherichia coli* and avian influenza virus (AIV). It is important to note that subclinical IBDV infection can also cause immunosuppression and be of economic importance due to secondary infection, growth retardation or the rejection of carcasses because of gross lesions.

15v.4.2 Gross and histopathology

Another disease that causes similar clinical signs to IBDV is acute coccidiosis. However, what sets IBDV apart is pathology in the BF. Inflammation leads to oedema and the BF may appear swollen and red from day 3 post-infection and there may be a yellow transudate or haemorrhages present. At later time points, destruction of B cells leads to bursal atrophy and the BF may be smaller than in uninfected birds. Therefore, an evaluation of the gross pathology of the BF should be performed at necropsy from a sample of the flock to aid diagnosis. Aside from the BF, there may be petechial haemorrhages in the pectoral or thigh muscles, increased mucus in the intestine and the spleen may be enlarged (Eterradossi and Saif, 2020).

Histopathological changes in the BF include a degeneration and necrosis of lymphocytes in the medulla of the bursal follicles from as early as day 1 post-infection. By days 3 and 4 post-infection, all lymphoid follicles may become affected and there may be significant loss of bursal follicle architecture. Lesions in the BF can be scored based on the extent and severity. Aside from the BF, the spleen, thymus, Harderian gland and caecal tonsils may also have lesions and evidence of lymphoid necrosis. It has also been reported that Marek's disease virus (MDV) (see Chapter 15xiii, this volume) and a type 8 adenovirus (see Chapter 15iii, this volume) can cause histopathological changes in the BF; however, the lesions are different to those seen for IBDV (Eterradossi and Saif, 2020).

15v.5 Diagnosis

A presumptive diagnosis is typically made based on a rapid onset of the described symptoms with a sharp increase in mortality in a flock that subsequently declines quickly. IBDV can be distinguished from other diseases that cause similar symptoms by examining the BF from a sample of the flock at necropsy for gross and histopathological lesions as described. However, it should also be noted that live vaccines can also induce bursal lesions, so vaccination history should be obtained (Eterradossi and Saif, 2020).

Serological tests for IBDV include an enzyme-linked immunosorbent assay (ELISA) and viral neutralization test (VNT), and a quantitative agar-gel precipitation (AGP) test is also used in the UK. ELISA is more rapid than VNT, and commercial kits are available; however, kits may vary in their sensitivity and specificity. Serological assays do not differentiate infected birds from those vaccinated with live vaccines, nor do they distinguish between a current and previous infection. Molecular tests such as reverse-transcription and polymerase chain reaction (RTPCR) and quantitative (q)RTPCR are useful for detecting a current IBDV infection with good sensitivity and specificity. However, they also cannot distinguish vaccinated from infected animals at present. Samples from the BF and/or spleen are the most useful when diagnosing IBDV, and the virus may be isolated in embryonated eggs when inoculated onto the chorioallantoic membrane (CAM) or into the yolk sac (Eterradossi and Saif, 2020).

15v.6 Epidemiology

IBDV is endemic worldwide and chickens and turkeys are the natural hosts. There are two serotypes, but only serotype 1 viruses cause disease in chickens. Serotype 1 virus strains have traditionally been grouped based on pathotype, as either 'subclinical', 'classical' or 'very virulent', depending on the disease severity and mortality percentages. 'Variant' strains refer to strains that emerged in the US in the 1980s and escaped the immunity conferred by conventional vaccines. However, other immune escape mutants have emerged due to antigenic drift in different regions, causing the formation of several subtypes within these groups. It has therefore been proposed to group IBDV strains based on the sequence of the capsid into seven different genogroups (Jackwood, 2017); however, this remains controversial in the field. In addition, it is important to sequence both segments A and B in order to monitor reassortment. Serotype 1 viruses have also been isolated from ostrich chicks, waterfowl, and a magpie, and samples from pigeons and guineafowl have been found to be RT-PCR positive. In addition, anti-IBDV antibodies have been found in birds of prey, pheasants, penguins, ducks, gulls, crows and falcons. In 1998, a serological survey of wild bird populations found neutralizing antibodies against IBDV serotypes 1 and 2 in a total of 15 (1.9%) and 36 (4.9%) of 793 birds, respectively. However, while IBDV serotype 1 strains are well known to cause disease and immunosuppression in chickens, little is known about how they affect wild birds. Moreover, although wild birds may be involved in the ecology and epidemiology of the disease, it remains unclear whether wild birds represent a reservoir from which poultry become infected, or whether they become infected due to spill-over from poultry units (Eterradossi and Saif, 2020).

15v.7 Control

There are no known antiviral therapies available for IBDV. Vaccination is therefore the cornerstone of IBDV protection and has been in use for decades in commercial settings. Traditional vaccines include inactivated and live attenuated platforms, with live vaccine viruses being attenuated through serial passage in cell culture or embryonated chicken eggs, though the mechanism of attenuation remains unknown. Typically, hens are vaccinated with the view to providing maternal antibodies that transfer to the egg and the hatched chick. Maternal antibodies, while protecting the chicks for its first few weeks of life, can neutralize live vaccine viruses and prevent them for providing protection. Maternal antibodies typically wane over the first couple of weeks of life, so farmers must wait until they have waned to a point where they will no longer neutralize the vaccine before administering. However, as maternal antibodies wane, chicks become more susceptible to circulating field strains, and there is a period where immune and susceptible birds coexist due to lack of uniformity in transmitted immunity. Farmers must therefore determine the optimal time for vaccination. In order to do this, it is necessary to quantify serum antibody titres, usually by ELISA, and use the 'Deventer formula' that aims to calculate when to vaccinate based on maternal antibody levels. Traditionally, weaker live vaccines were used, but the emergence of vv strains has necessitated the use of hotter vaccine strains, such that now 'intermediate' and 'intermediate-hot' vaccines are common. Hotter vaccine strains can 'break though' higher maternal antibody titres and can therefore be administered earlier, but they can cause bursal lesions and some degree of immunosuppression (Muller *et al.*, 2012).

Despite the need for appropriate timing of vaccination, live vaccines remain popular due to their cost-effectiveness and ease of administration, as they can be added to the drinking water. However, next generation vaccines have been licenced, for example vectored vaccines based on the herpesvirus of turkeys (HVT), into which the IBDV VP2 capsid gene is cloned, which can provide protection against MDV as well as IBDV. Immune complex vaccines, comprised of live IBDV vaccine strains mixed with antibodies that enable persistence of the antigen, are also licenced. These vaccines can be administered *in ovo* or to day-old chicks in the hatchery, despite the presence of maternal antibodies. Birds that are vaccinated with vectored vaccines have normal bursa architecture and it may be possible to distinguish vaccinated from infected birds, as only the VP2 protein from the IBDV is expressed, so birds will not have antibodies against other IBDV proteins, for example VP3 (Muller *et al.*, 2012).

Vaccines aim to protect against disease, but not infection. Consequently, vaccinated birds can still become infected with wild-type strains that continue to evolve. This has led to antigenic drift, and there is currently a drive for more matched vaccines against locally circulating strains as the antigenic diversity of commercial vaccines is limited (Jackwood, 2017). However, other factors may also contribute to vaccine failures, for example mistimed vaccines, inadequately dosed birds or poor overall flock health. Management practices should therefore be reviewed in cases of vaccine failure. In addition to vaccination, adequate biosecurity is paramount in preventing infection. The virus is very stable and more resistant to common disinfectants than other viruses. Poultry units should therefore be adequately disinfected with compounds with proven activity against IBDV, for an approved contact time. IBDV is also known to be carried by people, materials and machinery, so individuals should wear appropriate personal protective equipment and clothing that should also be disinfected properly (Eterradossi and Saif, 2020).

15v.8 Concluding Remarks

Despite being identified more than 50 years ago, and with decades of vaccination efforts, IBDV remains one of the top five infectious problems of poultry in almost every country surveyed. It is of economic impact because of the high morbidity and mortality caused, and because of immunosuppression exacerbating secondary infections and reducing the responsiveness of birds to other vaccination programmes. The virus is highly contagious and resistant to common disinfectants, and the successful control of clinical IBDV in a poultry unit requires co-operation between the veterinarian and the poultry producer. Vaccination regimens should be agreed, rigorous biosecurity measures taken and management practices should be of the highest quality to ensure adequate flock health.

15v.9 References

Alkie, T.N. and Rautenschlein, S. (2016) Infectious bursal disease virus in poultry: current status and future prospects. *Veterinary Medicine (Auckland)* 7, 9–18.

Dulwich, K.L., Giotis, E.S., Gray, A., Nair, V., Skinner, M.A., *et al.* (2017) Differential gene expression in chicken primary B cells infected ex vivo with attenuated and very virulent strains of infectious bursal disease virus (IBDV). *Journal of General Virology* 98(12) 2918–2930.

Eterradossi, N. and Saif, Y.M. (2020) Infectious bursal disease. In: Swayne, D.E. (editor-in-chief) *Diseases of Poultry*, 14th edn. Wiley-Blackwell, Hoboken, New Jersey, pp. 257–283.

Ingrao, F., Rauw, F., Lambrecht, B. and van den Berg, T (2013) Infectious bursal disease: a complex host-pathogen interaction. *Developmental Comparative Immunology* 41, 429–438.

Jackwood, D.J. (2017) Advances in vaccine research against economically important viral diseases of food animals: Infectious bursal disease virus. *Veterinary Microbiology* 206, 121–125.

Muller, H., Mundt, Eterradossi, E.N. and Islam, M.R. (2012) Current status of vaccines against infectious bursal disease. Avian Pathology 41, 133–139.

Qin, Y. and Zheng, S.J. (2017) Infectious bursal disease virus-host interactions: multifunctional viral proteins that perform multiple and differing jobs. *International Journal of Molecular Science* 18, 161. DOI: 10.3390/ijms18010161.

van den Berg, T.P., Eterradossi, N., Toquin D. and Meulemans, G. (2000) Infectious bursal disease (Gumboro disease). *Revue Scientifique Technique* 19, 509–543.

15vi Avian Astroviruses

Victoria J. Smyth*

Avian Virology Unit, Agri-Food and Biosciences Institute (AFBI), Stormont, Belfast, UK

15vi.1 Introduction

Avian astroviruses are a diverse group of small round viruses infecting poultry, game birds and many species of wild birds. They cause enteritis and growth retardation in young birds and some species can be vertically transmitted causing hatchery disease, e.g. avian nephritis virus (ANV; Biđin *et al*., 2012) and chicken astrovirus (CAstV; Smyth *et al*., 2013). Older birds are often refractory to the viruses and many strains are of low or no pathogenicity. These viruses are typically more associated with morbidity than mortality but some avian astroviruses of ducks and turkeys are associated with fatal diseases of organs outside of the gut, e.g. the liver and kidneys (Table 15vi.1).

Avian astroviruses are frequently also detected in healthy flocks, although usually in fewer numbers of birds, and appear more resistant to cleaning and disinfectant than other viruses, allowing them to persist in houses. Typically, astroviruses tend to infect one host species, although cross-over between host species can occur. There are many different enteric viruses of poultry, so mixed infections with other viruses of varying pathogenicities are common, e.g. avian orthoreovirus (see Chapter 15i, this volume) and fowl adenovirus (see Chapter 15iii, this volume), thereby complicating diagnoses.

15vi.2 Classification and Biological Properties

Avian astroviruses are grouped within the *Avastrovirus* genus of the *Astroviridae* family. The other genus, *Mamastrovirus*, containing mammalian astroviruses, includes at least eight serotypes of human astrovirus. Historically, most avian astroviruses have been named after their host species although an alternative naming system, currently consisting of Avastrovirus species 1, 2 and 3, is being implemented by the International Committee for Taxonomy of Viruses (ICTV). There are two astroviruses each of turkeys, chickens and ducks and a recently described astrovirus infecting geese (Table 15vi.1), although cross infection of hosts is known to occur, for example, turkeys, ducklings and geese can be infected with an astrovirus more commonly associated with chickens, ANV (Connor *et al*., 1987; Biđin *et al*., 2011; 2012). Furthermore, this new ICTV naming system will have to accommodate the more recently discovered novel astrovirus species in geese and those infecting wild birds.

Astroviruses are small, round viruses, similar in size and shape to other enteric viruses including picornaviruses, although a small proportion of avian astroviruses have a star shaped appearance under electron microscopy. They contain a positive-sense, single stranded RNA genome of ~6.6 to >7.7 kb in length, comprising three open reading frames (ORF), which primarily code for a protease (ORF 1a), an RNA-dependent RNA polymerase (ORF 1b) and a capsid polyprotein (ORF 2). There are untranslated regions (UTR) at both ends of the genome and a polyadenylated tail at the extreme 3' end, which allows the genome to act as a messenger RNA and speeds up the infection process. A ribosomal frameshift motif in the short overlapping region at the 3' end of ORF 1a and 5' end of ORF 1b, allows a shift in reading frame prior to translation of the polymerase gene on the joint ORF 1a/ORF 1b transcript and different astrovirus species employ different translation frame strategies. Non-structural proteins are translated from ORF 1a and from ORF 1a/1b on the genomic RNA, while the capsid polyprotein is expressed from a subgenomic transcript

*victoria.smyth@afbini.gov.uk

© CAB International 2021. *Poultry Health: A Guide for Professionals* (P. Barrow *et al*.)
DOI: 10.1079/9781789245042.0015

Table 15vi.1. Diseases associated with avian astroviruses.

Virus	Disease	Major tissue distribution
Turkey astrovirus type 1 (TAstV-1)	Enteritis, growth retardation	Intestine
Turkey astrovirus type 2 (TAstV-2)	Enteritis, growth retardation, PEC: poult enteritis complex, PEMS: poult enteritis and mortality syndrome	Intestine, bursa of Fabricius, thymus
Avian nephritis virus (ANV)	Nephritis, baby chick nephropathy, growth retardation	Intestine, kidney
Chicken astrovirus (CAstV)	Growth retardation, kidney disease, white chicks hatchery disease	Intestine, kidney, liver pancreas, spleen
Duck astrovirus type 1 (DAstV-1)	Hepatitis and variable mortality in young ducks	Liver, kidney, spleen
Duck astrovirus type 2 (DAstV-2)	Hepatitis and variable mortality in ducklings	Liver, kidney, spleen
Goose astrovirus (GoAstV)	Nephritis, growth retardation, extensive visceral gout and high mortality in young goslings, paralysis	Kidney, urate deposits on heart, liver, kidney and leg joint

of ORF 2 and cleaved into mature capsid proteins by cellular enzymes. Due to the lack of proofreading by the polymerase, the RNA genome constantly evolves during replication by acquiring nucleotide mutations that are not corrected, mostly in the capsid gene, leading to a wide range of strains with varying pathogenicities in circulation. Recombination of genomic material between strains further increases strain diversity (Palomino-Tapia *et al.*, 2020).

15vi.3 Epidemiology

Globally, avian astroviruses are very common viruses of commercial poultry which are contracted via the faecal–oral route. Since there are no specific treatments for their diseases, good biosecurity and husbandry are crucial and infections tend to be more common in lower status flocks. Most screening for the virus has been through the use of molecular tests since serological tests are few in number and very limited in terms of serotype diversity. Typically, the majority of published screening reports have had a regional slant, in that results for the more commonly farmed species in the countries of testing have been reported, e.g. turkeys in USA, chickens in Europe, ducks and geese in China, but it is probably safe to assume that many commercial poultry meat flocks have been penetrated by their respective astroviruses. Limited information in terms of the regionality of pathogenic strains is available; for instance, a highly pathogenic strain of CAstV resulting in kidney disease with visceral gout and mortality of up to 40% in young broiler flocks has only been reported in Asia, notably India (Bulbule *et al.*, 2013) and the Middle East (Figs 15vi.1a and b). More recently, several reports of novel astroviruses of geese, causing visceral gout in goslings, have come out of China (Zhang *et al.*, 2017; Zhang *et al.*, 2018).

15vi.4 Diseases Associated with Avian Astroviruses

Generally, avian astroviruses are associated with diarrhoea, enteritis and growth restriction in young birds although several are also associated with diseases outside of the gut (Table 15vi.1) and there are reports of encephalitis in game birds. Turkey astrovirus (TAstV) is the most prevalent virus in enteritis samples from turkey flocks with one study detecting TAstV in approximately 80% of affected flocks but also in 30% of healthy flocks showing that subclinical infections are also common (Reynolds *et al.*, 1986). Two TAstV species exist, types 1 and 2, of which the more prevalent, TAstV-2, is associated with two syndromes, poult enteritis and mortality syndrome (PEMS) and poult enteritis complex (PEC). Symptoms of PEMS include diarrhoea, enteritis, litter-eating, nervousness and listlessness ranging from mild to moderate and can last for up to 2 weeks, during which, growth is impacted (Reynolds *et al.*,1986). The virus replicates along the sides of intestinal villi which can lead to mild villous atrophy, crypt hyperplasia and infiltration by lymphohistiocytes. Other lesions can include dehydration, swollen, fluid-filled intestines with undigested feed and frothy caecal contents.

The two astrovirus species of chickens, avian nephritis virus and chicken astrovirus (CAstV), are mostly associated with morbidity and are both

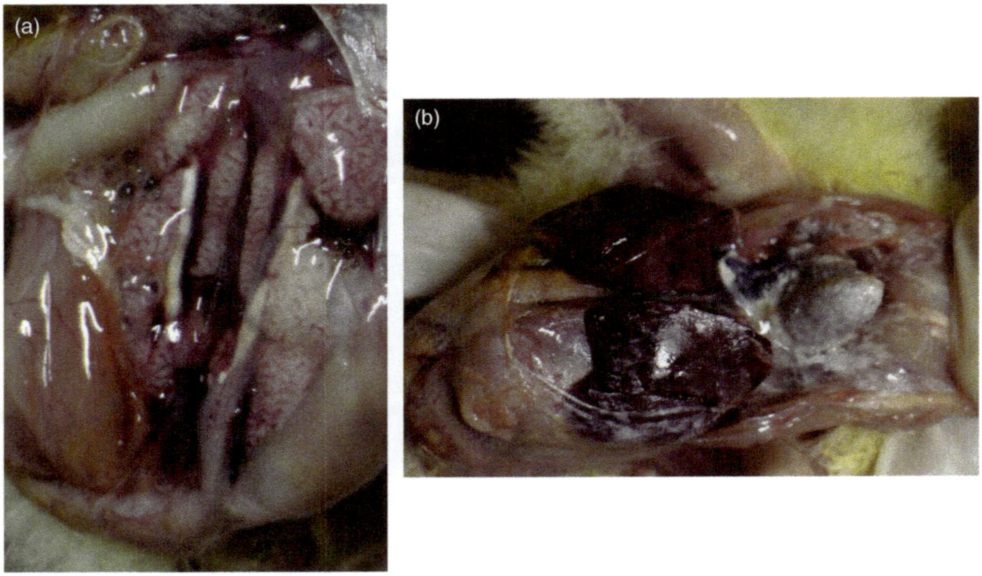

Fig. 15vi.1. (a) Broiler chick displaying severe renal swelling due to infection by a nephropathogenic strain of CAstV. (b) Broiler chick displaying urate deposition over heart and liver in a case of visceral gout due to CAstV infection. (Photographs reproduced with kind permission of Dr Hugo A. Pérez García. DVM, MAM.)

suspected of involvement in runting and stunting syndrome (RSS), a malabsorption disease of broilers, although other viruses have also been implicated in RSS and the exact aetiology remains to be determined. Runts hatch small, while stunted chicks fail to thrive and can be excessively small with retarded development by 2–3 weeks leading to high cull rates. Other symptoms of RSS can include diarrhoea, enteritis, undigested feed, wet litter, thin-walled and distended intestines and abnormal feathering, which is sometimes called 'helicopter' feathering. Characteristic lesions of RSS include cysts in the mucosa of the small intestine between days 6 and 12 but occasionally up to 3 weeks, and under experimental conditions, CAstV has been shown to cause these characteristic lesions (Kang *et al.*, 2018). Typically, either or both of these astroviruses may be involved in uneven flock growth and poor performance, and co-infection is common, along with other enteric viruses such as avian reovirus and fowl adenovirus.

In addition to the enteric maladies, both ANV and CAstV can cause kidney disease in young birds with extensive visceral gout (Figs 15vi.1a and b) (Shirai *et al.*, 1991; Bulbule *et al.*, 2013).

They are both associated with hatchery diseases, ANV with baby chick nephropathy and CAstV with white chicks hatchery disease. The latter is characterized by a short-lived hatchability drop lasting about 2 weeks, embryo dwarfing, excessive mid and late dead embryos and weak, pale, runted chicks that typically die within 24 h (Smyth *et al.*, 2013). The strains of CAstV that have been associated with the kidney disease and the hatchery disease have been typed as belonging to different subgroups of the B group, which are detectable using the commercially available CAstV B group ELISA. Less is known regarding disease caused by strains belonging to the CAstV A group, although an A group CAstV strain has also been associated with white chicks disease in Polish flocks (Sajewicz-Krukowska *et al.*, 2016).

There are two recognized astrovirus serotypes of ducks, termed duck astrovirus (DAstV)-1 and -2, that both cause fatal hepatitis in ducklings. Originally these were thought picornaviruses and were known as duck hepatitis virus (DHV)-2 (Asplin, 1965) and DHV-3 (Toth, 1969) respectively but were later characterized as astroviruses (Gough *et al.*, 1984; 1985). Infections by DAstV-1 resulted in mortalities of up to 50% in young ducklings under 2 weeks of age while mortality was lower in older ducklings. Death was rapid following the onset of illness often accompanied by opisthotonos.

Livers were haemorrhagic, punctate or striated, and kidneys were pale and swollen. Ducklings presented with polydipsia and white, loose droppings from urates (Gough *et al.*, 1985). Infections by DAstV-2 caused similar symptoms to DAstV-1 although mortality in very young ducklings (<2 weeks) is considered lower.

An emerging disease of young goslings known as gosling gout was reported in 2015 in China and had spread to most provinces in China by 2017 (Zhang *et al.*, 2018). The symptoms appear similar to the fatal kidney disease with extensive visceral gout seen in Indian broiler chickens that was reported by Bulbule and colleagues in 2013 as being caused by an astrovirus. Goose astrovirus has been identified as the responsible agent of gosling gout resulting in morbidity of 80–90% and mortality rates ranging from 20–70%. Urate deposits are extensive on the surface of multiple organs, the kidneys are enlarged and survivors are growth depressed and susceptible to secondary bacterial infections. It may also affect leg joints with swelling, urate deposits and immobilization (Zhang *et al.*, 2017).

15vi.5 Diagnosis Including Typing

There are difficulties regarding the diagnosis of avian astroviruses in certain syndromic diseases, such as RSS. The presence of multiple co-infections by other viruses, e.g. avian reovirus, which may be strains that are non-pathogenic, complicates the diagnosis, which is further confounded by the range of pathogenicities for avian astroviruses since many strains are non-pathogenic and astrovirus infections of healthy flocks are also common. Therefore, simply detecting an astrovirus in enteric diseases does not always mean it is the causal agent and other factors should be taken into consideration, such as the age of the flock since resistance to astroviruses increases rapidly with age. Maternal antibody status is also important for enteric disease syndromes of young chicks. Also, sampling should occur soon after the onset of disease which is often apparent soon after hatch when viral loads may be at their peak, but commonly samples aren't taken until the flocks are 2–3 weeks old so that astrovirus levels may have decreased substantially by the time of testing, making their significance less clear. Early faecal samples could be banked and frozen for later molecular testing. The involvement of avian astroviruses in diseases of organs outside the enteric tract is well established and more readily diagnosed, such as the fatal hepatitis in ducklings by DAstV or by CAstV in white chicks hatchery disease when exposure to other viruses is restricted. In addition to both ANV and CAstV, infectious bronchitis virus should be ruled out in cases of kidney disease of young chickens as all three viruses are nephropathogenic.

The most convenient method of diagnosing the presence of astroviruses is by reverse-transcription polymerase chain reaction (RT-PCR, see Chapter 22, this volume) since virus isolation of astrovirus is difficult and slow in cell culture. Additionally, many isolates do not possess the characteristic star shape under electron microscopy and cannot be distinguished from many other small, round viruses. Some RT-PCR tests are commercially available either as conventional (presence/absence) assays or real time, quantitative tests (RT-qPCR) in diagnostic laboratories and as off-the-shelf kits. Several research papers describe novel RT-PCR assays for the individual astrovirus species infecting poultry and some are multiplex, combined with tests for other common enteric pathogens, such as avian rotavirus (Day *et al.*, 2007). As there is such a high degree of genetic evolution associated with the replication of viruses with RNA genomes, it is important to determine the scope of individual tests (if known) as test development is typically limited by the amount and diversity of available sequences. In cases of enteric disease such as RSS, it is important to sample early, and advantageous to quantify the astrovirus as high loads of astrovirus are suggestive of a stronger association with disease. The disadvantage of most quantitative RT-PCR assays is that they do not permit typing, and yet it is also helpful to determine the strain in order to compare it with strains of known pathogenicity. An RT-PCR of the capsid gene is often the most useful test for this, as the region is not under the same functional constraints as the protease and polymerase genes, and furthermore, the capsid is under selective pressure to evade the bird's immune system, so it contains several hypervariable stretches of nucleotides that are useful for typing (Todd *et al.*, 2011). A testing strategy consisting of performing astrovirus RT-qPCR followed by typing RT-PCR of those astroviruses found at higher levels gives a fuller diagnosis.

Although several groups have developed ELISA (enzyme linked immunosorbent assay, see Chapter 22, this volume) tests for turkey, duck and chicken astroviruses (Tang *et al.*, 2005; Wang *et al.*, 2010;

Sellers *et al.*, 2010), there remains a lack of commercially available serological tests for the majority of avian astroviruses, with the exception of a commercial ELISA that detects strains in the CAstV B group (Skibinska *et al.*, 2015). Part of the difficulty in developing robust serology tests is the wide diversity of circulating strains, which are predominantly characterized by molecular means so that the serology is less well understood. For instance, in the case of ANV, only three serotypes have been determined empirically and yet there are estimated to be six more serotypes, based on similar degrees of genetic differences between the newer genotypes as there are between the existing serotypes. In the absence of robust astrovirus ELISA kits, immunofluorescence tests and serum neutralization tests may aid diagnosis, but it is important to ascertain from the laboratory the range of serotypes that are covered by the test, as these can be quite limited.

15vi.6 Control of Astrovirus Infections

Currently, commercial vaccines against avian astroviruses do not exist, although vaccines against TAstV and ANV are reportedly in development and anecdotal reports have suggested that an autogenous vaccine was effective against the CAstV strain causing kidney disease and visceral gout. In the case of chicken astroviruses, CAstV and ANV, it would be advantageous to ensure that broiler breeder flocks were protected against pathogenic strains before going into lay, in order to prevent vertical transmission to the embryos and to provide maternally derived antibodies to protect their offspring against horizontal transmission during the vulnerable brooding period. Given the high degree of mortality associated with duck and goose astroviruses and with PEMS in turkeys, suitable vaccines that could be administered at the hatchery, would be of immense benefit to the industry.

As there is no prophylaxis for diseases caused by astroviruses, improved levels of biosecurity and husbandry are currently the best protective measures available. Increasing downtime between crops and thorough cleaning of the houses before application of a robust disinfectant are to be encouraged. Astroviruses are more resistant to disinfectant that many other viruses and can persist in houses after cleaning and disinfection so all surfaces, including feeders and drinkers, must be well treated and the darkling beetles removed, as they can act as vectors for avian astroviruses. Fogging houses after cleaning has also been shown to be effective and should inactivate residual astrovirus.

15vi.7 References

Asplin, F.D. (1965) Duck hepatitis: vaccination against two serological types. *Veterinary Record* 77, 1529–1530.

Biđin, M., Lojkić, I., Biđin, Z., Tisljar, M., Majnarić, D., *et al.* (2011) Detection and characterization of avian nephritis virus in ducklings. *Avian Pathology* 40, 173–177.

Biđin, M., Lojkić, I., Tišljar, M., Biđin, Z. and Majnarić, D. (2012) Astroviruses associated with stunting and prehatching mortality in duck and goose embryos. *Avian Pathology* 41, 91–97.

Bulbule, N.R., Mandakhalikar, K.D., Kapgate, S.S., Deshmukh, V.V., Schat, K.A., *et al.* (2013) Role of chicken astrovirus as a causative agent of gout in commercial broilers in India. *Avian Pathology* 42, 464–473.

Connor, T.J., McNeilly, F., McFerran, J.B. and McNulty, M.S. (1987) A survey of avian sera from Northern Ireland for antibody to avian nephritis virus. *Avian Pathology* 16, 15–20.

Day, J.M., Spackman, E. and Pantin-Jackwood, M. (2007) A multiplex RT-PCR test for the differential identification of turkey astrovirus type 1, turkey astrovirus type 2, chicken astrovirus, avian nephritis virus, and avian rotavirus. *Avian Diseases* 51, 681–684.

Gough, R.E., Collins, M.S., Borland, E. and Keymer, L.F. (1984) Astrovirus-like particles associated with hepatitis in ducklings. *Veterinary Record* 114, 279.

Gough, R.E., Borland, E.D. and Keymer, I.F. (1985) An outbreak of duck hepatitis type II in commercial ducks. *Avian Pathology* 14, 227–236.

Kang, K.I., Linnemann, E., Icard, A.H., Durairaj, V., Mundt, E., *et al.* (2018) Chicken astrovirus as an aetiological agent of runting-stunting syndrome in broiler chickens. *Journal of General Virology* 99, 512–524.

Palomino-Tapia, V., Mitevski, D., Inglis, T., van der Meer, F., Martin, E. *et al.* (2020) Chicken Astrovirus (CAstV) Molecular Studies Reveal Evidence of Multiple Past Recombination Events in Sequences Originated from Clinical Samples of White Chick Syndrome (WCS) in Western Canada. Viruses 12, 1096. DOI: 10.3390/v12101096

Reynolds, D.L., Saif, Y.M. and Theil, K.W. (1986) A survey of enteric viruses of turkey poults. *Avian Diseases* 31, 89–98.

Sajewicz-Krukowska, J., Pać, K., Lisowska, A, Pikuła, A., Minta, Z., *et al.* (2016) Astrovirus-induced 'white chicks' condition – field observation, virus detection and preliminary characterization. *Avian Pathology* 45, 2–12.

Sellers, H., Linneman, E., Icard, A.H. and Mundt, E. (2010) A purified recombinant baculovirus expressed

capsid protein of a new astrovirus provides partial protection to runting-stunting syndrome in chickens. *Vaccine* 28, 1253–1263.
Shirai, J., Nakamura, K., Nozaki, H. and Kawamura, H. (1991) Differences in the induction of urate deposition of specific-pathogen-free chicks inoculated with avian nephritis virus passaged by five different methods. *Avian Diseases* 35, 269–275.
Skibinska, A., Lee, A., Wylie, M., Smyth, V.J., Welsh, M.D., *et al.* (2015) Development of an indirect enzyme-linked immunosorbent assay test for detecting antibodies to chicken astrovirus in chicken sera. *Avian Pathology* 44, 436–442.
Smyth, V.J., Trudgett, J., Wylie, M., Jewhurst, H., Conway, B., *et al.* (2013) Chicken astrovirus detected in hatchability problems associated with 'white chicks'. *Veterinary Record* 173, 403–404.
Tang, Y., Ismail, M.M. and Saif, Y.M. (2005) Development of antigen-capture enzyme-linked immunosorbent assay and RT-PCR for detection of turkey astroviruses. *Avian Diseases 49*, 182–188
Todd, D., Trudgett, J., Smyth, V.J., Donnelly, B., McBride, N., *et al.* (2011) Capsid protein sequence diversity of avian nephritis virus. *Avian Pathology* 40, 249–259
Toth, T.E. (1969) Studies of an agent causing mortality among ducklings immune to duck virus hepatitis. *Avian Diseases* 13, 834–836.
Wang, X., Wang, Y., Xie, X., Zhang, B. and Zhang, D. (2010) Expression of the C-terminal PORF-2 protein of duck astrovirus for application in a serological test. *Journal of Virological Methods* 171, 8–12.
Zhang, Y., Wang, F., Liu, N., Yang, L. and Zhang, D. (2017) Complete genome sequence of a novel avastrovirus in goose. *Archives in Virology* 162, 2135–2139
Zhang, X., Ren, D., Li, T., Zhou, H., Liu, X., *et al.* (2018) An emerging novel goose astrovirus associated with gosling gout disease, China. *Emerging Microbes and Infections* 7, 152–159.

15vii Avian Influenza

IAN H. BROWN*

Animal and Plant Health Agency-Weybridge, Addlestone, Surrey, UK

15vii.1 Introduction

Avian influenza (AI) is a severe infectious disease of birds which can affect a variety of mammalian species. It is a notifiable disease with the OIE (World Organisation for Animal Health) defining it as 'an infection of poultry caused by any influenza A virus of the H5 or H7 subtypes or by any AI virus with an intravenous pathogenicity index (IVPI) greater than 1.2 or, as an alternative, at least 75% mortality'. The viruses can be divided into high pathogenicity avian influenza (HPAI) and low pathogenicity avian influenza (LPAI).

Avian influenza has threatened poultry production over many decades historically through sporadic outbreaks but with increasing intensification of commercial poultry rearing, coupled with significant changes in the epidemiology and global spread it has become a high consequence disease for industry and anyone rearing birds. In the last 20 years, there have been huge increases in a number of cases and the disease now threatens global food security.

15vii.2 The Virus

AI is caused by influenza A virus. These are orthomyxoviruses, enveloped, negative-sense single strand (ss) RNA viruses. The genome is fragmented in eight linear fragments which replicate inside the nucleus of susceptible cells with proteins being synthesized and assembled in the cytoplasm prior to virus progeny release via budding from the cell surface. They are divided according to the characteristics of the nucleoprotein and matrix proteins into several types. Type A affects birds and mammals (including humans, pigs, horses, mink and sea mammals), type B infects humans, type C infects both humans and pigs and type D infects cattle and pigs.

In nature, 18 haemagglutinin (H) and 11 neuraminidase (N) distinct subtypes (each virus subtype possessing one H and one N) have been identified, of which 16 H subtypes have been detected in avian species, with predominantly 10 subtypes (H1–H10) having potential to cause infections in domestic poultry. There is much greater restriction on the range of H and N subtypes that are able to infect mammalian species including humans. Standard international nomenclature sets out how viruses are named and described. This in chronological order indicates the type, host, place of first isolation, reference number for the virus and the year of isolation, with the virus subtype included at the end in parenthesis e.g. A/chicken/Scotland/1/59 (H5N1).

Avian species are the reservoir for most influenza A viruses, in wild birds the viruses maintain largely in evolutionary stasis without causing undue harm to the host. Periodically the virus will come in contact and spill over to other host populations including domestic poultry. Furthermore, the origin of infection in mammalian species resides in the avian population. Transmission from birds to mammalian hosts is an infrequent event and rarely leads to the establishment of a stable virus population. Pigs are susceptible to viruses from avian, but also human influenzas and for this reason have been postulated to act as intermediary between birds and humans, since avian viruses generally are not efficient at replicating and infecting humans. Other animal populations such as horses and companion animals can maintain stable virus populations of influenza A as a result of transmission events from birds, however, most of these transmissions events are inefficient and the

*ian.brown@apha.gov.uk

© CAB International 2021. *Poultry Health: A Guide for Professionals* (P. Barrow *et al.*)
DOI: 10.1079/9781789245042.0015

viruses are not able to establish in their new mammalian host.

15vii.3 Zoonoses

Historically, avian influenza was not regarded as a zoonotic disease, however due to changes in the virus and increased awareness, zoonotic infections have been reported with increased frequency in recent years, and it is important that operatives working within the poultry sector are aware of the potential risks when handling and dealing with poultry or items that may be contaminated with poultry secretions. These zoonotic infections relate to strains maintained entirely within the avian population such as H5N1 HPAI viruses. Generally, humans are refractory to infections with avian viruses but those who have contact with infected birds may experience mild flu like illness since the virus usually is only able to replicate on local surfaces. Nevertheless, in a small number of cases the virus is able to cause a more productive respiratory infection and can lead to factors such as cytokine storm resulting in fatality. This has particularly been associated with emergence and spread of H5 HPAI viruses, however a characteristic of these avian strains is they lack the ability to spread from one human to another.

The potential for an avian influenza virus to genetically mix with a human strain resulting in progeny virus that carries novel H and N subtypes not known to the human population, but possess the property of high transmissibility, remains a major concern for pandemic emergence, since none of the human population will have any prior immunity to these novel subtypes traditionally present in avian species. The pathogenicity of the virus whether HPAI or LPAI for birds does not confer increased or reduced infectiousness for humans. On the contrary, several LPAI viruses, notably H9N2 and H7N9 have caused frequent infections in humans. LPAI H9N2 are ubiquitous in birds across many parts of the world with a resulting large interface to people. Nevertheless, when transmissions have occurred they generally resulted in mild flu like illness or conjunctivitis, often in children with uneventful outcome and full recovery. However, the emergence of H7N9 LPAI virus in poultry in China in 2013 was first detected through human cases, with the case fatality rate approaching 30%. After circulation for a few years Chinese authorities implemented a mandatory prophylactic vaccination programme in poultry and since this time human cases have been averted.

A series of pandemics of human flu have been recorded over time with isolates from cases in the last century having been typed. The 'Spanish flu' pandemic following the first World War for example was a classical H1N1 strain, followed in 1957 with H2N2, 1968 H3N2, 1977 H1N1 and in 2009 a different H1N1. The 1918 Spanish flu outbreak resulted in >40 million deaths worldwide, with the infection exacerbated by general poor health, which deteriorated in many countries during the war.

15vii.4 Subtypes and Genomic Fluidity

Influenza A viruses undergo change through two major mechanisms: antigenic drift and antigenic shift. In the case of antigenic drift point mutations in the external glycoproteins H and N mutate over time as viruses migrate through a population and new advantageous mutations become fixed in the population. This is largely driven by the errors during transcription of the RNA virus which occur more frequently than with DNA viruses. The rate of antigenic drift in influenza viruses in birds is at a low rate compared to other hosts since they exert much less population immunity to drive virus change. However, it should be noted that in the face of vaccination the rate of antigenic drift, particularly in the H gene, can be accelerated with long term implications for vaccine use. Antigenic shift is the mechanism whereby the virus can alter its gene composition by mixing and matching genes (due to the segmented nature of the genome) with influenza viruses from other sources. This has been shown to be important method for continued evolution of H5 HPAI viruses of the goose/Guangdong lineage, whereby the viruses maintain fitness (offering replicative advantage) and the ability to spread over time by continually inheriting genes from other avian influenza viruses circulating in wild birds.

The emergence of pandemic or panzootic (in birds) influenza occurs via the mechanism of either drift and shift or shift alone with two theories: circulation theory and a reassortment theory. In humans the 1918 virus is thought to have originated due to point mutations in the H1 gene of an avian virus over time, whereby it became adapted to humans. Whereas, in the pandemics of 1957 (H2N2) and 1968 (H3N2) the prevailing seasonal strain in humans underwent genetic reassortment with another virus from an avian host creating a new subtype. This mechanism of change in the H and N is an important correlate for spread within the human population. Furthermore, in 2009 a virus believed to have its origin in pigs caused a small pandemic in humans. This virus had acquired gene segments from multiple swine strains some, of which had direct ancestral links with bird strains. The panzootic of H5 HPAI in poultry is described later.

The ability of an influenza virus to persist and maintain within a host population requires it to have a high replicative fitness and the ability to efficiently transmit between individuals within that population. This property or trait is governed through all of the gene segments of the virus, which cover a range of functions from initial attachment to a cell surface receptor, to efficient replication within the target host cell. Some of these traits have been mapped but are not fully understood and precise correlates for fitness and transmission within avian species is relatively limited. However, attachment of avian influenza viruses to specific avian host cell receptors has been identified as a barrier for interchange between viruses. This probably gives a clue as to why mammalian influenza viruses are less able to transmit to avian species.

Strains are further divided according to their pathogenicity for birds (chickens). HPAI viruses produce severe disease with mortality often approaching 100% and so far have involved only viruses of H5 or H7 subtypes. LPAI viruses generally cause a mild respiratory infection with depression and often in laying birds egg reduction or poor-quality eggs, i.e. thin shell or misshapen. However, the severity of infection with LPAI viruses can be exacerbated by multi-factorial co-infection. All viruses that are not HPAI have the potential to cause disease problems in poultry but in practice this has been restricted to certain subtypes that more commonly occur than others, i.e. H1, H4, H5, H6, H7 and H9.

There are two main pathways for the emergence of HPAI: the classical pathway is where an H5 or H7 LPAI virus enters a poultry population directly or indirectly from wild birds and establishes stable spreading infection. During this adaptation and spread it is possible that an HPAI variant may emerge and be selected in the population. This switch can occur in a single farm or during series of events in a linked outbreak. Some particular subtype combinations of H and N appear to have a greater propensity to switch from low to high pathogenicity. For example, there are numerous examples across Europe with H7N7 virus entering laying birds as a low pathogenicity strain and rapidly switching to a high pathogenicity strain. In almost all of these cases there is a breach in biosecurity allowing entry of LPAI which is then able to freely transmit within susceptible birds and during this process an HPAI variant emerges due to infidelity in RNA transcription. Importantly most of these viruses do not transmit to, or are maintained independently in wild birds. The alternative pathway is whereby HPAI virus can spread from poultry to wild birds where they can be maintained for a period of time and if these populations of birds have migratory behaviour can carry the virus over some distance. This mechanism has been responsible for transglobal spread and panzootic with H5 HPAI viruses from Southeast Asia to the rest of the world.

15vii.5 Hosts and Epidemiology

The ultimate source of AI for poultry is wild birds and initial introduction to poultry can result in extensive secondary spread via a number of routes.

Influenza A viruses have been isolated for most orders of free-living wild birds. This includes in particular anseriformes (ducks, swans and geese) and charadiformes ('shorebirds'). From these major families, virus can readily spread to other species although long-term independent maintenance is less likely as they tend to be more of a dead-end species. With the expansion of H5 HPAI viruses a greater range of wild birds have been reported as infected, consequent with substantial global increases in wild bird surveillance activities for influenza viruses being used as early warning systems to detect spread of virus. However, it is not unusual in surveys when screening generally for LPAI viruses that incidence may be as high as 20% in certain target populations. Mallard ducks have been associated with much greater detection rates given their high susceptibility to viruses, but this equally applies to other species of dabbling duck. Clear distinction should be made between LPAI viruses circulating in their natural reservoir and spillover of HPAI viruses from poultry, the spread of which is mediated through wild birds for transient periods of time. Some species of free-living birds that are constantly found in close proximity to poultry systems such as pigeons and crows can occasionally become infected, but do have a degree of resistance.

Following infection high levels of infectious virus can be excreted with log $10^{8.7}$ infectious virus particles shed by infected ducks. Chickens will also excrete high viral loads with $>10^7$ infectious particles per gram of faeces and infectivity can be retained in the faeces for >6 weeks.

Since infected wild birds especially including ducks can produce high quantities of infectious virus, this will lead to virus being deposited into the environment where it can survive for considerable periods of time (many weeks) particularly with lower ambient temperatures and reduced UV radiation (i.e. winter months). Persistence of virus in this way is a common pathway whereby following indirect fomite introduction, virus can be carried into poultry production systems even in the apparent absence of local wild bird populations.

Avian influenza is spread by direct or indirect contact between infected and healthy birds. The virus is shed in secretions from the nares, buccal cavity and eyes of infected birds as well as their faeces. Though the virus can spread through airborne secretions, i.e. in dust, the disease itself is not generally an airborne infection over any distance. HPAI infection is spread to people often through direct contact with infected poultry, such as during slaughter or plucking.

Primary introduction to poultry from wild birds depends on a number of factors, including geographical location, extent of direct or indirect contact and farming practices. Domestic ducks have a key role in the long-term maintenance and spread of influenza A viruses since they are highly susceptible and are farmed in many parts of the world. Many domestic waterfowl (ducks and geese) are reared extensively in free-range format where they can have contact with wild waterfowl or other wild birds. Ducks are also reared intensively in houses but frequently with poor biosecurity, often inapparent infection including with HPAI virus in these hosts increases the risk for spread given the inability to easily detect the presence of disease. In fact, where mixed farming of multiple species occurs this increases the risk of introduction since anseriforme species will often act as the amplifiers of virus which then subsequently spreads to gallinaceous birds. Similarly, in live bird market settings present in many parts of the world, bringing together of many different species of different ages, sex and breeds increases the risk of virus transfer between hosts that would normally have limited close contact. These environments normally lack basic hygiene and can be an important source of virus that can then be disseminated to other production systems. However, it should be noted that outbreaks can occur randomly in any host population at any time including in the absence of domestic waterfowl species especially when viruses are endemic in poultry in a region.

Farming practices can increase the risk of spread of virus such as high-density poultry production with close proximity of farms, inefficient sanitation of surface water for drinking, improper control of food and equipment delivery vehicles, and lack of use of good hygiene practices by farm staff. The increasing number of backyard/hobby flocks poses a theoretical risk for initial virus introduction and multiplication but usually failures in the application of good biosecurity account for most incursions. Secondary spread occurs through activities associated with poultry production via fomite transmission including farmers and staff during husbandry, trucks and drivers moving birds, eggs or feed, groups of personnel involved in thinning or artificial insemination and also veterinarians.

15vii.6 Global Spread of H5Nx HPAI

The index case of most modern day H5 HPAI outbreaks occurred in geese in Guangdong province in China in 1996. Despite sporadic detection of H5N1 principally in live poultry markets, it was not until 2003 that serious outbreaks in various settings were reported with extensive mortality. The virus itself was well established in domestic ducks in southern China but rapid spread from December 2003 to many countries in South-east Asia including Laos, Cambodia, Vietnam, Thailand and Indonesia followed, with further spread radiating therefrom. The virus became entrenched in many of these countries despite numerous approaches to control. In some of these locations the virus still persists today in an endemic state, i.e. Indonesia, and in others the virus continually reoccurs despite efforts to control, including through vaccination. By late 2005 the virus had spread as far as the Middle East and subsequently into Europe and down into West Africa. The modes of transmission initially were highly contentious, but principally at local scale via movement of infected poultry, via poultry commodities or associated fomite transmission. However, transboundary spread over longer distances has definitively been proven to occur through migratory waterbirds resulting in the detection in Central Asia, Europe, North America and Africa. The epidemiology of these outbreaks is typified by numerous point introductions by wild birds but with some lateral secondary spread influenced by poultry production demographic and ability to implement effective local controls. This has occurred even in well developed 'biosecure' poultry productions systems especially where it involves species that do not present with clear clinical signs such as ducks and geese.

As the virus has spread around the globe it has diversified and evolved at different rates in different ecosystems. This has given rise to the so-called naming of genetic groups of viruses based on the H gene called clades. Since emergence in 1996, new clades have appeared, and others disappeared, whilst some have continued to evolve successfully. This large genetic diversity also translates into different phenotypic properties, i.e. clinical presentation in species such as ducks, and influences the utility of surveillance systems. Clades that have an improved fitness for their host and are able to infect a wider avian host range will often prevail. Furthermore, viruses may emerge escaping vaccinal immunity since many countries have actively used vaccination to control the panzootic, notably within China.

15vii.7 Pathogenesis and Infection Dynamics

As described above, cutting across the subtypes are two pathotypes, HPAI and LPAI, the latter of which induces a mild respiratory disease with problems in egg production. In contrast the clinical signs associated with HPAI can be sudden with rapidly rising mortality approaching 100% in a few days. Respiratory signs include gaping and difficulty in breathing, excessive lachrymation, oedema of the head, diarrhoea, neurological signs including paralysis and torticollis and subcutaneous haemorrhage (Fig. 15vii.1).

Egg laying may cease completely. Tissue damage is extensive affecting cardiovascular and visceral organs and the nervous system.

Experimental inoculation reproduces high mortality caused by several H5 strains. Quails are resistant to several H5 strains with some lines of domestic ducks being almost resistant to clinical effects although they do act as host to viral multiplication and shedding via the respiratory and intestinal tracts. Their relative resistance is thought to result from poor cytokine production in response to infection whereas chickens generate a cytokine storm itself causing huge tissue damage. However, some virus strains can cause acute disease involving systemic infection affecting multiple organ systems (Figs 15vii.2 and 15vii.3), neurological dysfunction and death.

There is variation in pathogenesis, and this will be influenced by the host and virus strain. In general, gallinaceous poultry are highly susceptible, but some hosts have a level of resistance, i.e. quail, or can have stronger resistance to clinical disease presentation including ducks and geese. It should be noted however, that the goose/Guangdong lineage viruses have a moderately high efficiency to replicate systemically in ducks and geese and in all species replicate to extremely high titre via the

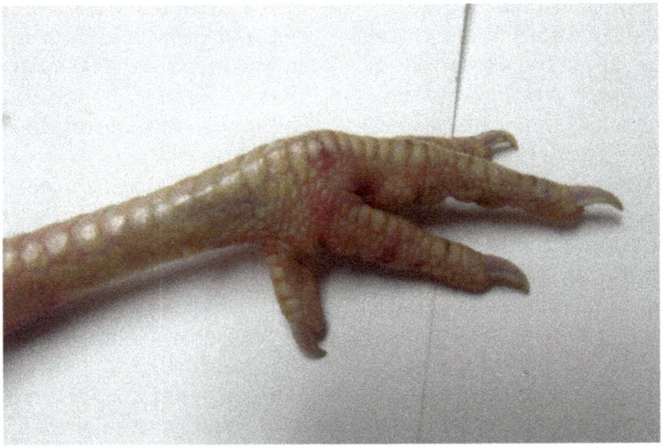

Fig. 15vii.1. Hyperaemia with HPAI in chickens. (Author's own image.)

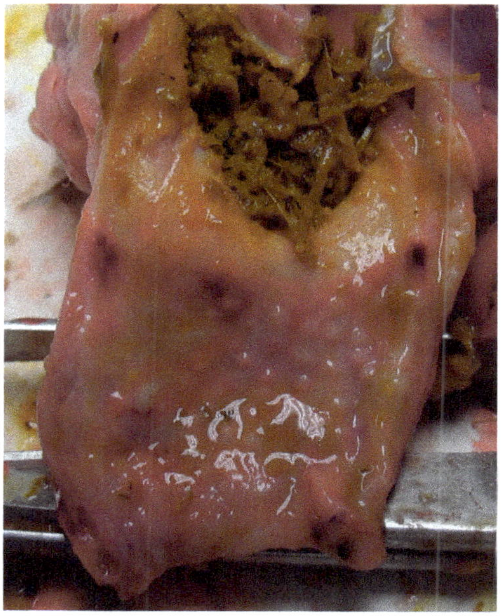

Fig. 15vii.2. Proventricular haemorrhages with HPAI. (Author's own image.)

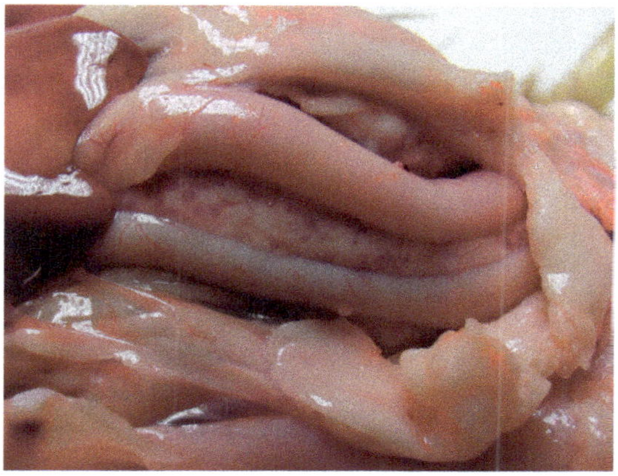

Fig. 15vii.3. Pancreatic necrosis with HPAI. (Author's own image.)

respiratory and intestinal tracts. Many birds will die of multiple organ failure since there is rapid systemic infection with neurological dysfunction, virus reaching the brain and death.

Three key factors must be achieved in order for the virus to replicate in a given host and particular cell type. This includes attachment via sialic acid receptors which are specific for avian and mammalian species, fusion of the haemagglutinin as the first part of the replication process and successful direction of the host cell to produce viral RNA and subsequent virus assembly. These factors need to be satisfied in order for successful infection, transmission across host barriers and explains the large host restriction amongst influenza viruses between birds and mammals. These factors are controlled and influenced by all the viral genes.

The mechanism of pathogenesis is initially mediated after cell attachment through the H glycoprotein mediating fusion with the host cell membrane. It is synthesized as an inactive precursor HA0 and is activated via cleavage by host proteases. The configuration of amino acids of the H cleavage site correlate with the tropism of the virus since it directs the ability of the HA0 to be cleaved by host enzymes. The presence of multiple basic amino acids at the HA0 cleavage site means the viruses are able to be cleaved by proteases present in all tissues, and permits spread systemically throughout the host. Without these basic amino acids, virus replication is restricted to multiplication in the respiratory and intestinal tracts due to the presence of trypsin-like enzymes in these locations which are able to cleave an HA0 motif lacking basic amino acids.

Pathogenicity does not directly correlate with transmissibility, however, HPAI viruses do have very low minimum infectious doses and are generally able to readily transmit within susceptible birds. Transmissions rates are broadly similar between all poultry types with virus shedding reaching elevated levels within 24 h before mortality.

15vii.8 The Cost of Avian Influenza

Avian influenza in the modern era has become entrenched in many areas of global poultry production with significant impact on food security. Transboundary spread of H5 HPAI (goose/Guangdong lineage) viruses of substantial diversity and the wide-ranging population it affects has had a huge societal impact. Precise estimates are not available, but at least 2 billion poultry have been culled or killed due to this group of viruses. The cost to the global economy again is uncertain, but total estimates have been of the order of \$50 billion. Outbreaks have been at the most intense in areas of densely populated poultry production systems of rearing that are extensive and not indoors, with active use of live bird markets and poor regulatory disease control mechanisms in the country. The outbreaks in size have increasingly enlarged.

However, it is not just this group of viruses that are capable of causing devastating outbreaks, previously large outbreaks occurred particularly in Europe and North America. One outbreak in northeastern Italy between 1999 and 2000 resulted in the death of 14 million birds. It affected all sectors of the chicken (39 broiler, 29 broiler breeder and 121 layer flocks) and turkey industries (177 turkey flocks and 5 turkey breeder flocks) but also quail and backyard flocks. In total there were 413 outbreaks. Total losses to the poultry and associated industries were €500 million with €51 million being paid in compensation.

The Netherlands was affected in 2003 involving 226 commercial and 15 backyard flocks. The number of birds culled to prevent further spread was 1425 commercial and 16,700 backyard flocks, a total of more than 30 million birds. The costs were €270 million in direct costs with an additional >€1 billion indirect. In the Netherlands farms can be distributed very densely with <50 farms/km^2 not uncommon and 12–15 farms/km^2 normal. This resulted in spread by caeca and feather dust especially during slaughter and clean up. In this particular outbreak, local farms were often owned by the same family so that extensive transmission was mediated by family and staff.

However, the largest HPAI epidemics in Europe in scale, geographical distribution and size occurred in 2016/17 and again in 2020/21 due to H5N8 HPAI. In 2016/17 28 EU member states were affected with a total of 1188 poultry outbreaks, 1583 detections in wild birds and 64 cases in captive or backyard birds. This resulted in the death or depopulation of approximately 35 million birds. Similarly in the 2020/21 epidemic (ongoing at time of writing) there have been 3555 reported HPAI detections (poultry and wild birds) with approximately 23 million affected poultry in 28 European countries.

LPAI of H9N2 subtype have become widespread and endemic in chickens in many countries, particularly Asia and Africa. Distinct H gene lineages and multiple genotypes are involved as might be expected for an endemic RNA virus. Although infection is generally mild (Figs 15vii.4a–d) high morbidity and mortality can occur.

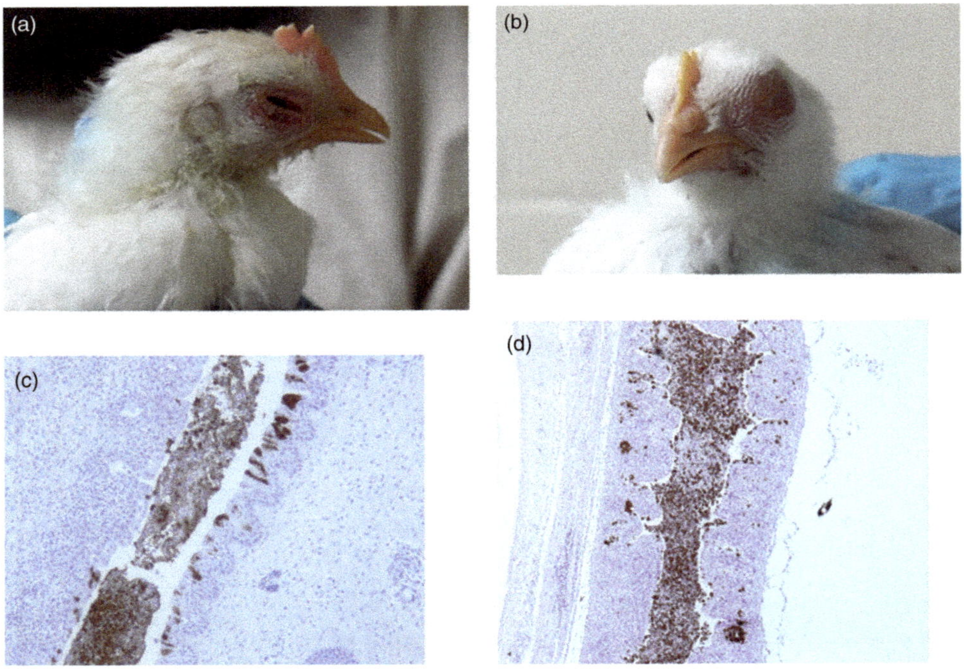

Fig. 15vii.4. Conjunctivitis observed in chickens directly inoculated with and contact-infected with H7N9 LPAIV (both wild-type and poultry adapted; examples in (a) and (b)). (c) Virus-specific IHC staining depicting viral antigen in epithelial cells lining the conjunctiva and cell debris within the conjunctival recess. (d) In addition, viral antigen was clearly abundant in cells within the lumen of the Harderian gland. The Harderian gland is located adjacent to the ocular cavity of the chicken. (Author's own image.)

Secondary infections with other infectious agents can occur making the clinical picture more severe. Local vaccination is often carried out to reduce shedding and prevent clinical signs although the importance of good biosecurity cannot be overemphasized.

15vii.9 Diagnosis

Clinical signs are not pathognomonic so laboratory diagnosis must be conducted. Presumptive diagnosis can be made on post mortem lesions which include respiratory inflammation, ovarian haemorrhage, necrosis of comb and wattles, subcutaneous oedema of head and neck and intestinal haemorrhage (Fig. 15vii.2) but also on the history of the flock and disease occurrence elsewhere. The method of choice for diagnosis is currently real time RT-PCR which will sensitively detect viral RNA in swabs collected from either the oral-pharynx or cloaca. Further work can be done to determine the virus subtype and pathotype by gene sequencing and/or using serological techniques having cultured the virus. Culture is conventionally done in embryonated fowl's eggs or cell culture, and virus isolated can be used to conduct standard *in vivo* pathogenicity tests by inoculating 4–6-week-old chickens intravenously. HPAI viruses have indices of >1.2 with the most pathogenic strains having a maximum score of 3.0 when all birds die within 24 h. The serological tests of choice are haemagglutination inhibition tests or ELISA.

15vii.10 Control

AI is regarded by the OIE as a disease of extreme severity for poultry and which requires legislative enforcement (see Chapter 23, this volume). Currently many countries including European states include all H5 and H7 subtypes (including LPAI forms) in their control policies. Control regimens are complex and may differ between countries with compartmentalization policies for different poultry sectors within individual countries. In EU countries the appearance of HPAI initiates a stamping-out procedure aimed at eradication as quickly as possible with the introduction of 3 and 10 km control zones. In countries where flock densities are very high, as in the Netherlands or Italy, pre-emptive mass culling may be used in addition.

Preventing secondary spread after initial introduction relies on good management and biosecurity (see Chapter 17, this volume). This particularly includes movement on and off the farm involving staff and personnel. Movement onto farms should be kept to a minimum and the highest levels of biosecurity for personnel must be instituted in high risk areas or control zones. Following an outbreak culling and complete depopulation should be carried out with incineration/complete burial of carcasses, litter and faeces carried out on site (if possible) followed by thorough cleaning and disinfection with a break of at least six weeks before repopulation.

Vaccination is prohibited in the EU (derogations possible under special conditions) but is sometimes used elsewhere, however although it reduces the severity and incidence of clinical signs, birds may still become infected, and virus can replicate in vaccinated birds. The OIE still therefore regards such birds as infected and require notification.

The conclusions from European outbreaks are that control of H5Nx HPAI is possible but requires strong veterinary infrastructure, cooperation between all stakeholder groups and is resource intensive. It requires restrictions in movement and trade and tight biosecurity. EU Directive 2005/94/EC recommends controlling outbreaks by immediate depopulation and implementation of 3 and 10 km control zones for HPAI. Strict regulations should be put in place to restrict movement within and out of zones, and movement out of the zones is only permitted under licence, with the option to provide test assurance in these circumstances. Further, surveillance should be conducted within the two control zones to establish that there has been no further spread of infection. In addition, tracing from infected premises to contacts outside the zones must be conducted with and, if necessary, requiring laboratory investigation to exclude infection.

15vii.11 Further Reading

Alarcon, P., Brouwer, A., Venkatesh, D., Duncan, D., Dovas, C.I., *et al.* (2018) Comparison of 2016–17 and previous epizootics of highly pathogenic avian influenza H5 Guangdong lineage in Europe. *Emerging Infectious Diseases* 24, 2270–2283.

European Community (2005) Commission decision 2005/95/EC of 20 December 2005 on community measures for the control of avian influenza and repealing Directive 92/40/EEC. *Official Journal of the European Union* L 10/16, 14.1.2006. Available at: https://eur-lex.europa.eu/legal-content/EN/ALL/?uri=CELEX:32005L0094 (accessed 9 March 2021).

Lycett, S., Pohlmann, A., Staubach, C., Calliendo, V., Woolhouse, *et al*. for the Global Consortium for H5N8 and Related Influenza Viruses (2020) Genesis and spread of multiple reassortants during the 2016/2017 H5 avian influenza epidemic in Eurasia. *Proceedings of the National Academy of Sciences* 117(34), 20814–20825.

OIE (World Organisation for Animal Health) (2018) Avian influenza. In: *Manual of Diagnostic Tests and Vaccines for Terrestrial Animals*, 8th edn. OIE, Paris. Available at : https://www.oie.int/fileadmin/Home/eng/Health_standards/tahm/3.03.04_AI.pdf (accessed 25 January 2021).

Sims, L.D. and Brown, I.H. (2016) Multi-continental panzootic of H5 highly pathogenic avian influenza (1996–2015). In: Swayne, D.E. (ed.) *Animal Influenza.* Wiley-Blackwell, Ames, Iowa, pp. 202–247.

Sutton, T.C. (2018) The pandemic threat of emerging H5 and H7 avian influenza viruses. *Viruses* 10, 461. DOI: 10.3390/v10090461.

Swayne, D.E., Suarez, D.L. and Sims, L.D. (2013) Influenza. In: Swayne, D.E. (editor-in-chief) *Diseases of Poultry*, 15th edn. Wiley-Blackwell, Danvers, Massachusetts, pp. 181–218.

15viii Newcastle Disease

Ian H. Brown*

Animal and Plant Health Agency-Weybridge, Addlestone, Surrey, UK

15viii.1 Introduction

Newcastle disease (ND) is a serious highly infectious systemic disease of birds first described in 1926/7 in Indonesia, and in Newcastle upon Tyne, UK. It caused several panzootics in poultry in the 1920s, 1960s and 1970s/80s, all originating in the Middle East. It results in a variable disease outcome linked to many factors but causes significant disease and economic burden.

The virulent virus (NDV) remains endemic in many countries in sub-Saharan Africa, the Middle East and several Asian countries. In some settings, particularly Africa and Asia where village poultry are an important part of local society, it is estimated that losses in backyard village chickens alone may reach 60%.

NDV is largely exotic in Europe and, following incursion, results in the implementation of statutory control measures (see Section 15viii.6 Control); however, in some countries in eastern and south-eastern Europe the virus is endemic, and surveillance can sometimes be limited, particularly where extensive use of vaccination is applied. Furthermore, there are emergent strains that may escape vaccine immunity. The challenge in endemically infected populations of birds where vaccination is usually prophylactically applied on scale, is to conduct effective surveillance to understand where the virus is present, since vaccination will often mask clinical disease. This can contribute to and exacerbate further endemic cycles of virus infection.

15viii.2 The Virus/Virology

NDV is one of the 21 currently identified strains of avian paramyxovirus belonging to the family *Paramyxoviridae*, genus *Orthoavulavirus*, which infect birds. NDV is a variant of *Avian paramyxovirus type 1* (APMV-1) which are negative-sense, single-stranded RNA viruses. APMV-1s are distinguishable from the other types (APMV-2 to 21) by serology. Like avian influenza, the viral RNA acquires its capsid in the cytoplasm and is enveloped as it leaves the infected cells. The viruses are pleomorphic. Other members of this family include the morbilliviruses (measles, rinderpest), the rubulaviruses, (including mumps virus), the henipaviruses (Nipah virus and Hendra virus) and respiroviruses (parainfluenza virus). NDVs have a range of virulence but all are lethal in fully susceptible birds. In contrast, many of the other types of *Avian paramyxovirus* (APMV-2 to -21), largely found in wild aquatic species, produce mild respiratory infections or have no known virulence in a range of poultry species (i.e. APMV-2, -3), but are also found in pigeons and psittacines. Avian paramyxoviruses may be distinguished by a number of serological tests but, increasingly, genetic sequencing methods are those of choice. This includes accurate differentiation of APMV type 1; however, it should be noted not all type 1 viruses are NDV, as type 1 also contains avirulent avian paramyxoviruses.

The genome is ca 15.5 kbp in length, encoding seven proteins: nucleocapsid (N), matrix (M), V protein, F, polymerase associated phosphoprotein (P), HN and L protein. Important structural features of the virus are the haemagglutinin-neuraminidase (HN) and fusion (F) genes. These two external glycoproteins on the surface of the virus are key virulence determinants and the major target of the host immune response, and are also used in virus classification. They are critical for virus attachment and penetration to the host cell, starting the process of virus replication. The HN mediates attachment

*ian.brown@apha.gov.uk

© CAB International 2021. *Poultry Health: A Guide for Professionals* (P. Barrow *et al.*)
DOI: 10.1079/9781789245042.0015

to the target host cell receptor, and the fusion protein facilitates fusion enabling integration of virus into the host cell prior to active viral RNA replication and virus assembly. The virus then buds through the host cell membrane before release. These two proteins are important for the induction of host cell immunity.

The F gene is synthesized as an inactive precursor F0 which is activated by cleavage by host proteases. The presence of multiple basic amino acids at the F0 cleavage site enables active cleavage of the fusion protein by ubiquitous proteases present throughout systemic tissues. This enables the virus to have a systemic tropism and is associated with high virulence. In contrast, viruses that lack multiple basic amino acids at the F0 cleavage site are only cleaved by trypsin-like enzymes at mucosal surfaces, which restricts replication to respiratory and intestinal tracts. By definition, these viruses are of lower virulence and are classified as avirulent avian paramyxovirus type 1; they are often used as live vaccine strains. The presence or absence of multiple basic amino acids is important for the classification and identification of NDV. Note, APMV-1s should not be referred to as NDV; NDV only refers to strains of APMV-1 that are virulent according to standard international definitions set down by the OIE (World Organisation for Animal Health). Further, APMV-1 and NDV are classified into genotypes based on the genetic characteristics of the F gene.

The OIE definition states:

> For the purposes of the *Terrestrial Code*, Newcastle disease (ND) is defined as an *infection* of *poultry* caused by Newcastle disease virus (NDV), which is an avian paramyxovirus serotype 1 (APMV-1) that meets one of the following criteria for virulence:
>
> a. the virus has an intracerebral pathogenicity index (ICPI) in day-old chicks *(Gallus gallus)* of 0.7 or greater; or
> b. multiple basic amino acids have been demonstrated in the virus (either directly or by deduction) at the C-terminus of the F2 protein and phenylalanine at residue 117, which is the N-terminus of the F1 protein. The term 'multiple basic amino acids' refers to at least three arginine or lysine residues between residues 113 and 116. Failure to demonstrate the characteristic pattern of amino acid residues as described above would require characterization of the isolated virus by an ICPI test.
>
> (OIE, 2019, p. 969)

15viii.3 Epidemiology

NDVs have a restricted tropism to avian species, and it is likely that all avian species may act as host to infection, but some may be more important than others. For example, it is known that waterfowl and *Columbiformes* are particularly susceptible to these viruses which may be important in viral ecology.

All species of domestic poultry are susceptible, although ducks appear to be less susceptible to clinical disease but can still shed virus. The susceptibility of bird species means that any geographical transfer of pet, exotic, game (including fighting cocks) or racing birds (pigeons), in addition to domestic poultry, can lead to transfer of infection. This includes internal spread of infection within a country that can be mediated through live bird markets. In these locations, multiple species of birds of different breed, genetic status and with variable infection status are traded with very high turnover, an environment that facilitates persistence and transmission of NDV.

Whilst it is known that a large range of wild birds may be infected and carry NDV, precise pathways and mechanisms whereby such viruses emerge in poultry are not well understood. For example, sporadic introduction of a single genotype NDV over many years in Sweden, a non-vaccinating country, with strict trade control is most probably explained by spillover from wild bird populations, and yet the primary host maintaining such strains is unclear.

The origin of outbreaks remains a major discussion point. It is possible that APMV-1 has been present in domestic fowl as a mild unrecognized disease, with virulent virus emerging as a result of mutation, or that it was also always present as a serious but unrecognized disease. Closely related but distinct APMV-1s have certainly been present in wild birds although this was not recognized until 1966. However, the mechanism for the emergence of virulent viruses from avirulent strains has been widely demonstrated. In principle, avirulent viruses which may be ubiquitous in many wild bird populations may occasionally transfer into domestic poultry. Following transmission to poultry, mutation events may follow that change the cleavage site motif on the F protein to one containing multibasic amino acids, which classifies the virus as virulent virus. Sometimes a relatively small number of point mutations (1–2) are required to switch avirulent to virulent virus, an event that may more easily occur after a host switch to gallinaceous poultry. Sequencing of the F gene provides insights into the origins of such viruses.

The major pathway for spread of Newcastle disease, other than direct movement of infected live birds, is through fomite transmission via human activity on contaminated footwear, clothing, vehicles, feed and equipment. The virus can persist in carcasses, faeces and the environment for several weeks, further complicating the risk pathways. Feral birds can spread virus via fomite transmission, i.e. birds that frequent farm environments can mechanically move between different farms thereby spreading virus. The main methods of transfer between infected birds include short distance droplet spread or via dust, particularly following respiratory infection. Respiratory and particularly intestinal infections can result in contaminated food or water which can lead to very rapid spread within a poultry house.

The panzootic of the 1980s was permeated mainly through the establishment of NDV in *Columbiforme* species. Particularly notable introduction occurred to the UK in the mid-1980s, whereby racing pigeons were infected with such viruses and rapidly spread the virus across the country with virus spillover into local indigenous feral pigeons. Furthermore, it was demonstrated that contamination of feed stored at docks was the source of virus for chickens that contracted the disease. This demonstrates the risk that *Columbiformes* present and, to this day, they maintain an active reservoir of infection with routine vaccination of racing pigeons practiced in many countries to reduce the infection risk. The virus in *Columbiformes* is termed pigeon paramyxovirus type 1, which when transmitted to domestic poultry is classified as Newcastle disease virus, owing to the virulent properties of the virus.

NDVs cause very clear and obvious clinical disease in gallinaceous poultry. However, in other hosts, including domestic waterfowl and gamebirds, clinical presentation may be less obvious. In the UK, two notable outbreaks were in pheasants in 2005 and grey partridges in 2006, and these occurred via different risk pathways. The outbreak in pheasants occurred in birds imported from France where the flock of origin was retrospectively confirmed NDV-positive but not initially recognized due to lack of clinical signs. The disease was a slow debilitating infection with low mortality, blindness and ataxia. Whilst the causative virus was common with many other viruses isolated across Europe, molecular epidemiology on virus detected in samples subsequently collected from the farm of origin in France, showed it to be indistinguishable from that in the UK outbreak. In an unrelated outbreak in East Lothian in Scotland in 2006, affected grey partridges were on a complex site containing many different species of gamebird. The source of infection was proved to be an infected pigeon loft, but the virus did not efficiently spread to other gamebirds kept on the site, showing that inefficient transmission of NDV can often be a characteristic in such hosts.

The prevailing strains in Europe are primarily of genotypes VII (reclassified and split into genotypes VII.1.1, VII.1.2 and VII.2) and VI (reclassified as VI.1 and VI.2 – pigeon paramyxoviruses). Some of the genotype VII viruses appear in some circumstances to evade vaccinal immunity. They are highly virulent, but in general if detected early, primarily through backyard bird infection, are not associated substantively with large outbreaks. This is probably due to extensive vaccination across many European counties against Newcastle disease prophylactically, especially in laying and breeding birds which are longer lived and have protective immunity during their lifespan. Sometimes viruses may only be detected when they reach non-vaccinated populations and cause disease, because of the challenges of conducting surveillance in vaccinated flocks in the absence of disease.

15viii.4 Clinical Outcomes and Pathology

Historically, virus strains were classified into groups by their virulence characteristics according to their clinical presentation in susceptible chickens. They correlate approximately with high, medium and low virulence: viscerotropic velogenic, causing acute lethal infections with haemorrhagic lesions in the intestines; neurotropic velogenic, also causing high mortality involving respiratory and neurological clinical signs but without gut lesions; mesogenic, involving respiratory and neurological signs but with low mortality; lentogenic, causing mild respiratory infections; and asymptomatic enteric, which cause avirulent infections with replication taking place primarily in the gut.

The course of disease is affected not only by the virulence of the strain involved but also by the host species, age and immunological status. Infection can be wide ranging with virulent velogenic strains being so acute that sudden death may be the first sign of disease. Less acute signs include depression, diarrhoea, oedema of the head (Fig. 15viii.1) and neurological signs including torticollis (Fig. 15viii.2) but with very high levels of mortality. Egg shells may be soft, or birds may stop laying altogether.

Moderately virulent (mesogenic) strains typically produce respiratory signs with neurological sequelae and levels of mortality <50%. Some strains, such as those from pigeons, may induce diarrhoea with neurological signs in fowl together with greatly reduced egg production. By definition, mesogenic strains can fulfil the international definition for virulence and therefore are classified as NDV and may be subject to statutory control in countries where they are exotic. They are normally used in vaccination programmes where endemicity is found, and they can potentiate boosting of immune responses.

Low virulence stains produce mild respiratory disease or none at all. Exacerbating circumstances including co-infection with other pathogens, and poor husbandry may cause apparent increases in

Fig. 15viii.1. Oedema of the head in NDV-infected chicken. (Author's own image.)

Fig. 15viii.2. Torticollis in NDV-infected chickens. (Author's own image.)

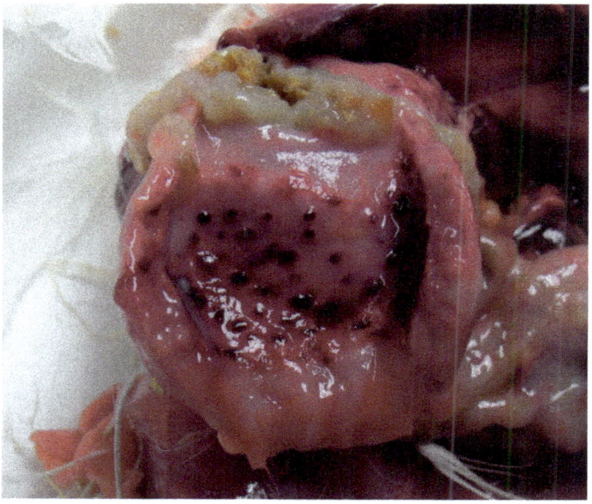

Fig. 15viii.3. Proventricular haemorrhages with NDV infection. (Author's own image.)

virulence. The clinical signs are not pathognomic. Infection with velogenic strains can result in necrotic lesions with haemorrhages in several organs, whilst respiratory infections can cause inflammation of the trachea sometimes with haemorrhages. The air sacs may also be inflamed and cloudy.

Intestinal infections may be characterized by haemorrhages including in the proventriculus (Fig. 15viii.3).

There is not a significant public health risk from NDV infection although the virus can replicate in a range of mammalian cell lines in addition to avian cell lines. Mild conjunctivitis may follow contact with infected birds or following exposure to live virus during mass vaccination processes.

15viii.5 Diagnosis (see also Chapter 22, this volume)

The standard approach (as defined by the OIE) to identify NDV is by isolation or detection of the virus followed by a virulence assessment using PCR/gene sequencing of the F0 cleavage site associated with high or low virulence, or *in vivo* tests in chickens. Optimally, both oropharyngeal and cloacal swabs should be tested from live sampled birds reflecting the breadth of tropism preferences amongst NDVs. If moribund or dead birds are available, a range of systemic tissues (including brain, lung, liver, heart, kidney and intestine) should be tested.

Following significant improvements in PCR methodology for the reliable and sensitive detection of all NDV genotypes, the use of real-time RT-PCR (rRT-PCR) is the primary method of choice for diagnosis. However, detection alone cannot be used to confirm NDV, and must be supplemented by sequencing of the F gene (to comply with the international definition). Genetic sequences can then be compared to databases of sequences providing information on virus characteristics useful for molecular epidemiology, but also for determining virulence by reference to known genetic correlates of virulence (i.e. presence of multibasic amino acids at the F0 cleavage site). A presumptive diagnosis can be made based upon clinical disease signs and positive PCR results in the absence of vaccination but, due to the ubiquitous nature of APMV-1 strains, virulence confirmation is required.

The virus can be cultured in a range of cells or embryonated fowl's eggs and identified by haemagglutination inhibition (HI) tests using monospecific antibodies (Chapter 22). Serological methods, including HI and ELISA (Chapter 22), are also used but interpretation of results can be confused by the use of vaccines. Fully susceptible non-vaccinated birds will not seroconvert if infected with NDV but may, of course, produce antibodies to avirulent APMV-1 that are indistinguishable in the assay. A common application of serology using the above methods is to monitor vaccinal status and efficacy of vaccination.

Given the widespread use of live vaccine, it is not uncommon for both live vaccine virus and NDV to be present in the same flock or bird, and it is particularly important that the diagnostic laboratory is able to correctly identify the presence of virulent virus in such circumstances. The traditional and international method of choice for determining virulence, which enables identification of virulent virus in a population of avirulent virus, is the *in vivo* pathogenicity test conventionally using the intracerebral pathogenicity index (ICPI). Following intracerebral inoculation of cultured virus in one-day-old chicks, clinical outcomes are monitored daily with virulent strains often causing 100% mortality in 24 h. Avirulent viruses result in no or very mild clinical signs. Another useful tool in the laboratory for quick assessment of virus virulence is to monitor the mean death time in infected chicken embryos. Viruses of high virulence typically have mean death times of less than 24 h, whilst avirulent viruses do not kill embryos, and therefore have mean death times in excess of 72 h.

Accurate differential diagnosis is required for other serious respiratory and enteric diseases with systemic clinical signs including infectious laryngotracheitis, infectious bronchitis, avian influenza, fowl cholera and *Mycoplasma* infections. Molecular diagnostic methods will differentiate NDV from these other pathogens.

15viii.6 Control

As a result of the serious economic nature of NDV, coupled with the severe economic losses associated with the panzootic in the 1970s, many countries that were normally free of infection developed schemes for disease control, enforced in some cases by legislation (see Chapter 23, this volume). This was supported by the OIE definition of NDV and international requirements to notify. Since outbreaks have been initiated by the transportation of exotic birds, rigid quarantine measures may be introduced. The association of NDV with pigeons has also resulted in some countries banning pigeon racing or enforcing vaccination involving birds from countries where the disease may be present.

Where outbreaks occur, countries may employ slaughter policies with disposal of carcasses onsite, imposition of poultry movement in affected areas, improved biosecurity and ring vaccination around the affected area. Approaches to vaccination at country level range from compulsory to optional to prohibited. Policies are generally linked to the enzootic nature of the disease or the perceived threat for new incursion. Vaccination is a viable option because one serotype is involved. It is the preferred option for countries where the disease is endemic and where eradication is not possible. In countries where ND is not endemic, the cost–benefit analysis of vaccination should be carried out. Laboratory-controlled and extensive field studies indicate vaccination can be highly effective at eliminating clinical signs and reducing virus shedding considerably. Vaccination results under field conditions can be more variable and may not prevent entry of infection into a flock, but will clearly reduce the severity of disease and likelihood of onward spread. Because virulent virus may still be present and multiply without clinical signs in vaccinated birds, ND as defined by OIE may still be confirmed. In many countries where vaccination is voluntary, only longer lived more valuable birds (such as egg layers or breeders or grandparent parent flocks) may be vaccinated.

Three main types of ND vaccines are commonly used: live, vectored and inactivated. Live ND vaccines are the most commonly used across the world, partly due to their ability to be administered via mass vaccination techniques. These strains, in common with ND field viruses, vary in their relative tropism for respiratory, enteric and nervous systems. To avoid significant adverse effects, the OIE recommends that the maximum ICPI be <0.7, whilst the EU defines a maximum ICPI of 0.4. Exposure to live vaccines results in a comprehensive immune response resulting in the generation of circulating, local (mucosal) and cell mediated immunity. In some endemically infected countries, mesogenic strains (intermediate virulence) are used as secondary vaccines. Although live vaccines are capable of reducing or eliminating clinical signs and mortality, they do not prevent infection with field virus or shedding of field virus. An alternative to live vaccines is vectored vaccines, usually another harmless virus containing an HN or F gene of NDV. As the vector replicates in the bird, the immune system is exposed to the key NDV antigens. Inactivated vaccines (often with adjuvant) need to be administered by injection of individual birds and are typically used to boost the immunity of older birds such as layers and breeders that have previously been primed by a live vaccine. There have been occasional reports of failure with standard vaccines in well-vaccinated birds upon exposure to antigenically diverse field strains and, where such strains persist, autogenous killed vaccines have been used against prevailing field strains.

15viii.7 Reference

OIE (2019) Newcastle disease (infection with Newcastle disease virus) In: *OIE Manual of Diagnostic Tests and Vaccines for Terrestrial Animals,* 9th edn. Office Internationale des Epizooties (OIE), Paris, p. 969.

15viii.8 Further Reading

Alexander, D.J. (2000) Newcastle disease and other avian paramyxoviruses. *OIE Revue Scientifique et Technique* 19, 443–462.

Brown I.H., Cargill, P., Woodland, R. and Van den Berg, T. (2021) Newcastle disease virus. In: Metwally, S., El Idrissi, A. and Viljoen, G. (eds) *Veterinary Vaccine for Livestock*. Wiley (in press).

Council Directive 92/66/EEC (1992) *Community measures for the control of Newcastle Disease, July 1992.* Available at: http://eur-lex.europa.eu/legal-content/en/TXT/?uri=CELEX%3A31992L0066 (accessed 25 January 2021).

Dimitrov, K.M., Abolnik, C., Afonso, C.L., Albina, E., Bahl, J., *et al.* (2019) Updated unified phylogenetic classification system and revised nomenclature for Newcastle disease virus. *Infection, Genetics and Evolution* 74, 103917. DOI: 10.1016/j.meegid.2019.103917

Suarez, D.L., Miller, P.J., Koch, G., Mundt, E. and Rautenschlein, S. (2020) Newcastle disease, other avian paramyxoviruses, and avian metapneumovirus infections. In: Swayne, D.E., Boulianne, M., Logue, C.M., McDougald, L.R., Nair, V., *et al.* (eds.) *Diseases of Poultry*, 14th edn. Wiley-Blackwell, Ames, Iowa, pp. 111–166.

15ix Avian Metapneumovirus Infection

Kannan Ganapathy*

Institute of Infection, Veterinary and Ecology Sciences, University of Liverpool, Leahurst Campus, Neston, Cheshire, UK

15ix.1 History of the Disease

In the late 1970s, a severe respiratory disease affecting turkeys was reported in South Africa. The onset of the disease was rapid with high morbidity and variable mortality. Clinical signs included sneezing, rales, sinusitis, conjunctivitis, ocular and nasal discharge, and a drop in egg production in laying birds. The disease was named turkey rhinotracheitis (TRT) and was later reported in most turkey-producing countries around the world. Since the 1980s, the causal agent of TRT has been isolated from chickens mostly showing respiratory symptoms, often with swollen heads. Antibodies were widely reported in many countries and species of birds, especially turkeys and chickens. The TRT causative agent, also previously known as avian rhinotracheitis (ART), is now known as avian metapneumovirus (aMPV) and is associated with egg losses.

15ix.2 Aetiological Agent

The aetiological agent of the disease was initially thought to be bacterial. *Bordetella avium*, an important and common turkey pathogen, was suspected. Later, through the use of embryonated eggs and tracheal organ cultures, the aetiological agent of TRT was isolated and identified as a virus. This virus and similar isolates from chickens were characterized as a pneumovirus. However, following the discovery of a similar virus isolated from humans, it was reclassified as an avian metapneumovirus (aMPV). The virus is classified as belonging to the family of *Paramyxoviridae*, subfamily *Pneumovirinae*, and the *Metapneumovirus* genus and is composed of an unsegmented single stranded, negative sense RNA. Electron-microscopic examination showed that aMPV is pleomorphic, fringed and roughly spherical in shape (Fig. 15ix.1).

It was assumed that aMPV was a single serotype. However, studies using monoclonal antibodies, and later using molecular methods, identified two distinct serotypes classed as subtype A and subtype B. In 1997, an outbreak of respiratory disease in turkeys in Colorado (US) led to another subtype being identified, subtype C. In an unrelated event, scientists in France discovered a subtype C-like aMPV virus in ducks. In 2000, a non-A, -B or -C subtype aMPV was isolated from turkeys in France and subsequently called subtype D. Avian MPV subtypes A and B have been reported worldwide, except in the US, Canada and Australasia. Subtype C has been found in US, France, South Korea and China.

15ix.3 Host

Avian MPV has been found in a range of avian species, but turkey is the main reservoir, followed by chicken. The virus has been detected in pheasants and guinea fowls showing signs of disease. Either antigen or antibodies against aMPV have been demonstrated in pheasants, ducks, guinea fowls, ostriches, herring gulls and other gull species, sparrows, swallows, pigeons and other wild birds. The subtype C virus has been detected in mice and rats in the US. To date, the importance of wild birds or animals in the spread of the virus is unknown.

15ix.4 Spread

Since the recognition of the disease and the detection of aMPV, horizontal spread has been strongly

*k.ganapathy@liverpool.ac.uk

© CAB International 2021. *Poultry Health: A Guide for Professionals* (P. Barrow *et al.*)
DOI: 10.1079/9781789245042.0015

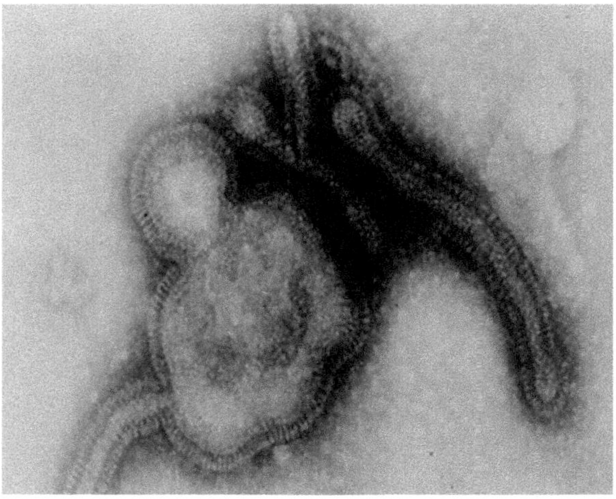

Fig. 15ix.1. Electron microscopy of avian metapneumovirus revealing irregularly shaped particles with a fringe of spikes. (Courtesy of R.C. Jones.)

suspected. The spread of disease is primarily through direct contact between infected and non-infected birds. Aerosol spread plays an essential role within and between the flocks or farms. Contaminated water, food and other materials found in the poultry houses and on farms can be a potential source of the virus. Movement of equipment, vehicles and personnel has also been implicated in the spread of the disease within and between farms. Other potential sources include the introduction of new birds or flocks onto farms, and wild birds (migratory or local) found in and around poultry houses. A number of external factors may increase susceptibility (see Section 15ix.5.4 below).

To date, there is no strong scientific evidence that aMPV is transmissible via a vertical route. However, aMPV has been detected in newly hatched day-old poults. It is likely that surface contamination of the eggshells (probably by infected oviducts) and other hatchery waste (e.g. faeces, dander and fluff), as well as direct contact between hatched chicks, may contribute to horizontal spread. Common disinfectants, when properly used, can kill the virus.

15ix.5 Disease Manifestations

Under field conditions, depending on the presence of exacerbating factors, mild to severe respiratory disease has been reported in aMPV-infected turkeys and chickens. If there are no complications, aMPV-infected chickens may recover without many clinical signs; however, turkeys may still show persistent substantial signs.

15ix.5.1 Turkeys

Young birds, less than 10 weeks old, are the most susceptible to aMPV infection and may show acute upper respiratory disease. The clinical signs may include watery eyes, nasal discharge, sneezing, coughing, respiratory noises, and general signs of depression and dullness. The morbidity may reach 100% with variable mortality rates, frequently over 50%, particularly in mixed infection cases. Egg production and quality is reduced in egg-laying turkeys, often in the absence of the respiratory signs.

15ix.5.2 Chickens

In chickens, the clinical signs caused by a single infection may go unnoticed. However, when complicated with other concurrent respiratory pathogens, such as infectious bronchitis virus (IBV), Newcastle disease virus (NDV), infectious laryngotracheitis virus (ILTV), *Mycoplasma gallisepticum*, *M. synoviae* (see Chapters 15x, 15viii, 15iv and 14viii respectively, this volume) or other bacterial/fungal infections, the disease may be more severe and prolonged (Fig. 15ix.2). In the last two decades, aMPV has been associated with swollen head syndrome (SHS) in chickens, which is characterized by swelling of periorbital and infraorbital sinuses (Figs 15ix.3 and 15ix.4).

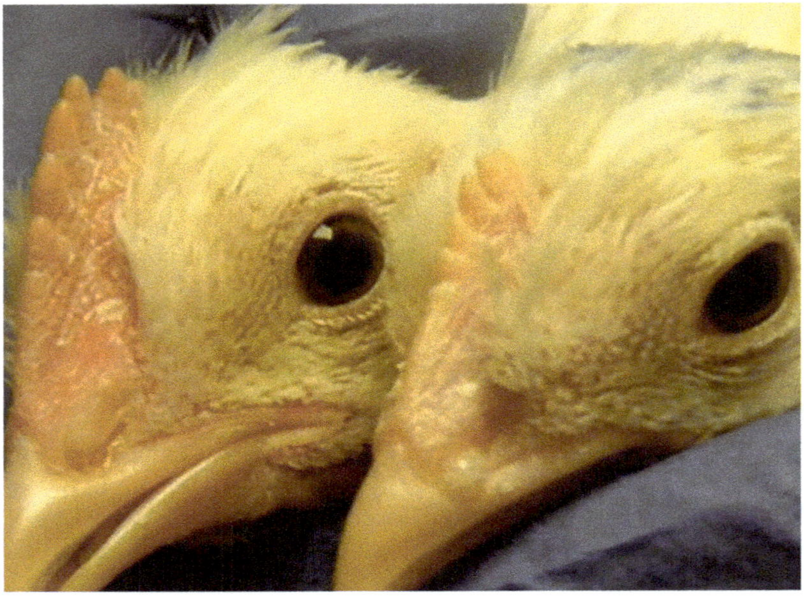

Fig. 15ix.2. Chicken with a single infection of aMPV, infected bird on the right showing nasal exudation compared to the normal bird. (Author's own image.)

Fig. 15ix.3. SHS in chickens can be associated with aMPV infection. (Author's own image.)

Other signs such as sneezing, coughing, nasal discharge and watery eyes may also be present. In some cases, torticollis, incoordination and opisthotonos have been reported. Morbidity and mortality remain below 4% and 2% respectively. Other pathogens, such as *Escherechia coli* (see Chapter 14ii, this volume) and IBV, have also been implicated with SHS.

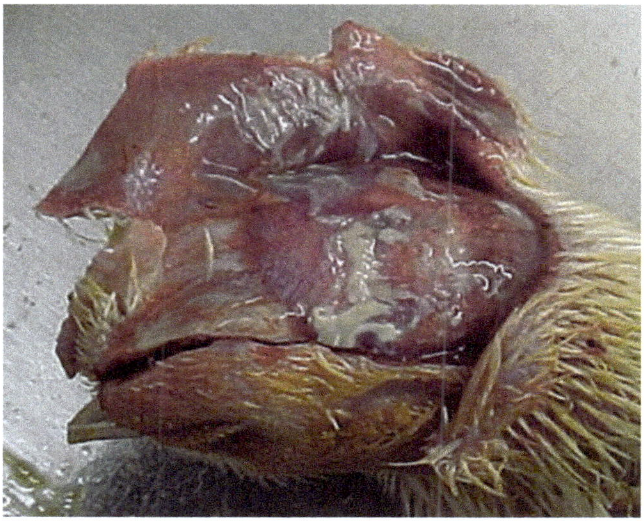

Fig. 15ix.4. Subcutaneous accumulation of gelatinous caseous exudation of swollen head. (Author's own image.)

Under experimental conditions, aMPV alone does not cause significant clinical signs in specific pathogen-free (SPF) chickens. No obvious respiratory signs have been observed, but when the nasal cavity is gently squeezed, clear to turbid exudate may be seen, usually between 3–9 days post infection. Younger birds and female birds are likely to show more severe clinical signs, particularly in broiler chickens. Such clinical signs may disappear within a few days. An infected bird may exhibit clinical signs for only one day with a full recovery thereafter. However, when virulent aMPV was concurrently administered with pathogenic *E. coli,* the resulting respiratory disease was exacerbated. To date, SHS has not been successfully reproduced in experimental birds.

In laying chickens kept in experimental conditions, egg quality and production were affected only when aMPV was administered intravenously. In the field, poultry veterinarians have observed that drops in egg production and loss of shell pigmentation were influenced by aMPV infection. Such losses have been prevented by the use of live and inactivated vaccines against aMPV infection.

15ix.5.3 Other species

Upper respiratory diseases resulting from aMFV infection simultaneously with *M. gallisepticum* (see Chapter 14viii, this volume), coronaviruses (see Chapter 15x, this volume), *E. coli* (see Chapter 14ii, this volume) and other infections can cause high mortality and losses in gamebirds.

15ix.5.4 Exacerbating factors

In turkeys, chickens and other species such as gamebirds, a number of infectious and non-infectious factors can increase the disease signs and lesions, and can contribute to production losses. Adverse management conditions, including poor ventilation, high levels of ammonia, high stocking density and stressful management practices (e.g. handling birds for vaccination, transportation to grower/layer sites) may increase disease incidence and severity. In addition, immunosuppression due to infectious or non-infectious causes may increase the susceptibility to infection and disease severity.

15ix.6 Gross and Microscopic Lesions

15ix.6.1 Turkeys

The external appearance of the head shows swelling of intraorbital sinuses, watery-sticky eyes, nares with watery-purulent discharge, tracheitis and lung congestions. In the abdomen, discrete peritonitis or, often, whole unbroken ova can be found (Fig. 15ix.5). In the oviduct, different levels of salpingitis may be present.

15ix.6.2 Chickens

Avian metapneumovirus alone rarely causes significant clinical signs, so very few pathological lesions are seen. However, when complicated with other concurrent

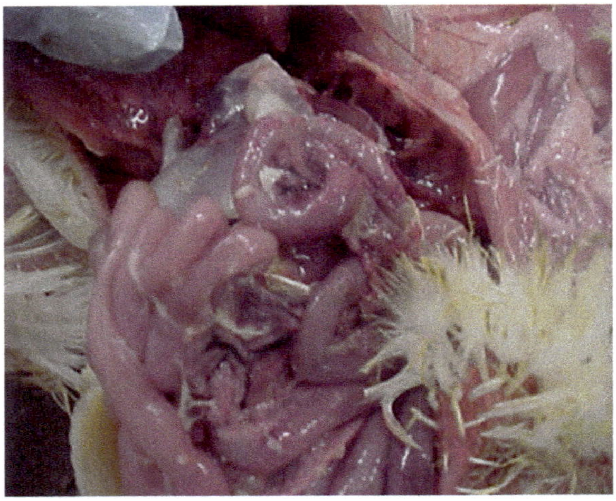

Fig. 15ix.5. Infectious peritonitis in an egg laying hen. (Author's own image.)

respiratory pathogens, lesions such as oedema in the subcutaneous tissues of the head and neck can be seen. This appears to be due to an intense cellulitis with subsequent accumulation of gelatinous to thick purulent exudate underneath the skin. Other findings include swollen intraorbital sinuses, often containing clear to turbid exudate. Examination of turbinates may reveal infiltration of exudate. In some cases, conjunctivitis and thickening of the eyelids may be present.

In both turkeys and chickens, histopathology has limited value for the diagnosis of aMPV infection as the lesions are not pathognomonic. Samples of turbinate and trachea often reveal localized changes such as deciliation of epithelium and infiltration of mononuclear inflammatory cells.

15ix.7 Case Investigation

When clinical signs associated with aMPV are reported in any type of poultry, all possible causes must be considered, including those related to management, husbandry and infectious diseases. In laying hens, a drop in egg quality/production may be seen. Often, a number of pathogens may occur concurrently and, frequently, management or husbandry irregularities play significant roles. These factors, as well as the interactions between them, should be considered in countries where multiple respiratory pathogens are commonly encountered. This is important because aMPV infection may be missed, and the clinical signs caused by aMPV infection may resemble other common diseases. Clinical investigations need to be undertaken to avoid confusion. Initially, diagnostic investigations can be focused on live birds, followed by post-mortem examination and sample collection.

For diagnosis of aMPV infection in live birds, oropharyngeal swabs or blood samples can be collected to demonstrate the presence of antigen or serum antibodies, respectively. Preferably, no less than 20 swab or blood samples should be collected from each house. The chance of aMPV detection is greatly enhanced when swabs are taken prior to the onset of clinical signs. As this is not always possible, swabs should be collected from a number of birds, including those showing no clinical signs and those exhibiting mild to severe clinical signs.

During post-mortem examination, samples of turbinate, trachea and lungs can be collected. If appropriate, swabs can be taken from the infraorbital sinuses and trachea. When it is not possible to undertake necropsies or to take swabs, it is advisable to take the head and neck as far as the thoracic inlet, pack it well in an ice-filled, insulated container and submit to a specialist laboratory.

Appropriate transportation and storage of samples would increase the chances of virus or antibody detection. Dry swabs, used for detection of antigen by RT-PCR, can be transported and stored at room temperature, but must be kept away from direct sunlight and heat. For virus isolation, the wet swabs are best transported and stored at refrigeration temperatures. The swabs can be packed on ice in insulated polystyrene containers. Whole blood in tubes or syringes can be stored at room temperature overnight before submitting to a laboratory. However, it is best to submit separated sera, transported and stored ideally at refrigeration temperature. The sera can be frozen and stored at –20°C. Tissues intended for virus isolation should be forwarded to a laboratory as soon as possible after collection, again, preferably on ice. When immediate submission is not possible, tissues can be frozen and stored at –70°C or at least at –20°C for later submission.

Clinical signs and lesions due to aMPV infection in turkeys and chickens are not pathognomic, and investigators need to consider many other diseases as differential diagnoses. These may include Newcastle disease; turkey coryza, infectious bronchitis; low pathogenic avian influenza (see Chapter 15vii, this volume); infectious laryngotracheitis (see Chapter 15iv, this volume); chronic respiratory disease; egg drop syndrome (see Chapter 15iii, this volume); avian encephalomyelitis (see Chapter 15ii, this volume); infectious coryza (see Chapter 14vi, this volume), vitamin A deficiency; ammonia gas; dusty environment and mycotoxicosis (see Chapter 12, this volume).

15ix.8 Laboratory Investigations (see also Chapter 22, this volume)

15ix.8.1 Virus detection

Swabs and tissues are processed for detection of the aMPV antigen, either by molecular or conventional methods. Most diagnosis of aMPV is by RT-PCR, which can be completed within two days. Unfortunately, this technique does not provide a viable live virus for any future work. Some laboratories may attempt isolation of aMPV by using tracheal organ cultures (TOCs). This method supports the growth of subtypes A and B, which is demonstrated by complete ciliostasis in the TOCs.

Subsequently, the presence of aMPV is confirmed by immunofluorescence or RT-PCR. Virus isolation of subtype C has been attempted in chicken embryo fibroblasts or Vero cell cultures. Other than TOC and cell lines, inoculation into susceptible birds (mostly turkey poults), yolk sac inoculation of embryonated eggs and other cell cultures has been demonstrated. Whilst most laboratories will be able to report the subtype of aMPV, few may be able to proceed to nucleotide sequencing to differentiate between the field and vaccine viruses of the same subtype.

For aMPV infection, interpretations of laboratory results are often complex and difficult. Poultry disease investigators must consider many factors – region/country/farm/flock history, clinical signs, lesions, vaccine, vaccination programme and administration methods – before reaching a conclusion. In general, on farms where vaccination against aMPV is not undertaken, positive virus detection either by RT-PCR or isolation, reflects exposure to field strains of aMPV. However, failure to detect aMPV does not necessarily indicate that the flock is free from the aMPV infection, since for detection of this virus it is essential that the correct samples are taken during the very early phase of infection. Thus, repeated sampling attempts are required to verify freedom from the aMPV, coupled with a lack of aMPV humoral antibodies.

In aMPV-vaccinated flocks, positive antigen/antibody detection should be considered in association with previous experiences (e.g. field and vaccine subtypes in the farm or area), current vaccine and vaccination schedules. Detection of subtypes other than the one used in the vaccine(s) reflects co-existence of other subtypes in the field. If the subtype detected is the same as the subtype of vaccine(s) used in the farm, further molecular tests, such as sequencing, may differentiate a vaccine strain from a field strain. It should be remembered that a vaccine strain might be detected for many weeks after a live vaccination.

15ix.8.2 Serology

Commercial ELISA kits are used regularly to detect serum aMPV antibodies, and the results need to be analysed and interpreted carefully. Whilst a positive detection reflects exposure to the aMPV, a negative result does not rule out that the birds have been exposed. This is because aMPV-infected chickens may not necessarily produce humoral antibodies, or the levels of antibodies may not have been at a detectable level at the time of the sampling. For optimum detection of aMPV antibodies, it is best to use ELISA plates that are coated with a homologous antigen. It has been reported that use of a homologous aMPV ELISA is superior to the heterologous system. In fact, for the detection of antibodies against aMPV subtype C, a homologous ELISA kit must be used.

In many countries, aMPV ELISA kits are used regularly to monitor antibody responses following vaccination. Unfortunately, in aMPV maternal antibody-positive chicks, single live vaccination does not normally induce an appreciable level of serum antibodies, at least for the first few weeks post vaccination. In contrast, breeder and layer chickens vaccinated with live vaccine followed by inactivated vaccine are likely to produce high levels of detectable humoral antibodies.

15ix.9 Immunity

In turkeys infected with aMPV, maternally derived antibodies (MDA) appear to have little or no role in protecting poults against clinical disease or infection. In chickens, no such work has been reported, but it is presumed that a similar scenario may exist. Vaccination against aMPV in MDA-positive chicks with live aMPV vaccines may not produce appreciable levels of humoral antibodies (detectable by an ELISA) for weeks. However, when the same vaccination was carried out in SPF chicks (aMPV MDA-negative), it induced good levels of humoral antibodies. Interestingly, when these groups were challenged with a virulent aMPV, both types of chicks were fully protected against clinical disease. This shows that local and cell-mediated immune responses are important in providing protection against clinical signs and against infection.

In laying birds, a number of experiments and field observations have demonstrated that high serum aMPV antibodies provide an excellent protection against loss of egg production and quality. Thus, it appears that particularly in this type of chicken, humoral antibodies are important in protecting the reproductive organs.

15ix.10 Control

The best preventive approach is to have a combination of measures, including improvements of biosecurity, management and vaccination strategies. Often such measures are aimed at reducing production losses, though some flocks may still have subclinical infections. There is no medication available for this viral infection.

15ix.10.1 Biosecurity (see Chapter 18, this volume)

As with other infectious diseases, a high standard of biosecurity is essential for infection prevention. Generally, the virus is sensitive to lipid solvents. However, in the presence of organic matter, the virus is able to survive for long periods. In the US, aMPV subtype C virus remained viable in poultry litter for up to 4 weeks at 20°C, and for up to 2 days at 37°C. Thus, thorough hygiene and disinfection procedures must be implemented to prevent the persistence of aMPV in the farming environment. Commonly used farm disinfectants are effective in destroying the virus, but the effective dilution must be checked.

15ix.10.2 Management

Good management of flocks such as avoiding overcrowding, feed/water deprivation, poor air quality (e.g. high dust, ammonia or both) and fluctuating house temperature, could contribute to reducing the impact of aMPV.

15ix.10.3 Vaccination

aMPV is the latest virus on the list of respiratory viral infections preventable by vaccination. A few years after the discovery of aMPV as the cause of TRT, a number of vaccines were developed to protect turkeys from this devastating disease. aMPV subtype A live attenuated vaccine viruses are effective in providing good protection, provided that the vaccine is administered correctly. Cross-protection studies have shown that subtype A vaccines are effective in protecting against virulent aMPV subtype B infections. For aMPV subtype C, vaccines are also available, but only in the US, where the subtype is predominantly found. Due to increasing evidence of aMPV infections in chickens, especially with regards to its association with swollen head syndrome (SHS) and drops in egg production, vaccines have been developed for chickens. Live vaccines can be sprayed on day-old chicks in the hatchery. On farms, the live vaccines can be administered either by spray or drinking water. In recent years, specifically developed avian vaccine spray machines allowing homogenous droplets of vaccine to be sprayed evenly over birds have been available. More veterinarians are advocating the spray method, which has been found to be efficient and cost effective. In countries where labour cost is not a restricting factor, aMPV live vaccines can be applied by oculo or nasal drops. The aMPV vaccine is sometimes given alongside other live respiratory vaccines, including ND and/or IB. For such combined application, it would be good to check with suppliers for details on compatibility of the aMPV with other live respiratory vaccines. Inactivated aMPV vaccines are generally given intramuscularly into the breast muscles.

Vaccination programmes to protect against aMPV vary according to many factors. Generally, a single live vaccination in broilers, and one or two live vaccinations followed by one inactivated vaccine in rearing birds of layers and breeders, are sufficient to provide protection against aMPV clinical signs and loss of eggs. In recent years, live vaccines of aMPV are administered alongside NDV and IBV live vaccines at day-old in hatchery or on the farm.

In general, following the introduction of aMPV vaccination, many producers have reported reduced mortality, higher weight gains, improved feed conversion ratio, steady egg production/quality and reduced respiratory incidents. However, in certain farms, such advantages may be masked by co-existence of other pathogens, poor biosecurity and/or by management-related problems. With our current knowledge of aMPV, it would be a mistake not to include preventive measures against this pathogen or to underestimate the 'elusive' ill effects of aMPV on the health and production of chickens.

15ix.11 Further Reading

Ball, C., Forrester, A., Herrmann, A., Lemiere, S. and Ganapathy, K. (2019) Comparative protective immunity provided by live vaccines of Newcastle disease virus or avian metapneumovirus when co-administered alongside classical and variant strains of infectious bronchitis virus in day-old broiler chicks. *Vaccine* 37(52), 7566–7575. pii: S0264-410X(19)31323-4. DOI: 10.1016/j.vaccine.2019.09.081.

Cook, J.K.A. and Cavanagh, D. (2002) Detection and differentiation of avian pneumoviruses (metapneumoviruses). *Avian Pathology* 31(2), 117–132.

Gough, R.E. and Pedersen, J.C. (2008) Avian metapneumovirus. In: Dufour-Zavala, L., Swayne, D.E., Jackwood, M.W., Pearson, J.E. Reed, W.M., *et al.* (eds) *Isolation and Identification of Avian Pathogens*. American Association of Avian Pathologists, Jacksonville, Florida, pp. 142–145.

Jones, R.C. (1996) Avian pneumovirus infection: questions still unanswered. *Avian Pathology* 25(4), 639–648.

Jones, R.C. (2007) Pneumovirinae. In: Pattison, M., McMullin, P., Bradbury, J. and Alexander, D.J. (eds) *Poultry Diseases*, 6th edn. Saunders-Elsevier, Philadelphia, Pennsylvania, pp. 309–316.

Jones, R.C. and Rautenschlein, S. (2013) Avian metapneumovirus. In: Swayne, D.E., Glisson, J.R., McDougald, L.R., Nolan, L.R., Suarez, D.L., *et al.* (eds) *Diseases of Poultry,* 13th edn. Wiley-Blackwell, Danvers, Massachusetts, pp. 112–138.

15x Infectious Bronchitis

Jane K.A. Cook*

Independent Consultant, Huntingdon, Cambridgeshire, UK

15x.1 Introduction

Infectious bronchitis (IB) is a highly infectious disease affecting mainly chickens, but also some other avian species. The initial target organ is the upper respiratory tract, and the virus causes an acute, highly infectious respiratory disease. It replicates in epithelial cells, not only in respiratory tissues, but also in oviduct, testes, kidney and the gastrointestinal tract. Infectious bronchitis virus (IBV) also affects egg laying performance in layers and breeders. Nephritis associated with IBV is a major and increasing problem. IB was first described in North Dakota, USA in 1930 and now has a worldwide distribution. It has high economic and welfare impact, but its relative importance depends on many factors including the prevalence of other diseases which may have greater impact, such as Newcastle disease (ND) and avian influenza (AI). IBV exists in the form of many variants (serotypes or genotypes), making it difficult to devise effective control strategies.

15x.2 Aetiology

IBV is a gammacoronavirus within the family *Coronaviridae*. It is a linear, positive sense, single stranded RNA virus. Coronavirus particles are enveloped, spherical or pleomorphic, 80–140 nm in diameter. The virus contains four structural proteins: a surface projection approximately 20 nm in length, known as the spike (S), a nucleoprotein, a membrane protein and an envelope protein. The S glycoprotein is responsible for attachment and fusion of the virus with the host cell and is of major importance in determining antigenic type of the virus and in inducing protective immunity.

15x.3 Susceptible Species

The chicken is the major host, but IBV, or IB-like viruses, also infect turkeys, pheasants, peafowl, guinea fowl and probably other galliforms. In some cases, analysis of their genome suggests they may be re-isolations of an IBV vaccine. Although coronaviruses detected in other avian species may not be associated with disease, infected birds are potential carriers and may play a role in transmission of infection.

15x.4 Pathology

15x.4.1 Respiratory infection

In susceptible chickens, infection of the upper respiratory tract is seen after an incubation period of 18–36 hours. The most common clinical signs include sneezing, coughing, tracheal rales, catarrhal exudate in the trachea, nasal cavity and sinuses, lachrymation, reduced weight gain and morbidity (up to 100%). Some mortality may occur, depending on the incidence of secondary infections. In an uncomplicated infection, recovery occurs within 10–14 days. However, secondary infections increase the duration and severity of clinical signs.

15x.4.2 Secondary bacterial infection (colisepticaemia)

Secondary bacterial infections, caused by, for example, *Escherichia coli* (see Chapter 14ii, this volume), occur in broilers when stocking density is high and ventilation levels suboptimal, leading to build up of dust and ammonia fumes. Other important predisposing factors include chilling at the brooding stage and immunosuppression. Good management is essential to reduce the incidence of colisepticaemia.

*jane@hough.waitrose.com

© CAB International 2021. *Poultry Health: A Guide for Professionals* (P. Barrow *et al.*)

DOI: 10.1079/9781789245042.0015

Post-mortem findings include lymphocytic infiltration and oedema of the epithelium, deciliation and sloughing off of the tracheal mucosa. Lungs may be congested. Airsacculitis, pericarditis and perihepatitis are common following colisepticaemia, and caseous plugs of mucus in the primary bronchi may occur, causing asphyxiation.

15x.4.3 Renal damage (nephritis)

Where this occurs it usually follows respiratory infection in broilers, commonly at 3–6 weeks, often affecting only a small percentage of the flock. Clinical signs include depression, scouring, and wet litter as a result of increased water intake. Mortality may be minimal but can reach 30%. Kidneys are pale, swollen and blotchy with distended tubules that appear white due to deposition of urates (Fig. 15x.1).

Deposition of urate crystals on internal organs (visceral gout) may occur. Histologically, interstitial lymphocytic infiltration is seen with granular degeneration, vacuolation and necrosis of the tubular epithelium. Similar problems may occur in breeders, often at onset of lay. For reasons that are not fully understood, nephritis associated with IBV is an increasing problem in many countries. Different IBV variants are involved and environmental factors also play an important role in the outcome of infection.

15x.4.4 IBV in laying birds

Respiratory signs may be seen, but more commonly IBV affects egg-laying performance. Drops of up to 70% in egg production may occur in fully susceptible hens, lasting at least 4–6 weeks (Fig. 15x.2).

In hens with some protective immunity, failure to lay at the full potential is more usual than major falls in production. Infection with some IBV variants at a very young age may result in permanent oviduct damage, including cystic oviducts often associated with 'false layers' (Benyeda *et al.*, 2009). The oviduct may appear normal, but deposits of yolk may accumulate in the abdomen – so called 'egg peritonitis'. Poor internal egg quality ('watery whites') and poor shell quality (thin, pale, misshapen and cracked eggs) are common; de-pigmentation of the shell may also occur (Fig. 15x.3).

On post-mortem examination, the oviduct may appear normal, or may have regressed with metaplasia of the epithelium, glandular dilation, lymphocytic infiltration of the subepithelium, proliferation of lymphoid follicles and fibroplasia. The ovarian follicle may be flaccid.

15x.5 Transmission

IBV is highly infectious, only a few virus particles being needed to initiate infection. During clinical infection large quantities of virus are shed from the respiratory tract and via the faeces. The virus spreads rapidly within and between groups via inhalation or direct contact with infected birds, contaminated litter, equipment or other fomites. Therefore, strict biosecurity is essential to minimize transmission. Virus is shed for several weeks

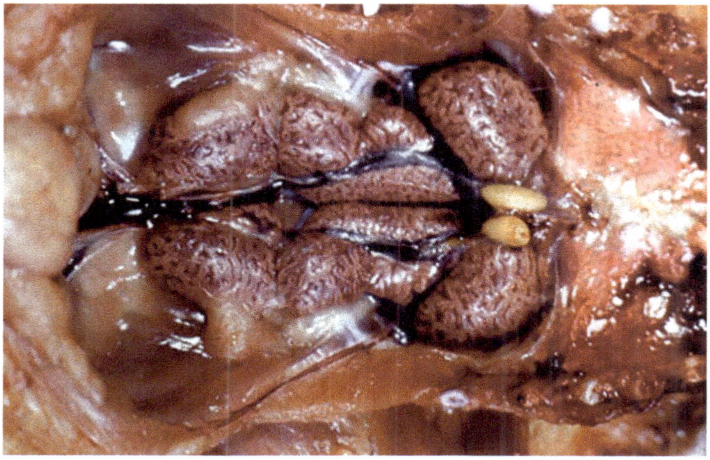

Fig. 15x.1. Pale and swollen kidneys from a chicken inoculated with IBV. (Courtesy of Prof. R.C. Jones, University of Liverpool.)

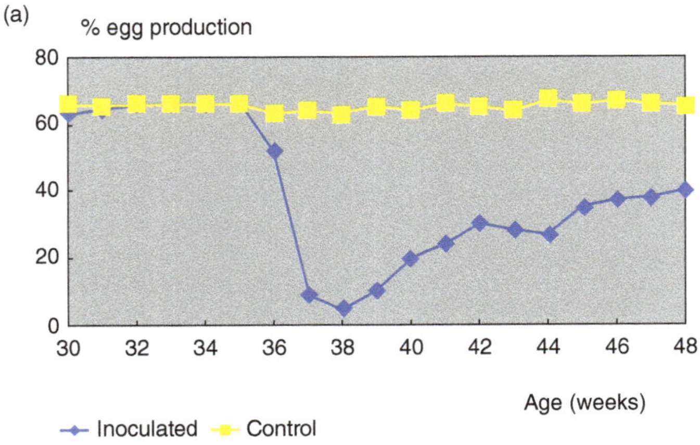

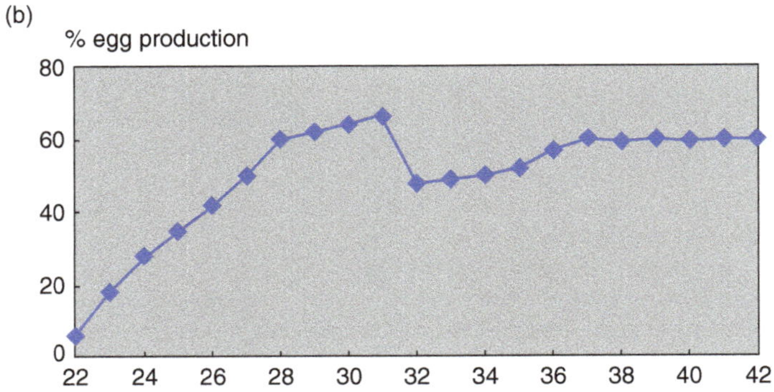

Fig. 15x.2. Drop in egg production following infection of laying hens with IBV. (a) Fully susceptible hens experimentally inoculated with IBV at 33 weeks of age. (b) Egg production of a flock of 8000 IBV-vaccinated hens from which an IBV variant antigenically different from the strains used in the vaccine was isolated at 32 weeks. ((b) Reproduced from Cook and Huggins, 1986, with permission from Informa UK Limited, trading as Taylor & Francis Group, www.tandfonline.com on behalf of Houghton Trust Ltd.)

Fig. 15x.3. The effect of IBV on egg shell colour. Eggs laid by five different hens (columns) prior to inoculation (top row) with an IBV variant and at 2–5 days post inoculation (rows 2–5). (Reproduced from Cook, 1984, with permission from Informa UK Limited, trading as Taylor & Francis Group, www.tandfonline.com on behalf of Houghton Trust Ltd.)

after infection and may persist in the intestinal tract, possibly the caecal tonsil, since the virus has been recovered from experimentally infected chickens for up to a year after infection. There is evidence that onset of lay may lead to virus re-excretion.

Whilst true egg transmission is not believed to occur, surface contamination of eggs from faecal material in the gastrointestinal tract occurs. Strict hygiene and biosecurity measures in the hatchery and the egg packing station are therefore vital. Vector transmission has not been reported.

Outside the host the virus is readily destroyed by lipid solvents, alkalis, many disinfectants, 1% formalin and heating at 56°C for 15 min.

15x.6 Different Types of IBV (commonly called variants)

The identification in Connecticut, USA in the 1950s of an IBV that did not protect against the original, Massachusetts (Mass) isolate was the first indication of antigenic variants. An increasing number of serotypic or genetic types of IBV continue to be described worldwide (de Wit *et al.*, 2011). Different variants may be prevalent in different areas and the dominant ones change with time. IBV variants arise as a result of random mutation or following genetic recombination between two different IBVs present in the same cell. They are recognized by molecular techniques (see below) and by *in vitro* virus neutralizing (VN) tests using monospecific antiserum raised to each serotype. It is important to be aware that serotyping and genotyping methods do not always give identical results. Variants are of epidemiological importance and must be considered when devising effective vaccination programmes. Because variants result from very small changes in the amino acid composition of the S glycoprotein, much of the virus genome is unchanged, and heterologous cross protection occurs and may be more broadly based than the results of VN tests (see below) indicate.

15x.7 Diagnosis (see also Chapter 22, this volume)

15x.7.1 Differential diagnosis

Because the respiratory signs are similar to those caused by other common pathogens, IBV infections cannot be diagnosed accurately solely on the basis of clinical signs. Likewise, poor egg-laying performance and renal damage both have other infectious and non-infectious causes. Diagnosis therefore depends on virus isolation/detection, serology or a combination of the two. For more detail see the review by de Wit (2000).

15x.7.2 Virus isolation/detection

The best chance of successful virus isolation is to examine upper respiratory tract material in the early stages of clinical infection, when virus replication is greatest. When investigating poor egg-laying performance or renal problems, kidney, faeces or intestinal tract material (caecal tonsil) are the samples of choice, however, success rates are generally low. Attempts to isolate IBV from the oviduct rarely succeed. Once a flock has recovered clinically, successful virus isolation is unlikely. Sentinel birds have been used to aid virus isolation.

IBV replicates in cell culture only after adaptation, therefore virus isolation is attempted by passage of swab fluid or homogenized tissue via the allantoic cavity of 9–11-day-old embryonated eggs, or by passage in tracheal organ cultures (TOC) and observing ciliostasis. Peak titres are seen approximately 48 h post inoculation in both systems and a number of 'blind passages' is required before a sample is assumed to be negative. Ciliostasis is not specific for IBV, nor are the embryo lesions seen – stunting and curling of the embryo and deposition of urates in the mesonephros – therefore the identity of the isolate as IBV must be confirmed by other means (Fig. 15x.4).

15x.7.3 Virus detection methods

Electron microscopy, immunoperoxidase and immunofluorescence may all be used to confirm the presence of IBV. This may be done directly on tracheal sections or after *in vitro* passaging. By incorporating type-specific monoclonal antibodies into an assay it may be possible to identify the IBV variant involved. However, molecular techniques such as real-time reverse transcriptase-polymerase chain reaction (RT-PCR) are becoming the norm. Reagents can be designed to identify either all known IBVs or specific genotypes. For more detail see Jackwood and de Wit (2020). Viral RNA for assay can be extracted directly from swab material or infected tissues; from allantoic fluid, or from

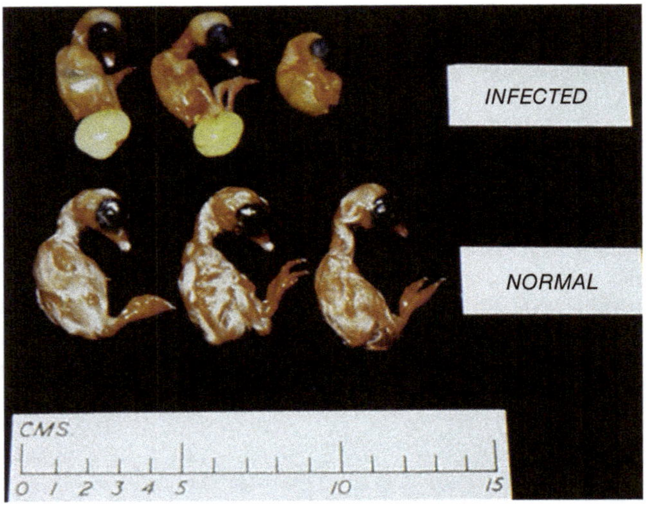

Fig. 15x.4. The effect of IBV on embryonated eggs. Eighteen-day-old embryos from eggs inoculated with IBV at 9 days (top row). Age matched controls (bottom row). (Author's own photograph.)

TOC supernatant of samples being used for virus isolation. Since viral nucleic acid is being detected, it is not necessary for live virus to be present and molecular assays detect the presence of the IBV genome for longer than is possible by virus isolation methods. The availability of FTA cards has greatly facilitated the collection and transport of samples, since IBV spotted onto the cards is inactivated and the cards can safely be posted to laboratories for examination.

Molecular techniques give results very quickly and have facilitated epidemiological studies to monitor the distribution of particular IBV types. However, because viral nucleic acid is being detected, a positive result may not indicate a current IBV infection.

It is important to remember that because of their high sensitivity, molecular techniques should be used under carefully controlled conditions by experienced workers and great care must be taken to avoid cross contamination. Many laboratories are now equipped to perform these assays.

15x.7.4 Serology

Several serological tests are available.

Agar gel precipitation (AGP), which detects antibodies to all IBV strains, is insensitive. However, as AGP detects antibody for only a short time after infection, a positive result is diagnostic, and the test has some use for this purpose.

The haemagglutination inhibition (HI) test can only be used with IBV that has been treated with the enzyme neuraminidase to cause it to haemagglutinate. Following single exposure to IBV, the HI response is generally type specific, but further exposure to different IBV types results in cross-reactions making interpretation of results difficult (Brown and Bracewell, 1988). However, it is a quick and useful diagnostic tool and if performed carefully by laboratories experienced in its use, it can differentiate serotypes.

ELISA is very sensitive and is widely used for diagnosis, flock profiling and to monitor vaccinal responses. Good quality commercial kits are available, and results are obtained very quickly. It is important to remember that ELISAs do *not* differentiate IBV serotypes.

Virus neutralization is expensive and time consuming because each IBV isolate must be tested against monospecific antisera to itself and other IBV types of interest. However, it is the best test for differentiation of serotypes. It can be performed in embryonated eggs, TOC or in avian cell culture using cell culture adapted virus.

ELISA and HI are the two tests commonly used for flock monitoring. Because most flocks will be antibody positive as a result of vaccination or earlier exposure to IBV, in order to confirm a recent infection, it is necessary to demonstrate a rising IBV antibody titre by testing paired serum samples, taken at the time infection is suspected and 2 or 3 weeks later. It is advisable to test the two sets of samples at the same time in order to minimize effects of variation within the assay.

15x.8 Immunity

This topic has been reviewed by Dhinakar Raj and Jones (1997).

Host effects. Some innate host resistance to infection occurs in the early stages of infection. Experimental data indicate differences between inbred chicken lines in their susceptibility to IBV, but there is no evidence of such differences in commercial breeds.

Maternally derived immunity may provide some passive, short-term protection against IBV challenge.

Local immunity in the upper respiratory tract is an important first line of defence, emphasizing the importance of careful vaccine application via the upper respiratory tract.

Humoral immunity (circulating antibody) is measured by serological tests (see above). It is present from about 10–14 days after infection or vaccination, but its level depends on the age of the bird and MDA levels at the time of inoculation and the possible involvement of immunosuppressive agents.

Cell mediated immunity is believed to be important in protection against IBV infections but is still not well understood and suitable assays to detect it are not yet available.

15x.9 Control of IBV Infections

Whilst good management and strict biosecurity are essential for IBV control and antibiotics may be required to combat secondary bacterial infections, adequate control is impossible without vaccination. Both live-attenuated and oil-adjuvanted inactivated vaccines are available. Live-attenuated vaccines are developed by attenuating the virulence of IBV by repeated passage in embryonated eggs. The number of passages is critical to achieve a strain which is not over attenuated by too many passages, but so poorly attenuated that it still causes disease. Inactivated vaccine, which is an essential part of IBV control in layers and breeders, is not effective without prior application of live-attenuated vaccines.

The majority of live-attenuated IBV vaccines are of the Mass serotype, for example H120, MM, Ma5 (Bijlenga, *et al.*, 2004). However, these will not protect against every variant, and vaccines developed using other types, for example Arkansas in USA, 793B (4/91; CR88) in Europe and elsewhere, BR1 in Brazil, may be included, but only where a local need has been clearly shown. There is evidence of heterologous cross protection between IBVs, since good protection against many variants has been demonstrated using a vaccination programme incorporating Mass and 793B-type live-attenuated IBV vaccines (Cook *et al.*, 1999; de Wit, *et al.*, 2011).

In the case of the inactivated vaccines, multivalent products are available, containing one or two different IBV antigens, together with antigens to other pathogens, such as NDV or IBDV (see Chapters 15viii and 15v respectively, this volume). Some bivalent live-attenuated vaccines, containing both IBV and NDV are used successfully. However, the mixing together of different monovalent live-attenuated vaccines is inadvisable because of the risk of interference between them.

There is a clear need for 'new generation' vaccines, developed using reverse genetics or vector vaccines, but it seems unlikely these will be available in the short term.

15x.9.1 Vaccination procedures

Broilers will receive live-attenuated vaccines from 1 day old (ideally in the hatchery) by spray, or via the drinking water. Although eye drop application is the most efficient method, it is not normally cost effective. One application may be sufficient, but revaccination is common. The age of first vaccination may be delayed in the presence of other pathogens, for example in areas where *Mycoplasma gallisepticum* (see Chapter 14viii, this volume) infection is prevalent. The presence of immunosuppressive agents, such as chicken anaemia virus (see Chapter 15xi, this volume) or IBDV may have a detrimental effect on the response to live-attenuated IBV vaccines.

Layers and breeders will receive several live 'priming' vaccinations during rear. These may also be of the Mass serotype, or may include vaccines against other serotypes, depending on the local situation (see above). This is followed by injection of inactivated vaccine prior to onset of lay. In order to maximize the immunity induced by the inactivated vaccine, it is advisable to leave 4–6 weeks between the final application of live vaccine and injection of the inactivated vaccine. In some areas live-attenuated IBV vaccines are sprayed regularly throughout lay, in already well-vaccinated flocks, in order to boost local respiratory tract immunity in the face of possible field challenge.

15x.10 Conclusions

Because IBV is so highly infectious, and because of the continual emergence of new, and often highly virulent variants, continued vigilance is necessary. Control of IBV depends on good management and hygiene procedures, strict biosecurity and the careful and correct use of the high quality live-attenuated and inactivated IBV vaccines available.

15x.11 References

Benyeda, Z., Mató, T., Süveges, T., Szabó, E., Kardi, V., *et al.* (2009) Comparison of the pathogenicity of QX-like, M41 and 793/B infectious bronchitis strains from different pathological conditions. *Avian Pathology* 38, 449–456.

Bijlenga, G., Cook, J.K.A., Gelb, J. Jr. and de Wit, J.J. (2004) Development and use of the H strain of avian infectious bronchitis virus from the Netherlands as a vaccine. A review. *Avian Pathology* 33, 550–557.

Brown, A.J. and Bracewell, C.D. (1988) Effect of repeated infections of chickens with infectious bronchitis viruses on the specificity of their antibody responses. *Veterinary Record* 122, 207–208.

Cook (1984) The classification of new serotypes of infectious bronchitis virus isolated from poultry flocks in Britain between 1981 and 1983. *Avian Pathology* 13, 733–741.

Cook, J.K.A. and Huggins, M.B. (1986) Newly isolated serotypes of infectious bronchitis virus: their role in disease. *Avian Pathology* 15, 129–138.

Cook, J.K.A., Orbell, S.J., Woods, M.A. and Huggins, M.B. (1999) Breadth of protection of the respiratory tract provided by different live-attenuated infectious bronchitis vaccines against challenge with infectious bronchitis viruses of heterologous serotypes. *Avian Pathology* 28, 477–485.

de Wit, J.J. (2000) Detection of infectious bronchitis. Technical review. *Avian Pathology* 29, 71–93.

de Wit, J.J., Cook, J.K.A. and van der Heijden, H.M. (2011) Infectious bronchitis virus variants: a review of the history, current situation and control measures. *Avian Pathology* 40, 223–235.

Dhinakar Raj, G. and Jones, R.C. (1997) Infectious bronchitis virus: immunopathogenesis of infection in the chicken. *Avian Pathology* 26, 677–706.

Jackwood, M. and de Wit, J.J. (2020) Infectious bronchitis. In: Swayne, D.E., Boulianne, M., Logue, C.M., McDougald, L.R., Nair, V., *et al.* (eds) *Diseases of Poultry*, 14th edn. Wiley-Blackwell, Ames, Iowa, pp. 167–188.

15xi Chicken Anaemia Virus and Circoviruses

JOAN A. SMYTH*

Department of Pathobiology and Veterinary Science, College of Agriculture, Health and Natural Resources, University of Connecticut, Storrs, Connecticut, USA

15xi.1 Introduction

Chicken anaemia virus (CAV) was originally classified as a circovirus together with porcine circoviruses 1 and 2, and psittacine beak and feather disease virus, and at that time was listed as the type species of the genus *Circovirus,* in the family *Circoviridae*. However, as genome organizations became better understood, it was realized that CAV is in fact very different from the other circoviruses. Accordingly, it was moved first to a newly created genus, the genus *Gyrovirus*, within the family *Circoviridae*, and then in 2017, the genus *Gyrovirus* was moved to the family *Anelloviridae*; thus, CAV is no longer considered a circovirus. However, there are other disease producing circoviruses within in the family *Circoviridae,* that infect farmed ducks, geese and pigeons and these are discussed in Sections 15xi.3.1 and 15xi.3.2 below.

15xi.2 *Anelloviridae*

15xi.2.1 Chicken anaemia virus

CAV is a significant cause of disease in chickens, but not in other poultry species. It causes clinical disease as a result of direct damage to haematopoetic cells in the bone marrow and thymic lymphoblasts during the viral replication phase. In older chickens, the virus apparently does not replicate well in the bone marrow, but the damage associated with viral replication in the thymus causes immunosuppression that renders chickens susceptible to a wide range of secondary infectious diseases. Some investigators have reported significant adverse economic effects in commercial poultry flocks with subclinical CAV infection.

Infections in specific pathogen free (SPF) flocks are problematic as these flocks are used for vaccine production and disease research, and it is difficult to eliminate CAV from infected SPF flocks. CAV has been found on multiple occasions as a vaccine contaminant, and avian vaccines are therefore monitored for the presence of CAV.

Virus, transmission and distribution

CAV is a very small (25–26.5 nm) non-enveloped single-stranded negative sense DNA virus. The genome (approximately 2.3 kb) encodes three viral proteins: VP1 (capsid protein), VP2 (a tyrosine phosphatase) and VP3 (a protein with apoptotic activity). CAV is currently the only listed member of the genus *Gyrovirus,* family *Anelloviridae*, but there are other tentatively proposed members (see Section 15xi.2.2). Some genetic variation and evidence of recombination between CAV strains has been reported.

CAV is transmitted both vertically and horizontally. Droppings, egg materials, feathers and other fomites may harbour virus. The virus has been found in broiler, layer and breeder chickens worldwide. It has also been found in some SPF flocks (see above).

Clinical signs

CAV causes clinical disease following vertical transmission; i.e. it produces clinical disease in the progeny of seronegative breeder hens that became

*joan.smyth@uconn.edu

© CAB International 2021. *Poultry Health: A Guide for Professionals* (P. Barrow *et al.*)
DOI: 10.1079/9781789245042.0015

infected during lay. Less commonly, CAV will cause clinical disease in young antibody negative chicks, or in chickens that have been immunosuppressed by other agents such as infectious bursal disease virus or Marek's disease virus (see Chapters 15v and 15xiii respectively, this volume). This reflects the fact that CAV replication is curtailed in the presence of antibodies; absence of maternally derived antibody or an inadequate antibody response to infection allows uncontrolled virus replication.

In horizontally infected immunocompetent chickens, infection is subclinical but immunosuppression results. Thus, CAV commonly underlies and/or exacerbates many of the other infectious disease problems encountered in poultry flocks.

Chickens which have been vertically infected first exhibit signs at approximately 10 days of age with a disease peak occurring at around 14–20 days. Signs include lethargy, pallor and reduced weight gain, with deaths occurring from approximately 12 days of age. The mortality rate is quite variable and reflects (i) the proportion of the broiler flock that is derived from the virus transmitting breeder flock, (ii) the presence/absence of other infectious agents that may enhance the pathological effects of CAV and (iii) the presence/absence of other infectious agents whose effects may be enhanced by the immunosuppressive effects of CAV. Thus, mortality rates will be much lower in broiler flocks where most chicks in the flock are derived from non-CAV-transmitting parents, and where good management practices minimize the presence of, and/or the effects of, other disease producing agents. In this author's experience, deaths among vertically infected broiler chickens are often due to secondary fungal pneumonia or gangrenous dermatitis. Interestingly, the gangrenous dermatitis commonly affects the wings, hence one of the original names for the disease, blue wing disease.

Subclinical infections are common and as noted elsewhere, they are important because these can cause immunosuppression.

Post-mortem and histological findings

The main findings in chickens dying from CAV infection, are (i) pale carcasses and pale to white bone marrow (Fig. 15xi.1) due to loss of haematopoetic tissue during viral replication and consequent anaemia, and (ii) marked atrophy of the thymus (Fig. 15xi.2) caused by viral replication in the thymic cortex.

Subcutaneous and intramuscular petechial and ecchymotic haemorrhages may be present. Atrophy of the bursa of Fabricius is widely reported in birds dead from CAV infection, but bursal atrophy in fact seems to be caused by other agents since (i) evidence of CAV replication is found in only a very small percentage of cells in the bursa of Fabricius, and (ii) B cells are considered refractory to CAV infection. Significant lesions caused by co-infecting agents may also be present. For example, as mentioned above, fungal pneumonia and gangrenous dermatitis are common in flocks vertically infected with CAV.

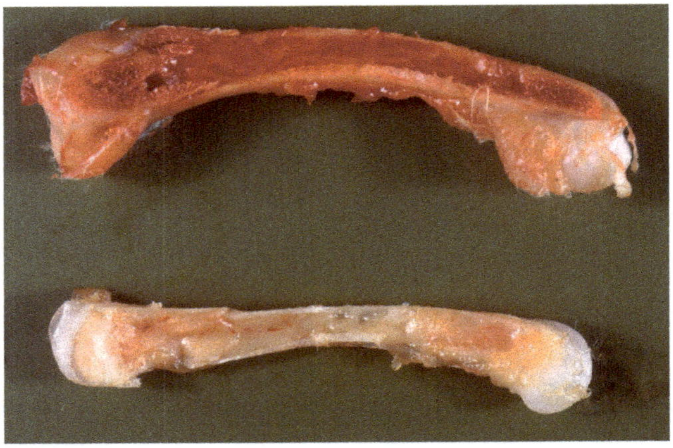

Fig. 15xi.1. Very pale bone marrow in a 14-day-old SPF chicken infected with CAV compared to that of a normal age matched control (top). The loss of haematopoietic tissue leads to anaemia, which can be profound. (Author's own image.)

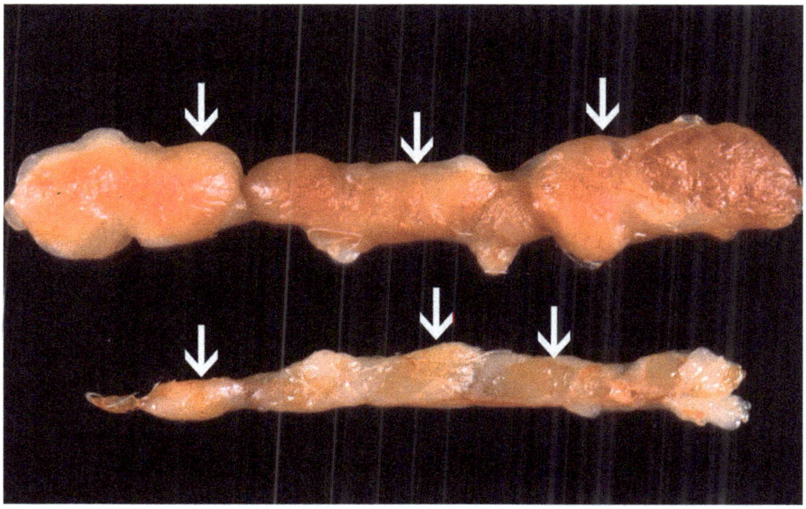

Fig. 15xi.2. Marked reduction in the size of the thymic lobules in a 14-day-old SPF chicken infected with CAV compared to those of a normal age matched control (top). Arrows point to individual thymic lobes. (Author's own image.)

Histologically, pathognomonic lesions develop but these are present transiently and are usually not detectable by the time chickens die from the disease. The pathognomonic lesions are enlarged thymic lymphoblasts and bone marrow haemocytoblasts which have enlarged nuclei with dispersed or coarsely granular chromatin and characteristic refractile circular eosinophilic nuclear inclusions (Fig. 15xi.3). The inclusions are only present during the phase of active viral replication.

At the time deaths are occurring, histological findings will include marked loss of haematopoetic tissue and marked lymphocyte depletion of the thymic cortex. Lymphocyte depletion may also be noted in the spleen and mucosa-associated lymphoid tissue. These later occurring changes are non-specific and so definitive diagnosis of CAV infection cannot usually be made during the clinical disease stage by histological evaluation alone.

In older immunocompetent chickens that become infected with CAV, the only detectable gross lesion is mild atrophy and reddening of the thymus; this change can be subtle and is usually only recognizable by comparison with age matched controls. Histological changes similar to those described in the thymus of young birds may be detectable, but these will be much more limited in extent. The virus does not replicate, or does so at a very low level, in the bone marrow of older immunocompetent chickens. Therefore, bone marrow aplasia and anaemia are not usual in older chicken. Once again, pathology caused by secondary infectious agents may be present.

In chickens that were immunosuppressed at the time of CAV infection, the full spectrum of gross and histological lesions described in young vertically infected chickens, may be present.

Diagnosis

Many methods exist for detection of CAV in birds. Detection of CAV antigen in the thymus of chickens is a very useful diagnostic tool, but since few labs have the antibodies necessary for antigen detecting tests, this approach is rarely used today. Instead, CAV DNA can be detected by *in situ* hybridization (ISH), PCR followed by amplicon sequencing or by quantitative PCR (qPCR). PCR-based methods are most widely used and are usually very sensitive for detecting CAV DNA, and qPCR can be helpful in distinguishing between subclinical infection and disease due to CAV. qRT-PCR can be used to detect RNA transcripts that are indicative of active infection. The sample of choice is thymus, but good success has been reported with liver, and also with feather pulp (80% detection rate at 14 days post inoculation). Cloacal swabs are less sensitive. It is important to realize that definitive diagnosis of CAV infection as a cause of disease can only be made based upon a combination of

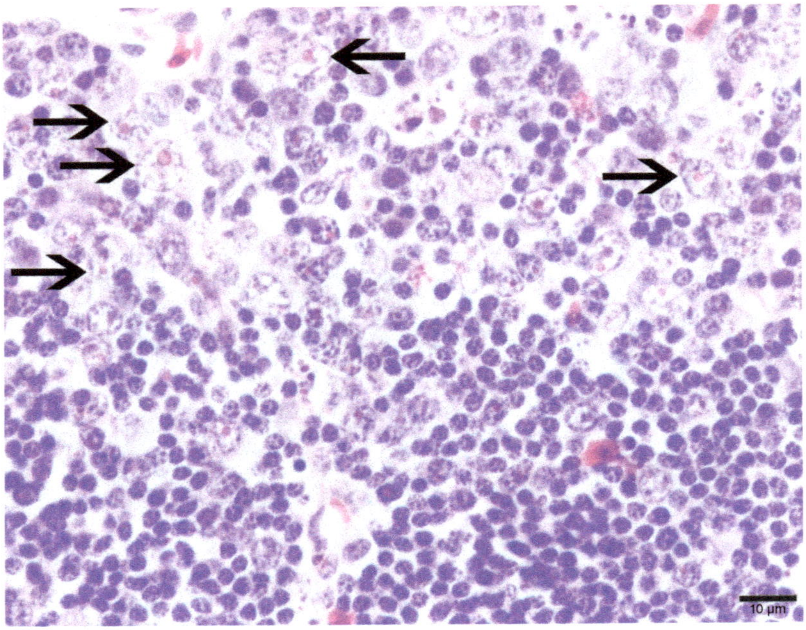

Fig. 15xi.3. Thymus from a 6-day-old chicken experimentally infected with CAV at 1 day old, i.e. day 5 post infection. Many of the thymic lymphoblasts in the outer cortex (top half of the image) have markedly enlarged pale staining nuclei. Several of these enlarged nuclei (arrows) contain one or more small refractile eosinophilic inclusions that are characteristic of CAV infection. Similar enlarged nuclei with inclusions can be found in both intra- and extra-sinusoidal haematoblasts, as well as within scattered cells in lymphoid aggregates throughout the body. Haematoxylin and eosin (H&E). Bar = 10 µm. (Author's own image.)

detection of the virus together with the presence of thymic atrophy with or without bone marrow aplasia.

Serological testing can be helpful. If CAV-induced disease is suspected in a flock, examination of sera from the contributing parent flocks should reveal at least some seropositive flocks. It is then important to examine previously collected blood samples from those flocks, to show that seroconversion (and therefore infection) occurred during the laying period. Such retrospective examination is usually possible because many large poultry producers routinely store frozen serum samples that were collected at around 18 weeks of age, i.e. pre- or point-of-lay samples.

Commercially available ELISA tests are commonly used for detection of CAV antibodies in poultry flocks. However, it is important for those working with SPF flocks to be aware that some ELISA tests can lack specificity. Thus, when testing SPF flocks, ELISA may be used for screening purposes, but another serological test should be used on positive samples. (See also Chapter 22, this volume.)

Control, prevention and treatment of disease

Like many non-enveloped viruses, CAV is a resistant virus and can be difficult to eliminate from the environment. It can be present in droppings and feathers, and contaminated equipment and bleeding needles could also introduce infection. Since vertical transmission is the most important route of infection in terms of clinical disease caused by CAV, clinical disease can be largely prevented by ensuring breeding flocks have developed immunity before they start to produce eggs. Many flocks will acquire immunity naturally during the rearing period. Some poultry companies collect blood samples from breeders at around 8–10 weeks of age to determine their status with respect to CAV antibodies. Antibody negative flocks can thus be identified and vaccinated well before onset of lay. There are several commercially available vaccines. It is important to be aware that some live attenuated vaccines may have residual pathogenicity.

There is no effective treatment for CAV infection. General supportive treatment measures have been tried but there is no information as to efficacy. Treatment for secondary bacterial infections may be indicated.

15xi.2.2 Other gyroviruses

There are at least three newly discovered viruses of birds that are currently tentatively classified as gyroviruses. Some of these gyroviruses are widespread in poultry, but since their pathological effects have not yet been characterized and their importance is not known, they will not be considered further.

15xi.3 *Circoviridae*

The family *Circoviridae* currently contains two genera, the genus *Circovirus* and the genus *Cyclovirus*.

15xi.3.1 Circoviruses

The most studied viruses of the genus *Circovirus* are the porcine circoviruses, which are known to cause several significant primary disease syndromes as well as predisposing to many secondary diseases because of their immunosuppressive effects. To date, circovirus infections are recognized as a cause of immunosuppression among farmed ducks, geese and pigeons, similarly predisposing their respective hosts to a wide range of secondary infectious diseases. There are also some reports of primary circoviral diseases in these species e.g. feathering abnormalities in geese and ducks, and sclerosing cholangitis in ducks. It is likely that more pathological effects, and more avian circoviruses, will be discovered in time as investigations continue in the various bird species. Indeed, the first chicken circovirus has just been isolated in China, from broilers with acute gastroenteritis. Its role in disease remains to be investigated.

Viruses, transmission and distribution

Currently there are 39 virus species in the genus *Circovirus*, and they tend to be host specific. Thus, duck circovirus (DuCV) has been found only in ducks, goose circovirus (GoCV) in geese, and pigeon circovirus (PiCV) in pigeons. Genetic diversity and evidence of recombination events have been reported within each of these three virus species. While multiple papers consider DuCV-1 and DuCV-2, currently only one duck circovirus species (DuCV) is recognized by the International Committee on Taxonomy of Viruses.

At 14–20 nm, members of the genus *Circovirus* are among the smallest known animal viruses. They are non-enveloped with single-stranded, ambisense, circular DNA. The 1.7–2.1 kb genome encodes for three major proteins; the capsid protein, a replicase protein and a protein with apoptotic activity.

DuCV, GoCV and PiCV can be transmitted both vertically and horizontally. By analogy, droppings, secretions, egg materials, feathers and fomites are likely sources of infection.

PiCV has been found in pigeons worldwide and has been detected in European meat pigeons. GoCV and DuCV have been found in farmed geese and ducks respectively, in countries throughout the world. Interestingly, there have been no reports of circovirus infection in farmed geese or ducks in Australia and New Zealand thus far, although circoviruses have been found in pigs, pigeons and other avian species in these countries.

Clinical signs

An array of clinical signs has been reported in flocks with naturally occurring circovirus infections, but there have been insufficient experimental studies of circovirus infection in pigeons, ducks and geese to establish which clinical signs are truly the result of circovirus infection, and which are the result of co-infecting agents and/or other nutritional and environmental factors. A common finding across circovirus infected flocks of all three species, is poor flock performance together with a high incidence of infectious diseases presumed to be secondary to circovirus-induced immunosuppression. Feathering abnormalities have been reported in infected goose and duck flocks. It has been shown experimentally that duck circovirus increases the incidence of goose parvovirus induced beak atrophy and dwarfism syndrome in ducks. In one study, diarrhoea was reported in all experimentally infected geese but not in the controls. In another study in ducks, no clinical signs were observed but weight gain was significantly lower in inoculated birds.

Field studies show that subclinical infections are common.

Post-mortem and histological findings

In naturally occurring circovirus infection in ducks, geese and pigeons, lymphocyte depletion of the bursa of Fabricius (Fig. 15xi.4) and thymus are commonly reported, and circoviral replication has been demonstrated in these organs, supporting the role of circovirus as the cause of the atrophy.

There have been few studies investigating pathology after experimental circovirus infection of ducks, geese and pigeons. In these, there have been either mild non-specific changes or no gross lesions. Surprisingly, atrophy of the bursa of Fabricius or thymus has not been seen in some of these studies.

Histologically, lymphocyte depletion and characteristic intracytoplasmic inclusion bodies are found in the bursa of Fabricius of pigeons and geese (Fig. 15xi.5), and the presence of circovirus in these inclusions has been demonstrated by ultrastructural examination or by *in situ* hybridization (Fig. 15xi.6).

While circoviral DNA can be found in virtually every tissue in the body, it is not always associated with obvious histological change, or, it is associated with non-specific pathological change. Circoviral DNA has been demonstrated in bile ducts of several species, and duck circovirus has recently been proven to cause primary sclerosing cholangitis in ducks. More studies are needed to

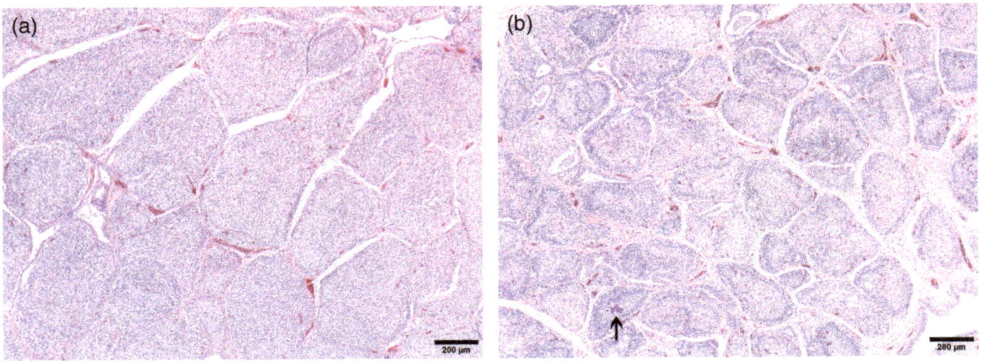

Fig. 15xi.4. (a) Bursa of Fabricius (BF) from a normal pigeon showing large well populated follicles. (b) BF from a circovirus infected pigeon, showing small follicles due to lymphocyte depletion. A cluster of cells (arrow) that contain large botryoid inclusions is just visible at this very low magnification. H&E. Bars = 200 µm. (Author's own image.)

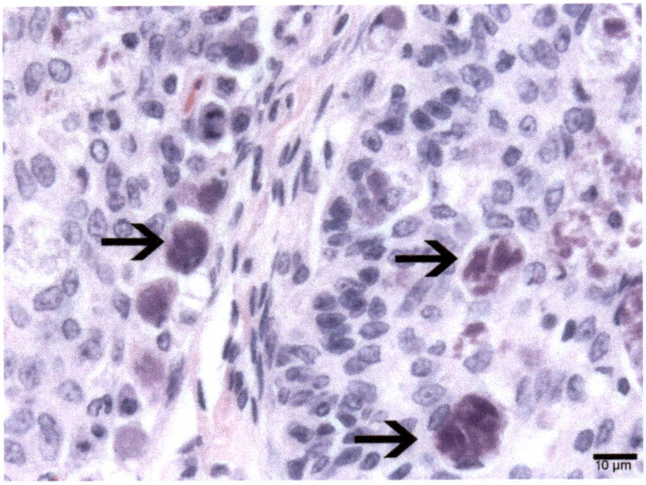

Fig. 15xi.5. Bursa of Fabricius from a circovirus infected pigeon with characteristic botryoid inclusions (arrows) in the cortex (left arrow) and medulla (right arrows) of adjacent follicles. H&E. Bar = 10 µm. (Author's own image.)

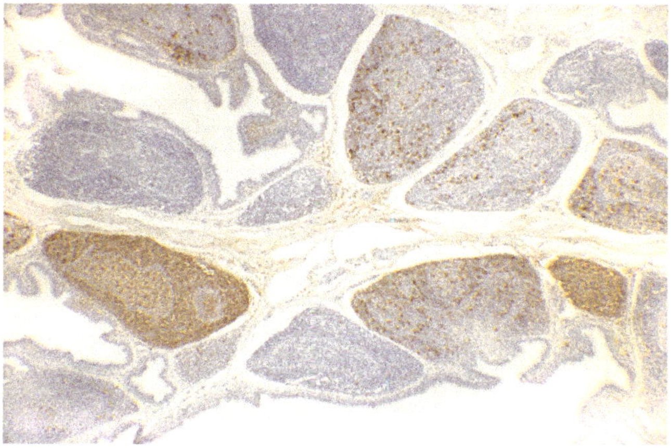

Fig. 15xi.6. Circoviral DNA (brown) in the bursa of Fabricius of a goose demonstrated by *in situ* hybridization. Haematoxylin counterstain. (Author's own image.)

determine the full range of histological changes in ducks, geese and pigeons caused by their respective circoviruses.

Diagnosis

Several methods exist for the detection of circovirus infection in birds. The most common methods are PCR based, but metagenomic approaches have also been used to identify infections (see Chapter 22, this volume). Testing by *in situ* hybridization and immunohistochemistry is only available in specialist labs. Serological tests have been described but currently, there are no commercially available tests.

As was the case for CAV, the significance of identifying circovirus infection in a flock or individual bird, can only be determined by considering together with flock performance, pathological findings, the presence/absence of other infectious agents and flock management.

Control, prevention and treatment of disease

PiCV, DuCV and GoCV are transmitted both vertically and horizontally, and infected flocks are widespread. The circoviruses have proven resistant to removal by disinfection. There are currently no commercially available vaccines against the circoviruses of ducks, geese or pigeons.

Thus, prevention of infection will prove difficult. There is currently insufficient information about the biology of circovirus infection in ducks, geese and pigeons to know whether it is best to try to eliminate infected stock or to try to ensure that breeding birds have been exposed before they come into lay. Good management practice to minimize exposure to environmental stressors and other infectious agents, will help to minimize the impacts of circovirus infection.

As with CAV infection, there is no effective treatment for elimination of circoviruses from birds; supportive treatment may be beneficial.

15xi.3.2 Cycloviruses

A cyclovirus (genus *Cyclovirus*, family *Circoviridae*) has been identified in chicken faeces, but to date there is no information about its pathological effects. Therefore, cycloviruses will not be considered further in this Chapter.

15xi.4 Further Reading

Gimeno, I.M. and Schat, K.A. (2018) Virus-induced immunosuppression in chickens. *Avian Diseases* 62, 272–285.

Schat, K.A., Woods, L.W., Van Santen, V.L. and Latimer, K.S. (2013) Chicken infectious anemia virus and other circovirus infections. In: Swayne, D.E., Glisson, J.R., McDougald, L.R., Nolan, L.K., Suarez, D.L., *et al.* (eds) *Diseases of Poultry*, 13th edn. Wiley-Blackwell, Ames, Iowa, pp. 247–288.

Smyth, J.A. and Schat, K.A. (2016) Chicken anemia virus. In: Williams, S.M., Dufour-Zavala, L., Jackwood, M.W.,

Lee, M.D., Lupian, B.I, *et al.* (eds.) *Isolation, Identification and Characterization of Avian Pathogens,* 6th edn. American Association of Avian Pathologists, Madison, Wisconsin, pp. 183–188.
Smyth, J.A. and Schat, K.A. (2013) Virus induced immunosuppression: chicken infectious anemia. In: Gimeno, I. (ed.) *Immunosuppressive Diseases of Poultry.* Servet, Zaragoza, Spain, pp. 89–121.
Todd, D. (2000) Circoviruses: immunosuppressive threats to avian species: A review. *Avian Pathology* 29, 373–394.

15xii Avian Leukosis and Reticuloendotheliosis

VENUGOPAL NAIR*

The Pirbright Institute, Woking, Surrey, UK

15xii.1 Overview

Avian leukosis refers to a group of diseases comprising transmissible tumours of chickens caused by avian leukosis viruses (ALV), members of the family *Retroviridae* (Fauquet *et al.*, 2005). The term 'leukosis' embraces several different leukaemia-like proliferative diseases of different haemopoietic cell types resulting in lymphoid, myeloid or erythroid tumours. While most of the modern commercial poultry breeding industry has been successful in eradicating ALV from the breeding flocks, avian leukosis continues to be a problem in many countries such as China (Gao *et al.*, 2012; Payne and Nair, 2012). Economic losses from avian leukosis arise from tumour mortality and loss of production. Reticuloendotheliosis (RE) represents a group of syndromes caused by another common, but not ubiquitous, retrovirus called reticuloendotheliosis virus (REV). The syndromes include runting disease, chronic lymphoid neoplasia and acute reticulum cell neoplasia (Zavala and Nair, 2020).

15xii.2 Nature of Pathogens

ALVs are placed in the genus *Alpharetrovirus* in the family *Retroviridae*. They are classified into ten different subgroups designated A to J based on their envelope properties including neutralization, host range and interference (Nair, 2020). Chickens are infected by ALV subgroups A, B, C, D, E and J, of which the subgroup E includes endogenous retroviruses not associated with tumours. In addition to this grouping based on the viral envelope, ALV strains can also be classified as: (i) slowly transforming viruses (e.g. RAV-1) that carry a fully infectious viral genome and (ii) acutely transforming viruses (e.g. MC29) with their defective genome carrying transduced oncogenes such as v-*myc* (Kung and Liu, 1997). ALV consists of 80–120 nm particles with the two copies of the viral RNA packed in the nucleocapsid surrounded by the plasma membrane into which the viral glycoproteins are embedded. The two copies of the viral RNA allow reverse transcriptase complex to switch templates during replication. The ~7.3 kb long viral RNA genome includes the *gag/pro-pol-env* genes which encode for the virion group-specific (gs) antigens/protease, reverse transcriptase (RT) enzyme and the envelope glycoprotein, respectively.

ALV enters the cells by binding on the cell surfaces through specific viral receptors, which include the TVA receptor used by the Subgroup A, TVB receptor used by the subgroup B and the NHE-I receptor used by subgroup J (Federspiel, 2019). Upon entry into the cells, the viral RNA is reverse transcribed into linear DNA molecules that become integrated at random locations into the host genome as proviral DNA, which has the same gene order as the viral RNA but is flanked by identical sequence structures referred to as the long terminal repeats (LTR). Transcription of the viral genomic RNA from the LTR results in production of infectious viruses that are released by budding from the plasma membrane.

REV belongs to the genus *Gammaretrovirus* in the family *Retroviridae*. The REV genome, with a similar structure to ALV, is about 9.0 kb in length. However, acutely transforming strain REV-T has a much shorter genome of about 5.7 kb due to the

*venugopal.nair@pirbright.ac.uk

© CAB International 2021.
DOI: 10.1079/9781789245042.0015

large deletion of the gag-pol region, and insertion of v-rel oncogene. REV belongs to a single serotype, although subtypes have been reported. Unlike ALV, no REV-related endogenous sequences have been recognized in the avian genomes.

15xii.3 Transmission and Epidemiology

ALV-infected chickens carry integrated proviruses with the capability to produce infectious viruses for life, acting as carriers and sources of horizontal transmission through droppings and other fomites. However, since ALV has a relatively short half-life outside the host, the infection does not readily spread through indirect contact. Infected birds can also transmit the virus vertically through the eggs, and the chicks hatched from vertically infected eggs are immunologically tolerant and remain viraemic and infectious after hatch, serving as a major nucleus of infection for most chickens in the flock.

Depending on the status of ALV infection, birds in the infected flocks can be grouped into different categories such as: (i) V−A− (no viraemia, no antibody), (ii) V−A+ (no viraemia, with antibody), (iii) V+A+ (viraemia, with antibody) and (iv) V+A− (viraemia, no antibody). Most of the V+A− hens transmit ALV infection vertically to their progeny, while a few of the V−A+ hens may also transmit the virus to the progeny, at least intermittently. Birds from infected flocks, as well as the products such as eggs and meat, can spread infection to other flocks and locations. Because of the vertical transmission potential, ALV infection can spread through hatching eggs and day-old chicks, in addition to through the semen.

REV infection can also be transmitted vertically through eggs, resulting in persistent infection of the progeny. Egg albumen and semen from such persistently infected birds contain high titres of REV. Horizontal transmission through close contact also occurs in different poultry species. Several insect species have also been implicated in transmission of the virus. Contaminated poultry vaccines are a common source of new outbreaks of REV as well as ALV infection.

15xii.4 Nature of the Disease

The incubation period of ALV infections is highly variable as the pathogenic effects of the disease occur when ALV integrates into the critical regions of the genome dysregulating the expression of important oncogenes such as c-*myc* (Bishop, 1990) or microRNAs such as miR-155 (Tam *et al.*, 2002). Because of the insertional activation of ALV genome into cellular genes that are necessary for the induction of tumours, ALV-induced tumours are slow in onset and are seen in older birds. However, in some of the tumours resulting from the activation of oncogenes, acutely transforming viruses with transduced oncogenes can be generated. Such viruses can induce more rapid onset tumours (Kung and Liu, 1997).

REV infection is common in chickens, turkeys and ducks in countries such as United States, China, Japan and Egypt, as demonstrated by seroprevalence rates. While lymphomas have been reported in infected birds, the most common form of the disease is characterized by immunosuppression, runting and chronic neoplasia. Acute reticulum cell hyperplasia associated with REV-T has very rapid onset with mortality often reaching 100%.

15xii.5 Clinical Signs

The clinical signs of avian leukosis are not specific and include loss of appetite, weakness, emaciation and weight loss, diarrhoea and dehydration, with pale comb and wattles. When large lymphoid tumours occur in visceral organs, there can be clinical signs of abdominal enlargement. In some of the diseases such as erythroblastosis and myeloblastosis, there can be signs of haemorrhage from areas such as the skin and the feather follicles. In cases of myelocytomatosis, such as those caused by viruses belonging to ALV subgroup J, skeletal myelocytomas on the ribs and skull may be visible from the outside (Figs. 15xii.1a and b).

Sarcomas and other connective tissue tumours may also be visible on the skin and musculature. Similarly, in cases of osteopetrosis, the long bones of the limbs may show diffuse or irregular thickening that can be palpable during inspection. In cases of 'fowl glioma' associated with ALV, neuronal symptoms associated with cerebellar hypoplasia can also be seen.

REV infected birds with runting disease syndrome show stunted growth and significant loss of weight. Some of the infected chickens may display abnormal feather development, referred to as 'nakanuke', characterized by focal adhesion of the barbs to the shaft in the wing feathers. Chronic lymphomas in REV-infected birds have a slow onset with disease manifestation several weeks after infection.

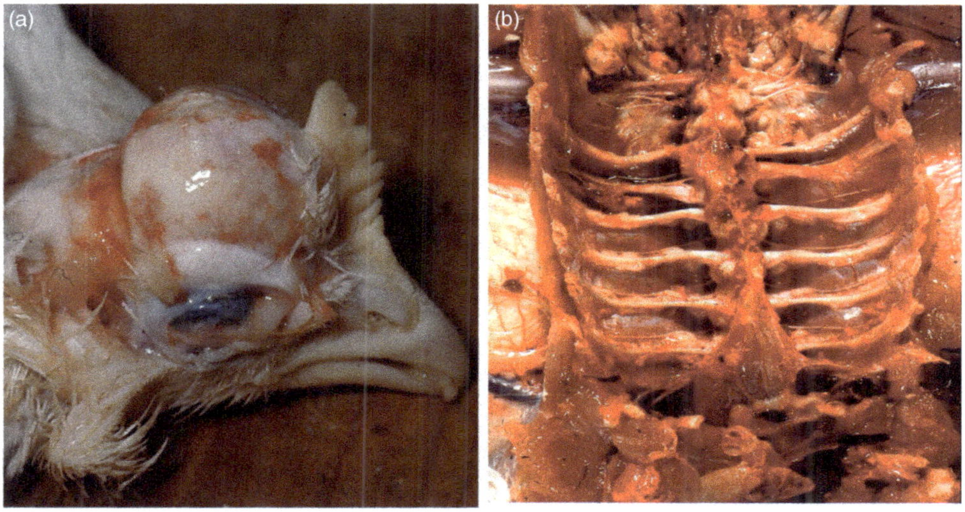

Fig. 15xii.1. Skeletal myelocytomas on the skull (a) and ribs (b). (Author's own photograph.)

15xii.6 Lesions

In ALV infections where tumours are absent, lesions of stunting and atrophy of the lymphoid organs, and anaemia are visible. In fully developed cases of lymphoid leukosis, which usually occur in birds older than 4 months, gross tumours are usually seen in liver, spleen, bursa of Fabricius and other organs. The tumours are generally soft, smooth and glistening with a greyish or white cut surface with no evidence of necrosis. Tumours can occur either as diffuse or as miliary nodules. In cases of erythroblastosis, the liver and kidneys are usually swollen, with an enlarged spleen which is usually cherry red in colour. The bone marrow of affected birds is hyperplastic with red colour and semisolid consistency. In cases of myelocytomatosis, usually associated with ALV-J infections in meat-type chickens, characteristic myelocytomas of multiple bone tissues are visible. These lesions are usually nodular and creamy in colour, developing at the costochondrial junctions of the ribs as well as in the sternum, pelvis and skull. In addition to these tumours, haemangiomas appearing as blood-filled cystic masses or blisters, can be seen on the skin and visceral organs. Characteristic microscopic lesions of different types of tumours are also very valuable in understanding of the disease pathogenesis and for accurate diagnosis.

REV-infected birds showing runting disease may show thymic and bursal atrophy, enlarged nerves, proventriculitis and abnormal feathering. Birds with chronic lymphomas show proliferating lymphoblasts in multiple organs including the bursa of Fabricius. Such birds may also show peripheral nerve enlargement, adenocarcinomas or sarcomas.

15xii.7 Diagnostic Approaches

Avian leukosis is a complex disease involving multiple subgroups, with neoplastic lesions involving multiple cell types. While the demonstration of viral antigens, antibodies or virus-specific nucleic acids is useful, detection and typing of the causative agent are also important. Virus isolation from clinical samples such as blood, cloacal swabs, egg albumen and tumours is considered the 'gold standard' for diagnosis. Virus isolation can be carried out on primary chicken embryo fibroblast (CEF) cultures or the DF-1 cell line, and the isolates can be stored for further characterization using standard tests such as virus neutralization, host range and interference studies. Molecular biological tests based on polymerase chain reaction (PCR) have been developed for differentiating between endogenous and exogenous retroviruses as well as for differentiating ALV subgroups (Gao *et al.*, 2014). Serological tests, such as virus neutralization and group-specific ELISA tests, are also used extensively in diagnosis and flock monitoring of ALV infections (Fadly, 2000).

Because of the similarities of the lesions with other avian neoplastic diseases, diagnosis of RE requires the demonstration of REV or specific antibodies, and exclusion of other oncogenic viruses such as ALV and MDV. While isolation of REV and demonstration of specific antigens are valuable, the most common method of diagnosis is the use of PCR tests. Amplification of REV envelope or 3′ LTR sequences using conventional PCR tests, or loop-mediated isothermal amplification (LAMP), are widely employed for specific diagnosis of REV.

15xii.8 Control and Prevention

As ALV infections result in lifelong carrier status from the integrated proviruses, with the potential of vertical and horizontal transmission to other birds, eradication of the virus from the breeding flocks is considered the best option for control and prevention. Programmes for ALV eradication from infected flocks are aimed at removal of infected carrier birds from the flocks as efficiently as possible to break the transmission cycle from the hens to the progeny. This requires the application of highly sensitive diagnostic tests that can detect infected birds for removal from the flocks to reduce the chances of them transmitting the virus to new birds. In order to make sure that no infected birds are missed, diagnostic tests are applied at different stages of the life cycle of the bird including testing the meconium from the newly hatched chicks, blood and cloacal swabs at different stages of growing up, and the egg albumen from the newly laid eggs. In order to establish an ALV-free flock, it is important to remove any positive or potentially exposed birds to break the virus transmission cycle. ALV eradication procedures in infected flocks involve selection of fertile eggs from hens negative in the egg albumen or vaginal swab tests, hatching of chicks in isolation in small groups and removing any positive groups, and monitoring the infection at the flock level. Increased biosecurity measures to prevent virus transmission and introduction of infections through contaminated vaccines or other sources are also very important. Selective breeding for genetic resistance has also been successful in disease control. More recently, the feasibility of introducing *de novo* genetic resistance through gene editing approaches has also been demonstrated as another potential approach in controlling avian leukosis.

Methods applied for ALV eradication are applicable for controlling RE in infected flocks, although such methods are rarely applied because of the sporadic and self-limiting nature of the disease. However, such eradication programmes are required in endemic disease flocks. Prevention of REV is mostly accomplished through biosecurity measures for controlling insects and fowlpox infections, and improved quality assurance of vaccines to prevent introduction of the virus.

15xii.9 References

Bishop, J.M. (1990) Nobel lecture. Retroviruses and oncogenes II. *Bioscience Reports* 10, 473–91.

Fadly, A.M. (2000) Isolation and identification of avian leukosis viruses: a review. *Avian Pathology* 29, 529–535.

Fauquet, C.M., Mayo, M.A., Maniloff, J., Desselberger, U. and Ball, L.A. (2005) *Virus Taxonomy: VIIIth Report of the International Committee on Taxonomy of Viruses*. Elsevier Academic Press, San Diego, California.

Federspiel, M.J. (2019) Reverse engineering provides insights on the evolution of subgroups A to E avian sarcoma and leukosis virus receptor specificity. *Viruses* 11, 497. DOI: 10.3390/v11060497.

Gao, Y., Yun, B., Qin, L., Pan, W., Qu, Y., *et al.* (2012) Molecular epidemiology of avian leukosis virus subgroup j in layer flocks in china. *Journal of Clinical Microbiology* 50, 953–60.

Gao, Q., Yun, B., Wang, Q., Jiang, L., Zhu, H., *et al.* (2014) Development and application of a multiplex PCR method for rapid differential detection of subgroup A, B, and J avian leukosis viruses. *Journal of Clinical Microbiology* 52, 37–44.

Kung, H.J. and Liu, J.L. (1997) Retroviral oncogenesis. In: Nathanson, N. (ed.) *Viral Pathogenesis*. Lippincott-Raven Publishers, Philadelphia, Pennsylvania.

Nair, V. (2020) Leukosis/Sarcoma group. In: Swayne, D.E., Boulianne, M., Logue, C.M., McDougald, L.R., Nair, V., *et al.* (eds) *Diseases of Poultry*, 14th edn. Wiley, Hoboken, New Jersey, pp. 587–625.

Payne, L.N. and Nair, V. (2012) The long view: 40 years of avian leukosis research. *Avian Pathology* 41, 1–9.

Tam, W., Hughes, S.H., Hayward, W.S. and Besmer, P. (2002) Avian bic, a gene isolated from a common retroviral site in avian leukosis virus-induced lymphomas that encodes a noncoding RNA, cooperates with c-myc in lymphomagenesis and erythroleukemogenesis. *Journal of Virology* 76, 4275–86.

Zavala, G. and Nair, V. (2020) Reticuloendotheliosis. In: Swayne, D.E., Boulianne, M., Logue, C.M., McDougald, L.R., Nair, V., *et al.* (eds.) *Diseases of Poultry*, 14th edn. Wiley, Hoboken, New Jersey, pp. 625–637.

15xiii Marek's Disease

VENUGOPAL NAIR*

The Pirbright Institute, Woking, Surrey, UK

15xiii.1 Overview

Marek's disease (MD) is a common highly contagious lymphoproliferative disease of poultry associated with T-cell lymphoid tumours in multiple visceral organs, immunosuppression and paralysis due to mononuclear infiltration into the peripheral nerves. Named after the Hungarian veterinarian Dr Jozsef Marek who first reported the disease, MD causes major economic losses to the farmers worldwide (Nair *et al.*, 2020). MD remains a major concern for the poultry industry in several countries due to the unpredictability of the outbreaks and the continuing evolution of virulence among MDV strains.

15xiii.2 Nature of Pathogen

The causative agent of MD is Marek's disease virus (MDV-1, also known as *Gallid herpesvirus 2*, GaHV-2) which belongs to the genus *Mardivirus* in the subfamily *Alphaherpesvirinae* of the family *Herpesviridae*. MDV-1 comprises a group of viruses that include avirulent attenuated vaccine strains such as Rispens (CVI988) at one end of the spectrum, to very virulent (vvMDV) and very virulent plus (vvMDV+) pathotypes such as Md5 and 675A strains at the other end. The genus *Mardivirus* also consists of the non-pathogenic *Gallid herpesvirus* 3 (GaHV-3) strains such as SB-1 and *Meleagrid herpesvirus*-1 (MeHV-1) that includes the herpesvirus of turkey (HVT) strain Fc-126, which are used as vaccines to protect against MD. Similar to other alphaherpesviruses, MDV-1 particles (150–160 nm) consist of an icosahedral capsid containing the viral genome, and the proteinaceous tegument surrounded by the lipid envelope bilayer into which several viral glycoproteins are embedded. The MDV genome consists of 160–180 kb double stranded DNA that includes the unique long (U_L) and unique short (U_S) regions each flanked by inverted repeat regions referred to as terminal and internal (TR_L, IR_L, IR_S and TR_S) repeats. The MDV-1 genome has more than 100 genes that encode several structural and non-structural herpesvirus homologues as well as a unique set of MDV-encoded proteins such as Meq, vIL-8, pp38 and others that are associated with pathogenesis. MDV has a strictly cell-associated replication, and experimental infections or vaccinations must be carried out using live infected cells.

15xiii.3 Epidemiology

Birds become infected via the airborne route by the inhalation of infected poultry house dust contaminated by the infectious virus shed from the feather follicles of infected birds. Because of the ability of the virus to survive for long periods in the poultry house dust, birds are exposed to infection early in life. Onset of clinical disease depends on the maternal antibody levels and vaccination status, as well as genetic resistance of the birds. Although vaccines are effective in preventing clinical disease, they do not protect birds from infection, and this is considered to be one of the factors driving MDV virulence (Read *et al.*, 2015) and emergence of vvMDV and vv+MDV pathotypes (Witter, 1997).

15xiii.4 Nature of the Disease

In infected birds, MDV has a complex life cycle involving lytic replication in multiple cell types, resulting in severe immunosuppression characterized by bursal and thymic atrophy. The latent infection in lymphocytes that follows, often leads to neoplastic disease characterized by T-cell lymphomas in multiple organs and paralysis due to infiltration of peripheral

*venugopal.nair@pirbright.ac.uk

© CAB International 2021. *Poultry Health: A Guide for Professionals* (P. Barrow *et al.*)
DOI: 10.1079/9781789245042.0015

nerves. MDV replication in the feather follicle epithelial cells leads to the shedding into the environment of infectious virus that acts as a source of infection of other chickens.

15xiii.5 Clinical Signs

The clinical signs of MD usually occur from around 3–4 weeks of age, although early mortality can also be seen in younger chicks especially in the absence of maternal antibodies. Clinical disease, with tumours in multiple visceral organs, can frequently be seen between 12 and 24 weeks causing huge economic losses to the farmers. In the classical form of the disease, affected birds show paralytic clinical signs due to the lymphocytic infiltration into the peripheral nerves. Other clinical signs include evidence of blindness. In addition, infected birds may also show signs of transient paralysis, characterized by sudden development of ataxia and paralysis of the legs, wings and neck. These clinical signs usually only last for 24–48 h and are thought to be due to brain oedema.

15xiii.6 Lesions

Gross pathological lesions include the lymphomatous lesions in multiple organs including the gonads, kidney, liver, heart and spleen (Fig. 15xiii.1a).

These can occur as diffuse enlargement of the organs or as focal nodular growths of varying sizes. In organs such as ovary where the lymphomas are common, the normal folliculated appearance may be obliterated. In most of the infected birds, the proventriculus is affected with marked thickening. In cases where neuronal involvement is observed, sciatic and brachial nerves show diffuse enlargement and can appear much thickened. Gross ocular lesions with loss of pigmentation in the iris give a 'grey eye' appearance. In the acute stages of the disease, atrophy of the thymus and bursa of Fabricius are common with splenic enlargement. Histopathological lesions of the lymphomas show proliferating tumour cells characterized by large pleomorphic nuclei and expressing CD4 (see Chapter 2, this volume). Enlarged peripheral nerves (Fig. 15xiii.1b) show lymphoproliferative lesions with light to moderate levels of lymphocyte infiltration. Affected nerves may also show demyelination and Schwann cell proliferation.

15xiii.7 Diagnostic Approaches

The characteristic clinical signs and the lesions of MD are usually sufficient for making a diagnosis in flocks suffering from clinical disease. However, differential diagnosis from other avian tumour diseases,

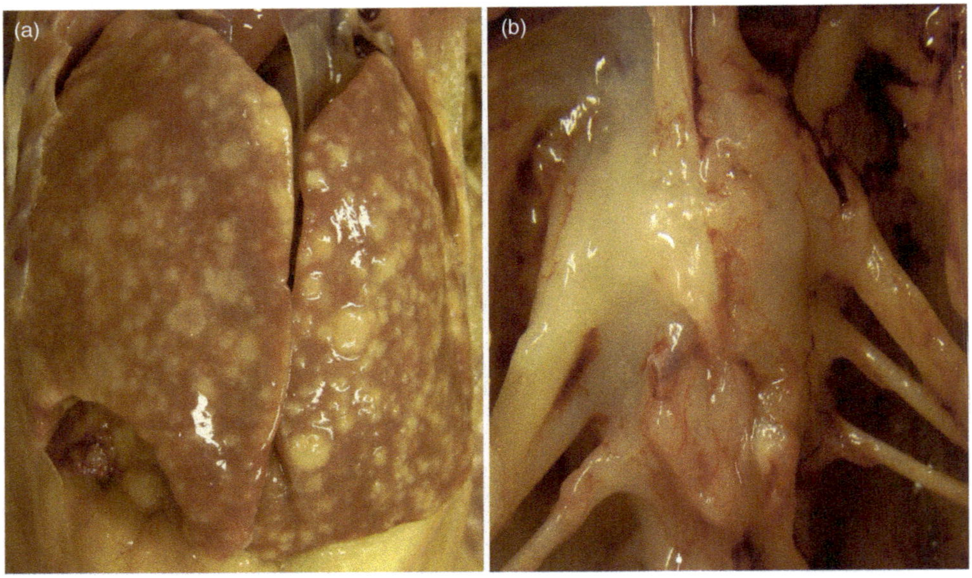

Fig. 15xiii.1. (a) Lymphomatous lesions in liver. (b) Enlarged peripheral nerves in sciatic plexus (left) with normal nerves (right). (author's own images.)

such as lymphoid leukosis or reticuloendotheliosis, requires laboratory diagnosis. However, as MDV is ubiquitous in poultry farms, detection of the presence of MDV is often not sufficient for the diagnosis of MD. Principal methods of the identification of viral infections include virus isolation or detection of viral DNA or antigens in the tissues. MDV can be isolated from the infected birds at any stage of infection. Inoculum for virus isolation can be heparinized blood, lymphocytes, splenocytes or tumour cells from the infected birds. However, intact viable cells are required for the successful virus isolation because of the avidly cell-associated nature of the infectivity.

Commonly used cell culture systems for virus isolation include primary cultures such as chicken or duck embryonic fibroblast (CEF/DEF) or chicken kidney cell (CKC) cultures which can be inoculated with 1–2 × 10^6 cells from spleen, blood or tumours. These cultures will demonstrate characteristic MDV plaques usually in 3–6 days of incubation, but in some instances the cell culture systems may have to be passaged at least once to visualize the plaques. Confirmation of the specificity of the virus plaques can be determined by staining with specific antibodies.

Availability of nucleotide sequences of whole viral genomes of several MDV strains has enabled the development of specific polymerase chain reaction (PCR) tests that can be used to differentiate between virulent strains and the different vaccine strains (Silva, 1992). Loop-mediated isothermal amplification (LAMP) methods for rapid detection of MDV genome (Wozniakowski *et al.*, 2013) and quantitative PCR (qPCR) tests that can accurately determine the genome copy number of the vaccine and virulent MDV strains, have also been developed (Baigent *et al.*, 2016). Availability of specific monoclonal antibodies against different viral proteins has also helped in the detection of MDV-specific antigens in infected tissues using different immuno-histochemical and immuno-fluorescent approaches.

15xiii.8 Control and Prevention

The ubiquitous nature of the virus and its capability for long-term survival in the infected birds, as well as in the contaminated poultry house environment, makes the eradication of virus infection impossible. Hence the control of the disease is primarily dependent on preventive vaccination, although improvement of the farm management practices for reducing exposure to the virus and increasing the proportion of birds with increased genetic resistance can also help. Vaccination with different types of live attenuated vaccines is the cornerstone of the control strategy. The strains of vaccine viruses currently used to protect against MD include the antigenically related HVT strain Fc-126, non-pathogenic GaHV-3 strain SB-1 and the naturally attenuated MDV-1 strain CVI988. While these vaccine strains vary in their ability to protect against different MDV-1 pathotypes, they are also used in combination as bivalent vaccines to make use of their synergistic effects (Witter, 2001). Vaccine strains such as HVT and SB-1 are also used widely as recombinant viral vectors to induce protection against other avian diseases (Bublot *et al.*, 2007; Sadigh *et al.*, 2018). MD vaccines are usually inoculated at the hatchery to one-day-old chicks or increasingly as *in ovo* vaccines at embryonic day 18 (ED18) using automatic machines with increased precision. As cell-associated viral vaccines, proper reconstitution of the vaccine during thawing and administration is crucial to ensure adequate protection.

Although proper vaccination at the hatchery is very valuable for protection against the disease, management practices that will help in reducing high levels of exposure to the virus, especially at the early stages of a chick's life, are equally important. Similarly, efforts to reduce stress and exposure to other immunosuppressive diseases are also valuable in inducing a strong protective immune response against MD. Use of strains of birds with higher levels of genetic resistance to MD can also help in achieving better responses to vaccines.

15xiii.9 References

Baigent, S.J., Nair, V.K. and Le Galludec, H. (2016) Real-time PCR for differential quantification of CVI988 vaccine virus and virulent strains of Marek's disease virus. *Journal of Virological Methods* 233, 23–36.

Bublot, M., Pritchard, N., Le Gros, F.X. and Goutebroze, S. (2007) Use of a vectored vaccine against infectious bursal disease of chickens in the face of high-titred maternally derived antibody. *Journal of Comparative Pathology* 137 Suppl 1, S81–4.

Nair, V., Gimeno, I. and Dunn, J. (2020) Marek's disease. In: Swayne, D.E., Boulianne, M., Logue, C.M., McDougald, L.R., Nair, V., *et al.* (eds) *Diseases of Poultry,* 14th edn. Wiley, Hoboken, New Jersey, pp. 550–587

Read, A.F., Baigent, S.J., Powers, C., Kgosana, L.B., Blackwell, L., *et al*. (2015) Imperfect vaccination can enhance the transmission of highly virulent pathogens. *PLoS Biology,* 13(7), e1002198.

Sadigh, Y., Powers, C., Spiro, S., Pedrera, M., Broadbent, A., *et al*. (2018) Gallid herpesvirus 3 SB-1 strain as a recombinant viral vector for poultry vaccination. *NPJ Vaccines* 3, 21.

Silva, R.F. (1992) Differentiation of pathogenic and non-pathogenic serotype 1 Marek's disease viruses (MDVs) by the polymerase chain reaction amplification of the tandem direct repeats within the MDV genome. *Avian Diseases* 36, 521–528.

Witter, R.L. (1997) Increased virulence of Marek's disease virus field isolates. *Avian Diseases* 41, 149–163.

Witter, R.L. (2001) Marek's disease vaccines – past, present and future (Chicken vs virus – a battle of the centuries). In*:* Schat, K.A., Morgan, R.W., Parcells, M.S. and Spencer, J.L. (eds) *Current Progress on Marek's Disease Research.* American Association of Avian Pathologists, Kennett Square, Pennsylvania.

Wozniakowski, G., Samorek-Salamonowicz, E. and Kozdrun, W. (2013) Comparison of loop-mediated isothermal amplification and PCR for the detection and differentiation of Marek's disease virus serotypes 1, 2, and 3. *Avian Diseases* 57, 539–43.

15xiv Fowlpox

Richard C. Jones*

Institute of Infection, Veterinary and Ecological Sciences, University of Liverpool, Leahurst Campus, Neston, Cheshire, UK

15xiv.1 Introduction

Fowlpox is a disease of avian species, and most importantly, the chicken, characterized by cutaneous lesions in the form of thick scabs on the unfeathered parts of the skin and caused by poxviruses. It has been recognized for many years and was one of the first diseases of poultry to be investigated. In addition to the form resulting in skin lesions, there is a less common manifestation, usually described as wet pox, characterized by lesions in the mouth and upper respiratory tract. Fowlpox is more common in older birds, and rare in broilers. It is slow spreading, usually by direct contact such as pecking and scratching, and is also spread by biting insects. The incidence of fowlpox is dramatically reduced by vaccination. The disease is worldwide but prevalence is more common in tropical climates.

15xiv.2 Aetiology

The first investigations into the cause of the disease were conducted in the early 1930s and were relatively easy by virtue of the fact that the agent grew readily in fertile eggs and later, tissue cultures. The virus is one of the largest known, with brick-shaped virions measuring some 250 × 100 nm. It is a DNA virus of complex symmetry with characteristic 'Turkish towel'-like protein structures on its surface (Fig. 15xiv.1).

The electron microscope shows the characteristic bi-concave internal structure of the virion and, in infected cells, aggregates of virions appear as Bollinger bodies which can be seen with the light microscope in the cytoplasm in stained sections.

Fowlpox is the type species of the genus *Avipox*, and members have been isolated from 280 species of birds. Three clades have been accepted as belonging to different classes of birds: fowlpox-type viruses (mainly from gallinaceous birds), canarypox-like viruses (mainly from passerines) and psittacine viruses. Recent work has revealed others from aquatic birds. The true classification still needs further work, and host definition is particularly complicated where birds of many species are kept, such as in zoos. It seems likely that much cross-species infection occurs, perhaps resulting in subclinical infection in many cases. Strains from different species differ antigenically but show cross-reactions.

Poxviruses are among the most resistant viruses and can survive for very long periods in the scabs of dead birds.

Poxviruses can be easily cultivated on the chorio-allantoic membrane of the fertile chicken egg (see later). This provides a simple way of quantitating the viruses.

Poxviruses have a very long genome (up to 300 kbp) and have been widely used as vectors for genes from other poultry viral pathogens, including infectious bronchitis, infectious laryngotracheitis and Newcastle disease viruses. The benefits of these vectored vaccines are that they are thermostable, induce cell-mediated as well as humoral antibodies to the target pathogens and are not zoonotic. Canarypox virus is used as a vector for mammalian vaccines.

15xiv.3 Disease

15xiv.3.1 Cutaneous fowlpox

This form predominates. Infection occurs through broken skin, but not intact skin, after scratching or biting during fighting or by biting insects, the latter

*jonesrc@liverpool.ac.uk

© CAB International 2021. *Poultry Health: A Guide for Professionals* (P. Barrow *et al.*)
DOI: 10.1079/9781789245042.0015

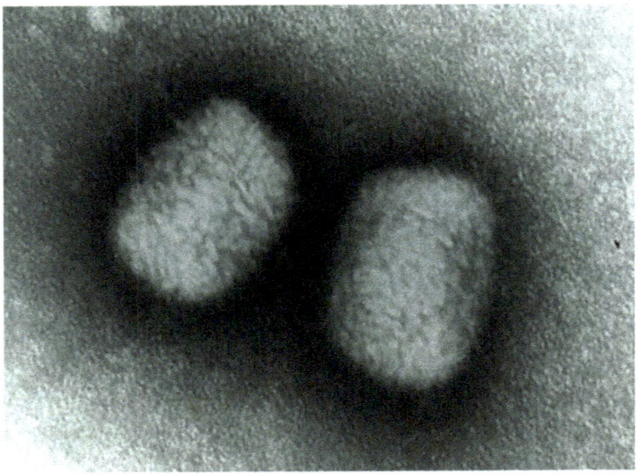

Fig. 15xiv.1. Fowlpox virus. Electron micrograph showing typical 'Turkish towel' appearance of the surface proteins, ×500,000. (Author's own image.)

especially in warm climates. Spread is much faster where mosquitoes are present. Bad sanitation aids spread as the virus is unusually resistant to desiccation and is able to survive in scabs for many months. Virus enters an epithelial cell and spreads locally with cell proliferation. The sequence is: papule, vesicle, pustule, scab. Viraemia occurs but there is apparently little damage to internal organs, although there are reports of virus in the liver and spleen. The incubation period is normally between 4 and 10 days and disease is unnoticed until cutaneous lesions appear. Lesions form on the unfeathered skin of the head, neck, legs and feet and atypically, as feather folliculitis (Figs 15xiv.2 and 15xiv.3).

There may be nasal discharge and eye closure. Disease results in inappetence and depression, poor growth and, in laying flocks, reduced egg production.

In this form of the disease, mortality is usually low, but can range from 0 to 50% with morbidity between 10 and 95%.

15xiv.3.2 Diphtheritic fowlpox

Inhalation and ingestion of infected droplets can result in caseous lesions in the oropharynx, pharynx and trachea, and is commonly known as 'wet pox' (Fig. 15xiv.4).

Here, because of problems of respiration or digestion, mortality is higher than in cutaneous pox, particularly if associated with bacterial infection. Wet pox can present problems in diagnosis, especially in differentiation from infectious laryngotracheitis (see Chapter 15iv, this volume).

Histological examination of scabs demonstrates the presence of large eosinophilic intracytoplasmic inclusion bodies ('Bollinger bodies') which are pathognomonic for fowlpox (Fig. 15xiv.5).

15xiv.4 Diagnosis

Clinically, fowlpox can be diagnosed when a significant number of birds have cutaneous lesions on the unfeathered skin. Histologically, basophilic intracytoplasmic Bollinger bodies are pathognomonic for cutaneous fowlpox. In very mild outbreaks, confirmation of the agent can be carried out by demonstration of discrete pocks on the dropped chorioallantoic membrane of a fertile hen's egg after 11 days of incubation. The virus induces the growth of discrete pink pocks. PCR can also be used and is rapid. Negative staining of samples for electron microscopy is a rapid means of demonstrating the presence of the very large viruses and can be done in minutes, if the instrument is available.

It is very important to distinguish wet pox from infectious laryngotracheitis, caused by a herpesvirus. The caseous lesions may be very similar with both viruses but can be distinguished by EM, PCR or immunostaining. Trichomonas is another agent which may need to be ruled out.

Serum antibodies for fowlpox are rarely tested for, but this can be done with commercial ELISA kits or the very simple but insensitive agar gel precipitation test.

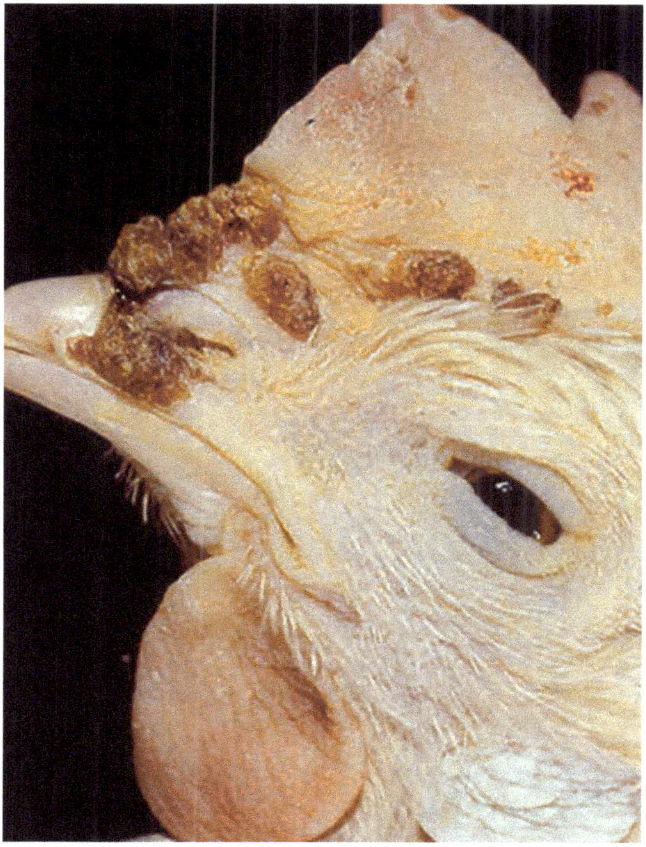

Fig. 15xiv.2. Pox lesions on head of a chicken. (Author's own image.)

15xiv.5 Control

Control of fowlpox is achieved by vaccination. The early investigations of the causative virus showed that it could easily be cultivated, and vaccines were among the earliest to be developed and are the forerunners of those used today. Vaccines are used in attenuated live form after multiple passage in fertile chicken eggs or, less commonly, in tissue culture. Tissue culture origin (TCO) vaccines are more attenuated than chick embryo origin (CEO) vaccines. As a consequence, TCO vaccines can be used in day-old chicks while CEO vaccines cannot be used until the birds are around 6 weeks of age. However, the lower immunogenicity of the CEO vaccines requires that they need to be applied again at about 12 weeks.

Fowlpox vaccines require intradermal injection since usual mass-medication methods, such as spray or drinking water applications, are not successful. The vaccines are applied to chicks using a double pointed needle and the skin is examined 7–10 days later to assess the 'take'.

Turkeys are vaccinated by the 'thigh stick' method and vaccinated at 7–10 days.

An unusual aspect of control of fowlpox is that where it is endemic, when the first affected birds have been culled, the rest of the flock can be vaccinated. This is an example of where vaccination in the face of disease can be successful and is possible because spread of infection is slow.

15xiv.6 Reticuloendotheliosis Virus (see also Chapter 15xii, this volume)

Fowlpox viruses have a very long genome, and it has been found that the pathogenic field strains often

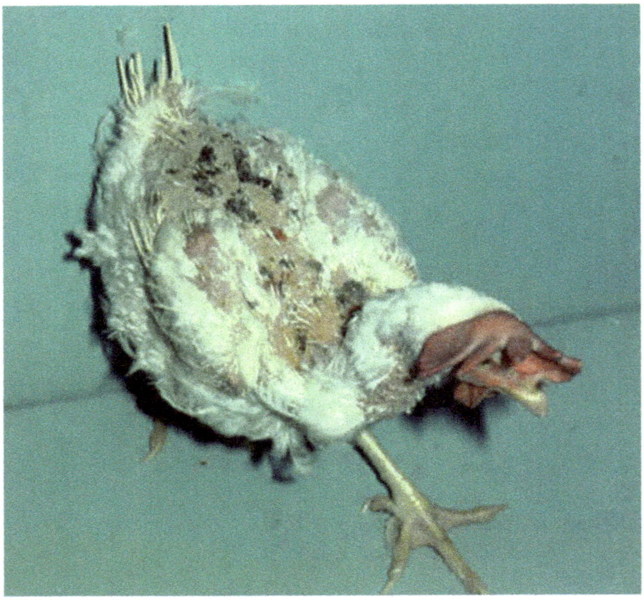

Fig. 15xiv.3. Fowlpox scabs on the unfeathered skin of a chicken. (Author's own image.)

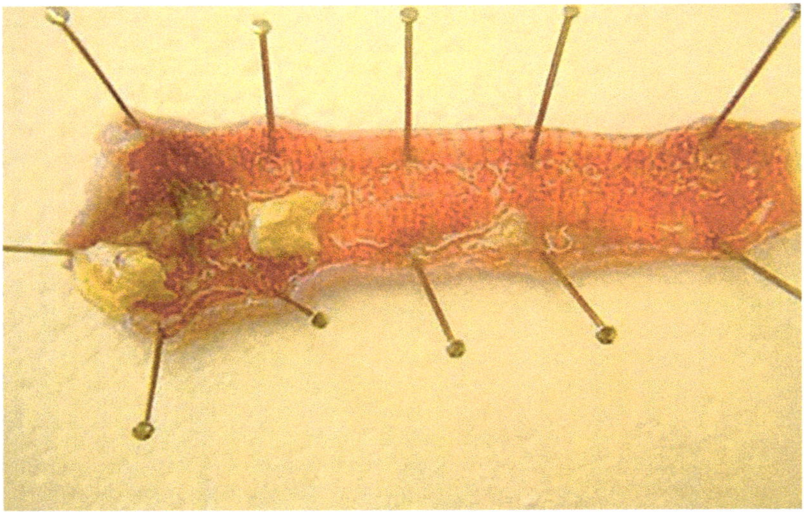

Fig. 15xiv.4. Diphtheritic fowlpox or 'wet pox' in the pharynx and trachea. May be clinically indistinguishable from infectious laryngotracheitis. (Author's own image.)

possess an integrated copy of the reticuloendotheliosis virus (REV) genome. Highly passaged viruses, and particularly the vaccine strains, appear to retain only a vestige of the REV provirus and this may be due to their laboratory attenuation. Those viruses which contain the REV material may be more virulent or more resistant to vaccinal immunity. This characteristic requires further investigation.

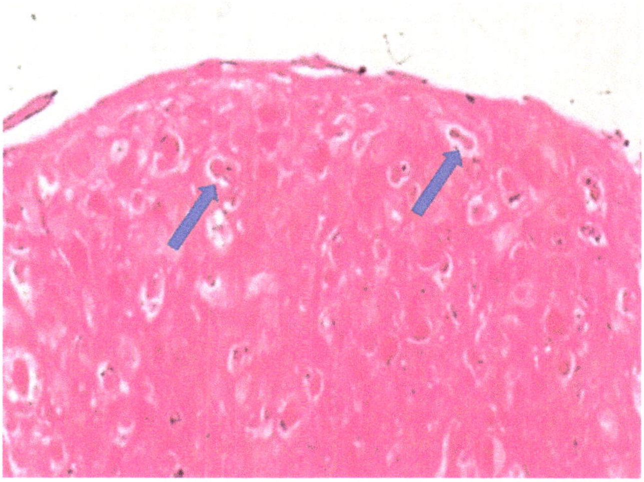

Fig. 15xiv.5. Bollinger bodies (arrows) in a section of comb tissue (H&E stain). (Author's own image.)

15xiv.7 Further Reading

Giotis, S. and Skinner, M.A. (2019) Spotlight on avian pathology: fowlpox virus. *Avian Pathology* 48, 87–90.

Tripathy, D.N. and Reed, W.M. (2013) Pox. In: Swayne, D.E., Glisson, J.R., McDougald, L.R., Nolan L.K., Suarez, D.L., *et al.* (eds) *Diseases of Poultry*, 13th edn. Wiley-Blackwell, Hoboken, New Jersey, pp. 333–350.

16i Coccidiosis

Damer Blake*

Royal Veterinary College, Hawkshead Lane, North Mymms, Hertfordshire, UK

16i.1 Introduction

In excess of 72 billion chickens are produced in the world each year, all of which are immunologically naïve to challenge by *Eimeria* species parasites at the time of hatch. In the absence of effective control many chickens will become infected with *Eimeria* and some will suffer clinical disease, called coccidiosis.

Eimeria are protozoan parasites, part of the phylum *Apicomplexa* and closely related to pathogens such as *Cryptosporidium*, *Plasmodium* and *Toxoplasma gondii*. Almost all *Eimeria* species exhibit absolute host specificity, such that those species which infect chickens can only successfully replicate in chickens (Vrba and Pakandl, 2015). Many other *Eimeria* species are capable of infecting other poultry or ruminant species, but those that infect chickens are economically most important. The global cost attributed to *Eimeria* has been estimated to exceed $10 billion every year, including losses attributed to subclinical and clinical disease, as well as the costs of anticoccidial control. Mortality caused by coccidiosis can be significant, but the greatest impact is commonly due to compromised performance in terms of body weight gain, food conversion ratio and flock homogeneity.

16i.2 *Eimeria* Lifecycle

Eimeria lifecycles are relatively simple, featuring a single definitive host with no intermediate or vector hosts. *Eimeria* infection is initiated by ingestion of one or more sporulated oocysts (Fig. 16i.1).

For those species that infect poultry the oocyst is robust, featuring a tough outer wall which can support survival within the environment for many months. A sporulated oocyst encloses four sporocysts, each of which includes a Stieda body and contains two genetically identical sporozoites.

Once ingested, the oocyst wall is disrupted by grinding in the crop or gizzard, releasing the sporocysts (Fig. 16i.2).

When sporocysts reach the intestine the Stieda body is eroded under the action of trypsin and bile, permitting the sporozoites to exit. Sporozoites, the first motile stage of the lifecycle, then migrate through the intestine until they find a gut cell to invade, forming a parasitophorous vacuole. The precise location of invasion varies by *Eimeria* species, as described below. Immediately following invasion, the sporozoite rounds up to become a trophozoite, before developing into a schizont. During the process of schizogony, merozoites are formed asexually within each schizont until, once mature, the merozoites escape into the intestinal lumen. In poultry, schizogony is repeated three or four times (depending on *Eimeria* species), after which the final merozoites differentiate into gametes. Hundreds of male gametes, termed microgametes, develop within individual microgametocytes. Single female gametes, known as macrogametes, develop within each macrogametocyte. Once mature, the motile microgametes escape from their microgametocytes and fertilize macrogametes, which subsequently develop into zygotes and become oocysts. Each progeny oocyst, which contains a single sporoblast and is called unsporulated (and thus non-infectious) at the time of excretion, undergoes sporulation in the environment. Sporulation is a metabolically active process that requires temperatures in excess of 20°C, oxygen and humidity. Given appropriate conditions each oocyst can sporulate within 2–3 days,

*dblake@rvc.ac.uk

© CAB International 2021. *Poultry Health: A Guide for Professionals* (P. Barrow *et al.*)
DOI: 10.1079/9781789245042.0016

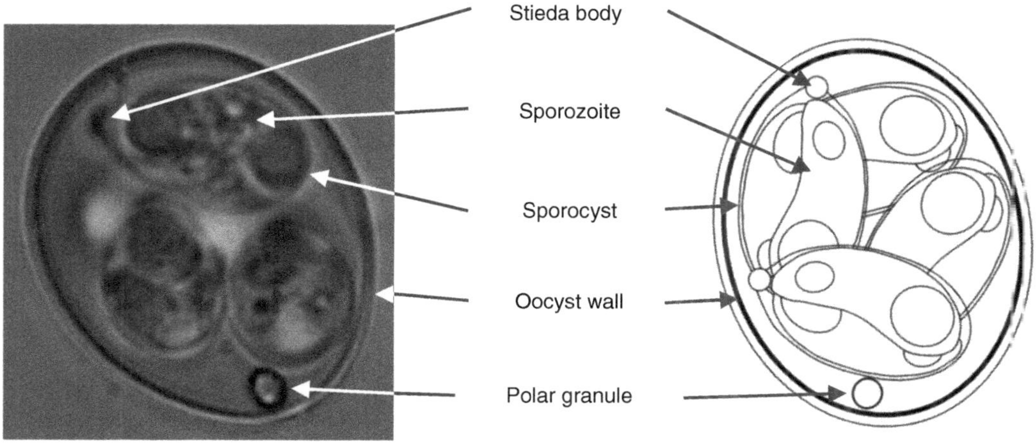

Fig. 16i.1. Structure of the eimerian oocyst.

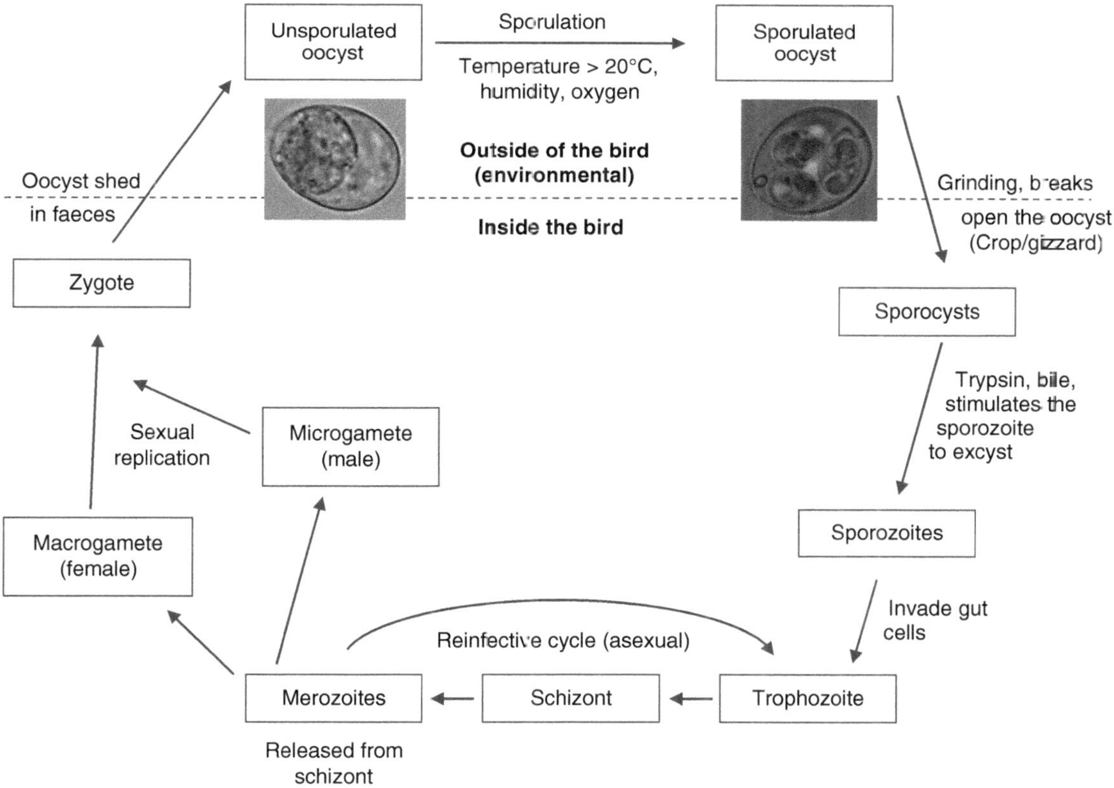

Fig. 16i.2. The lifecycle of *Eimeria* that infect chickens.

becoming infectious when completed. Sporulated oocysts can survive and remain infectious for several months in the environment, lasting longer in cool and damp conditions. With a single host and an obligatory environmental phase, *Eimeria* follow a faecal–oral lifecycle.

16i.3 *Eimeria* Species That Infect Poultry

Seven *Eimeria* species have been recognized to infect chickens: *Eimeria acervulina*, *E. brunetti*, *E. maxima*, *E. mitis*, *E. necatrix*, *E. praecox* and *E. tenella*. All seven can be pathogenic, although the nature and severity of infection varies by species, each falling loosely into one of two disease manifestations (Table 16i.1). Malabsorptive coccidiosis, caused by *E. acervulina*, *E. maxima*, *E. mitis* or *E. praecox*, rarely results in mortality unless the level of challenge is overwhelming. Instead, the consequences of infection include villous atrophy and mucoid enteritis, primarily due to excessive numbers of gametes, zygotes and developing oocysts during the latter stages of the lifecycle. *E. praecox* has frequently been considered of negligible significance, although pathogenic strains capable of causing disease equivalent to *E. acervulina* have been reported (Williams *et al.*, 2009). If undetected and uncontrolled, malabsorptive coccidiosis can become a chronic problem defined by suboptimal performance. Haemorrhagic coccidiosis, caused by *E. brunetti*, *E. necatrix*, or *E. tenella*, can be considerably more pathogenic, with mortality common during heavy infections. The haemorrhagic enteritis is associated with merozoite release, especially release from larger, deeper schizonts such as the second generation of schizogony for *E. tenella*. The severity of disease is influenced by a wide range of variables including the magnitude and age of the infecting dose, host breed and immune status (i.e. primary or re-infection). Historical reports of additional species

Table 16i.1. Summary of *Eimeria* species characteristics.

Species Pathogenicity (disease type[a])	Sporulated oocyst	Mean oocyst size[b]	Location	Lesion score[c] 0	1	2	3	4[d]
E. acervulina ++ (M)		L: 18.3 W: 14.6 L/W: 1.25	SI (upper)	No gross lesions	Few elongated white lesions	More lesions, normal content	Linked lesions, watery content	Ladder lesions, creamy exudate
E. brunetti +++ (H)		L: 24.6 W: 18.8 L/W: 1.31	SI (lower) caeca, rectum	No gross lesions	Microscopy to detect parasites	Grey, pink flecks sloughed	Catarrhal exudate, mucus plug, red	Necrotic membranes
E. maxima +++ (M)		L: 30.5 W: 20.7 L/W: 1.47	SI (mid)	No gross lesions	Some orange mucus	Copious orange mucus	Pinpoint blood clots, mucus	Ballooned, putrid odour
E. mitis ++ (M)		L: 15.6 W: 14.2 L/W: 1.10	SI (lower)	No gross lesions	No gross lesions	No gross lesions	No gross lesions	No gross lesions
E. necatrix +++++ (H)		L: 20.4 W: 17.2 L/W: 1.19	SI (mid) caeca[e]	No gross lesions	Serosal white spots	White spots ballooning	White plaques ballooning	Ballooned
E. praecox ++ (M)		L: 21.3 W: 17.1 L/W: 1.25	SI (upper)	No gross lesions	No gross lesions	No gross lesions	No gross lesions	No gross lesions
E. tenella ++++ (H)		L: 22.0 W: 19.0 L/W: 1.16	Caeca	Normal caecal content	Normal caecal content	Little/no caecal content	Blood/ caseous core	Blood/caseous core

[a]Disease types, M = malabsorptive pathology, H = haemorrhagic pathology.
[b]Oocyst morphology as described by Long *et al.* (1976). Note, morphology not given for *E. mitis*.
[c]Lesion scoring criteria as described by Johnson and Reid (1970). Note, lesions not described for *E. mitis* and *E. praecox*. Lesion scoring pie charts shown left to right per *Eimeria* species/score indicate the appearance of petechiae (black); non-haemorrhagic lesions (brown); thickening of the intestinal wall (blue); and the appearance of mucus (green) or blood (red) in the intestinal contents.
- = not referred to.
[d]Dead birds scored at 4.
[e]Gametogony occurs in the caeca.

such as *E. hagani* or *E. mivati* have not been widely recognized and, in the absence of type specimens, are now generally acknowledged to be dubious (Vrba *et al.*, 2011).

Lifecycle duration is specific to each *Eimeria* species. The time between infection and excretion of the first oocysts, termed the pre-patent period (PPP), is shortest for *E. praecox* at ~84 h (Long *et al.*, 1976). *E. acervulina* (89 h) and *E. mitis* (91 h) have similarly short PPPs, while *E. maxima* has the longest PPP of the malabsorptive species (120 h). The haemorrhagic species tend towards longer PPPs, including *E. brunetti* (120 h), *E. tenella* (132 h) and *E. necatrix* (138 h). The period of oocyst excretion, known as the patent period, can last up to six or more days, influenced by the immune status of the host. In the absence of re-infection, oocyst shedding stops at the conclusion of the patent period, resulting in a self-limiting infection that leaves the host substantially immune to subsequent challenge.

Surveys for the occurrence of all seven *Eimeria* species that infect chickens indicate they can be found wherever chickens are present, although the proportions of each species can vary enormously (Clark *et al.*, 2016). Additionally, three novel parasite genotypes originally described in Australia have been detected across much of the southern, but not the northern, hemisphere (Clark *et al.*, 2016). The reason(s) for such a dichotomous distribution is not clear. Preliminary sequence analyses targeting a small number of genomic and mitochondrial locations suggest that these cryptic genotypes do not conform to any of the known *Eimeria* species, but in the absence of type specimens their status (and the risk they pose) remains to be confirmed.

Descriptions of those *Eimeria* species that infect turkeys are rather less well defined. At least seven species have been recognized to infect turkeys with capacity to cause disease: *E. adenoeides*, *E. dispersa*, *E. gallopavonis*, *E. innocua*, *E. meleagridis*, *E. meleagrimitis* and *E. subrotunda*. However, type isolates for some species remain controversial or absent with historic pathognomonic descriptions possibly derived from mixed species infections. For example, it has been suggested that *E. adenoeides* may be a synonym for either *E. meleagridis* or *E. gallopavonis* (Vrba and Pakandl, 2014), while isolates for *E. subrotunda* remain scarce. Unusually, species such as *E. dispersa*, *E. meleagridis* and *E. innocua* have been found to be capable of successful replication in other gallinaceous birds such as grey partridge and bobwhite quail (Vrba and Pakandl, 2015).

16i.4 Sites of Development Within the Gut

Those *Eimeria* species that infect the chicken are known to be absolutely host specific. Further, each species targets and replicates within distinct sections of the intestine (Table 16i.1). *E. acervulina* and *E. praecox* can be found in the upper intestine, primarily the duodenum. *E. maxima* replicates throughout the middle portion of the intestine, including both the jejunum and ileum. Early infection and the asexual phases of *E. necatrix* replication also occur in the mid-intestine, although the parasite migrates to the caeca to complete the sexual phase of its lifecycle. *E. mitis* replicates within the lower intestine. *E. tenella* replicates exclusively within the caeca, while *E. brunetti* is found in the lower small intestine and the rectum, with some overflow into the caeca. The factors which control such precise specificity are not known, although it is clear that each parasite can be defined by a complex repertoire of proteins, many of which are secreted or located on the surface of the parasite and may contribute to each parasite's apparent preferences. The extreme site-specificity of each *Eimeria* species, combined with species-specific differences in pathogenicity, produce distinct pathognomonic signatures.

16i.5 Immunity

Natural *Eimeria* infection induces a robust immune response against subsequent homologous challenge. Infection with as little as five *E. maxima* oocysts can induce apparently complete immunity to subsequent low-level challenge by the same isolate (Blake *et al.*, 2005). In contrast, for species like *E. tenella*, several rounds of infection are required to induce a comparable level of immunity. However, the immunity induced by infection is absolutely parasite species-specific. Infection with one species will only induce immune protection against challenge by the same species. A chicken must have been infected by all seven species if it is to become immune to all seven species. For some species there is evidence for additional strain-specific antigenic diversity, with examples of escape from immunity reported for *E. acervulina*, *E. brunetti*, *E. maxima*, *E. mitis* and *E. tenella* (e.g. Smith *et al.*, 2002).

Immunity induced during primary *Eimeria* infection includes potent antibody and T-cell mediated responses, although immune protection is primarily mediated by the T cell component featuring a prominent role for interferon gamma (Shirley *et al.*, 2005). CD4+ T cells appear to be important to the response against many, but not all *Eimeria* species. The secondary immune response to re-infection is different, with a more limited role for interferon gamma. All stages of the eimerian lifecycle within the chicken appear to be immunogenic, with the early stages capable of inducing immunity that is protective against subsequent challenge.

16i.6 Diagnosis

Detection of *Eimeria* infection and determination of species identity can be achieved using microscopic, pathological or molecular biological methods. The presence of a patent *Eimeria* infection can be assessed most simply by microscopy, using faecal or litter samples, intestinal contents or scrapings. Direct microscopy of a smeared sample can permit non-quantitative detection. Oocysts can be enriched for increased sensitivity by flotation in solutions such as saturated saline or sucrose, and quantified using a modified McMaster protocol (e.g. https://www.rvc.ac.uk/review/Parasitology/Index/Index.htm). Identification of the infecting species is more challenging. Oocyst morphology can be used to differentiate those *Eimeria* species that infect chickens, using differences in length, width and length:width ratio as a guide (Table 16i.1). However, while examples such as *E. maxima* can readily be identified based upon their relatively large size, many of the other species present overlapping profiles and can be challenging, even to the expert. One approach has been to categorize oocysts into small (*E. acervulina* and *E. mitis*; termed AM), medium (*E. necatrix*, *E. tenella* and *E. praecox*; NTP) or large (*E. brunetti* and *E. maxima*; BM) oocyst types (Haug *et al.*, 2008). This approach works well, although the inability to distinguish highly pathogenic *E. necatrix* and *E. tenella* from low pathogenic *E. praecox* is problematic. A small number of experts routinely identify six or all seven species, although *E. necatrix* and *E. praecox* remain challenging. *Eimeria* infections commonly involve multiple species, exacerbating the problem.

In addition to oocyst morphology, the location of *Eimeria* replication within the gut can be a valuable diagnostic tool. As described above, each *Eimeria* species is predisposed to replicate in specific, albeit overlapping, sites within the intestine (Table 16i.1). Microscopic examination of intestinal smears to detect *Eimeria* lifecycle stages from different sections of the intestine can provide additional information relevant to identification. For example, *Eimeria* detected in the duodenum are likely to be *E. acervulina* or *E. praecox*, species which can be differentiated by oocyst morphology. Pre-patent as well as patent infections can be detected in this manner (i.e. before and after the production of oocysts). The more pathogenic *Eimeria* species cause distinctive pathognomonic lesions within the intestine. Details defining these lesions can be used to identify *Eimeria* species and have been developed into semi-quantitative lesion scoring strategies to assess the severity of infection. Several scoring systems exist, but the best established is that published by Johnson and Reid (Johnson and Reid, 1970). Characteristics such as the location of pathology, appearance of mucus and/or blood, and thickening of the intestinal wall are used to determine severity on a scale from 0 (apparently healthy) to +4 (severe disease and/or dead), as summarized in Table 16i.1. Routine lesion scoring is of greatest value during investigation of unexpected mortality or post-mortem of culled sentinel chickens.

Examination of the chicken's environment can provide some evidence of eimerian infection. Detection of blood or mucus in faeces can be indicative of infection by haemorrhagic or malabsorptive group *Eimeria* species, although diagnosis cannot be definitive given the multi-factorial nature of enteric dysbiosis.

The addition of molecular diagnostic tools to detect and speciate *Eimeria* has provided opportunities for routine screening in medium-throughput protocols. Polymerase chain reaction (PCR) assays specific for the *Eimeria* genus, or individual *Eimeria* species, have been available for more than 20 years, together with methods for field sampling and DNA extraction (Kumar *et al.*, 2014). The specificity and sensitivity of PCR encourage their use; however, uptake within the poultry production industry has been slow, likely a consequence of difficulties in DNA extraction from oocysts and the requirement for quality control. Currently, PCR-based diagnostics are offered by a small number of commercial and academic providers. More recent development of techniques such as quantitative PCR for the *Eimeria* genus and individual species offers considerable advantages over standard PCR, although use has largely been restricted to research.

16i.7 Control

Control of *Eimeria* commonly relies on a combination of good husbandry, chemoprophylaxis (or therapy) and/or vaccination. Understanding of the eimerian lifecycle, in particular the obligate requirement for sporulation of oocysts in the environment, has offered opportunities to disrupt faecal–oral transmission between chickens. Good litter quality, lower stocking densities and adequate ventilation combine to reduce environmental contamination with oocysts, and compromise sporulation of those oocysts that are present. However, husbandry alone is insufficient to control *Eimeria* in modern intensive and free-range production systems.

Chemoprophylaxis is routine for control of *Eimeria* in modern broiler production throughout much of the world, including most of Europe. Primarily administered through feed, effective application of chemoprophylaxis is designed to establish a balance between infection and immunity such that chickens can be produced in balance with *Eimeria*. However, no drugs are completely effective with resistance to all now widespread (Chapman, 1997), frequently resulting in imbalance and the occurrence of subclinical infection or clinical disease. Two types of anticoccidial drugs are used: chemicals and ionophores, the latter products of fermentation. At present, multiple different drugs are available for use, most of which are considered to exhibit different modes of action and mechanisms of resistance. The problem of resistance has been addressed through the use of combinations and regular shuttling between products, although monitoring of efficacy is required to inform optimal drug choice and avoid economic or welfare costs. Details of anticoccidial drugs licensed for use in the UK can be found in the NOAH Compendium (http://www.noahcompendium.co.uk/). Ionophores dominate the anticoccidial drug market in the UK and Europe since they limit, but do not completely prevent, eimerian replication. Allowing a low level of parasite replication permits induction of an immune response which can protect the recipient from pathogenic *Eimeria* challenge during the latter stages of production, especially during any drug withdrawal period. Importantly, while the ionophore anticoccidials can be considered to be antimicrobials, they are not currently regarded as antibiotics in the UK and rest of the EU. In direct contrast, ionophores are regulated as antibiotics in the USA, where the emergence of 'No antibiotics – ever' production systems has resulted in a dramatic reduction in routine drug use. Similarly, routine anticoccidial drug use is now precluded in countries such as Norway, where alternatives are required.

Vaccination is the leading alternative to chemoprophylaxis. Live parasite vaccines dominate the sector, including either virulent (wild-type, i.e. unmodified since isolation from the field) or attenuated *Eimeria*. Wild-type vaccines such as Coccivac-B and -D and Immucox for chickens, or Coccivac T for turkeys, include multiple *Eimeria* species. When administered to poultry, each vaccine initiates a natural infection, inducing a robust immune response that is protective against those species included in the formulation. Live vaccines are only protective against those species that are included in the formulation since immunity is species-specific (as described earlier). Controlled and even vaccine uptake is essential, since over-dosing can result in disease, while under-dosing leaves individuals unprotected when the live vaccine recycles. Wild-type vaccines are used widely, including in the USA where they are increasingly being employed in place of drugs (Chapman and Jeffers, 2014), but they are not currently used in the EU. Recognition of the relative risk posed by wild-type vaccines prompted development of a second generation of live attenuated anticoccidial vaccines. With few exceptions, attenuated vaccines include live *Eimeria* lines that have been selected for precocious development. Attenuation is achieved over ten or more parasite generations through recovery and serial passage of the first oocysts excreted at the beginning of the patent period, resulting in an abbreviated or 'precocious' pre-patent period. Parasites attenuated in this manner exhibit fewer and/or smaller rounds of schizogony, resulting in reduced reproductive capacity and pathogenicity without compromising immunogenicity (McDonald *et al.*, 1986). In the UK and EU, almost all breeding and laying chickens are vaccinated using live attenuated anticoccidial vaccines such as Paracox, Hipracox and HuveGuard, although broiler stock are only rarely vaccinated. At present, the cost (compared to drugs) and availability preclude routine vaccination of European broilers. Production of live *Eimeria* vaccines can only be achieved by infection of chickens and recovery of progeny oocysts under controlled conditions, creating an inherent limit on production capacity, especially for vaccines based on less productive attenuated parasite lines. Alternatives include a vaccine consisting of purified gametocyte antigens, named Coxabic, although uptake has been very limited.

16i.8 Prospects for the Future

As public concerns and legislation regarding the use of drugs in production of food for human consumption intensify, it is likely that routine anticoccidial chemoprophylaxis will come under increasing scrutiny. Demand for novel methods to control *Eimeria* is now greater than ever, with a range of probiotics, prebiotics and feed supplements appearing on the market. Some poultry breeding companies are responding, exploring the capacity to select chickens with enhanced resistance to *Eimeria* infection or disease. Efforts to develop new recombinant or vectored vaccines that are cost-effective, scalable and easy to deliver continue, although to date no product has reached the market. In their absence, it is likely than more live parasite vaccines will be produced and marketed. It is important to note that production of cheap poultry products has been facilitated by effective control of *Eimeria*, and that in the absence of control poultry products are likely to become more expensive.

16i.9 References

Blake, D.P., Hesketh, P., Archer, A., Carroll, F., Shirley, M.W., *et al.* (2005) The influence of immunizing dose size and schedule on immunity to subsequent challenge with antigenically distinct strains of *Eimeria maxima*. *Avian Pathology* 34, 489–94.

Chapman, H. (1997) Biochemical, genetic and applied aspects of drug resistance in *Eimeria* parasites of the fowl. *Avian Pathology* 26, 221–244.

Chapman, H.D. and Jeffers, T.K. (2014) Vaccination of chickens against coccidiosis ameliorates drug resistance in commercial poultry production. *International Journal of Parasitology Drugs and Drug Resistance* 4, 214–7.

Clark, E.L., Macdonald, S.E., Thenmozhi, V., Kundu, K., Garg, R., *et al.* (2016) Cryptic *Eimeria* genotypes are common across the southern but not northern hemisphere. *International Journal of Parasitology* 46, 537–544.

Haug, A., Gjevre, A.G., Thebo, P., Mattsson, J.G. and Kaldhusdal, M. (2008) Coccidial infections in commercial broilers: epidemiological aspects and comparison of *Eimeria* species identification by morphometric and polymerase chain reaction techniques. *Avian Pathology* 37, 161–70.

Johnson, J. and Reid, W.M. (1970) Anticoccidial drugs: lesion scoring techniques in battery and floor-pen experiments with chickens. *Experimental Parasitology* 28, 30–6.

Kumar, S., Garg, R., Moftah, A., Clark, E.L., Macdonald, S.E., *et al.* (2014) An optimised protocol for molecular identification of *Eimeria* from chickens. *Veterinary Parasitology* 199, 24–31.

Long, P., Joyner, L., Millard, B. and Norton, C. (1976) A guide to laboratory techniques used in the study and diagnosis of avian coccidiosis. *Folia Veterinaria Latina* 6, 201–217.

McDonald, V., Rose, M.E. and Jeffers, T.K. (1986) Eimeria tenella: immunogenicity of the first generation of schizogony. *Parasitology* 93, 1–7.

Shirley, M.W., Smith, A.L. and Tomley, F.M. (2005) The biology of avian *Eimeria* with an emphasis on their control by vaccination. *Advances in Parasitology* 60, 285–330.

Smith, A.L., Hesketh, P., Archer, A. and Shirley, M.W. (2002) Antigenic diversity in *Eimeria maxima* and the influence of host genetics and immunization schedule on cross-protective immunity. *Infection and Immunity* 70, 2472–9.

Vrba, V. and Pakandl, M. (2014) Coccidia of turkey: from isolation, characterisation and comparison to molecular phylogeny and molecular diagnostics. *International Journal of Parasitology* 44, 985–1000.

Vrba, V. and Pakandl, M. (2015) Host specificity of turkey and chicken *Eimeria*: controlled cross-transmission studies and a phylogenetic view. *Veterinary Parasitology* 208, 118–24.

Vrba, V., Poplstein, M. and Pakandl, M. (2011) The discovery of the two types of small subunit ribosomal RNA gene in *Eimeria mitis* contests the existence of *E. mivati* as an independent species. *Veterinary Parasitology* 29, 47–53.

Williams, R.B., Marshall, R.N., Pages, M., Dardi, M. and del Cacho, E. (2009) Pathogenesis of *Eimeria praecox* in chickens: virulence of field strains compared with laboratory strains of *E. praecox* and *Eimeria acervulina*. *Avian Pathology* 38, 359–66.

16ii Histomoniasis (Blackhead Disease)

Hafez Mohamed Hafez[1]* and Rüdiger Hauck[2]

[1]Institute of Poultry Diseases, Free University Berlin, Berlin, Germany;
[2]Department of Pathobiology and Department of Poultry Science, Auburn University, Auburn, Alabama, USA

16ii.1 Introduction

The disease caused by the protozoan parasite *Histomonas meleagridis* has been given many names. Colloquially, it is known by the misnomer 'blackhead disease'. Other names based on the typical pathological lesions are 'infectious enterohepatitis' or 'infectious typhlohepatatitis'. Nowadays, the systematic names histomoniasis or histomonosis are used more often.

Infection with *H. meleagridis* can cause a severe disease in gallinaceous birds. It is thought that *H. meleagridis* was introduced with pheasants from China to the US, where the disease was first described in the late 19th century in turkeys. For the following decades, histomoniasis was the most important cause of mortality in turkey flocks until several highly effective drugs against the disease were discovered. In addition, improved management practices, like separation of turkey and chicken flocks, as well as the trend toward confinement rearing, substantially decreased the incidence of histomoniasis. Starting in 1995, the EU and the USA successively banned all drugs used to prevent or treat histomoniasis due to food safety concerns. In consequence, histomoniasis is increasingly responsible for considerable economic problems to the poultry industry, causing sometimes disastrous economic losses in chickens, turkeys and game birds.

16ii.2 Causative Agent

H. meleagridis is a flagellated amoeboid protozoan parasite. It is a member of the *Parabasalia*, order *Tritrichomonadida*, family *Dientamoebidae*. Within the genus *Histomonas* are two species, *H. meleagridis* and *H. wenrichi* (Cepicka *et al.*, 2010). *H. wenrichi* is described as non-pathogenic and possessing four flagella. The latter feature can be used for differentiation from *H. meleagridis*. Two morphologies of the *H. meleagridis* are known, namely the lumen-dwelling form with one flagellum, which the parasite takes in the caecal lumen, and the tissue form during invasion of tissues, which lacks the flagellum and has an irregular, amoeboid shape (Hess and McDougald, 2013).

16ii.3 Host Spectrum

Many, probably all, gallinaceous birds are susceptible to natural and/or experimental infections with *H. meleagridis*, but susceptibility of gallinaceous hosts varies considerably (Hauck and Hafez, 2013). Chickens and pheasants seem to be relatively resistant, while turkeys and peafowl are extremely susceptible.

In addition, the host spectrum of *H. meleagridis* extends beyond the order *Galliformes*. Swan geese (*Cygnopsis cygnoides*), mallards (*Anas platyrhynchos*) and Muscovy ducks (*Cairina moschata*) can harbour *H. meleagridis* for some time after experimental infection (Lund *et al.*, 1974; Callait-Cardinal *et al.*, 2006). *Histomonas*-like parasites were repeatedly described in ostriches (*Struthio cameius*) and other ratites (McDougald, 2005); however, the diagnoses relied only on the morphology of the observed parasites. Pigeons were refractory to experimental infection (Hauck and Hafez, 2012).

*Corresponding author: hafez.mohamed@fu-berlin.de

© CAB International 2021.
DOI: 10.1079/9781789245042.0016

16ii.4 Mode of Infection and Transmission

Infected birds shed *H. meleagridis* in their faeces. However, the unprotected parasite cannot survive for a prolonged time in the environment; its survival time in contaminated water or faecal matter is only 9 h, depending on the temperature (Lotfi *et al.*, 2012). This limits its transmission between houses or farms by indirect transmission. Oral infection with unprotected trophozoites does not appear to be an important route of infection, but birds can be infected by sitting down on liquid faeces containing the parasite and taking up small amounts through the cloaca. This mechanism called 'cloacal drinking' seems to be responsible for the quick spread of the parasite through turkey flocks (Hu *et al.*, 2004).

In contrast, *H. meleagridis* can survive for months in eggs of the caecal worm *Heterakis gallinarum*, in which it is shed from hosts infected with both parasites. Earthworms in turn can ingest eggs of *H. gallinarum*, acting as paratenic hosts for *H. meleagridis*. Thus protected, *H. meleagridis* can remain infective in the environment for years. Within the worm eggs, *H. meleagridis* will also survive passage through the proventriculus and gizzard, and infects hosts after oral uptake of the eggs or earthworms.

Cyst-like stages of *H. meleagridis* have been described. They develop outside the host under suboptimal conditions, and the described amorphous outer layer might give better protection than the single cell membrane of the trophozoites. Such stages might be involved in transmission or persistence on a farm (Munsch *et al.*, 2009).

16ii.5 Clinical Signs

Clinical signs are not specific but include loss of appetite, increased thirst, droopiness and drowsiness (Fig. 16ii.1).

Sulfur-coloured droppings are seen in the later stages of disease when liver function is severely damaged, and bile pigments are excreted through the kidneys. The darkening of the facial regions, which led to the name blackhead disease, is rarely observed. After intra-cloacal infection, clinical signs, including mortality, can start as early as 6 days after infection, and mortality typically peaks between 13 and 15 days after infection. After oral infection with *H. gallinarum* eggs containing *H. meleagridis*, clinical signs will be visible 9 days after infection and first mortality occurs after 12 days, peaking between 19 and 21 days after the infection (Hauck and Hafez, 2013).

In chickens, morbidity may be high, but mortality seldom exceeds 15%. In addition, infection of laying hens can cause a drop in egg production of

Fig. 16ii.1. Turkey showing severe depression and coloured droppings. (Author's own image.)

more than 50% (Liebhart *et al.*, 2013). Differences in severity of the disease between chicken lines are minor (Zahoor *et al.*, 2011; Lotfi *et al.*, 2014). Mortality in turkeys is often close to 100% after experimental infection. In field outbreaks, very high mortality in turkey flocks is not uncommon; usually flocks are euthanized once mortality hits a certain threshold and it becomes clear that there would be very few, if any, surviving birds. On the other hand, mortality does not exceed 10% in most outbreaks in turkeys, and cases in which only one single bird died due to the infection have been described (Callait-Cardinal *et al.*, 2007; Aka *et al.*, 2011). As with chickens, differences between various turkey lines including wild turkeys, are very minor (Reynaud *et al.*, 2005; Lotfi and Hafez, 2009).

There are indications that *H. meleagridis* strains may vary in their virulence and pathogenesis, but the underlying mechanisms are poorly understood (Grafl *et al.*, 2015).

16ii.6 Gross and Histopathological Lesions

In most cases, lesions are confined to the caeca and liver. Livers are swollen and display circular depressed areas of necrosis. Lesions are yellowish to yellow-green and extend deeply into the underlying liver tissue (Fig. 16ii.2).

The caeca are ballooned with thickened walls, severe diphtheroid inflammation and ulcerations. The lumen is filled by caseous cores that may be blood tinged (Fig. 16ii.3).

Further gross lesions can be found in other organs such kidney, bursa of Fabricius and spleen.

Histopathology shows the severe inflammation of the caecal wall with hyperaemia, sometimes, small haemorrhages and large numbers of heterophils and mononuclear cells. Fibrin and cellular debris form the core in the caecal lumen (Fig. 16ii.4a).

The parasites reside in the cleft between core and caecal wall as well as throughout the entire caecal wall from the mucosa almost to the serosa. In the liver, parasites can be detected clustering together in lacunae at the periphery of the lesions (Fig. 16ii.4b). Haematoxylin and eosin (H&E) stain *H. meleagridis* cells eosinophilic. Periodic acid-Schiff stain (PAS) and Grocott's stain will stain them intensely red or brown-to-black, respectively, facilitating detection and identification.

16ii.7 Diagnosis (see also Chapter 22, this volume)

Field diagnosis can be carried out on the basis of clinical signs and the highly suggestive gross lesions. However, *Tetratrichomonas gallinarum* (trichomonad, see Chapter 16iii, this volume) can cause identical lesions in the caeca and liver and can be difficult to differentiate from *H. meleagridis* by histopathology (Liebhart *et al.*, 2014; Hauck *et al.*, 2019). Lesions in the caeca may be confused with coccidiosis or salmonellosis, while similar liver lesions may also be due to infections with neoplastic viruses like Marek's disease virus (see Chapter 15xiii, this volume), lymphoproliferative disease of turkeys virus or reticuloendotheliosis virus (see Chapter 15xii, this volume) (Hess and McDougald, 2013).

16ii.7.1 Direct demonstration

Diagnosis can be based on the microscopical demonstration of moving flagellate parasites in caecal smears from freshly killed or recently dead birds. The lumen dwelling form of the parasite is most easily observed with phase-contrast microscopy of

Fig. 16ii.2. Enlarged liver with numerous multifocal pale yellow foci. (Author's own image.)

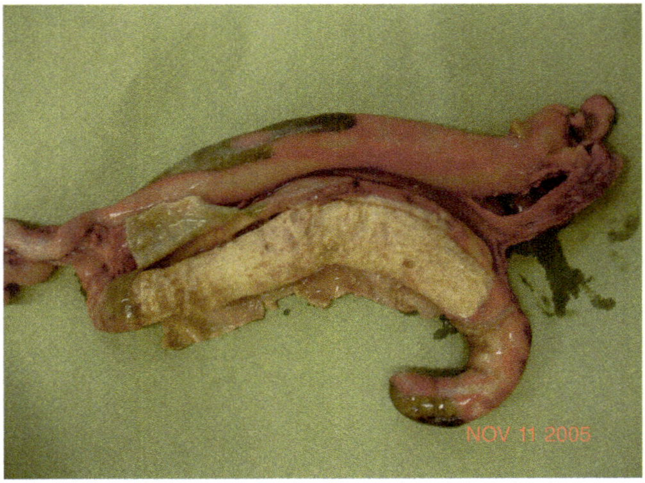

Fig. 16ii.3. Caeca with caseous cores and petechial haemorrhages. (Author's own image.)

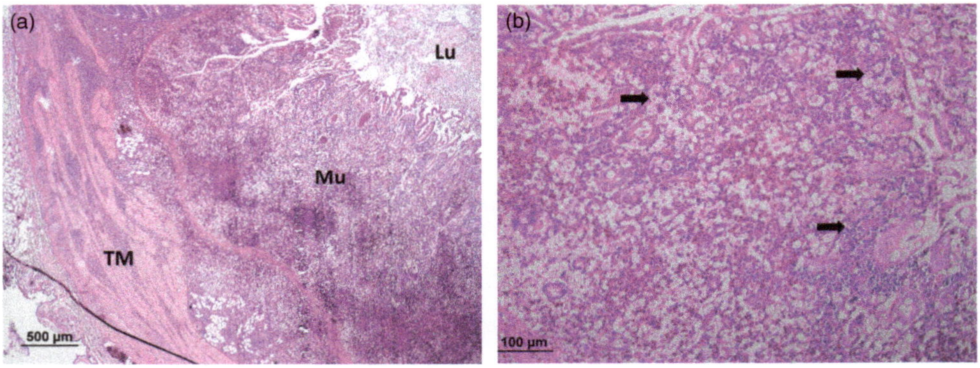

Fig. 16ii.4. (a) Histopathology – fibrin and cellular debris form the core in the caecal lumen (Lu). Mucosa (Mu) and Tunica muscularis (TM) are thickened and infiltrated by inflammatory cells. (b) Histopathology – liver showing extensive areas of necrosis. Arrows point out *Histomonas* trophozoites in lacunae. (Author's own images.)

fresh specimens. However, evaluation of caecal smears can be very difficult, due to the presence of other pathogenic and non-pathogenic flagellates like *H. wenrichi* or *T. gallinarum* (Hess and McDougald, 2013).

16ii.7.2 Isolation

For isolation, only material from birds recently killed or dead should be used. Caecal content and/or pieces of liver are inserted into a pre-warmed medium. Rapid shipment of samples to the laboratory, preferably with a heat source, is paramount for successful isolation (Gerhold *et al.*, 2010). Several culture media for *H. meleagridis* have been described. Probably the most commonly used medium is Dwyer's medium (Dwyer, 1970) consisting of cell culture medium M199 with 10% horse serum, 5% chicken embryo extract and 10 mg/culture rice flour. Other protozoans, bacteria and fungi will grow easily in these media; in fact, the presence of living bacteria is necessary for culture of *H. meleagridis*.

16ii.7.3 Polymerase Chain Reaction (PCR)

Several PCR assays for the detection of *H. meleagridis* have been developed. The most common target is the small subunit (ssu) ribosomal rRNA gene (Bleyen *et al.*, 2007). The ssu rRNA gene is a multi-copy gene with about 250 copies; this increases the sensitivity considerably over PCR assays targeting other genes.

Molecular typing based on sequencing various genes has been described (Hauck *et al.*, 2010; Bilic *et al.*, 2014). At the most, four types were distinguished, and it is unclear if the detected types relate to differences in virulence or host spectrum.

16ii.7.4 Detection of antibodies using ELISA

A sandwich ELISA using hyperimmune serum against *H. meleagridis* purified by absorption with bacterial and rice antigens, a competitive ELISA using monoclonal antibodies against *H. meleagridis* and an ELISA using recombinant *H. meleagridis* antigen have been described (Windisch and Hess, 2009; van der Heijden *et al.*, 2010; Lotfi *et al.*, 2014). The ELISAs have been used for basic research and in epidemiological studies; their use in routine diagnostics is limited.

16ii.8 Control

The likelihood of introduction into a farm in caecal worm eggs can be greatly decreased by routine procedural biosecurity like change of footwear and disinfecting the tyres of incoming vehicles. The role of wild birds as a reservoir for *H. gallinarum* and *H. meleagridis* is unknown, but preventing contact between poultry and wild birds should be essential to all biosecurity programmes.

The disease often stays confined to one house, and separation by wire mesh is usually sufficient to prevent spread between compartments in the same house, but outbreaks can affect several houses on one farm.

When an outbreak is ongoing, topdressing the litter to cover infectious faeces and prevent cloacal drinking has been tried, but often this measure is not successful. After depopulation, complete removal of litter and careful cleaning and disinfection with substances effective against worm eggs are important.

Due to the persistence in caecal worm eggs and earthworms, houses with dirt floors are more at risk than houses with concrete floors. Covering the floor with plastic liner before adding litter prevented reoccurrence of the disease for only a few subsequent flocks.

16ii.9 Treatment

Drugs and feed additives previously used against *H. meleagridis* have been banned in the EU and the USA.

Since 2015, paromomycin sulfate has been registered for use in some EU member states to prevent histomoniasis in turkeys. However, its efficacy is too low for therapy of ongoing infections, so success of the application of paromomycin is highly dependent on early diagnosis and start of metaphylactic treatment (Bleyen *et al.*, 2009; Hafez *et al.*, 2010).

A variety of anticoccidials, antibiotics and plant extracts were tested over the years, usually without success.

16ii.10 Vaccination

Commercial vaccines against histomoniasis are currently not available. Experimental vaccination using *H. meleagridis* attenuated *in vitro* by serial passaging effectively protects chickens and turkeys from histomoniasis (Liebhart *et al.*, 2013, 2017). Inactivated vaccines did not induce protective immunity.

16ii.11 References

Aka, J., Hauck, R., Blankenstein, P., Balczulat S. and Hafez, H.M. (2011) Wiederauftreten von Histomonose auf einer Putenelterntierfarm. *Berliner Münchner Tierärztliche Wochenschrift* 124, 2–7.

Bilic, I., Jaskulska, B., Souillard, R., Liebhart, D. and Hess, M. (2014) Multi-locus typing of *Histomonas meleagridis* isolates demonstrates the existence of two different genotypes. *PloS One* 9, e92438. DOI: 10.1371/journal.pone.0092438.

Bleyen, N., De Gussem, K., De Gussem, J. and Goddeeris, B.M. (2007) Specific detection of *Histomonas meleagridis* in turkeys by a PCR assay with an internal amplification control. *Veterinary Parasitology* 143, 206–213.

Bleyen, N., De Gussem, K., Pham, A.D., Ons, E., Van Gerven, N., *et al.* (2009) Non-curative, but prophylactic effects of paromomycin in Histomonas meleagridis-infected turkeys and its effect on performance in non-infected turkeys. *Veterinary Parasitology* 165, 248–255.

Callait-Cardinal, M.P., Chauve, C., Reynaud, M.C., Alogninouwa, T. and Zenner, L. (2006) Infectivity of *Histomonas meleagridis* in ducks. *Avian Pathology* 35, 109–116.

Callait-Cardinal, M.P., Leroux, S., Venereau, E., Chauve, C.M., Le Pottier, G., *et al.* (2007) Incidence of histomonosis in turkeys in France since the bans of dimetridazole and nifursol. *Veterinary Record* 161, 581–585.

Cepicka, I., Hampl, V. and Kulda, J. (2010) Critical taxonomic revision of parabasalids with description of one new genus and three new species. *Protist* 161, 400–433. DOI: 10.1016/j.protis.2009.11.005

Dwyer, D.M. (1970) An improved method for cultivating *Histomonas meleagridis*. *Journal of Parasitology* 56, 191–192.

Gerhold, R.W., Lollis, L.A., Beckstead, R.B. and McDougald, L.R. (2010) Establishment of culture conditions for survival of Histomonas meleagridis in transit. *Avian Diseases* 54, 948–950.

Grafl, B., Weise, H., Le Bris, J., Liebhart, D., Bilic, I., *et al.* (2015) Aberrant clinical appearance and pathomorphology noticed during an outbreak of histomonosis indicates a different pathogenesis of Histomonas meleagridis genotype 2. *Avian Diseases* 59, 452–458.

Hafez, H.M., Hauck, R., Gad, W., De Gussem, K. and Lotfi, A. (2010) Pilot study on the efficacy of paromomycin as a histomonostatic feed additive in turkey poults experimentally infected with Histomonas meleagridis. *Archive Animal Nutrition* 64, 77–84.

Hauck, R. and Hafez, H.M. (2012) Pigeons are not susceptible to intracloacal infection with *Histomonas meleagridis*. *Pakistani Veterinary Journal* 32, 589–592.

Hauck, R. and Hafez, H.M. (2013) Experimental infections with the protozoan parasite *Histomonas meleagridis*: a review. *Parasitology Research* 112, 19–34.

Hauck, R., Balczulat, S. and Hafez, H.M. (2010) Detection of DNA of *Histomonas meleagridis* and *Tetratrichomonas gallinarum* in German poultry flocks between 2004 and 2008. *Avian Diseases* 54, 1021–1025.

Hauck, R., Stoute, S., Savaris, T. and Shivaprasad, H.L. (2019) Typhlohepatitis and amyloidosis associated with high mortality in Chukar partridges (*Alectoris chukar*). *Avian Diseases* 63, 446–451.

Hess, M. and McDougald, L.R. (2013) Histomoniasis (blackhead) and other protozoan diseases of the intestinal tract. In: Swayne, D.E., Glisson, J.R., McDougald, L.R., Nolan, L.K., Suarez, D.L., *et al.* (eds) *Diseases of Poultry. Wiley-Blackwell, Ames, Iowa*, pp. 1172–1182.

Hu, J., Fuller, L. and McDougald, L.R. (2004) Infection of turkeys with *Histomonas meleagridis* by the cloacal drop method. *Avian Diseases* 48, 746–750.

Liebhart, D., Sulejmanovic, T., Grafl, B., Tichy, A. and Hess, M. (2013) Vaccination against histomonosis prevents a drop in egg production in layers following challenge. *Avian Pathology* 42, 79–84.

Liebhart, D., Neale, S., Garcia-Rueda, C., Wood, A.M., Bilic, I., *et al.* (2014) A single strain of *Tetratrichomonas gallinarum* causes fatal typhlohepatitis in red-legged partridges (*Alectoris rufa*) to be distinguished from histomonosis. *Avian Pathology* 43, 473–480.

Liebhart, D., Ganas, P., Sulejmanovic, T. and Hess, M. (2017) Histomonosis in poultry: previous and current strategies for prevention and therapy. *Avian Pathology* 46, 1–18.

Lotfi, A. and Hafez, H.M. (2009) Susceptibility of different turkey lines to *Histomonas meleagridis* after experimental infection. *Parasitology Research* 105, 113–116.

Lotfi, A., Abdelwhab, E.M. and Hafez, H.M. (2012) Persistence of *Histomonas meleagridis* in or on materials used in poultry houses. *Avian Diseases* 56, 224–226.

Lotfi, A., Hauck, R., Olias, P. and Hafez, H.M. (2014) Pathogenesis of histomonosis in experimentally infected specific-pathogen-free (SPF) layer-type chickens and SPF meat-type chickens. *Avian Diseases* 58, 427–432.

Lund, E.E., Chute, A.M., Vernon, M.E. (1974) Experimental infections with *Histomonas meleagridis* and *Heterakis gallinarum* in ducks and geese. *Journal of Parasitology* 60, 683–686.

McDougald, L.R. (2005) Blackhead disease (histomoniasis) in poultry: a critical review. *Avian Diseases* 49, 462–476.

Munsch, M., Lotfi, A., Hafez, H.M., Al-Quraishy, S. and Mehlhorn, H. (2009) Light and transmission electron microscopic studies on trophozoites and cyst-like stages of *Histomonas meleagridis* from cultures. *Parasitology Research* 104, 683–9.

Reynaud, M.C., Zenner, L., Alogninouwa, T. and Chauve, C.M. (2005) Comparison of the susceptibility to *Histomonas meleagridis* infection of two strains of turkey (*Meleagris galloplavo*): preliminary study. *Revue Médecine Vétérinaire* 156, 620–623.

van der Heijden, H.M., Stegeman, A. and Landman, W.J.M. (2010) Development of a blocking-ELISA for the detection of antibodies against *Histomonas meleagridis* in chickens and turkeys. *Veterinary Parasitology* 171, 216–222.

Windisch, M. and Hess, M. (2009) Establishing an indirect sandwich enzyme-linked-immunosorbent-assay (ELISA) for the detection of antibodies against *Histomonas meleagridis* from experimentally infected specific pathogen-free chickens and turkeys. *Veterinary Parasitology* 161, 25–30.

Zahoor, M.A., Liebhart, D. and Hess, M. (2011) Progression of histomonosis in commercial chickens following experimental infection with an in vitro propagated clonal culture of *Histomonas meleagridis*. *Avian Diseases* 55, 29–34.

16iii Other Important Parasites

FIONA TOMLEY*

Department of Pathobiology and Population Sciences, The Royal Veterinary College, University of London, North Mymms, Hatfield, Hertfordshire, UK

16iii.1 Introduction

Parasitic diseases have significant impacts on the welfare and production of poultry in most parts of the world. Many classes of parasites infect poultry, and they target a variety of host organs and tissues, mostly of the digestive, respiratory and sensory systems, causing many different pathologies.

First line control should combine good management, hygiene and biosecurity practices to minimize entry of parasites and vectors, confine birds away from potential sources of infection and provide good control of ventilation, moisture and temperature. Regular inspection is important to recognize early signs of infestation and keeping parasites at low levels is usually the goal. Interventions to prevent or treat specific diseases are best applied early to avoid escalation and serious problems. Such interventions rely mainly on the use of anti-parasitic drugs, dusts, lubricants and barrier products.

Parasites can be divided into those that feed on the host but develop and live in the environment (ectoparasitic), and those that live at least partly inside the animal host (endoparasitic). Some poultry parasites have direct life cycles where horizontal bird to bird spread is the major route of transmission; others are heteroxenous and can be acquired from alternative hosts such as arthropods, worms, wild birds and even small mammals. Ectoparasites of poultry include mites, lice, ticks, flies and fleas; endoparasites include classes of worms and protozoa, all of which are described in detail by Taylor *et al.* (2015). Brief summaries of what are currently considered to be the most important species are given in Table 16iii.1.

16iii.2 Ectoparasites

In terms of prevalence and severity, mites and lice are globally the most important ectoparasites of poultry, although larger arachnids (ticks) and insects (flies, beetles, ants) are an increasing problem for chicken production in hot climates, especially if manure is not well managed. Ectoparasites can get into all rearing systems but have greatest impact on longer-lived birds especially intensively farmed layer hens where heavy infestations develop during the lifetime of the flock. Control of all types of ectoparasites in poultry follows broadly similar lines and it is important to avoid overcrowding, minimize stress, thoroughly disinfect premises between flocks, maintain good hygiene and biosecurity, and provide control of ventilation, lighting and temperature. Signs of infestation may include restlessness, itching, aggression, matted or dirty feathers, feather pulling, skin lesions, weight loss, reduced egg production, anaemia and reluctance to enter nesting boxes or hen houses. There is a limited choice of insecticidal drugs available to treat ectoparasitic diseases (see Table 16iii.2) and populations of the most serious pests have acquired genetic resistance to commonly used classes of drugs including synthetic pyrethroids, organophosphates and carbamates (e.g. Mullens *et al.*, 2017; Thomas *et al.*, 2018; Pugliese *et al.*, 2019). There are also a variety of non-chemical treatment options that aim to reduce parasite numbers through desiccation, suffocation, trapping or predation. It is important to consider whether to treat only the birds, or if there is a need to also treat contaminated environments.

*ftomley@rvc.ac.uk

© CAB International 2021. *Poultry Health: A Guide for Professionals* (P. Barrow *et al.*)
DOI: 10.1079/9781789245042.0016

Table 16iii.1. Most important parasites of poultry.

Ectoparasites	Host system: site	Main features
Red mite (*Dermanyssus gallinae*)	Sensory: whole body	Nocturnal mites blood feed for up to ~2 h. Adults, grey <1 mm, red/brown when fed. Live in cracks/crevices so can go undetected but progression from egg to adult can occur in 7–10 days and infestations build up fast. Causes severe itching, dermatitis, anaemia, egg-drop, sometimes death. Can transmit other agents. Can survive for months without feeding so control methods target environment as well as the bird. Can bite poultry workers.
Northern fowl mite (*Ornithonyssus sylvarum*)	Sensory: vent	Blood feeder that lives on the bird and rapidly reaches high numbers. Adults, grey ~1 mm, red/brown when fed. Clumps of debris visible at base of vent feathers. Can survive off the bird for ~3 weeks. Causes thickened skin, irritation, anaemia, egg-drop, sometimes death. Can transmit other agents. Control requires treating birds and leaving houses empty for 1 month between flocks.
Scaly leg mite (*Cnemidocopes mutans*)	Sensory: legs, feet (comb, wattles)	Lives in the ground or on the floor of damp houses. Adults <0.5 mm, white/grey. Burrows under the scales of legs or feet causing severe irritation, crusting, lameness. Legs become thickened and lumpy with raised scales and may smell musty. Older birds and feathered leg breeds are most susceptible. Control requires repeat treatments and house disinfection.
Depluming mite (*Cnemidocoptes gallinae*)	Sensory: head and neck	Close relative of the scaly leg mite. Feeds on skin and feather debris and burrows deep into skin at base of the feather. Causes irritation and pain leading to feather pulling, weight loss and egg-drop. Difficult to treat.
Common chicken louse (*Menopon gallinae*)	Sensory: vent and under wings	Common pest that lives constantly on the bird, feeding on skin and feather debris. Flat, yellow, fast moving ~2 mm long. Causes irritation but generally not bleeding and is a problem only in large numbers. Topical insecticides kill adults but not eggs so regular application needed.
Nematodes (roundworms) Gapeworm (*Syngamus trachea*)	Respiratory: trachea, lungs	Transmitted directly and by earthworms; larvae and adults migrate from gut via lungs to trachea causing pneumonia, blockage, gasping and death. Adult males (5 mm) and females (20 mm) are permanently conjoined forming Y-shaped red-coloured 'forked worms' Particularly problematic in pheasants and young turkeys.
Threadworms (*Capillaria species*)	Digestive: oesophagus, crop, intestine	Fine, filamentous worms up to 1.5 cm. Mild or moderate infections show a variety of non-specific symptoms; heavy infections can cause diphtheritic lesions, diarrhoea, anaemia, weight loss, egg drop and death.
Gizzard worms (various genera)	Digestive: gizzard	Transmitted directly and by a variety of arthropods; 2–4cm long, cause ulceration and necrosis, loss of condition and slow growth. Particularly problematic in geese.
Strongyl worm (*Trichostronglyus tenuis*)	Digestive: caeca	Small, hair like worms; can cause severe, even fatal, enteritis. Particularly problematic in game birds.
Large roundworms (*Ascaris species*)	Digestive: duodenum, ileum	Very common in outdoor-reared birds; can reach ~12 cm in length and heavy infestations cause malabsorption, wasting, impaction, diarrhoea, anaemia, blockage and death.
Caecal worms (*Heterakis gallinae*)	Digestive: caeca	White, 1.5 cm long with a pointed tail, typically cause very little pathology in chickens but can carry *Histomonas meleagridis* that causes blackhead which is a major gut/liver pathogen in turkeys and occasionally in chickens.

Continued

Table 16iii.1. Continued.

Ectoparasites	Host system: site	Main features
Trematodes (flatworms) Flukes (various genera)	Digestive: intestine	Transmitted by snails; heavy infections can cause haemorrhage and diarrhoea. Mainly a problem in ducks, geese or in foraging birds.
Cestodes/Tapeworms (various genera)	Digestive: intestine	Transmitted by earthworms and arthropods. Highly varied in size and pathology depending on the genus, these can occasionally cause problems in outdoor reared birds.
Protozoa Trichomonads (*Trichomonas gallinae*)	Digestive: oesophagus, crop, proventriculus	Transmitted from wild birds, especially columbiforms and can be problem in foraging flocks. Heavy infections cause severe necrotic lesions in the oesophagus leading to weight loss and high morbidity.
Coccidia (*Eimeria* species)	Digestive: various sites of intestine	Highly prevalent in all systems where birds have contact with faeces. Severe enteritis with malabsorption, diarrhoea, weight loss, haemorrhage and death if not controlled. Current prophylaxis with anticoccidials (chemicals and ionophore) and live vaccines.
Hexamita (*Spironucleus meleagridis*)	Digestive: Intestine	Transmitted through faeces, contaminated feed and water, a problem in turkeys and game birds. Adults act as carriers so it is a problem in mixed-age flocks. Causes severe watery diarrhoea in young birds with high mortality.
Histomonads (*Histomonas meleagridis*)	Digestive: Caecum, Liver	Transmitted by *Heterakis* worms that infect the caecum. Complex morphology, life cycle and pathology. Particularly pathogenic in turkeys, especially poults where it causes blackhead with severe liver and caecal damage and high mortalities.

16iii.2.1 Poultry red mite: an emergent and serious problem in layer hens

Dermanyssus gallinae, the poultry red mite, is the most damaging ectoparasite of poultry worldwide. It is a small (<1 mm) blood-feeding ectoparasite (phylum *Acarina*, order *Mesostigmata*) with a short (7–10 day) life cycle that can rapidly become a major problem on commercial layer farms. Adults and several larval stages are nocturnal feeders that spend most of their lives away from the chicken in multi-stage colonies where they breed and develop. In heavy infestations colonies are visible due to their association with mite debris (faeces, dust, larval sheddings) and are found, for example, on the undersides of perches, nest boxes and cage fittings, and in cracks and crevices around the hen house (Fig. 16iii.1).

D. gallinae has been recognized as a significant pest for decades, but its importance has increased in the past ~20 years in parallel with expansion of commercial poultry production. This rise in prevalence is well charted in Europe, where >80% of laying flocks are infested (George *et al.*, 2015) at a recently estimated cost of >€230 million (van Emous, 2017). All types of units can be affected but it is widely believed that changes in layer husbandry from 2009 onwards in preparation for the 2012 EU ban of traditional 'battery' cages has contributed significantly to increased prevalence (Sigognault Flochlay *et al.*, 2017). Specifically, the shift to more complex and enriched housing environments provides abundant refugia within which mites can live and multiply away from hens and treatments. Europe is not alone in seeing increased prevalence: *D. gallinae* is a global problem with infestation rates of, for example, 75% in S. Korea (Oh *et al.*, 2020), 88% in China (Wang *et al.*, 2010) and 40% in Egypt (Eladi *et al.*, 2018). Other factors favouring mite survival and reproduction in modern layer systems include increased sizes of flocks, climate (heat and humidity), genetic resistance to commonly used drugs, legislative removals of acaricides and lack of new control methods including vaccines (Sigognault Flochlay *et al.*, 2017; Tomley and Sparagano, 2018).

Table 16iii.2. Some antiparasitic treatments to control ectoparasites and worms in poultry[a].

Class of drug	Mode of action	Examples of use in poultry[b]
Benzimidazoles	Metabolic – binds and disrupts microtubular structures	Flubendazole – roundworms, flatworms
Carbamates	Respiratory/neurotoxic – reversibly inhibits acetylcholinesterase	Carbaryl – mites, lice, ticks
Formamidines	Neurotoxic – octopamine receptor antagonist	Amitraz – mites, lice, ticks
Hydroxybenzonitriles	Mitochondrial – uncouples oxidative phosphorylation	Nitroxinil - gapeworm
Imidazothazoles	Neurotoxic – mimetic of acetylcholinesterase	Levamisole – roundworms
Isoflavones	Mitochondrial – blocks oxidative phosphorylation	Rotenone – lice
Isoquinolines	Not precisely known; affects calcium ion permeability	Praziquantal – flatworms
Isoxazolines	Neurotoxic – GABA receptor antagonist, binds chloride ion channels	Fluralaner – mites
Macrocyclic lactones	Neurotoxic – GABA agonist, binds chloride ion channels	Ivermectin – mites, lice, round worms
Neonicotinoids	Neurotoxic – nicotinic acetylcholine receptor agonist	Imidacloprid – lice, insects
Organo-phosphates	Neurotoxic – irreversibly inhibits acetylcholinesterase	Phoxim – mites, lice, insects
Phenylpyrazoles	Neurotoxic – GABA inhibitor, blocks chloride ion channels	Fipronil – mites, lice, insects
Piperazine	Neurotoxic – GABA agonist, reversibly inhibits acetylcholinesterase	Piperazine – large roundworms
Pyrethroids	Neurotoxic – blocks closure of sodium channels	Permethrin/lambda-cyhalothrin – mites, lice, ticks
Salicylanilides	Mitochondrial – uncouples oxidative phosphorylation	Rafoxanide/Closantel – flatworms
Silica	Desiccant – accelerates loss of body water	Diatomaceous earth – mites, lice
Spinosyns	Neurotoxic – not completely known, acts on GABA and nicotinic receptors	Spinosad – mites, lice, flies
Sulfur dust	Unknown	Various formulations – mites, lice

[a]In the UK and many other countries, few drugs are directly authorized for treatment of parasitic diseases in poultry but can be prescribed 'off label' according to 'The cascade: prescribing unauthorized medicine' for which there is regularly updated guidance. https://www.gov.uk/guidance/the-cascade-prescribing-unauthorised-medicines.
[b]An excellent guide to the active ingredients in antiparasitic veterinary drugs including access to technical datasheets and guidance on withdrawal periods can be found at Parasitipedia.net (https://parasitipedia.net/index.php?option=com_content&view=article&id=2448&Itemid=2715).

D. gallinae is of public health concern because these mites do bite humans with effects that range from mild irritation and itching to gamasoidosis, a serious and underdiagnosed dermatological condition invariably caused by a specific L1 lineage of *D. gallinae* associated predominantly with pigeons (Pezzi *et al.*, 2017). There is also a growing list of viral and bacterial pathogens, including several that are zoonotic, for which *D. gallinae* is implicated as a reservoir and transmission vector (Sigognault Flochlay *et al.* 2017). Whilst much evidence to date comprises PCR detection of pathogen nucleic acid in mites, with rather few biological demonstrations of disease transmission between hosts, there are significant and valid concerns about the potential of *D. gallinae* to transmit viral or bacterial pathogens between hens and to humans (George *et al.*, 2015).

Control of red mite in layer hens is challenging and requires continued monitoring to spot early infestations. A variety of acaricidal chemicals are available including synthetic pyrethroids, carbamates, organophosphates and formamidines, all broad-spectrum products used to control a range of arthropod pests; these are not all licenced for use but may be used off-label (see Table 16iii.2). Other effective chemicals, such as the phenylprazole Fipronil, cannot be used to treat laying hens because it can accumulate to toxic levels in eggs; its illegal use in laying birds in 2017 prompted a food safety alert in several EU countries (Ruzza *et al.*, 2020). Populations of *D. gallinae* with resistance to commonly used acaricides are widely reported, with resistance due to over-expression of mite P450 monooxygenase *cyp-3* detoxification genes (Wang *et al.*, 2020) and mutations in voltage-gated sodium

Fig. 16iii.1. *Left:* Aggregation of *Dermanyssus gallinae* infesting the hen house of a backyard flock. Multiple stages of *D. gallinae* are observed in the colony. Eggs are clumped together in the centre and have a pearly white colouration (marker 1). As larvae do not feed before moulting, they retain this white colouration (marker 2). Protonymphs and deutonymphs are noticeably smaller than adult *D. gallinae* and when recently engorged are bright red (marker 3). A colour spectrum ranging from bright to dark red is observed in adult *D. gallinae* (markers 4–6). This colouration is dependent on the status of blood digestion and egg development (females only). *Right:* Three adult *D. gallinae* captured by direct light microscopy at 100× magnification. (Photos courtesy of Paul Barrow (left) and Eleanor Karp-Tatham (right).)

channels (Katsavou *et al.*, 2020). All older products, as well as the more recently introduced insecticide Spinosad, are applied as sprays, mists and dusts. This is not ideal as it requires large amounts of chemicals to achieve acaricidal concentrations that can kill large refuged colonies of mites and poses risks to workers of exposure to pesticides and residue-containing dusts.

There are two systemic products; both are mite neurotoxins that target gated chloride channels. The first is the isoxaxoline-substituted benzamide derivative fluralaner launched in 2017 as a novel licenced acaricide for control of *D. gallinae*, which is effective in drinking water (Thomas *et al.*, 2017). The second is the macrocyclic lactone avermectins, which are active against roundworms and many ectoparasites. Ivermectin has been used off-label in poultry for several years mainly to treat heavy infestations with large roundworms or scaly leg mites; however recent evidence shows that several different avermectins administered orally to chicks offer effective control also of *D. gallinae* (Xu *et al.*, 2019).

In addition to chemicals there is a wide range of other complementary or alternative treatments available that offer some support for management of *D. gallinae* infestations (reviewed by Pritchard *et al.*, 2015; Sigognault Flochlay *et al.*, 2017). For example, diatomaceous earth can be effective within small poultry houses. Moreover, much research is currently focused on new or improved strategies for mite control which includes development of vaccines; evaluation of natural oils, volatiles and predators; improved formulations for delivering antiparasitic dusts; and better methods for removing mites from the environment between flocks.

16iii.3 Endoparasitic Worms: Increasing Burdens in Outdoor Rearing

Many parasitic roundworms and flatworms infect poultry and when birds have access to contaminated litter, faeces, earth or pasture, it is likely they will ingest eggs or larvae. In most cases, if birds acquire small numbers of parasites these are reasonably well tolerated and natural immunity develops with few clinical disease symptoms. For poultry housed indoors in cages, on slats, or on solid floors subjected to thorough disinfection and cleaning between flocks, it is rare for worms to cause significant problems. Nevertheless, they do have impacts on performance; laying hens experimentally infected with low burdens of *Ascaris galli* and *Heterakis gallinarum* showed significantly reduced feed conversion, lay rate, egg weight and egg quality traits with a high performing layer Lohmann Brown Plus genotype more severely affected than the Lowmann Dual genotype (Stehr *et al.*, 2019).

Clinical disease due to worms is more likely in outdoor reared poultry especially in warm and moist conditions that favour survival of worm eggs. In such situations, parasite burdens can be high and cause severe pathologies, as listed in Table 16iii.1. Several recent studies show high incidences of parasites in such conditions with chickens commonly infested with both cestodes (mainly *Raillietina* and *Hymenolepsis* species) and nematodes (mainly *Ascaris* and *Heterakis* species) for example in Kenya (Wamboi *et al.*, 2020), Vietnam (Van *et al.*, 2020), Brazil (da Silva *et al.*, 2018), India (Jayentakumar Singh and Mohilal, 2017) and Bangladesh (Ferdushy *et al.*, 2016). In temperate zones worm burdens in free range and organic layers are significantly higher than in caged layers or broilers (Permin *et al.*, 1999) and several recent studies show high levels of infection particularly with the large roundworm *Ascaris galli* (e.g. Sharma *et al.*, 2019). A UK study of commercial free-range layers showed at least one gut or respiratory nematode in every flock tested, with no significant differences between organic and non-organic units. In this study there was no correlation of faecal egg counts with productivity, hen mortality or any other welfare measures, suggesting that worm burdens were at a low level (Sherwin *et al.*, 2013). In contrast analysis of 55 organic flocks in eight European countries indicated levels of parasites likely to cause clinical disease (Thapa *et al.*, 2015) and a longitudinal study in Danish organic layer farms showed statistically significantly increased summer mortality in hens with high levels of infestation (Hinrichsen *et al.*, 2016).

For birds with access to outdoors, regular deworming with chemical anthelminthic (see Table 16iii.2) is recommended especially for young birds at highest risk (see Chapter 7, this volume). Repeat doses are usually needed as most products kill adult worms but are not effective against eggs; also, in heavily contaminated environments reinfection is common. There are currently no vaccines available to protect poultry against parasitic worms. So far there is little evidence for significant resistance of poultry worms to major classes of drugs although increasing usage is likely to select resistant genotypes, as is the case in ruminants (Kenyon *et al.*, 2017).

16iii.4 Protozoa

Compared to ectoparasites and worms, there are few species of protozoa that infect chickens; however the economic and health impacts of these agents are the most important in modern poultry production (Table 16iii.1). Chief amongst these are species of *Eimeria* that cause coccidiosis (see Chapter 16i, this volume). Most other protozoa are of relatively minor significance in poultry, with the exception of *Histomonas meleagridis* which causes serious damage to the caeca and liver of turkeys with resulting high morbidity and mortality (see Chapter 16ii, this volume).

16iii.5 Conclusion

Poultry, especially those raised intensively, are exposed to many disease-causing microbes including various classes of parasites. Only a small number of parasitic diseases currently pose serious threats, but the overall global burden of disease from parasites is high and will increase as intensification of indoor and outdoor of broiler and layer chickens continues. Lack of effective vaccines, increasing resistance to antiparasitic and insecticidal drugs and lack of research into these neglected diseases are all issues of concern for future sustainable production of poultry meat and eggs.

16iii.6 References

da Silva, G.S., Romera, D.M., da Silva, C.G., Soares, V.E. and Meireles, M.V. (2018) Helminth infections in chickens (*Gallus Domesticus*) raised in different production systems in Brazil. *Veterinary Parasitology: Regional Studies and Reports* 12, 55–60. DOI: 10.1016/j.vprsr.2018.02.003

Eladi, A.H., Hamed, H.R. and El-Shafei, R.A. (2018) Prevalence of mites and their impact on laying hen (Gallus gallus domesticus) farm facilities in Egypt, with an analysis of deltamethrin residues in eggs and tissues. *Avian Pathology* 47, 161–171.

Ferdushy, T., Hasan, M.T and Golam Kadir, A.K. (2016) Cross sectional epidemiological investigation on the prevalence of gastrointestinal helminths in free range chickens in Narsingdi district, Bangladesh. *Journal of Parasitic Diseases* 40, 818–22.

George, D.R., Finn, R.D., Graham, K.M., Mul, M., Maurer, V., *et al.* (2015) Should the poultry red mite Dermanyssus gallinae be of wider concern for veterinary medical science. *Parasites and Vectors* 8, 178. DOI: 10.1186/s13071-015-0768-7.

Hinrichsen, L.K., Labouriau, R., Engberg, R.M., Knierim, U. and Sørensen, J.T. (2016) Helminth infection is associated with hen mortality in Danish organic egg production. *Veterinary Record* 179, 196. DOI: 10.1136/vr.103614.

Jayentakumar Singh, L. and Mohilal, N. (2017) Gastrointestinal parasitic infection in diverse species of domestic birds of Manipur, India. *Journal of Parasitic Diseases* 41, 142–146.

Katsavou, E., Vlogiannitis, S., Karp-Tatham, E., Blake, D.P., Ilias, A., *et al.* (2020) Identification and geographical distribution of pyrethroid resistance mutations in the poultry red mite *Dermanyssus gallinae*. *Pest Management Science* 76(1), 125–133.

Kenyon, F., Hutchings, F., Morgan-Davies, C., van Dijk, J. and Bartley, D.J. (2017) Worm control in livestock: bringing science to the field. *Trends in Parasitology* 33, 669–677.

Mullens, B.A., Murillo, A.C., Zoller, H., Heckeroth, A.R., Jirjis, F., *et al.* (2017) Comparative in vitro evaluation of contact activity of Fluralaner, Spinosad, Phoxim, Propoxur, Permethrin and Deltamethrin against the northern fowl mite, *Ornithonyssus Sylviarum*. *Parasites and Vectors* 20, 358. DOI: 10.1186/s13071-017-2289-z.

Oh, S.I., Do, Y.J., Kim, E., Yi, S.W. and Yoo, J.G. (2020) Prevalence of poultry red mite (*Dermanyssus Gallinae*) in Korean layer farms and the presence of avian pathogens in the mite. *Experimental and Applied Acarology* 81, 223–238.

Permin, A., Bisgaard, M., Frandsen, F., Pearman, M., Kold, J., *et al.* (1999) Prevalence of gastrointestinal helminths in different poultry production systems. *British Poultry Science* 40, 439–43.

Pezzi, M., Leis, M., Chicca, M. and Roy, L. (2017) Gamasoidosis caused by the special lineage L1 of *Dermanyssus gallinae* (Acarina: Dermanyssidae): a case of heavy infestation in a public place in Italy. *Parasitology International* 66, 666–670.

Pritchard, J., Kuster, T., Sparagano, O. and Tomley, F. (2015) Understanding the biology and control of the poultry red mite *Dermanyssus Gallinae*: a review. *Avian Pathology* 44, 143–53.

Pugliese, N., Circella, E., Cocciolo, G., Giangaspero, A., Horvatek, T.D., *et al.* (2019) Efficacy of λ-cyhalothrin, amitraz, and phoxim against the poultry red mite *Dermanyssus gallinae* De Geer, 1778 (Mesostigmata: Dermanyssidae): an eight-year survey. *Avian Pathology* 48(sup1), S35–S43.

Ruzza, M., Tiozzo, B., Rizzoli, V., Giaretta, M, D'Este, L., *et al.* (2020) Food risks on the web: analysis of the 2017 Fipronil alert in the Italian online information sources. *Risk Analysis* 40, 2071–2092.

Sharma, N., Hunt, P.W., Hine, B.C. and Ruhnke, I. (2019) The impacts of *Ascaridia galli* on performance, health, and immune responses of laying hens: new insights into an old problem. *Poultry Science* 98, 6517–6526.

Sherwin, C.M., Nasr, M.A.F., Gale, E., Petek, M., Tafford, K., *et al.* (2013) Prevalence of nematode infection and faecal egg counts in free-range laying hens: relations to housing and husbandry. *British Poultry Science* 54, 12–23.

Sigognault Flochlay, A., Thomas, E. and Sparagano, O. (2017) Poultry red mite (*Dermanyssus Gallinae*) infestation: a broad impact parasitological disease that still remains a significant challenge for the egg-laying industry in Europe. *Parasites and Vectors* 10, 357. DOI: 10.1186/s13071-017-2292-4.

Stehr, M., Grashorn, M., Dannenberger, D., Tuchscherer, A., Gauly, M., et al. (2019) Resistance and tolerance to mixed nematode infections in relation to performance level in laying hens. *Veterinary Parasitology* 275, 108925. DOI: 10.1016/j.vetpar.2019.108925.

Taylor, M.A., Coop, R.L. and Wall, R.L. (2015) *Veterinary Parasitology*, 4th edn. Wiley, Chichester, UK.

Thapa, S., Hinrichsen, L.K., Brenninkmeyer, C., Gunnarsson, S., Heerkens, J.L., *et al.* (2015) Prevalence and magnitude of helminth infections in organic laying hens (*Gallus gallus domesticus*) across Europe. *Veterinary Parasitology* 214, 118–24.

Thomas, E., Chiquet, M., Sander, B., Zschiesche, E. and Flochlay, A.S. (2017) Field efficacy and safety of fluralaner solution for administration in drinking water for the treatment of poultry red mite (Dermanyssus gallinae) infestations in commercial flocks in Europe. *Parasites and Vectors* 10, 457. DOI: 10.1186/s13071-017-2390-3.

Thomas, E., Zoller, H., Liebishch, G., Alves, L.F.A., Vettorato, L., *et al.* (2018) In vitro activity of fluralaner and commonly used acaricides against *Dermanyssus gallinae* isolates from Europe and Brazil. *Parasites and Vectors* 11, 361. DOI: 10.1186/s13071-018-2956-8.

Tomley, F.M. and Sparagano, O. (2018) Spotlight on avian pathology: red mite, a serious emergent problem in layer hens. *Avian Pathology* 47, 533–535.

Van, N.T.B., Cuong, N.V., Yen, N.T.P., Nhi, N.T.H., Kiet, B.T., *et al.* (2020) Characterisation of gastrointestinal helminths and their impact in commercial small-scale chicken flocks in the Mekong delta of Vietnam. *Tropical Animal Health and Production* 52, 53–62.

Van Emous, R. (2017) Verwachtte schade bloedluis 21 miljoen euro. *Pluimveeweb.nl*. Available at: https://www.pluimveeweb.nl/artikel/163578-verwachtte-schade-bloedluis-21-miljoen-euro/ (accessed 26 January 2021).

Wamboi, P., Waruiru, R.M., Mbuthia, P.G., Nguhiu, J.M. and Bebora, L.C. (2020) Haemato-biochemical changes and prevalence of parasitic infections of indigenous chicken sold in markets of Kiambu county, Kenya. *International Journal of Veterinary Science and Medicine* 13, 18–25.

Wang, C., Xu, X., Huang, Y., Yu, H., Li, H., *et al.* (2020) Transcription profiling and characterization of *Dermanyssus gallinae* cytochrome P450 genes involved in beta-cypermethrin resistance. *Veterinary Parasitology* 283, 109155. DOI: 10.1016/j.vetpar.2020.109155.

Wang, F.F., Wang, M., Xu, F.R., Liang, D.M. and Pan, B.L. (2010) Survey of prevalence and control of ectoparasites in caged poultry in China. *Veterinary Record* 167, 934–937.

Xu, X,, Wang, C., Zhang, S., Huang, Y., Pan, T., *et al.* (2019) Acaricidal efficacy of orally administered macrocyclic lactones against poultry red mites (*Dermanyssus gallinae*) on chicks and their impacts on mite reproduction and blood-meal digestion. *Parasites and Vectors* 12, 345. DOI: 10.1186/s13071-019-3599-0.

17 The Chicken Microbiota and How to Modulate It

Fien De Meyer[1], Annatachja De Grande[2], Richard Ducatelle[1] and Filip Van Immerseel[1*]

[1]*Livestock Gut Health Team (LiGHT), Department of Pathology, Bacteriology and Avian Diseases, Faculty of Veterinary Medicine, Ghent University, Merelbeke, Belgium;* [2]*Flanders Research Institute for Agriculture, Fisheries and Food, Animal Sciences Unit – Poultry and Rabbit Husbandry, Melle, Belgium*

17.1 Introduction

Microbiota is defined as the microbial community, including commensal, symbiotic and (opportunistic) pathogenic microorganisms which usually colonize an area within or on a host organism (Clavijo and Florez, 2018). The microbiome describes the genetic information from all microorganisms found in a particular environment. Unraveling the development of the chicken microbiome and how it is affected by different factors, including dietary factors, is of great value as the microbiota composition and functionality is linked with animal performance and health, and can be modulated using dietary interventions. Until recently, only a minority of the bacterial diversity could be recovered by cultivation. Due to the implementation of 16S rRNA-based next generation sequencing (NGS) and various -omics technologies, research on the chicken microbiome has exploded, whereby we increasingly start to understand biological functions of the microbiota and thus the importance of the microbiota in overall health, development of the gut and its immune system, and maintenance of intestinal homeostasis (Oakley *et al.*, 2014, Shang *et al.*, 2018).

The chicken hosts a range of microbial communities located in different places in the body. The main sites carrying the most abundant microbiota are the skin, respiratory and reproductive tract and most importantly the gastrointestinal tract (GIT). Since this latter is the area with highest bacterial abundance and diversity, the GIT is generally used to describe the protective role of microbiota to infectious and non-infectious diseases.

17.2 Microbiota in Different Organs

17.2.1 The skin microbiota

The skin is the organ which is most exposed directly to environmental bacteria. Therefore, the housing environment and management factors (ventilation, hygiene) play an important role in the microbial composition found on the skin. The unique physical and chemical properties of the skin select for a unique composition of the microbiota on various locations. Therefore, the skin is not characterized by one microbial composition, but determined by the number of gland cells, hairs, feathers, production of secretions and temperature, which differs along the skin. The skin, in particular the epidermis, forms an important barrier against invading pathogens. Animal skin is likely to come in contact with fecal material and can be colonized with intestinal bacteria. This plays an important role in the development of foot pad dermatitis and breast blisters in broilers, and on some occasions in wound infections. There is relatively little information available on the avian skin microbiota and there are no data on the presence of a protective microbiota unlike the situation in humans.

*filip.vanimmerseel@ugent.be

© CAB International 2021. *Poultry Health: A Guide for Professionals* (P. Barrow *et al.*)

DOI: 10.1079/9781789245042.0017

17.2.2 The respiratory tract microbiota

Several studies show that the respiratory tract is not sterile. The lower respiratory tract is considered to be relatively sterile, although the upper respiratory tract (URT,) especially the nose and nasopharynx, shows a rich microbial composition, (Johnson *et al.*, 2018). These bacteria originate from the environment of the animal (e.g. stable, dust, other animals) and the gastrointestinal tract. The broiler trachea microbiota is related to the microbiota in the nasal cavity, but also to the microbiota in the gut (ileum and cecum) and the environment (litter) (Ngunjiri *et al.*, 2019). The URT is dominated mainly by Gram-positive bacteria with *Lactobacillus* being the most prevalent genus. Other highly prevalent genera are *Staphylococcus*, *Escherichia*/*Shigella*, *Corynebacterium*, *Ruminoccus* and *Blautia*.

It is assumed that in analogy with the microbiota of the GIT, the respiratory tract microbiota play an important role in the resistance against colonization of pathogens and play a role in the maturation of the immune system. Imbalance of normal microbial composition may lead to overgrowth of pathogens that may already have been present in the upper respiratory tract. There are few references in the literature describing the microbial composition of the respiratory tract in poultry and the interaction between commensals, facultative pathogens and pathogens. It has been shown that birds infected with avian influenza viruses are often carriers of *Mycoplasma gallisepticum*, *M. synoviae* (for both see Chapter 14viii, this volume), *Ornithobacterium rhinotracheale* (see Chapter 14vi, this volume), *Escherichia coli* (see Chapter 14ii, this volume) or *Staphylococcus* (see Chapter 14ix, this volume). The interaction of pathogens and facultative pathogens at the same infection site could be either synergistic or antagonistic. Viral respiratory infections can also augment secondary bacterial infections, even by commensal bacteria, as a result of mechanical damage to the ciliated and goblet cells.

17.2.3 The reproductive tract microbiota

The microbiota composition of the urinary and reproductive tract depends on the specific organs. In general, the upper urinary (kidney, ureter, bladder) and reproductive (ovaries) tract are sterile. Infection of the upper urinary tract are mostly ascending, while infections of the upper reproductive tract are believed to mainly occur via the blood stream (Lee *et al.*, 2019). The microbial composition and relative abundance of bacterial genera is thought to be stable throughout the entire reproductive tract of the chicken and shows a relatively high abundance of *Lactobacillus* species. Other less abundant genera were *Pseudomonas*, *Megamonas* and *Bacteroides*. *Lactobacillus* species confer a protective role against pathogen colonization, by ensuring a low pH and production of antibacterial substances. The most well-known pathogen that can colonize the reproductive tract and contaminate eggs is *Salmonella* (see Chapter 14iv, this volume). This bacterium can colonize the upper oviduct and be incorporated into forming eggs, and survive in egg white, and thus cause zoonotic transmission to humans. The avian serovars *S.* Gallinarum and *S.* Pullorum also produce persistent infection of the ovary. *M. gallisepticum* also can cause salpingitis and other pathologies in the reproductive tract. *E. coli* and *Gallibacterium anatis* (see Chapter 14vi, this volume) have been reported as two major pathogens which can cause reproductive tract disorders and are both able to penetrate the eggshell.

17.3 The Intestinal Microbiota

17.3.1 Development

The GIT is composed of different segments that should be considered separate ecosystems, despite the fact they are strongly interconnected (Clavijo and Florez, 2018). The chicken GIT includes the upper segment (crop, proventriculus and gizzard), small intestine (duodenum, jejunum and ileum), caeca, colon and cloaca. The GIT of newly hatched birds is colonized rapidly by environmental bacteria, not derived from the mother animal, given the relative sterile hatching conditions, but derived from feed, water and the environment (Shang *et al.*, 2018). The microbial composition in the crop, duodenum, ileum and caeca are very similar during the first 4 days of life but are differentiated by about day 7. The crop of birds over 2 weeks of age harbours 10^8–10^9 cfu/g bacteria and is usually dominated by *Lactobacillus* spp. whereas lactobacilli and enterococci are detected dominant, although still in low numbers, in the gizzard. Of the small intestine, the duodenum has the lowest bacterial density due to the short transit time and dilution by pancreatic enzymes and bile acids, but the composition is similar to the crop microbiota. Among the small intestinal segments, the ileum (10^9–10^{11} cfu/g bacteria) is most studied, where *Lactobacillus* species dominate, followed by *Streptococcus, Enterococcus* and various *Clostridiaceae* (Oakley *et al.*, 2014). In comparison with any other part of the chicken gut, the caeca have been extensively studied as it is a fermentation chamber and contains high bacterial diversity and complexity. The caeca have an important role in carbohydrate fermentation and recycling nitrogen using uric acid. Compared to the other intestinal segments, the caecal bacterial composition is very different (Stanley *et al.*, 2016) and harbours up to 10^{12}–10^{13} cells/g. In the first few days of life, there is a low diversity dominated by Gram-negative *Enterobacteriaceae* and a small number of *Enterococcus* species. After some days, the number of species increases significantly followed by an increase in anaerobic *Ruminococcaceae* during the first week of life, followed by other *Firmicutes*. From 2 weeks of age onwards, *Firmicutes* outnumber *Enterobacteriaceae*. In general, *Firmicutes*, *Bacteroidetes* and *Proteobacteria* are the most dominant phyla in the adult chicken caeca (Oakley *et al.*, 2014). *Actinobacteria* and *Verrumicrobia* are less abundant. It is clear from numerous studies that age is one of the most differentiating factors when it comes to microbial development with a shift from facultative anaerobic Gram-negative bacteria (*Proteobacteria)* in the beginning to mainly Gram-positive strictly anaerobic *Firmicutes* at later ages.

17.3.2 Functions

A brief description of the function of the microbiota

The GIT has a role in homeostasis, providing the host the ability to withstand psychological, environmental and physical stresses. More than 900 bacterial species inhabit the GIT and are involved in digestion of feed and defence against pathogens by forming a protective barrier by a variety of suggested mechanisms, including attachment to the epithelial cells and preventing the opportunity for the colonization of enteric pathogens, production of antimicrobial factors and nutrient competition. Another major feature of the gut microbiota is that commensal bacteria stimulate the early development of the immune system, including both the innate and adaptive immune response, and regulate mucosal immunity (tolerance vs inflammation), all depending on the microbial composition (Clavijo and Florez, 2018; Shang *et al.*, 2018) (see also Chapter 2 this volume).

Microbial metabolites

The mouth contains glands that secrete saliva which contains enzymes such as amylase to start the digestion process. In the crop, breakdown of starch with the formation of lactate and lactic acid production is initiated by several *Lactobacillus* species (Borda-Molina *et al.*, 2018). Lactobacilli also dominate the proventriculus, gizzard, duodenum and ileum together with *Streptococcus, Enterococcus* and various *Clostridiaceae* in the latter two segments. The small intestine is the main site for nutrient absorption through epithelial cells (Clavijo and Florez, 2018) where amino acids and peptides, and also monosaccharides, are taken up by the host epithelium. Protein can on some occasions also reach the distal intestinal tract where they can be degraded by proteolytic bacteria. Amino acid degradation can occur through deamination with the production of short chain and branched chain fatty acids (isobutyrate, isovalerate, 2-methylbutyrate) and ammonia (NH_3). A second route of bacterial amino acid conversion is through decarboxylation, by which a variety of amines and polyamines are produced whereby sulfur-containing amino acids (cysteine, methionine) can cause H_2S formation. It is a common belief that excessive protein fermentation is harmful through the production of toxic molecules (e.g. NH_3, H_2S, phenolic derivatives) although strikingly, no information is available for many of the molecules produced. Protein fermentation is mainly associated with lactobacilli, *Clostridia* and genera such as *Escherichia, Proteus, Klebsiella, Desulfovibrio* and others (mostly *Proteobacteria*).

The caecum is the most diverse gut section with a great abundance of the *Clostridiaceae*, *Bacteroidaceae*, *Lactobacillaceae*, *Lachnospiraceae* and *Ruminococcaceae* families, the two latter containing a variety of butyrate producing bacteria (Borda-Molina *et al.*, 2018, Broom and Kogut, 2018). The caeca are also characterized by the longest retention time making it a good reservoir for breakdown of soluble fibres such as inulin and xylans, insoluble fibres such as cellulose and oligosaccharides (OS) (e.g. fructo-, arabinoxylan- and xylo-OS). This results in production of OS of variable chain length. These oligosaccharides can then be used by other bacterial groups to form short chain fatty acids (acetic, propionic and butyric acid), lactic acid and gases (CO_2, H_2). Butyric acid is anti-inflammatory, promotes proliferation of epithelial cells in the gut and strengthens the epithelial barrier by affecting tight junctions and increasing cell proliferation.

Intestinal health and microbial composition

Despite the fact that intestinal health has been the focus of many studies, the term is not yet clearly defined. Kogut and Arsenault (2016) define gut health as the absence/prevention/avoidance of disease so that the animal is able to perform its physiological functions in order to withstand exo- and endogenous stressors. Whereas Ducatelle *et al.* (2018) define intestinal health as a combination of macroscopic, morphological and microbiological factors and state that a 'good gut health' could be defined as the absence of macroscopic intestinal lesions and a gut characterized by long slender villi, short crypts, an adequate number of inflammatory cells in the propria mucosae, with an intestinal microbiome with a high microbial and functional diversity. Both definitions are valid and connected with each other.

In the gut of chickens, the most important disease is coccidiosis, caused by the *Eimeria* parasite (see Chapter 16i, this volume). Necrotic enteritis (see Chapter 14v, this volume) is the most well-known intestinal disease of bacterial origin, and has many predisposing triggers, including coccidiosis, fast growth and high-energy diets, mucosal damage caused by mycotoxins and many others. The most important digestive problems with performance losses are however not associated with specific pathogens, but merely a result of an imbalance in the feed–host–microbiota relationship (Johnson *et al.*, 2018). The term 'dysbiosis' is generally used in the poultry industry and is expressed as a reduced intestinal barrier function, poor nutrient digestibility (see also Chapter 12, this volume) leading to increased risk of bacterial translocation and inflammatory responses (Shang *et al.*, 2018).

Rather well-described shifts in microbial composition have been reported in the gut of animals with necrotic enteritis and after mycotoxin exposure. Studies that try to correlate microbial composition with animal performance, however, have been rather inconclusive. Butyrate-producing bacteria are often found to be depleted in inflammation and disease models, while high levels of *Proteobacteria*, including the *Enterobacteriaceae*, are often found in inflammatory conditions. Trends towards depletion in butyrate producing bacteria have been described in animals with coccidiosis and other predisposing triggers for necrotic enteritis.

While luminal bacteria can be important for breakdown of substrates in the gut, clearly mucosa-associated bacteria are important because of the close proximity of the epithelium with which they can interact. Examples are the segmented filamentous bacteria (*Candidatus Arthromitus*) that seem to be crucial in protecting against pathogens because of stimulation of innate immune mechanisms in the host and butyrate producing anaerobes, such as *Butyricicoccus pullicaecorum*. The latter were shown to protect against necrotic enteritis and increased performance in a feed-driven inflammation model in broilers.

17.4 Strategies for Improving Health and Performance (see also Chapter 12, this volume)

In the last decade there has been an expansion in the research on the development of feed additives as alternatives for antimicrobial growth promoters (AGP) and on tools to prevent disease and thus reduce the use of therapeutic antibiotics. Many of them try to steer the microbial composition to control pathogens, reduce excess inflammation, strengthen epithelial integrity and improve animal performance. Different kinds of additives, including probiotics, prebiotics, acidifiers and phytobiotics amongst others, are considered to regulate and adjust the microbial composition to improve health and performance of the host.

Probiotics have been defined as live microorganisms that, when administered to animals, confer a health benefit on the host. Among all probiotics utilized in poultry production, *Bacilli* are the most commonly used because of their stability (spores) as a feed-additive, combined with a variety of potential functions that they can exert. Lactobacilli and mixes of strains are also available commercially. It is not always clear what the mode of action is, and what the indications for using probiotics actually are, but reports on effects on disease and performance are widespread in scientific literature.

Prebiotics are defined as ingredients (substrates) that stimulate increased beneficial microbial activity in the digestive system in order to improve the health of the host. Prebiotics are non-digestible poly- and oligosaccharides, such as inulin, fructo-oligosaccharides (FOS), xylo-oligosaccharides

(XOS) and galacto-oligosaccharides (GOS). Some of these have been shown to increase the population of *Bifidobacterium* and *Lactobacillus* and reduce *E. coli* and *C. perfringens* populations in the GIT (Shang *et al.*, 2018). An advantage of prebiotics is that they have a low risk of undesirable side effects in the host and the production process and administration can be easy, although this depends on the type of product (Clavijo and Florez, 2018).

Organic acids and their salts have been used in poultry diets to inhibit growth of intestinal bacteria (or kill bacteria in the drinking water and the crop in case of drinking water additives) through acidification. Short chain fatty acids, medium chain fatty acids and other organic acids exhibit antimicrobial activity of which the effect depends on the concentration of the acid and the bacterial species to which the acid is exposed. Organic acids are weak acids that are known to penetrate the bacteria cell wall and dissociate inside the cell and thus disturb intracellular pH and ion balance. Furthermore, organic acids can modulate the gastrointestinal microbial population and reduce the level of pathogenic bacteria such as *Salmonella*, the latter by a specific effect on virulence gene expression.

Phytobiotics are described as primary or secondary components of plants that contain bioactive compounds that exert a positive effect on the growth and health of animals. Primary components include base nutrients such as fat, protein and carbohydrates, whereas secondary components are described as essential oils, phenolic compounds and colourants (Clavijo and Florez, 2018). The term phytobiotics comprises of a wide range of substances, and based on biological origin, formulation, chemical description and purity they can be divided in four groups: (i) herbs (products from flowering or non-woody plants), (ii) botanicals (entire or processed parts of plants), (iii) essential oils (hydro-distilled extracts) and (iv) oleoresins (extracts based on non-aqueous solvents). Several growth and health promoting properties have been attributed to phytobiotic use in poultry production by improving intestinal health, improving nutrient digestibility and reducing inflammation. The exact mechanisms on how phytobiotics work differ between the compounds and are not elucidated for many, but some mechanisms have been suggested including disruption of the cellular membrane of pathogens, modification of the surface of cells affecting the hydrophobicity and therefore their virulence capacity, stimulating the immune system (activation of lymphocytes, macrophages and NK cells) and promoting the growth of beneficial bacteria such as lactobacilli and bifidobacteria (Diaz-Sanchez *et al.*, 2015).

From all the additives described above, multiple beneficial effects have been proposed, including stimulation of the development of beneficial microbiota, reduction and prevention of colonization by enteric pathogens, modulation of immunological activity, stimulation of epithelial health, increased digestive capacity and help in the maturation of intestinal tissue. Given the huge variety of feed additives that exist, the above list is far from complete.

17.5 References

Borda-Molina, D., Seifert, J. and Camarinha-Silva, A. (2018) Current perspectives of the chicken gastrointestinal tract and its microbiome. *Computational and Structural Biotechnology Journal* 16, 131–139.

Broom, L.J. and Kogut, M.H. (2018) The role of the gut microbiome in shaping the immune system of chickens. *Veterinary Immunology and Immunopathology* 204, 44–51.

Clavijo, V. and Florez, M.J.V. (2018) The gastrointestinal microbiome and its association with the control of pathogens in broiler chicken production: a review. *Poultry Science* 97(3), 1006–1021.

Diaz-Sanchez, S., D'Souza, D., Biswas, D. and Hanning, I. (2015) Botanical alternatives for use in organic poultry production. *Poultry Science* 94, 1419–1430.

Ducatelle, R., Goossens, E., De Meyer, F., Eeckhaut, V., Antonissen, G., *et al.* (2018) Biomarkers for monitoring intestinal health in poultry: present status and future perspectives. *Veterinary Research* 49(1), 43.

Johnson, T.J., Youmans, B.P., Noll, S., Cardona, C., Evans, N.P., *et al.* (2018) A Consistent and predictable commercial broiler chicken bacterial microbiota in antibiotic-free production displays strong correlations with performance. *Applied and Environmental Microbiology,* 84(12), e00362.

Kogut, M.H. and Arsenault, R.J. (2016) Editorial: gut health: the new paradigm in food animal production. *Frontiers in Veterinary Science* 3, 71.

Lee, S., La, T-M., Lee, H-J., Choi, I-S., Song, C-S., *et al.* (2019) Characterization of microbial communities in the chicken oviduct and the origin of chicken embryo gut microbiota. *Scientific Reports* 9, 6838. DOI: 10.1038/s41598-019-43280-w.

Ngunjiri, J.M., Taylor, K.J.M., Abundo, M.C., Jang, H., Elaish, M., *et al.* (2019) Farm stage, bird age, and body site dominantly affect the quantity, taxonomic composition, and dynamics of respiratory and gut microbiota of commercial layer chickens. *Applied and Environmental Microbiology,* 85(9), e03137.

Oakley, B.B., Lillehoj, H.S., Kogut, M.H., Kim, W.K., Maurer, J.J., *et al.* (2014) The chicken gastrointestinal microbiome. *Fems Microbiology Letters* 360, 100–112.

Shang, Y., Kumar, S., Oakley, B. and Kim, W.K. (2018) Chicken gut microbiota: importance and detection technology. *Frontiers in Veterinary Science* 5, 254.

Stanley, D., Hughes, R.J., Geier, M.S. and Moore, R.J. (2016) Bacteria within the gastrointestinal tract microbiota correlated with improved growth and feed conversion: challenges presented for the identification of performance enhancing probiotic bacteria. *Frontiers in Microbiology* 7, 187. DOI: 10.3389/fmicb.2016.00187.

18 Biosecurity

Richard Jennison*

Poultry Health Services, Leominster, Herefordshire, UK

18.1 Introduction

Biosecurity can be generically defined as a set of procedures or measures designed to protect the population in question against harmful biological agents. Biosecurity can be considered in two different ways, i.e. bio-exclusion, which for most aspects of poultry rearing is what we normally regard as biosecurity (i.e. keeping contamination out) and biocontainment (i.e. keeping contamination in). This is very important in other animal sectors such as for experimental infection studies. However, it may be important to consider what should be done to contain contamination, for example for flocks where a disease may be present.

Biosecurity is important for reasons of welfare, economics, food safety and to maintain public confidence. Most people will naturally think of foot dips, but the development of a biosecurity programme requires the development of a holistic approach to disease exclusion and should ideally start with an open mind and a HACCP (Hazard Analysis and Critical Control Point) approach to identifying threats to production and how best to counter these threats.

In the development of a comprehensive biosecurity programme it is important to consider the following major issues. In some cases, these are points which require addressing during a biosecurity risk analysis of a site, but which should also be included in the development of a new site *de novo*.

18.2 Nature of Pathogens to be Excluded

Although all forms of potential pathogens, including viruses, bacteria, protozoa and other endo/ectoparasites, are usually considered, more emphasis may be placed on one type compared with others. Consideration needs to be given to whether these agents are endemic within a region or exotic. How the pathogens being considered are transmitted must be taken into account, i.e. whether this is primarily through the air (droplets but also dust), via the water source, on or in the food, via contact with wild birds, vermin or pets which might have access to the birds/accommodation, fomites and also people, whether these are regular staff or contractors.

18.3 The Site

The risks associated with buildings that are older, and some of which may be of wooden construction, are clearly much greater because of limitations in avoiding entry of dust and air from the outside (Fig. 18.1), but also reduced efficiency in cleaning and disinfection associated with wooden structures.

It is potentially much more straightforward to design a new site with high biosecurity precautions (Fig. 18.2) than to 'retro-fit' enhanced biosecurity to an existing site. Within the site perimeter, the buildings accommodating the birds should be constructed solidly and be as inaccessible as practicable to wild birds, vermin (such as rodents) and other undesirable pest species (such as earthworms and flies).

For a new building, the site should ideally be geographically isolated from other poultry sites. Separation of 0.5–1 km is ideal (Lister, 2008), mainly in respect of airborne disease transmission. Larger distances, such as to prevent a site falling into a 3 km protection zone or a 10 km surveillance

*richard.jennison@poultryhealthservices.com

© CAB International 2021. *Poultry Health: A Guide for Professionals* (P. Barrow *et al.*)
DOI: 10.1079/9781789245042.0018

Fig. 18.1. Examples of poor biosecurity in old and deteriorating poultry houses showing daylight shining through cracks in building infrastructure (a)–(c) and cracks in floor allowing access to pests (d). (Author's own images.)

zone in the event of a notifiable disease outbreak, are sensible considerations. However, in many places, such distances may not be achievable, owing to high densities of poultry around poultry production centres.

In addition, management of local disease 'risk' can be challenging owing to an increase in the keeping of small 'backyard' poultry flocks. Nearby risk factors, such as lakes and watercourses, which may attract waterfowl, might also affect the desirability of a particular location for use as a poultry site.

18.4 Access and Physical Security

Physical security of the overall site should ideally include a robust, intact site perimeter, although a large number of poultry sites are located close to roads or public footpaths and may have tracks/footpaths running through the middle of the farm. The perimeter should be enclosed by a fence with a gate which should be closed and locked at all times and should only be opened briefly to allow essential vehicles to access the site. Minimizing human access to the site is essential to biosecurity. Most visitors, including postmen and couriers, that visit a poultry site do not need to enter the site perimeter. It is certainly also feasible for other visitors, such as egg collection drivers (for breeding or laying farms) to collect eggs or trolleys without entering the site perimeter. An off-site car park should be provided to reduce the risk of vehicles driving onto the site. Of the small proportion of visitors that do need to enter the site perimeter, not all will require access to the bird area.

Some sites have taken a very robust approach to minimizing site visitors, such as enabling feed to be delivered from an off-site location (Fig. 18.3), and by placing a post box on the site boundary for mail and parcels (Fig. 18.4).

A gatehouse should be provided at the site boundary to completely separate the area outside the site perimeter from its inside for visitors. The gatehouse should provide rooms for changing into

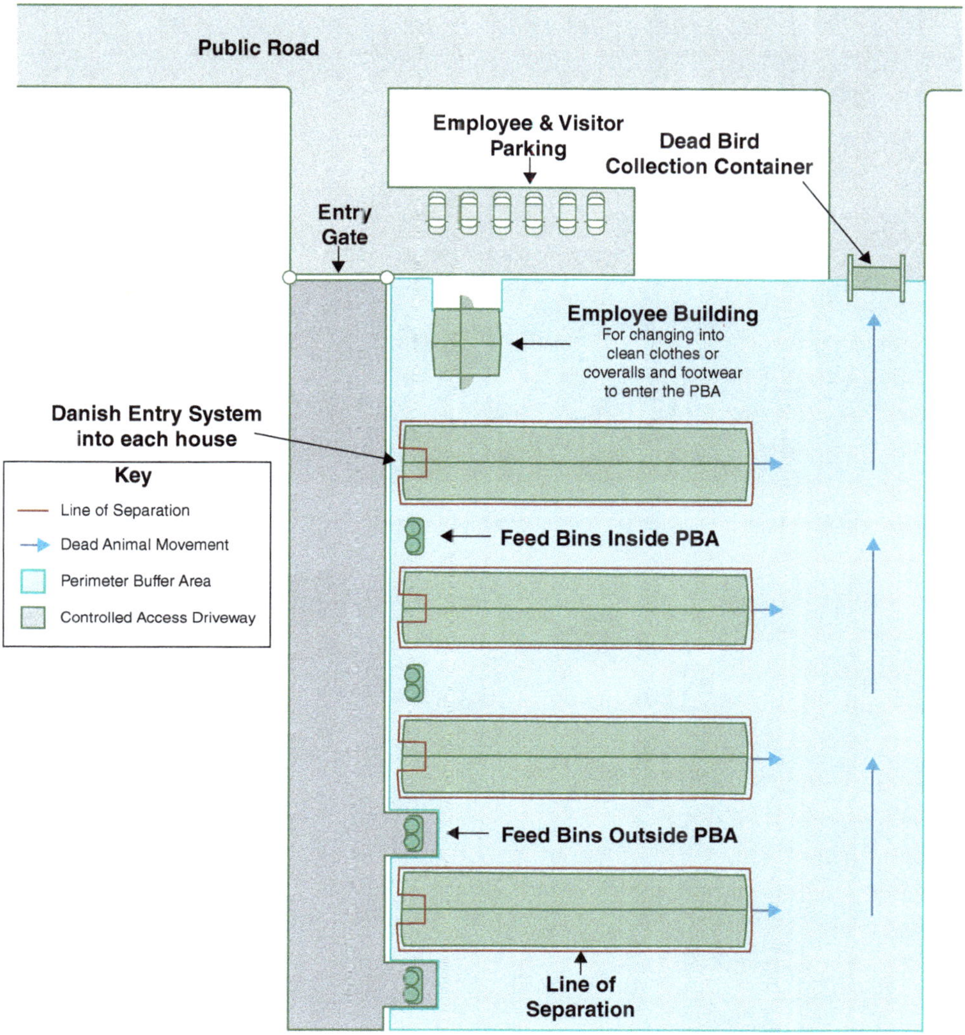

Fig. 18.2. A poultry site with key biosecurity features. The line of separation (red) is a critical control point for preventing exposure to incoming disease. The perimeter buffer area (PBA) (blue) is aimed at reducing pathogen load in the environment immediately outside the poultry houses. (Reproduced with permission from J. Roth Iowa State University and Poultry Health Services.)

dedicated site clothing and footwear. Access should be through a locked door (as an integral part of the site boundary) and should incorporate a barrier to change across. Ideally, the gatehouse should provide shower facilities, for use prior to changing into site clothing and footwear. Vehicles that must access the site should be cleaned and disinfected effectively prior to entry. As a minimum, this should be wheels and wheel arches (Figs 18.5 and 18.6). However, other areas of contamination, such as the driver's footwell, should also be checked and disinfected if necessary.

The drivers of such vehicles should be required to wear dedicated site overalls and footwear, or disposable overalls and overboots. Increasingly, sites are requesting the use of face masks and gloves.

A visitor book should be provided to gather information on visitors to site. This should record date, name of visitor, vehicle registration plate

Fig. 18.3. Delivery of feed from off-site location. (Author's own image.)

Fig. 18.4. External parcel box to minimize unnecessary visitors. (Author's own image.)

details, and possibly dates and locations of recent poultry sites visited. Some farms now request indication of whether the visitor will enter bird areas (as opposed to merely entering the site perimeter). The visitor book is also important to create a record of 'dangerous contacts'.

Entry requirements for access to a site should be adhered to strictly. One major risk factor for transmitting infection from one site to another is by human contact, moving the contamination between farms. For example, *Mycoplasma gallisepticum* (see Chapter 14viii, this volume) has been reported to survive in the human nasal cavity for 24 h and on human hair for 3 days (Christensen *et al.*, 1994). This provides a rationale for the periods of exclusion from other poultry (ranging from 24–72 h) that are required by poultry breeding and hatching sites to reduce the risk of disease transmission. In addition, higher health status sites housing elite breeding stock normally require a shower-in and shower-out regimen to avoid introduction and onward transmission of infectious agents, and will require the wearing of dedicated site clothing and footwear.

Fig. 18.5. Drive-through wheel dip. (Author's own image.)

Fig. 18.6. Sparge-type drive-over sprayer. (Author's own image.)

On growing farms, there may be limitations to such restrictions, particularly where staff are involved in other farming activities with other livestock species, such as pigs or sheep, which introduces additional risk. Some farms have been known to have a game bird shooting business close to the poultry farm. These factors must be considered before setting an unattainable entry requirement.

Routine maintenance within the bird area should ideally be undertaken at depopulation/turn around, when no birds are present. It is also important to evaluate how far these requirements can be maintained during weekends and holiday periods.

Entry into the bird area requires a number of disinfection measures. Foot dips remain a cornerstone of biosecurity prior to access to a bird area (Fig. 18.7).

However, they are not a panacea, and a number of factors can reduce their effectiveness including: (i) deliberate avoidance of their use by staff; (ii) inactivation of the disinfectants by sunlight and organic matter, such as faeces on footwear; (iii) dilution of the disinfectant by rain if the containers are left uncovered; and (iv) the requirement for a contact time of up to several minutes for inactivation, particularly in cold weather.

Barrier changing is increasingly being employed. Footwear worn inside the building is not allowed to be worn outside and *vice versa*. A 'step over' barrier reinforces the separation. The Danish System has recently been introduced as a higher standard of barrier changing in which the outer and inner and outer zones are separated by a buffer zone, to be crossed in stockinged feet and reduce the risk of visitors stepping over a simple barrier and compromising the biosecurity (Fig. 18.8). Colour changes on the floors can also reinforce behaviour compliance.

Changing overalls between houses on a site should be done but is rarely carried out. There is increasing focus on hand hygiene in control room areas, prior to entering the bird areas. Some sites provide sinks for handwashing, while others may provide disinfectant hand sanitizers (Fig. 18.9a,b).

18.5 The Poultry and Production Method

It is important to consider the poultry species and type that will be reared. Turkeys, for example, seem particularly susceptible to a variety of diseases, including avian influenza, compared with ducks. Consideration needs to be given to the required level of biosecurity for higher value birds, such as elite breeding stock, compared with free-range hens or commercial broilers. This is simply a matter of economics.

Also, consider whether the site is rearing younger birds (such as broilers) – which have a

Fig. 18.7. (a) and (b) Different types of foot dip. (Author's own images.)

Fig. 18.8. Danish system for barrier changing (a); also shown in operation (b). (Author's own images.)

Fig. 18.9. (a) and (b) Options for hand sanitizing and washing. (Author's own images.)

relatively immature immune system and are more susceptible to infection for this reason – or more mature birds. The proposed type of production (e.g. indoor, compared with free-range) will affect the risk of birds coming into contact with disease contamination.

In addition, most large-scale commercial poultry production will operate an 'all-in-all-out' system, which allows a period of time where the site is empty for cleaning and disinfection. However, some businesses operate a multi-age model, where the site is never completely empty of birds. This creates different disease risks and poses an increased challenge to biosecurity.

18.6 Water

The source of the water being offered to the birds can be a biosecurity risk. Untreated water from open bodies, such as lakes and rivers, has been associated with outbreaks of avian influenza. However, even mains or borehole water, if poorly sanitized, can be a carrier of infectious agents such as *Enterococcus* or *Escherichia coli.*

18.7 Vermin and Other Animals

Some diseases rely on vectors or intermediate hosts in their transmission (for example, wild birds, rodents, earthworms, flies, etc.). Domestic animals, whether these are food animals or pets, carry a number of pathogens capable of infecting poultry. Cats are sometimes used to control rodents but themselves carry pathogens, so this practise should be avoided.

It is important to reduce the attractiveness of a site for 'pest' species. Use of modern housing, preventing access, is an ideal situation and all doors should be closed, including doors to feed and bedding stores and rooms housing machinery. Promptly cleaning up feed spills following deliveries and using dust traps to catch dust liberated during feed blowing will reduce the risk of transmission by this route.

Rodent control should be considered holistically, rather than reliance solely on baiting. So, for example, rodents prefer not to cross open, uncovered areas and a wide expanse of concrete is preferable outside the buildings. Concreting also improves the effectiveness of disinfection, increases desiccation and microbial killing by UV light and reduces standing water which other animals can drink. Long vegetation should be removed, and material should not be stored alongside houses. The siting of bait boxes for rodents is crucial, with entry holes facing in the direction of a rodent run.

It is clear that earthworms also act as vectors of disease (see Chapter 16ii, this volume) and their entry into poultry houses can be limited by liming of expansion joints and doorways. Doors and walls should be kept in good condition.

Free-range birds should be fed and watered indoors.

18.8 Cleaning and Disinfection

Microorganisms can be found in dust, feathers and faeces during and after poultry rearing. Removal of this material after depopulation and cleaning, followed by disinfection, reduces the risk of reinfection of a new flock. Both are required since it is thought that there are approximately 500 million bacteria per gram of used litter, of which 92% are removed by mechanical cleaning, 6% by disinfectants and 1% by fumigation. It is not just the inside of the house, but all areas and all parts that require cleaning and disinfection including the water system, where biofilms may form, food bins and feeder systems and also the records room.

For some agents, the period of time without susceptible poultry on site can be sufficient for some infectious agents, such as *Mycoplasma*, to die. However, for most microbes, this is not the case, and a process of 'dilution' by physical and chemical cleaning, followed by killing by contact with appropriate disinfectants, is required.

An ideal cleaning and disinfection regime would include a physical clean and removal of all material (mucking out) coupled with blowing down and washing of contaminated areas. The physical clean should include a detergent step, partly to improve the effectiveness of the physical clean by aiding removal of grease and gross organic debris, and also to directly inactivate some of the infectious organisms that are present.

A disinfection step should follow the cleaning stage. Ideally, prior to application of disinfectant, adequate time should be allowed for any standing water to dissipate or be removed (to prevent dilution of the disinfectant). Bear in mind that a disinfectant is likely to be inactivated by residual organic material, so a poor physical clean may well lead to less effective disinfection.

There is no one disinfectant that is equally effective against all types of infectious agent. Selection should be made to address the infectious agents causing greatest concern: bacteria, such as *Salmonella* (see Chapter 14iv, this volume); viruses, where consideration needs to be given to the differing susceptibility of enveloped versus non-enveloped viruses since the latter tend to be more resistant and difficult to inactivate; and protozoa, such as coccidia (see Chapter 16i, this volume), which are particularly resistant to many kinds of chemical disinfectant.

Fumigation is the process of using 'fumes' (i.e. a vapour or gas form of disinfectant) as a 'terminal' disinfectant step. It can be used in small chambers (e.g. egg stores) but is also widely used in large poultry buildings.

It can be very effective in achieving additional kill of any remaining infectious microorganisms. However, its efficacy is wholly reliant on an effective cleaning process removing as much organic material as possible, as the volumes of disinfectant are relatively low, and penetration of organic deposits cannot be expected.

Chemicals used for fumigation include formaldehyde, chlorine dioxide and vapourized hydrogen peroxide. The means of creating disinfectant gases include:

1. 'Reaction' of the disinfectant material with another agent to create a gas (e.g. reacting formalin with potassium permanganate will release formaldehyde gas).
2. Prills/cans, with the gas liberated by heating or burning.
3. Use of heat to 'evaporate' a liquid state product, either using hot surfaces (often used for whole house disinfection with formaldehyde) or by specialist vapour generating equipment.
4. Use of pressure to create a fine 'mist' from a liquid, and a fan to distribute the mist (e.g. an orchard sprayer)

Note that some of these chemicals – particularly formaldehyde – are very toxic.

Appropriate personal protective equipment (PPE) must be employed when the product is being used. The air space should be thoroughly ventilated prior to staff entering the building.

Consideration should be given to less obvious materials and structures such as the weight from a bell drinker (Fig. 18.10a), augers and 'sleeves' within feeder systems (Fig. 18.10b).

Fig. 18.10. (a) Uncleaned weight from a bell drinker. (b) Poorly cleaned sleeve from a feeder system. (Author's own images.)

18.9 Carcass Disposal

Carcasses of birds that have died from disease pose an obvious biosecurity risk to other birds on site. Fatalities should be removed promptly from the bird area. Visits to the site by off-site carcass collection services may pose a significant biosecurity risk, owing to the lack of knowledge or of control of the sites already visited by the service provider. Many sites operate on-site freezing and storage of carcasses, with collection occurring after depletion. At the very least, carcasses should be collected from a locked receptacle held outside the site perimeter to which rodents cannot gain access. On-site disposal of birds by incineration is an attractive option, but incinerators can be challenging to operate owing to cost and licensing requirements. Another area that is under increasing focus is biosecure removal of carcasses from the house environment, such as by installation of hatches in doors (Fig. 18.11).

18.10 Depopulation

The biosecurity risk from catching and depletion for slaughter must be considered. Catching teams have been implicated in *Campylobacter* contamination of broiler flocks. Farms for other species, e.g. pigs, have loading ramps, with the vehicular access technically being outside the site perimeter, reducing the biosecurity risk from catchers and transport vehicles.

18.11 Mechanical Vectors of Disease (Fomites)

Sharing of tools/equipment between sites (such as vaccination equipment, but also larger machinery such as feed spreaders or straw choppers), should be avoided as far as practicable. Strong consideration should be given to each site having a selection of dedicated tools, to reduce the infection risk from the tools of external contractors, when dealing with essential maintenance.

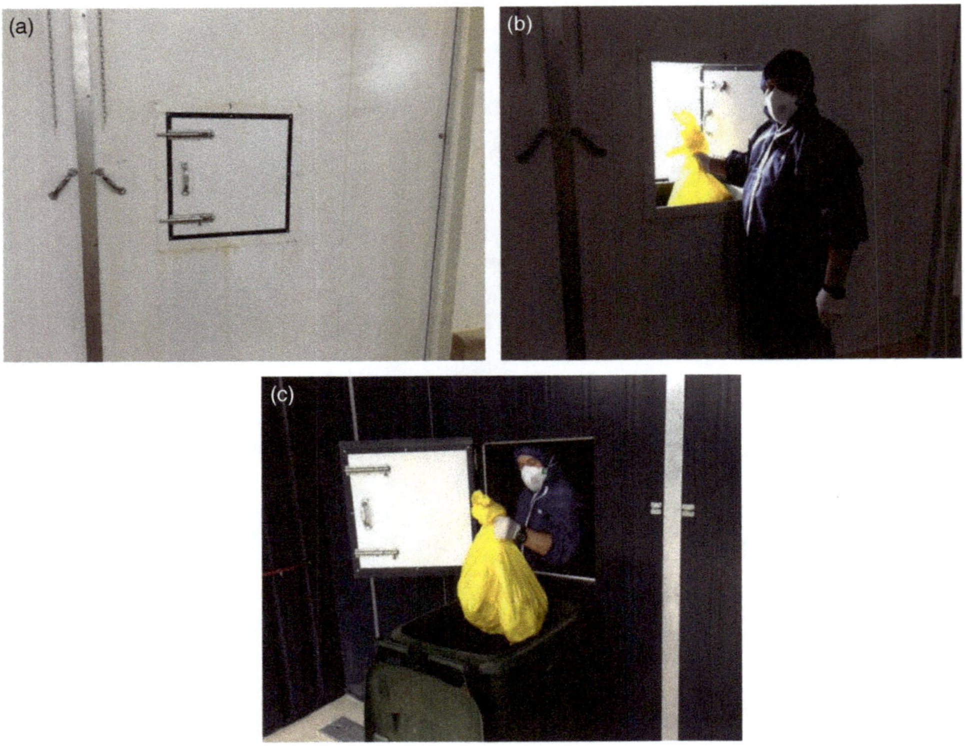

Fig. 18.11. (a)–(c) Hatches for carcass disposal. (Author's own images.)

18.12 Conclusions

Biosecurity must be seen as a major component in reducing the risk of introducing infection to poultry in all types of production system. It must be initiated rationally and holistically, ideally using a HACCP approach covering all realistic possible avenues of infection introduction mitigated by any limitations, either from the geographical location or other factors that need to be considered. The development of a comprehensive biosecurity plan is not only economically sensible but improves animal welfare, reduces public health risks and eases the challenge of antibiotic stewardship.

18.13 References

Christensen, N.H., Yavari, C.A., McBain, A.J. and Bradbury, J.M. (1994) Investigations into the survival of *Mycoplasma gallisepticum*, *Mycoplasma synoviae* and *Mycoplasma iowae* on materials found in the poultry house environment. *Avian Pathology* 23, 127–143.

Lister, S.A. (2008) Biosecurity in poultry management. In: Pattison, M., McMullin, P.F., Bradbury, J.M. and Alexander, D.J. (eds) *Poultry Diseases*, 6th edn. Elsevier, London, pp 48–65.

18.14 Further Reading

Collett, S.R. (2013) Principles of disease prevention, diagnosis and control. In: Swayne, D.E. (editor-in-chief) *Diseases of Poultry*. Wiley-Blackwell, Hoboken, New Jersey, pp. 1–23.

McMullin, P.F. (2004) *A Pocket Guide to Poultry Health and Disease*. 5M Enterprises Ltd., Sheffield, UK

Morishita, T.Y., Greenacre, C.B. and Souza, M. (2015) Biosecurity and zoonotic diseases. In: Greenacre, C.B. and Morishita, T.Y. (eds) *Backyard Poultry Medicine and Surgery: A Guide for Veterinary Practitioners*. Wiley, Ames, Iowa, pp. 117–132.

Office International des Epizooties (2019) Biosecurity procedures in poultry production. *Terrestrial Animal Health Code,* Volume 1. OIE, Paris, pp. 245–250.

19 Poultry Chemotherapy and Antimicrobials

MICHAEL CLARK*

School of Veterinary Medicine and Science, University of Nottingham, Sutton Bonington, Loughborough, Leicestershire, UK

19.1 Introduction

The global rise in intensive poultry production has required the use of therapeutics. To better comprehend their use it is important to review the function of treatments in poultry production. Antimicrobials, particularly antibiotics, have different actions which need to be understood. Evaluating the different classes of antibiotics allows an understanding of whether they have a use in poultry production. Just because an antibiotic can be used in poultry production does not necessarily mean it ought to be. Poultry clinicians have many pressures placed upon them when prescribing and dispensing medications and these need to be considered. Antimicrobial resistance is probably the biggest single factor in the changing trends in poultry antibiotic use. With this growing pressure there has been renewed focus on alternative therapeutics.

The purpose of medication is to reduce the presence of clinical signs of disease and to alleviate any welfare compromises associated with disease. Antibiotics have been used as treatments where all medicated birds are known to have bacterial infection. With large flock sizes associated with commercial poultry production, there are instances when a metaphylactic approach is taken. This is when it is known that there are some individuals in the flock showing clinical signs of disease but there are also clinically normal birds that are also receiving treatment. Prophylactic antibiotic treatment has historically been extensively used in poultry production. An example would have been the use of 'starter medications' such as lincomycin/spectinomycin used in the first 3 days of life for broiler production. This was known to have a beneficial effect in reducing the prevalence of *Escherichia coli* yolk sac infection. However, this undoubtedly resulted in many healthy flocks receiving unnecessary medication and the practice is not compatible with responsible use of antibiotics (see Section 19.6).

19.2 Pharmacology Review

Antibiotic treatment outcomes are dependent on three key factors. There is the pharmacodynamic consideration. This is the study of the biochemical, physiologic and molecular effect of drugs on the body and involves receptor binding (including receptor sensitivity), post-receptor binding effects and chemical interactions (https://www.msdmanuals.com/en-gb/professional/clinical-pharmacology/pharmacodynamics/overview-of-pharmacodynamics). The pharmacokinetics determine how drugs are absorbed, distributed and excreted by the bird. Medications do not work in isolation, there are also host defence mechanisms working at the same time.

Bacteriostatic antibiotics work by suppressing bacterial multiplication, whereas bactericidal antibiotics work by killing bacteria. Their killing action can either be time dependant or concentration dependant or both. If bacteriostatic and bactericidal treatments are used concurrently there may be an antagonistic effect. Whereas two bactericidal compounds of different categories can be synergistic e.g. lincomycin and spectinomycin.

To determine an antibiotic's sensitivity an *in vitro* test is done, routinely performed by the disc diffusion (Kirby–Bauer) method. Serum levels will need

*michael.clark2@nottingham.ac.uk

© CAB International 2021. *Poultry Health: A Guide for Professionals* (P. Barrow *et al.*)
DOI: 10.1079/9781789245042.0019

to be higher when antibiotics are used *in vivo*, to be efficacious. The size of the growth-free zone determines whether the bacteria are considered to be susceptible, resistant or intermediate to a particular antibiotic by comparison with the zones produced with a known sensitive strain of the same microorganism.

The minimum inhibitory concentration (MIC) is the lowest concentration (in µg/ml) of an antimicrobial that will inhibit the visible growth of a given microorganism after 24 h of incubation. An antibiotic break point is the dilution where bacteria begin to show resistance. Together they can facilitate antibiotic selection. Pulse dosing (where there are escalating antibiotic levels followed by a prolonged dose free period) is only suitable for bactericidal antibiotics as, in a bacteriostatic regime, bacterial populations will recover during the moments when medication is not being used. There is a phenomenon called the post antibiotic effect (PAE) which relates to antibiotic impact long after treatment ceases. An example of this is the enhanced phagocytic effect after Pulmotil (tilmicosin) treatment (Kirst, 1997). Pharmacodynamic properties of the common antimicrobial medicines and indications are shown in Table 19.1.

19.3 Modes of Treatment

Individual application: this is not often used in commercial poultry flocks due to large flock sizes and normally no individual bird identification. However, a treatment for an individual bird may be indicated with a small hobby flock or with expensive pedigree birds high up the breeding pyramid.

In-feed medication: this was commonly used in the UK with veterinary surgeons using a Medicated Feed Stuffs (MFS) prescription. It has fallen out of favour in recent years. With a strong emphasis on responsible use of antibiotics it is difficult to justify prophylactic/metaphylactic antibiotics being presented to birds for up to 10 days in their feed. In duck production, in-feed medication is often preferable to in-water application. This is because a significant amount of ducks' daily water usage is for preening and not for drinking. Coccidiostats (both chemicals and ionophores) are used in commercial broiler, commercial turkey and gamebird rations. In the UK these products are listed as zootechnical feed additives (ZFAs) and as such do not require veterinary prescriptions for their use.

Drinking water application: the vast majority of antibiotics prescribed to commercial poultry are applied through the drinking water. It is quick to start dosing by this route and correspondingly it is easy to terminate treatment. In water medication can be administered into the bulk water tank with some practical considerations taken into account. The operator needs to know the volume of water held by the tank to correctly dose. If the tank is very large and the chosen medication has a poor solubility, then there can be problems in keeping the product in suspension. On starting treatment, the mains supply into the tank needs to be turned

Table 19.1. Antimicrobials with a defined MRL (maximum residue limit) for eggs.

Products with a defined MRL in eggs		Spectrum of activity[a]
Chlortetracycline	200 µg/kg	*Mycoplasma*, *Salmonella*, *E. coli*, *Pasteurella* and *Clostridium perfringens*
Colistin[b]	300 µg/kg	*E. coli* (poor intestinal absorption)
Erythromycin	150 µg/kg	*Mycoplasma*, *Pasteurella* and *E. coli*
Lincomycin	500 µg/kg	*Staphylococcus*, *Erysipelothrix*, *Mycoplasma* and *C. perfringens* (poor intestinal absorption)
Neomycin	500 µg/kg	*E. coli* (poor intestinal absorption)
Oxytetracycline	200 µg/kg	*Mycoplasma*, *Salmonella*, *E. coli*, *Pasteurella* and *Staphylococcus*
Phenoxymethylpenicillin[b]	25 µg/kg	*C. perfringens*
Tiamulin[b]	1000 µg/kg	*Mycoplasma* and *Brachyspira*
Tylosin[b]	200 µg/kg	*Mycoplasma* and *C. perfringens*

[a]See individual relevant chapters for specific pathogens.
[b]Antimicrobials currently authorized in the UK with zero-egg withdrawal preparations available.

off, to ensure a consistent concentration of product in the tank. The stockperson needs to know the water consumption of the flock so the flow rate from the tank is known. The mains supply must resume prior to the tank running dry. Often tanks are bypassed when treatments are not being administered and because of this infrequent use they can become contaminated. Most in water treatments are now applied through water proportioners. The operator needs to know at what inclusion rate the proportioner is set at. A suitable sized container for the stock solution is required. The equipment needs to be regularly serviced.

Antibiotics can be administered *in ovo*. Such treatments often accompany *in ovo* vaccination. There is a voluntary ban on antibiotics being given to poultry embryos via this route in the UK.

Though a bacterial infection may be present in a flock of commercial birds and the prescribing vet knows there is a licenced efficacious treatment the decision whether or not to medicate is multifactorial. In any flock of birds with a bacterial infection there will be a proportion that have the diseases and will die of the infection. There will be moribund birds that may improve or deteriorate. Of the clinically normal birds some of this subgroup will be infected and some non-infected (see Fig. 19.1). The proportion of the flock in each of these groups will influence the prescriber's decision whether to treat or not.

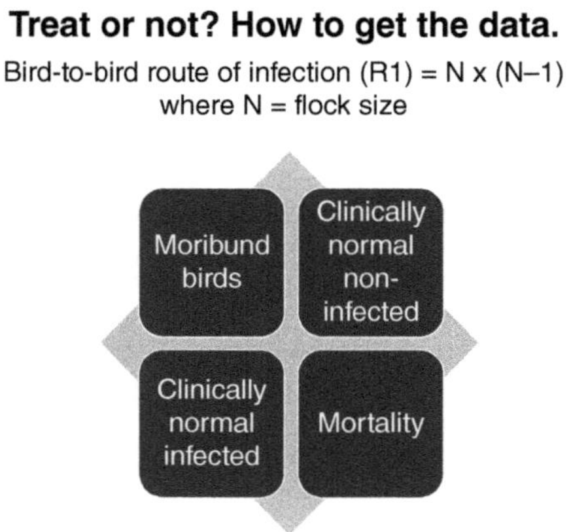

Fig. 19.1. Proportions of birds in different clinical groups in infected flocks. (Courtesy of Poultry Health Services.)

19.4 Assessment of Antimicrobials in Poultry Treatment

Antimicrobial sensitivity tests (ASTs) are essential to help make an informed decision on treatments. Sensitivity plates are still routinely used despite their limitations. It must be remembered that although there may be no growth of an isolate around a particular disc this *in vitro* finding may not hold true *in vivo*. Samples are taken commonly from a post-mortem lesion and plated directly for sensitivity. This facilitates a result within 24 h but can be compromised if there is a mixed/contaminated growth. Blood agar and MacConkey agar plates should be used simultaneously. If the direct sensitivity plates are corrupted, then a pure culture can be taken from the blood agar or MacConkey plates with a 24 h lag time. Even at this juncture identification of the organism may not be possible on morphology alone and further analysis such as serological testing may be required. Secondly the significance of the isolate may require further laboratory work. A good example is *E. coli*. Many *E. coli* are commensals with only some being avian pathogenic *E. coli* (APEC). Thus, serotyping should be carried out to confirm the presence of a pathogenic *E. coli* strain prior to contemplating treatment. Numerous biotechnology companies are developing rapid sensitivity tests. Biomerieux has equipment in the market place, though the kit requires a pure culture. Therefore, the time lag from post-mortem examination to sensitivity result is constrained by the duration needed to grow an isolate. It is not only plate antibiotic sensitivity that influences a clinician's treatment decision. The minimum inhibitory concentration (MIC) is also important, though MICs are more frequently sought in epidemiological studies rather than diagnostic cases. There are discs that give an MIC score; however, interpretation can be difficult.

In the EU and UK, if a clinician wishes to use a medication under the cascade, which is a longstanding legal flexibility providing a rational balance between the legislative requirement for veterinary surgeons to prescribe and use authorized veterinary medicines where they are available and the need for professional freedom to prescribe other products where they are not, the veterinary surgeon must ensure that the active ingredient(s) are listed in the Table of Allowed Substances in the Commission Regulation (EU) No 37/2010. The majority of antimicrobials authorized for use in poultry do not have established maximum residue limits (MRLs) for eggs, but there are some (Table 19.1). For non-egg producing poultry there are several products available with meat withdrawal times. Furthermore, many of these antimicrobials have explicit notes on the Table of Allowed Substances to explain that they are not to be used in birds producing eggs for human consumption (https://www.bsavalibrary.com/content/chapter/10.22233/9781905319862.chap15).

Most licenced products have a 3- to 7-day treatment period. There are some products for which an MRL cannot be established and therefore must not be used in any food producing animals (Annex 4). These include products previously used in the poultry industry such as dimetridazole and furazolidone.

Response to treatment is normally assessed by the impact of treatment on clinical signs and flock performance indicators. If a flock is known to be immunocompromised and there is a bacterial infection that requires treatment a bactericidal medication is preferable to a bacteriostatic one.

19.5 Adverse Reactions and Side Effects

There are a few drugs with a narrow therapeutic margin (lethal dose/effective dose, LD_{50}/ED_{50}) in poultry medicine. An example would be potentiated sulfonamides. Turkeys are very taste sensitive to this product, so it is very easy to inadvertently breach the effective dose with dehydration occurring as a result of the birds not drinking thus reaching a lethal dose.

Though it may appear counterintuitive, flocks testing positive for *Salmonella* are not permitted to be treated under the National Control Plan (NCP) for *Salmonella*. This is because this could inhibit routine testing if flocks are undergoing treatment and antibiotics in a *Salmonella* positive flock could increase the chance of selecting for antibiotic resistance, a very undesirable outcome against an organism of importance in veterinary public health.

Should a veterinary surgeon or a producer encounter an adverse reaction with a veterinary medicine it must be reported to either the Veterinary Medicine Directorate (in the UK) and/or the pharmacovigilance team holding the Marketing Authorisation (MA) for the product.

19.6 Responsible Use of Antimicrobials

Extensive use of antibiotics and other chemotherapeutics in veterinary or human medicine has resulted in increasing levels of resistance in commensal and pathogenic bacteria and parasites with exchange of resistant zoonotic bacteria between man and animals.

One of the main concerns in bacterial resistance is not just resistance per se but its transmissibility between related and unrelated bacterial species and genera. Transmissibility occurs most frequently as a result of the resistance genes being located on self-transmissible plasmids, but transmission can also occur by means of bacteriophage activity or by take up of the genes as naked DNA.

Resistance genes may accumulate on plasmids so that some strains can be multi-resistant, in some cases to seven or more unrelated antibiotics. This can present huge problems. Recent developments have seen the plasmid transmissibility of antibiotics such as colistin and quinolones which were previously chromosomally mediated. Transmissible resistance is not an issue in parasites such as *Eimeria* (see Chapter 16i, this volume) although resistance to several drugs has accumulated over the years.

Bacterial resistance has been selected by medicinal use in poultry production but also historically by their use for growth promotion. In the UK in the 1960s chemotherapeutic antibiotics were used and were banned which led to the development by the pharmaceutical industries of new antibiotics which were not used in human or veterinary medicine. However, their gradual use during the 1980s for treating MRSA in human medicine meant that they were once again regarded as chemotherapeutic with the result that in 2006 antimicrobial use for growth promotion was banned in the European Union although they are still used for this reason in many countries. This coincided with the establishment of Responsible Use of Medicines in Agriculture Alliance (RUMA). RUMA has the aim of producing a coordinated and integrated approach to best practice in animal medicine use. It produces guidelines for various livestock sectors including poultry and game production (https://www.ruma.org.uk/wp-content/uploads/2014/09/poultry-antimicrobials-long.pdf). Beyond the UK, there is the European Platform Responsible Use of Medicines in Animal (EPRUMA), which is a multi-stakeholder initiative. Though previously used as a support to production, antibiotics are not an alternative to good husbandry, biosecurity measures and preventative programmes. When treatments are indicated polypharmacy (the use of many medicines) should be avoided. All prescribing and dispensing must be done in accordance with the law. In the UK this is enshrined in the Veterinary Medicines Regulations (2009) (https://www.legislation.gov.uk/uksi/2009/2297/pdfs/uksi_20092297_en.pdf), which is transposed from the current European Directive. When a veterinary medicine is unlicensed for the poultry species treated or used not in accordance with its SPC (Summaries of Product Characteristics) a 28-day meat withdrawal and a 7-day egg withdrawal is the minimum that must be applied by the prescribing vet. (https://www.gov.uk/guidance/the-cascade-prescribing-unauthorised-medicines#food-producing-species). Prescribing veterinarians and poultry producers should also be mindful of any restrictions placed upon them by any assurance schemes e.g. Assured Chicken Production, Lion Code and Freedom Food.

19.7 Decreasing Antibiotic Usage

As far back as 2010, the Dutch government issued the goal of a 50% reduction in the use of antibiotics by 2014 compared to the 2009 usage. In Denmark veterinarians can prescribe but not dispense antimicrobials, with many calling for this to be extended to the UK. Following on, there has been an aim to have a common European Union surveillance programme for antibiotic consumption and antimicrobial resistance. Another aim is a reduction in antibiotic consumption among both humans and animals with the focus on the critically important antibiotics which are those essential for the treatment of serious infections (https://www.who.int/foodsafety/cia/en/). The UK has taken some voluntary measures, taking the lead from the British Poultry Council's Antibiotic Stewardship (https://www.britishpoultry.org.uk/british-poultrys-successful-stewardship-on-antibiotic-use/). The measures are:

- The withdrawal of the use of cephalosporins in the breeding pyramid supplying UK produced birds.
- The cessation of any prophylactic fluoroquinolone use.
- The reduction in all prophylactic medication use applying a risk based approach.
- The cessation of colistin use in broiler chicken and turkeys.

The BPC Antibiotic Stewardship Report 2019 (https://www.britishpoultry.org.uk/bpc-antibiotics-report-2019/) had the following highlights:

- 30.2% reduction in the total use of antibiotics from 2012 to 2018.
- 82.6% reduction in the use of critically important antibiotics 2012 to 2018.

In 2018, the sector used:

- 16.2 tonnes of antibiotics resulting in a 12.4% increase in year-on-year usage.
- 7.1% of the total antibiotics licensed for food producing animals in 2017 as compared to 21% in 2012.

By 2017 data demonstrate that both duck and broiler chickens were already well below the UK Government's multispecies target for 2018 of 50 mg/PCU. This resulted in the 2018–2020 target for broiler chickens being set at 25 mg/PCU (ruma.org.uk/wp-content/uploads/2017/10/RUMA-Targets-Task-Force-Report-2017-FINAL.pdf).

19.8 Common Misconceptions

Applying withdrawal times to prescribed medications is important. It is a common misconception that if they are adhered to, then those veterinary medicines cannot contribute to resistance in people. However, as indicated, there is a complex system by which bacteria share and spread antibiotic resistance genes.

Some staunch supporters of the poultry industry exist that claim there is no evidence that antibiotics in the poultry industry have caused resistance in people. However, there is clear evidence to show that there are some cephalosporin resistant genes that originated in the chicken breeding pyramid that are causing mortality in people in the EU (Collignon *et al.*, 2013).

Many observers would assume that antibiotics are only used when a bacterial disease had been diagnosed. However, up to about 2014 it was not uncommon for broiler chickens and turkeys to routinely receive 'starter' antibiotic medications. There were many laying hens that received antibiotics routinely around peak production. Also, in an attempt to control enteritis many broiler chickens and turkeys received prophylactic antibiotics.

It is no doubt a truism that intensive poultry production was able to develop with relatively high stocking levels because of the use of antimicrobials. This is most evident in the use of ionophores in the control of coccidiosis. It might be assumed that Europe has the toughest antimicrobial legislation, but in the USA ionophores are banned in poultry production, though currently they are permitted in the EU. Whilst there was a knowledge gap, antimicrobials allowed producers and veterinarians to cope with management deficiencies in these new production systems.

19.9 Therapeutics Other Than Antibiotics

19.9.1 Vitamin supplementation (see also Chapter 12, this volume)

There is an argument that if a flock is receiving a balanced ration then there is no need for vitamin supplementation. Using water soluble supplements could even be counter-productive, as they could be substrates for microbial proliferation and hence contamination of drinking lines. The vast sales of water-soluble vitamins would suggest that there are many producers who perceive a benefit in their use. Supplementary vitamins could well help an inappetent flock that is not consuming its normal daily feed ration. If the feed is known to be suboptimal or the birds are intestinally compromised, then supplementation could also help.

19.9.2 Analgesics and anti-inflammatories

Non-steroidal anti-inflammatory drugs (NSAIDs) are rarely used in commercial or backyard poultry. This is despite many infections causing pyrexia and there being many causes of inflammation in poultry. As all poultry are relatively stoic in their response to discomfort there is frequently a lack of awareness that birds are in pain. Sodium salicylate is indicated as an antipyretic treatment of acute respiratory diseases in combination with an appropriate anti-infective treatment at a dose of 100 mg/kg for 3 days. Meloxicam has been used in backyard poultry at a dose rate of 0.5–1 mg/kg IM or PO, once or twice daily. Prescribing veterinary surgeons must adhere to cascade prescribing principles and ensure a Special Import Certificate (SIC) is obtained for products licenced in an EU member state but not the UK.

19.9.3 Competitive exclusion products

The ethos behind competitive exclusion is that early in a chick's development its immature gut is seeded with commensal bacteria that are known to be pathogen free. These beneficial bacteria are encouraged to colonize the intestines, effectively squeezing out any pathogens the young birds may ingest early in life. This forms a pillar to the 'Seed, Feed and Weed' principle (www.seedfeedweed.co.uk). Once this seeding has taken place, these commensals can be fed with short chain fatty acids that encourage their adherence and replication. Pathogens can be further discouraged (weeded out) with the use of such products as organic acids in either the drinking water or feed. By reducing the pH of feed and water with organic acids, the pathogen burden birds consume can be reduced (see Chapter 17, this volume).

19.9.4 Anthelmintics (see Chapter 16iii, this volume)

There is little need for anthelmintics in short lived, intensively reared meat birds. The longer lived and the more extensive the flock, the more likely there is to be an endoparasite burden. In the UK flubendazoles and fenbendazole are licensed. Flubenvet (flubendazole) is used widely in feed in commercial poultry and is also available in a 60 g pot suitable for backyard poultry. The product has no egg withdrawal and is deemed efficacious against the common poultry nematodes. Panacur Aquasol (fenbendazole) is only really appropriate for commercial poultry, but also has zero egg withdrawal.

19.9.5 Ectoparasiticides (see Chapter 16iii, this volume)

Until recently there was no licenced product for red mite (*Dermanyssus gallinae*) in poultry. There is now MSD's Exzolt (10 mg/ml fluralaner). This product has zero egg withdrawal, but cost may preclude its use in backyard poultry.

19.10 References

Collignon, P., Aarestrup, F.M., Irwin, R. and McEwen, S. (2013). Human deaths and third-generation cephalosporin use in poultry, Europe. *Emerging infectious diseases* 19(8), 1339–1340. DOI: 10.3201/eid.1908.120681.

Kirst, H.A. (1997) Macrolide antibiotics in food-animal health. *Expert Opinion on Investigational Drugs* 6(2), 103–118. DOI: 10.1517/13543784.6.2.103

19.11 Further Reading

Farinde, A. (2019) Overview of Pharmacodynamics. Available at: www.msdmanuals.com/en-gb/professional/

clinical-pharmacology/pharmacodynamics/overview-of-pharmacodynamics (accessed 26 January 2021).

Gov.uk Veterinary Medicines Directorate (2015) The cascade: prescribing unauthorised medicines – Food-producing species. Available at: www.gov.uk/guidance/the-cascade-prescribing-unauthorised-medicines#food-producing-species (accessed 26 January 2021).

Griffiths, R. (2017) British Poultry Council British poultry's successful stewardship on antibiotic use. British Poultry Council. Available at: www.britishpoultry.org.uk/british-poultrys-successful-stewardship-on-antibiotic-use/ (accessed 26 January 2021).

McMullin, P. (2004) *A Pocket Guide to Poultry Health & Diseases*. 5M Enterprises Ltd., Sheffield, UK.

Nind, F. and Mosedale, P. (eds) (2020) *Backyard Poultry*. In: BSAVA Guide to the Use of Veterinary Medicines. British Small Animal Veterinary Association. Available at: https://www.bsavalibrary.com/content/chapter/10.22233/9781905319862.chap15 (accessed 26 January 2021).

RUMA Alliance Poultry Working Group (1999) Responsible Use of Antimicrobials in Poultry Production. Available at: www.ruma.org.uk/wp-content/uploads/2014/09/poultry-antimicrobials-long.pdf (accessed 26 January 2021).

RUMA Alliance (2017) *Targets Task Force Report* 2017. Available at: www.ruma.org.uk/wp-content/uploads/2017/10/RUMA-Targets-Task-Force-Report-2017-FINAL.pdf (accessed 26 January 2021).

Seed Feed Weed (n.d.) Available at: www.seedfeed-weed.co.uk (accessed 26 January 2021).

The Stationery Office (2009) Statutory Instrument No. 2297 – The Veterinary Medicines Regulations 2009. Available at: https://www.legislation.gov.uk/uksi/2009/2297/pdfs/uksi_20092297_en.pdf (accessed 11 March 2021).

20 Vaccination Strategies and Application of Vaccines

PETER CARGILL*

Wyatt Poultry Services, part of CVS (UK) Ltd., Hereford, UK

20.1 Introduction

The modern poultry industry is complex. As such, successful disease prevention and control relies on collaboration and understanding of all staff involved in the production system. While total disease prevention is desirable, this is often unattainable for epidemiological or economic reasons and, often, disease control measures are aimed at reducing the level of impact on birds rather than complete prevention. There are two prime requisites for disease-free poultry production:

1. Good biosecurity – the most powerful tool in preventing exposure to disease agents.
2. High management standards – a term incorporating:
   - the selection of high quality chicks;
   - housing and equipment of a high standard;
   - good environmental control;
   - high quality feed;
   - clean air and water;
   - high standards of cleaning and disinfection; and
   - an appropriate programme of vaccination.

Vaccination should not be used as an alternative to good biosecurity or high management standards.

20.2 Formulating Vaccination Programmes for Poultry

Commercial poultry production is, in most countries, a high-volume industry and, for this reason, the types of vaccines employed and vaccination techniques required must be fully understood before formulating a vaccination programme. Most diseases encountered are respiratory diseases, and most have a viral aetiology.

There are some basic principles to consider and knowledge required when formulating vaccination programmes. All birds belonging to the same production system should be considered as a single epidemiological unit regardless of geography. Fundamental changes to programmes should be made only after considering the health of the entire operation and ALL diagnostic data available and changes should be made in individual steps and their effects evaluated before making further changes.

Essential knowledge required:

- basic knowledge of poultry diseases (reference books are available);
- local disease types and incidence;
- bird production parameters (some diseases are age related);
- technical knowledge of vaccines available; and
- the current vaccination programme.

But, most importantly, the process must be approached logically.

20.3 Vaccine Types Available

Vaccines are available for most of the infectious agents identified as affecting poultry: viral, bacterial, protozoal and even some ectoparasites. One feature common to all vaccine types is that, for each product, a 'minimum protective dose' is required to be delivered to every bird in the group in order for the product to be effective. This 'minimum protective dose', often referred to as 'full dose', is defined for each product in its development and regulatory process.

There are two basic types of vaccine currently available for poultry although many new technologies are applicable to poultry vaccine development.

*peter.cargill@wyattpoultry.com

© CAB International 2021. *Poultry Health: A Guide for Professionals* (P. Barrow *et al.*)
DOI: 10.1079/9781789245042.0020

Live vaccines:

- naturally occurring apathogenic strains;
- attenuated strains (traditional, auxotrophs, temperature sensitive, precocious);
- vector vaccines; and
- gene-deleted.

Inactivated (killed) vaccines:

- oil adjuvanted; and
- sodium hydroxide adjuvanted.

Due to their nature, there are some differences between these vaccine types. Many live vaccines can be deployed effectively by means of mass vaccination techniques, such as via the drinking water or spray application, whereas others require administration via eye drop, transfixion scarification or injection. Inactivated vaccines require application via individual injection, with both subcutaneous and intramuscular routes commonly in use.

Although there are exceptions, most live vaccines are available in physically compact freeze-dried or frozen preparations, with a long shelf life, whereas inactivated vaccines are bulkier, liquid presentations generally with a relatively short shelf life.

With the exception of live vector vaccines, live vaccines expose birds to the 'normal' pathogenesis of the organism involved and, as such, interact with the birds' immune system in a more diverse manner generating local, cell mediated and humoral immunity. Inactivated vaccines merely present non-viable organisms or fragments thereof that are presented to the immune system over time due to the adjuvant included. They do not follow the 'normal' pathogenesis of the organisms included, although they are generally capable of generating a longer duration of immunity than most live vaccines. One consequence of the fundamental differences between these two vaccine types is that use of live vaccines may expose birds to the potential clinical effects of the organism involved. The effect may or may not be apparent and will depend upon the vaccine in question. However, there are few potential clinical effects of the components of inactivated vaccines other than the physiological effect of the adjuvants commonly included.

Potential interference between live vaccine strains and complex regulatory systems results in a limited number of multivalent live products being available. This is not generally the case with inactivated vaccines, and numerous multivalent products are available.

20.4 Aims of Vaccination for Poultry

The nature of commercial poultry production is such that economic efficiency is paramount, and essential in order to ensure the long-term viability of the industry and its place in providing a high-quality affordable protein source for the local population. To this end, vaccination must have the aim of protecting birds from both clinical and subclinical disease, reduce human risk to zoonotic pathogens such as *Salmonella* (see Chapter 14iv, this volume) and should impact on the following parameters:

- minimize mortality;
- improve growth rate or egg numbers;
- optimize shell quality;
- optimize chick quality;
- improve food conversion ration/utilization;
- minimize factory condemnations; and
- improve food safety.

Our ability to achieve this aim is dependent on the disease level and type, and the choice of vaccine and the method and efficiency of its administration. Some degree of 'interaction' between live vaccines and the bird is essential in order to stimulate an immune response; however, 'adverse' reactions are undesirable and serve no useful purpose in terms of protection. Adverse reactions can manifest in the form of:

- clinical signs (sneezing/coughing etc);
- increased mortality;
- decreased growth rate;
- increased feed conversion ratio;
- increased medication costs; and
- increased factory condemnations.

Factors that can predispose to adverse reactions to live vaccines are:

- failure of a full dose of vaccine being delivered to the entire flock on the same day;
- the vaccine strain deployed and its method of application;
- level of relevant maternal antibody in the vaccinates;
- poor chick quality;
- concurrent immunosuppression;
- age at vaccination;
- down-time between crops and level of terminal hygiene achieved; and
- water, litter and air quality.

20.5 Achieving Effective Vaccination of Poultry

Effective vaccination is achieved by delivering a full dose of vaccine, to all birds within a flock, in a single operation. If this is achieved, it will generate optimal protection from the product concerned, with minimum effect on the biological performance of the flock. However, the ability to achieve this aim is determined by the technical and practical aspects of the administration technique employed.

20.6 Common Methods of Vaccine Administration in Poultry

20.6.1 Administration by spray/aerosol

This route is commonly used to administer live vaccines to birds both at day-old (either in the hatchery or on farm), and during the growing phase on farm. Published studies related to the ideal particle size for administering vaccines report a wide variation which is related to the age of the birds used in the studies, and the use in some studies of solid microspheres which lack the physical properties of water such as polarity and surface tension. From the available data, it is generally accepted that particles less than 10 µm in diameter are undesirable as they may be inhaled far enough into the respiratory tract to cause an adverse reaction to the vaccine strain in use, although some publications report the successful use of particles 2–5 µm in diameter with day-old chicks. The process of evaporation of water droplets can be calculated mathematically and, considering a 'typical' poultry house environment, in order to avoid particles less than 10 µm in diameter at the time birds are exposed, spray equipment that generates particles 50–70 µm in diameter is probably ideal. It should be noted that in hot climates with extremely low humidity, particles generated in this range are likely to have totally evaporated before birds are exposed.

Sprays/aerosols can be generated by several means, the main methods employed in poultry are:

- Pressure – forcing water though a small aperture generating shearing forces on water that results in a wide variation in particle sizes.
- Spinning disc/controlled droplet application – centrifugal technology generating a very consistent particle size.
- Ultrasonic – currently only experimental use generating extremely small consistent particles.

Pressure spray equipment is generally operated at between 2 and 4 bar, and at this pressure a particle range of 30–600 µm is usually generated with the majority of the particles being greater than 100 µm (Figs 20.1 and 20.2).

Due to the relationship between volume and diameter of spheres, increasing the diameter of a droplet tenfold results in an increase in volume 1000-fold. Inhalation of particles in excess of 100 µm in diameter is not possible and such particles are

Fig. 20.1. High speed photograph of particles generated by a pressure nozzle. (Photograph used with permission from Micron Sprayers Ltd.)

most likely to be deposited on the floor, on the feathers of birds or possibly in the eye. Due to the innate behaviour of poultry, droplets that are readily accessible will be taken up orally by birds. When used in a poultry house, the nature of this process results in a large proportion of wasted water and, as such, water volumes are often detailed as a number of litres per 1000 birds when this method is employed in a poultry house. This introduces a practical concern, that of the weight of water required to be carried by the operator which can be in the order of 20 kg. An additional consideration should be that, due to the nature of the process, particles can only travel 50–70 cm from the nozzle so, in order to achieve effective vaccination, the operative must ensure that the nozzle comes within this range of all the birds in the house. In practical terms this is difficult and often results in a poor level vaccination of a flock.

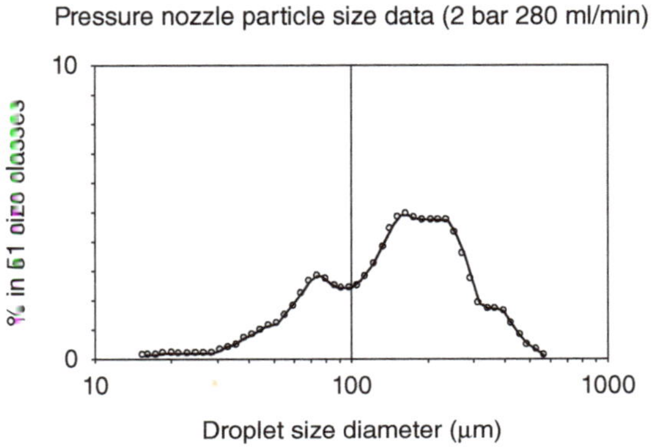

Fig. 20.2. Particle size distribution – pressure nozzle at 2 bar. (Author's own figure.)

Spray administration to day-old chicks in boxes in the hatchery is almost universal. In this situation, pressure equipment can be used successfully as particle size is relatively unimportant, and the main objective is to apply water droplets to the outside of the chicks where they are able to take up the vaccine orally. Effectiveness of the process is determined by the volume of water applied to each box (7.5–25 ml) and the evenness of coverage of the box, as this better facilitates lateral uptake of the drops. Coverage of boxes is variable and depends on the type of equipment in use and the nozzle specification (Fig. 20.3).

Spinning disc/controlled droplet application (CDA) (Fig. 20.4) is technology originally developed for application of insecticides to certain types of crops and is aimed at generating a very specific range of particle size, and minimizing the volumes of water required for application.

The technology is in common use for vaccinating poultry in the housed environment, generates particles

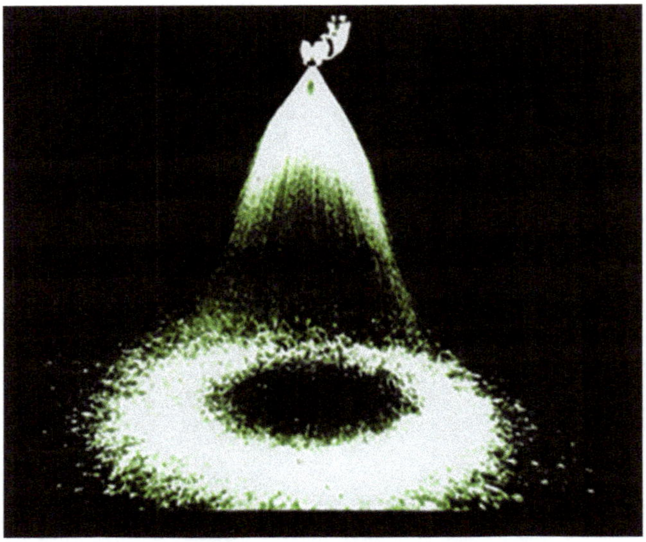

Fig. 20.3. Photograph illustrating a typical physical spray pattern generated by a hollow cone nozzle. Doughnut shaped rather than disc shaped. (Photograph used with permission from Micron Sprayers Ltd.)

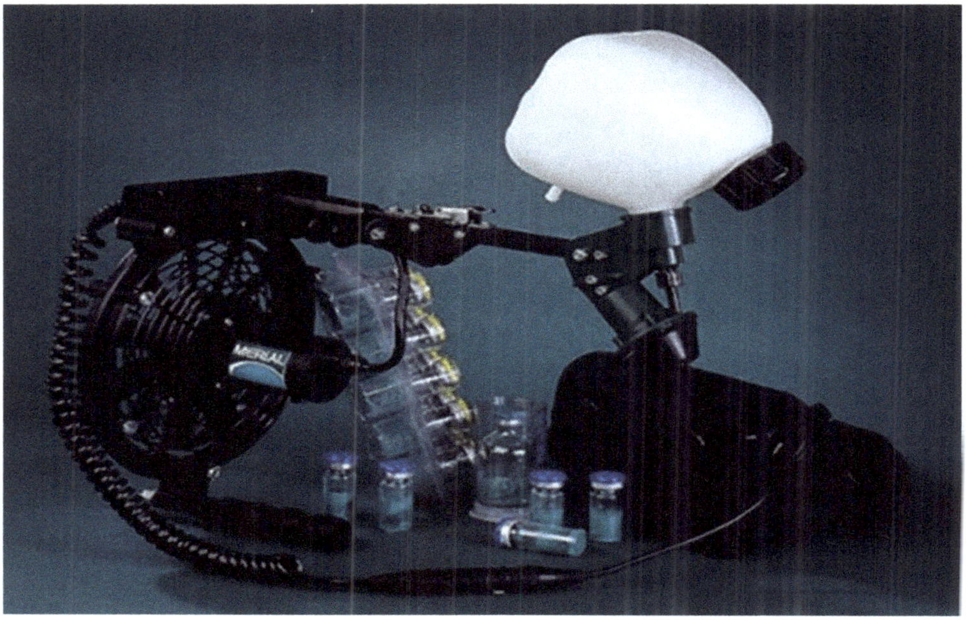

Fig. 20.4. Fan-assisted CDA equipment. (Courtesy of Micron Sprayers.)

in the 70–100 μm range, propels particles approximately 3 m from the equipment and utilizes relatively low volumes of water (1000 ml per 30,000–50,000 birds) (Figs 20.5 and 20.6). The nature of this equipment removes the practical limitations of pressure equipment, as the weight of water required is low and the equipment need only come within 3 m of each bird in order to deliver the vaccine effectively.

Maintaining good hygiene of all spray equipment is essential. Inadvertent bacterial contamination of respiratory disease vaccines results in a synergy that commonly results in acute bacterial septicaemia and associated mortality. *Escherichia coli* (see Chapter 14ii, this volume) and *Pseudomonas* spp. are a particular concern.

Ultrasonic nebulizers (Fig. 20.7) – currently only used experimentally, this type of equipment produces a particle size range of 2–5 μm and has been shown to be effective in immunizing birds with Newcastle disease vaccine (see Chapter 15viii, this volume) and Marek's disease vaccine (see Chapter 15xiii, this volume). Commercial application is complicated by the requirement for an exposure period of circa 2 min, but this technology may be of use in the future.

20.6.2 Administration of vaccines via the drinking water

This method is universally employed for a wide range of live vaccines. In order to be effective, there are some basic principles that should be followed to maximize the vaccine viability and ensure that all birds in the group receive a full protective dose of vaccine:

- Ensure that ALL water that will come in contact with the vaccine is treated with an appropriate stabilizer that is capable of deactivating chlorine and metal ions that are detrimental to vaccine viability.
- Aim to deliver the vaccine to birds over a pre-determined time period, appropriate for the vaccine in use.
- Deliver the vaccine in a pre-determined volume of water that should be calculated from the water consumption recorded during a similar time period the day prior to vaccine administration.

These principles can be achieved in many ways, and the practical method employed should consider the drinker design, plumbing/pipe system, water tank and automatic dosing machine if available. Ideally, drinker systems should be primed with water containing vaccine prior to bird access (Fig. 20.8).

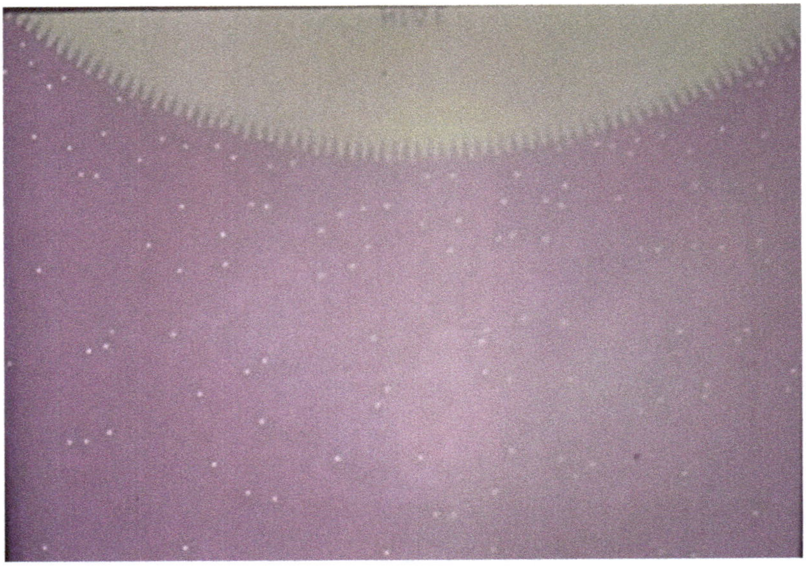

Fig. 20.5. Photograph of particles generated by CDA equipment. (Photograph used with permission from Micron Sprayers Ltd.)

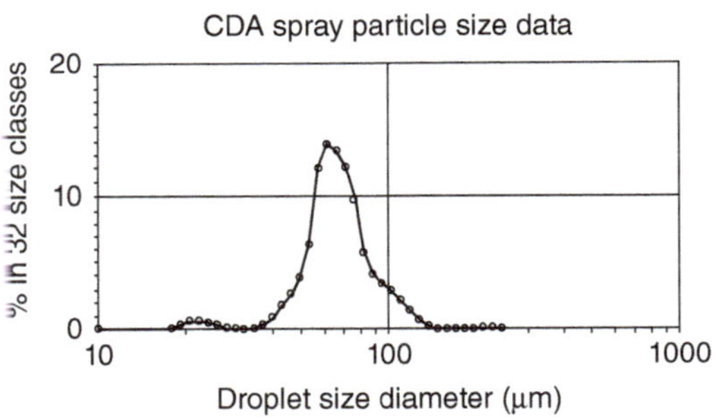

Fig. 20.6. Particle size distribution, CDA equipment. (Author's own figure.)

Water deprivation may encourage the flock to drink over a short period of time. However, deprivation period in excess of 1.5 h or in hot climates is usually detrimental to vaccine uptake. A good standard of water hygiene is desirable in order to avoid potential bacterial disease, and bell drinker systems can present significant hygiene issues (Fig. 20.9) and should be cleaned prior to vaccine administration.

20.6.3 Administration by injection

This method is mainly relevant to the use of inactivated vaccines. However, several live vaccines require injection. As a parenteral route, high quality equipment and needle hygiene are essential in order to avoid bacterial lesions. The most common route is intramuscular into the leg or breast muscles; however, subcutaneous injection into the neck is also common.

Automatically-filling syringes are available, and vaccine is usually available in 1000-dose vials that must be shaken thoroughly before use in order to homogenize the product which may settle during storage. Inactivated vaccines have a high thermal capacity, particularly oil adjuvant products, and should be warmed slowly prior to use in order to minimize the thermal shock to birds. The process should not be rushed, as birds may not receive a full dose of vaccine, and inadvertent injection into the liver or periosteal needle damage should be avoided (Fig. 20.10).

Vaccine preparations may settle on storage and will require thorough mixing prior to use (Fig. 20.11).

When injecting into the neck it is important to avoid damage to essential structures. Needles should be changed at least every 1000 birds, and more frequently for valuable and primary breeding stock.

Unlike most live vaccines, inactivated vaccines present some degree of safety risk to humans if self-injected, or subsequent to needle scratches. Medical attention should be sought after any accidental

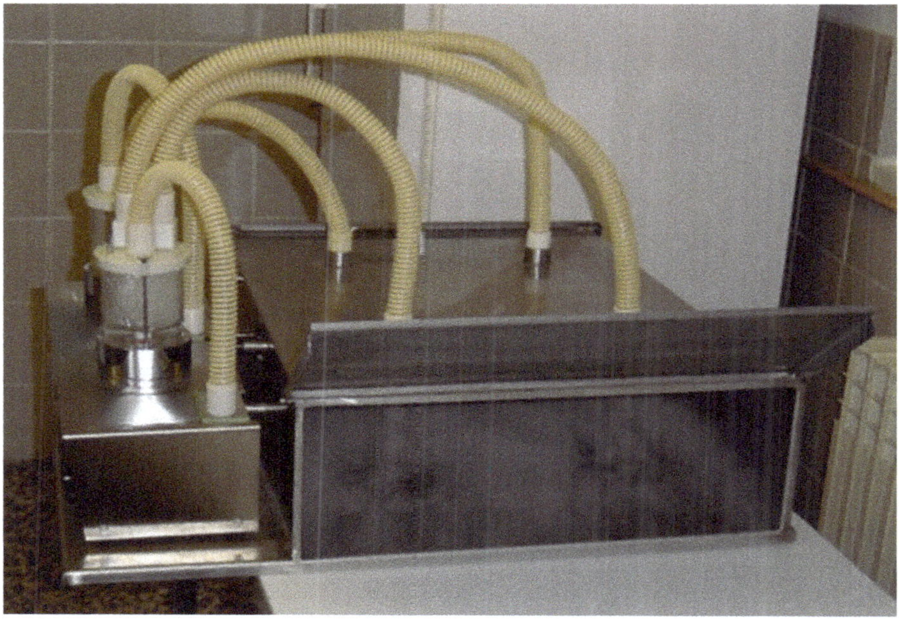

Fig. 20.7. Ultrasonic particle generator (left) and exposure chamber (right). (Author's own photograph.)

Fig. 20.8. Drinker lines should be primed with vaccine prior to allowing bird access. (Author's own photograph.)

injection, as oil emulsion vaccines in particular can result in extensive tissue necrosis and loss of digits. The appropriate vaccine leaflet should always be consulted which will detail the appropriate treatment required.

20.6.4 Administration by eye drop

This is not universally employed due to the cost of labour involved. However, this route is the most effective for all live respiratory vaccines and many others. The process involves individual handling of

Fig. 20.9. Bell drinkers should be cleaned prior to vaccination. (Author's own photograph.)

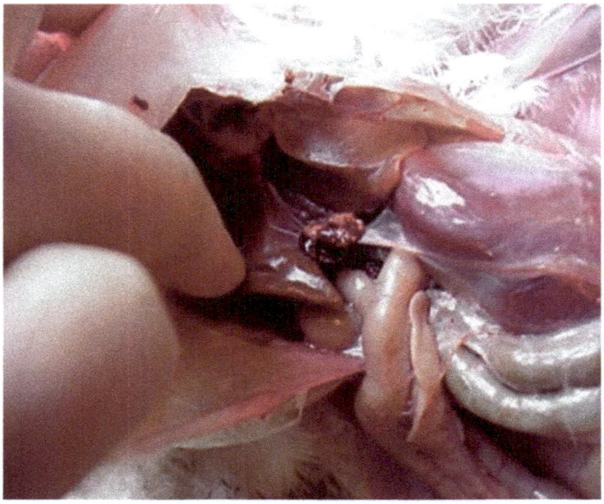

Fig. 20.10. Injecting vaccine into the liver usually results in sudden death. (Author's own photograph.)

each bird (Fig. 20.12) in the group and the administration of more than the minimum protective dose of vaccine due to the nature of vaccine titres. The process must not be rushed, and care must be taken to ensure that the drop disperses across the eye rather than 'rolling off' due to surface tension effects. Specific diluent and dropper tips are made available by vaccine manufacturers, and dyes can be included in order to audit the effectiveness of the process if required. Dye should be found throughout the nasal and buccal cavities and often in the crop indicating widespread delivery of vaccine to the essential target tissues.

20.6.5 Transfixion and scarification

Often referred to as 'wing web stab', this method of application is used exclusively for administering fowlpox vaccines. However, combined fowlpox/avian encephalomyelitis vaccines (see Chapters 15xiv and 15ii, respectively, this volume) are available in some areas of the world. The wing web is the most common site used (although the thigh or foot may also be used as a suitable site) and application is accomplished with the use of a dedicated high-grade stainless steel, two-pronged device. The process is labour intensive and, in order to avoid classical fowlpox lesions, care must be taken to avoid the vaccine coming into contact with birds' eyes or mouth. Use of the wing web as a site of administration commonly can lead to issues with clinical lesions when birds place their head beneath the wing when sleeping.

Fig. 20.11. Normal settlement of inactivated oil vaccine during storage. (Author's own photograph.)

20.6.6 *In ovo* administration

A novel concept in vaccine administration was developed in the late 1980s–early 1990s, this technique delivering vaccine through the shell of an embryonating egg and into the amniotic fluid or directly into the embryo. The process is automated and currently there are several different types of equipment available each with their advantages and disadvantages. Primarily used for Marek's disease vaccination, there is a variability in use of this technique due to the routine or non-routine vaccination for Marek's disease between different countries. However, due to the increase in availability of vector vaccines based on Marek's disease vaccine, the use of *in ovo* vaccination is likely to increase in the near future.

Vaccination is usually carried out during the transfer process from setters to hatcher, and the equipment available is complex in order to provide a fully automated process (Figs 20.13 and 20.14). However, this complexity leads to increased risk, in particular related to bacterial and fungal contamination of eggs. Various means of sanitizing the needles involved have been developed by the various manufacturers in order to minimize bacterial contamination and transfer of pathogens between eggs. Accidental contamination of the process/equipment with live egg-attenuated vaccine types such as

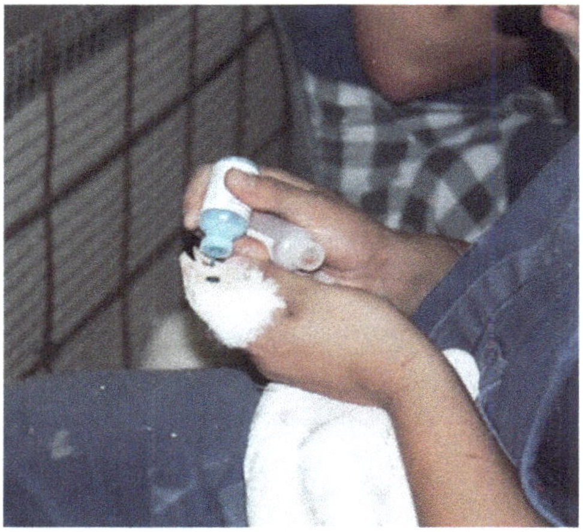

Fig. 20.12. Manual eye dropping of vaccine. (Author's own photograph.)

Fig. 20.13. Eggs stabilized prior to injection. (Author's own photograph.)

infectious bronchitis (see Chapter 15x, this volume) results in devastating drops in hatchability, as does extensive bacterial contamination.

20.6.7 Administration using gels

Aimed at vaccinating day-old chicks, this is a relatively new concept whereby the vaccine is disseminated in a thick viscous carrier that is dribbled on to birds via a multi-nozzle manifold (Figs 20.15 and 20.16).

The surface tension properties of the gel facilitate lateral oral uptake from neighbouring chicks. All droplets are consumed by chicks in less than 2 min and studies have demonstrated widespread distribution of the gel in the nasal and oral cavities, oesophagus, crop and gizzard within 5 min of ingestion. Several different products are now available, some containing dye to allow auditing of uptake. Overall, the process improved the efficiency of vaccine uptake and reduced waste, although some machinery available for administration is complex and can be difficult to manage from a hygiene perspective. An added benefit of this process is that chicks do not risk chilling from the evaporative effect of water sprays (Fig. 20.17).

Fig. 20.14. Equipment is complex and presents hygiene and maintenance issues. (Author's own photograph.)

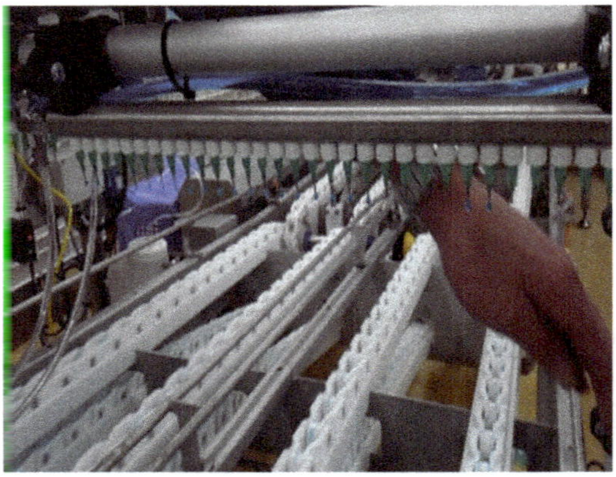

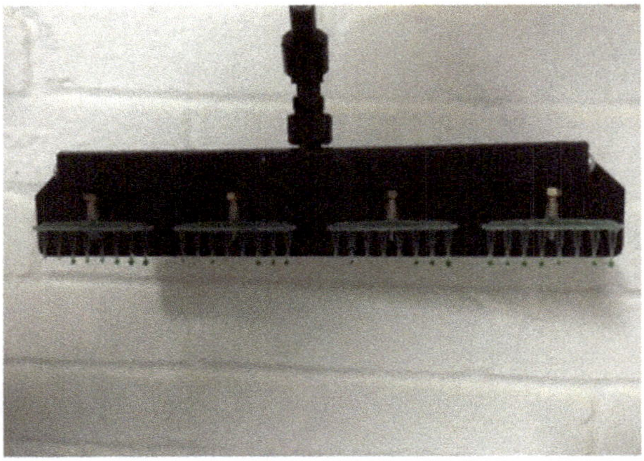

Figs 20.15 and 20.16. Examples of gel manifolds in use. (Author's own photographs.)

Fig. 20.17. Chicks shortly after application of gel. (Author's own photograph.)

20.7 Conclusion

There are numerous techniques and varied equipment available for vaccine administration. Vaccine suppliers are usually able to offer advice on the best method and equipment for administration of their products. However, it is important to consider both the technical attributes of any technique or equipment together with the practical benefits/limitations of them in the environment in which the product will be used prior to making any decision.

20.8 Further Reading

Cserep, T. (2008) Vaccines and vaccination. In: Pattison, M., McMullin, P.F., Bradbury, J.M. and Alexander, D. (eds) *Poultry Diseases*, 6th edn. Elsevier, London, pp. 66–81.

Collett, S.R. (2013) Principles of disease prevention, diagnosis and control: Introduction. In: Swayne, D.E. (ed.-in-chief) *Diseases of Poultry,* 13th edn. Wiley, Hoboken, New Jersey, pp. 34–38.

21 How to Carry Out a Field Investigation

PAUL MCMULLIN*

Poultry Health International, Thirsk, North Yorkshire, UK

21.1 Introduction

While a great deal of our work in poultry medicine is focused on preventative medicine, including good management, pathogen eradication or exclusion programmes, vaccination and health monitoring, things will go wrong from time to time and require investigation. Some such investigations can readily be carried out by receiving appropriate samples for examination, but field visits can provide the opportunity for a more thorough investigation. Carrying out such investigations effectively offers many opportunities for professional development and learning, as well as supporting a client at a difficult time. Field investigations can require not just the, for us, conventional skills of the clinician, microbiologist, epidemiologist and pathologist, but also those of a psychologist, detective and puzzle enthusiast! While some investigations will identify a simple single-disease cause, the effective controls already applied for such diseases increase the likelihood that it will be something more complex, and may even be, in some respects at least, something new. The client may not care about the technical niceties (though clients in the poultry industry are often the most technically savvy of all veterinary clients), but they will be particularly interested in what they can do to solve the problem.

21.2 How Can the Request for a Field Investigation Arise?

This will nearly always happen when someone in the poultry production system has recognized that there is a problem and has decided they need an answer. This may be because submission of samples for laboratory investigation have not arrived at that answer, or at least not suggested a route to a solution.

Sometimes a problem has been recognized but no laboratory investigation has been carried out, perhaps because no facilities for this are locally available.

It may be because an investigation has arrived at an answer, but a second opinion is requested. This may, for instance be because a dispute is underway or anticipated.

21.3 Industry Structure and Quality Systems

The poultry industry varies in structure within and between countries. There is a general 'production chain' stretching from primary breeding organizations, through commercial breeding companies and hatcheries to those farms producing final product – meat birds or eggs, and then the processor or egg packer which are often the interface with retailers. The degree of integration across multiple segments of this chain varies. When carrying out field investigations it is important to have a good grasp on the relationships that are involved, because solutions may sometimes require actions by different participants and have different possible timelines. It is also useful to understand the nature, objectives and requirements of quality assurance schemes because of their potential to highlight issues and provide a framework for arriving at the required solutions. Examples of assurance schemes operated in the UK include organic standards (https://www.gov.uk/government/publications/organic-certification-list-of-uk-approved-organic-control-bodies/approved-uk-organic-control-bodies), the Defra Poultry Health Scheme (mainly adopted by breeding and hatcheries –

*paulmcmullin@poultryhealthinternational.net

© CAB International 2021. *Poultry Health: A Guide for Professionals* (P. Barrow *et al.*)
DOI: 10.1079/9781789245042.0021

https://assets.publishing.service.gov.uk/government/uploads/system/uploads/attachment_data/file/377556/phs-handbook.pdf) , the British Lion scheme for egg production (https://www.egginfo.co.uk/british-lion-eggs) and the Red Tractor Scheme (https://assurance.redtractor.org.uk/) for meat production.

A well-recognized system for applying scientific principles to quality improvement in industry and agriculture is the 'Shewhart/Deming Cycle' or 'PDCA (Plan Do Check Adjust) Cycle' (Fig. 21.1). This is simply the application of scientific methodology to the task of improving productivity and quality in industry and agriculture. It makes sense to consider an investigation, starting with a question and, hopefully, resulting in an answer, to be one side of a PDCA cycle. If the 'answer' does not make it possible to make an adjustment, plan and implement a solution, then the objective has probably not been achieved. Even if it does suggest a solution, it will usually be necessary to carry out further checks to ensure that the solution has worked.

21.4 Steps in Carrying Out a Field Investigation

21.4.1 Step 1: Describe the problem/question

It can be helpful to start off the process (usually as part of an initial consultation) by taking a brief history of the circumstances with a view to formulating a concise description of the nature of the problem to be investigated. It will often be something new, or at least newly recognized, though it may be something seen historically which has recurred. Describing timelines (When did it start? Has it become worse at a particular time?) may help focus subsequent data collection and analysis on the most relevant period. It would be worthwhile determining whether there are any differences of opinion as to the existence or manifestation of the problem.

Try to describe the problem in general or, if appropriate, in detail without considering a diagnosis e.g. loss of weight gain, increased liver lesions, etc. If it is a complex issue it may be helpful to break it into its component parts.

Sometimes it is helpful to look at the 'flip-side' of the question, or change the focus from what is happening to what is not happening. Alternatively, try shifting the frame of reference and ask how the bird sees/appreciate the problem, i.e. whether it is in some way dissatisfied with its environment, or has it just 'decided not to lay'!

Having identified the basic question, it will be a good point to clarify if there are particular time constraints on field investigations, logistics and farm contact details, and provide an estimate of when it can be carried out and a time frame for preliminary and final reporting.

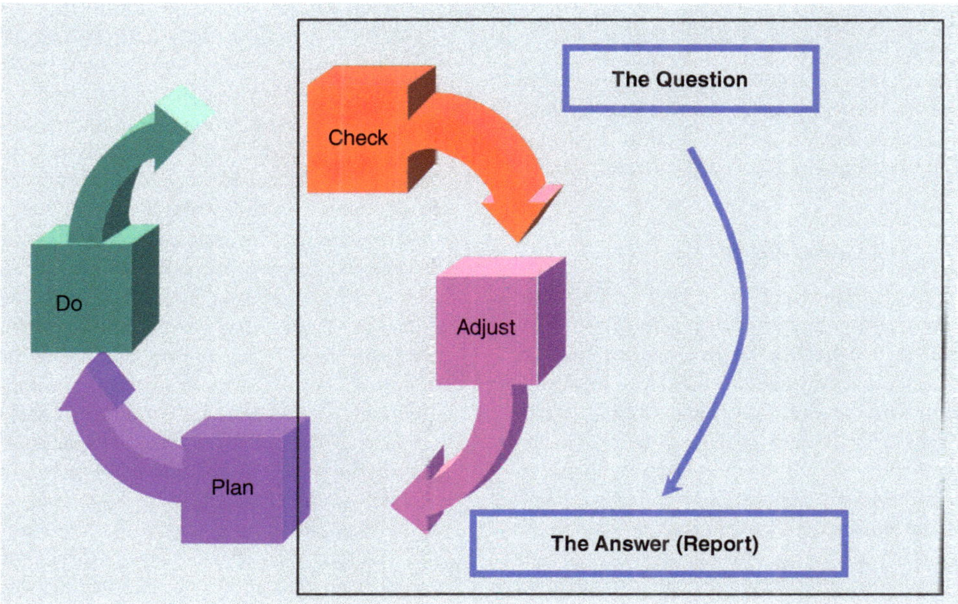

Fig. 21.1. The Shewhart/Deming or PDCA cycle. (Author's own image.)

If it is a problem involving different parties, particularly if there is an actual or potential legal dispute, the investigator must be clear as to who he/she is acting for and the appropriate chain of communication.

21.4.2 Step 2: Make observations and collect data

Prepare for field visit

It is usually preferable to check in advance biosecurity policies, availability of protective clothing, etc. It is wise, however, to have spare disposable overalls and overboots just in case. Check in advance any policies in relation to mobile phone/camera use on site. Sometimes the site will need to get approval to allow this and/or be required to provide an on-site camera. Site preparedness for hosting the visit may give an indication of how well they understand and put into practice the principles of biosecurity. It will often be necessary to bring along a 'post-mortem (PM) kit' including gloves, shears, and sampling materials – typically containers, transport swabs for bacteriology, buffered formalin pots and FTA cards. Depending on the environmental conditions and the sort of samples to be collected, it may be helpful to have cool-boxes with ice-packs available. If the investigator is unfamiliar with the detail of the production system that will be visited, it may be helpful to seek guidance from colleagues who are more familiar. Farm staff will expect a visiting veterinarian to have a reasonable understanding of normal production processes, bird movements, hatcheries, breeding, etc., but are nearly always keen to help by providing detailed information.

Site arrival

Contact farm management on arrival and be prepared to provide identification as required. Establish a methodical, cordial working environment, as farm staff will have very useful knowledge and their cooperation will be mutually beneficial. Confirm that any birds that have been culled or died in the 24 h prior to the visit will be held securely in a cool location (not frozen).

Follow the biosecurity procedures as instructed, usually starting with the sign-in, possibly one or more showers-in, and changes into protective clothing. The PM kit will usually be left in a suitable location for PM examinations.

Take the history

As in all veterinary investigations, it is helpful to have a structured approach to collecting background information. Poultry farms will usually have Veterinary Health and Welfare plans; at their best these will include details of management and veterinary actions throughout the flock history. Production charts will also usually be available in various formats. Enquire whether this information can be made available electronically as this may avoid the need to re-enter data if detailed analysis is required. It is still helpful to photograph the relevant documents on farm, particularly as they may have detailed annotations not present on the electronic versions.

Figure 21.2 shows a sample submission form for post-mortem examination. This can also be helpful when collecting history during a field investigation.

Carry out flock visit

Take note of general tidiness *en route* from the site entrance to the poultry house, in particular any evidence of biosecurity hazards such as rodent harbourages and wild bird activity.

Follow the standard biosecurity precautions as practiced on site for entry into the service area, and thence into bird areas. Entry directly into bird areas may be encountered in some countries but signifies a lower level of biosecurity. Further history taking may be relevant in the service area (records not encountered in previous history taking).

In carrying out the flock inspection, follow the lead of farm staff. Value their observations and knowledge, but use all senses to observe both the environment and the birds. It may be necessary to request that light intensity is increased to facilitate the process. Observe the general distribution of the flock within the available space prior to entry, then walk the floor area slowly and methodically, observing general behaviour and individuals who 'stand out' because they are behaving differently in some way. Observe the litter quality, faecal consistency, any evidence of rodent or ectoparasite activity and anything else which might be relevant to the problem under investigation. Question observations throughout the visit. Try to establish the 'Who, What, Why, When?' Ensure that any questioning is neutral and open. Be alert for things that feel 'not quite right'. While bringing all experience and knowledge to bear, take care not to close out

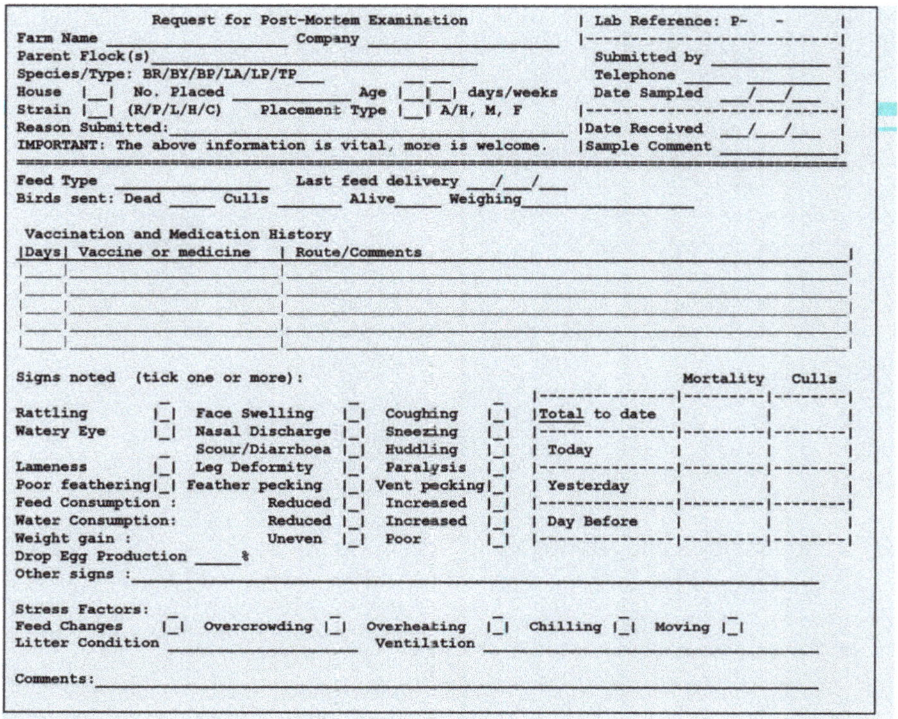

Request for Post-Mortem Examination | Lab Reference: P- -
Farm Name ____ Company ____
Parent Flock(s) ____ Submitted by ____
Species/Type: BR/BY/BP/LA/LP/TP ___ Telephone ____
House |_| No. Placed ____ Age |_|_| days/weeks Date Sampled __/__/__
Strain |_| (R/P/L/H/C) Placement Type |_| A/H, M, F
Reason Submitted: ____ |Date Received __/__/__
IMPORTANT: The above information is vital, more is welcome. |Sample Comment ____

Feed Type ____ Last feed delivery __/__/__
Birds sent: Dead ____ Culls ____ Alive ____ Weighing ____

Vaccination and Medication History

Days	Vaccine or medicine	Route/Comments

Signs noted (tick one or more):

Rattling |_| Face Swelling |_| Coughing |_|
Watery Eye |_| Nasal Discharge |_| Sneezing |_|
Scour/Diarrhoea |_| Huddling |_|
Lameness |_| Leg Deformity |_| Paralysis |_|
Poor feathering |_| Feather pecking |_| Vent pecking |_|
Feed Consumption : Reduced |_| Increased |_|
Water Consumption: Reduced |_| Increased |_|
Weight gain : Uneven |_| Poor |_|
Drop Egg Production ___%
Other signs : ____

	Mortality	Culls
Total to date		
Today		
Yesterday		
Day Before		

Stress Factors:
Feed Changes |_| Overcrowding |_| Overheating |_| Chilling |_| Moving |_|
Litter Condition ____ Ventilation ____

Comments: ____

Fig. 21.2. Example of a post-mortem (PM) submission form. (Author's own image.)

lines of thought. Have full regard for the accumulated wisdom and knowledge of other technical staff, veterinary, agricultural and nutritionist, as well as that for farm management and even junior members of staff. On the other hand, a fresh pair of eyes is a distinct advantage, so it is wise to be kind when pointing out something simple which has been missed in the hurly-burly of day-to-day operations.

Wherever possible, document observations with photographs. Pick up any recently dead birds and segregate birds that should be culled on humane grounds or with significant disease for diagnostic purposes. Any segregated live birds should be kept in a container identified to the flock and transported to the location used for on-site PM examinations. On-site investigations enable accurate selection of the samples most likely to be relevant to the type of problem under investigation.

Post-mortem examination

Field PM examinations can present some challenges in terms of the available facilities, but on the other hand they have the advantage of self-selected very fresh material, and farm staff are often interested in the process so it can provide some training opportunities. Aim to carry it out in a location protected from weather, but with good illumination. Treat the carcasses and any fluids as potentially infectious so ensure that carcasses and fluids are contained, and materials disinfected as required.

Cull live birds humanely, weigh carcasses and proceed with a standard post-mortem approach, working methodically to examine all relevant systems. This should include external examination prior to opening the body cavity and may require more detailed work on the skeletal or nervous system in some circumstances.

Collect samples for bacteriology from organs showing lesions prior to opening intestines (bone marrow culture is usually preferable in birds that have already died, because of post-mortem spread of bacteria from the gut to viscera).

If intending to collect samples for histopathology, take care to collect and fix the samples as soon as possible – particularly if the sample is from the intestine. Handle tissues gently, and cut small samples (up to 1 cm^3, including areas of normal tissue and lesion where evident. Immerse in neutral buffered formal saline at a ratio of 1:10 v/v. Small samples should be fully fixed in 1–2 days. Store at room temperature while fixing.

When collecting materials take care not to contaminate the outside of containers.

Record weight, sex, whether culled or dead, and the findings encountered in each bird on a suitable form adapted to the IT system to be used to generate a report.

Note: If at any point in the investigation it is suspected that notifiable disease is present on site, then the veterinary authorities should be notified, and no material should be removed from site unless specifically licensed.

In all other situations, samples should be packed appropriately in a manner to avoid leakage and any contamination (double-bagged, including absorbent material when liquid is involved).

21.4.3 Step 3: Turn the data into knowledge

The post-visit phase involves collating the information collected at the time, often analysis of other data sets requested during or after the visit, integrated with general and clinical observations, and results of further testing. This phase is highly variable and can range from a simple PM report with some laboratory confirmation to extensive data analysis. It is often helpful to review photographs taken on site at leisure, sometimes it is possible to note things not observed during the visit. Identification of the site on Google Earth may allow confirmation of when houses were built, changing vegetation patterns, etc.

Throughout the process, maintain the main focus on the question being investigated. Working through the analysis and as a hypothesis emerges, identify data that support or illustrate the analysis, but also data that argue against it. Does the analysis confirm that the original question illustrates a problem? Do the data show something else? Where possible, plan to illustrate the information graphically.

If enough information is not obtained from the investigation, is it available elsewhere? Don't forget to consider 'Who knows more about it than I do?'. This may be colleagues in practice, in diagnostic laboratories, research organizations and in the pharmaceutical industry.

Be on the look-out for 'accidental experiments', perhaps because a vaccine was not applied, or equipment failure resulted in some birds or even flocks being subject to an unintentional change. Identifying this may point towards causation, and sometimes even solutions.

It may be necessary to ask whether a field trial is useful, or, perhaps, essential.

21.4.4 Step 4: Formulate the answer

'*Remember there are 3 solutions to every problem, and usually the first one you think of is not the optimal one*' (Keith Gooderham).

The report of the investigation is the product and, hopefully will be eagerly anticipated and provide the client with a solution or at least a way forward towards a solution. It should address the following simple questions:

What is a one sentence description of the problem?
Who identified the problem?
Is the problem real?
What evidence is available? (as recorded data or anecdotal evidence).
What further questions need to be asked?
How can the answers to these be obtained?
Are further investigations necessary?
Are any solutions possible/available?
Was the question the right one? (An opportunity to point towards other issues which might benefit from investigation.)

21.5 Conclusions

The better the investigator is at proactively implementing effective preventative medicine, the fewer high-profile investigations will be needed. However, the same principles apply for routine site visits for health monitoring, so the skills are important to cultivate and practice. Because of success in controlling text-book disease, the investigator is more likely to be dealing with multifactorial problems with elements of environmental control, management, parasites, infections, nutrition, genetics, etc. With complex issues it may be helpful to collaborate with colleagues nationally and internationally to increase the pool of knowledge to our mutual benefit.

21.6 Acknowledgement

This chapter is based on the presentation originally developed by Keith Gooderham for the Poultry Health Course. Sadly, he died shortly before this was written. Nevertheless, he contributed both in providing the original presentation and his generous sharing of experience and his optimistic philosophy over many years.

22 Laboratory Diagnosis of Poultry Diseases

Susan Baigent[1]*, Vivien Coward[2], Scott Reid[2], Rowena Hansen[2], Vanessa Ceeraz[2] and Paul Barrow[3]

[1]*Viral Oncogenesis Group, The Pirbright Institute, Woking, Surrey, UK;* [2]*Avian Virology Investigation Unit, APHA, Addlestone, Surrey, UK;* [3]*School of Veterinary Medicine, University of Surrey, Guildford, UK*

22.1 Overview

When investigating a case, the clinician may consider the use of laboratory-based tests as part of the diagnostic process. Clinical signs and gross lesions alone are usually insufficient for unambiguous diagnosis of an infectious disease as few diseases of poultry elicit pathognomonic signs, and indeed concomitant infection or disease syndromes are not uncommon. Some infections may simply manifest as subclinical and only become apparent after the interrogation of production records. Differential diagnosis and confirmation require demonstration of the presence of the causative pathogen(s). The main types of laboratory tests are classical tests (conventional methods to detect the pathogen, and serological methods to detect antibodies against the pathogen) and molecular methods to detect the pathogen's genetic material. Sensitivity and specificity of the methods vary. Molecular tests have many advantages (and some disadvantages) over conventional methods (Table 22.1) but, often, an integrated approach, using a combination of these methods, is used for rapid and conclusive identification of a pathogen. Rapid diagnosis is essential, allowing control measures to be put in place to prevent spread of disease. Validation and standardization of tests and compliance with national accreditation bodies is essential to demonstrate that tests are reliable, reproducible and fit for purpose. For all methods, use of positive and negative controls is essential to confirm test specificity. This chapter acquaints the reader with the tests, optimal sample types and storage requirements for laboratory diagnosis of avian diseases, and opportunities for differential diagnoses. The principles underpinning the tests and the advantages and limitations of each are described.

This chapter contains references to many pathogens mentioned in greater detail in other chapters in this book and the reader should refer to individual chapters where appropriate.

22.2 Sample Types, Sample Handling and Storage

Care is required during sampling, as zoonotic agents could potentially be present. Samples should reflect clinical presentation and the replication or shedding sites of the pathogen: tracheal/oropharyngeal swabs or lung samples for respiratory pathogens, cloacal swabs or intestinal tract for enteric pathogens, blood or organs for systemically replicating pathogens, brain for neurological pathogens and feathers for viruses which replicate in the skin. Samples for isolation of live pathogen *must* be collected fresh and aseptically to minimize contamination, and preferably during the acute phase of the disease. Organ samples should be collected from freshly culled or recently dead birds while swabs and feathers can be collected from live birds. Poultry house 'dust' is a particularly useful environmental sample for molecular detection of multiple pathogens that are shed by infected birds; it is easy

*Corresponding author: sue.baigent@pirbright.ac.uk

© CAB International 2021.
DOI: 10.1079/9781789245042.0022

Table 22.1. Comparison of conventional and molecular methods for pathogen detection.

Conventional methods for pathogen detection	Molecular methods for pathogen detection
Fresh samples required to ensure pathogen remains live	No need for fresh samples (frozen or fixed samples may be used)
Time-consuming	Reduced time – rapid results
Labour-intensive (low throughput)	Reduced labour (high throughput)
Equipment relatively inexpensive	Equipment relatively expensive for most methods
Less sensitive	Highly sensitive
Can be quantitative	Can be quantitative, over many orders of magnitude
Only detect live infectious pathogen	Detect presence of non-viable pathogen, as well as infectious pathogen
Do not detect latent pathogen	Detect latent pathogen
Distinction between strains or serotypes is more difficult	Distinction between strains or serotypes is usually straightforward
Differentiation of vaccinated and infected birds can be difficult	Differentiation of vaccinated and infected birds is relatively straightforward for most pathogens
Pen-side tests often not possible	Some pen-side tests available
Isolation yields viable pathogen for further studies	Does not yield viable pathogen for further studies

to collect and gives an overall picture of contamination of the birds' environment.

Serum samples taken during the convalescent phase are used to detect an immune response. Removal of serum from the clot prior to submission helps maintain serum integrity and avoid haemolysis. For effective antigen detection and isolation, swabs used for sampling should have plastic or wire-shafts as the components of wooden-shafted swabs interfere with the polymerase chain reaction.

To preserve antigen integrity, clinical samples should be despatched to the diagnostic laboratory in the appropriate medium, usually on ice or at 4°C. Should delays in shipment be anticipated, samples should be kept frozen. Transportation of the samples and correct packaging should be taken into consideration and should comply with road/air transport regulations and guidelines associated with biological material transfer.

22.3 Conventional Methods

22.3.1 Bacterial isolation and identification

Culture is historically the 'gold-standard' method and always associated with Koch's postulates. However, in many cases for the veterinary and human medical fields, this is being replaced by molecular methods, either entirely by analysing the DNA content of tissue samples, or by replacing the time-consuming role of biochemistry in species identification followed frequently by additional typing methods, including serotyping (based on serological agglutination) and phage typing to identify individual strains. Even with more conventional approaches to diagnosis, culture may not always be used. Microorganisms such as the mycobacteria are slow growing, requiring 2–4 weeks for colonies to become sufficiently visible for further identification. In this case, a combination of pathology and microscopy provides a more rapid diagnosis, tentative but sufficient for further decisions on treatment, slaughter, etc.

Reference should be made to the relevant chapters for the most appropriate method for culture and identification for the major bacterial pathogens. Table 22.2 shows the main cultural approaches for the bacterial pathogens covered by this book.

It must also be remembered that serological tests, particularly agglutination or ELISA (Section 22.4.4), are used frequently for monitoring flocks for the presence of organisms such as *Salmonella* and *Mycoplasma*.

22.3.2 Parasite identification

In the vast majority of cases, morphological approaches are still the main means of parasite identification, whether this be microscopy of oocysts for *Eimeria* spp., or gross morphology for helminths. These are covered in Chapters 16i–16iii.

22.3.3 Virus isolation (VI)

Pathogens require a living host or living cultured cells in order to replicate. For VI, fresh viable samples

Table 22.2. Cultural and morphological approaches to bacterial diagnosis.

Bacterial pathogen	Sample	Culture medium	Other	Chapter reference
Mycobacterium avium	Lesions	Supplemented Middlebrook agar, slow growing	Ziehl–Neelsen staining of lesions	14i
Avian pathogenic *Escherichia coli* (APEC)	Lesions	MacConkey or Eosin-Methylene Blue agar	Serology of colonies for serotype	14ii
Campylobacter	Faeces	CCDA agar, microaerophilic, 42°C	Bacterial morphology	14iii
Salmonella	Faeces (all serotypes) Also liver and spleen for *S.* Gallinarum and *S.* Pullorum	Brilliant Green or XLD agar, enrichment with Rappaport-Vassiliadis or Selenite broth	Serology for serotype important	14iv
Clostridium perfringens	Faeces or mucosa	Blood agar, anaerobic (haemolytic)	PCR for *netB*, numerous large Gram+ rods in lesions	14v
Pasteurella multocida	Blood or liver	Blood agar improved by 5% heat-treated serum	Live smears for capsulate bacteria	14vi
Ornithobacterium rhinotracheale	Trachea, lungs, air sacs	Sheep blood agar, microaerophilic	Colony PCR or ELISA for confirmation	14vi
Avibacterium paragallinarum	Trachea and respiratory tract	Sheep blood, 5–10% CO_2	Colony or tissue PCR for confirmation	14vi
Gallibacterium anatis	Reproductive tract	Blood agar	Biochemistry or PCR	14vi
Riemerella anatipestifer	Respiratory tract, brain, bone marrow	Blood or chocolate agar, 5–10% CO_2	Colony PCR for confirmation	14vi
Brachyspira	Faeces or mucosa	Blood agar, anaerobic	Morphology by microscopy, PCR for confirmation	14vii
Mycoplasma	Nasal swabs and respiratory tract	Complex media with yeast and heat-inactivated serum, slow growing	Confirm by immunofluorescence or PCR	14viii
Erysipelas	Liver, spleen, haemorrhagic lesions	Blood agar and variety of media to suppress contaminants, microaerophilic	Gram stain and microscopy	14ix
Staphylococcus	Lesions	Blood agar, haemolytic	Gram stain and microscopy	14ix
Chlamydophila	Respiratory tract	Embryonated eggs	PCR for confirmation Cell lines including Vero and HeLa used for culturing	14x
Bordetella avium	Mid-trachea	Blood or brain heart infusion agar	PCR or immunofluorescence for confirmation	14x

from chickens are inoculated into a live host (*in vivo*), live embryonated eggs (*in ovo*), live tissue culture (*ex vivo*) or live cell culture (*in vitro*) for ongoing propagation of the virus. The virus isolated by VI can then be harvested, and stocks prepared and frozen for further investigation. Table 22.3 provides a summary of avian viruses, sample types for diagnostic investigation, and available classical tests.

Table 22.3. Overview of avian viruses, optimal sample types for diagnostic investigation and available classical tests.

Viral pathogen (family) and example	Sample	Test(s) available	Chapter reference
Reoviridae; Avian rotavirus	Faeces, intestinal contents	Direct electron microscopy (EM), cell culture	15i
Reoviridae; Avian reovirus	Swabs, serum, tendons	Cell cultures (preferred)/VI in eggs, EM, agar gel immunodiffusion test (AGIDT)	15i
Picornaviridae; Duck hepatitis virus type 1	Swabs, serum, kidney, viscera, spleen	Cell cultures, virus neutralization test (VNT)	15ii
Adenoviridae; Egg drop syndrome virus	Swabs, faeces, serum, pharynx, kidney	Virus dependent Cell cultures (preferred)/VI in eggs, EM, AGIDT, haemagglutination inhibition test (HAIT)	15iii
Pneumoviridae; Avian metapneumovirus	Nasal secretions or tissue scraped from the sinuses of affected birds, serum	VI in eggs, tracheal organ cultures, ELISA	15ix
Birnaviridae; Infectious bursal disease virus	Serum, muscle, intestines, kidney, spleen, bursa	Immunofluorescence, immunostaining, VI in eggs, VNT, ELISA, AGIDT	15v
Astroviridae; Avian nephritis virus	Swabs, serum, intestinal contents	VI in eggs, ELISA, EM	15vi
Orthomyxoviridae; Avian influenza A virus	Swabs, serum, brain, lung, trachea, intestinal contents, viscera	VI in eggs, HAIT, ELISA, AGIDT	15vii
Paramyxoviridae; Avian paramyxovirus type 1 (APMV-1)	Swabs, serum, brain, lung, trachea, intestinal contents, viscera	VI in eggs/cell culture, HAIT, AGIDT	15viii
Circoviridae; Beak and feather disease virus	Serum, feathers, liver, bile and faeces	HAIT, ELISA	15xi
Retroviridae; Avian sarcoma leukosis virus	Serum, liver, spleen, bursa	Immunohistochemistry, ELISA	15xii
Coronaviridae; Infectious bronchitis virus	Swabs, serum, trachea, caecal tonsil, kidney	VI in eggs, tracheal organ cultures, HAIT	15x
Herpesviridae; Duck viral enteritis virus	Swabs, serum, liver, pancreas, lungs, kidney, caeca, oesophagus, spleen	Cell cultures (preferred)/VI in eggs, VNT	9, 15xiii
Parvoviridae; Goose parvovirus	Swabs, serum, heart, bursa, liver, spleen, pancreas	Cell cultures/VI in eggs, VNT	
Poxviridae; Fowlpox virus	Tissues containing lesions, swabs	VI in eggs, EM	15xiv

Virus isolation in eggs

VI in specific pathogen-free (SPF) or specific antibody-negative (SAN) embryonated fowls' eggs is the gold standard and remains the most relied-upon isolation method for certain viruses such as avian influenza virus (AIV) and Newcastle disease virus (NDV) (OIE, 2019). However, embryonated eggs can be used to isolate viruses responsible for a wide range of exotic and endemic avian viral diseases including paramyxoviruses, adenoviruses, poxviruses, infectious bronchitis virus (IBV), herpesviruses, reoviruses, duck hepatitis virus (DHV) and goose parvovirus (GPV).

At the veterinary laboratory, tissue samples are homogenized and added to phosphate buffered saline (PBS) containing antibiotics to reduce the risk of bacterial growth. Samples are then incubated for an hour, clarified and inoculated into embryonated eggs (Fig. 22.1). Swabs are processed into brain heart infusion broth (BHIB) containing antibiotics for 2 min prior to inoculation.

The source of the embryonated eggs depends on the virus/disease under investigation, for example: for isolation of AIV, avian paramyxovirus type 1 (APMV-1) and IBV, embryonated chicken eggs are required, whereas embryonated duck eggs are more appropriate for isolation of DHV or GPV. Importantly, the age of the embryonated eggs must be appropriate for the disease under investigation. For the propagation of AIV and APMV-1, 9–11-day-old chicken embryos must be used. The route of inoculation into the embryonated egg (shown in Fig. 22.1) and the maximum number of passages required is also disease specific.

Inoculated eggs are incubated for up to 10 days and examined regularly by candling for signs of mortality and abnormality. Embryo mortality can occur by needle stick injury, which, if this happens, will show within the first 24 h and be evident by the visualization of a small blood clot near the site of inoculation. In the hands of an experienced operator, needle stick injuries are rare. Visual observations whilst candling include discolouration of egg fluid, shrinking of blood vessels, haemorrhagic lesions, stunting or inertia of the embryo, or embryo death. VI typically involves two or three passages (the transfer of a propagating virus into a new egg), depending on the virus investigated.

Upon completion of the desired propagation period, as a method of embryo euthanasia, the eggs are chilled by storing at 4°C for at least 4 h prior to virological investigation. This begins with the harvesting of the allantoic fluid and/or the embryo if abnormalities were observed (Fig. 22.2). For example, if 'clumping down' of the embryonic feathers and white kidney lesions are observed, this may indicate the presence of IBV.

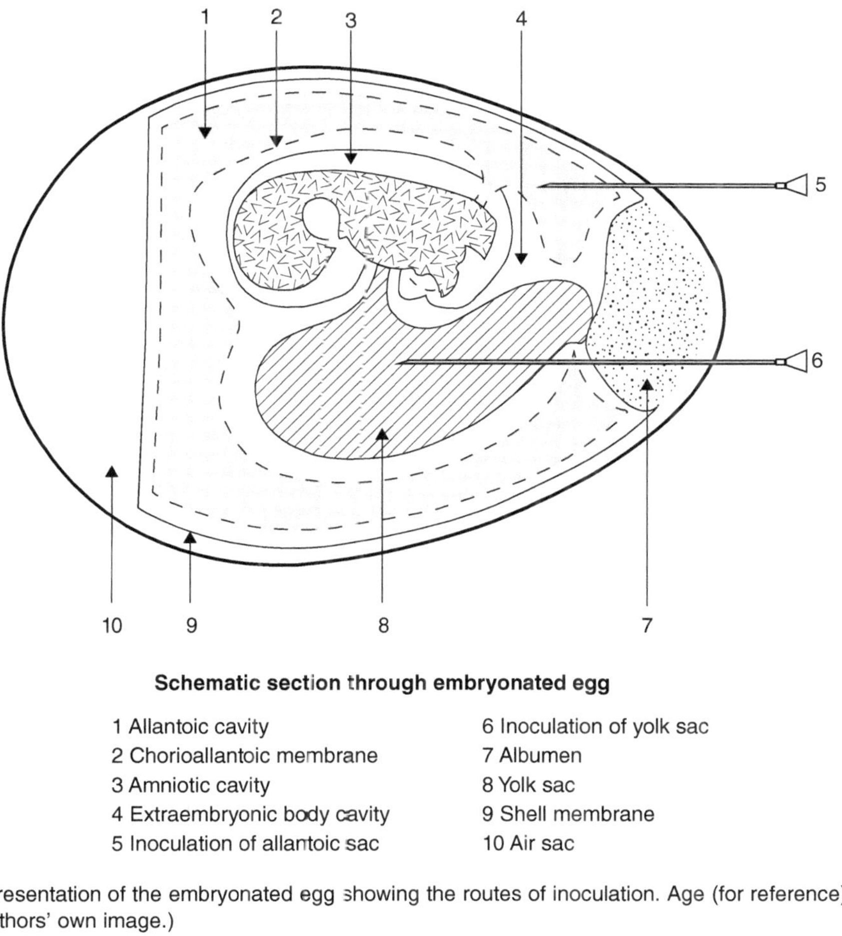

Fig. 22.1. Representation of the embryonated egg showing the routes of inoculation. Age (for reference) is 9–11 days. (Authors' own image.)

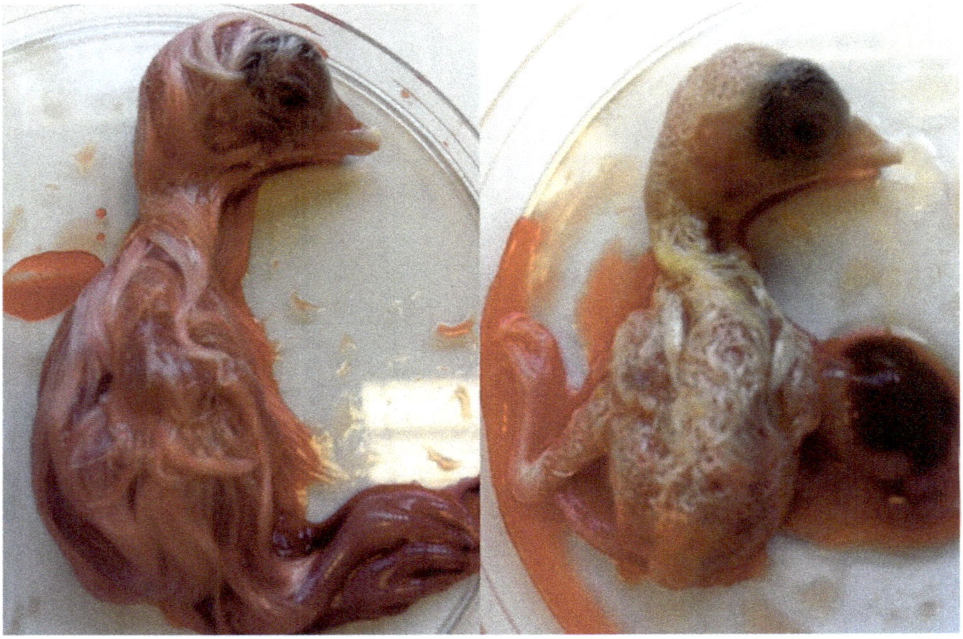

Fig. 22.2. Fifteen-day-old embryo uninfected (left) and infected (right) with infectious bronchitis virus showing the stunted growth and feather dystrophy (clubbing). (Authors' own images.)

The allantoic fluid may be tested to ascertain the haemagglutination of chicken red blood cells (RBCs) (Section 22.3.4). A positive result indicates the presence of a virus with haemagglutinating activity, enabling further confirmatory testing to be performed on the amplified virus. However, this test is time-consuming and expensive, and requires specialist facilities. Not all viruses (e.g. poxvirus and adenovirus) haemagglutinate RBCs, and as such require alternative methods of identification.

Virus isolation in cell or tissue culture

VIRUS ISOLATION IN CELL CULTURE A selection of cell culture systems is available for propagation of avian viruses (Table 22.4). The choice of primary cell culture or continuous cell lines is governed by the suspected virus under investigation as some viruses will propagate more successfully in specific cell cultures or lines.

Tissues or swabs are processed into PBS with antibiotics, as described for egg inoculation. Prior to infection, the cell monolayer should be at least 80% confluent. The sample suspension is inoculated directly onto the cell culture or cell line, overlaid with warm media after an hour, and incubated for up to 7 days. The flasks are examined daily for the presence of cytopathic effect (CPE) using a light microscope. This is a degenerative visual change in the cell monolayer. Different types of CPE can be observed, including granular formation, clustering, detachment and elongation of cells within the monolayer. A CPE indicates virus replication. Figure 22.3a depicts the CPE resulting from reovirus infection and shows the cells detaching from the cell monolayer. Figure 22.3b shows cell-associated Marek's disease virus (MDV) cytopathic plaques.

Sample quality is crucial as contaminants can adversely affect the cell monolayer. Caution must be taken to ensure that aseptic technique is maintained throughout due to the exquisite sensitivity of cell cultures. Bacterial or fungal growth can be misinterpreted as CPE. Filtering the sample with a 0.45 µm filter prior to addition to the cell monolayer can reduce the risk of bacterial contamination.

Negative stain electron microscopy (EM) can confirm the presence of virions causing CPE in cell culture. For this procedure, the cell culture flask contents are subjected to freeze-thaw, ultra-centrifuged and the resulting pellet is suspended in a small volume

Table 22.4. Summary of cell culture options for virus isolation.

Type of cell culture (most sensitive)	Tissue	Virus investigated
Primary chicken embryo epithelial cells	Liver and kidney	Herpesvirus, reovirus, adenovirus, avian influenza A virus, avian paramyxovirus-1(APMV-1)
Primary duck embryo epithelial cells	Liver	Duck viral enteritis virus
Primary chicken embryo fibroblast cells	Torso and limbs	Avian paramyxovirus type 1, avian metapneumovirus virus, birnavirus, avian poxviruses, Marek's disease herpesvirus
Mammalian cell lines – African grey monkey kidney cells. Baby Hamster kidney cells	Kidney	Reoviruses, avian metapneumoviruses

of deionized water. The sample is adsorbed onto a carbon coated copper grid or similar substrate, and a stain is applied, blotted and dried to produce a thin layer of electron dense stain which may be examined with an electron microscope.

In certain cases, samples can be directly examined by negative stain EM without prior need for cell cultivation. These samples are initially processed in deionized water for direct examination. As some viruses possess similar morphology, care should be taken to ensure correct interpretation; however, virus families can be differentiated by particle size by an experienced operator. Figure 22.4 shows electron micrographs of common avian viruses.

VIRUS ISOLATION IN TRACHEAL ORGAN CULTURES Tracheal organ cultures are highly sensitive for the detection of avian respiratory viruses and are used for isolation of IBV and avian metapneumovirus (AMPV). Segments of the chicken tracheal tissue are harvested and placed in media. Cultures are incubated in suspension within a slowly rotating drum and examined for ciliostasis using low power microscopy for up to 3 weeks. If virus is present, the epithelial cells are destroyed. Successful virus detection is confirmed by either genotyping or EM.

22.3.4 Haemagglutination test

This is a method of quantifying viruses which can agglutinate RBCs. Haemagglutination is a property of many enveloped viruses (e.g. AIV and APMV-1). The haemagglutinin (HA) proteins on the virus surface bind to sialic acid receptors on the RBCs, forming a lattice of agglutinated RBCs holding the RBCs in suspension. The method measures virus particles but does not confirm infectivity.

The species of animal from which the RBCs are derived must be appropriate for the virus under test (e.g. chicken RBC are ideally used to detect avian influenza viruses). The diluted sample is added to diluted whole blood in a microtitre plate, then incubated for 60 min at 4°C. If a haemagglutinating virus is absent (or too dilute) the RBCs form a compact pellet in the bottom of the well; if haemagglutinating virus is present, the RBCs remain in suspension (Fig. 22.5). See also Section 22.4.1 Haemagglutination inhibition test/assay.

22.3.5 Antigen detection

Antigenic proteins of pathogens can be detected using agar gel immunodiffusion on tissues (infectious bursal disease virus (IBDV), poxviruses), antigen capture ELISAs (AIV, reticuloendotheliosis virus (REV)) and immunofluorescent or immunohistochemical staining of frozen or fixed tissue sections or infected cultured cells (APMV-1, AIV, infectious laryngotracheitis virus (ILTV), avian encephalomyelitis virus (AEV)).

For immunohistochemistry (IHC) (Ramos-Vara, 2005), fixation of tissues is vital to preserve cell morphology and tissue architecture for staining. Some antigens can be successfully detected in formalin-fixed paraffin-embedded tissue sections, but other antigens cannot tolerate aldehyde fixation. In this case, fresh tissues should be rapidly frozen in liquid nitrogen, or by first embedding in a substance such as OCT (optimal cutting temperature) compound, before cutting sections using a cryostat. However, compared with paraffin-embedded sections, frozen sections have relatively poor morphology, are more difficult to cut, and require frozen storage.

For high quality immunostaining, care must be taken to minimize non-specific background staining, by optimizing fixation, and pre-treatment with blocking agents. Sections are then incubated with an antibody or antiserum which is specific for an

(a)

(b)

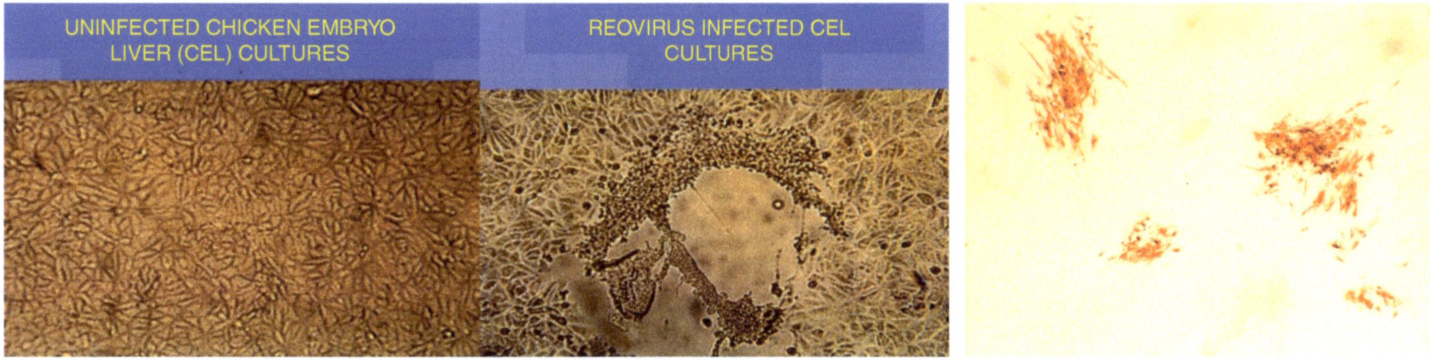

Fig. 22.3. Depiction of CPE resulting from reovirus infection in cultured chicken embryo liver cells (a), and Marek's disease virus infection in cultured chicken embryo fibroblast cells (stained to detect MDV gB protein) (b). (Authors' own images.)

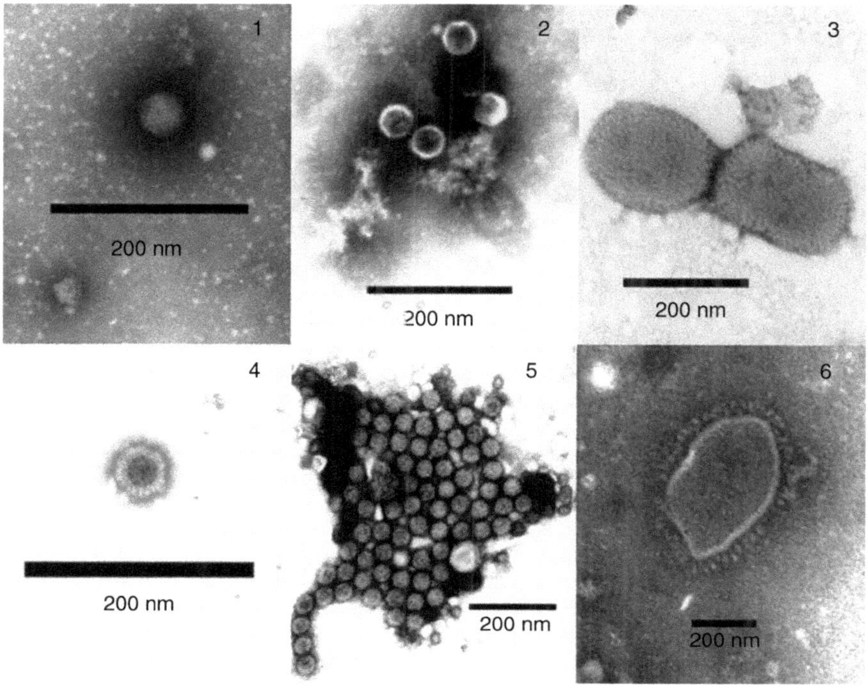

Fig. 22.4. Electron micrographs of common avian viruses – 1: adenovirus, 2: poxvirus, 3: herpesvirus, 4: rotavirus, 5: coronavirus, 6: reovirus. (Authors' own images.)

antigen produced by the pathogen of interest. If the specific antigen is present in the tissue section, the antibody binds to that antigen. Following washing to remove unbound antibodies, an enzyme-conjugated secondary antibody is added, then a chemical substrate for the enzyme. The enzyme converts the substrate to a detectable form (coloured or fluorescent product) that is easily detected by light microscopy or fluorescent microscopy to show presence of the pathogen in the tissue section (Fig. 22.6).

22.4 Serological Methods

Serological methods are used to test blood serum samples to identify antibodies, that are present specifically after infection with a certain pathogen, to confirm that an animal is (or has been) infected with that pathogen. All are based on the principle of specific antigen–antibody binding. Serological tests may be performed using commercially available kits and assays, and these may target early or late immune responses, e.g. detection of IgM and/or IgG antibody, respectively. Some tests also differentiate between antibody responses to vaccine and field strains (so-called 'DIVA' [differentiating infected from vaccinated animal] tests), and, while some tests are suitable for multi-species, others are species-specific.

Whilst results must be interpreted with care and with the vaccination history of the bird/flock in mind, serology is useful for monitoring response to vaccination, virus epidemiology, and for detecting exotic viruses. The majority of the World Organisation for Animal Health (OIE) recommended tests for international trade utilize serology assays.

Serum is convenient to collect and may be stored for several days at 4°C, or for longer periods at –20°C without significant loss of anti-viral antibody titre. An appropriate vein is identified, and blood is withdrawn aseptically using a needle and syringe (vacuum vials may cause collapse of fragile veins in small birds). Blood samples are allowed to clot, serum is collected, then preferably heated at 56°C for 30 min, and sent to the laboratory at 4°C. For each serological test, quality control should include a known negative serum and a known positive serum.

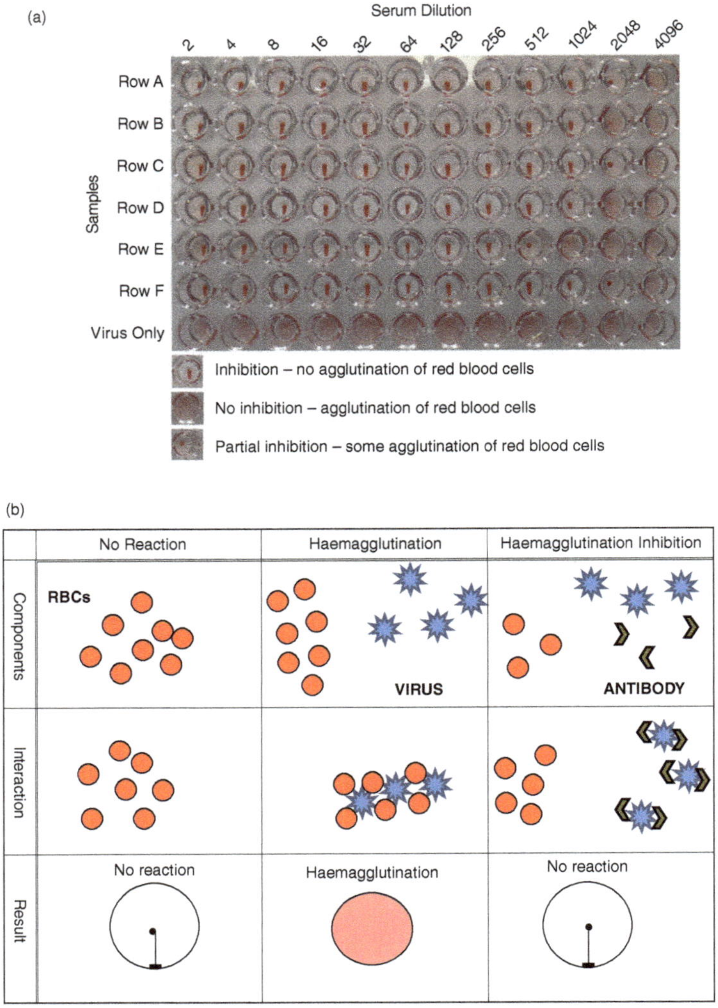

Fig. 22.5. (a) Haemagglutination of chicken red blood cells by avian influenza virus (H5N1), and inhibition of haemagglutination by serum samples from vaccinated chickens. Rows A to F represent individual bird sera. (Figure produced by, and used with permission from, Rebecca Daines and Munir Iqbal, The Pirbright Institute.) (b) Schematic showing mechanism of haemagglutination and haemagglutination inhibition.

22.4.1 Haemagglutination inhibition test/assay (HIT/HAIT)

Haemagglutination (22.3.4) can be inhibited by the addition of serum that contains antibodies against surface proteins of the test virus because these antibodies neutralize the virus by preventing its attachment to RBCs. If the serum does not contain antibodies against test virus, haemagglutination will occur. The HAIT is widely used for diagnosis of infection caused by influenza viruses and APMV-1. The presence of virus in test samples is detected by haemagglutination; the identity of the virus, or of antibodies in a bird's serum, is determined by specific inhibition of that haemagglutination. HAIT does not differentiate between antibodies to APMV-1 specific subtypes. However, HAIT is particularly useful for detecting HA subtype-specific antibodies to AIV strains.

A standardized quantity of HA antigen is mixed with serially diluted test serum in a microtitre plate. Following incubation, a fixed concentration of RBCs is added and the degree of binding of antibody to the HA antigen may be assessed. The HI

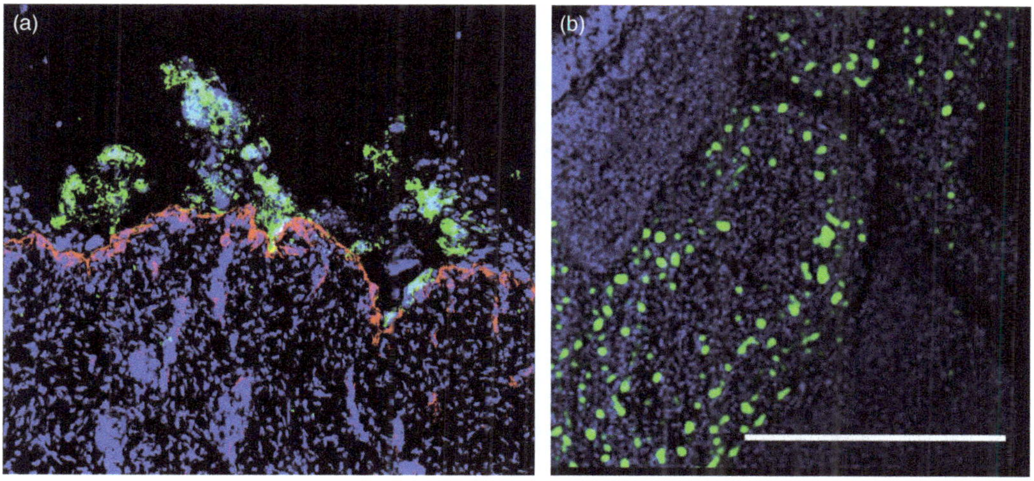

Fig. 22.6. (a) Immunofluorescent staining of infectious laryngotracheitis virus-induced plaques on conjunctival mucosa. ILTV antigens are stained with green fluorescence showing the virus plaques; collagen IV is stained with red fluorescence showing the basement membrane; blue fluorescence shows the cell nuclei. (Image produced by, and used with permission from, Vishwanatha R.A.P. Reddy, The Pirbright Institute.) (b) Immunofluorescent staining for infectious bursal disease virus in a cryo-section of the bursa of Fabricius of an experimental chicken, 3 days after infection. Green fluorescence shows the IBDV antigens; blue fluorescence shows the cell nuclei. (Image produced by, and used with permission from, Andrew Broadbent, The Pirbright Institute.)

titre is the highest dilution of serum that prevents haemagglutination (Fig. 22.5).

HAITs are easy to perform and inexpensive; however, accurate and consistent reading of the plate requires an experienced operator. Other limitations of the HAIT include the propensity of some viruses to cross-react with related viral antigens leading to less specific results. Naturally occurring non-specific inhibitors are capable of binding to the viral HA and may interfere with virus-RBC agglutination thus leading to incorrect interpretation of results. Serum controls (positive and negative) must therefore be present and if any haemagglutination occurs in the negative control well, the inhibitors must be removed by adsorption or by another treatment method. Furthermore, HAIT is not suitable for those viruses which do not haemagglutinate RBCs.

22.4.2 Agar gel immunodiffusion test (AGIDT)

This method detects antibodies by passive diffusion of antigens and antibodies toward each other in an agarose gel matrix. A positive control antigen is added to a central well in a gel plate, while test sera are added to surrounding wells. On incubation overnight at 37°C, the antigens and antibodies diffuse out of their respective wells. Where they meet, the antibodies specifically react with a corresponding antigen forming large antigen–antibody complexes which are visible as opaque precipitation lines in the gel (positive result). The assay is simple, rapid, inexpensive and semi-quantitative, but lacks sensitivity and is open to subjective interpretation. It is further limited in that not all avian species develop demonstrable precipitating antibodies.

22.4.3 Virus neutralization test (VNT)

When an animal is infected with a virus, antibodies are produced against multiple parts of many virus proteins. Some of these antibodies can block virus infection by neutralization – the principle of the VNT. Serial doubling dilutions of heat-inactivated test sera are incubated with a known quantity of reference virus before addition to cell culture in microtitre plates (*in vitro*) or inoculation into SPF embryonated eggs (*in ovo*). Over a set period of time, CPE or embryo deaths are recorded accordingly.

If antibodies specific to the virus are present, they will neutralize the virus, thus preventing it from causing infection and CPE or embryo death.

The serum antibody titre is the reciprocal of the highest dilution that does not show CPE or cause embryo deaths. The VNT is the 'gold standard' test to detect antibodies to cytopathic and embryo-lethal poultry viruses that do not cause haemagglutination (herpesviruses, adenoviruses, reoviruses, IBDV, AMPV, poxviruses). The method can be used to detect antibodies to specific serotypes or strains of virus, and to identify virus isolates using known positive antisera, but it is more labour- and time-intensive, and the *in ovo* version is not suitable for mass serological screening of flocks.

22.4.4 Enzyme-linked immunosorbent assay (ELISA)

There are several types of ELISA (direct, sandwich, competitive and reverse ELISAs), and commercial ELISA kits are available for most major viral pathogens of poultry and some bacteria including *Salmonella, Mycoplasma, Ornithobacterium rhinotracheale* (ORT) and *Riemerella*. The advantage of using commercial kits is that they are standardized and quality-assured by the manufacturer. ELISA is fast, highly sensitive and specific and offers high throughput, high reproducibility and quantitative datasets, often detecting antibody earlier than other methods. However, ELISA cannot differentiate between serotype-/subtype-specific antibody responses and requires sophisticated equipment for measuring chromogenic output.

Commercially available kits comprise microtitre wells coated with specific antigens into which diluted test sera are added. If reactive antibodies are present, these form a complex with the coated antigens, sparking a further binding process to form a secondary antibody/enzyme/substrate complex, the product of which provides a chromogenic reaction which is read using a plate reader. ELISA is useful for assessing distribution and frequency of infection, and for flock profiling to examine the quality of vaccine-induced immunity in a flock.

22.4.5 Complement fixation test (CFT)

The CFT can determine the presence of antigen-specific antibody by incubating serum with antigen and complement. This method is labour-intensive and relatively insensitive, and its use has largely been superseded by the serological tests detailed above.

22.5 Molecular Methods

Molecular methods rely on detection of genetic material of the pathogens rather than the antigens encoded by them. With development of new technologies, sample throughput is increasing, cost of equipment is decreasing, and tests are becoming more specific and sensitive (Suarez *et al.*, 2007). This section provides a brief introduction to nucleic acids and the principles of molecular tests, then covers molecular methods that are well established for diagnosis, and some newer methods. Table 22.5 provides a summary and comparison of the molecular techniques covered in this chapter.

22.5.1 DNA and RNA

Genetic material of pathogens

The full set of genetic information of any organism (its genome) is carried in its nucleic acids. Most pathogens have deoxyribonucleic acid (DNA); some have ribonucleic acid (RNA). All bacteria, fungi and parasites have a DNA genome. Many virus families (including herpesviruses, poxviruses, circoviruses and adenoviruses) also have a DNA genome, but other virus families (including paramyxoviruses, orthomyxoviruses, retroviruses, birnaviruses and coronaviruses) have an RNA genome that is less stable than DNA. Detection of RNA requires an additional step – conversion of RNA to a complementary DNA copy (cDNA) in an enzymatic process called reverse transcription. This cDNA can then be subjected to molecular tests. Nucleic acids are composed of units called nucleotides (NT), connected and arranged in a linear, non-overlapping sequence. The four NTs are adenine (A), cytosine (C), guanine (G) and thymine (T) for DNA. In RNA, T is replaced by uracil (U). Nucleic acids may exist as single-stranded DNA or RNA (ssDNA, ssRNA) for some virus genomes, but more usually as double-stranded DNA or RNA (dsDNA, dsRNA). The two strands (a complementary pair) are held together by hydrogen bonds: C pairs with G, and A pairs with T (or U). This property of specific hybridization of complementary nucleic acid sequences is key to the mechanism of all molecular methods. Nucleic acid sequences may be hundreds of NT long. They are packaged as chromosomes, sub-divided into genes. The genetic information carried by any organism defines the characteristics of that organism and gives a unique molecular signature by which they can be distinguished from closely related organisms.

Table 22.5. Comparison between molecular methods.

	End-point PCR	Real-time PCR	Sequencing	LAMP	DNA fingerprinting	Microarrays	MLST
Can be quantitative	No	Yes	N/A	Yes	N/A	N/A	N/A
Equipment relatively inexpensive	Yes	No	No	Yes	Yes	No	No
Specialist training needed	Yes	Yes	Yes	No	Yes	Yes	Yes
Specificity	High	High	High	High	High	High	High
Sensitivity	Good	High	Good	Very high	Good	High	Good
Prior knowledge of pathogens present needed	Yes	Yes	Yes	Yes	Yes	No	Yes
Simultaneous surveillance of multiple pathogens	No	No	No	No	No	Yes	No
Detect new pathogens, complex diseases, unexpected causes	No	No	No	No	No	Yes	No
Identify new strains, track pathogen epidemiology	No	No	Yes	No	Yes	Yes	Yes
Potential as pen-side test	No	No	No	Yes	No	No	No

22.5.2 Nucleic acid isolation

To use molecular methods to detect pathogens, the first step is usually to isolate nucleic acid from the sample (although some commercial kits allow certain molecular tests to be performed directly on samples). Only small quantities (e.g. 20 mg) of sample are needed to isolate the nucleic acid. Commercial nucleic acid isolation kits are based on silica spin-column technology and can be used for small numbers of samples on a single-column basis or for high sample throughput using 96-well or 384-well plates, and they may also be automated. The process yields pure ready-to-use DNA or RNA in less than 2 h.

In a nucleic acid sample prepared from chicken tissue, the chicken-origin sequences will vastly outnumber the sequences of any pathogens that are present (>99.99% vs <0.01%). Therefore, molecular methods must specifically identify and amplify these small amounts of pathogen nucleic acid to enable detection.

22.5.3 Common principles of molecular tests

Taking steps to confirm reaction specificity, prevent contamination, and confirm reaction success are important for all molecular tests.

Sequence complementarity for specific amplification

The principle of complementarity of nucleotides is key to the mechanism of all molecular methods. The NT sequence of all or part of the genome of the pathogen of interest (or closely related pathogen) must be known, with the selected sequence being unique to the pathogen of interest. Then, the laboratory analyst can design short complementary NT sequences (oligonucleotides, designed using readily available software, then manufactured commercially) that specifically bind to the pathogen's nucleic acid, permitting selective amplification and detection of the pathogen of interest so it is easily identified in the vast pool of total nucleic acid. To detect all members of a pathogen family, a conserved gene sequence is selected. To distinguish between subtypes within a family, a variable gene sequence is selected.

Contamination control

To prevent false positive results, contamination of molecular reactions by foreign DNA must be avoided. Additionally, contamination by DNase or RNase enzymes, which destroy DNA or RNA, must also be prevented. Sterile DNase- or RNase-free plasticware and disposable gloves should be used.

Negative control DNA or RNA as appropriate (extracted from a representative sample which is negative for the pathogen) should be included in each batch of reactions along with a 'no template control' (NTC) negative control (deionized water) to check that no contamination has arisen post-extraction of the nucleic acid, during the amplification step.

Quality control to confirm successful reaction

Where possible, positive control DNA (extracted from a sample which is positive for the pathogen) should be included in each batch of reactions to confirm specificity for the pathogen.

22.5.4 Polymerase chain reaction (PCR)

Principle of PCR

PCR is a reliable and robust procedure for amplifying nucleic acid from the target pathogen, making large (detectable) amounts of selected nucleic acid sequence from very small starting amounts. It involves multiple cycles, the number of copies of the target DNA/cDNA being doubled at every cycle.

Two types of PCR are covered in this section: conventional end-point PCR and real-time quantitative PCR. The principle of amplification is the same for both, but the method of detection of reaction products differs. Reactions may be set up in single microtubes, strips of microtubes, or 96-well plates.

Specificity of PCR

Two short oligonucleotides (usually 18–25 NT in length, known as forward and reverse primers), containing sequences complementary to the DNA target region are required. These primers should lie at the outer edges of the sequence to be amplified; this amplified sequence is called the amplicon. For real-time PCR, a third nucleic acid fragment (a probe, lying in a region of the amplicon between the two primers) is also needed.

Conventional end-point PCR

In end-point PCR, amplification products are not analysed until completion of all PCR cycles. Reactions are performed in a thermocycler, an intelligent heating block programmed to perform repeated cycles of alternating heating and cooling to a defined series of temperature steps, to copy the target nucleic acid sequence. The following steps are repeated 30–40 times: 95°C (denaturing – the two complementary DNA strands are separated); 50–60°C (hybridization – primers specifically bind to target sequence and DNA polymerase attaches complementary NTs to assemble the new DNA strand); 72°C (extension – DNA polymerase synthesizes the new DNA strand by adding further NTs to the primers). The new DNA strand itself is used as a template in the next cycle, so the number of DNA molecules doubles at each cycle.

Nucleic acid amplified by end-point PCR is not visible to the naked eye so is visualized by gel electrophoresis. Samples are scored positive or negative depending on whether an amplicon band is visible. Although intensity of the amplicon bands gives an indication of relative quantity of target pathogen nucleic acid in each sample, PCR product cannot be accurately quantified.

Real-time quantitative PCR (qPCR)

Inclusion of a fluorescently tagged probe in the reaction, and use of a real-time thermocycler which measures fluorescence, enables measurement of PCR product generated throughout the reaction so the read-out is in real-time, not at the end point. The probe emits fluorescence, which increases as the target nucleic acid is amplified. This, coupled with choice of a short amplicon and rapid temperature cycling, makes real-time PCR faster, more reproducible, and more sensitive than end-point PCR. The PCR cycle at which fluorescence passes a defined threshold (C_T value) is inversely proportional to initial amount of target sequence (Fig. 22.7). C_T value can be converted to number of pathogen genomes using a standard curve, making real-time PCR accurately quantitative, rather than just giving positive/negative results. Use of real-time PCR in virology is reviewed by Mackay (2004). Detection and characterization of many other avian viruses by PCR are reviewed by Cavanagh (2001).

22.5.5 Loop-mediated isothermal amplification (LAMP)

LAMP is a simple, rapid technique for nucleic acid amplification (reviewed by Wong *et al.*, 2018). It uses four (or six) primers, designed to recognize six (or eight) distinct regions on the target gene, so specificity and amplification efficiency (and therefore sensitivity) are much higher than in PCR. However, even using commercial software packages, it can be difficult to design appropriate LAMP primers for some target genes. Nucleic acid amplification proceeds at constant temperature and the process does not require highly trained scientists or sophisticated, expensive or fragile instruments.

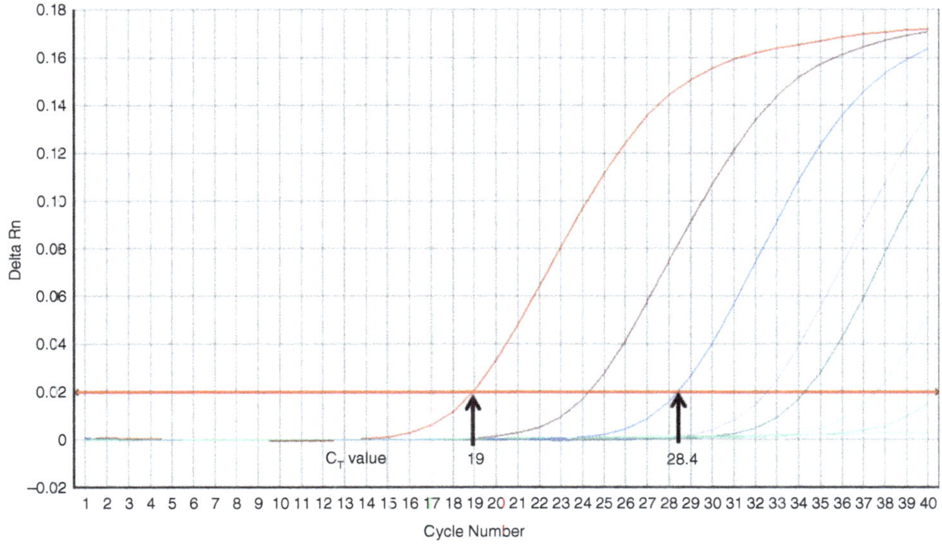

Fig. 22.7. Raw data from real-time PCR. At each PCR cycle (X axis), fluorescent light is emitted (Y axis). Each fluorescence curve represents a different sample reaction (i.e. a different well of the 96-well plate). The C_T value for each sample is the PCR cycle at which fluorescence passes a fixed threshold (horizontal line). C_T values are shown for two samples. The lower the C_T value, the greater the amount of target DNA in the sample. (Author's own image.)

The whole process takes 15–60 min to amplify the DNA 10^9 times.

Reverse transcription loop-mediated isothermal amplification (RT-LAMP) is a one-step nucleic acid amplification method to multiply specific sequences of RNA from the target pathogen. Current availability of commercial kits makes it possible to combine both RT and LAMP in one reaction.

Amplification product can be detected at endpoint, or in real-time, by the naked eye via an increase in turbidity or by inclusion of dyes that give a colour change in positive samples. Alternatively, an instrument can be used to measure increase in turbidity or fluorescence allowing correlation with the number of copies initially present, making the reactions quantitative.

There is also potential to perform LAMP assays on a chromatographic lateral flow device (LFD), a sealed single-use disposable test unit in which a coloured band confirms presence of the pathogen. LAMP and RT-LAMP are rapid, specific, sensitive, simple, robust, cost-effective and are less often subject to inhibition by components present in complex samples. Therefore, LAMP has potential for use as an alternative methodology to PCR, as a simple screening assay for detection of certain pathogens in farm settings or at the point of care by clinicians.

Specific and sensitive LAMP assays have been developed and validated for detection of chicken *Eimeria* species, MDV, avian pathogenic *E. coli*, *Salmonella* and *Enterococcus* species.

22.5.6 Nucleic acid sequencing

Sequencing is the process of determining the precise physical order of the four nucleotides A, C, G and T within nucleic acid molecules. A selected gene, PCR product, whole chromosome or complete genome can be sequenced. The process uses sequence-specific primers, DNA polymerase enzyme and fluorescently labelled NTs. Development of modern fluorescence-based sequencing technologies, and associated equipment (next generation sequencing, NGS), has increased throughput and reduced costs, enabling sequencing of whole genomes. Such technologies include 454 Pyrosequencing, Nanopore DNA sequencing, and Illumina (Solexa) sequencing.

Most NGS approaches require amplification of the nucleic acid by PCR or cloning before sequencing. Modern sequencing technologies use specific primer extension by DNA polymerase and fluorescently labelled NTs. These are detected as they are added to the new DNA chain one at a time and a camera takes images of the NTs to determine sequence. Thousands of fragments are sequenced individually but concurrently (massively parallel sequencing) in an automated process, and computational analysis of huge quantities of sequence data enables electronic assembly of individual sequences into a long, contiguous sequence based on overlapping regions.

Sequencing can distinguish between variants within a pathogen family, identify and classify known and new pathogens, and track pathogen epidemiology.

A phylogenetic tree is a branching diagram showing evolutionary relationships between organisms, based on similarities and differences in their genetic characteristics. Computational analyses compare and align gene sequences from different strains of an organism to calculate 'genetic distance' between strains.

Sequencing has been used to identify a novel natural recombinant avian leukosis virus (ALV), to group fowl adenovirus (FAdV) into five species based on sequence of the hexon gene, and to type strains of *Mycoplasma synoviae*.

22.5.7 DNA fingerprinting

DNA fingerprinting, also called restriction fragment length polymorphism (RFLP) analysis, finds unique patterns that occur in DNA to identify similarities and differences. Small variations (polymorphisms) in DNA sequences account for variations in characteristics. DNA fingerprinting exploits polymorphisms to distinguish variants within a pathogen family, identify new strains and track pathogen epidemiology. The process is labour-intensive, time-consuming and requires a large amount of sample DNA.

A polymorphic region of DNA is 'digested' into small fragments using one or more restriction enzymes, which each selectively cleave a DNA molecule wherever a short, specific sequence is recognized. As variant pathogens of the same species can have different DNA sequences, the number and length of fragments differs between variants. The fragments are separated by length using agarose gel electrophoresis, transferred to a membrane, then visualized on X-ray film. A RFLP occurs when the length of a fragment varies between individuals, indicating non-identical sequences.

Pegg *et al.* (2016) used RFLP to study isolates of *Eimeria* parasites in UK and Ireland. The method has also been used to track epidemiology of ILTV field isolates and their relationship with vaccine strains (Graham *et al.*, 2000).

22.5.8 DNA microarray

A DNA microarray, reviewed by Ojha and Kostrzynska (2008), is a collection of ~20,000 microscopic DNA spots printed on a glass or silicon chip in an organized grid layout. Each spot (probe) is a sequence (~70 NT) complementary to a pathogen gene. A sample can be screened for the presence of multiple pathogens simultaneously, and there is no need for prior knowledge of what pathogens might be present. Microarrays are useful for discovering unknown pathogens, detecting pathogens that might otherwise be overlooked, surveillance, and investigating outbreaks, complex diseases and unexpected causes. However, chips are relatively expensive.

The sample DNA (the 'target') is subjected to random PCR to amplify thousands of sequences, and the amplicons are labelled with fluorescent dye. The labelled DNAs are incubated with the microarray for ~24 h, during which the labelled DNA fragments hybridize to any probe to which they are complementary, generating a fluorescent signal at the location of those specific probes. Data are collected using a microarray scanner consisting of a laser, a computer and a camera. As the pathogen origin of each probe is known, a fluorescent signal demonstrates presence of sequences from that pathogen in the target DNA. Generation of many complex results needs time-consuming analysis.

There are commercially available microarrays for diagnosis of some human infections, but microarrays for poultry pathogens are not widely used. Microarrays have been developed to detect *Salmonella* and *E. coli*, and for simultaneous detection and differentiation of NDV and AIV.

22.5.9 Multiple locus sequence typing (MLST)

MLST involves the amplification by PCR of specific fragments of DNA from a chromosome, which are then sequenced. This is usually done for bacteria for which typing systems have been difficult to develop, such as the food-poisoning *Campylobacter jejuni*. Sequence information is obtained for several house-keeping genes with the sequences from different strains being compared. Although the sequence information generated encompasses a relatively small percentage of the whole chromosome, it has been valuable in tracing the source of outbreaks of human campylobacteriosis to individual poultry farms.

22.6 Differential Diagnoses and Discussion

As many avian infectious diseases present with similar clinical signs, differential diagnosis must always be considered, and, as such, a battery of tests including both conventional and molecular tests may be selected. For example, common clinical signs such as coughing and sneezing could indicate either avian influenza (AI) or ILTV. Likewise, reduction in egg production is observed with infectious bronchitis, AI and egg drop syndrome. Mixed infections involving both bacteria and endemic avian viruses are not uncommon. In rare cases, exotic viral diseases such as low pathogenicity AI (LPAI) may be masked within a disease syndrome.

Laboratory diagnosis of avian diseases starts with the clinical history of the bird or flock which will inform the optimal sample collection and testing algorithm. In cases where clinical disease is apparent, a detailed post-mortem examination is extremely useful and should be performed on fresh carcasses or recently euthanized birds when the opportunity arises. Where there are no overt clinical signs, as is the case with international trade testing, screening of birds for the presence of either antigen or antibody is stipulated by the importation/exportation certification of the country.

Molecular tests are increasingly being used in veterinary diagnostic investigation, as alternative and/or additional methodologies to the numerous conventional tests. As the number of genetic tests for the detection of RNA or DNA virus pathogens has expanded rapidly over recent years, so have the different types of genetic testing methodologies used.

Differential diagnostic routes should also be considered should the described VI and serological methods fail to isolate live virus or detect an immune response, respectively, to any one of the listed viruses under investigation from the submitted sample types (Table 22.3). The microarray is one additional option for screening original clinical material or extracted nucleic acid from the test samples. Fundamentally, constant communication flow with the practitioner as clinical signs/disease presentation develop will influence the consideration of differential diagnostic routes including bacterial infection, parasitology and environmental factors.

22.7 References

Cavanagh, D. (2001) Innovation and discovery: the application of nucleic acid-based technology to avian virus detection and characterization. *Avian Pathology* 30, 581–598.

Graham, D.A., McLaren, I.E., Calvert, V., Torrens, D. and Meehan, B.M. (2000) RFLP analysis of recent Northern Ireland isolates of infectious laryngotracheitis virus: comparison with vaccine virus and field isolates from England, Scotland and the Republic of Ireland. *Avian Pathology* 29, 57–62.

Mackay, I.M. (2004) Real-time PCR in the microbiology laboratory. *Clinical Microbiology and Infection* 10, 190–212.

OIE (2019) *Aves: Manual of Diagnostic Tests and Vaccines for Terrestrial Animals*. OIE, Paris.

Ojha, S. and Kostrzynska, M. (2008) Examination of animal and zoonotic pathogens using microarrays. *Veterinary Research* 39, 4.

Pegg, E., Doyle, K., Clark, E.L., Jatau, I.D., Tomley, F.M., *et al.* (2016) Application of a new PCR-RFLP panel suggests a restricted population structure for *Eimeria tenella* in UK and Irish chickens. *Veterinary Parasitology* 229, 60–67.

Ramos-Vara, J.A. (2005) Technical aspects of immunohistochemistry. *Veterinary Pathology* 42, 405–426.

Suarez, D.L., Das, A. and Ellis, E. (2007) Review of rapid molecular diagnostic tools for avian influenza virus. *Avian Diseases* 51(1 Supplement), 201–208.

Wong, Y.P., Othman, S., Lau, Y.L., Radu, S. and Chee, H.Y. (2018) Loop-mediated isothermal amplification (LAMP): a versatile technique for detection of micro-organisms. *Journal of Applied Microbiology* 124, 626–643.

23 Legislation

Richard Jennison[1]* and Paul Barrow[2]

[1]*Poultry Health Services, Leominster, Herefordshire, UK;* [2]*School of Veterinary Medicine, University of Surrey, Guildford, UK*

23.1 Introduction

Poultry, like other livestock, are subject to national and international legislation which is focused predominantly on four main areas:

1. To define minimum standards, and to promote good practice, for protection of animal welfare.
2. For animal health reasons.
3. For marketing purposes, and to protect product quality.
4. For consumers, to protect human health from the risk of zoonoses.

In general, as poultry production has tended to become more intensive, increasing levels of welfare legislation have been introduced in many countries.

Globalization of trade has increased the risks of key, potentially economically devastating, notifiable diseases, such as avian influenza and Newcastle disease, requiring coordinated action, and there is an increased expectation to control food-borne pathogens and reduce antibiotic use.

Export has been a driving force in introducing improved welfare and other legislation in the key exporting countries which is generally mandatory for export, involving Good Manufacturing Practice (GMP), Good Production Practice (GPP), Hazard Analysis Critical Control Points (HACCP) and Standard Operating Procedures (SOPs), which then has a trickle-down effect on domestic production in the country.

European legislation is generally regarded as the most prescriptive, covering all aspects of breeding, hatching, rearing and slaughter. This will be presented together with comparison for the USA and some of the major producers such as China, Brazil and Thailand. The OIE has established a network of expertise to provide guidance to countries to improve welfare standards (https://www.oie.int/en/what-we-do/animal-health-and-welfare/animal-welfare/).

23.2 Animal Welfare

23.2.1 Welfare – an introduction

Interest in welfare is increasing, with introduction of national and international legislation and a number of welfare assurance schemes. Higher welfare standards can improve not only the quality of life of the animals but also the final product. Infectious disease impacts welfare as do aspects of husbandry that affect behaviour and stress, and which may themselves affect susceptibility to disease.

Within the EU, the Treaty of Lisbon (which came into force in 2009) recognized that animals are sentient beings. As a result, Community legislation concerning the welfare conditions of farm animals has been produced, which lays down minimum standards.

Measurement of welfare has developed over many years and it is recognized that it is best assessed using animal-based parameters. Assessment systems should be species- and production-type-relevant, and attempts to standardize systems and parameters have been made.

Within the EU several groups have responsibility for reviewing animal health and welfare, including the Scientific Committee on Animal Health and Animal Welfare (https://ec.europa.eu/food/sci-com/scah_en) and the Animal Health and Welfare Panel of the European Food Safety Authority (https://www.efsa.europa.eu/en/panels/ahaw), resulting in a series of principles embodied in the European Convention for the Protection of Animals kept for Farming Purposes (https://www.coe.int/en/web/conventions/full-list?module=treaty-detail&treatynum=087).

*richard.jennison@poultryhealthservices.com

© CAB International 2021. *Poultry Health: A Guide for Professionals* (P. Barrow *et al.*)

DOI: 10.1079/9781789245042.0023

The EU has produced a number of pieces of legislation with relevance to poultry welfare. In general, each tends to cover different types (e.g. broilers, layers) and different systems of production (e.g. cage, colony). EU 98/58 provides broad overarching principles relevant to all stages of poultry production.

The UK Animal Welfare Committee (AWC – formerly Farm Animal Welfare Committee, FAWC) has issued guiding principles for assessing welfare embodied in the five freedoms, namely freedom from (i) hunger and thirst, (ii) discomfort, (iii) pain, injury or disease, (iv) fear and distress and (v) freedom to express normal behaviour.

Different HACCP-based systems have been developed in the USA (www.grandin.com/welfare.audit.using.haccp.html) where no legislation covers all aspects of poultry production but where commercially accepted voluntary standards are specified in the National Chicken Council (NCC) Animal Welfare Guidelines (www.nationalchickencouncil.org). These cover issues of stocking density, litter quality, light intensity and NH_3/CO_2 levels.

Other major producing countries, including China, Brazil and Thailand, are introducing national legislation. In most cases, compliance is mandatory for export and voluntary for the domestic market.

China introduced the Animal Husbandry Law (2005, amended in 2015) covering domestic livestock, laboratory and wild animals. Historically poultry have not been regarded as sentient, with minimal attention to welfare, but the Management Regulations of Practising Veterinarians (2008) begins to provide some protection for poultry. The aims are to improve poultry production and product quality in China, particularly in poorer regions. There is considerable attention to protection of genetic resources and relatively little detail on measures to protect against notifiable diseases and improve food safety by reducing food-borne pathogens. However, record keeping of all aspects of production is regarded as important.

The Brazilian Poultry Association is responsible for liaising with central government to introduce measures, driven by the need to export, towards GMO-free and vegetable-material-based feed, ethics, welfare and environmental issues with a push towards greater transparency within the industry.

In Thailand the introduction of welfare issues is the preserve of the government Department of Livestock Development. Legislation covers all aspects of production, including feed quality, drinking water and drug use.

23.2.2 Welfare related to transport of chicks and adults

European Regulation 01/2005 and associated national legislation protect animals transported in association with 'economic activity', and this includes chicks but not hatching eggs. Standards are set on transporter authorizations, vehicle approval, certificates of competence, loading containers, specific feed and water requirements, specified space allowances and also include an assessment of fitness to travel, particularly on journeys over 65 km with provision of food and water to which birds must have access if a journey exceeds 12 h. The exception to this is for chicks, where feed and water are not required to be provided for journeys of less than 24 h, provided that the journey is completed within 72 h after hatching. Stocking densities according to size are specified.

In the USA, the accepted voluntary standards require that animals are fit to travel, although animals may travel for 28 consecutive hours without food or water. There is also no specific requirement for space, except that birds must be able to sit as a single layer.

China requires compliance with local by-laws and regulations which cover provision of adequate food and water for transport.

23.2.3 Legislation related to rearing

Council Directive 98/58/EC specifies general provisions for keeping farm livestock. These provisions, within the UK, are enacted under different pieces of legislation in England, Scotland, Northern Ireland and Wales.

Council Directive 1999/74/EC, with the 2007 amendment, provides minimum standards for laying hens and banned conventional battery cages across the European Union in 2012. The EU Directive allows 'enriched' or 'furnished' cages to be used. Non-enriched cages are still in use in many countries. In the last 20–30 years, particularly in the laying chicken sector, there have been increases in free-range and barn production. Production methods with marketing applications, such as Free-Range or Organic, are also the subject of EU Legislation (e.g. EC 543/2008, EC 889/2008, EC 589/2008).

Regulation EC 589/2008 provides marketing standards for eggs sold in the EU, including egg grading, labelling, hen living conditions and record keeping.

Directive 2007/43/EC applies to intensively reared broiler flocks of 500 or more birds. It sets limits on stocking densities, and makes a number of specific technical requirements, such as duration and intensity of lighting period, feeders, drinkers, ventilation, heating and noise. Fresh litter must be available. Birds must be inspected twice daily, with sick birds being removed or treated immediately. Feed withdrawal immediately prior to slaughter must be less than 12 h. Detailed record keeping is also required for genotype, bird numbers, area used, numbers dead and culled and reason, and birds remaining after thinning takes place.

Under EU Regulation 889/2008, organic poultry meat birds are required to have daily access to the outdoors for at least one third of their lives. Birds are reared to a lower stocking density than free-range and for a longer period of time.

23.2.4 Welfare legislation related to specified surgical procedures

The UK *Veterinary Surgery Exemptions Order 2015* specifies procedures that would be expected to be performed by a veterinary surgeon but are permitted to be performed by trained non-veterinary surgeons.

Within the UK, the application of some mutilations (e.g. castration, pinioning) is banned in farmed birds. Some mutilations are currently permitted (e.g. beak trimming, dubbing), but their use is tightly regulated under UK and EU Law. Furthermore, there is increasing scrutiny on the permitted mutilations of farmed animals (such as beak trimming). Some areas within the EU have applied bans on their use.

23.2.5 Forced moulting

Laying flocks are sometimes force-moulted, rather than being slaughtered, to reinvigorate laying. This involves withdrawal of food (and sometimes water) for 7–14 days or sufficiently long to cause a body weight loss of 25–35%. This stimulates the hen to lose her feathers, but also increases egg-production. Flocks may be force-moulted several times in some countries. In 2003, more than 75% of all flocks were moulted in the USA. Forced moulting is illegal in the UK and EU because complete withdrawal of feed and water is not permitted.

23.2.6 Welfare immediately prior to and for slaughter

EU Regulation 1099/2009 covers killing of birds at the slaughterhouse, in the hatchery or on farm.

For slaughterhouses, standard operating procedures must be developed. Certificates of competence are required for people involved in handling animals at any stage until the animal is legally dead.

Under the UK Welfare of Animals at the Time of Killing (WATOK) Regulations, the legally permitted methods of killing poultry include:

- cervical dislocation;
- exposure to gases (CO, CO_2, N_2, argon);
- captive bolt;
- electrical stunning;
- maceration (embryos and chicks up to 72 h old); and
- lethal injection.

Regulation 1099/2009 allows killing by manual percussion, but this is banned within the UK.

Cervical dislocation may be performed:

- Manually – for birds up to 3 kg (although operators may only kill 70 birds per day by this method).
- Mechanically – for birds up to 5 kg.
- Heavier birds must be killed by other methods.

Electrical stunning is permitted for poultry. After stunning, birds must be killed by bleeding. This is usually achieved by cutting the major blood vessels in the neck. Blood loss must be complete before any further processing, such as plucking. Bleeding out may take up to 90 s for chickens and 2 min for turkeys and geese.

For backyard and hobby flocks, the issue is complex and may depend on whether killing is for humane reasons or for consumption (https://assets.publishing.service.gov.uk/government/uploads/system/uploads/attachment_data/file/695225/fawc-opinion-welfare-of-animals-killed-on-farm-march2018.pdf).

Animals may not be killed at home according to religious rites.

No stunning methods are specified as part of slaughter in the USA.

23.3 Animal Health: Notifiable Avian Diseases

Notifiable avian diseases (NAD) are those which are of such seriousness that they affect international trade and may affect public health or wider society. Affected countries may be unable to export animals or animal products, and importation may require certificates demonstrating freedom from these diseases.

For poultry, the current NAD are avian influenza (see Chapter 15vii, this volume), governed by Directive 2005/94/EC and by The Avian Influenza (Preventive Measures) (England) Regulations (2006), and Newcastle disease (see Chapter 15viii, this volume) governed by Directive 92/666/EC. The causative viruses (AIV and NDV), as well as paramyxovirus 1 in pigeons, are governed by the Diseases of Poultry (England) Order 2003. The primary enabling UK legislation for both is the Animal Health Act (1981).

On discovery of/suspicion of a NAD, a farmer or attending veterinary surgeon is obliged to notify the veterinary authorities (DEFRA within the UK) of a so-called 'report case'.

Upon laboratory confirmation of the presence of NAD (e.g. by an OIE reference laboratory, such as the Veterinary Laboratories Agency – VLA – within the UK), the country is required to notify international organizations, such as the OIE and European Commission.

Both diseases (AI and ND) require compulsory movement restrictions within a protection zone of 3 km, and a surveillance zone of 10 km. All animals on infected farms must be killed ('stamping out policy'). These regulations will be supplemented by additional detail covering a wide range of animal diseases in EU 2016/429 to be applied in 2021.

The UK has also developed a scheme of 'testing to exclude' NAD, where a clinician has detected signs that may be consistent with these diseases, but NAD is relatively low on the differential diagnosis list. This allows testing to occur without the need to implement the statutory disease control measures (such as movement restrictions) that are associated with a 'report case'.

The US Federal Government has the authority to define control areas for eradication. Strategies may vary between states from immediate 'stamping-out' to a longer-term eradication strategy.

Clearly these diseases are major disruptors of trade and have been major drivers towards improved health and welfare in poultry meat exporting countries. In Brazil, the 1994 National Program for Poultry Health set standards for biosecurity, disinfection, sample collection and analysis with National Plans to control avian influenza and Newcastle disease but also *Mycoplasma gallisepticum* (see Chapter 14viii, this volume) and the Gallinarum, Pullorum, Enteritidis and Typhimurium *Salmonella* serovars (see Chapter 14iv, this volume). In Thailand, a National Strategic Control Plan was introduced in 2004 in response to the threat of avian influenza. This requires pre-catching-for-slaughter testing for AI, and now also for *Salmonella*.

In 2007, China enacted a law to control infectious epidemics including reporting and notification, destruction, disinfection and disposal of infectious material and dead animals, etc. with mandatory vaccination, depending on the nature of the epidemic. There has been considerable attention in recent years to the role of wet markets involving on-site slaughter of birds which increases the risk of spread of AI.

23.4 Legal Requirements Regarding Medication

Antibiotic use is tightly regulated in many countries although this is not universal (see also Chapter 19, this volume).

Since 2006 (Regulation (EC) 1831/2003), antibiotic growth promoters have been banned in the EU and, for permitted antibiotics metaphylaxis is discouraged.

Licensing drugs for use in food-producing animals is complex and must address any concerns for consumer safety from residues in food.

In the USA incorporation of antibiotics for growth stimulation has also been prohibited since 2016. The WHO lists the Highest Priority Critically Important Antibiotics for which use is restricted to severe infections in man (https://www.who.int/foodsafety/cia/en/).

In the UK, the Responsible Use of Medicines in Agriculture Alliance (RUMA) provides recommendations on antimicrobial use requiring prescription by a veterinary surgeon. The Welfare of Farm Animals Regulations (2007) and Veterinary Medicines Regulations (2013) require accurate record keeping of antimicrobial use.

There is also increasing regulation in other countries. The Chinese government recently launched a regulation to withdraw medicated feed additives, to fulfil the National Action Plan to Combat Antimicrobial Resistance from Animal Resources (2017–2020). This involves withdrawal of antibiotics for growth-promotion, although the currently free online availability of antibiotics will require implementation and enforcement. Thailand has also seen a recent tightening of procedures for antibiotic use.

23.5 Food-borne Zoonoses Legislation

This relates primarily to *Salmonella* and *Campylobacter* (see Chapter 14iii and 14iv, respectively, this volume), although the UK Zoonoses Order (1989), which arose out of the *Salmonella* Enteritidis pandemic in the 1980s, covered a number of specified zoonoses. The pandemic also led to European and national legislation to monitor and control *S.* Enteritidis and *S.* Typhimurium, some of which has been superseded by more recent legislation. The Zoonoses Order is now covered by EU Regulation 2160/2003. *Salmonella* control in the UK and other EU countries is carried out under the aegis of Salmonella National Control Programmes (NCP) with separate sections for breeders, layers and broilers, including turkeys but not ducks.

The NCP for *Salmonella* in breeding flocks of domestic fowl sets out the requirements contained in EU Regulations (EC) No 2160/2003, (EC) No 1003/2005 and 200/2010. The UK legislation covering this is the Control of Salmonella in Poultry Order 2007 which sets out, among other things, the requirements for registration and sampling. The Regulations set a target of not more than 1% of adult breeding flocks being infected with *Salmonella* of public health significance by the end of 2009. In line with Regulation (EC) 1003/2005, and in contrast to laying and broiler flocks, the programme for breeding flocks also includes *S.* Hadar, *S.* Infantis and *S.* Virchow, in addition to *S.* Enteritidis and *S.* Typhimurium which were initially of greatest public health significance.

Rearing flocks require testing on three occasions: on the day of arrival, when the chicks are 4 weeks old, and again 2 weeks before moving to the laying phase or laying unit; samples collected are chick box liners, dead or culled chicks, boot swabs or composite faeces. During the laying period, every breeding flock on the holding should be sampled every 2 weeks. Samples may consist of boot swabs or composite faeces samples.

The legislation applies to commercial hatcheries with sampling of pooled soiled hatcher basket liners or broken eggshells.

The NCP measures for broilers are based on the target levels set out in EU Regulation 646/2007 and which were for no more than 1% of flocks to remain positive for *S.* Enteritidis and *S.* Typhimurium. These do not include birds reared for private consumption, to local establishments supplying directly to the final consumer, or to smaller farms with <2000 birds. Sampling involves boot swabs, faeces or dust taken within 3 weeks before slaughter or before removal at thinning.

For laying flocks, the NCP sets out the statutory requirements contained in EU Regulations No 2160/2003 and No 1168/2006 (see https://www.gov.uk/guidance/salmonella-get-your-egg-laying-hens-tested). The regulations do not apply for production for private use or for flocks of fewer than 350 hens which supply directly to the consumer. Eggs from flocks known to be infected with *S.* Enteritidis or *S.* Typhimurium can only be sent for consumption if they are treated to eliminate *Salmonella* infection (generally pasteurization). Testing includes chick box liners or 60 carcasses of dead-on-arrival birds, boot swabs for floor-rearing or composite faeces sample for cage-rearing. Samples are taken between 22–26 weeks of age and then every 15 weeks during production.

NCP samples must not be taken from broiler and layer flocks for a short period after antibiotic administration.

In addition, the UK operates an Assured Chicken Production scheme requiring members to follow comprehensive specific hygiene standards including those related to staffing, traceability and records, housing and vermin control, biosecurity, nutrition and responsible use of agrochemicals. The UK British Egg Industry Council also runs a 'Lion Code' egg-specific assurance scheme covering the entire production chain, which exceeds NCP requirements including more frequent testing. In the UK there are both duck and turkey assurance schemes with *Salmonella* testing components.

In the USA *Salmonella* control falls under the National Poultry Improvement Plan (NPIP), adherence to which is mandatory for inter-state and export trade. Testing is carried out in breeding flocks, although this is variable depending on the nature of the flock. There is also some extension of testing into broilers but with no specific requirement. Feed components regulations are also not as specific, with meat and bonemeal allowed in feed. Many carcass decontaminants (which are not permitted in the EU) are permissible in the USA to reduce food-borne pathogen contamination.

Other countries have started surveillance for *Salmonella*, including Thailand. In Brazil, technical rules are now in place for monitoring *S.* Typhimurium and Enteritidis. Russia, Ukraine and the CIS tend to follow EU rules on monitoring and controlling food-borne pathogens.

The production of *Salmonella*-free poultry feed in the UK is covered by a Code of Practice based on Regulations (EC) 183/2005 and 2160/2003 and EU Zoonoses Directive 2003/99 and national statutory instruments. These require feed businesses to comply with standards for facilities and equipment. Feed production systems should be based on HACCP principles defined in Codex Alimentarius CoP CAC/RCP 1 1969, Rev 4 – 2003. Procedures are specified for sampling infrastructure, equipment, feed and components together with procedures if *Salmonella* is isolated.

An NCP is also available in the UK for turkeys with the Animal and Plant Health Agency (APHA) providing advice on controlling *Salmonella* in ducks.

Campylobacter control is covered by EU Regulation 2017/1495 to reduce levels of infected carcasses during slaughter and processing. It also covers sampling procedures.

Index

Note: Page numbers in **bold** type refer to **figures.** Page numbers in *italic* type refer to *tables*

This book is published by **CABI**, an international not-for-profit organisation that improves people's lives worldwide by providing information and applying scientific expertise to solve problems in agriculture and the environment.

CABI is also a global publisher producing key scientific publications, including world renowned databases, as well as compendia, books, ebooks and full text electronic resources. We publish content in a wide range of subject areas including: agriculture and crop science / animal and veterinary sciences / ecology and conservation / environmental science / horticulture and plant sciences / human health, food science and nutrition / international development / leisure and tourism.

The profits from CABI's publishing activities enable us to work with farming communities around the world, supporting them as they battle with poor soil, invasive species and pests and diseases, to improve their livelihoods and help provide food for an ever growing population.

CABI is an international intergovernmental organisation, and we gratefully acknowledge the core financial support from our member countries (and lead agencies) including:

UKaid from the British people

Ministry of Agriculture People's Republic of China

Australian Government – Australian Centre for International Agricultural Research

Agriculture and Agri-Food Canada

Ministry of Foreign Affairs of the Netherlands

Schweizerische Eidgenossenschaft / Confédération suisse / Confederazione Svizzera / Confederaziun svizra – Swiss Agency for Development and Cooperation SDC

Discover more

To read more about CABI's work, please visit: **www.cabi.org**

Browse our books at: **www.cabi.org/bookshop**,
or explore our online products at: **www.cabi.org/publishing-products**

Interested in writing for CABI? Find our author guidelines here:
www.cabi.org/publishing-products/information-for-authors/

www.ingramcontent.com/pod-product-compliance
Lightning Source LLC
LaVergne TN
LVHW070848210926
848482LV00016B/892

* 9 7 8 1 7 8 9 2 4 5 0 4 2 *